EMOTIONS IN HISTORY

General Editors
UTE FREVERT   THOMAS DIXON

The History of Emotions

An Introduction

JAN PLAMPER

Translated by
KEITH TRIBE

OXFORD
UNIVERSITY PRESS

OXFORD

UNIVERSITY PRESS

Great Clarendon Street, Oxford, OX2 6DP,
United Kingdom

Oxford University Press is a department of the University of Oxford.
It furthers the University's objective of excellence in research, scholarship,
and education by publishing worldwide. Oxford is a registered trade mark of
Oxford University Press in the UK and in certain other countries

First published in German as *Geschichte und Gefühl.*
Grundlagen der Emotionsgeschichte

By Jan Plamper

© 2012 by Siedler Verlag, a division of Verlagsgruppe
Random House GmbH, München, Germany.

The translation of this work was funded by Geisteswissenschaften
International – Translation Funding for Humanities and Social Sciences
from Germany, a joint initiative of the Fritz Thyssen Foundation,
the German Federal Foreign Office, the collecting society VG WORT,
and the Börsenverein des Deutschen Buchhandels
(German Publishers & Booksellers Association).

© in this English translation Oxford University Press 2015

The moral rights of the author have been asserted

First Edition published in 2015

Impression: 3

Published in the United States of America by Oxford University Press
198 Madison Avenue, New York, NY 10016, United States of America

British Library Cataloguing in Publication Data
Data available

Library of Congress Control Number: 2014940239

ISBN 978–0–19–966833–5

Printed and bound by
CPI Group (UK) Ltd, Croydon, CR0 4YY

To the Berlin Feel Tank

Acknowledgements

Rather than me coming to this book, it is as if this book came to me. I was working on another study about the history of fear among soldiers when conceptual problems began piling up so fast that I found myself forced to call a halt, so that I might have some time to think them through. This happened during the academic year 2007/8, when I was a Junior Fellow at the Historisches Kolleg in Munich. Lothar Gall, the board's chairperson at the time, was accommodating when I told him about my diversion. For a productive year at this unique institute for advanced study, I owe a debt of gratitude to him, Karl-Ulrich Gelberg, Elisabeth Hüls, and Elisabeth Müller-Luckner, as well as my co-fellows Albrecht Cordes, Jörg Fisch, Georg Schmidt, and Martin Wrede. I am also grateful to Michael Hoch-geschwender, Benjamin Schenk, and Martin Schulze Wessel for good conversation and much more during my year in Munich.

The book was written under conditions that were similarly idyllic while I was on a multi-year Dilthey Fellowship, funded by the Fritz Thyssen Foundation, at Ute Frevert's Centre for the History of Emotions at the Max Planck Institute for Human Development in Berlin—my 'feel tank'. My colleagues there provided stimulating discussion, critical readings of my texts, and afforded glimpses of their own work-in-progress. Without all this the final book would have been much worse, perhaps it would have never become a book. I am extraordinarily grateful to Jose Antony, Christian Bailey, Christina Becher, Magdalena Beljan, Gaby Bend-mann, Anja Berkes, Clare Bielby, Rob Boddice, Philippe Bongrand, Juliane Brauer, Daniel Brückenhaus, Moritz Buchner, Kate Davison, Sabine Donauer, Christiane Eifert, Pascal Eitler, Dagmar Ellerbrock, Merih Erol, Monika Freier, Ute Frevert, Benno Gammerl, Alice Goff, Joachim Häberlen, Christa Hämmerle, Bettina Hitzer, Philipp von Hugo, Uffa Jensen, Christine Kanz, Ursula von Keitz, Mana Kia, Anja Laukötter, Susanne Michl, Salil Misra, Sven Oliver Müller, Sophie Oliver, Stephanie Olsen, Tine van Osselaer, Margrit Pernau, Josef Prestel, Till van Rahden, Imke Rajamani, Karola Rockmann, Shweta Sachdeva, Mohammad Sajjad, Daniela Saxer, Monique Scheer, Maritta Schleyer, Anne Schmidt, Mark Seymour, Nadeem Shah, Kerstin Singer, Franziska Timm, Karen Vallgarda, Nina Verheyen, Gian Marco Vidor, Claudia Wassmann, and Helen Watanabe-O'Kelly. Working in a new field that was booming, and was in fact being seriously hyped, was exhilarating: the general atmosphere in which we worked, the rapid develop-ment of concepts and terminology, the rapid publication and then citation of research work was a singular experience. The chances that any of us will ever repeat this experience in our academic careers are slim.

The presence of experimental psychologists at the Max Planck Institute for Human Development was a major advantage for a humanities person like myself. Ulman Lindenberger made time for a thorough and constructive critique of my life science chapter, Isabel Dziobek and Hauke Heekeren gave me important leads.

I was also able to benefit from discussions with and comments made by Ray Dolan, Klaus Fiedler, and Tania Singer during multidisciplinary conferences at the Institute. Among those more loosely connected with the Institute I should like to highlight Ruth Leys. My intellectual debt to her work is enormous, she engaged me in critical argument on various occasions, and she kept me from giving up at a critical juncture. Rüdiger Zill read the Introduction's philosophical excursus with the sharp eye of a specialist in the philosophy of emotions. To all of them I am most grateful.

Margrit Pernau invited me to co-teach a summer school of the Studienstiftung des Deutschen Volkes, and I ended up learning so much from the students in our group, especially those from the life sciences. The life scientists at the September 2010 'History of Emotions' summer school in Görlitz were Aram Kehyayan und Marco Schmidt. Marco read and criticized my third chapter, as did another participant at our summer school, Philipp Gerlach. Philipp was also my intern in early 2011, and he did indispensable preliminary work for the philosophical part of the introduction. Many thanks!

Ingo Gildenhard, Jochen Hellbeck, and Karl Schlögel took time out of their own work to listen to me while I was writing, and also to ask questions. That was very helpful. The reading of the entire finished manuscript by Dietrich Beyrau, Klaus Gestwa, Christa Hämmerle, and Barbara H. Rosenwein was similarly helpful. Barbara H. Rosenwein has been a wonderfully generous mentor from the very beginning of this project, responding reliably and rapidly to every one of my email questions. Stefanie Gert and Eva Sperschneider, as well as Hartmut Burggrabe and Johanna Rocker, provided first-rate research assistance. I owe a huge debt of gratitude to them all.

The recommendations of Anselm Doering-Manteuffel, Eli Bar-Chen, and Igal Halfin were crucial in placing the original of this book with Siedler Publishers at German Random House. Working with Siedler was a smooth and, indeed, reassuring encounter with the publishing business. My editors Heike Specht, who commissioned the book, Antje Korsmeier, who provided substantive feedback from a philosopher's perspective, and Tobias Winstel, who always looked further than I could think, were not only highly professional, but also friendly and approachable. The same is true for Dietlinde Orendi from the illustrations department. In the end, Christiane Fritsche edited the revised manuscript with a mind-boggling sense for German style. Ditta Ahmadi performed miracles during the typesetting of the book.

The translation of the book was made possible by a Geisteswissenschaften International Prize. I am grateful to Keith Tribe, my translator. Karola Rockmann of the Max Planck Institute for Human Development in Berlin painstakingly checked the translation. Anika Fiedler helped track down English quotations. She was funded by a grant from the History Department at Goldsmiths, University of London, where I feel privileged to have been teaching since September 2012. My department also kindly paid for the rights for the illustrations and let Kerstin Feule take time off her administrative job to track them down. I am happy the English version of the book found a home in Ute Frevert and Thomas Dixon's 'Emotions in History' series at Oxford University Press, where Rowena Anketell meticulously copy-edited and Emily Brand, Robert Faber, Emma Slaughter, Cathryn Steele, and Christopher Wheeler expertly shepherded the manuscript through production. My friend Ilya Vinkovetsky kindly checked the first proofs.

This book starts with my visit to an anatomy course. It was Johannes Vogel of the Anatomical Institute at the Charité Hospital who generously invited me to his anatomy course on 7 December 2009 at the Rudolphi Room. Irina Kremenetskaia worked just 100 metres away in the Charité neurosurgical laboratory. Our marriage proves that the bridging of the gap between the humanities and the life sciences, between social constructionism and universalism, is possible—at least on a personal level. To be sure, things are easier when one is blessed with two daughters of exceptional emotional intelligence, Olga and Lisa Plamper. To my family go not only my thanks, but also my love.

Contents

List of Figures

History and Emotions

An Introduction

Hardly more than a dark, oval shadow, about the size of a raisin, merging into other brain matter of a lighter colour—the amygdala. I immediately thought: perhaps you cannot even separate it out. It is not an organ like the liver or the kidney. These you can remove from a plastic model of the human torso, and then simply put them back. I was shown the amygdala in a sectioned brain that looked just like someone had sliced up a cauliflower. A student had checked a number of buckets filled with formaldehyde until she found a brain sectioned so that the amygdala was visible, carefully separating the slices to show me.

This was early one December morning in 2009, in the Rudolphi Room of the Anatomical Institute of the Berlin Charité, Europe's largest university clinic. I had emailed them to say that I was working on a history of fear among First World War Russian soldiers and would like to see a human amygdala, since it governed the human response of fearfulness and I had kept on coming across references to it in neuroscientific writings. The response was quick: I could attend the anatomy course for medical students the coming Monday, and I would be shown an amygdala. Arriving before the lecturer, I told the others about my interest—they were all fourth semester students, wearing white coats. While they fished out one brain after another from the plastic buckets in search of one that was suitable—brains dripping with formaldehyde—I glanced at the neighbouring table. Two female students were just heaving a body bag onto the table. They removed the blue plastic covering, then the gauze bandages covering the head, turned the skinned, prepared corpse onto its front, propped the head up with a wooden block, removed the sawn top of the skull, and began fishing around deep inside the cavity with pincers and a scalpel. It suddenly occurred to me that the path these two students were taking into these regions below the cortex which governed cognition was just like that of my own historical studies. These students would at some point come across the amygdala, the inner sanctum of fear, the most basal point of the most fundamental of all feelings.

The amygdala was so named in 1819 by its discoverer, the German anatomist Karl Friedrich Burdach (1776–1847), because of its almond-shaped form, as in the Greek αμύγδλο ('almond').[1] By the 1930s, animal experiments and studies of

---

[1] David Sander, 'Amygdala', in Sander and Klaus R. Scherer (eds), *The Oxford Companion to Emotion and the Affective Sciences* (Oxford: Oxford University Press, 2009), 28–32, here 28.

human patients had shown that this was the area of the brain where all neuronal processes caused by and responding to threats took place (for example, the threat represented by a venomous snake), processes which activated the nervous system out of its state of relaxation (enhancing muscle tone, accelerating the pulse, in short, everything needed to flee from the snake), and which were generally categorized as 'fear' or 'anxiety'. From the 1980s on, new imaging procedures associated with computer tomography reinforced this view. I asked the students working at the anatomy table under a harsh neon light what they considered to be the prevailing view about the function of the amygdala, and they agreed: 'negative emotions, especially fear'.

Popular knowledge of the amygdala's significance may be attributed to a best-seller written by a New York neuroscientist, Joseph LeDoux's *The Emotional Brain: The Mysterious Underpinnings of Emotional Life* (1996), a book which has been translated into many languages. LeDoux, who plays 'Heavy Mental' electric guitar with other members of his lab in a band called *The Amygdaloids*, talks of two roads to fear: a fast one via the amygdala, and a somewhat slower one via the cerebral cortex.[2] According to LeDoux, when a threat (the snake) is registered, this information takes 12 milliseconds to reach the amygdala, which then prepares the nervous system for a fight-or-flight reaction rooted in evolutionary biology. This quick response can decide upon life or death, and the body is prepared to run from the threat, or to stand and fight. In twice that length of time the same information is conveyed to the cortex, which calculates: is that really a snake, or perhaps a piece of wood that looks like a snake? If it really is a snake, is it alive or dead? If it is alive, is it a venomous snake, or instead one that is quite harmless? If there is no actual danger, the cortex signals to the amygdala, and the nervous system calms down.[3] The suggestive power of the illustration in LeDoux's book depicting this process is considerable. Since 1996 it has been used more often than any others in works devoted to fear (Fig. 1).[4]

Since then, the amygdala has become so well known that I can hardly mention my historical work on fear among soldiers without being asked about it. There are very few emotions to which an anthropological constant—today dressed up in neuro-biological terminology—is applied in such an automatic way as happens with the fear felt by soldiers. Underlying this is the idea that there is a solid neurobiological (almond) kernel at the centre of the fear felt by all animals across time and culture, from the laboratory mouse to *Homo sapiens*. And this has been one pole in the study of emotion since the nineteenth century: solid, unchanging, culturally universal, inclusive of all species, transcending time, biological, physiological, essential, basic, hard-wired. The placement of the amygdala deep in the brain's core—a site which the students at the next table were setting out to explore—says it all.

But what is the amygdala? It is a mass of nerve cells activated in particular operations of the brain, emotion being one of these operations—at least most

---

[2] See <http://www.amygdaloids.com> accessed 25 February 2014.
[3] Joseph E. LeDoux, *The Emotional Brain: The Mysterious Underpinnings of Emotional Life* (New York: Simon and Schuster, 1996), ch. 6, esp. 163–8.
[4] The illustration is also included in LeDoux, *The Emotional Brain*, 166.

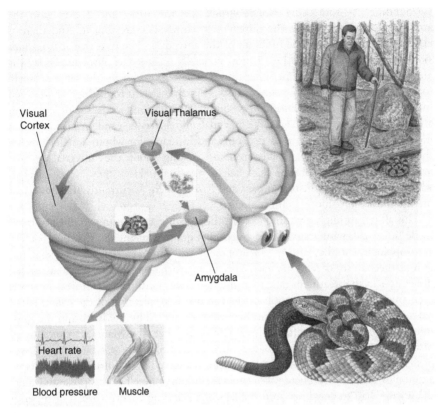

Fig. 1 Joseph LeDoux and The Two Roads to Fear

Source: Joseph E. LeDoux, 'Emotion, Memory and the Brain', *Scientific American*, 270/6 (1994), 50–6, here 38, illustration by Robert Osti.

researchers do still agree on this. But argument begins as soon as one asks: which nerve cells belong to the amygdala? For the neighbouring regions are also composed of nerve cells, some of which are thought to be relevant to emotion.[5] The gradual transition between the dark spot in the brain section and the less-dark area

[5] A survey article claims that 'The amygdala consists of functionally distinct nuclei (i.e. 13 main nuclei, each having further subdivisions), which have extensive internuclear and intranuclear connections'; Tim Dalgleish, Barnaby D. Dunn, and Dean Mobbs, 'Affective Neuroscience: Past, Present, and Future', *Emotion Review*, 1/4 (2009), 355–68, here 358. Another paper disputes that there is a unitary structure of nerve cells called the amygdala, and refers instead to a 'structurally and functionally heterogeneous region of the cerebral hemispheres'; Larry W. Swanson and Gorica D. Petrovich, 'What is the Amygdala?', *Trends in Neurosciences*, 21/8 (1998), 323–31, here 330. Yet others argue that nerve cells from other parts of the brain belong to an 'extended Amygdala', among which is the *substantia innominata* of the basal forebrain; John P. Aggleton (ed.), *The Amygdala: A Functional Analysis* (2nd edn, Oxford: Oxford University Press, 2000), 8–9; M. Davis and P. J. Whalen, 'The Amygdala: Vigilance and Emotion', *Molecular Psychiatry*, 6/1 (2001), 13–34.

surrounding it—something which struck me the first time I ever saw the amygdala—itself represents the difficulty in clearly demarcating it. And there is also disagreement about the function of the amygdala. The idea that it is responsible only for negative emotions is now generally regarded as obsolete. Today the amygdala is considered among other things to be responsible for the sense of smell, for visual perception, and for the capacity of jazz musicians to distinguish between music played from a score and improvisation.[6] In addition to this, the organization and connection of nerve cells in the amygdala differ between rodents, upon which most of the experiments are carried out, and humans, for whom conclusions are then drawn.[7] And finally, strictly speaking, talking about 'the' amygdala is misleading, since there is one in each half of the brain. How they are connected, whether they perform distinct tasks, and if so, which, is currently the subject of intense discussion among neurobiologists.[8]

This all ran through my mind as I left the institute and found myself once more in Berlin's weak winter sun. I had run across quite different things when reading anthropological studies of fear. Anthropology had not been seeking a general and unique mechanism of fear that had a specific neuroanatomical site, but had noticed differences in the treatment of fear at different times in different cultures. This was even true of soldierly fear, as was evident in one example: that of the Maori tribes native to New Zealand, who until they were conquered by the British in the mid-nineteenth century were often at war with each other. If a Maori warrior showed physical signs of fear before a battle, such as trembling, it was said that he was possessed by *atua*, a kind of spirit that had been angered by an infringement of *tapu*, a canon of social rules. There was a ritual for ridding oneself of this possessed state: the warrior had to crawl between the legs of a standing Maori woman of superior social status. The sexual organs of the woman, especially the vagina, had special powers which could free the warrior of *atua*. If the warrior crawled between the woman's legs without shaking then he was freed of *atua*, and went off to battle liberated from fear. But if he still shook, the ritual cleansing was judged a failure, and the warrior could stay at home unpunished. Apparently no one thought it possible for someone to be afflicted with *atua* during a battle; and so we can assume that Maori warriors just did not feel fear. Hence the model of soldierly fear for the Maori warrior is one that locates it outside the body. Fear originates not in his

[6] For the sense of smell see Geoffrey Schoenbaum, Andrea A. Chiba, and Michela Gallagher, 'Neural Encoding in Orbitofrontal Cortex and Basolateral Amygdala during Olfactory Discrimination Learning', *Journal of Neuroscience*, 19/5 (1999), 1876–84; for visual perception see Ralph Adolphs, Daniel Tranel, Hanna Damasio, and Antonio R. Damasio, 'Fear and the Human Amygdala', *Journal of Neuroscience*, 15/9 (1995), 5879–91; for the distinction by jazz musicians between improvised and scored music, see Annerose Engel and Peter E. Keller, 'The Perception of Musical Spontaneity in Improvised and Imitated Jazz Performances', *Frontiers in Auditory Cognitive Neuroscience*, 2/83 (2011), 1–13.
[7] See Richard J. Davidson, 'Seven Sins in the Study of Emotion: Correctives from Affective Neuroscience', *Brain and Cognition*, 52/1 (2003), 129–32, here 130.
[8] Daan Baas, André Aleman, and René S. Kahn, 'Lateralization of Amygdala Activation: A Systematic Review of Functional Neuroimaging Studies', *Brain Research Reviews*, 45/2 (2004), 96–103.

'soul', or his 'psyche', or his 'brain', but instead in a transcendent sphere of *tapu* norms and higher beings.[9]

This example quite significantly modifies any idea of the universality of a soldier's fear. And here we come to the second polarity for all research on feelings: soft, anti-essentialist, anti-determinist, social constructivist, culturally relative, culturally specific, culturally contingent. Since the mid-nineteenth century at the very latest, academic discussion of emotion has revolved around these two polarities: hard and soft, essentialist and anti-essentialist, determinist and anti-determinist, universal and culturally conditioned. The concepts grouped at either end of this spectrum are not complementary. What their relation to each other is; how, when, and where they emerged; what distinguishes them; how they might be precisely mapped—none of this is clear. Research is only in its earliest phases. Anyone who during the first decade of the third millennium has taken part in multidisciplinary conferences involving neuroscientists and specialists in the humanities—there is little point here in talking of *inter*disciplinarity—will know just how sensitive these polarities are, and how quickly camps form around them that become bitter foes. The polarization between universalism and social constructivism has often been noted: Barbara H. Rosenwein has written that 'some scholars view emotions as innate whereas others consider them to be "social constructions".'[10] For Ingrid Kasten the question is 'where and how boundaries are to be drawn between universals and variables'.[11] Peter and Carol Stearns talk of the challenge of sorting 'the durable (animal) from the transient (culturally caused)'.[12] According to Rüdiger Schnell, 'today's historical research into emotions involves two basic and contrary positions: according to the one, human feelings have remained the same for millennia (only the means of expressing them having changed); and according to the other, each emotion has its own history determined by general historical changes'. Schnell also considers that 'universalists and evolutionary theorists' are in one camp, 'constructivists in the other'.[13] Armin Günther asks whether 'emotions have a history at all, or are they anthropological constants?'[14] And finally, Catherine Lutz and Geoffrey White conclude that 'A number of classic theoretical or epistemological tensions are found in the emotion literature. These include...

[9] Jean Smith, 'Self and Experience in Maori Culture', in Paul Heelas and Andrew Lock (eds), *Indigenous Psychologies: The Anthropology of the Self* (London: Academic Press, 1981), 145–59, here 149.

[10] Barbara H. Rosenwein, 'Introduction' in Rosenwein (ed.), *Anger's Past: The Social Uses of an Emotion in the Middle Ages* (Ithaca, NY: Cornell University Press, 1998), 2.

[11] Ingrid Kasten, 'Einleitung', in C. Stephen Jaeger and Ingrid Kasten (eds), *Codierungen von Emotionen im Mittelalter: Emotions and Sensibilities in the Middle Ages* (Berlin: De Gruyter, 2003), xiii–xxviii, here xiv.

[12] Peter N. Stearns and Carol Z. Stearns, 'Emotionology: Clarifying the History of Emotions and Emotional Standards', *American Historical Review*, 90/4 (1985), 813–36, here 824.

[13] Rüdiger Schnell, 'Historische Emotionsforschung: Eine mediävistische Standortbestimmung', *Frühmittelalterliche Studien*, 38 (2005), 173–276, here 180, 213.

[14] Armin Günther, 'Sprache und Geschichte: Überlegungen zur Gegenstandsangemessenheit einer historischen Psychologie', in Michael Sonntag and Gerd Jüttemann (eds), *Individuum und Geschichte: Beiträge zur Diskussion um eine 'Historische Psychologie'* (Heidelberg: Asanger, 1993), 34–48, here 35.

universalism and relativism.'[15] Even where the binary opposition of social constructivism and universalism does not arise, it is usually considered necessary to
mention explicitly that this opposition is not being employed, as for instance when
a collection relating to medical ethnology notes that 'The papers do *not* focus on
debates about the universality or cultural specificity of particular emotions'.[16]

It has likewise been noted that this division between universalism and social
constructivism has done little to help develop our ideas.[17] Even a quick glance at
writings from the eighteenth and nineteenth centuries shows that this distinction is
far from God-given, but instead made by humans. It comes from another dichotomy: that of nature versus culture. For much of the seventeenth century 'nature'
was for European thinkers still an open category: often the subject of allegory (as
the goddess Diana) and widely worshipped (in temples to Nature), it was capable of
transformation and moved flexibly to a goal, instead of simply existing, solid and
immutable. Nature was 'an intention never fully realized in actuality'; it was 'still
understood as a pliable set of potentialities, not as a reality inexorably, unalterably
fixed'.[18] Nature was something that could be modelled, something mutable.

This all changed with the Enlightenment. In the course of the early eighteenth
century the contrast of nature to culture crystallized. Henceforth, nature was no
longer changeable, and it assumed new properties. First of all, the 'state of nature'
became for political theorists such as Thomas Hobbes the period before the
existence of any state, and for John Locke and Jean-Jacques Rousseau the period
before the existence of society. Secondly, nature became defined as 'primitive', a
developmental description for alien, non-European peoples. Thirdly, Enlightenment thinkers began to equate nature with the human body, especially with its
internal and less mutable aspects, among which were the instincts (for example in
the work of Julien Offray de La Mettrie and other 'mechanical' philosophers).
Fourthly and lastly, the semantics of nature fused with the environment in general,
so that flora and fauna became 'nature'.[19] These last two meanings—nature as the
body and nature as the environment—first of all became a pre-religious form of
legitimation; and then, following a process that we can for the sake of simplicity,

[15] Catherine Lutz and Geoffrey M. White, 'The Anthropology of Emotions', *Annual Review of Anthropology*, 15 (1986), 405–36, here 406. See also Helena Flam, for whom there are 'constructivist and positivist approaches': Helena Flam, *Soziologie der Emotionen: Eine Einführung* (Konstanz: UVK Verlagsgesellschaft, 2002), 118. According to Owen Lynch 'the Western hierarchical distinction of reason over emotion implies the further hierarchical distinctions of human over animal and culture over nature': Owen M. Lynch, 'The Social Construction of Emotion in India', in Lynch (ed.), *Divine Passions: The Social Construction of Emotion in India* (Berkeley and Los Angeles: University of California Press, 1990), 3–34, here 10.
[16] Mary-Jo Delvecchio Good, Byron J. Good, and Michael M. J. Fischer, 'Introduction: Discourse and the Study of Emotion, Illness and Healing', *Culture, Medicine and Psychiatry*, 12/1 (1988), 1–7, here 2, emphasis in original.
[17] See Lutz and White, 'Anthropology of Emotions', 406, 429–30.
[18] Lorraine Daston and Gianna Pomata, 'The Faces of Nature: Visibility and Authority', in Daston and Pomata (eds), *The Faces of Nature in Enlightenment Europe* (Berlin: BWV, 2003), 1–16, here 14.
[19] Maurice Bloch and Jean H. Bloch, 'Women and the Dialectics of Nature in Eighteenth-Century French Thought', in Carol P. MacCormack and Marilyn Strathern (eds), *Nature, Culture and Gender* (Cambridge: Cambridge University Press, 1980), 25–41, here 27.

but with no small amount of reservation, call 'secularization', they became a unique and absolute legitimating instance. Nature was poured and cast as a solid *fundamentum absolutum*, and became the new ultimate certainty. During the nineteenth century this process was associated with the diffusion of Francis Galton's ideas and their vulgarization as 'eugenics', as well as with the professionalization and institutionalization of the modern natural sciences.[20] The contrast of nature to culture was also inscribed in discussion about scientific methods. In 1894 for example, in his inaugural lecture as rector of the University of Strasbourg, the neo-Kantian philosopher Wilhelm Windelband made a distinction between nomothetic and idiographic study that remains in use to this day: the nomothetic natural sciences seek generally valid laws and favour the method of reductionist experiment, while by contrast idiographic human sciences seek not the universal, but the specific and unique in their objects of study.[21]

The historian of science, Lorraine Daston, considers that the contrasting of nature to culture, of universalism to social constructivism, is so deeply rooted that any attempt to move beyond such polarities would involve group therapy for all scientific disciplines. Only on the psychiatrist's couch, as it were, might the ideological heritage of the nineteenth century be 'worked through'.[22] In this book I have time and again sought to get up off the couch, throw open the window and reveal a new perspective, a post-therapeutic study of emotion, the study of emotion beyond the dichotomy of universalism and social constructivism.

I have two objectives in this book. First of all, it is an introduction to the history of emotions, and so a synthesis of the current state of knowledge on the subject. An introduction of this kind is not easy to write, for at present the history of emotions is taking off in all directions. Metaphorically, it is rather like tracking photographically each instant of the acceleration of a rocket from its launching pad. I think that this is still feasible for the history of emotions, while it is now too late for the psychology, ethnology, and philosophy of emotions. What has been published so far in the history of emotions can still be pulled together, even if we will eventually come to a point of no return, where knowledge reaches a critical mass beyond which no single person will have the capacity to absorb it. In conformity with this work of review, this book will summarize and order, myths regarding recent studies will be cleared away, and there will be a great deal of direct quotation, so that readers writing their own histories have a sound basis for developing their own work

[20] For Galton's contribution to the nature–culture dyad, see Donald A. MacKenzie, *Statistics in Britain: 1865–1930: The Social Construction of Scientific Knowledge* (Edinburgh: Edinburgh University Press, 1981).

[21] Wilhelm Windelband, *Geschichte und Naturwissenschaft: Rede zum Antritt des Rectorats der Kaiser-Wilhelm-Universität Strassburg, gehalten am 1. Mai 1894* (3rd edn, Strasbourg, 1904). See also the ethnologist John Leavitt, who argues that the study of emotion has been hindered by an unproductive division between a nature investigated by nomothetic sciences and a culture for which 'ideolectic' sciences are responsible; John Leavitt, 'Meaning and Feeling in the Anthropology of Emotions', *American Ethnologist*, 23/3 (1996), 514–39, here 515.

[22] Lorraine Daston in conversation with the author (25 June 2009). See also Jan Plamper and Benjamin Lazier, 'Introduction: The Phobic Regimes of Modernity', *Representations*, 110/1 (2010), 58–65, here 59.

on the history of feeling. As in any survey of this kind, the bird's-eye view is just a bird's-eye view, and all readers are encouraged to follow up the literature to which I refer so that they might, instead of a coarse-grained overview, gain a sense of detail.

Nonetheless, this book is not just an overview; it is also an intervention in a rapidly developing research field. This will be plain in each chapter: I have sought to maintain neutrality in summarizing the material, while at the same time making my own opinion as transparent as possible. This is especially true for my critical assessment of the way in which some of the human and social sciences—primarily relating to the study of literature and images, but also political science—make casual use of the neurosciences, which are today so much in vogue. These borrowings often look like a binge that will be closely followed by the most dreadful hangover—I am quite certain of that. And I would place emphasis here upon *casual* borrowings, since in principle borrowings of this kind can lead to important innovations. One needs a degree of literacy in the neurosciences to understand what one is borrowing from, when one borrows. And this book seeks to promote such literacy—in Chapter Three both objectives, overview and intervention, are inseparable. Other works have shown me how it might be possible to bridge the gap between a balanced assessment of a field as a whole and wholehearted involvement in this field; that this might even be done with elegance is something that they have shown me, and without such exemplars I might never have begun this book.[23]

The book is divided into four chapters. Chapter One presents a chronology of historical studies of emotion from the start of the history of emotions in the late nineteenth century. This developmental process is placed in the context of social and political events, together with that of other scientific disciplines that had an influence upon the history of emotions. I show in this way that even the history of emotions has a history. Chapter Two turns to the social constructivist end of the spectrum in the debate over emotion, dealing with the discipline that has contributed more than any other to our understanding that feelings are dealt with differently in different cultures: anthropology. Chapter Three switches attention to the other, essentialist, end of the spectrum, and provides an overview of the study of emotion in experimental psychology from the end of the nineteenth century, focusing especially on recent research in the neurosciences. Here I must make a clarification: I use the term 'life sciences' for psychology, physiology, medicine, neurosciences, and related disciplines. This term first emerged in the 1980s as an extension of the more restricted sense of 'biology', introducing areas such as cognitive psychology, brain research, or computer-based neurological research that dealt with living organisms. 'Life sciences' represents the fluidity existing between these separate disciplines. Chapter Four then opens up a perspective upon those areas in the historical study of emotions that might have a future. The dedication of Chapter Two to social constructivism and Chapter Three to universalism does retain the dyadic structure that has prevailed. This contrast has

[23] Terry Eagleton's *Literary Theory: An Introduction* (Minneapolis: University of Minnesota Press, 1983) served as my most important model.

had too much influence upon everything that has been written about feeling and emotion, and a book which seeks at least in part to be a synthesis cannot do entirely without it. But if *The History of Emotions: An Introduction* can raise questions about this dyad, and ultimately assist in reconciling the two camps, that would be something of an achievement.

This Introduction, however, is devoted to the most fundamental questions raised by the history of emotions: What is emotion? Who has emotion? Do emotions have a history? Assuming that they do have a history, how does the discipline of history deal with this history? Any approach to answering these questions demands exploration of many scientific domains, above all, two and a half millennia of philosophy. This is firstly because philosophical investigations were especially influential and so form a necessary framework for this book; secondly, because in the following chapters they are overshadowed by work in anthropology and the life sciences; and thirdly, because they were often preoccupied with themes and dichotomies other than the opposition of universalism to social constructivism, and thus demonstrate the real prospect of moving beyond this distinction dominating recent work on the study of emotion.[24]

1 WHAT IS EMOTION?

'What Is an Emotion?' is the title of a famous essay by the American psychologist William James (1842–1910) that appeared in 1884.[25] James did answer his own question—we will come to that—but it is significant that both question and answer come from a psychologist. This leads us to the prior question of who defines what emotions are. For the discourse on emotion is not always dominated by the same discipline; successive disciplines have addressed the issue, and some of these, like William James's own discipline of psychology, had not existed in previous centuries. Very roughly, it can be said that in the West, from antiquity until about 1860, it was primarily philosophy and theology that defined thinking about emotions, together with rhetoric, medicine, and literature, and while after 1860 experimental

---

[24] We can thank the ethnologist Catherine A. Lutz for what is probably the most concise account of the history of emotions, in just two sentences: 'The extensive discussions of the concept of the emotions that have occurred in the West for at least the past 2,000 years have generally proceeded with either philosophical, religious, moral, or, more recently, scientific-psychological purposes in mind. This discourse includes Plato's concern with the relation between pleasure and the good; the Stoic doctrine that the passions are naturally evil; early Christian attempts to distinguish the emotions of human frailty from the emotions of God; Hobbes's view that the passions are the primary source of action, naturally prompting both war and peace; the argument of Rousseau that natural feelings are of great value and ought to be separated from the "factitious" or sham feelings produced by civilization; the nineteenth-century psychologists' move to view emotions as psychophysiological in nature, with consciousness seen less and less as an important component of the emotions'; Catherine A. Lutz, *Unnatural Emotions: Everyday Sentiments on a Micronesian Atoll & Their Challenge to Western Theory* (Chicago: University of Chicago Press, 1988), 53.
[25] William James, 'What Is an Emotion?', *Mind*, 9/34 (1884), 188–205. This title has been alluded to many times since, as for instance by the psychologist Jerome Kagan in his *What Is Emotion? History, Measures, and Meanings* (New Haven: Yale University Press, 2007).

psychology became dominant, this dominance shifted to neuroscience in the late twentieth century.[26]

A statement as general as this needs to be qualified. To start with, we can introduce what could be called a meta-history of emotions, dealing with who could speak with authority about emotions, where and when they might speak, how these speakers related to each other over time. A history of this kind has been initiated and written for particular periods, but we only have more or less reliable evidence for ancient Greece, eighteenth-century colonial North America, and nineteenth-century Great Britain.[27] This book cannot provide an *histoire totale* of emotion, nor even a complete meta-history of emotions, piecing the islands of knowledge that we have into an archipelago and then filling in the ocean that separates it. All that can be done here is to provide some suggestions regarding what we might need if we were to construct such a meta-history. In any case, the idea that more than two and a half millennia of Western theological and philosophical thought about emotion has simply been displaced by one hundred and fifty years of research into the psychology of emotion is deeply problematic, for we also need to take account of thinking about feelings in non-Western parts of the world, where it has also played an important role. Besides, transfers from West to East and vice versa were so diverse and multidirectional even before the rise of psychology that it no longer makes any sense to talk in terms of 'Western' and 'non-Western' categories.[28]

There is another prior question that we cannot avoid. Are we really talking about the same object when we refer to 'emotion' as understood by Joseph LeDoux in the neurosciences of 1996 and 'emotion' as used by Klaus Scherer for experimental developmental psychology in 1979? Or Barbara Rosenwein's use of the term for historical studies in 2002 and 'emotion' for Jaak Panksepp's neuroscience in 1998? Or the use of the term 'emotions' by Charles Darwin in 1872, and the entry for

[26] Philip Fisher provides a description of the fields that dealt with emotion, although he gives no chronology: 'What we know or how we think about the passions was, from the beginning, a complex product of overlapping and sometimes mutually encumbering work in philosophy, in literature—especially epic and tragedy—in medicine, in ethics, in rhetoric, in aesthetics, in legal and political thought. In our own time, new work in evolutionary biology, psychology, anthropology, and most recently in the neurobiology of the brain, along with work in game theory and economics, and, above all, in philosophy, continues the interwoven texture of shared, interdependent, sometimes interfering, even damaging, and sometimes enhancing collaborative thought'; Philip Fisher, *The Vehement Passions* (Princeton: Princeton University Press, 2002), 7.

[27] For Greece, see David Konstan, *The Emotions of the Ancient Greeks: Studies in Aristotle and Classical Literature* (Toronto: Toronto University Press, 2006); for colonial North America, see Nicole Eustace, *Passion Is the Gale: Emotion, Power, and the Coming of the American Revolution* (Chapel Hill: University of North Carolina Press, 2008), 481–6; for Great Britain in the 19th century, see Thomas Dixon, *From Passions to Emotions: The Creation of a Secular Psychological Category* (Cambridge: Cambridge University Press, 2003).

[28] For this process of transfer, see the example of the emotional dimension of 'hysteria' in the Greek-Persian-Arabic-Indian triangle: Guy N. A. Attewell, *Refiguring Unani Tibb: Plural Healing in Late Colonial India* (New Delhi: Orient Longman, 2007), 225–37; for emotion itself, and its localization in the body in the Greek-Persian-Arabic-Indian-British relationship, see Margrit Pernau, 'The Indian Body and Unani Medicine: Body History as Entangled History', in Axel Michaels and Christoph Wulf (eds), *Images of the Body in India* (London: Routledge, 2011), 97–108, esp. 104–6.

'affection' in the *Encyclopaedia Britannica* of 1910/11 which states that affection 'does not involve anxiety or excitement, that it is comparatively inert and compatible with the entire absence of the sensuous element'? Is there anything in common between *les affects* as understood by Gilles Deleuze and Félix Guattari in 1980, the Indonesian *perasaan hati* in the mid-1980s, 'affect' as used in English by the philosopher Brian Massumi in 2002, and the *emozioni* as described by Cesare Lombroso in 1876?[29] In brief: is there a unity of meaning sufficient to permit us to deal with these very different terms originating in very different fields, times, and cultures as 'emotion'?

At first glance it certainly does not look like it. Even in such a limited field as English-language experimental psychology, ninety-two different definitions of emotion have been counted between 1872 and 1980.[30] The sheer difficulty of defining emotion is often treated as its leading characteristic, for instance when in 1931 an American cardiologist described emotion as a 'fluid and fleeting thing that like the wind comes and goes, one does not know how'; or when two psychologists half a century later argued that 'everyone knows what an emotion is, until asked to give a definition'.[31]

There are, however, three reasons to bring all these definitions together under 'emotion'. First of all, many concepts of emotion are etymologically connected. If you trace back the German terms *Emotion* and *Gemüthsbewegung* ('stirring of one's soul'), for example, then you find that they both relate to the Latin *movere*. Showing and tracing all these connections in a large number of languages would be a major project for conceptual history (*Begriffsgeschichte*), one that could only be pursued on a collaborative basis. Besides this, even cultures whose languages having nothing like a concept of emotion often import the word. The Tibetan language does this, where non-Tibetans were so frequently asked why there was no word for emotion that a neologism—*tshor myong*—was invented to cover the term.[32] Secondly,

[29] See LeDoux, *Emotional Brain*; Klaus R. Scherer, 'Nonlinguistic Vocal Indicators of Emotion and Psychopathology', in Carroll E. Izard (ed.), *Emotions in Personality and Psychopathology* (New York: Plenum Press, 1979), 495–529; Barbara H. Rosenwein, 'Worrying about Emotions in History', *American Historical Review*, 107/3 (2002), 821–45; Jaak Panksepp, *Affective Neuroscience: The Foundations of Human and Animal Emotions* (New York: Oxford University Press, 1998); Charles Darwin, *The Expression of the Emotions in Man and Animals* (London: John Murray, 1872); 'affection', in *The Encyclopædia Britannica: A Dictionary of Arts, Literature, and General Information*, i. *A to Androphagi* (11th edn, Cambridge: Cambridge University Press, 1910), 299–300, here 300; Gilles Deleuze and Félix Guattari, *Mille plateaux* (Paris: Éditions de Minuit, 1980), 314; Karl G. Heider, *Landscapes of Emotion: Mapping Three Cultures of Emotion in Indonesia* (Cambridge: Cambridge University Press, 1991), 41; Brian Massumi, *Parables for the Virtual: Movement, Affect, Sensation* (Durham, NC: Duke University Press, 2002); Cesare Lombroso, *L'uomo delinquente in rapporto all'antropologia, alla giurisprudenza ed alle discipline carcerarie* (Turin: Bocca, 1876), 651.

[30] Paul R. Kleininna Jun. and Anne M. Kleininna, 'A Categorized List of Emotion Definitions, with Suggestions for a Consensual Definition', *Motivation and Emotion*, 5/4 (1981), 345–79.

[31] Stewart R. Roberts, 'Nervous and Mental Influences in Angina Pectoris', *American Heart Journal*, 7/1 (1931), 21–35, here 23; Beverley Fehr and James A. Russell, 'Concept of Emotion Viewed from a Prototype Perspective', *Journal of Experimental Psychology: General*, 113/3 (1984), 464–86, here 464.

[32] Georges Dreyfus, 'Is Compassion an Emotion? A Cross-Cultural Exploration of Mental Typologies', in Richard J. Davidson and Anne Harrington (eds), *Visions of Compassion: Western*

comparison and draft translations throw up similarities, and also of course differences. In fact, draft translations are extremely productive, and make up the majority of definitional science. Thirdly, and lastly, scholarship without meta-concepts—a nominalist human science—would relapse into a radically random enterprise. In itself, there would be nothing against that. But since there is a market for anti-nominalist scholarship, and currently also for a history of emotions, this scholarship will be produced.

I have decided to use 'emotion' as a meta-concept. As a synonym I will also use 'feeling'. At the same time I will not shy away from the necessary labours of historicization: I will therefore address myself to the clarification of specific terminological usage when and wherever it occurs. I will deal with the word 'affect' in a different manner. Influenced by the neurosciences, the notion has in recent years increasingly assumed the sense of purely physical, prelinguistic, unconscious emotion. For this reason, it will not be deployed as a meta-concept in this book. If I had used 'affect' as a meta-concept I would have had to use up a lot of space in rowing against the currently dominant usage, introducing considerations of evaluation, language, and consciousness.

But back to my original question: what is emotion? Today, much of the public and transdisciplinary scholarly discourse concerning emotion is dominated by a psychology which is heavily coloured by the neurosciences. A general collective amnesia prevails concerning the history of psychological, not to mention philosophical, ideas regarding emotion—even if there are today voices raised in the neurosciences suggesting that the entire history of philosophy represents an anticipation of the modern natural sciences.[33] Only a rough outline of two and a half thousand years of philosophical thinking about emotion can be given here. A constant feature of this history is the reception process, including the psychology of today, and here the 'unspoken' reception is important, in which the actual philosophical connections are no longer recognized. If at the conclusion of this account some elements of the wealth and complexity of the philosophy of emotion are recognizable, then the following pages will have served their purpose.

One of the earliest recorded definitions, also one of the most enduring and influential, comes from Aristotle (384–322 BC).[34] He described the Greek term *pathos* (*pathē* in the plural) as follows:

> The emotions are all those affections which cause men to change their opinion in regard to their judgements, and are accompanied by pleasure and pain; such are anger, pity, fear, and all similar emotions and their contraries.[35]

Scientists and Tibetan Buddhists Examine Human Nature (Oxford: Oxford University Press, 2002), 31–45, here 31.

[33] Antonio R. Damasio, *Looking for Spinoza: Joy, Sorrow, and the Feeling Brain* (Orlando, FL: Harcourt, 2003), 15.

[34] The most concise introduction to thinking on emotion from Plato to Augustine can be found in Barbara H. Rosenwein, *Emotional Communities in the Early Middle Ages* (Ithaca, NY: Cornell University Press, 2006), ch. 1.

[35] Aristotle, *The 'Art' of Rhetoric*, trans. John Henry Freese (Cambridge, MA: Harvard University Press, 1959), 173. More generally, see Michael Krewet, *Die Theorie der Gefühle bei Aristoteles* (Heidelberg: Winter, 2011).

This quotation comes from his *'Art' of Rhetoric*, in a passage that deals with the way that emotion fogs judicial powers of judgement. The target group of the text were those whose work in politics or in the courts of law involved the use of eloquence to exert emotional influence. Aristotle gave them a kind of instruction manual. In this first of many catalogues of affects, Aristotle does not simply distinguish between positive and negative emotions, as is usual today, but treats each emotion as itself having a negative and a positive sense, and as being capable of producing pleasure or pain.

Interpretations of this passage diverge greatly: some think it untypical of Aristotle and thus as being limited to the pragmatic context of rhetoric; others regard it as quite typical of Aristotle's conception of emotions, and more generally that of the city states of Classical Greece (*c.*500–336/323 BC), where emotions were understood to be reactions, reactions not to events but to actions or situations that resulted from actions, the consequences of which affect one's relative status, or the relative status of others.[36] For some, Aristotle's list reminds them of the basic emotions which Paul Ekman identified in the later twentieth century; others on the other hand believe that Aristotle's conception of emotion, and his emphasis upon the element of judgement, is a forerunner of the experimental psychology of cognitive appraisal that is opposed to Ekman but which belongs to the same period; yet others point to contemporary social psychology with its emphasis upon the intersubjective and communicative function of emotion.[37] It is quite apparent that even very old ideas about emotion are eagerly projected upon the key cleavages in recent research.

But let us stick with Aristotle and one particular emotion, that of anger (*orgē*). We can read the following in Aristotle's *The 'Art' of Rhetoric*:

> Let us then define anger as a longing, accompanied by pain, for a real or apparent revenge for a real or apparent slight, affecting a man himself or one of his friends, when such a slight is undeserved. If this definition is correct, the angry man must always be angry with a particular individual (for instance, with Cleon, but not with men generally), and because this individual has done, or was on the point of doing, something against him or one of his friends; and lastly, anger is always accompanied by a certain pleasure, due to the hope of revenge to come. For it is pleasant to think that one will obtain what one aims at; now, no one aims at what is obviously

---

[36] William W. Fortenbaugh, *Aristotle on Emotion: A Contribution to Philosophical Psychology, Rhetoric Poetics, Politics and Ethics* (2nd edn, London: Duckworth, 2002), 114 treats the passage as untypical, and limited to rhetoric; while the contrasting position can be represented by Konstan, *Emotions of the Ancient Greeks*, 40.

[37] For Aristotle as a precursor of Ekman, see Carol Tavris, 'A Polite Smile or the Real McCoy?', review of Paul Ekman, *Emotions Revealed: Recognizing Faces and Feelings to Improve Communication and Emotional Life* (New York: Times Books, 2003), in *Scientific American*, 288/6 (2003), 87–8. For Aristotle as the forerunner of the appraisal approach of cognitive psychology: Randolph R. Cornelius, *The Science of Emotion: Research and Tradition in the Psychology of Emotion* (Upper Saddle River, NJ: Prentice Hall, 1996), 115; Kagan, *What Is Emotion?*, 11–12; Richard Lazarus, 'Relational Meaning and Discrete Emotions', in Klaus R. Scherer, Angela Schorr, and Tom Johnstone (eds), *Appraisal Processes in Emotion: Theory, Methods, Research* (Oxford: Oxford University Press, 2001), 37–67, here 40. For Aristotle as forerunner of social psychology, Konstan, *Emotions of the Ancient Greeks*, 31, citing the social psychologist Agneta Fischer.

impossible of attainment by him, and the angry man aims at what is possible for himself. Wherefore it has been well said of anger, that 'Far sweeter than dripping honey down the throat it spreads in men's hearts' for it is accompanied by a certain pleasure, for this reason first, and also because men dwell upon the thought of revenge, and the vision that rises before us produces the same pleasure as one seen in dreams.[38]

Hence anger is neither an exclusively positive nor an exclusively negative emotion. Anger is of course painful, but also involves the expectation of 'sweet' revenge. In addition, Aristotle's conception of anger had a temporal dimension: anger had an endpoint, whereas hatred had no end and was temporally unlimited. The power of imagination is also an element of anger: revenge is sweet, and the sweetness of revenge is something imagined; here, expectation blossoms in the domain of imagination.

Aristotle generally associated *pathē* with the world of imagination, providing the basis for further reflection upon aesthetics and feelings: is there any difference between the sympathy I feel for someone whom I rush to assist after he falls off his bike, and that which I feel for Oliver Twist, the hero of a novel? And if so, in what way? Can emotional reactions to 'real' events that affect me directly be compared or even equated with emotional reactions to cultural products such as novels, films, or computer games? And what has that got to do with my fear of spiders, keeping me captive in a windowless room? Aristotle considers that feelings devoid of any connection with reality—the pure products of *phantasia*—have a lesser force than feelings which are related in some way with the real world.[39]

In fact, *pathē* was used first by Plato (424/3–348/7 BC) and his pupil Aristotle to refer to circumstances that originated of themselves. This had not always been so. 'Homer's literary figures saw themselves as more or less helpless in the face of the power of feelings', and the pre-Socratic philosophers also defined emotions as something that was external, and not something produced within men themselves—the parallel here with the Maori warriors who attributed their fear to *atua*, noted above, is quite clear.[40] Perhaps it is because of the long shadow cast by Classical Greek theories of emotion that many of the metaphors we today use to express our feelings correspond to the idea that emotion is something external: we are 'overcome with rage', 'seized by pleasure', and 'love-struck'.[41] But this does not

[38] Aristotle, *'Art' of Rhetoric*, 173–5.
[39] Simo Knuuttila, *Emotions in Ancient and Medieval Philosophy* (Oxford: Clarendon Press, 2004), 37, 40.
[40] Christoph Demmerling and Hilge Landweer, *Philosophie der Gefühle: Von Achtung bis Zorn* (Stuttgart: Metzler, 2007), 2. See also Bruno Snell, *The Discovery of the Mind: The Greek Origins of European Thought*, trans. T. G. Rosenmayer (New York: Harper & Row, 1960) [Ger. orig., *Die Entdeckung des Geistes: Studien zur Entstehung des europäischen Denkens bei den Griechen*, 1946].
[41] 'We talk about being "paralyzed" by fear, "smitten" by love, "struck" by jealousy, "overwhelmed" by sadness, and being "made mad" with rage'; Robert C. Solomon, *True to Our Feelings: What Our Emotions Are Really Telling Us* (Oxford: Oxford University Press, 2007), 190. See, for a discussion of the philosophy of emotion in antiquity, Rüdiger Zill, *Meßkünstler und Rossebändiger: Zur Funktion von Metaphern und Modellen in philosophischen Affekttheorien*, PhD diss., Freie Universität Berlin, Berlin, 1994.

mean that Greek philosophers thought in terms of a unidirectional schema of stimulus and response that left no room for considerations of judgement and calculation. On the contrary: Aristotle defined fear as 'a painful or troubled feeling caused by the impression of an imminent evil that causes destruction or pain' and did not conceive this as an automatic (also physical) reaction to imagined future adversity, but instead as something which admitted the power of conviction, opinion, and belief to interrupt the course of emotion.[42] Aristotle would have traced my fear of the snake I saw in the woods to the imagined harm I suffered from the threat of its bite, but ascribed to me the capacity of suppressing any preprogrammed emotion before it started because I had, as a 6-year-old visiting the terrarium in the Boston Zoo, developed a real love of snakes, or stopping it because as a 40-year-old I had engaged in behavioural therapy that kept my phobia in check.

Besides that, because of their inherent element of judgement Aristotelian emotions can be altered not only in oneself, but in others as well, especially the young. In Aristotle's eyes the young needed to develop their feelings so that proper judgement became second nature.[43] Those philosophers associated with Stoicism agreed with Aristotle until it came to the element of judgement in his definition of emotion.[44] They went their own way once it came to the education of young people: their pantheism led them to emphasize the bigger picture and the irrelevance of emotion. The aim was to achieve an emotionless or calm state of apathy (*apatheia*), followed by ataraxia.[45] Love and marriage were to be avoided because of their relative lack of significance in their general pantheistic perspective. This form of control over emotion echoed long afterwards—the Roman emperor Marcus Aurelius (121–180) wrote about the ataraxic ideal in his *Meditations* and above all recommended that politicians be calm, while the American philosopher Martha Nussbaum, who sees herself as a 'neo-Stoic', consequently has an understanding of emotion that lays emphasis upon one's own well-being—hence the Stoic emphasis on peace of mind—but she still views emotion as 'appraisal'.[46]

---

[42] Aristotle, *'Art' of Rhetoric*, 201. See also Knuuttila, *Emotions in Ancient and Medieval Philosophy*, 35, 37.

[43] A. W. Price, 'Emotions in Plato and Aristotle', in Peter Goldie (ed.), *The Oxford Handbook of Philosophy of Emotion* (Oxford: Oxford University Press, 2010), 121–42, here 137–8.

[44] The Stoics who were most interested in emotion were Zeno of Kition (*c*.333/2–262/1 BC), Chrysippos (281/276–208/204 BC), Poseidonios (135–51 BC), Seneca (*c*.1–65), and Epiktetos (*c*.50–*c*.125). See e.g. on the Stoics and their attitude to emotion Richard Sorabji, *Emotion and Peace of Mind: From Stoic Agitation to Christian Temptation: The Gifford Lectures* (Oxford: Oxford University Press, 2000); Margaret R. Graver, *Stoicism and Emotion* (Chicago: University of Chicago Press, 2007); Barbara Guckes (ed.), *Zur Ethik der älteren Stoa* (Göttingen: Vandenhoeck & Ruprecht, 2004); but also the older text by Maximilian Forschner, *Die stoische Ethik: Über den Zusammenhang von Natur-, Sprach- und Moralphilosophie im altstoischen System* (2nd edn, Darmstadt: Wissenschaftliche Buchgesellschaft, 1995).

[45] On ataraxia and apathy see Joachim Ritter (ed.), *Historisches Wörterbuch der Philosophie*, i (Basel: Schwabe, 1971), 429–33, 593.

[46] Martha Nussbaum, *Upheavals of Thought: The Intelligence of Emotions* (Cambridge: Cambridge University Press, 2001), 4–5, ch. 1. Nussbaum goes beyond the Stoics in detail, admitting to animals the capacity of emotion. She generally distinguishes between a descriptive and a normative Stoic programme, embracing the former and rejecting the latter. See Jules Evans, 'An Interview with Martha

	Hot Strong Will	Cold Weak Will
Dry Strong Feelings	Yellow Gall Choleric: irritable	Black Gall Melancholic: sad and reflective
Wet Weak Feelings	Blood Sanguine: lively and active	Passive Phlegmatic: passive and difficult

Fig. 2 Galen's Doctrine of the Four Fluids and The Related Emotional Types

In the course of the second century AD a Greek physician emerged who had been influenced by Plato and whose ideas of emotion influenced generations of Arabic and European physicians, right up to the Italian Renaissance. Galen (*c.*130–*c.*200) put forward a doctrine of human temperament which ascribed particular properties to blood, phlegm, yellow gall, and black gall.[47] Galen thought that an excess of one of these fluids caused one's humour to belong to one particular sphere (see Fig. 2).

Galen did not see any therapeutic potential in chemical or physical media, but instead in moral education and moderation. His doctrine of the four fluids, and especially the related pathology of humours (choleric, sanguine, melancholic, and phlegmatic)—hence the characteristics of external, excess emotions—can still be found, albeit in modified form, in the writings of Immanuel Kant and also those of some psychologists of the late nineteenth and early twentieth centuries.[48]

Fundamental to most thought about emotion since Plato has been the idea of a tripartite soul. Plato considered that the soul was formed by rational (*logistikon*), spirited (*thymoeides*), and appetitive (*epithymetikon*) elements. This idea was modified by Aristotle and the Stoics, but most lastingly by Augustine (354–430), who was influenced by early Christian writings on emotion.[49] Augustine created a hierarchical, staged model of souls, where the lowest stage was purely vegetative and physical, and the highest stage, the seventh, was beatitude or divine epiphany.[50] The top two stages were reserved for men. Augustine also replaced the Aristotelian and Stoic division of the emotional process—which conceives of it as a more physical initial movement (*primus motus*) and a second, cognitive and moral

Nussbaum', *Philosophy for Life* (5 February 2009) <http://philosophyforlife.org/an-interview-with-martha-nussbaum/> accessed 21 February 2014.

[47] For an introduction to Galen's doctrine of the four fluids see Jutta Kollesch and Diethard Nickel (eds), *Antike Heilkunst: Ausgewählte Texte aus den medizinischen Schriften der Griechen und Römer* (Stuttgart: Reclam, 1994), 25–7.

[48] Rosenwein, *Emotional Communities in the Early Middle Ages*, 41; Knuuttila, *Emotions in Ancient and Medieval Philosophy*, 93–8; Sorabji, *Emotion and Peace of Mind*, 253–60.

[49] See on these early Christian monks, the so-called Desert Fathers, and their ideas about emotion: Rosenwein, *Emotional Communities in the Early Middle Ages*, 46–50.

[50] Dixon, *From Passions to Emotions*, 34.

evaluation—with a unitary category of the emotions (*motus*) subordinated to the will:

> What is important here is the quality of a man's will. For if the will is perverse, the emotions will be perverse; but if it is righteous, the emotions will be not only blameless, but praiseworthy. The will is engaged in all of them; indeed, they are all no more than acts of the will. For what is desire and joy but an act of will in agreement with what we wish for? And what is fear and grief but an act of will in disagreement with what we do not wish for?[51]

However, because of original sin, man's will generally guides him in the wrong direction. Only he who had accepted God's mercy and oriented his will to the fixed point of God could render his feelings positive. In this Augustine's ideas fundamentally conflicted with those of Classical Greek philosophers. For unlike the Stoics, whose pantheistic conceptions led them to discover the divine in earth and nature, Augustine located divinity in an unreachable, transcendent sphere. For him, emotions were thus oriented towards life after death. Everything temporal, including the human body, was defiled and transitory.[52] This was quite different to Aristotle, for whose thought the emotional and the cognitive were inseparable. Augustine had thus already anticipated the duality of emotion and reason for which Descartes is usually blamed.[53] And as a further contrast with the Stoics, whose ideal for life was emotional serenity, Augustine welcomed emotionality in life, so long as it was subordinated to the will and aimed at divinity.[54]

Emotional thinking during the Middle Ages is not so well researched as that in antiquity, and furthermore had little influence on subsequent centuries; the Scholastics, and in particular Thomas Aquinas (1225–74), are usually treated as an appendix to Aristotle and Augustine.[55] It is always said that René Descartes (1596–1650) was the real innovator. He is not only regarded as the most influential philosopher of modernity, but as the founder of dualism, above all of mind–body

---

[51] Augustine, *The City of God against the Pagans*, ed. and trans. R. W. Dyson (Cambridge: Cambridge University Press, 1998) [Lat. orig., *De civitate dei*, 426], 590.

[52] Rosenwein, *Emotional Communities in the Early Middle Ages*, 50–1.

[53] Robert C. Solomon, *The Passions: Emotions and the Meaning of Life* (Indianapolis: Hackett, 1993). According to Thomas Dixon, Robert Solomon is wrong to hold Christian thinkers like Augustine and Thomas Aquinas responsible for the separation of emotion and reason. In fact, they dealt in terms of passion and reason, in which reason, just like passion, could be 'moved' (*motus*), although this was only as a positive movement such as love; Dixon, *From Passions to Emotions*, 53–4.

[54] Augustine dealt with voluntaristic control of emotion autobiographically in his *Confessions*, which for the most part concerns his efforts to repress his own lust (*libido*); Dixon, *From Passions to Emotions*, 51–2.

[55] An introduction to medieval emotional thinking can be found in Peter King, 'Emotions in Medieval Thought', in Goldie (ed.), *Oxford Handbook of Philosophy of Emotion*, 167–87; Knuuttila, *Emotions in Ancient and Medieval Philosophy*, chs. 3–4; Piroska Nagy and Damien Boquet (eds), *Le Sujet des émotions au Moyen Âge* (Paris: Beauchesne, 2009), esp. pt. I. On Thomas Aquinas see Nicholas E. Lombardo, *The Logic of Desire: Aquinas on Emotion* (Washington, DC: Catholic University of America, 2011). On the medieval and early modern periods, from Thomas Aquinas to Descartes and Spinoza, see Dominik Perler, *Transformationen der Gefühle: Philosophische Emotionstheorien 1270–1670* (Frankfurt am Main: Fischer, 2011).

dualism, which also involved a contrast between emotion and reason.[56] His 'I think, therefore I am' is often understood in this way, as, for example, in this statement from the neuroscientist Antonio Damasio, who summarizes *Descartes' Error* (the title of his best-seller) in this way:

> Taken literally, the statement illustrates precisely the opposite of what I believe to be true about the origins of mind and about the relation between mind and body. It suggests that thinking, and awareness of thinking, are the real substrates of being. And since we know that Descartes imagined thinking as an activity quite separate from the body, it does celebrate the separation of mind, the 'thinking thing' (*res cogitans*), from the nonthinking body, that which has extension and mechanical parts (*res extensa*). . . . This is Descartes' error: the abyssal separation between body and mind, between the sizable, dimensioned, mechanically operated, infinitely divisible body stuff, on the one hand, and the unsizable, undimensioned, unpush-pullable, nondivisible mind stuff; the suggestion that reasoning, and moral judgment, and the suffering that comes from physical pain or emotional upheaval might exist separately from the body. Specifically: the separation of the most refined operations of mind from the structure and operation of a biological organism.[57]

Recently it has been argued against this position that Descartes, by rationalizing God, by making Him the epitome of reason—clearly differentiating himself from Christian philosophers such as Augustine and Thomas Aquinas—likewise loaded reason with emotion. For example, he treated fear as an element of will, treating the control of fear not as the suppression of passion, but as the victory of one passion over another: 'useful thoughts designed to generate one passion (e.g. courage) to counteract another (e.g. fear)'.[58] All the same, such revisionism should not distract from the sheer novelty of Descartes, as when he announces in *The Passions of the Soul* his intention of investigating emotions as 'a physician' and separating them from the soul, so that they might be studied as mechanisms, like all living organisms

---

[56] Nicolas Malebranche (1638–1715) radicalized the mind–body dualism. For his theory of emotion see Tad Schmaltz, 'Malebranche: Neigungen und Leidenschaften', in Hilge Landweer and Ursula Renz (eds), *Klassische Emotionstheorien: Von Platon bis Wittgenstein* (Berlin: de Gruyter, 2008), 331–49.

[57] Antonio R. Damasio, *Descartes' Error: Emotion, Reason, and the Human Brain* (New York: Putnam, 1994), 248–9. Various critics have noted that Damasio has used Descartes as a straw man, without taking account of studies of Descartes's work: see Henrik Lagerlund, 'Introduction: The Mind/Body Problem and Late Medieval Conceptions of the Soul', in Lagerlund (ed.), *Forming the Mind: Essays on the Internal Senses and the Mind/Body Problem from Avicenna to the Medical Enlightenment* (Dordrecht: Springer, 2007), 1–15; Timo Kaitaro, 'Emotional Pathologies and Reason in French Medical Enlightenment', in Lagerlund (ed.), *Forming the Mind*, 311–25.

[58] Deborah Brown, 'The Rationality of Cartesian Passions', in Henrik Lagerlund and Mikko Yrjönsuuri (eds), *Emotions and Choice from Boethius to Descartes* (Dordrecht: Kluwer Academic Publishers, 2002), 259–78, here 270. On Descartes's contribution, important but less original than usually assumed, see Anthony Levi, *French Moralists: The Theory of the Passions, 1585 to 1649* (Oxford: Clarendon Press, 1964). On the prehistory of the upgrading of emotions in early modernity see Wilhelm Dilthey, 'Die Funktion der Anthropologie in der Kultur des 16. und 17. Jahrhunderts', in *Gesammelte Schriften*, ii. *Weltanschauung und Analyse des Menschen seit Renaissance und Reformation* (6th edn Stuttgart: Teubner, 1960), 416–92.

(with the exception of the human soul).[59] He used the example of the finger of another person which is getting close to one's eye; even if our mind knows that this finger belongs to a friend, our body responds with the mechanisms of fear and self-protection, and we blink. In such a circumstance our mind proves useless, since 'the machine of our body is so formed that the movement of this hand towards our eyes excites another movement in our brain, which conducts the animal spirits into the muscles which cause the eyelids to close'.[60]

The court artist to Louis XIV, Charles Le Brun, also made use of Descartes's theory of emotion in his anatomical sketches of emotion, inaugurating a connection between emotion and medially represented (sketched, photographed, computer-generated) faces (and brains) that would prove enormously influential.[61] Le Brun created a sketched taxonomy of facial expression showing particular emotions that remained in use until the nineteenth century. But even in his lifetime critics argued that the ideal-typical faces were too static: they both lacked the processual character of emotion, and appeared simultaneously, rather than in clear succession. This objection, that emotion might not be treated in its pure forms, reappeared in the later twentieth century as a regular criticism of the theory of basic emotions.[62]

Baruch de Spinoza (1632–77) is often treated as the opposite of Descartes if the latter is understood as a dualist, and has in the last few years experienced a breathtaking renaissance in the study of embodiment in the social sciences, literary studies, and the study of images (see Chapter Three). This boom can be read out of the titles of Damasio's popular books, which run from the critical *Descartes' Error* to the affirmative *Looking for Spinoza*. It could be said that the alacrity with which the modern neurosciences have adopted Spinoza can be blamed upon the ambiguity and disorderliness of his thinking. One might also trace the Spinoza renaissance to his rejection of dualism—he is often called a monist because of his belief in a single divine substance—a rejection which leads him to see feeling and soul as two sides of the same reality. The connection in his main work, *Ethica: Ordine geometrico demonstrata* (1677; Eng. *Ethics*), of natural scientific, geometric reflection with emotional thinking is also a bonus that only adds to his attraction for literary

[59] René Descartes, 'Préface to "Passions de l'âme": Letter of Descartes to the editor, 14 August 1649', in Roger Ariew (ed.), *Descartes in Seventeenth-Century England*, ii. *Descartes's Works in Translation* (Bristol: Thoemmes Press, 2002), B3.

[60] Descartes, 'Préface to "Passions de l'âme" ', 37. The example is cited in Daniel M. Gross, *The Secret History of Emotion: From Aristotle's Rhetoric to Modern Brain Science* (Chicago: University of Chicago Press, 2006), 23.

[61] [Charles] Le Brun, *A Method to Learn to Design the Passions: Proposed in a Conference on the General and Particular Expression: Written in English, and Illustrated with a Great Many Figures Excellently Designed by M. Le Brun, Chief Painter to the French King, Chancellor and Director of the Royal Academy of Painting and Sculpture: Translated and all the Designs Engraved on Copper by, John Williams* (London: n.p., 1734) [1st Fr. edn 1698].

[62] Anne Schmidt, 'Showing Emotions, Reading Emotions', in Ute Frevert et al., *Emotional Lexicons: Continuity and Change in the Vocabulary of Feeling 1700–2000* (Oxford: Oxford University Press, 2014), 62–90. The mixed character of emotions is today emphasized by, amongst others, Kagan, *What Is Emotion?*

scholars interested in the neurosciences and for neuroscientists interested in literature.[63]

Spinoza considered that the mind, and hence also feelings, were part of nature; as
such, they obeyed generally valid laws:

> I shall, then, treat of the nature and strength of the emotions, and the mind's power
> over them, by the same method I have used in treating of God and the mind, and
> I shall consider human actions and appetites just as if it were an investigation into lines,
> planes, or bodies.[64]

He also divided feelings into actions and passions, such that actions have their
origin in us, while passions have an external origin. Self and the external are not
however categorically distinct, since both are part of nature. At the same time he
assumed there to be only three basic feelings: joy, sadness, and the higher feeling of
cupidity/desire (*cupiditas*). These building blocks in his treatment of feeling (as
elsewhere) were combined in a complicated manner into laws expressed as axiomatic aphorisms, such as

> Proposition 38: If anyone has begun to hate the object of his love to the extent that his
> love is completely extinguished, he will, other things being equal, bear greater hatred
> toward it, than if he had never loved it, and his hatred will be proportionate to the
> strength of his former love.[65]

The physical and law-like nature of these propositions gained the attention of
physiologists during the nineteenth century, and later the admiration of experimental psychologists.[66] The current fashion for Spinoza focuses in particular on
his monism. Writers in the social sciences and literary studies invoke him so that
they might valorize matter, whether these be everyday objects, trees, or Arctic
ice. Matter has feeling and ultimately agency just like the human being; hence
matter is also within range of our empathy and deserving of protection, even
requiring protection, something which makes these ideas attractive to ecological
projects and other post-Marxist political endeavours.[67] Social scientists and

---

[63] Baruch de Spinoza, 'Ethics', in *Spinoza: Complete Works*, ed. Michael L. Morgan, trans. Samuel
Shirley (Indianapolis: Hackett, 2002), 213–382.

[64] Spinoza, 'Ethics', 278. On Spinoza in general see what remains the most complete compendium
of thought on emotion in one volume, even if it is organized according to the perspective of 1930s
experimental psychology (two of the authors were psychologists): H. M. [*sic* Harry Norman] Gardiner,
Ruth Clark Metcalf, and John G. Beebe-Center, *Feeling and Emotion: A History of Theories* (New York:
American Book Company, 1937), 192–205. See also Steven Nadler, 'Baruch Spinoza', in Edward
N. Zalta (ed.), *The Stanford Encyclopedia of Philosophy (Spring 2011 Edition)* <http://plato.stanford.
edu/archives/spr2011/entries/spinoza> accessed 22 February 2014.

[65] Spinoza, 'Ethics', 298.

[66] See e.g. the physiologist Johannes Müller, *Handbuch der Physiologie des Menschen: Für
Vorlesungen*, ii (Koblenz: Hölscher, 1840), 543–52.

[67] See Jane Bennett, *Vibrant Matter: A Political Ecology of Things* (Durham, NC: Duke University
Press, 2010), x–xi: 'I try to bear witness to the vital materialities that flow through and around us.
Though the movements and effectivity of stem cells, electricity, food, trash, and metals are crucial to
political life (and human life per se), almost as soon as they appear in public (often at first by disrupting
human projects or expectations), these activities and powers are represented as human mood, action,
meaning, agenda, or ideology. This quick substitution sustains the fantasy that "we" really are in charge

literary scholars are also attracted to monism because it makes possible the embodiment of thought processes.[68]

Neuroscientists also took an interest in Spinoza's monism since they saw in it an anticipation of their own work, for example, in the idea 'That mind and body are parallel and mutually correlated processes, mimicking each other at every crossroad, as two faces of the same thing', and 'That deep inside these parallel phenomena there is a mechanism for representing body events in the mind'.[69] Spinoza can also be assimilated to evolutionary theory and the idea of homeostasis—that living beings seek to maintain themselves in existence—and neuroscience has also endorsed his theory of virtue: it can be said that 'We have to work hard at formulating and perfecting the human decree but to some extent our brains are wired to cooperate with others in the process of making the decree possible'.[70] In a word: Spinoza was 'the protobiologist'.[71]

Thomas Hobbes (1588–1679) never wrote a separate text on the emotions, but he constantly referred to emotions in his writing, from his early *Elements of Law, Natural and Politic* through *Leviathan* to *De Homine*: 'No writer of the period attributes to them such significance for the whole life of man as he.'[72] Hobbes described the state of nature as a terrible living-out of passions: 'no Arts; no Letters; no Society; and which is worst of all, continuall feare, and danger of violent death;

---

of all those "its"—its that, according to the tradition of (nonmechanistic, nonteleological) materialism I draw on, reveal themselves to be potentially forceful agents. Spinoza stands as a touchstone for me in this book, even though he himself was not quite a materialist. I invoke his idea of conative bodies that strive to enhance their power of activity by forming alliances with other bodies, and I share his faith that everything is made of the same substance.... This same-stuff claim, this insinuation that deep down everything is connected and irreducible to a simple substrate, resonates with an *ecological sensibility*, and that too is important to me.' Emphasis in original.

[68] See William E. Connolly, *Neuropolitics: Thinking, Culture, Speed* (Minneapolis: University of Minnesota Press, 2002), 7–8: 'Humans, as embodied, thinking beings, form two irreducible perspectives on themselves. Spinoza introduced this view, treating thought and extension as two aspects of the same substance rather than two kinds of stuff from which the universe is composed. I adopt a modified version of Spinoza's "parallelism" ... In my judgment, neither that thesis nor those contending against it have been proved. But a modified Spinozism can marshal points in its favor. First, it expresses the understanding of those who contend that human life evolved from lower forms without divine intervention, and it does so without reducing human experience to third-person accounts of it. Second, it encourages cultural theorists to explore accumulating evidence of significant correlations between the observation of body/brain processes and the lived experience of thinking. Third, it encourages us to come to terms actively with a variety of *techniques*—many of which already operate in everyday life—that can stimulate changes in thinking without adopting a reductionist image of thought in doing so. Fourth, it allows us to explore how thinking itself can sometimes modify the microcomposition of body/brain processes, as a new pattern of thinking becomes infused into body/ brain processes. For, as Gerald Edelman and Giulio Tonino, two leading neuroscientists, put the point pithily, "Neurons that fire together wire together." The version of parallelism adopted here encourages exploration of opaque, ubiquitous relations between technique and thinking without reducing the experience of thinking itself to a series of observational states. It appreciates the complexity of thinking while encouraging us to deploy technique to become more thoughtful. Technique is part of culture, and thinking is neurocultural.' Emphasis in original.

[69] Damasio, *Looking for Spinoza*, 217. Other life scientists who invoke Spinoza are listed in the same work, 300 n. 7.

[70] Damasio, *Looking for Spinoza*, 173–4. [71] Damasio, *Looking for Spinoza*, 14.

[72] Gardiner, Metcalf, and Beebe-Center, *Feeling and Emotion*, 184.

and the life of man, solitary, poore, nasty, brutish, and short'.[73] But this condition involved a hope: that for a short while this living-out of passions and fear balanced each other, and made rational decisions possible. This equilibrium, Hobbes argued, came from the social contract, which was the only means for humankind to escape the state of nature.

For Hobbes all feelings were bodily manifestations, connected to the will and directed at external objects. There were only two directions for such movements: towards an object, appetite; or away from an object, aversion. If we neither desire nor are averse to an object we despise it and keep our body (our heart) in between the two movements. The two directions create a short catalogue of 'simple' emotions, such as love, sorrow, and joy, and, when combined with other factors, an endless catalogue of further emotions.[74] With Hobbes, we need to bear in mind that 'His main interest . . . is not psychological analysis, but the development of a conception of human nature which would explain men's actions and afford an intelligible basis for civil institutions and political government'.[75]

The eighteenth-century Scottish moral philosophers reacted to Hobbes and his adversary John Locke (1632–1704) in elaborating a system of moral sentiments, introducing a conception of empathy that remains much discussed today. Anthony Ashley-Cooper, Earl of Shaftesbury (1671–1713), closely connected to the Scottish moral philosophers, inquired into the utility of emotions, and treated them in a far more relational manner than Hobbes. For Hobbes, one part of the emotions, natural affections, was directed mainly to one's fellow beings, whereas unnatural affections were antisocial, involving only one's own advantage.[76] In contrast to Hobbes, Shaftesbury also saw that in human nature 'virtue and interest may be found at last to agree'.[77] Emotions were valuable a priori, and the pursuit of happiness has to be understood in accordance with this. The different feelings men had related to one another like the 'strings of a musical instrument', which strived for natural harmony.[78]

Francis Hutcheson (1694–1746) went one step further. Also a moral philosopher, he considered that emotions were 'by Nature ballanced against each other,

---

[73] Thomas Hobbes, *Leviathan*, ed. Richard Tuck (rev. edn, Cambridge: Cambridge University Press, 1996), 89.

[74] Hobbes, *Leviathan*, ch. 6. Generally, Hobbes's treatment of emotion is scattered through a number of texts: chs. 7, 9, and 12 of *The Elements of Law, Naturals and Politic* (1640/50); *De Cive* (1642); chs. 6 and 13 of *Leviathan* (1651); ch. 25.12–13 of *De Corpore* (1655); ch. 11 of *De Homine* (1658).

[75] Gardiner, Metcalf, and Beebe-Center, *Feeling and Emotion*, 187–8.

[76] In addition, Shaftesbury 'for the first time discovered feeling as a unique and independent capacity or sentiment. He considered feelings—contrary to his teacher John Locke—not as something deriving from sensations and reflections, but as a mental phenomenon *sui generis*'; Angelica Baum and Ursula Renz, 'Shaftesbury: Emotionen im Spiegel reflexiver Neigung', in Landweer and Renz (eds), *Klassische Emotionstheorien*, 351–69, here 353.

[77] Anthony Ashley-Cooper, 3rd Earl of Shaftesbury, *Characteristics of Men, Manners, Opinions, Times*, ed. Lawrence E. Klein (Cambridge: Cambridge University Press, 1999), 167.

[78] Gardiner, Metcalf and Beebe-Center, *Feeling and Emotion*, 212.

like the *Antagonistic Muscles* of the Body'.[79] David Hume, who described himself as a 'pagan' philosopher, made the passions into something that controlled reason: 'reason is, and ought only to be the slave of the passions, and can never pretend to any other office than to serve and obey them'.[80] For Hume, reason had in itself no particular 'evaluative and representational content', so that even a murder can be thoroughly rational.[81] A murder only became immoral once our passions were engaged. Hume himself emphasized that

> Tis not contrary to reason to prefer the destruction of the whole world to the scratching of my finger. Tis not contrary to reason for me to chuse my total ruin, to prevent the least uneasiness of an Indian or person wholly unknown to me. Tis as little contrary to reason to prefer even my own acknowledg'd lesser good to my greater, and have a more ardent affection for the former than the latter.[82]

Besides the passions as an instance that controlled reason there was another strand of Hume's thinking on emotion, one that has recently gained an increasing amount of attention: that of sympathy. According to Hume, sympathy works as a process whose complexity is only imperfectly grasped by the medical metaphor of 'contagion': if we observe external signs of emotion in our fellow men (tears, for example, when someone is sorrowful), we construct a mental image of the feelings experienced by this person which can enter into association with one's own feelings and so in turn give rise to feelings that can determine our own action (for example, giving the person a hug to comfort them).[83] This area of Hume's thinking about emotion, together with that of Adam Smith (1723–90), today casts a lengthy shadow extending from philosopher Max Scheler's idea of 'emotional contagion', to the conception of emotional intelligence advanced by John Mayer and Peter Salovey and popularized by Daniel Goleman, as well as to contemporary Theory of Mind and neuroscientific research on mirror neurons.[84]

With the arrival of the Enlightenment the emotional scenery was shifted once more. The canonization of reason demanded sacrifices, and the strict separation of reason and feeling was one such sacrifice. Consequently emotion was defined as

---

[79] Francis Hutcheson, *An Essay on the Nature and Conduct of the Passions and Affections: With Illustrations on the Moral Sense*, ed. Aaron Garrett (Indianapolis: Liberty Fund, 2002), 119, emphasis in original.

[80] David Hume, *A Treatise of Human Nature: Being an Attempt to Introduce the Experimental Method of Reasoning into Moral Subjects*, ii. *Of the Passions* (London: John Noon/Thomas Longman, 1739), 248 (pt. 3, sect. 3).

[81] Sabine A. Döring, 'Allgemeine Einleitung: Philosophie der Gefühle heute', in Döring (ed.), *Philosophie der Gefühle* (Frankfurt am Main: Suhrkamp, 2009), 12–65, here 16. For Hume as a 'self-styled "pagan" philosopher' see Solomon, *True to our Feelings*, 100.

[82] Hume, *Treatise of Human Nature*, ii. 249–50 (pt. 3, sect. 3).

[83] Rachel Cohon, 'Hume's Moral Philosophy', in Edward N. Zalta (ed.), *The Stanford Encyclopedia of Philosophy (Fall 2010 Edition)* <http://plato.stanford.edu/archives/fall2010/entries/hume-moral> accessed 22 February 2014.

[84] Max Scheler, *The Nature of Sympathy*, trans. Peter Heath (New Brunswick, NJ: Transaction, 2008), 14–17; Peter Salovey and John D. Mayer, 'Emotional Intelligence', *Imagination, Cognition and Personality*, 9/3 (1989–90), 185–211; Daniel Goleman, *Emotional Intelligence: Why It Can Matter More Than IQ* (New York: Bantam Books, 1995). On Theory of Mind and mirror neurons see Chapter Three.

unreason, celebrated as such by some, damned as such by others. The former camp held sway during the Age of Sentimentalism (*c.*1720–1800), during which Jean-Jacques Rousseau (1712–78) became the pathfinder for a cult of emotional authenticity. He took the view that men in the ideal state were naturally equal and unsullied by the lamentable influence of culture. As he wrote in his novel *Émile*, 'The man who has lived the most is not he who has counted the most years but he who has most felt life.'[85] The formation of feeling thus signified the reintroduction of man to his original state, leading him away from the influences of culture. It was therefore no wonder that Rousseau agitated against the expression of feeling in the theatre, which was simulated and therefore inauthentic. In addition, the feelings represented by actors addressed those of the audience in a dangerous manner. Since 'all the passions are sisters and one alone suffices for arousing a thousand', the social body was threatened with overstimulation and, ultimately, loss of self-control.[86]

This Enlightenment separation of reason and feeling was most clearly expressed in the work of Immanuel Kant (1724–1804)—and, unlike with Rousseau, in a strongly negative fashion. Kant never developed a coherent theory of feeling, but he did talk a great deal about emotion and, towards the end of his life, ascribed it a significant place as the Other of reason. His first thoughts about moral sentiments were linked to Hume, but from the 1790s on he adopted a distinctly anti-emotional standpoint, expressing *emotio* and *ratio* as a binary opposition that has survived to this day. In his 1798 *Anthropologie in pragmatischer Hinsicht* (Eng., *Anthropology from a Pragmatic Point of View*, 1974) he subdivided emotion into affects and passions, defining emotion as beyond the control of reason, thus uncoupling it from any kind of ethics. For Kant, affect was something sudden, 'the feeling of a pleasure or displeasure in the subject's present state that does not let him rise to *reflection* (the representation by means of reason as to whether he should give himself up to it or refuse it)'.[87] Whereas affects could become a 'temporary surrogate of reason', passions lay far beyond the range of an ethics governed by reason: an 'Inclination that can be conquered only with difficulty or not at all by the subject's reason is *passion*'.[88] This meant for Kant that being 'subject to affects and passions is probably always an *illness of the mind*, because both affect and passion shut out the sovereignty of reason'.[89] Inner freedom was founded upon self-control,

[85] Jean-Jacques Rousseau, *Emile, or, On Education (Includes Emile and Sophie, or, The Solitaries)*, trans. and ed. Christopher Kelly and Allan Bloom (Lebanon, NH: Dartmouth College Press, 2010) [Fr. orig., *Émile, ou de l'éducation*, 1762], 167.

[86] Jean-Jacques Rousseau, 'J. J. Rousseau, Citizen of Geneva, to M. d'Alembert: Letter to d'Alembert on the Theater', in *Letter to d'Alembert and Writings for the Theater*, trans. and ed. Allan Bloom, Charles Butterworth, and Christopher Kelly (Hanover, NH: University Press of New England, 2004), 251–352, here 265. See also Sidonia Blättler, 'Rousseau: Die Transformation der Leidenschaften in soziale Gefühle', in Landweer and Renz (eds), *Klassische Emotionstheorien*, 435–56, esp. 440–1.

[87] Immanuel Kant, *Anthropology from a Pragmatic Point of View*, trans. and ed. Robert B. Louden (Cambridge: Cambridge University Press, 2006), 149, emphasis in original.

[88] Kant, *Anthropology from a Pragmatic Point of View*, 152, 149, emphasis in original.

[89] Kant, *Anthropology from a Pragmatic Point of View*, 149, emphasis in original.

and nothing was such a threat to this as feelings.[90] In a word: 'no human being wishes to have passion. For who wants to have himself put in chains when he can be free?'[91]

What is emotion? This outline of responses by important writers to this question must break off here. From about 1800 on there was a steadily expanding pool of writing concerning emotion in different disciplines, which will be examined in the following chapters: history (Chapter One), anthropology (Chapter Two), and experimental psychology (Chapter Three), the latter two being newly founded around the turn of the nineteenth century. Since then, philosophy has retained its interest in emotions: Arthur Schopenhauer (1788–1860), Søren Kierkegaard (1813–55), Friedrich Nietzsche (1844–1900), Martin Heidegger (1889–1976), and Jean-Paul Sartre (1905–80), to name but a few, were joined in the past two decades by a rapidly developing analytic philosophy of emotion, all of which have contributed to an understanding of feelings in a way that permeates the following chapters. It should also be said that this is no more than a sketch, and that there is every reason for work to develop quickly in this or that area if theories of emotion from the past are examined with a greater degree of intensity. Quite apart from this, a sketch of this kind provides very little indication of the relevance of emotion to everyday thinking in their contemporary cultures and periods. For example, ancient history has only just begun to move the study of Greek emotional culture beyond the work of Plato and Aristotle, using hitherto unused stone, clay, and papyrus sources.[92]

2 WHO HAS EMOTION?

This review of philosophical thought on emotion demonstrates that not all persons are thought capable of feeling to the same extent, and in the same way; as with Aristotle, for example, who made youths the object of the deliberate inculcation of feeling, having to practise proper judgement until it became second nature. No attention was paid to the question of whether animals might or might not be capable of feelings.[93] Today it is usual to treat feelings as something common to all humans, inherent and intimate, the inner sanctum of autonomy, the site in which human subjectivity crystallizes in its purest form. The generation and stabilization

[90] 'But two things are required for inner freedom: being one's own master in a given case (*animus sui compos*), and ruling oneself (*imperium in semetipsum*), that is, subduing one's affects and governing one's passions'; Immanuel Kant, *The Metaphysics of Morals*, trans. and ed. Mary Gregor (Cambridge: Cambridge University Press, 1996) [Ger. orig., *Metaphysik der Sitten*, 1797], 166.

[91] Kant, *Anthropology from a Pragmatic Point of View*, 151.

[92] Since 2009 a research group in Oxford, originally formed around the ancient historian Angelos Chaniotis (now Institute for Advanced Study, Princeton), has studied these: *The Social and Cultural Construction of Emotions: The Greek Paradigm*. For a first volume from this group see Angelos Chaniotis (ed.), *Sources and Methods for the Study of Emotions in the Greek World* (Stuttgart: Steiner, 2012).

[93] See, in regard to Aristotle, Amélie Oksenberg Rorty, 'Structuring Rhetoric', in Amélie Oksenberg Rorty (ed.), *Essays on Aristotle's Rhetoric* (Berkeley and Los Angeles: University of California Press, 1996), 1–33, here 18–19; Konstan, *Emotions of the Ancient Greeks*, 22.

of such unique qualities requires marking off, distinctions, differences—in short, the production of an Other. The production of this Other has left textual traces whose variety and extent is owed to the fact that the process of production is never completed—it remains unfinished, unstable, seeking to create ever new differences. Anyone who seeks an answer to the question 'who feels?' would do well to consider the textual traces of this production of the Other. Here we will consider two: first of all, the distinction between human and animal, and then the differentiation between humans and humanoid machines.

There is a long tradition of associating animals with the body and emotion, and humans with mind and reason. Using as a source German-language dictionaries, the historian Pascal Eitler has shown how increasingly difficult it became, from the late eighteenth century on, to sustain this tradition unbroken. In 1745, for example, *Zedler*, the most important of eighteenth-century dictionaries, made a distinction between 'sensations' (*Empfindungen*) on the one hand, and 'feelings' (*Gefühle*) and 'affect' (*Affekte*) on the other. Animals were thought to be capable of perceiving sensations, but feelings and affect were reserved for human beings alone: 'beasts are free of all of these [feelings]. They can sense present things; but they lack reflection and consideration, which is why they cannot be much moved by affect.'[94] Eitler argues that fifty years later, at the zenith of Sentimentalism, the concept of 'sensation' underwent a process of revaluation such that this boundary between human feeling/affect and animal sensation became porous.[95]

During the second half of the nineteenth century there were two new developments that destabilized the distinction of human from animal in respect to feelings. First of all, the theory of evolution placed in question the existence of any distinction between man and animal. Charles Darwin's *The Expression of the Emotions in Man and Animals* of 1872 drew parallels in the expression of feeling between visitors to his house and his own pets. Secondly, the rising science of physiology, including the physiology of emotion, conducted laboratory experiments on animals and from this developed far-reaching theories of emotion related to the brains and organs of animals, as some reactions that were observed came very close to those of humans. This led to a great debate over vivisection—surgical interventions on living animals—a debate which turned on the question of whether this practice harmed animal feelings. This also involved human feelings with respect to animals, in particular sympathy and empathy.[96] The line that distinguished human beings as feeling beings, and which separated them from animals, had to be repeatedly redrawn.

A similar process has taken place with humanoid machines—automata, robots, androids—as represented in cultural products such as novels and films. This also followed an uncertain path, and so has left useful textual traces in the form of a long tradition depicting humans who develop feelings for machines, and machines that

[94] Pascal Eitler, 'The "Origin" of Emotions—Sensitive Humans, Sensitive Animals', in Frevert et al., *Emotional Lexicons*, 91–117, here 95.
[95] Eitler, 'The "Origin" of Emotions', 98.
[96] Eitler, 'The "Origin" of Emotions', 99–105, 109.

develop their own emotional lives. As a literary tradition this goes back to E. T. A. Hoffmann's story *Der Sandmann* (1816; Eng. *The Sand-Man*), in which a young man loses his heart to a mechanical doll, continuing on to Mary Shelley's *Frankenstein* (1818), in which the monster created by a scientific experiment, an artificial human being, develops feelings. Humanoid machines are endemic in the history of film, for example in *Star Trek: The Next Generation* (1987–94), where Android Data's lack of emotion continually leads to strange decisions, or in Steven Spielberg's *A.I.: Artificial Intelligence* (2001), which deals with a deceptively human 11-year old robot in the twenty-second century who feels emotion, and who is loved by his human family, a love which is sustained until their own human son, who had been in a coma, wakes up.[97] This suggests that anyone who does not have some sort of feelings with regard to humanoid machines is somehow emotionally deficient, or not entirely human. Experimental psychologists have studied the capacity for empathy on experimental subjects, testing their sympathy for avatars by giving them painful electric shocks in a Milgram-type experimental situation:

> in spite of the fact that all participants knew for sure that neither the stranger nor the shocks were real, the participants who saw and heard her tended to respond to the situation at the subjective, behavioural and physiological levels as if it were real.[98]

Experiments of this kind often presume a conception of a mirror image, whereby I can only have sympathy if I can imagine that my other is similar to myself, a conception which in turn presupposes that I have an idea of my self. Since the mid-1990s neuroscientific research into mirror neurons has lent support to the rapid diffusion of this conception (see Chapter Three, Section 3). Ergo, my capacity for sympathy with other human beings, and also with inanimate humanoid objects, becomes the measure of my humanity per se.

There is an interesting side effect of this empathy with humanoid machines that has been observed: if the machine is too much like a human being, all empathy vanishes and is replaced by disgust. How one might go about designing a machine that maximizes sympathy without going too far and provoking disgust is therefore an entirely practical question—not only for engineers designing robots for daily use in household and personal care in ageing societies like Japan and Germany, but also for the makers of computer-animated films. The production team for the film *Shrek* (2001), for example, felt themselves constrained to render Princess Fiona less anthropomorphic 'because "she was beginning to look too real, and the effect

[97] Catrin Misselhorn, 'Empathy and Dyspathy with Androids: Philosophical, Fictional and (Neuro-)Psychological Perspectives', *Konturen*, 2 (2009), 101–23, here 101–2. See also Thomas Thiel, 'Fühlt die Maschine? Die Androidenrobotik an der Grenze zur Utopie', *Frankfurter Allgemeine Zeitung* (7 July 2010), N4; Wolfgang Gessner, Gesine Lenore Schiewer, and Alex Ringenbach, 'Why Androids Will Have Emotions: Constructing Human-Like Actors and Communicators Based on Exact Sciences of the Mind', in Denis Lalanne and Jürg Kohlas (eds), *Human Machine Interaction: Research Results of the MMI Program* (Heidelberg: Springer, 2009), 133–63.
[98] Mel Slater et al., 'A Virtual Reprise of the Stanley Milgram Obedience Experiments', *PLoS ONE*, 1/1 (2006), e39, here 1.

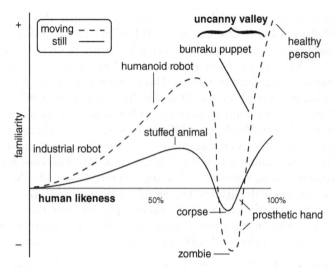

Fig. 3 Masahiro Mori and 'The Uncanny Valley'

Source: Simplified version of Mori's original graph in Karl F. MacDorman, 'Mortality Salience and the Uncanny Valley', *IEEE-RAS International Conference on Humanoid Robots*, Tsukuba, Japan (5–7 December 2005) [conference paper], 399–405 here 399.

was getting distinctly unpleasant"'.[99] The robot specialist Masahiro Mori identified this effect in 1970 and dubbed it 'uncanny valley', which is best presented as a graph (Fig. 3).[100]

The philosopher Catrin Misselhorn explains this phenomenon in analogy with faulty visual perception. The greater the degree to which man and machine share typical and apparent characteristics, the greater the identification of object and idea of the object. At the same time, habitual emotional dispositions with respect to this object are activated. Knowledge of the lack of authenticity also plays a role, something that switches off empathy. According to Misselhorn, this involves 'a kind of very fast oscillation between four situations': first, an object is perceived and the process of identification with an idea appropriate to the object triggered; then one enters the threshold where object and idea coincide; this coincidence misfires; the identification of object and idea is broken off, but is then initiated once more, because the object is still perceived. 'This reminds a bit of a radio receiver trying to tune into a transmitter in bad conditions when the reception of one station is always interfered with by another one and sheer noise.'[101] This interference is expressed emotionally as disgust.

[99] Cited in Misselhorn, 'Empathy and Dyspathy with Androids', 103.

[100] Masahiro Mori, 'The Uncanny Valley', trans. Karl F. MacDorman and Norri Kageki, *IEEE Robotics & Automation Magazine*, 19/2 (2012), 98–100 [Jap. orig., 'Bukimi no tani', 1970].

[101] Catrin Misselhorn, 'Empathy with Inanimate Objects and the Uncanny Valley', *Mind and Machines*, 19/3 (2009), 349–59, here 357.

So who has emotion? It should be clear that there is no definitive answer to this fundamental question. People in different times and different places have given varying responses to it, and to a great extent these answers allow us to make inferences about the ideas and feelings of these people—this is evident in the case of the distinction between the human and the animal, and in that of anthropomorphic machines. Answers to this question depend for the most part on the major asymmetries in human history—social differences, gender differences, ethnic differences. The indigenous peoples of European colonial empires, together with women and members of the lower social strata in Europe itself, were all in nineteenth-century Britain, Germany, and France assumed a priori to have different kinds of feeling. Instead of taking the question 'who feels?' as a point of departure, seeking apodictic clarification, we should make the historically changing responses to this question themselves the object of our investigation.

3 WHERE IS EMOTION?

The question of where emotions are localized is not trivial. If they are located outside humans, in spirits or gods, then men and women can become the playthings of transcendental forces, suddenly overwhelmed and just as suddenly freed from them. An idea of this kind is often associated with the sense that men and women have very little influence over feelings. So, for example, the volatile temperament of a North Cheyenne Native American Indian would be explained by her tribe by saying that she once looked out of her window at night, which is taboo among the North Cheyenne. The woman felt herself assailed by an alien force, and quickly fainted. When she came to, she was a different person.[102] If on the other hand emotions are located within the human body, these locations and the properties ascribed to them (for instance, those of an organ) have an effect upon the resulting theory of emotion. We have already seen this with Galen's pathology of humours, and the associated emotional prototypes—choleric, sanguine, melancholic, and phlegmatic.

This location of emotion in the body often has practical consequences. Since the Egyptians thought that the brain was responsible for the blood supply, and the heart for feelings, they thought nothing of introducing a hook into the brain through the nose during the mummification of a corpse, cutting the brain into pieces and then removing them through the nostrils with a spatula. The heart, on the other hand, was left in the body.[103] As opposed to the Egyptians, the neuroscientist Joseph LeDoux was the child of a time and place in which the brain is seen as being the centre of emotion, mind, and much more. As a small boy in Louisiana

---

[102] Anne S. Straus, 'Northern Cheyenne Ethnopsychology', *Ethos*, 5/3 (1977), 326–57, here 341–2.

[103] This practice was most widespread during the time of the New Kingdom, *c.*1569–1076 BC. See Ann Rosalie David, 'Mummification', in Donald B. Redford (ed.), *The Oxford Encyclopedia of Ancient Egypt*, ii (Oxford: Oxford University Press, 2001), 439–44, here 440–1.

he faltered when his father, a butcher, asked him to search by hand through the brain matter of a slaughtered cow for the bullet that had killed it. His father's customers 'were not fond of chomping down on lead while enjoying their sweet-breads'. Joseph found it very hard to run his 'fingers through a brain. You have to put aside any idea that the cow's brain was the home of the cow's mind, and just treat it as a piece of meat.'[104]

The location of emotion in the body also has consequences for its linguistic articulation, above all with respect to imagery and metaphor. As in many cultures, the Australian Pintupi aboriginals associate childhood with a presocial stage char-acterized by unchecked emotion, a limited ability to control oneself, a difficulty in foreseeing the consequences of one's own action, and a marked individualism instead of a consciousness of the self as part of a social network. Children are described as 'lacking knowledge', 'unselfconscious', also interestingly as 'deaf' (*patjarru, ramarama*). Why 'deaf'? Because for the Pintupi, thought is the key to maturation, a way out of wild emotionality; because 'thinking', 'understanding', and 'hearing' are for them all associated with one verb, *kulininpa*, which literally means 'to hear'; and because for them the sanctum of thought lies in the ear, whereas that of feeling is to be found in the stomach.[105]

We can also learn something from comparing ideas of the eye and its significance for emotion. In many languages, among them English and German, light serves as a metonym for happiness and contentment, and so a happy person is described as someone with 'bright' or 'shining' eyes. By contrast, the Chinese talk of 'stretched' or 'broadened eyebrows' (*yang-shou shen-mei*).[106] The precise way in which the Chinese describe eyebrows is found in very few other languages. To give only one example: *chou-mei bu-zhan* means 'brows contracted without relaxation' or 'knit-ting one's brows in anxiety'; *chou-mei ku-lian* means 'wear a worried look'; *yang-mei tu-qi* means 'feel elated after unburdening oneself of resentment'; *mei-fei se-wu* means 'with dancing eyebrows and radiant face—enraptured'.[107] In China eye-brows are the 'most obvious indicators of internal feelings', hence windows into the soul.[108]

At the same time there is no fixed relationship between the conception of emotion, including its localization, and its oral, written, aural, and imagistic representation; the relation is highly variable. So for instance, even where facial expression did play a great role in conceptions of the body, we find in the court painting of sixteenth- and seventeenth-century North Indian Islam no indication of the face as the site of emotion. Here the decisive means for the expression of feeling

---

[104] Joseph LeDoux, 'Brains Through the Back Door', in John Brockman (ed.), *Curious Minds: How a Child Becomes a Scientist* (New York: Pantheon Books, 2004),142.

[105] Fred R. Myers, *Pintupi Country, Pintupi Self: Sentiment, Place, and Politics among Western Desert Aborigines* (Washington, DC: Smithsonian Institution Press, 1986), 107.

[106] Ning Yu, 'Body and Emotion: Body Parts in Chinese Expression of Emotion', *Pragmatics and Cognition*, 10/1 (2002), 341–67, here 343.

[107] Yu, 'Body and Emotion', 345.

[108] Ning Yu, 'Metaphorical Expressions of Anger and Happiness in English and Chinese', *Metaphor and Symbolic Activity*, 10/2 (1995), 59–92, here 79. See also Zoltán Kövecses, *Metaphor and Emotion: Language, Culture, and Body in Human Feeling* (Cambridge: Cambridge University Press, 2000), 172.

was bodily movement, colour, brush-strokes, and pictorial composition.[109] More-over, the semantics of the bodily expression of emotion is rarely universal, but is instead ambiguous: while a smile in many cultures means pleasure and content-ment, it can also signify shame, a polite invitation for the initiation of contact, even a reaction to death or loss.[110]

And another thing: one should not treat that which is non-European as timeless. None of the examples introduced so far are set in stone. In his fieldwork in Tahiti during the 1960s, the anthropologist Robert Levy found that the majority of his interviewees supposed the origin of feelings to be in their abdomen, although a few talked of the heart, something which Levy attributed to Christian missionaries and Bible study.[111] The shift of emotion from one place to another in the body is always a question of historical knowledge. It would be quite wrong to think of the body as something timeless and pancultural. If one seeks to form a more exact sense of the construction of the body, the first issue is whether emotion is located outside the body (in spirits or gods for instance) or within it: is the body really just the plaything of transcendental influences, or are spirits within the body? With what kind of cosmology is the body bound up?

One does not even have to leave Europe to get an idea of the instability with which feelings are localized in the body. We need only go back to Descartes, who wrote in 1649 'that the last and most proximate cause of the passions of the soul is nothing other than the agitation with which the spirits move the little gland in the middle of the brain', meaning the pineal gland or the epiphysis.[112] David Hartley (1705–57), the founder of associationist psychology who sought to make a con-nection with John Locke and Isaac Newton (1642–1727), was positive that emotions were formed by external stimuli. He thought that they caused the medullary substance of the nerves to vibrate, a vibration that was then conveyed to the brain via 'ether', where the increasingly faint oscillations were felt as 'vibratiuncles'. Emotions were therefore 'vibratiuncles'.[113] And so it is evident that, even in the canonical Western culture, shifts in the localization of emotions in the human body can be very major. Following on from this, we could consider the reciprocal effects between the way emotions are localized and bodily move-ments, and in particular, those that are considered to be quite fundamental movements such as the heartbeat, the pulse, and gastric juices. Is it possible for

---

[109] Monica Juneja, 'Visualising Emotional States in Indian Court Painting of the Early Modern Period', Lecture at the Max Planck Institute for Human Development, Berlin (8 June 2009); Monica Juneja, 'Translating the Body into Image: The Body Politic and Visual Practice at the Mughal Court during the Sixteenth and Seventeenth Centuries', in Michaels and Wulf (eds), *Images of the Body in India*, 235–60, here 239, 243.

[110] William M. Reddy, *The Navigation of Feeling: A Framework for the History of Emotions* (Cambridge: Cambridge University Press, 2001), 101.

[111] Robert Levy, *Tahitians: Mind and Experience in the Society Islands* (Chicago: University of Chicago Press, 1973), 271.

[112] René Descartes, *The Passions of the Soul*, trans. Stehen M. Voss (Indianapolis: Hackett, 1989) [Fr. orig., *Les Passions de l'âme*, 1649], 50.

[113] Gardiner, Metcalf, and Beebe-Center, *Feeling and Emotion*, 222.

local conceptions of emotion to affect these bodily movements? If I come from a culture in which an accelerated pulse is treated as a sign of anger, does my pulse beat faster than it would if I had been socialized in a culture in which this was not the case? For the time being we shall leave this important question open, but we will return to it repeatedly.

4 DO EMOTIONS HAVE A HISTORY?

As we have seen with philosophical thinking about emotion, responses to the question of what emotions are have changed significantly over time. It could be objected that each response is only an answer to different conceptions and characterizations of something that has nonetheless remained constant in all eras. If this were true, emotions would have no history, only the conception of emotion would alter historically. Many theories at the universalistic end of the scale do claim exactly this: they do not dispute that emotions are conceptualized in different ways, but maintain that emotions possess a constant, transhistorical, and culturally generalized foundation. Fear in the face of the enemy would therefore be common to the Roman legionary, the medieval halberdiers, the private soldier on the Verdun battlefield, or the Congolese child soldier, and accompanied by the same physical signs: raised pulse, dilated pupils, thumping heart, cold sweat. The example of the Maori warrior who is freed of *atua* and goes fearlessly into battle does not contradict this, since the body's programmed response of fear is simply shifted to the period before battle, but is in itself no different to that experienced in all cultures and eras.

This might well be true. But it is also true that conceptions of emotion have an impact upon the way emotion is experienced in the self-perception of the feeling subject—the qualia, as it is called in psychology. In the instance of the Maori warrior the impact of the conception of emotion was so marked that he quite possibly did react fearlessly to stimuli assumed to be of a generally threatening character—the opponent facing him seeking to take his life. It is evidence of the power of a cultural framework to neutralize an inborn, automatically-triggered emotional response. Moreover, we have just heard of the key question regarding the reaction of local conceptions of emotion upon basic physical processes such as the pulse. Anticipating arguments to be introduced in Chapter Four of this book, we can here introduce a preliminary answer supplied by recent research in the neurological sciences and cognitive psychology, which has drawn attention to a feedback effect between the articulation of an 'emotional word' and the sensation of emotion. If I say 'I am happy', a mechanism of self-examination can be set in motion to determine whether I do really feel happy at this moment. This is an open-ended mechanism: this self-exploratory process of self-examination can conclude that I do not feel happy and so conflict with the expressed feeling; or I might come to the opposite conclusion and overwrite other emotions felt at the same time. The current vogue in popular psychology for Neuro-Linguistic Programming (NLP) is to a large extent based upon this latter postulate, as is counselling that founds everything upon the transformative power of verbalized feelings.[114] William Ian Miller, a legal theorist and a specialist in the emotions of Icelandic sagas, comments 'that once we name an emotion it takes on a life of its own'.[115]

Let us assume that the body presents us with real and insurmountable boundaries in the expression of emotion, that, for example, the fear of an opponent felt by a warrior in battle (or in the case of the Maori, before battle) can never be associated with a slowing pulse. What does this amount to? Since the human sciences are interested in cultural variability, the universal is often uninteresting, involving 'trivially true' universals.[116] Besides, what is universal amounts to a molehill when compared to the mountain of data on cultural difference. One characteristic of historical studies is that they emphasize this variety of emotional conceptions and cultural patterns. For the time being this will have to serve as an answer to the question of whether emotions have a history. This is the central question, and this book provides both a compendium of answers given by others, as well as an attempt to formulate its own.

5 WHAT SOURCES MIGHT WE USE IN WRITING THE HISTORY OF EMOTIONS?

At first sight it might seem that the history of emotions can only be written using sources in which people talk about their emotions. And since feelings have belonged to the domain of the inward and intimate since the Romantic era at the latest, these sources were not originally intended for publication. They have a marked relation to the self, and take the form of diaries, autobiographies, and memoirs. This can be extended to include private communication as a source, as in (love) letters, emails, text messages, or telephone conversations that (for instance) security services listen in to. This approach would render impossible the history of emotions across the centuries and cultures in which these sources did not exist, quite apart from the greater part of humanity that did not write. Fortunately we are not constrained in this way, since the history of emotions today uses almost all the sources available to historical study; and if there are limits, these limits are little different to those encountered in other historical subdisciplines.

This starts with archaeology, which is able to rely on very few written sources. Despite this, in recent years archaeologists have sought to establish how the emotions of historical actors in prehistoric and ancient epochs might be reconstructed; or more precisely, how we might describe the framework within which historical actors could have had emotions. Attempts are then made, for example, to

---

[114] See for this feedback mechanism Jan Plamper, 'The History of Emotions: An Interview with William Reddy, Barbara H. Rosenwein, and Peter Stearns', *History and Theory*, 49/2 (2010), 237–65, esp. 242.

[115] William Ian Miller, *The Anatomy of Disgust* (Cambridge, MA: Harvard University Press, 1997), 31.

[116] Gross, *Secret History of Emotion*, 34.

reconstruct the spatial organization of a burial site, then speculating upon the manner in which the spatial qualities of this site might have affected the feelings of those actors present at the rituals relating to the deceased.[117] Of course, such a procedure is built upon many presuppositions: first of all, it is assumed that Celts, Romans, or Mongolians did have feelings; second, that the spatial organization of the burial site did in some way influence Celts, Romans, and Mongolians. But archaeology is no stranger to such difficult issues, so that there is no basic objection to these new questions from the history of emotions.

The same is true from the sources of diplomatic history, which no longer defines itself as the history of the external affairs of a particular nation state. During the 1960s and 1970s social history had supposedly more or less killed off diplomatic history. But it survived, and has in the past couple of decades been reborn as the 'cultural history of diplomacy', a history that directs attention to the symbolic and ritual dimensions of diplomacy, and as international history, which researches the historical interweaving of persons and institutions of different countries.[118] If one looks closely then one cannot help but be struck by how prominent emotions are in the testimony of high international politics, meetings between kings and kaisers, between generals and general secretaries, between presidents and party leaders. For example, after Queen Victoria gave birth to an heir in 1841, her husband, Prince Albert, named Friedrich Wilhelm IV godparent. Friedrich Wilhelm consented, prompting protest from both Victoria's and Albert's families, who by age and relationship had precedence over the Prussian king, and who had been overlooked. Duke Ernst von Coburg, the German father of Victoria's husband Albert, wrote a letter in which he told his son that he did not understand

> why the King of Prussia has been granted this honour which, excuse me if I state it plainly, I find quite inappropriate; . . . Prussia [is] the *arch enemy of our House* . . . and, having swallowed half of all our hereditary possessions, constantly threatens to take the remainder. Moreover, the present king has shown himself most *disobliging, most arrogant*, and unjust in respect of our present demands . . . If it is therefore possible, I would there ask you to withdraw this matter, which must leave the most unpleasant impression in Germany, especially in the whole of Saxony. I must observe with deepest

---

[117] Sarah Tarlow, 'Emotion in Archaeology', *Current Anthropology*, 41/5 (2000), 713–46.

[118] See e.g. Akira Iriye, 'Culture and International History', in Michael J. Hogan and Thomas G. Paterson (eds), *Explaining the History of American Foreign Relations* (2nd edn, Cambridge: Cambridge University Press, 2004), 241–56; Ursula Lehmkuhl, 'Diplomatiegeschichte als internationale Kulturgeschichte: Theoretische Ansätze und empirische Forschung zwischen Historischer Kulturwissenschaft und Soziologischem Institutionalismus', *Geschichte und Gesellschaft*, 27/3 (2001), 394–423, referring explicitly to emotion on p. 414; Jessica C. E. Gienow-Hecht and Frank Schumacher (eds), *Culture and International History* (New York: Berghahn Books, 2003); Markus Mösslang and Torsten Riotte (eds), *The Diplomats' World: A Cultural History of Diplomacy, 1815–1914* (Oxford: Oxford University Press, 2008). In 2010 a conference on diplomacy was held in London which focused on emotion: see Heidi Mehrkens, Review of 'Persönliche Beziehungen zwischen Staatsmännern als Kategorie der Geschichte des Politischen (1815-1914)', H-Soz-u-Kult, H-Net Reviews (November 2010) <http://www.h-net.org/reviews/showrev.php?id=31864> accessed 23 February 2014.

sorrow how little regard you have shown for the *honour* and the *interests* of the House to which you belonged, and *still belong*.[119]

'Most arrogant' and 'unjust', 'sorrow' and 'honour': this is emotionally charged language in the correspondence of the European nobility, whose dynastic ties determined in so many ways the politics of the mid-nineteenth century. From the point of view of the history of emotions it would be worth examining the use of an emotional vocabulary in various types of official documents—in letters from one head of state to another, letters from a head of state to aristocratic relatives, diplomatic bags, ceremonial protocol, announcements to the press. Here we might not only consider the rhetorical use of sorrow or of honour, but also their locally specific constructions. Diplomatic sources, often written in a lingua franca such as French or English, but switching constantly into other languages, allow for a microscopic examination of the differences and disjunctions, ambiguities and misunderstandings between distinct cultures of emotion.[120]

Diplomatic rituals often involve honour, respect, and face-saving. In 1898 the president of France, Felix Fauré, paid a visit to Queen Victoria while she was staying near Nice. By that time she was nearly 80, and not in the best of health. For both parties the ceremonial greeting went badly, and the way this happened says a great deal about the emotional encoding of the conflict between two distinct forms of state—monarchy and republic. Instead of meeting President Fauré on the front steps of her villa, as protocol required, Victoria sent her son, the Prince of Wales. She noted in her diary:

> At 1/2 p[ast] 3, Mr. Faure, the President of the Republic, who has been spending some days at the Riviera Palace came to see me. Bertie received him below, & brought him up & the 3 Princesses with the Ladies were at the top of the stairs. I stood at the door of the Drawing Room & asked him to sit down. He was very courteous & amiable, with a charming manner, so 'grand seigneur' & not at all 'parvenu'. He avoided all politics, but said most kindly how I was 'aimé par la population',—that he hoped I was comfortably lodged.[121]

After her death, Victoria's diary was transcribed and cleaned up, the original being destroyed. Another source suggests that in fact the British queen thought the French president to be quite the parvenu, that she expressed this belief through

[119] Letter from Ernst I to Albert of 28 November 1841, cited in Johannes Paulmann, *Pomp und Politik: Monarchenbegegnungen in Europa zwischen Ancien Régime und Erstem Weltkrieg* (Paderborn: Schöningh, 2000), 277–8, emphasis in original.

[120] On the misunderstandings arising from emotionally charged diplomacy see Susanne Schattenberg, 'The Diplomat as "an Actor on a Great Stage before all the People"? A Cultural History of Diplomacy and the Portsmouth Peace Negotiations of 1905', in Mösslang and Riotte (eds), *Diplomats' World*, 167–94; Susanne Schattenberg, 'Die Sprache der Diplomatie oder Das Wunder von Portsmouth: Überlegungen zu einer Kulturgeschichte der Außenpolitik', *Jahrbücher für Geschichte Osteuropas, Neue Folge*, 56/1 (2008), 3–26; Susanne Schattenberg, 'Die Angst vor Erniedrigung: Die U-2-Krise und das Ende der Entspannung', in Bernd Greiner, Christian Th. Müller, and Dierk Walter (eds), *Angst im Kalten Krieg* (Hamburg: Hamburger Edition, 2009), 220–51.

[121] Paulmann, *Pomp und Politik*, 229.

her neglecting to greet him personally at the steps, and that furthermore Fauré certainly got the message. In memoirs published posthumously in 1952 the assistant private secretary to the queen described the arrival of the president in the hall as follows:

> he looked around to see who was there to meet him, and seeing neither the Queen nor the Prince of Wales, kept his hat on to imply that the visit had not properly begun. He shook hands with the three ladies still with his hat on, and of course did the same with the men. Such a proceeding was hardly dictated by the Protocol, and it surprised us all. When Paris heard of this afterwards I was told that everyone said it was outrageous and very bad manners. The President was then conducted upstairs, and the Prince of Wales came hurrying down as if he were late. It was then and only then that the President took his hat off.[122]

In the course of the twentieth century the public realm and the media gained in influence, even in the case of communication between actors of quite different levels.[123] In 1957 for example the British prime minister Anthony Eden probably lost his office because of a public display of strong feelings, or rather, because of a display of feeling that happened behind closed doors but which then became public. His successor, Harold Macmillan, appeared to demonstrate self-control and was thus the contrary of Eden, hence better representing the contemporary manly 'culture of restraint'.[124]

The next example shows the diversity of the target audience for emotional diplomacy in the era of mass media. In January 2007 the Russian president Vladimir Putin met the German chancellor Angela Merkel for bilateral talks at his government dacha at Sochi on the Black Sea. It can be supposed that Putin knew that Merkel had been bitten by a dog when a child, and had a fear of dogs. At the first meeting he had given her a stuffed toy dog.[125] From the very first minute of the state visit in Sochi Putin's very large Labrador Koni kept close to him, and of course Merkel. Even during their negotiations she was lying under the oval table, which was in itself an infringement of diplomatic manners. But there was more: Putin remarked maliciously, 'I hope the dog does not frighten you.'[126] The success of Putin's deliberate attempt to unsettle the chancellor is clear from her body language (Fig. 4).

---

[122] Paulmann, *Pomp und Politik*, 230.

[123] At the same time it has become increasingly common to deposit intimate documents such as diaries and personal memoirs in private and state archives. See for the emotional history of the Cold War Frank Costigliola's study, based on this kind of source: ' "Unceasing Pressure for Penetration": Gender, Pathology, and Emotion in George Kennan's Formation of the Cold War', *Journal of American History*, 83/4 (1997), 1309–39; Frank Costigliola, ' "I Had Come as a Friend": Emotion, Culture, and Ambiguity in the Formation of the Cold War, 1943–1945', *Cold War History*, 1/1 (2000), 103–28.

[124] Martin Francis, 'Tears, Tantrums, and Bared Teeth: The Emotional Economy of Three Conservative Prime Ministers, 1951–1963', *Journal of British Studies*, 41/3 (2002), 354–87, here 357.

[125] Christoph Schwennicke, 'Die Herrin von Schloss Ungefähr', *Der Spiegel*, 49 (2007), 34–42, here 40–1.

[126] 'Merkel verlangt von Putin "bessere Kommunikation" ', *Frankfurter Allgemeine Zeitung* (22 January 2007), 1.

Fig. 4 Angela Merkel, Vladimir Putin, and Koni in Sochi, 21 January 2007

Sources: image above © DMITRY ASTAKHOV/AFP/Getty Images; image below © Picture-Alliance/dpa-Report/ Guido Bergmann.

For his own TV audience Putin presents himself as the familiar animal-loving president receiving a visitor in the kind of relaxed atmosphere that Camp David represents. The message for Angela Merkel is one coded in the threatening manner of the former 'Big Brother' of the Soviet Union: 'Here I am, and I know your country like the back of my hand, since I spent five years in the KGB in Dresden. For me you are part of the underground Christian, dissident-loving clique of the GDR, and I will show you who is boss here. And I can behave quite differently.' This second message seems to have been received and understood. It is said that Putin is one of the few international politicians whom she regards as an equal, and who represents an unequalled challenge to her spirit of resistance.[127]

What 'really' happens between actors in diplomatic meetings, what influence sense perceptions might have in personal encounters—historians find all of this hard to reconstruct. But this should not prevent them at least considering inter-personal communication when analysing the political consequences of encounters, seeking to disentangle their causes. The emotional history of diplomacy in no respect completes the list of potential fields with untapped sources for the study of emotion in history. There is no shortage of sources for the history of emotions.

So what conclusions might we draw from all of this for those who seek a historical mapping of *Homo sentiens*?[128] One thing is already clear, and here we can shift from synthesis to intervention, anticipating Chapter Four: it is not enough to define emotion according to the manner in which historical actors define it. Historical study is naturally diachronic, and, giving away another of the book's conclusions in advance, the periods that studies addressing the history of emotions deal with are often far more extended than in other branches of history. In order to determine its object of study, historical investigation has need of a transtemporal category, which presupposes that much is shared in common. If there is very little shared in common between the feelings that Napoleon expressed as *sentiments* in his French love letters to Josephine around 1800, and what in English was considered 'emotional' in the letter that Barack Obama sent to his daughters, then a relapse into pure contingency can hardly be avoided.[129] The writing of history is only possible if a meta-category exists—even if this meta-category clashes from time to time with the concepts employed in the source language. This represents my renunciation of any radical social constructivism.

Historians of emotion therefore need a working definition of emotion. There would be no point in formulating one here; the entire book is intended as a navigational aid in the search for such a working definition. We do not need a

[127] Schwennicke, 'Die Herrin von Schloss Ungefähr'; Christoph Schwennicke, 'Die schwarze Witwe', *Spiegel Online* (20 October 2009) <http://www.wiso-net.de/webcgi?START=A60& DOKV_DB=SPON&DOKV_NO=SPON20091020-656141&DOKV_HS=0&PP=1> accessed 23 February 2014.

[128] Flam, *Soziologie der Emotionen*, 173.

[129] *Lettres de Napoléon à Joséphine pendant la première campagne d'Italie, le Consulat et l'Empire et lettres de Joséphine à Napoléon et à sa fille*, ii (Paris: Didot Frères, 1833), 33, 73, 106, 124; Ed Pilkington, 'Obama Writes Emotional Letter to Daughters Malia and Sasha', *The Guardian* (15 January 2009). <http://www.guardian.co.uk/world/2009/jan/15/obama-letter-children-malia-sasha> accessed 23 February 2014.

definition analogous to those in the natural sciences, a definition that only relates to certain very restricted fields in order to be all the more exact. It would also be a good idea to begin, sooner rather than later, to come to terms with particular central aspects that have been a preoccupation for philosophers and other thinkers since antiquity.

First of all, we need to form an idea of whether emotions do involve a kind of automatic response, as in the framework of stimulus-response, where stable responses follow from external stimuli, or whether imagination might play a role. As a rule, the history of emotions attributes a greater role to the imaginary sphere than is usual in the life sciences and other disciplines.

Secondly, we need to be clear about the relation of the body to emotion. Here it is important to begin by examining local and historical ideas about feeling and physicality in the context of our object of investigation. The physical can only be defined once we have turned our attention to the description of non-verbal bodily practices (like *shokeling*, the way in which Orthodox Jews rock when praying), or to embodied verbal behaviour (like the writing of letters between fathers and sons living in the same household, characteristic of the early modern French aristocracy in which feelings and inclinations that had been written down were thought more significant than those expressed verbally).[130]

Thirdly, it is worthwhile to consider the emotional components of judgement or evaluation. The amount of agency afforded to actors in the past, whether they were more reacting than acting, whether they distinguished between the objects of their emotion according to culture, membership of particular groups, or their individual formation—these are all important questions for the histories of emotion.

Finally, it makes sense to develop a position upon the relation of emotion to morality. If historical actors give ethical reasons for their actions, expressing in this way the interconnection of feeling and morality, this lends their emotions a meaning distinct from that in societies where emotion and morality are treated as unrelated. If we can clarify these four points we will have made an important step forward in developing a working definition of emotion; the foundation will have been laid, and we can set about furnishing the space of emotional history.

---

[130] Orest Ranum, 'The Refuges of Intimacy', in Philippe Ariès and Roger Chartier (eds), *A History of Private Life*, iii. *Passions of the Renaissance* (Cambridge, MA: Belknap Press, 1989), 207–63, here 259–61.

One

The History of the History of Emotions

1 LUCIEN FEBVRE AND THE HISTORY OF EMOTIONS

In the beginning of the history of emotions there was one solitary man: Lucien Febvre (1875–1956). This is at any rate the way things have been seen by most of the attempts made to historicize the history of emotions.[1] In 1929 Febvre and Marc Bloch (1886–1944) founded the journal *Annales d'histoire économique et sociale*, around which one of the most important schools of historiography of the twentieth century was formed. Historians writing in the *Annales* shifted the study of history from the domain of high politics, kings, and diplomacy into the world of ordinary people, peasants, and craftsmen; they grounded history in the environment, demography, economy, society, and mentalities. It is no surprise, therefore, that it was *Annalistes* who were among the first to take feelings into account.

Febvre had made his name with studies of Martin Luther and the history of the Rhine. In June 1938 he took part in a conference organized by Henri Berr entitled 'Sensibility in Man and Nature', and in 1941 he published his revised paper in the *Annales*.[2] In this article he appealed to fellow historians to place emotions at the centre of their work, encouraging them to overcome any hesitation concerning the

---

[1] Surveys that treat the history of emotions as originating with Febvre are, e.g. Barbara H. Rosenwein, 'Worrying about Emotions in History', *American Historical Review*, 107/3 (2002), 821–45, esp. 821–3; and Joanna Bourke, 'Fear and Anxiety: Writing About Emotion in Modern History', *History Workshop Journal*, 55 (2003), 111–33, esp. 113–14.

[2] Lucien Febvre, 'La Sensibilité et l'histoire: Comment reconstituer la vie affective d'autrefois?', *Annales d'histoire sociale*, 3/1–2 (1941), 5–20. Lucien Febvre, 'Sensibility and History: How to Reconstitute the Emotional Life of the Past', in *A New Kind of History: From the Writings of Febvre*, ed. Peter Burke, trans. K. Folca (New York: Harper & Row, 1973), 12–26. Febvre's actual lecture manuscript was not published until 1943, i.e. after the revised *Annales* version: Lucien Febvre, 'La Sensibilité dans l'histoire: Les "Courants" collectifs de pensée et d'action', in Henri Berr (ed.), *La Sensibilité dans l'homme et dans la nature* (Paris: Presses Universitaires de France, 1943), 77–100. See, for the background to this, Peter Schöttler, 'Lucien Febvre, die Renaissance und eine schreibende Frau: Nachwort', in Lucien Febvre, *Margarete von Navarra: Eine Königin der Renaissance zwischen Macht, Liebe und Religion* (Frankfurt am Main: Campus, 1998), 361–2, here 377–8 n. 63. There is another essay by Febvre, dating from 1938, in which emotion is discussed. He there proposes to borrow from psychology, stating that 'we refrain from projecting the present, that is our present, into the past'; 'we give up psychological anachronism, the worst sort of anachronism, and the most insidious and harmful of all'; 'For historical psychology is faced with a special problem. When psychologists, in their essays and learned articles, talk to us about the emotions, decisions and reasonings of "man", what they are really telling us about are our own emotions, decisions and reasonings, our own particular situation as West European white men integrated into groups with long-standing cultures'; Lucien Febvre, 'History and Psychology', in *A New Kind of History: From the Writings of Febvre*, ed. Burke, 1–11, here 9, 5.

discipline of psychology when studying feelings of the past. What might that look like? 'I spoke of death', wrote Febvre,

> Just open volume IX of Henri *Bremond's Histoire littéraire du sentiment religieux en France*...Open it at the chapter which bears the title 'L'art de mourir'. Not three hundred years ago; what an abyss between the morals and sentiments of the men of that age and ours![3]

For Febvre, it was this abyss between the past and the present that formed the point of departure for all history of emotions, along with the need to find a language within which this abyss could be measured.

Febvre's essay is first and foremost a plea for the study of emotions—whatever criticism there might be. Against all of those who disputed the legitimacy of the history of emotions Febvre argued that they did already include emotions in their histories, except that they did so in an unconscious and anachronistic manner, imposing ideas of emotion drawn from their own time on former periods, without considering whether there might have been a shift in conceptions related to any one feeling in the meantime.[4] Febvre was scornful of the psychologizing popular histories of the day:

> Psychology—let us just consider Bouvard or Pécuchet, strong in the experience gained from acquaintance with the milliners and shop girls of their district and using it as a basis to explain Agnès Sorel's feelings for Charles VII, or Louis XIV's for Madame de Montespan, in such a way that their relations and friends exclaimed: 'Oh, how true!'[5]

Febvre asked: 'And when the historian has told us, "Napoleon had a fit of rage" or "a moment of intense pleasure", is his task not complete?'[6] Not at all: for we have no idea what 'rage' meant in Napoleon's time, and what public displays of rage looked like.

Febvre went on to call for the analysis of representations of feeling in writing and image over time. This implied something that we would today call a conceptual history (*Begriffsgeschichte*) of emotion, the description of shifts of the meaning of concepts of emotion through decades and centuries.[7] Febvre was the first to delineate the contours of a field of research that would occupy the greater part of the future history of emotions. He was extremely far-sighted in identifying the difficulty of distinguishing one emotion from another, and in emphasizing the ambivalence and complexity of feelings. He was quite clear that many emotions could often emerge simultaneously, even diametrically opposed feelings occurring in one and the same individual.[8]

There was a great deal at stake for Febvre in all of this. 'No history of love, just remember that. We have no history of death.' This, he suggested, was a fatal lacuna, 'as long as they [these histories] have not been done *there will be no real history*

---

[3] Febvre, 'Sensibility and History', 24–5.   [4] Febvre, 'Sensibility and History', 14.
[5] Febvre, 'Sensibility and History', 19.   [6] Febvre, 'Sensibility and History', 14.
[7] On images of emotion see Febvre, 'Sensibility and History', 20–3; and on conceptual history see Febvre, 'Sensibility and History', 20.
[8] Febvre, 'Sensibility and History', 18.

possible.[9] But where did this sense of urgency come from, and why did Febvre consider a history of emotions to be so important?

It is quite plain that Febvre was influenced by the work of French anthropologists and psychologists writing during the 1920s and 1930s—Lucien Lévy-Bruhl's *La Mentalité primitive* of 1922; Charles Blondel's *Introduction à la psychologie collective* of 1928; and a 1938 article on emotion by Henri Wallon in the *Encyclopédie française*, which was edited by Febvre.[10] But there are firm indications that it was the spread of fascism in Europe that played the greatest role in Febvre delivering his lecture and publishing his essay.[11] First of all, his conception of emotion is heavily intersubjective, in which the emotions of one person arouse emotions in others and enter into a mutual relationship—or as Febvre put it, 'Emotions are contagious.'[12] There was also the influence of the still popular contemporary crowd theorist Gustave Le Bon, and it is not hard to see behind his words the enraptured faces of the masses and the Nazi Party rallies on the other side of the Rhine.[13] Secondly, he also thought that the linear historical narrative of 'the gradual suppression of emotional activity through intellectual activity' was being undermined by 'most recent history' and the 'revived primitive feelings'.[14] This retreat from *ratio* to *emotio* was linked to the unsettling sense that there was an 'emotional life within us which is always ready to inundate intellectual life and to carry out a sudden reversal of that evolution we were so proud of from emotion to thought, from emotional language to articulate language'.[15] Thirdly, the emotions that Febvre suggested be studied were primarily negative: 'the history of hate, the history of fear, the history of cruelty'. As Febvre noted: 'The subject of such empty talk, which has so little to do with humanity, will tomorrow have finally made our universe into a stinking pit of corpses.'[16] The threat of European Fascism and the seductive emotional potential of National Socialism therefore prompted Febvre's approach.[17] Seen in this way, there are not one, but at least three men who stand at

[9] Febvre, 'Sensibility and History', 24; emphasis in original.
[10] Alain Corbin notes this background to Febvre's essay in his 'A History and Anthropology of the Senses', in Corbin (ed.), *Time, Desire and Horror: Towards a History of the Senses*, trans. Jean Birrell (Cambridge: Polity Press, 1995), 181–95; as does Rosenwein, 'Worrying about Emotions in History', 822–3.
[11] Despite what is often claimed, the experience of Vichy cannot be treated as a motive, since the original version of the *Annales* essay came from the conference organized by Henri Berr in 1938. I thank Peter Schöttler for pointing this out to me.
[12] Febvre, 'Sensibility and History', 14.
[13] Febvre, 'Sensibility and History', 14–15. Febvre also emphasized the intersubjectivity of emotions so that he might parry those critics for whom the history of emotions might be thought too individual and insufficiently representative; Febvre, 'Sensibility and History', 14. For the influence of Le Bon on Febvre see Corbin, 'History and Anthropology of the Senses', 181.
[14] Febvre, 'Sensibility and History', 15–16, 26. Febvre, e.g. described literary or artistic occupations as 'means of sentimental anaesthesia' of feeling. He did not think of this so much in Freud's sense of sublimation, but rather as simple substitution; Febvre, 'Sensibility and History', 15.
[15] Febvre, 'Sensibility and History', 25.   [16] Febvre, 'Sensibility and History', 26.
[17] See also a 1939 book review by Febvre of Edmond Vermeil's *Doctrinaires de la révolution allemande 1918–1938*: 'Doctrine and the doctrinaires: so be it. But can one really approach National Socialism in terms of doctrine?...Hatred, aggression, passion: should one not instead investigate how in the past not Nazi intellectuality and doctrine but instead the sensibility and sentimentality of National Socialism were formed? Nazism, a revolution. Fine. But what is a

the beginning of the history of emotions: Lucien Febvre, Benito Mussolini, and Adolf Hitler.

2 THE HISTORY OF EMOTIONS PRIOR TO FEBVRE

But were Febvre, Mussolini, and Hitler really at the beginning? Not many people today find Great Man stories or the search for a zero hour very convincing. Just as at the Conclusion of this book we will end up at the current condition of the history of emotions, so here we start at the very beginning, as presently understood.[18] 'As presently understood' because we still lack a systematic treatment of the historiography of emotions, especially of the period up to 1900. For this reason the description that follows will be necessarily episodic, limiting its sketch of the place of emotion in historical studies before the work of Febvre to a few particular instances.

Let us first of all consider a very early instance. For the historian Thucydides (454–c.399 BC) emotion was one, if not *the sole*, impulse to human action in the past. Fear and other powerful feelings made the Athenians and Spartans do what they did to each other between 431 and 404 BC in the Peloponnesian War. The Spartans 'voted that the treaty had been broken and that they must go to war . . . because they feared further increase in the power of the Athenians', while the Corinthians acted 'out of hatred for the Corcyreans'.[19] The ancient historian Ramsay MacMullen, who outlined a panorama of the emotional history of antiquity, believes that for Thucydides it is feelings that 'make people break out of their routines, they destroy the status quo. Yet they [feelings] are not irrational.'[20] They form the basis 'of ordinary and surely reasonable behavior—reasonable in the sense that he [Thucydides] and his readers or anyone at all could easily understand them'.[21]

According to MacMullen, for other historians after Thucydides emotions were merely a rhetorical device, used to grab the reader's attention, or as a means of persuasion. It was only with Polybius (c.200–c.120 BC) that emotions once more

revolution? A transformation of doctrines? I would say for my part, more a change in the range of morally-accepted affective reactions, and hence a social change. I have for some time demanded that a history of sensibilities, a history of sentiment, be written' Lucien Febvre, 'Sur la doctrine nationale-socialiste: Un conflit de tendances', *Annales d'histoire sociale* 1/4 (1939), 426–8, here 427.

[18] A brief outline of the history of emotions before Febvre can be found in John Corrigan, 'Introduction' in *Religion and Emotion: Approaches and Interpretations* (Oxford: Oxford University Press, 2004), 3–31, here 28–9, 20.

[19] Thucydides, *The Peloponnesian War*, trans. Steven Lattimore (Indianapolis: Hackett, 1998), 43 (1.88), 15 (1.25).

[20] Ramsay MacMullen, *Feelings in History, Ancient and Modern* (Claremont, CA: Regina Books, 2003), 9. MacMullen's book is divided into three chapters: ch. 1 deals with the manner in which ancient historians wrote about feelings; ch. 2 highlights the work of a few authors and theories in experimental psychology, from James Lange to Antonio Damasio; ch. 3 examines more closely the place of emotions in some of the writings of the *Annales* School, and closes with a case study of the feelings that motivated the North American anti-slavery movement of the early 19th century.

[21] MacMullen, *Feelings in History, Ancient and Modern*, 9.

became a motivating factor in human decision-making and action. The feelings of kings had very particular consequences—'Personal feelings turn into history when they are regal'—but Polybius thought them hard to decipher, and he continually asked himself how it was that a monarch could descend into tyranny.[22]

With collective actors such as the Roman Senate or the Carthaginians, emotions such as hope, despair, and courage did govern action, but historians found them easier to understand, given that they were not the effects of an individual personality like a king, but could be explained by external circumstances.[23] And so there were two ancient historians who considered the power of feelings to be a decisive impulse—at least according to the first reconstructions of the ancient history of emotions that we currently have.[24]

Apart from ancient historical writing, most of what we know about the history of emotions before Febvre relates to the late nineteenth century, when discussion among historians of the role of feelings developed. This was as much as anything an effect of the separation out of different sciences into independent disciplines, academic study in both Europe and North America being influenced by the rise of the natural sciences.[25] Originally the humanities, the natural sciences, and the social sciences had all found a home together in the Philosophy Faculty of the university. From the later nineteenth century on, however, they all went their separate ways. Philosophy had to surrender its status as the master science to the natural sciences, whose claim to objectivity (something of special interest here) placed the humanities under very great pressure to review their own methods. Here 'objectivity' always meant the rationality of the scientist, understood to be a neutralization of emotion.

In Germany, Wilhelm Dilthey (1833–1911) responded to the challenge of the natural sciences by writing *Einleitung in die Geisteswissenschaften* (1883; Eng. *Introduction to the Human Sciences*), providing the human sciences with a theoretical foundation. He placed in question the idea that the natural sciences had a monopoly on an objective representation of the world, claiming a greater degree of objectivity for the human sciences, on the grounds that they were capable not only of a rational apprehension of the world, but also one which related to the senses and

---

[22] MacMullen, *Feelings in History, Ancient and Modern*, 15.

[23] MacMullen, *Feelings in History, Ancient and Modern*, 17.

[24] It becomes apparent that MacMullen's idiosyncratic book cannot be the last word on the role of feelings in the writing of ancient history once we understand his motivation: to refute the doyen of ancient history Ronald Syme (1903–89), who in his book *The Roman Revolution* (1939) treated ancient historical figures as if they were motivated by rational calculation; MacMullen, *Feelings in History, Ancient and Modern*, 50. MacMullen concludes with the methodological demand that historians should empathize with the emotions of their historical actors, using as an example writers of fiction who have often suffered and wept with their protagonists; MacMullen, *Feelings in History, Ancient and Modern*, 134–5.

[25] In the following I rely on Jakob Tanner, 'Unfassbare Gefühle: Emotionen in der Geschichtswissenschaft vom Fin de siècle bis in die Zwischenkriegszeit', in Uffa Jensen and Daniel Morat (eds), *Rationalisierungen des Gefühls: Zum Verhältnis von Wissenschaft und Emotionen 1880–1930* (Munich: Fink, 2008), 35–59; Daniel Morat, 'Verstehen als Gefühlsmethode: Zu Wilhelm Diltheys hermeneutischer Grundlegung der Geisteswissenschaften', in Jensen and Morat (eds), *Rationalisierungen des Gefühls*, 101–17.

feelings. Work in the human sciences had 'the whole of human nature' for its object, and made use of 'full, untruncated experience'.[26] By contrast, natural scientists were wedded to the 'impossibility of deriving mental or spiritual facts from those of the mechanical order of nature'.[27] Dilthey continued:

> Social states are intelligible to us from within; we can, up to a certain point, reproduce them in ourselves on the basis of the perception of our own states; our representations of the historical world are enlivened by love and hatred, by passionate joy, by the entire gamut of our emotions.... Accordingly, the play of causes which operate blindly is replaced by the play of representations, feelings, and motives.[28]

The decisive hermeneutic step involved the historian merging into the historical actor. Since the historical scholar was capable of mobilizing all his perceptive powers, including those relating to the emotions, he was capable of understanding human beings in the past in their totality:

> The decisive fact for the study of mental structure is that *the transitions from one state to another, the effect of one on another are part of inner experience. We experience this structure.* We understand human life, history, and all the hidden depths of the human mind because we experience these transitions and effects and so become aware of this structure which embraces all passions, sufferings and human destinies.[29]

The usual interpretation of Dilthey's writings talks of a break around 1900, when he turned away from his theorization of the human sciences and devoted himself entirely to the formulation of a historical hermeneutic. Correspondingly, emotions were lost from view. However, it has recently been shown that Dilthey placed great value on emotions in the hermeneutics that he developed from 1900 onwards. Daniel Morat is entirely right to characterize Dilthey's hermeneutic as a *Gefühls-methode*, a 'method of feeling'.[30]

Dilthey's contemporary Karl Lamprecht (1856–1915) was also interested in emotions, borrowing from psychology and anthropology. In his 1897 essay 'Was ist Kulturgeschichte?' ('What is Cultural History?') he advocated that the achievements 'of modern psychology as an exact science of the laws of inner life' be taken into account, enriching in this way the historical explanation of the 'inner

---

[26] Wilhelm Dilthey, *Introduction to the Human Sciences: Selected Works*, i, ed. Rudolf Makkreel and Frithjof Rodi (Princeton: Princeton University Press, 1989), 51, 173.

[27] Dilthey, *Introduction to the Human Sciences*, 63.

[28] Dilthey, *Introduction to the Human Sciences*, 88–9.

[29] Wilhelm Dilthey, 'Ideas about a Descriptive and Analytical Psychology', in *Selected Writings*, ed. and trans. H. P. Rickman (Cambridge: Cambridge University Press, 1976), 88–97, here 94, emphasis in original.

[30] See Morat, 'Verstehen als Gefühlsmethode'. Morat demonstrates the limitations of a concentration upon Dilthey's distancing from the concept of empathy (*Einfühlung*). Dilthey's terminology of 'putting oneself in the place of another' (*Hineinversetzen*), 'reimagining' (*Nachbilden*), and 're-experiencing' (*Nacherleben*) retains, according to Morat, an emotional content, although these are not privileged over other elements; Morat, 'Verstehen als Gefühlsmethode', 114–15.

motivations of personal conduct'.[31] In particular, Lamprecht thought in terms of a division of labour between the sciences, whereby anthropology dealt with 'affect and acts of conscious will', with 'feelings and drives', whose varied manifestations in different eras would be studied by historians.[32] As employed by Lamprecht, what resulted was a narrative of national progress with emotional aspects, distanced from a teleology of increasing control of affect by one thing only: in developed nations affect was not restrained; rather, the 'principle of progressive psychic intensity' prevailed. Hence the painting 'of an individualistic era, of Dürer for instance . . . was more intense than that of the conventionalistic era, as, for example, in the miniatures of the *Hortus deliciarum*; while Adolph Menzel, part of the subjectivist era, is almost more intense as a painter than Dürer'.[33]

Following on from Dilthey and Lamprecht, Georg Steinhausen (1866–1933) and Kurt Breysig (1866–1940) likewise saw no problem in treating the nation as a unit of analysis and as an emotional collective actor. Steinhausen's *Der Wandel deutschen Gefühlslebens seit dem Mittelalter* (1895) presented five 'developmental phases of German feeling and sensibility', setting up a series of contrasts: 'natural versus artificial', 'constant versus volatile', 'German versus alien', 'people versus elites', a positive value being imputed to the first term in each dyad.[34] But what did Steinhausen's emotional history look like? In Phase Two, 'at the beginning of the fourteenth century the German was a sober, simple person, almost devoid of sentiment (*Gemüt*)' whose life was characterized by 'very limited feeling'.[35] Phase Four, from the later eighteenth century to the early nineteenth, was by contrast 'the time of sensibility and feeling' during which Germany descended into a sea of 'feelings' and 'tears'.[36]

Kurt Breysig put forward a similar schema in his *Geschichte der Seele im Werdegang der Menschheit* (1931). He began from the assumption 'that in each and every developmental era of humanity different inner forces (*Seelenkräfte*) ruled the mind and deed of peoples'.[37] Breysig continued publishing during the 1930s, and as Jakob Tanner notes, in his writings 'Teutonic clarity, combined with a narrowly national perspective, reached vertiginous heights'.[38] But neither Breysig and Steinhausen, nor Dilthey and Lamprecht—none of these four—show up in the older literature on the historicization of emotion. Since they had little time for the lability of feelings, none of them today offer anything with which a modern history of emotions can work.

All the same, there are many threads leading from these four writers to the foremost thinkers of the early twentieth century who had something to contribute

---

[31] Karl Lamprecht, 'Was ist Kulturgeschichte? Beitrag zu einer empirischen Historik', *Deutsche Zeitschrift für Geschichtswissenschaft NF*, 1 (1896/7), 75–150, here 86. My remarks on Lamprecht and emotion here are inspired by Tanner, 'Unfassbare Gefühle', 41–4. On Lamprecht see also Rüdiger Schnell, 'Historische Emotionsforschung: Eine mediävistische Standortbestimmung', *Frühmittelalterliche Studien*, 38 (2005), 173–276, here 222–3.
[32] Lamprecht, 'Was ist Kulturgeschichte?', 118.
[33] Lamprecht, 'Was ist Kulturgeschichte?', 132.   [34] See Tanner, 'Unfassbare Gefühle', 46.
[35] Tanner, 'Unfassbare Gefühle', 45.   [36] Tanner, 'Unfassbare Gefühle', 45.
[37] Kurt Breysig, *Geschichte der Seele im Werdegang der Menschheit* (Breslau: Marcus, 1931), viii.
[38] Tanner, 'Unfassbare Gefühle', 46.

to a history of emotions.[39] The art historian Aby Warburg (1866–1929) had studied cultural history with Lamprecht in the 1880s. In 1905 he introduced the idea of a *Pathosformel* into the study of art history, characterizing emotionally charged gestures or facial expressions in painting and sculpture.[40] He suggested that powerful emotions were reduced to 'formulas of pathos' which re-emerged, perhaps centuries later, as movements of the hand or facial expression in works of art. *Pathosformeln* are, if you like, an image of emotional intertextuality. In 1958 an associate of Warburg, Gertrud Bing, argued that when painters of the Italian Renaissance adopted emotionally charged gestures from ancient sculpture 'they sought to make their own the classical expression of the deepest disturbance of the human condition'.[41] Georg Simmel, once described by José Ortega y Gasset as a 'philosophical squirrel, jumping from one nut to the other', found feelings difficult to avoid.[42] There was always something emotional for Simmel about social relationships and processes that fostered community:

> Whatever external events we might also identify as social, it would be like a marionette play, not any more conceivable and meaningful than the interpenetration of clouds or the interweaving development of tree branches, if we were not to recognize fully as a matter of course psychological motivations, feelings, thoughts, and needs, not only as bearers of those events but as their essential vitality and us really as only interested parties.[43]

Simmel had no doubt that feelings such as trust, honour, and loyalty—but also enmity, envy, jealousy, anger, hatred, contempt, and cruelty—not only divided individuals and groups but also brought them together; and that in this way feelings

---

[39] The idea that the grand theories of Marx, Weber, Durkheim, and Simmel also imply a grand narrative of the historical development of emotion, can be found in Eva Illouz, *Cold Intimacies: The Making of Emotional Capitalism* (Cambridge: Polity Press, 2007), 1–2.

[40] See Aby Warburg, 'Dürer and Italian Antiquity (1905)', in *The Renewal of Pagan Antiquity: Contributions to the Cultural History of the European Renaissance*, trans. David Brett (Los Angeles: Getty Research Institute for the History of Art and the Humanities, 1999), 553–8.

[41] Gertrud Bing, 'Aby M. Warburg: Vortrag von Frau Professor Bing anläßlich der feierlichen Aufstellung von Aby Warburgs Büste in der Hamburger Kunsthalle am 31. Oktober 1958', in Aby M. Warburg, *Ausgewählte Schriften und Würdigungen*, i, ed. Dieter Wuttke (3rd edn, Baden-Baden: Koerner, 1992), 455–64, here 461. See for Warburg's *Pathosformel*: Kurt W. Forster, 'Energie, Emotion und Erinnerung in Aby Warburgs Kulturwissenschaft', in Johannes Fehr and Gerd Folkers (eds), *Gefühle zeigen: Manifestationsformen emotionaler Prozesse* (Zurich: Chronos, 2009), 283–303; Ute Frevert, 'Angst vor Gefühlen? Die Geschichtsmächtigkeit von Emotionen im 20. Jahrhundert', in Paul Nolte, Manfred Hettling, Frank-Michael Kuhlemann, and Hans-Walter Schmuhl (eds), *Perspektiven der Gesellschaftsgeschichte* (Munich: Beck, 2000), 95–111, here 102–3; Tanner, 'Unfassbare Gefühle', 47–9. Warburg was influenced by Darwin's emphasis upon the physical expression of signs of emotion and also by his 1872 book, *The Expression of the Emotions in Man and Animals*. See Carlo Ginzburg, 'From Aby Warburg to E. H. Gombrich: A Problem of Method', in *Clues, Myths, and the Historical Method*, trans. John and Anne C. Tedeschi (Baltimore: Johns Hopkins University Press, 1989), 17–59, esp. 20.

[42] José Ortega y Gasset cited by Lewis Coser, *Masters of Sociological Thought: Ideas in Historical and Social Context* (New York: Harcourt, Brace, Jovanovich, 1977), 199.

[43] Georg Simmel, *Sociology: Inquiries into the Construction of Social Forms*, i (Leiden: Brill, 2009), 35. For more details about Simmel and the emotions, see Helena Flam, *Soziologie der Emotionen: Eine Einführung* (Konstanz: UTB, 2002), 16–43.

worked to promote the formation of social groups.[44] It is no wonder therefore that the 'connection between the history of politics and anthropology in regard to "emotion" was a topic of discussion at the second annual meeting of the German Sociological Society in 1912'.[45]

Moreover, Max Weber's *The Protestant Ethic and the Spirit of Capitalism* (1930; Ger. orig., *Die protestantische Ethik und der Geist des Kapitalismus*, 1904–5/1920) can also be read as an account of feelings. Weber ranged the various forms of Protestantism along an emotional thermometric scale: Calvinists were in the ice blue zone, believing themselves to be the 'tool[s] of the divine will', tending towards 'ascetic action' and 'worldly asceticism', only recognizing the unsentimental, such as commercial success, as signs of God's mercy. Weber placed Lutherans somewhere in the middle, seeing themselves as 'vessel[s] of the Holy Spirit', being inclined to 'mysticism and emotionalism'. 'The Lutheran faith thus left the spontaneous vitality of impulsive action and naïve emotion more nearly unchanged.' Pietists by contrast teetered on the red-hot domain of Catholicism: 'in the peculiar piety of Herrnhut, the emotional element held a very prominent place', foregrounding the 'principle that the childlikeness of religious feeling was a sign of its genuineness'.[46]

The Dutch historian Johan Huizinga (1872–1945) was also interested in childlike emotions, publishing *Herfsttij der middeleeuwen* (1919; Eng. *The Autumn of the Middle Ages*, 1996) in the wake of the horrors of the First World War.[47] In Huizinga's Middle Ages there was a great deal of unrestrained weeping and anger, feelings were 'of unrefined exuberance, sudden cruelty'; 'In his description of the peace congress at Arras in 1435, Jean Germain makes the audience fall to the ground filled with emotions, speechless, sighing, sobbing and crying during the moving addresses by the delegates.'[48] The emotional dimension of all spheres of social life was characterized by extremes and lack of restraint. As in politics, of which Huizinga remarked: 'During the fifteenth century the immediate emotional affect is still directly expressed in ways that frequently break through the veneer of utility and calculation.'[49] And the law? Huizinga emphasizes that 'The sense of justice was still three quarters heathen and dominated by a need for vengeance.'[50]

[44] Simmel, *Sociology*, 256; see also for trust (*Vertrauen*), 315–16; for honour (*Ehre*), 387–9; for loyalty (*Treue*), 517–22; for enmity, envy, jealousy (*Feindseligkeit, Neid, Eifersucht*), 255–8.

[45] Ursula Lehmkuhl, 'Diplomatiegeschichte als internationale Kulturgeschichte: Theoretische Ansätze und empirische Forschung zwischen Historischer Kulturwissenschaft und Soziologischem Institutionalismus', *Geschichte und Gesellschaft*, 27/3 (2001), 394–423, here 414. I thank Jörn Happel for bringing this article to my attention.

[46] Max Weber, *The Protestant Ethic and the Spirit of Capitalism*, trans. Talcott Parsons (New York: Charles Scribner's Sons, 1958), 114, 120, 113, 114, 126, 135. See also Flam, *Soziologie der Emotionen*, 44–60; Tanner, 'Unfassbare Gefühle', 49.

[47] '[E]very experience had that degree of directness and absoluteness that joy and sadness still have in the mind of a child'; Johan Huizinga, *The Autumn of the Middle Ages*, trans. Rodney J. Payton and Ulrich Mammitzsch (Chicago: University of Chicago Press, 1996), 1. The first English translation was published as *The Waning of the Middle Ages* in 1924. Huizinga shared with Marc Bloch a negative view of powerful collective emotions as a consequence of the experiences of the First World War.

[48] Huizinga, *The Autumn of the Middle Ages*, 2, 8.

[49] Huizinga, *The Autumn of the Middle Ages*, 15.

[50] Huizinga, *The Autumn of the Middle Ages*, 20.

And religion? Huizinga took the view that 'A comfortable lack of religious awe and the complacencies of everyday life alternated with periods of the most intense displays of the passionate piety that spasmodically seized the people.'[51] The persecution of witches represented for Huizinga 'disgust, fear, and hatred of intolerable transgressions, even such things outside of the direct realm of faith'.[52]

Besides that, in Huizinga we constantly encounter terms such as 'susceptibility', 'blind passion', and 'painful supersensitivity'.[53] What he wrote about feelings had less of a historiographic impact than the period with which he dealt: the late medieval era of the fourteenth and fifteenth centuries, on the threshold of early modernity. Subsequently Humanism, the Renaissance, and Protestantism closed the valve of emotional control. In brief: Erasmus and Luther made modern men out of hyperemotional medieval children. Huizinga's master narrative of the linear progression of emotional control, while stripped of its lifetime metaphors, proved extremely tenacious, and at the end of the 1930s it was given its most elegant—and seductive—form.

3 THE HISTORY OF EMOTIONS IN THE TIME OF FEBVRE AND AFTER

Unnoticed by Febvre, during 1939 a book was published in Switzerland written by a young and little-known historical sociologist, Norbert Elias (1897–1990): *Über den Prozeß der Zivilisation: Soziogenetische und psychogenetische Untersuchungen* (Eng. *The Civilizing Process*, 1969).[54] Elias had begun writing this in 1933 after he had emigrated from Germany, first to Paris and then to London; it only became more widely known in the 1960s and 1970s after it was republished in German, and especially after it was translated into English.[55] Today it is a classical sociological text, obligatory reading for historians and students of literature, presenting a grand theory of a European modernity initiated around 1600 which involves an

---

[51] Huizinga, *The Autumn of the Middle Ages*, 203.
[52] Huizinga, *The Autumn of the Middle Ages*, 288–9.
[53] Huizinga, *The Autumn of the Middle Ages*, 8, 20, 226.
[54] Besides Febvre, there were others in the *Annales* School who sought a scholarly approach to emotions. In *Les Rois thaumaturges* (1924; Eng. *The Royal Touch: Monarchy and Miracles in France and England*, 1961) Marc Bloch (1886–1944) described the shamanistic powers attributed to medieval kings as an element forming the 'feeling of loyalty' that subjects had for their rulers; see Tanner, 'Unfassbare Gefühle', 55. In *Apologie pour l'histoire, ou Métier d'historien* (1949; Eng. *The Historian's Craft*, 1953), his methodological testament written shortly before he was murdered by the Gestapo in 1944, Bloch noted the significance of feelings: 'What religious historian would be satisfied by examining a few theological tracts or hymnals? He knows full well that the painting and sculpture of sanctuary walls and the arrangement and furnishings of tombs have at least as much to tell him about dead beliefs and feelings as a thousand contemporary manuscripts'; Marc Bloch, *The Historian's Craft* (Manchester: Knopf, 1992), 56.
[55] Norbert Elias, *The Civilizing Process: Sociogenetic and Psychogenetic Investigations*, trans. Edward Jephcott, ed. Eric Dunning, Johan Goudsblom, and Stephen Mennell (rev. edn, Oxford: Blackwell, 2010) [Ger. orig., *Über den Prozeß der Zivilisation: Soziogenetische und psychogenetische Untersuchungen*, 2 vols, 1939].

ultimately linear process of the increasing control of affect.[56] To be a modern man means: to be disgusted by the poor table manners of fellow diners, to be ashamed of a relative who spits on his floor, to find embarrassing the sight of a naked person in a public place. Before modernity everything was different: premodern people hardly ever had table forks, 'Table utensils are still limited; on the left the bread, on the right the glass and knife.'[57] Premodern people had no problem about blowing their nose with their fingers while at the table, helping themselves with their bare hands from a common plate, or throwing chewed bones on the floor; disapproval was reserved for those who used the tablecloth to blow their nose, got food on their nose and ears or in their eyes, or finished up the contents of the common plate.[58] Premodern men had no superego. Before the onset of modernity there was no 'invisible wall of affects which seems now to rise between one human body and another, repelling and separating'; instead, emotion had freer rein, it was expressed 'more freely, more directly, more openly than later'.[59]

Elias's central metaphor was the 'affect-econom[y]'.[60] He assumed that it had to be kept permanently in equilibrium so that a feeling which disappeared from one place had to reappear at another. According to Elias, emotions that medieval men and women could freely express became, in the transition to modernity, overlaid with taboos. These taboos were internalized, external compulsion became self-compulsion. This warped the soul, at best being damped by the use of sport to ventilate the brutal, unmediated expression of emotion, at worst leading to 'compulsive actions and other symptoms of disturbance'.[61] Whereas today's historians spurn psychoanalysis, the influence of Freud is unmistakable.[62] The lasting merit of Elias is that he supplied the conceptual armoury for the emergent field of the history of emotions. He coined a new terminology for the description of emotional reality, using terms that all critique an essentialist conception ('affect structure';

---

[56] Lip service to the idea that the civilizing process 'does not follow a straight line', but is characterized by 'the most diverse criss-cross movements, shifts and spurts in this or that direction', can be found in Elias's book, *Civilizing Process*, 157. Peter Ludes also disputes that the civilizing process is linear in conception; Peter Ludes, *Drei moderne soziologische Theorien: Zur Entwicklung des Orientierungsmittels Alternativen* (Göttingen: Schwartz, 1989), 152, 354 n. 12. There has been a great deal of criticism of Elias's thesis: see e.g. Hans-Peter Duerr, *Der Mythos vom Zivilisationsprozeß*, i. *Nacktheit und Scham* (Frankfurt am Main: Suhrkamp, 1988); further volumes in 1990, 1993, 1997, and 2002. A summary can be found in Gerd Schwerhoff, 'Zivilisationsprozeß und Geschichtswissenschaft: Norbert Elias' Forschungsparadigma in historischer Sicht', *Historische Zeitschrift*, 266 (1998), 561–606; Michael Hinz, *Der Zivilisationsprozess: Mythos oder Realität? Wissenschaftssoziologische Untersuchungen zur Elias-Duerr-Kontroverse* (Opladen: Leske und Budrich, 2002); Axel T. Paul, 'Die Gewalt der Scham: Elias, Duerr und das Problem der Historizität menschlicher Gefühle', *Mittelweg 36*, 16/2 (2007), 77–99.

[57] Elias, *Civilizing Process*, 91.   [58] Elias, *Civilizing Process*, 55–6.

[59] Elias, *Civilizing Process*, 60, 168.   [60] Elias, *Civilizing Process*, 29.

[61] Elias, *Civilizing Process*, 376. See also his remarks on the internalization of drives, the transformation of taboos into self-restraint, and for sport as a safety valve. Also on neuroses: 'It may be "that there have always been" "neuroses". But the "neuroses" we see about us today are a specific historical form of psychic conflict which needs psychogenetic and sociogenetic illumination.' Elias, *Civilizing Process*, 127.

[62] For more discussion of psychoanalysis and emotions in Elias see Barbara H. Rosenwein, 'Thinking Historically about Medieval Emotions', *History Compass*, 8/8 (2010), 828–42, esp. 829.

'structure of affects'; 'affect formation'; 'emotional life').[63] He also introduced composite terms, words that capture the real construction of emotions ('social structure and the structure of affects', 'social regulation and management of the emotions', 'affect-modelling').[64]

Considering the period during which Elias was writing, the way that he dealt with the conception of emotion was remarkably open. He wrote, for example:

> And this raises the question of the limit of the transformability of the psychic economy. Without doubt, it possesses specific regularities that may be called 'natural'. The historical process modifies it within these limits.[65]

Or:

> The formation of feelings of shame and revulsion and advances in the threshold of repugnance are both at once natural and historical processes. These forms of feeling are manifestations of human nature under specific social conditions, and they react in their turn on the socio-historical process as one of its elements.... So far as the psychical functions of humans are concerned, natural and historical processes work indissolubly together.[66]

These ideas include elements of both essentialism and social constructivism. They anticipate synthetic conceptions of emotions discussed in the 1990s by William M. Reddy, who considered emotions to be formed culturally and historically, but who never denied their universal corporeal core.

There are very many parallels between Elias and Febvre. Both assumed that feelings were subject to historical transformation; both advocated the use of psychology in history; both had an intersubjective concept of emotion; both considered that a history of emotions must make use of the depiction of feelings in paintings; and both were very sensitive to the thin skin of emotional control, to how quickly, in the Europe of Mussolini and Hitler, *emotio* threatened to break free of *ratio*.[67]

Nonetheless, Elias's progressive, intersubjective conception of emotion as the outcome of a reciprocal relationship between a fixed nature and a changing environment won no converts and had little impact when it was first published. His contemporaries and successors worked with an ahistorical and universalistic conception of emotion. In the late 1970s Jean Delumeau did register in his multi-volume book on fear in medieval and early modern Europe the widespread anxiety

---

[63] Elias, *Civilizing Process*, 28, 98, 169, 29.   [64] Elias, *Civilizing Process*, 169, 158, 29.

[65] Elias, *Civilizing Process*, 135.

[66] Elias, *Civilizing Process*, 135. On a single emotion, fear: 'To be sure, the possibility of feeling fear, just like that of feeling joy, is an unalterable part of human nature. But the strength, kind and structure of the fears and anxieties that smoulder or flare in the individual never depend solely on his or her own "nature" nor, at least in more complex societies, on the "nature" in the midst of which he or she lives. They are always determined, finally, by the history and the actual structure of his or her relations to other people, by the structure of society; and they change with it'; Elias, *Civilizing Process*, 442.

[67] For the opening towards psychology see Elias, *Civilizing Process*, 120–1.

of the epoch, but he treated this as a product of its time, since he did not ultimately consider emotion to be a cultural-historical variable.[68]

Theodore Zeldin, a British historian of Russian background who specializes in the history of France, took a different approach. His four-volume history of France from 1848 to 1945 turns upon 'six passions: ambition, love, anger, pride, taste, and anxiety'.[69] Taking the first of these emotions, what does Zeldin understand by ambition?

> The study of ambition—of hope and envy, of desire and frustration, of self-assertion, greed and imitation—puts class conflict, the bug held responsible for so many of society's ailments, under a microscope.[70]

It was therefore economic history and the history of labour movements that was about to be rewritten. Although Zeldin maintained that he would give equal weight to the observation of the private (family life and the like) and the public (political life), in practice the first predominated. The greatest part of his book is devoted to the emotional consequences of the individual's search for meaning in an era of individualism, where the foundations once provided by religion, family, and village no longer bound the social fabric together. More precisely, Zeldin creates a medical language for the description—and invention—of the ailments of individualism; of psychiatry and psychoanalysis in general, and fear and hysteria in particular.[71]

Zeldin was, like Elias, ahead of his time.[72] His turn to emotions can be read as a reaction to contemporary social history, which in the 1970s was dominated by a search for regularities, strict causality, quantification, and large-scale structures. A biographical explanation for Zeldin's far-sightedness can be found in the catastrophic history of Russian Jewry in the first half of the twentieth century which, like Febvre's account of Mussolini and Hitler, gave him insight into the supremacy of *emotio* over *ratio*. Zeldin's methodological credo was that human 'behaviour is muddled and obscure'; and this was in 1973, a good fifteen years before the poststructural reinterpretation of the individual as a many-layered, ambivalent, and

---

[68] Delumeau makes use of a stimulus-response framework drawn from contemporary experimental psychology. The historical study of fear does not for him involve the study of an emotion subject to change, but instead the analysis of historically changing fearful subjects and objects: 'who was afraid of what?'; Jean Delumeau, *La Peur en Occident (XVIe–XVIIIe siècles): Une cité assiégée* (Paris: Fayard, 1978), 21.

[69] Theodore Zeldin, *France, 1848–1945*, i. *Ambition and Love* (Oxford: Oxford University Press, 1979), vii. The passage quoted was inserted into the Preface of the 2nd edn and is missing from the 1st edn published in 1973. See also Zeldin's instructive reflections on his multi-volume work in 'Personal History and the History of Emotions', *Journal of Social History*, 15/3 (1982), 339–47; and also Zeldin, *An Intimate History of Humanity* (New York: HarperCollins, 1994).

[70] Zeldin, *France, 1848–1945*, i. *Ambition and Love*, vii.

[71] Zeldin, *France, 1848–1945*, ii. *Intellect, Taste and Anxiety* (Oxford: Clarendon Press, 1977), esp. ch. 3, 'Worry, Boredom and Hysteria'. See also ch. 2, 'Individualism and the Emotions', in which Zeldin outlines the search for meaning, and its associated emotional costs, in the work of writers from the Romantics to Flaubert and Proust.

[72] Zeldin was not entirely alone. In the later 1970s his doctoral student Judith Devlin studied the remnants of superstition in French 19th-century popular culture, and in this context also touched on emotions; Judith Devlin, *The Superstitious Mind: French Peasants and the Supernatural in the Nineteenth Century* (New Haven: Yale University Press, 1987).

elastic entity began to gain ground among anti-positivist historians who took an interest in theory.[73] Zeldin also took the view that human conduct manifested itself in enormous variety, and 'each activity moved around its own axes, was absorbed by its own preoccupations and divided on lines peculiar to itself'—a position that was close to that of the sociologists Pierre Bourdieu and Niklas Luhmann, who at that time had little influence among historians.[74] Contemporary historians who worked in terms of Marxism or modernization theory assumed that the economy was predominant, treating all other social spheres (religion, science, sport, and so on) as subordinate manifestations; but for Bourdieu each 'field' had its own logic, and followed its own rhythm, while Luhmann talked in terms of 'systems' and 'subsystems'.[75] And Zeldin was one of the first who understood the historian to be a subject, someone whose action was determined by emotion and whose orientation to research and its aims is itself emotionally charged, a research object being selected in terms of emotional prejudices and predispositions. According to Zeldin, Jean Delameau had initiated

> his study because he wished to understand the terror he felt at the age of ten when a friend suddenly died; a terror so intense that he stayed away from school for three months; . . . so this history is very much a reflection on individual experience, giving birth to a massive reflection on the experience of others.[76]

During the 1970s and quite separately from the work of Zeldin, Febvre, or Elias, there also developed a new 'psychohistory', whose principal representatives were Peter Gay, Lloyd deMause, and Peter Loewenberg. Despite their differing approaches to a psychologizing history, they quickly agreed upon the importance of emotions.[77] Ute Frevert has suggested that Gay's multi-volume *The Bourgeois Experience* (1984–98)

[73] Zeldin, *France, 1848–1945*, i. *Ambition and Love*, vii.

[74] Zeldin, *France: 1848–1945*, ii. *Politics and Anger* (Oxford: Oxford University Press, 1979), ix.

[75] Pierre Bourdieu, *Distinction: A Social Critique of the Judgement of Taste*, trans. Richard Nice (Cambridge, MA: Harvard University Press, 1984); Niklas Luhmann, *Social Systems*, trans. John Bednarz, Jr with Dirk Baecker (Stanford, CA: Stanford University Press, 1995). There is an excellent comparison of Bourdieu's conception of 'field' and Luhmann's use of 'system' in a quite unexpected place: George Steinmetz, 'German Exceptionalism and the Origins of Nazism: The Career of a Concept', in Ian Kershaw and Moshe Lewin (eds), *Stalinism and Nazism: Dictatorships in Comparison* (Cambridge: Cambridge University Press, 1997), 251–83, esp. 269–71.

[76] Zeldin, 'Personal History and the History of Emotions', 345.

[77] See the description of childhood anxieties as the outcome of a lack of parental love and the practice of swaddling babies in Lloyd deMause, 'The Evolution of Childhood', in deMause (ed.), *The History of Childhood* (New York: Harper & Row, 1974), 1–73, esp. 49–50. See also Peter Gay, *The Bourgeois Experience: Victoria to Freud*, 5 vols (New York: Oxford University Press/Norton, 1984–98); Peter Loewenberg, 'Emotion und Subjektivität: Desiderata der gegenwärtigen Geschichtswissenschaft aus psychoanalytischer Perspektive', in Nolte et al. (eds), *Perspektiven der Gesellschaftsgeschichte*, 58–78. On the premodern period: Lyndal Roper, *Oedipus and the Devil: Witchcraft, Sexuality and Religion in Early Modern Europe* (London: Routledge, 1994); and Roper on the advantages of using psychoanalytical categories in the history of emotions: 'I find psychoanalytic theories the most helpful, because they offer a way of thinking about emotions as connected to internal states and conflicts. Psychoanalytic insights can help us think about the causes of particular emotions, and about both the unconscious and conscious processes at work in our relations with others. . . . The major challenges which any use of psychoanalytic ideas faces are twofold. First, psychoanalysis is much better

writes the history of the nineteenth century as a history of drives and their forms of expression in a way that subsumes not only the intimate pillow talk of the bourgeois couple, but also Theodore Roosevelt's passion for hunting and the pre-First World War diplomacy of calculated risk.[78]

However, the more general criticism of psychohistory is addressed to its interpretation of feelings—emotions are forced ahistorically into psychoanalytic or psychological categories that are in fact specific to particular times and places. This was, for instance, how Erik Erikson's explanation of Martin Luther's doctrine of justification by faith came about:

> The interpretation is plausible that Martin was driven early out of the trust stage, out from 'under his mother's skirts', by a jealously ambitious father who tried to make him precociously independent from women, and sober and reliable in his work. Hans succeeded, but not without storing in the boy . . . a deep nostalgia for a situation of infantile trust. His theological solution—spiritual return to a faith which is there before all doubt, combined with a political submission to those who by necessity must wield the sword of secular law—seems to fit perfectly his personal need for compromise.[79]

From this perspective it was also predictable that Stalin 'as a leader, . . . was responsible for the deaths of millions of his countrymen' following 'frightful beatings' as a child from his alcoholic father;[80] and likewise the Velvet Revolution during the later 1980s in Eastern Europe became the outcome 'of an earlier growth of love toward children'.[81] The psychohistorical account of emotion and its history is thus full of glaring anachronisms. Psychoanalysis can serve a purpose where historical actors do speak its language, and provide some insight into the history of feelings. Hence, for example, the emotional history of West Germany's leftist experiments in communal living during the 1970s and 1980s could not be written without using emotional categories mediated by psychoanalytical terminology.[82]

---

at explaining individuals than it is at dealing with groups; and historians usually want to understand collective behaviour. The second danger is that unless we historicize its use very carefully, psychoanalysis can end up being reductive, so that all kinds of different historical processes can be reduced back to oedipal feelings and aggressions, or to unresolved ego differentiation from the mother. When psychoanalysis starts to flatten our explanations, so that they become predictable, they fit too easy, then they cease to make the subjectivity of people in the past truly riveting—the only point of using such theories'; 'Forum: History of Emotions', *German History*, 28/1 (2010), 67–80, here 71.

[78] Frevert, 'Angst vor Gefühlen?', 97.

[79] Erik H. Erikson, *Young Man Luther: A Study in Psychoanalysis and History* (New York: Norton, 1962), 255–6.

[80] Lloyd deMause, 'The Gentle Revolution: Childhood Origins of Soviet and East European Democratic Movements', *Journal of Psychohistory*, 17/4 (1990) <http://www.kidhistory.org/gentle.html> accessed 11 February 2014.

[81] deMause, 'The Gentle Revolution'.

[82] Cf. Sven Reichardt, *Authentizität und Gemeinschaft: Linksalternatives Leben in den siebziger und frühen achtziger Jahren* (Berlin: Suhrkamp, 2014); Sven Reichardt, '"Wärme" als Modus sozialen Verhaltens? Vorüberlegungen zu einer Kulturgeschichte des linksalternativen Milieus vom Ende der sechziger bis Anfang der achtziger Jahre', *Vorgänge*, 44/3–4 (2005), 175–87; Sven Reichardt, 'Authentizität und Gemeinschaftsbindung: Politik und Lebensstil im linksalternativen Milieu vom

From the late 1970s German and American early modern historians (Hans Medick, David Sabean, Louis Tilly), British demographic historians (linked to Jack Goody), and French anthropologists all turned their attention to family history and emotions, without any reference to psychology and psychoanalysis. Institutionally, this multidisciplinary group was anchored at the Max Planck Institute for History in Göttingen and the Maison des Sciences de l'Homme in Paris. Substantively, they sought to break with the dichotomous thinking of many contemporary social scientists, polarized between disinterested (affective) mother–child relationships on the one hand, and self-interested (non-affective) relationships among male family members on the other. Instead, they sought to reinstall the relationship between emotion and purposive rationality.[83] There was 'no simple association between arrangements of family roles and the emotional commitment to them', and that meant, according to Esther Goody, that relationships between mother and child, as well as those between father and child, could in no respect be regarded as disinterested, or devoid of feeling.[84] Researchers based in Göttingen and Paris also questioned the narrative of family history constructed by Edward Shorter and others, a narrative that presumed a steadily increasing emotional content to relationships between couples from the eighteenth century onwards, since for the preceding period it was true that if 'we encounter young men passing up fat dowries to wed their heart's desire, we shall know we're standing before romance'.[85] Before the onset of early modernity, relations between couples and within families were by no means limited to purposive rationality.

The rise of gender history during the 1970s followed a similar path to the arguments being developed in Göttingen and Paris.[86] They too reacted against Shorter's argument that the rise in the number of illegitimate births between 1750 and 1850 could be used to show that women were becoming increasingly involved in relationships based upon love rather than practical considerations, and that modernity could therefore be read as a progressive history of the romanticization of conjugality.[87] Gisela Bock and Barbara Duden objected that this idea of

---

Ende der 1960er bis zum Anfang der 1980er Jahre', *Forschungsjournal Neue Soziale Bewegungen*, 21/3 (2008), 118–30.

[83] Hans Medick and David Warren Sabean, 'Introduction' in Medick and Sabean (eds), *Interest and Emotion: Essays on the Study of Family and Kinship* (Cambridge: Cambridge University Press, 1984), 1–8, here 4. More than twenty years later Susan Broomhall extended the perspective from the family to the entire household; Susan Broomhall (ed.), *Emotions in the Household, 1200–1900* (Basingstoke: Palgrave Macmillan, 2008).

[84] Esther Goody, 'Parental Strategies: Calculation of Sentiment? Fostering Practice among West Africans', in Medick and Sabean (eds), *Interest and Emotion*, 266–77, here 277.

[85] Edward Shorter, *The Making of the Modern Family* (New York: Basic Books, 1975), 17.

[86] For an introduction to gender history and emotions, and especially love, see Ingrid Bauer, Christa Hämmerle, and Gabriella Hauch, 'Liebe widerständig erforschen: Eine Einleitung', in Bauer, Hämmerle, and Hauch (eds), *Liebe und Widerstand: Ambivalenzen historischer Geschlechterbeziehungen* (Vienna: Böhlau, 2005), 9–35.

[87] Shorter, *Making of the Modern Family*, 80–3, 148–61. See also the chapter on familial affective relationships in Lawrence Stone, *The Family, Sex and Marriage in England, 1500–1800* (New York: Harper & Row, 1977), 102–19.

romanticization had recast female domestic labour as non-labour, and so consoli-
dated the subordination of women in the early modern marriage:

> In the customary institution of family and marriage the wife surrendered to the
> husband both her capacity for physical work and her sexuality for life, or the duration
> of the marriage; her activity was attributed to love, and was paid for with love—even if
> the facts tell a very different story, and that in the marriage market it was not only love
> that was exchanged for love, but the work of love for subsistence.[88]

And so it is evident that in the early days of gender history, which was primarily
women's history, and even called itself so, emphasis was laid upon the instrumentalization of feelings to reinforce established gender inequalities and create new
ones. The supposedly biological and essential quality of a natural 'mother love' was
also a target for this new history of gender.[89]

During the 1980s and 1990s, and influenced by the 'linguistic turn', gender
historians problematized the category of gender, discovering increasing evidence
that what were thought to be fixed physical differences between men and women
were in fact historical constructs. Gender history fragmented into the history of the
body, the history of sexuality, men's history, and a number of other subdivisions. In
none of these was emotion made an independent object of study.[90] As in the early
modern family history developed in Göttingen and Paris, emotion remained
peripheral, so that in 1997 Edith Saurer (1942–2011) argued that it was 'about
time that the history of love was taken as a point of departure for a history of gender
relationships'.[91] All the same, the contribution made by the women's movement of

---

[88] Gisela Bock and Barbara Duden, 'Arbeit aus Liebe—Liebe als Arbeit: Zur Entstehung der
Hausarbeit im Kapitalismus', in Gruppe Berliner Dozentinnen (eds), *Frauen und Wissenschaft:
Beiträge zur Berliner Sommeruniversität für Frauen, Juli 1976* (Berlin: Courage, 1977), 118–99, here
121. Shorter's arguments had already been criticized by early feminists; Simone de Beauvoir (1908–86)
wrote in 1949: 'The word love has by no means the same sense for both sexes, and this is one cause of
the serious misunderstandings that divide them. Byron well said: "Man's love is of man's life a thing
apart, 'Tis woman's whole existence." ' Since the woman 'is anyway doomed to dependence, she will
prefer to serve a god rather than obey tyrants—parents, husband, or protector. She chooses to desire
her enslavement so ardently that it will seem to her the expression of her liberty; she will try to rise
above her situation as inessential object by fully accepting it; through her flesh, her feelings, her
behaviour, she will enthrone him as supreme value and reality: she will humble herself to nothingness
before him. Love becomes for her a religion.' Authentic love can only exist between two equal and
autonomous persons: 'Genuine love ought to be founded on the mutual recognition of two liberties;
the lovers would then experience themselves both as self and as other'; Simone de Beauvoir, *The Second
Sex*, ed. and trans. H. M. Parshley (Harmondsworth: Penguin, 1972), 652, 653, 677.

[89] See e.g. Elisabeth Badinter, *Mother Love: Myth and Reality: Motherhood in Modern History*
(New York: Macmillan, 1981); Yvonne Schütze, *Die gute Mutter: Zur Geschichte des normativen
Musters 'Mutterliebe'* (Bielefeld: Kleine, 1986).

[90] Typical of the marginal status of emotion in gender history is the way in which feelings are dealt
with only in passing in a well-known introduction to gender history—see Claudia Opitz-Belakhal,
Geschlechtergeschichte (Frankfurt am Main: Campus, 2010), 110—and where the issue is only raised at
the end of a summary of the 4th vol. of Philippe Ariès and George Duby (gen. eds), *A History of Private
Life*: iv. *From the Fires of Revolution to the Great War*, ed. Michelle Perrot, trans. Arthur Goldhammer
(Cambridge, MA: Belknap Press, 1994) [Fr. orig., *Histoire de la vie privée*, iv. *De la révolution à la
grande guerre*, 1987].

[91] Edith Saurer, 'Liebe, Geschlechterbeziehungen und Feminismus', *L'Homme*, 8/1 (1997), 6–20,
here 20.

the 1970s to the ennoblement of stereotypical female emotions, even as objects of study on the part of experimental psychology, cannot be underestimated.

In the mid-1980s the history of emotions made a major advance thanks to the work of Peter N. Stearns, the founding editor of the *Journal of Social History*, and Carol Zisowitz Stearns, a historian and psychiatrist. In a widely read article in the *American Historical Review* they proposed a strict distinction between the individual experience of emotion and emotional norms, making the latter the prime object of study. They coined the term 'emotionology' as the name for this work, and defined it as

> the attitudes or standards that a society, or a definable group within a society, maintains toward basic emotions and their appropriate expression; ways that institutions reflect and encourage these attitudes in human conduct.[92]

Historians should direct their attention to the regulatory apparatus that governed the expression of feelings in society as a whole, or its elemental social groups. The institutions they had in mind here were kindergartens, schools, and armies, but also marriage and the family. In schools, for instance, young people were taught to respect their elders, military service taught soldiers to conceal their fear, and within the family parents presented to children an ideal relationship based upon the model of romantic love. Of course, emotional norms were not frozen and static, but subject to historical change. Hence the anti-authoritarian education of the 1960s mutated into love between equals; military reforms in the US Army during the Vietnam War promoted a more open acknowledgement of a soldier's fears, although this really turned out to be a new way of dealing with such fears; and romantic love turned out to be a recent historical construct dating from the period after the French Revolution.

The Stearns regarded emotion and emotionology as distinct analytical entities, but mutually related. The relationship between emotion and emotionology was reorganized in regard to the range of feelings that historical actors had. If in one period it had been socially acceptable for there to be expressions of rage in marital disputes, but not in a subsequent period, then a continuing feeling of rage became, in a new historical constellation, a feeling of guilt, accessible to historians through diaries.[93] This brings us to the problem of sources, something that the history of emotions highlights and to which the Stearns drew attention. Their first article in 1985 employed personal sources such as diaries and autobiographies as well as belles-lettres; also the classical socio-historical sources of social protest (strikes, demonstrations, revolutions) that could, with care, be used as evidence of emotion; later they focused upon self-help literature.[94] From the very beginning they were as social historians very concerned about the difficulty of gaining access to the

---

[92] Peter N. Stearns and Carol Z. Stearns, 'Emotionology: Clarifying the History of Emotions and Emotional Standards', *American Historical Review*, 90/4 (1985), 813–36, here 813.
[93] Stearns and Stearns, 'Emotionology', 825.
[94] See e.g. Carol Zisowitz Stearns and Peter N. Stearns, *Anger: The Struggle for Emotional Control in America's History* (Chicago: University of Chicago Press, 1986).

emotions of the working classes, especially those who were illiterate.[95] The later focus upon self-help literature led to the accusation that they had abandoned this concern, and that they overestimated the social reach of their sources. Barbara H. Rosenwein argued, for example, that whatever they gleaned from books of etiquette regarding anger, envy, or fear was unrepresentative of society as a whole, but related only to one part of the middle class.[96]

Peter and Carol Stearns thought of the history of emotions as an extension of social history. This might seem surprising today, as at the beginning of the twenty-first century many would place the history of emotions as part of the new cultural history, even perhaps of discourse analysis, the history of the body, or of gender history. But from the perspective of the later 1970s and 1980s the Stearns, together with Huizinga, Febvre, Elias, Delumeau, and Zeldin, looked to Anglo-American and French social history as it had developed since the 1960s, including its many offshoots, especially family history. Here, among the early modern historians in Göttingen and Paris, as well as in contemporary gender history, at issue were primarily the emotions of love, fear, anger, and envy. In addition, John Demos had cast socio-historical light upon the relationships between the original Pilgrim settlers, where the promotion of love between spouses can be seen as a way of forestalling the destructive social potential of marital disputes. Abram De Swann had also shown that the quantitative decline in workers' protests in the Western world during the second half of the twentieth century could be related to the strategic management of personnel: he argued that the introduction of foremen who were more flexible and positively disposed to employers 'optimized' the 'emotional management' of employees in a company, choking off protest before it had time to develop.[97] At the same time, the Stearns marked themselves off from New Left historians like Charles Tilly and George Rudé who, in turn marking themselves off from Le Bon, described human masses in revolt and in other collective forms of protest as acting from rational grounds: as actors who were goal-oriented and who acted in their own self-interest, and not chaotically, unpredictably, and at times contrary to their own self-interest.[98] By contrast, the Stearns' declared aim was to provide some historical insight into the turbulent nature of collective protest.[99] Following their programmatic 1985 paper, over the next two decades the Stearns published a considerable number of monographs: on anger and emotional control in American history, on envy, on 'coolness' as an emotional style in twentieth-century America, and on fear.[100] For them, the central caesura in the

[95] Stearns and Stearns, 'Emotionology', 830.
[96] Rosenwein, 'Worrying about Emotions in History', 824–5.
[97] Stearns and Stearns, 'Emotionology', 818 (Demos); 832 (De Swaan).
[98] George F. E. Rudé, *The Crowd in History: A Study of Popular Disturbances in France and England, 1730–1848* (New York: Wiley, 1964); Charles Tilly, Louise Tilly, and Richard H. Tilly, *The Rebellious Century, 1830–1930* (Cambridge, MA: Harvard University Press, 1975); Charles Tilly, *From Mobilization to Revolution* (Reading, MA: Addison-Wesley, 1978).
[99] Stearns and Stearns, 'Emotionology', 816–17.
[100] Stearns and Stearns, *Anger*; Peter N. Stearns, *Jealousy: The Evolution of an Emotion in American History* (New York: New York University Press, 1989); Peter N. Stearns, *American Cool: Constructing a Twentieth-Century Emotional Style* (New York: New York University Press, 1994); Peter N. Stearns

history of emotional norms could be identified with the onset of modernity in 1600. This led subsequently to the accusation that they had uncritically adopted Elias's chronology; they had simply left it intact and started their studies *after* the illusory watershed proposed by Huizinga, Febvre, and Elias.[101] Despite the Stearns' academic influence, and some evidence of institutionalization with the book series *The History of Emotions* edited by Peter N. Stearns and Jan Lewis from 1993, the history of emotions did not at this time achieve the kind of breakthrough that gender history, the history of the body, post-colonial history, and other variants had done in the later 1980s and the 1990s.[102]

Nonetheless, writing on the history of emotions that did get published was subject to a change of theoretical paradigm. While in the mid-1990s the linguistic turn was only beginning to have an impact in Germany on disciplines such as history, in the USA a much more consequential shift was affecting a whole spectrum of disciplines: the rise of the life sciences to predominance. Chapter Three deals in greater detail with this tectonic shift. For the moment, it can be said that from an epistemological point of view the rise of the life sciences reinvigorated domains that had been sidelined by the linguistic turn: objectivity, empiricism, universalism (both temporal and cultural), serious, non-ironic modes of exposition. Free-floating signs and changing meanings, fluid identities, postmodern 'anything goes', language games and irony—all of this came under enormous pressure. American historical writings, including those which dealt with feelings, quickly showed the impact of this transformation. The tendency to deal with emotions in terms of research results drawn from the life sciences increased, especially since emotion formed one of the core domains of the life sciences, unlike, say, social inequality or political culture. William M. Reddy, an American historian, anthropologist, and specialist on France, was in the early 1990s the first to use ideas drawn from the life sciences in his work on emotions, making particular use of cognitive psychology. The result was a series of programmatic essays, among them 'Against Constructionism', and *The Navigation of Feeling*.[103] The latter, presented in detail in Chapter Four, brings together social constructivist approaches to the anthropology of emotion with the universalism of cognitive psychology, proposing a synthetic history of emotions that is then applied to the history of eighteenth-century France and the Terror during the French Revolution.

---

and Jan Lewis (eds), *An Emotional History of the United States* (New York: New York University Press, 1998); Peter N. Stearns, *American Fear: The Causes and Consequences of High Anxiety* (London: Routledge, 2006).

[101] Rosenwein, 'Worrying about Emotions in History', 826.

[102] See also the conference on 'The Historicity of Emotions' (1998), developed out of a six-month seminar at the Institute for Advanced Studies of the Hebrew University, Jerusalem. Among those participating in the conference were Natalie Zemon Davis and Anthony Grafton; it was organized by Michael Heyd and Yosef Kaplan; email from Michal Altbauer-Rudnik (10 June 2007).

[103] William M. Reddy, 'Against Constructionism: The Historical Ethnography of Emotions', *Current Anthropology*, 38/3 (1997), 327–51; William M. Reddy, *The Navigation of Feeling: A Framework for the History of Emotions* (Cambridge: Cambridge University Press, 2001).

4 THE HISTORY OF EMOTIONS AND 9/11

The Navigation of Feeling was published on 10 September 2001.[104] The next day came to be 9/11. A coincidence, of course, but there is a connection between the two events. While 9/11 was an abrupt wake-up call, it also became a catalyst that accelerated the development of longer-term processes: both the instant and the catalysis contributed to the present global boom in the study of the history of emotions.

At first, 9/11 seemed to realize dramatically the force of fanatical negative emotions. Dan Rather, the veteran anchorman of American TV news, described the motivation of the terrorists as 'deep, abiding hate' in the edition of David Letterman's *Late Show* broadcast on 17 September, the first since the attack on the Twin Towers. He broke down in tears twice.[105] Directly after 9/11 many others identified hatred and envy as the leading motivation of the suicide bombers.[106] Hence, when the American Senate opened its hearing into 'terrorist organizations and motivations' on 15 November, the invited security expert, a psychiatrist and senior adviser to President Bush, began by attacking this very thesis: 'The first thing to emphasize is that terrorists are not seriously psychologically disturbed. These are not crazed fanatics. In fact, terrorist groups expel from their midst emotionally disturbed individuals just as a Green Beret squad would.'[107]

Simultaneously 9/11 triggered a tsunami of overwrought communication, both in the USA and elsewhere. Because this was mainly through electronic media—texts, mobile phone clips, chat room conversations, blogs, and emails—historians talked of 'history in e-motion'.[108] A central question that emerged here was whether or not the communicative fallout from 9/11 raised the profile of emotionally saturated communication in general, and related to men in particular. There is no doubt that the elevation to the status of national hero of men such as the firefighters at Ground Zero did not preclude description in the national media of

[104] Cf. *Amazon* <http://www.amazon.com/Navigation-Feeling-Framework-History-Emotions/dp/0521004721/ref=sr_1_1?ie=UTF8&s=books&qid=1216212175&sr=1-1> accessed 12 February 2014.
[105] 'Media Monitor', *The Hotline* (18 September 2001).
[106] James F. Williamson, 'Properly Fought, A Just War is Defensible', *Commercial Appeal* (12 October 2001), B5: 'Because hatred, jealousy and religious fundamentalism motivate them, terrorists are oblivious to the scorn of the community of nations'. On the average Afghan encountered by Allied forces: 'These clearly are people who are not filled with the hatred that motivates terrorists'; 'World Must Pitch in to Rebuild Afghanistan', *Press and Sun Bulletin* (18 November 2001), 14A.
[107] Jerrold Post, Clinical Professor, Psychiatry and Behavioral Sciences, George Washington University, cited in 'U.S. Senator Mary Landrieu (D-LA) Holds Hearing on Terrorist Organizations and Motivations', *Federal Document Clearing House (FDCH) Political Transcripts* (15 November 2001).
[108] The phrase 'history in e-motion' refers to the chronological chaos unleashed by the electronic communication related to 9/11, in which the actual sequence of events, and a clear sense of before and after, became blurred. See Despoina Valatsou, 'History, Our Own Stories and Emotions Online', *Historein: A Review of the Past and Other Stories*, 8 (2008), 108–16, here 114. The main source for this paper is the September 11 Digital Archive of the Center for History and New Media (CHNM), George Mason University, USA.

their emotional world, with its sense of loss and grief.[109] As 2001 came to an end, the word 'closure' came to be commonly used in op-ed pieces, hitherto a specialist term relating to the emotional processing of a traumatic event; although every time the term was used, actual 'closure' was postponed.[110] In American annual retrospectives at the end of December 2001 it was said that 'These images stay with us as we stumble into 2002, learning a vocabulary of new emotions, straddling the fine line between revenge and the pursuit of justice.'[111]

What of the long-term consequences of 11 September 2001? One effect was acceleration away from the linguistic turn, something already well under way in the American academy. The eleventh of September worked here as a catalyst. On all sides people asked what post-structuralism, in vogue since the 1980s, had to say about the raw violence involved in steering a plane full of passengers into a skyscraper full of people. What did discourse analysis have to say about phenomena like religious ecstasy and hatred, which after 11 September seemed so direct and prelinguistic that they were repeatedly referred to in terms of adjectives like 'archaic' and 'elemental'? The attacks in New York, Washington DC, and Pennsylvania cast the analytical armoury of post-structuralist history in doubt, and furthered the rise of the life sciences. This sudden perception that post-structuralism was irrelevant had an additional aesthetic effect. With one blow, the cultural-historical arsenal of the 1990s seemed trivial, ethically questionable, the ironic tone in which it was written inappropriate. The result was 'ironoclasm' in the writing of history and in other artistic domains, even if this turn away from irony was short-lived.[112]

Ultimately, 9/11 accelerated the bio-revolution that had begun in the second half of the 1990s. This revolution involved the final displacement of physics as the leading science by biology, and the appropriation by the new 'life sciences' of what had for centuries been considered the 'eternal' questions of humanity—free will, the nature of the self, also of feelings—and dealt with by the human sciences. One burning issue became: how guilty is a murderer who, detached from his environment, more or less automatically fulfils what he has been genetically programmed to do? How can he say 'I have murdered' if the 'I' cannot be detached from his

---

[109] '9/11: We Will Never Forget', *New York Post* (31 May 2002), 4; Terry Corcoran, 'Officers Recall the Cheers', *Journal News* (Westchester County, NY) (10 September 2002), 1A.

[110] Shaila K. Dewan, 'Closure? A Buzzword Becomes a Quest', *New York Times* (25 November 2001), section 1A, 41.

[111] Patrick May, '2001: A Year of Uncertainty', *San Jose Mercury News* (30 December 2001).

[112] This tectonic shift was also registered by these cultural seismographs, the feuilleton pages: see Edo Rents, 'Mehr Ironie wagen!', *Frankfurter Allgemeine Sonntagszeitung* (28 October 2001), 21; Susanne Ostwald, 'Ende der Ironie: Jedediah Purdy und die Halbwertszeit der Kulturkritik', *Neue Zürcher Zeitung* (21 January 2003), 51; MaryAnn Snyder-Körber, 'Was kommt nach dem 11. September? Die Terroranschläge des Jahres 2001 in den USA haben die Alltagskultur Nordamerikas nachhaltig verändert', *Der Tagesspiegel* (8 August 2007), Sonderthemen. It was the 'ironoclasm' of 2001 that made possible a historical retrospective upon the events of 1989 and the impulse it had given to irony; Dirk von Petersdorff, 'Die Schule der Ironie: 1789, 1989', *Merkur*, 64/732 (2010), 403–12, here 407. On the return of irony in the second half of the noughties, Andrian Kreye, 'Die leicht Verzweifelten: In den USA kehrt die Ironie zurück—als neue Ernsthaftigkeit', *Süddeutsche Zeitung* (28 February 2005), 13; Burkhard Müller, 'Sei niemals nicht ironisch: Empirisch gesichert: Kurssturz für das uneigentliche Reden', *Süddeutsche Zeitung* (26 November 2008), 13.

62   *The History of Emotions*

brain, if therefore the statement 'my brain has murdered' is inadmissible, since it presumes that a position exists outside the brain and involves speaking about the brain in the third person? And should the capacity for sympathy be treated as a positive characteristic of a person if sympathy is driven by mirror neurones? From the later 1990s the solution to these and other quite simplistic questions was sought in the opinions of neurobiologists, rather than of legal and ethical philosophers.

Generally speaking, the end of the twentieth century was a dizzying time: all the New Economy hype, apparently unending growth after the collapse of real existing socialism, and a time in which Craig Venter, the owner of a firm decoding the human genome who was widely regarded by natural scientists as a charlatan, got more coverage in the culture section's op-ed columns of the *Frankfurter Allgemeine Zeitung* than Jürgen Habermas.[113] It was a time when love was expressed in the language of evolutionary biology, as in Michel Houellebecq's *Les Particules élémentaires* (1998; Eng. *The Elementary Particles*, 2000).[114] Long passages of this novel read like a basic biology textbook. The relationship between the sexes is reduced to a struggle for the optimization of the male gene pool. *The Elementary Particles* also provided a scientific warrant for all men who, despite ideas of 'working on relationships' and 'socially constructed' conceptions of beauty, still felt themselves drawn to attractive young women, and broke up many a heterosexual couple from Paris to Prague. The eleventh of September brought about the end of this New Economy and biotech boom, but at the same time impelled the ideas and theories of the life sciences into the heart of a domain traditionally the preserve of the human sciences. All of these threads came together in 9/11. In sum: if one adheres to the fiction of a zero hour, and seeks a history that starts with a clear beginning, if therefore we are to look for the birthplace of today's history of emotions, then it is in Manhattan on the morning of 11 September 2001.

The history of emotions has enjoyed a boom ever since. Evidence for this can be found in conferences that take place all around the world, with research groups on three continents—America, Australia, and Europe.[115] The nature of emotion has

---

[113] Frank Schirrmacher, 'Die Patente der Fliege: Eine Begegnung mit J. Craig Venter', *Frankfurter Allgemeine Zeitung* (18 April 2000), 49.

[114] Michel Houellebecq, *The Elementary Particles*, trans. Frank Wynne (New York: Knopf, 2000). Frank Wynne's translation of the book was published in the UK as *Atomised* in the same year.

[115] Examples of conferences are: 'Representing Emotions: Evidence, Arousal, Analysis' with Peter Burke, Otniel Dror, and others (University of Manchester, May 2001); 'Emotions in Early Modern Europe and Colonial North America' (German Historical Institute, Washington DC, November 2002); four conferences of the working group Geschichte + Theorie (AG+T): 'Medien und Emotionen: Zur Geschichte ihrer Beziehungen seit dem 19. Jahrhundert' (Bochum, February 2005), 'Rationalisierungen des Gefühls: Zum Verhältnis von Wissenschaft und Emotionalität, 1880–1930' (Berlin, October 2006), 'Die Präsenz der Gefühle: Männlichkeit und Emotion in der Moderne' (Berlin, September 2007), and 'Eine Geschichte der Tiere—Eine Geschichte der Gefühle: Historische Perspektiven auf das 18. bis 20. Jahrhundert' (Berlin, May 2010); 'Emotsii v russkoi istorii i kul'ture' (Centre franco-russe de recherche en sciences humaines et sociales de Moscou and Deutsches Historisches Institut Moscow, April 2008); 'Interpreting Emotion in Eastern Europe, Russia, and Eurasia' (University of Illinois, Urbana-Champaign, June 2008); 'The Cultural History of Emotions in Premodernity' (Umeå University, October 2008). The most important research groups are the Institute for the Study of Emotion, Florida State University (with Reddy und Stearns as opening speakers 2002); the section 'Die Rolle der Emotion: Ihr Anteil bei menschlichem Handeln und bei der

become a common topic of discussion in the media. Nedko Solakov, a Bulgarian contemporary artist, created an installation in the Bonn Museum of Art which he simply called 'Emotions'.[116] In the international competition to stage the 2018 Ryder Cup Germany has adopted as its slogan 'Emotions made in Germany'.[117] Advertising copy writers talk of football as 'pure emotion'.[118] There is a popular magazine called *Emotion*. Cars are bought because of their emotional surplus value. And if someone seems likeable and sensitive to others we talk of their 'emotional intelligence' (EQ); or we complain if once again our neighbour lets his dog run around off the lead, referring to their low level of EQ.[119] It is no wonder that there is so much talk among academics and scientists of an 'emotional turn', or of an 'affective turn'.[120] Whether this will gel into a new historical subdiscipline, with professorships, journals, organizations, and conferences, remains to be seen. But the following scenario is certainly possible: unlike, for example, economic history, the history of emotions could be absorbed into other subdisciplines. Emotion adds a new dimension to gender, sexuality, the body, environment, and space, extending national, global, social, or even economic history.

What can be said about the outcome of this boom in the history of emotions? What results do we have, what can be added to the detailed reports on the 'state of the art' in 2010 and 2011 by Bettina Hitzer, Susan J. Matt, and Nina Verheyen?[121]

Setzung sozialer Normen' at the Collegium Helveticum, Zurich (since 2004); the programme based at the Universities of Aix-Marseille and Québec à Montréal, 'Les Émotions au Moyen Âge' (EMMA) (from 2006); the International Network for the Cultural History of Emotions in Premodernity (CHEP) at the University of Umeå (since 2007); the Excellence Cluster/Research Center 'Languages of Emotion' at the Freie Universität Berlin (since 2007); the Centre for the History of Emotions at the Max Planck Institute for Human Development in Berlin (from 2008); the Queen Mary Centre for the History of Emotions at the University of London (from 2008); the section 'Emotional Culture and Identity' (CEMID) at the Institute for Culture and Society, University of Navarra (from 2010); and the Australian Research Council Centre of Excellence for the History of Emotions (from 2011).

[116] Rainer Burkard, 'Ekelige Verführung', *Die Zeit*, 41 (22 October 2008), 55.

[117] *Golf Time* 12 (July/August 2009), 33.

[118] 'Tränen als pure Emotion', *Fifa.com* (23 April 2010) <http://de.fifa.com/worldfootball/news/newsid=1198668.html> accessed 20 February 2014.

[119] Daniel Goleman, *Emotional Intelligence: Why It Can Matter More Than IQ* (New York: Bantam Books, 1995).

[120] Thomas Anz, 'Emotional Turn? Beobachtungen zur Gefühlsforschung', *literaturkritik.de* (18 January 2007) <http://www.literaturkritik.de/public/rezension.php?rez_id=10267> accessed 20 February 2014; Rainer Schützeichel, 'Emotionen und Sozialtheorie: Eine Einleitung', in Schützeichel (ed.), *Emotionen und Sozialtheorie: Disziplinäre Ansätze* (Frankfurt am Main: Campus, 2006), 7–26, here 7; Patricia Ticineto Clough and Jean Halley (eds), *The Affective Turn: Theorizing the Social* (Durham, NC: Duke University Press, 2007); Vanessa Agnew, 'History's Affective Turn: Historical Reenactment and Its Work in the Present', *Rethinking History*, 11/3 (2007), 299–312; Ute Frevert, 'Was haben Gefühle in der Geschichte zu suchen?', *Geschichte und Gesellschaft*, 35/2 (2009), 183–208, here 183–4; Jürgen Kaube, 'Tränenkunde: Die Dämpfe des Herzens', review of Beate Söntgen and Geraldine Spiekermann (eds), *Tränen* (Munich: Fink, 2008), in *Frankfurter Allgemeine Zeitung* (10 June 2009), N3: 'Following on from what no-one has yet called an "emotional turn", but is exactly that, following on from the contemporary enthusiasm in the cultural sciences for feeling, presence, emotion, passion, affect and other conditions of arousal'; Jan Plamper, 'Introduction' in *Emotional Turn? Feelings in Russian History and Culture* [Special Section], *Slavic Review*, 68/2 (2009), 229–37.

[121] Bettina Hitzer, 'Emotionsgeschichte: Ein Anfang mit Folgen', *H-Soz-u-Kult* (23 November 2011) <http://hsozkult.geschichte.hu-berlin.de/forum/2011-11-001> accessed 20 February 2014;

Although it is difficult to map a rapidly expanding and shifting terrain, I will try to describe its contours and limits as they stand in 2012.

One limitation is immediately obvious: the history of emotions is overwhelmingly a European and North American history, even if there are a few essays and monographs dealing with the world beyond—for instance, on the theories of emotion embedded in early Chinese medicine and philosophy, or on anger in medieval Arab-Islamic literature.[122] The Japanese code of honour has also been studied from the perspective of the history of emotions, as has the wave of public sympathy induced by the media for a Chinese mass murderer of the 1930s.[123] The same is true for some aspects of colonial history, for instance, Dutch Islamophobia and the mutually related cultures of fear shared by the original inhabitants of California and the Spanish colonial masters.[124] And for India there have been in the last few years a number of important histories published dealing with love, linguistic nationalism, and emotion, and the interconnection of the history of the body and of emotion.[125] Also among these works can be included the various

Susan J. Matt, 'Current Emotion Research in History: Or, Doing History from the Inside Out', *Emotion Review*, 3/1 (2011), 117–24; Nina Verheyen, 'Geschichte der Gefühle [Version: 1.0]', *Docupedia-Zeitgeschichte* (18 June 2010) <http://docupedia.de/zg/Geschichte_der_Gef%C3%BChle> accessed 20 February 2014. See also the literature which has a more restricted remit, or is older: William M. Reddy, 'Historical Research on the Self and Emotions', *Emotion Review*, 1/4 (2009), 302–15; Florian Weber, 'Von der klassischen Affektenlehre zur Neurowissenschaft und zurück: Wege der Emotionsforschung in den Geistes- und Sozialwissenschaften', *Neue Politische Literatur*, 53 (2008), 21–42; Alexandra Przyrembel, 'Sehnsucht nach Gefühlen: Zur Konjunktur der Emotionen in der Geschichtswissenschaft', *L'Homme*, 16 (2005), 116–24; Schnell, 'Historische Emotionsforschung'.

[122] Angelika C. Messner, 'Emotions, Body, and Bodily Sensations within an Early Field of Expertise Knowledge in China', in Paolo Santangelo and Ulrike Middendorf (eds), *From Skin to Heart: Perceptions of Emotions and Bodily Sensations in Traditional Chinese Culture* (Wiesbaden: Harrassowitz, 2006), 41–63; Angelika C. Messner, 'Making Sense of Signs: Emotions in Chinese Medical Texts', in Paolo Santangelo and Donatella Guida (eds), *Love, Hatred, and Other Emotions: Questions and Themes on Emotions in Chinese Civilization* (Leiden: Brill, 2006), 91–109; Curie Virág, 'Emotions and Human Agency in the Thought of Zhu Xi', *Journal of Song Yuan Studies*, 37 (2007), 49–88; Zouhair Ghazzal, 'From Anger on Behalf of God to "Forbearance" in Islamic Medieval Literature', in Barbara H. Rosenwein (ed.), *Anger's Past: The Social Uses of an Emotion in the Middle Ages* (Ithaca, NY: Cornell University Press, 1998), 203–30.

[123] Eiko Ikegami, 'Emotions', in Ulinka Rublack (ed.), *A Concise Companion to History* (Oxford: Oxford University Press, 2011), 333–53; Eugenia Lean, *Public Passions: The Trial of Shi Jianqiao and the Rise of Popular Sympathy in Republican China* (Berkeley and Los Angeles: University of California Press, 2007).

[124] Michael Laffan, 'White Hajjis: Dutch Islamophobias Past and Present', in Laffan and Max Weiss (eds), *Facing Fear: The History of an Emotion in Global Perspective* (Princeton: Princeton University Press, 2012), 202–16; Lisbeth Haas, 'Fear in Colonial California and within the Borderlands', in Laffan and Weiss (eds), *Facing Fear*, 74–90.

[125] Daud Ali, 'Anxieties of Attachment: The Dynamics of Courtship in Medieval India', *Modern Asian Studies*, 36/1 (2002), 103–39; Francesca Orsini, 'Love Letters', in Orsini (ed.), *Love in South Asia: A Cultural History* (Cambridge: Cambridge University Press, 2006), 228–58; Sumathi Ramaswamy, *Passions of the Tongue: Language Devotion in Tamil India, 1891–1970* (Berkeley and Los Angeles: University of California Press, 1997); Lisa Mitchell, *Language, Emotion, and Politics in South India: The Making of a Mother Tongue* (Bloomington: Indiana University Press, 2009); Scott Kugle, *Rebel Between Spirit and Law: Ahmad Zarruq, Sainthood and Authority in Islam* (Bloomington: Indiana University Press, 2006); Joseph S. Alter, *Gandhi's Body: Sex, Diet and the Politics of Nationalism* (Philadelphia: University of Pennsylvania Press, 2000). See also colonial history written from the perspective of the history of emotions: Margaret Critchlow Rodman, 'The Heart in the Archives:

publications of Margrit Pernau, who has studied Indian-Muslim literature on etiquette and gendering, in which guidance is given on feeling and the expression of emotion, together with the related Indian-Muslim discourse of civility and its emotional elements.[126]

What do the classical eras of European history have to tell us? I have already talked about emotions and archaeology in the Introduction.[127] For ancient history, Egon Flaig has, among others, shown how Roman politicians made deliberate use of emotionally coded gestures.[128]

An example: in 133 BC the Tribune Tiberius Gracchus introduced a draft for a new agrarian law. When one of the other tribunes opposed it, as usually happened with attempts to reform the laws governing aristocratic landownership, this amounted to an almost insuperable veto. Tiberius Gracchus therefore refused to carry out his administrative functions, and brought the work of the Senate to a halt. Two senators then interrupted one of his public meetings and sought, in front of thousands of Roman citizens, to persuade him to change his mind by using emotional gestures, the Greek historian Plutarch describing the affair as follows: 'Manlius and Fulvius, men of consular dignity, fell down before Tiberius, clasped his hands, and with tears besought him to desist.'[129] Since the rules of public political communication dictated that the addressee of such gestures had to act, Tiberius Gracchus went straight to the Senate. Since the senators continued to

---

Colonial Contestation of Desire and Fear in the New Hebrides, 1933', *Journal of Pacific History*, 38/3 (2003), 291–312.

[126] Margrit Pernau, 'Male Anger and Female Malice: Emotions in Indo-Muslim Advice Literature', *History Compass*, 10/2 (2012), 119–28; Margrit Pernau, 'An ihren Gefühlen sollt Ihr sie erkennen: Eine Verflechtungsgeschichte des britischen Zivilitätsdiskurses (ca. 1750–1860)', *Geschichte und Gesellschaft*, 35/2 (2009), 249–81; Margrit Pernau, 'Teaching Emotions: The Encounter between Victorian Values and Indo-Persian Concepts of Civility in Nineteenth-Century Delhi', in Indra Sengupta and Daud Ali (eds), *Knowledge Production, Pedagogy, and Institutions in Colonial India* (New York: Palgrave Macmillan, 2011), 227–47; Margrit Pernau, *The History of Emotions in India* (forthcoming). Pernau has also supervised a number of doctoral students within Ute Frevert's Centre for the History of Emotions at the Max Planck Institute for Human Development in Berlin, and from this work has since been published: Monika Freier, 'Cultivating Emotions: The Gita Press and Its Agenda of Social and Spiritual Reform', *South Asian History and Culture*, 3/3 (2012), 397–413; M. Sajjad Alam Rizvi, 'Conceptualizing Emotions: Perspectives from South Asian Sufism', *Economic and Political Weekly* (forthcoming); Maritta Schleyer, '*Ghadr-e Dehli ke Afsane*', *Annual of Urdu Studies*, 27 (2012), 34–56.

[127] Sarah Tarlow, 'Emotion in Archaeology', *Current Anthropology*, 41/5 (2000), 713–46.

[128] Egon Flaig, 'Wie man mit Gesten zwingt: Der Einsatz des Emotionalen in der Politik des antiken Rom', *Sozialwissenschaftliche Information: Geschichte Politik Wirtschaft*, 30/3 (2001), 72–83. See also Alfred Kneppe, *Metus temporum: Zur Bedeutung von Angst in Politik und Gesellschaft der römischen Kaiserzeit des 1. und 2. Jhdts. n. Chr.* (Stuttgart: Steiner, 1994); Dirk Barghop, *Forum der Angst: Eine historisch-anthropologische Studie zu Verhaltensmustern von Senatoren im Römischen Kaiserreich* (Frankfurt am Main: Campus, 1994); Christian Meier, 'Die Angst und der Staat: Fragen und Thesen zur Geschichte menschlicher Affekte', in Hans Rössner (ed.), *Der ganze Mensch* (Munich: DTV, 1986), 228–46. From the perspective of ancient philology, David Konstan and N. Keith Rutter (eds), *Envy, Spite and Jealousy: The Rivalrous Emotions in Ancient Greece* (Edinburgh: Edinburgh University Press, 2003), and on Rome and Cicero's *Tusculanae disputationes*, Robert Kaster, *Emotion, Restraint, and Community in Ancient Rome* (New York: Oxford University Press, 2005).

[129] Plutarch, *Lives*, x. *Agis and Clemones, Tiberius and Caius Gracchus, Philopoemen and Flaminius*, trans. Bernadotte Perrin (Cambridge, MA: Harvard University Press: 1988), 171.

oppose his draft law, Tiberius threatened to hold a public vote over the political fate of his principal opponent, Octavius: should he retain the office of People's Tribune? A vote to remove him from office would be something completely new, and would result in exile—in other words, social death. Before the vote was taken, Tiberius therefore sought to persuade Octavius, with word and gesture, to approve the new law: 'In the first place, however, he begged Octavius in public, addressing him with kindly words and clasping his hands, to give in and gratify the people.'[130] Tiberius' emotionally charged gesture did not work, and Octavius lost the vote. Shortly before the end of the count, when only one more vote would have meant that his opponent would have lost the vote, Plutarch reported that Tiberius paused,

> and again entreated Octavius, embracing and kissing him in the sight of the people, and fervently begging him not to allow himself to be dishonoured, and not to attach to a friend responsibility for a measure so grievous and severe. On hearing these entreaties, we are told, Octavius was not altogether untouched or unmoved; his eyes filled with tears and he stood silent for a long time. But when he turned his gaze towards the men of wealth and substance who were standing in a body together, his awe of them, as it would seem, and his fear of ill repute among them, led him to take every risk with boldness and bid Tiberius do what he pleased.[131]

Ultimately Octavius refused to relent in his opposition to the agrarian law; he lost the vote and narrowly escaped being lynched. Tiberius' law was then passed by the popular assembly.

All the evidence regarding the bodily expression of Tiberius and his opponents come from a single historian, from Plutarch, but Flaig is able to draw upon other writings and sources that allow a 'culturally specific inventory of affective gestures' to be reconstructed: 'The semantics of gesture derives not from invariant psychic or relational dispositions, but from the seriality of events, from their variance and their embedment in confrontations that are always also disputes over imputed meanings.'[132] Given the 'habitual orientation to consensus' in the politics of the Roman elite, Tiberius' embrace and kisses meant the following for Octavius:

> If it is true that there was strong pressure upon Roman senators to arrive at a consensus, or, at least, remain open to the idea that a consensus could be achieved—and not only for them, but also for Romans in general, whether in their families or in public situations—then the embrace and kiss of Tiberius had a dual semantic valence: on the one hand, it made it easier for his opponent to relent in his bitter opposition, it built a bridge for him across which he could leave an untenable position without losing face.... On the other hand, this gesture signalled to the people that Octavius was immoveable, that he had a moral defect, because he was not capable of giving in, even though he knew that what he stood for was unjust, that he had departed from the basic rules of Roman behaviour, that he infringed the basic norms of a harmonious communal life.[133]

[130] Plutarch, *Lives*, x. 171.   [131] Plutarch, *Lives*, x. 173.
[132] Flaig, 'Wie man mit Gesten zwingt', 74.
[133] Flaig, 'Wie man mit Gesten zwingt', 76, 77.

Flaig here combines Pierre Bourdieu's praxeology with semiotics to produce a genuinely novel reading, a clear analysis of non-verbal political communication which had been previously treated by ancient historians as the idiosyncrasies of an individual, or as the result of unconscious motivations. He is also able to draw a comparison with Greek history, permitting him to identify what is new in Roman politics, and so in this way discover the traces of historical change.

5 BARBARA H. ROSENWEIN AND EMOTIONAL COMMUNITIES

Medieval studies were in the vanguard of the history of emotions.[134] This is in part because medieval scholars have for almost a century worked with a key text that is also a work fundamental to the history of emotions: Johan Huizinga's *Herfsttij der middeleeuwen* (1919; Eng. *The Waning of the Middle Ages*, 1924 and *The Autumn of the Middle Ages*, 1996). Foremost among the historians who have studied this text is Barbara H. Rosenwein. In 1998 she published a collection of essays dealing with anger, in which Huizinga's idea of an unmediated, childlike expression of emotion in the Middle Ages was placed in question. In a way rather similar to Flaig's work on antiquity, Gerd Althoff here showed that outbreaks of rage on the part of Merovingian kings were not the product of immaturity, or of hyperemotionality, but of something quite different: they were strategic signs in a process of symbolic communication. The open display of anger was aimed at both followers and foes, emphasizing the determination of the king to go to war.[135] Rosenwein discovered a conception of feeling in Johan Huizinga and Norbert Elias that could be called a 'pneumatic' or 'hydraulic' model:[136] universally conceived emotions are contained within the body and 'well up', 'boil over', 'break out', 'bubble over'—in short, they become visible. This happens in the most varied ways: physically, through verbal and non-verbal signs, or in the shape of art (the hydraulic model underlies the Freudian theory of the sublimation of drives). Rosenwein investigated the origin of hydraulic imagination, locating it in the medieval pathology of humours as well as in the 'nerve-force' that Darwin situated in the body's interior, manifesting itself as 'intense sensations', among which were emotions.[137]

---

[134] It is plain that study of the history of medieval emotions and the extensive development in medieval literary studies of a focus upon emotion has been mutually reinforcing. See e.g. Peter Godman, *Paradoxes of Conscience in the High Middle Ages: Abelard, Heloise, and the Archpoet* (Cambridge: Cambridge University Press, 2009).

[135] Gerd Althoff, '*Ira Regis*: Prolegomena to a History of Royal Anger', in Rosenwein (ed.), *Anger's Past*, 59–74.

[136] Rosenwein, 'Worrying about Emotions in History', 834; Jan Plamper, 'The History of Emotions: An Interview with William Reddy, Barbara H. Rosenwein, and Peter Stearns', *History and Theory*, 49/2 (2010), 237–65, here 250–2. The concept of a 'hydraulic model' can be traced back to Robert Solomon, among others: see Robert C. Solomon, *The Passions: Emotions and the Meaning of Life* (Indianapolis: Hackett, 1993), 77–88.

[137] Charles Darwin, *The Expression of the Emotions in Man and Animals*, with an introduction, afterword, and commentaries by Paul Ekman (3rd edn, New York: Oxford University Press, 1998), 74, cited in Rosenwein, 'Worrying about Emotions in History', 835.

In 2002 Rosenwein published an article that synthesized historical research on emotion.[138] This became an instant classic because of the way that it countered what she called the 'grand narrative' of the history of emotions: that 'the history of the West is the history of increasing emotional restraint'.[139] According to Rosenwein, this assumption had been shared by all previous historical theories of emotion—from Huizinga, through Elias and Febvre, to Dulumeau and the Stearns, from Weber's origin of capitalism via Freud's 'culture' to Foucault's modern disciplinary regimes that developed in early modernity.[140] The success of the 'grand narrative' presented by Huizinga and Elias was matched only by the erroneousness of their basic assumption, the hydraulic model. Any validity that it might have once had was ended by cognitive psychology in the 1960s, and anthropological social constructivism in the 1970s at the very latest. The former had replaced the idea of feelings as internal fluid processes by that of rational processes of cognition in the brain, while the latter had done away with the idea of universalism.

But what alternative was there to the 'grand narrative' of incremental emotional control? Rosenwein put forward her own way of thinking about the social foundation of emotion: emotional communities. She argued that

> These are precisely the same as social communities—families, neighborhoods, parliaments, guilds, monasteries, parish church memberships—but the researcher looking at them seeks above all to uncover systems of feeling: what these communities (and the individuals within them) define and assess as valuable or harmful to them; the evaluations that they make about other's emotions; the nature of the affective bonds between people that they recognize; and the modes of emotional expression that they expect, encourage, tolerate, and deplore.[141]

One had therefore to abandon any unconscious ahistorical transfer of the modern category of nation to periods where there was no such conception. During the Middle Ages people belonged to and moved between several, often overlapping communities that often embodied quite different emotional norms.[142]

Rosenwein has since further developed her idea of emotional communities, applying it to historical sources. Her book *Emotional Communities in the Early Middle Ages* (2006) explains how emotional communities are groups of persons who share the same norms regarding the expression of feelings, valuing the same feelings (or not).[143] Graphically, emotional communities form

[138] Rosenwein, 'Worrying about Emotions in History'.
[139] Rosenwein, 'Worrying about Emotions in History', 827.
[140] Rosenwein, 'Worrying about Emotions in History', 828.
[141] Rosenwein, 'Worrying about Emotions in History', 842.
[142] Rosenwein has developed her thoughts on the question of how diverse norms of feeling might be between the different emotional communities to which an individual could belong during the Middle Ages. Today she regards the degree of possible variation to be less great than she had thought in the 1990s and the early 2000s; Plamper, 'History of Emotions', 256–7.
[143] Barbara H. Rosenwein, *Emotional Communities in the Early Middle Ages* (Ithaca, NY: Cornell University Press, 2006), 2.

a large circle within which are smaller circles ... The large circle is the overarching emotional community, tied together by fundamental assumptions, values, goals, feeling rules, and accepted modes of expression. The smaller circles represent subordinate emotional communities, partaking in the larger one and revealing its possibilities and its limitations. They too may be subdivided. At the same time, other large circles may exist, either entirely isolated from or intersecting with the first at one or more points.[144]

It seems that this model was quite consciously formulated as being universally applicable, for all times and cultures, even if Rosenwein nowhere makes this explicit.

As a rule, Rosenwein considers emotional communities to be social communities with close relationships (i.e. with personal contact). They can however also be 'textual communities', in which people are linked together through media, without ever meeting. Rosenwein drew attention to the mnemonic techniques of the Middle Ages, in which texts were not only learned by heart, but also embodied and to an extent made part of the self, with which one could communicate in much the same way one did with a friend.[145] Emotional communities could therefore have affinities with Foucault's 'discourse', Bourdieu's 'habitus', and Reddy's 'emotives'. No emotional communities could be built upon one single emotion; only upon several, upon 'constellations'.[146]

How then in practice did Rosenwein identify emotional communities?[147] She did not usually begin from the sources, but started with a group of individuals already living a communal life—in a monastery, guild, or village.[148] For this group she then assembled a broad array of sources—as a medievalist, primarily ecclesiastical texts, deeds, hagiographies, letters, histories, chronicles.[149] She extracted emotion words from them, paying attention to pattern, narrative, and the distinction of male from female. Similar emotion words were assembled into dossiers. To avoid anachronism (any assumption that an emotion word was a constant, meaning the same in the past as it does today), Rosenwein studied the contemporary emotional theories of the emotional community (Thomist theories in the medieval case, psychological theories in the case of twentieth-century Western societies). Since emotions are not only represented explicitly by emotion words, she paid due attention to borrowings and imagery in emotional language (metaphors or figures

---

[144] Rosenwein, 'Worrying about Emotions in History', 24.

[145] At a lecture given on 6 July 2009 at the Centre for the History of Emotions at the Max Planck Institute for Human Development in Berlin Rosenwein noted that modern mass media also made possible the construction of emotional communities in which there was no direct contact between members.

[146] Rosenwein, *Emotional Communities in the Early Middle Ages*, 26.

[147] On Rosenwein's methodology see Plamper, 'History of Emotions', 253–4; Rosenwein, 'Thinking Historically about Medieval Emotions', 833–6; Barbara H. Rosenwein, 'Problems and Methods in the History of Emotions', *Passions in Context: Journal of the History and Philosophy of the Emotions*, 1 (2010), 12–24.

[148] She made this clear in her Berlin lecture of 6 July 2009.

[149] She also regarded images and music to be possible sources; see Plamper, 'History of Emotions', 254–5.

of speech, such as 'he exploded' when referring to rage). In putting the dossiers together she considered the frequency of particular emotion words, and evaluated these frequencies quantitatively. She argued that many emotion words had explicit or implicit normative functions and were to be understood as 'emotional scripts' whose temporal change should be a central object of historical investigation.[150]

In the introduction to *Emotional Communities* Rosenwein sought to counter possible criticism. She dealt here with the objection that source texts were themselves subject to the conventions of a particular genre. To avoid the possibility that the characteristics of a genre might be read as those of an emotional community, Rosenwein argued that it was necessary to use a very broad range of sources from diverse genres, making plain the rules governing the reproduction of any one genre. For the conventions of a genre are themselves historical constructs, whose principles of construction are open to analysis by the historian. She also addressed the argument that formulations in the sources that seemed to be saturated with emotion were often no more than conventional phrases, and not expressions of emotion. For example, the mode of address 'Dear X' or 'I am pleased to be able to accept new challenges' were simply turns of phrase that had little to do with love or with pleasure. Of course, responded Rosenwein, but these phrases were themselves subject to historical change that indicated something of the changing status of particular emotions. For Rosenwein, one always needs to keep historical relevance in mind when considering if, where, and in what period the common greeting is 'greetings!', 'great to see you!', or 'good day!'.[151]

The conception of emotional communities is an attractive way of approaching the way in which emotional bonds are formed and reproduced. It avoids the individualizing trap of psychohistory, which never succeeded in making the leap from the individual to the collective. It avoids the problem of aggregation in Elias, whose search for the emotional tone of an entire epoch leaves us with a very coarse image. It goes further than the individual emotions which represented more or less the limit of the Stearns' approach. And it also avoids the Stearns' fatal assumption that norms as represented in texts upon etiquette can be equated with actually-existing emotional norms. But it is an open question whether it has greater potential than Reddy's 'emotional regime', as Rosenwein claims.[152] This demarcation seems a little forced; for the entire conceptual vocabulary of the history of emotions is still too new to make such hard-and-fast distinctions, rather than creatively combining such theoretical building blocks. Many scholars will thus in

---

[150] Stated in her Berlin lecture of 6 July 2009.

[151] Rosenwein, *Emotional Communities in the Early Middle Ages*, 26–9.

[152] This will be dealt with in Chapter Four. Rosenwein argues that Reddy's emotional regimes are modern and binary (on the one hand, the court or the state as an emotional regime; on the other, society [or salons and Freemasons' lodges] as an emotional refuge). She maintains that her conception of emotional communities is more plural and open. Moreover, in Reddy's theoretical framework emotional regimes are adapted to emotional navigation, emotional suffering, and emotional freedom, whereas the idea of emotional community is not freighted with such ballast. See Rosenwein, *Emotional Communities in the Early Middle Ages*, 23.

fact employ emotional communities and emotional regimes as synonyms.[153] But one could argue instead that the conception of emotional community itself suffers from the problems of any theory of societization, and that it is insufficiently open and radical: for are not the boundaries of an emotional community so porous and transient that one should rather be compelled to move away from the terminology of 'boundary', and hence of 'community'?

Nonetheless, Rosenwein is right in one respect: Elias's idea that premodern emotions were childlike stops historians of all moulds from examining the centuries before 1600. Instead of looking for possible continuities, they can simply presume that there was a caesura. Since Elias there has been no history of emotions that has had to deal with the period 1500 to 2000.

But even if we take the period from 1600 to the present it can be established that emotions have been subject to constant change, as demonstrated in recent years by a number of fascinating studies of historical change.[154] Susan C. Karant-Nunn has, for example, examined the emotional fallout of the Reformation in Catholic, Protestant, and Calvinist sermons, showing how in the post-Reformation sixteenth and seventeenth centuries each of these tendencies had developed their own 'emotion scripts'. The Catholic script was oriented to the physical suffering of Jesus on the Cross, Lutherans focused upon the spiritual, and the Calvinist script matched feelings to a strict God who could look into one's soul and immediately discriminate between genuine and inauthentic religious fervour.[155] Ute Frevert has used the transition from absolutism to enlightened absolutism to demonstrate the gradual shift in emotional communication between ruler and ruled during the lengthy reign of Frederick the Great. To quote Anna Louisa Karsch, a contemporary poet, 'subject children' became 'citizens now delighted to find themselves to be persons'.[156] These citizens 'learned that the love of subjects generated claims. If love was more than the obedience that a child owed to a strict father, and if it were to be dispensed freely with all their heart, and not "coldly" and "mechanically", this opened up a new space of communication.'[157] Martina Kessel has studied boredom and shown that, in the eighteenth century, it was still a feeling 'primarily of temporal meaning, indicating simply a lengthy period', whereas the Industrial Revolution was associated 'with too much free time, or with too little work', and

---

[153] Rosenwein herself sought explicitly to reserve a place for Reddy's 'emotives' in her emotional communities; Rosenwein, *Emotional Communities in the Early Middle Ages*, 25.

[154] On the early modern history of emotions see Gail Kern Paster, Katherine Rowe, and Mary Floyd-Wilson (eds), *Reading the Early Modern Passions: Essays in the Cultural History of Emotion* (Philadelphia: University of Pennsylvania Press, 2004); Nicole Eustace, *Passion Is the Gale: Emotion, Power, and the Coming of the American Revolution* (Chapel Hill: University of North Carolina Press, 2008); Andreas Bähr, *Furcht und Furchtlosigkeit: Göttliche Gewalt und Selbstkonstitution im 17. Jahrhundert* (Göttingen: V&R unipress, 2013); Vera Lind and Otto Ulbricht (eds), *Emotions in Early Modern Europe and Early America* (in press).

[155] Susan C. Karant-Nunn, *The Reformation of Feeling: Shaping the Religious Emotions in Early Modern Germany* (New York: Oxford University Press, 2010), 7, 60–2, 96–9, 128–31, 254–5.

[156] Cited in Ute Frevert, *Gefühlspolitik: Friedrich II. als Herr über die Herzen?* (Göttingen: Wallstein, 2012), 126.

[157] Frevert, *Gefühlspolitik*, 126.

so boredom became an emotional problem.[158] Susan J. Matt has studied changes in the way in which homesickness has been dealt with in America. In the nineteenth century it was still a legitimate emotion and openly acknowledged by adults, whereas by the twentieth century it had become a sign of insufficient maturity and attributed to children who were separated from their parents during summer camp for a long period.[159]

Another example of changes in emotion comes from Alain Corbin. He shows how the torture and burning in August 1870 of a young nobleman in a south-western French village, witnessed by hundreds of villagers, prompted public outrage in the rest of France, while one hundred years earlier a very similar spectacle was not really considered to be cruel, and in 1760 had brought women and children to the marketplace. For it was then still true that 'Executions were also occasions for celebration. People gambled, drank, and brawled in the shadow of the gallows. Minutely orchestrated, torture played on a well-tempered scale of emotions.'[160] It was the process of desacralization brought about by the Enlightenment that first undermined the impact of ritual and sacrilege, rendering spectacles of this kind 'horrifying'; then the development of anaesthetics lowered the pain threshold; and the 'emergence of *l'âme sensible*' in sentimental literature did the rest.[161] Joanna Bourke has written a cultural history of fear which shows that the objects of fearful behaviour are constantly changing,[162] while Ute Frevert has examined the decay of feelings—emotions lost and found. For example, one of the deadly sins is *acedia* (idleness, indolence), but this no longer plays a role in modernity. Modern men and women often sense a lack of commitment and drive, but they do not suffer from the symptoms that the medieval monk believed that someone suffering from *acedia* would have: fever and aching joints. Nor would the root of the evil be traced to demons, or the devil.[163]

Other works search not for diachronic differences, but synchronic compari-sons.[164] William M. Reddy, for example, was struck by the relative lack of interest

[158] 'Boredom' in German is *Langeweile*, literally 'long while'; Martina Kessel, *Langeweile: Zum Umgang mit Zeit und Gefühlen in Deutschland vom späten 18. bis zum frühen 20. Jahrhundert* (Göttingen: Wallstein, 2001), 19, 26.

[159] Susan J. Matt, *Homesickness: An American History* (New York: Oxford University Press, 2011), 198–200, 254–5. For much of her book Matt's account reads like a history of migration with an emotional focus. A similar text is Sonia Cancian, *Families, Lovers, and their Letters: Italian Postwar Migration to Canada* (Winnipeg: University of Manitoba Press, 2010).

[160] Alain Corbin, *The Village of Cannibals: Rage and Murder in France, 1870*, trans. Arthur Goldhammer (Cambridge, MA: Harvard University Press, 1992) [Fr. orig., *Le Village des cannibals*, 1991], 90. I would like to thank Marc Elie for this reference. See also the interview with Corbin by Paule Petitier and Sylvain Venayre, 'Entretien avec Alain Corbin', *Écrire l'histoire: Dossier émotions*, 2 (2008), 109–14.

[161] Corbin, *Village of Cannibals*, 91, 119.

[162] Joanna Bourke, *Fear: A Cultural History* (London: Virago, 2005).

[163] Ute Frevert, *Emotions in History: Lost and Found* (Budapest: Central European University Press, 2011), 31–2.

[164] Instead of distinguishing between diachronic studies tracing the historical change of feelings and synchronic studies which examine the difference of emotions in one and the same period, one could select physical signs of emotion—such as crying, laughing, and smiling—as the leading organizational principles. On weeping see Elina Gertsman (ed.), *Crying in the Middle Ages: Tears of History*

in love as an object of study on the part of historians of gender and sexuality—at least by comparison with a flourishing industry around questions of lust and sexuality. This led him to the study of the historical roots of the distinction between romantic love and sexual pleasure. He located these roots around 1200: at this time courtly love was increasingly idealized, while the volume of theological tirades against powerful desire, lust, *concupiscentia*—above all by Thomas Aquinas—was ever louder. Just how unusual this European separation was becomes evident if one considers Japan and India, where there never was this dualism of pleasure and love—nor is there today. According to Reddy, the case of prostitution shows that this decoupling of pleasure from love is still absent in Japan. For instance, it can be shown that Japanese prostitutes have far fewer sexual contacts per day than French prostitutes. The services which the former offer cover many forms of sociability, as 'sexual intercourse is not necessary to the type of release, or consolation' that stressed-out Japanese businessmen look for in a visit to a prostitute.[165] Árpád von Klimó and Malte Rolf have compared National Socialist intoxication (*Rausch*) and Stalinist enthusiasm (*entuziazm*) and established that in the former, intoxication was understood to have no object and aimed to break down barriers, while for Stalinism enthusiasm always had a goal.[166]

We can already clearly see the emergence of two issues that will be dealt with in the next chapters of this book. First of all, the emotional history of modernity will to a great extent have to be written as a history of the sciences. Once the sciences made emotions an object of study, they not only produced knowledge about emotions, but also had a significant social influence. Secondly, it will be necessary to deal with the emotional history of the twentieth century mostly as a history of media and communication. As early as 1941 Lucien Febvre called for the reconstruction of past ideas of emotion through medieval and Renaissance art, although it is true that he subscribed to the view that the visual representation of emotion in a painting by Van Eyck lent us direct and 'authentic' access to the emotional life of fifteenth-century Flanders, as if there were no representational genres and

---

(New York: Routledge, 2011); Anne Vincent-Buffault, *The History of Tears: Sensibility and Sentimentality in France* (New York: St Martin's Press, 1991); Thomas Dixon, 'The Tears of Mr Justice Willis', *Journal of Victorian Culture*, 17/1 (2012), 1–23. On laughing and smiling see Gerd Althoff, 'Vom Lächeln zum Verlachen', in Werner Röcke and Hans Rudolf Velten (eds), *Lachgemeinschaften: Kulturelle Inszenierungen und soziale Wirkungen von Gelächter im Mittelalter und in der Frühen Neuzeit* (Berlin: de Gruyter, 2005), 3–16.

165 William M. Reddy, 'The Rule of Love: The History of Western Romantic Love in Comparative Perspective', in Luisa Passerini, Liliana Ellena, and Alexander C. T. Geppert (eds), *New Dangerous Liaisons: Discourses on Europe and Love in the Twentieth Century* (New York: Berghahn Books, 2010), 50. See also William M. Reddy, *The Making of Romantic Love: Longing and Sexuality in Europe, South Asia, and Japan, 900–1200 CE* (Chicago: University of Chicago Press, 2012).

166 Árpád von Klimó and Malte Rolf, 'Rausch und Diktatur', *Zeitschrift für Geschichtswissenschaft*, 51/10 (2003), 877–95. See also Árpád v. Klimó and Malte Rolf, 'Rausch und Diktatur: Emotionen, Erfahrungen und Inszenierungen totalitärer Herrschaft', in Klimó and Rolf (eds), *Rausch und Diktatur: Inszenierung, Mobilisierung und Kontrolle in totalitären Systemen* (Frankfurt am Main: Campus, 2006), 11–43. See for more comparative emotional history Susanne Michl and Jan Plamper, 'Soldatische Angst im Ersten Weltkrieg: Die Karriere eines Gefühls in der Kriegspsychiatrie Deutschlands, Frankreichs und Russlands', *Geschichte und Gesellschaft*, 35/2 (2009), 209–48.

conventions. By contrast, the mass media of the twentieth century are qualitatively new; and in this era, the majority of human desires and appetites are first aroused by mass media. There is hardly a feeling that is not framed and pre-structured by media.[167] Let us return once more to 11 September 2001, the day which launched the new history of emotions. The enormous emotional impact of 9/11 is unthinkable without television; in fact, if the terrorists had not been so certain that their atrocity would be filmed, broadcast globally, and then extracts repeated for days and days, they would probably never have chosen this form of terror. Hence without the media we would have had a quite different history, which would then have to be written quite differently.

In the mid-twentieth century Febvre described the 'history of feelings' as 'almost virgin territory', for the most part *'terra incognita'*.[168] More than fifty years later, at the beginning of the second decade of the twenty-first century, this terra incognita is being measured and mapped, claims are being staked out. There is a veritable boom in the history of emotions. This chapter has linked early historical studies of feelings to space and time, to persons and institutions. It has demonstrated that the history of emotions also has a history. Wherever we begin, we always run up against an important distinction between essentialist, culturally universal, transhistorical conceptions of emotion on the one hand, and socially constructed, culturally contingent, relativistic, historical conceptions of emotion on the other. Students of emotion rely upon the existence of this binary opposition—indeed, the entire history of the history of the history of emotions could be written in terms of the nature–nurture dyad. Let us now turn to the second pole, the relativistic nurture, represented by social anthropology.

---

[167] There are already some studies of the issues involved here: Frank Bösch and Manuel Borutta (eds), *Die Massen bewegen: Medien und Emotionen in der Moderne* (Frankfurt am Main: Campus, 2006). See also Oliver Grau and Andreas Keil (eds), *Mediale Emotionen: Zur Lenkung von Gefühlen durch Bild und Sound* (Frankfurt am Main: Fischer, 2005).
[168] Lucien Febvre, 'Pour l'histoire d'un sentiment: Le Besoin de sécurité', *Annales: Économies, Sociétés, Civilisations*, 11/2 (1956), 244–7, here 247.

Two

Social Constructivism
Anthropology

1 THE VARIETIES OF EMOTIONS

The *Diagnostic and Statistical Manual of Mental Disorders* (DSM), a system of classification used by the American Psychiatric Association (APA), describes depression as an emotional disorder brought about by genetic or negative external events, expressed in symptoms such as apathy, lack of appetite, lack of motivation, and suicidal thoughts. Before the existence of 'depression' there were many other models, from the Hippocratic 'black gall' ($\mu\epsilon\lambda\alpha\gamma\chi o\lambda\iota\alpha$) to the 'melancholia' of the nineteenth century; but as an illness in the clinical sense, depression has only existed since the early twentieth century. The clear formulation of the symptoms of 'depression' might have more to do with the professionalization of American psychiatry and the taxonomic imperative of the DSM than anything else, but this medicalization did have some benefits. People who felt themselves to be suffering were no longer thought to be possessed by the devil, or as being marked from birth as degenerates of weak character, but were given a medical diagnosis by experts. On humanitarian grounds alone the quotation marks should be omitted when talking of depression. This must have been similar to the way in which the psycho-anthropologist Gananath Obeyesekere thought about depression when, during the 1980s, he addressed the issue in Sri Lanka, where he was born and grew up.

Obeyesekere found something rather different in Sri Lanka. He first realized just how different when an American friend, a trained psychologist visiting him during his fieldwork, said, just as he was about to return to the United States: 'Gananath, your friend is a classic case of depression.'[1] Neither Obeyesekere nor the wife and doctors of the Sri Lankan friend in question had ever considered him to be 'depressive'—quite apart from the man himself. Certainly, he had a pessimistic outlook on life. But it was also known that as a practising Buddhist he was always going off into the hills to meditate. Meditation made it possible for him to place his suffering in a disjointed world outside himself, displacing it metaphysically. After

---

[1] Gananath Obeyesekere, 'Depression, Buddhism, and the Work of Culture in Sri Lanka', in Arthur Kleinman and Byron Good (eds), *Culture and Depression: Studies in the Anthropology and Cross-Cultural Psychiatry of Affect and Disorder* (Berkeley and Los Angeles: University of California Press, 1985), 139. See also Gananath Obeyesekere, *The Work of Culture: Symbolic Transformation in Psychoanalysis and Anthropology* (Chicago: University of Chicago Press, 1990).

that, the more Obeyesekere thought about the matter, the clearer the outlines of a cultural framework became, one in which there was no such thing as a disturbance of emotional equilibrium called 'depression'.

In Buddhist ontology our presence on earth is just one of several preliminary stages on the way to nirvana. The human world in which we live is thus considered especially filled with suffering, the human body as particularly dirty. Metaphors of decay and faeces do the psycholinguistic work of separating body and self. A 61-year-old Sri Lankan said about his body:

> I try to control my body. I think: my hair, teeth, nails, nerves, bones, and so forth are impermanent. Why? They are not mine. They are of no use. There is no point in all of this. Though one enjoys life and dresses well while living in the world it is of no use for the other world. . . . My body is revulsive like a corpse, like feces.[2]

And an 85-year-old emphasized:

> My body is revulsive. I think: when my bowels are stretched out, my, how long they are! I feel I want nothing of the human body.[3]

Could these metaphors be any further removed from the obsession with beauty and youth so typical of post-industrial Western societies? It is the same with any number of Sri Lankan Buddhist myths and rituals described by Obeyesekere, and which taken together he characterized as 'the work of culture'; he concluded that his supposedly depressive friend 'had generalized his hopelessness into an onto-logical problem of existence, defined in its Buddhist sense as "suffering"'.[4] To describe him as 'depressive' would merely be ethnocentric. To make the point more clearly, Obeyesekere developed 'a piece of reverse ethnocentrism':

> Take the case of a South Asian male (or female) who has the following symptoms: drastic weight loss, sexual fantasies, and night emissions and urine discoloration. In South Asia the patient may be diagnosed as suffering from a disease, 'semen loss'. But on the operational level I can find this constellation of symptoms in every society, from China to Peru. If I were to say, however, that I know plenty of Americans suffering from the disease 'semen loss', I would be laughed out of court even though I could 'prove' that this disease is universal.[5]

Obeyesekere's anthropology of emotion is only one of many; take for example Margaret Trawick's study of the concept of love among south Indian Tamils. Here the highest form of love—mother love (*tāy pācam*)—forbids the mother to look at her child lovingly, particularly when it is asleep, since a devoted glance from a mother could permanently harm the child. If a mother loves her child very much she is supposed to demean it, by for instance giving it a horrible name like 'Baldy' or 'Nosey', or playfully wind it up by saying things like, 'Are you going to die? Are you

---

2 Cited in Obeyesekere, 'Depression, Buddhism, and the Work of Culture in Sri Lanka', 141–2.
3 Obeyesekere, 'Depression, Buddhism, and the Work of Culture in Sri Lanka', 142.
4 Obeyesekere, 'Depression, Buddhism, and the Work of Culture in Sri Lanka', 139.
5 Obeyesekere, 'Depression, Buddhism, and the Work of Culture in Sri Lanka', 136.

going to die?'[6] Jane Fajan's study of the Baining in Papua New Guinea finds something similar, in that they experience loneliness as hunger. For them hunger is not an expression of a physical need, but an emotional deficiency, since sociability is thought to be essential to life, eating in common being the expression of sociability.[7] In a similar vein is Greg Urban's work on the travel diaries of Europeans who, in the sixteenth century, were greeted by the Tupinamba with wailing and lamenting. This people of the Amazon rainforest basin (today part of Brazil) usually greeted both strangers and acquaintances who had not been seen for a while with tears of welcome.[8] Finally, particularly striking is Unni Wikan's study of laughter on Bali, taking the case of the young Suriati, who has suddenly been informed by telegram of the death of her fiancé Isham. She returns home quite calmly from the burial, with two files of photographs of the deceased in her luggage. Suriati's friends gathered together, looked at the photos, and began to laugh:

> This was nothing to be sad about! The boy was dead, so what would be the use? Where one stick is broken, another will grow! Didn't he have brothers? Oh, so there was a ready substitute! The world is full of men. No use grieving over one. Go on, be happy, let bygones be bygones![9]

These cases from the anthropological study of emotion have one major message: they destabilize any idea of pancultural emotions. The way in which feelings are organized in different cultures definitively undermines any idea that feelings are common to humanity, even that feelings unite us as humans. Movement across the globe, along longitude and latitude, is one thing; movement along the timeline of decades and centuries is another. What kind of perspective opens up on feelings when we include time as a vector in the algorithm?

Two examples. Icelandic sagas are literary products that recount prose tales of heroic deeds and family feuds. Despite their status as works of art, they are repeatedly used by historians seeking information about everyday life in the Middle Ages. These sagas describe one thing frequently and in detail: emotions, above all, the somatics of emotion. The persons involved redden, or turn white as a sheet; they laugh, smile, weep, and raise their eyebrows. So far, so good. A little less frequently than blushing, surges of feeling also cause the bodies of the protagonists to swell up. When in the *Brennu-Njáls Saga* Thorhall Asgrimsson finds out about the murder of his guardian, 'his body swells up, blood flows from his ears, and he

---

[6] Margaret Trawick, 'The Ideology of Love in a Tamil Family', in Owen M. Lynch (ed.), *Divine Passions: The Social Construction of Emotion in India* (Berkeley and Los Angeles: University of California Press, 1990), 37–63, here 42, 44.

[7] Jane Fajans, *They Make Themselves: Work and Play Among the Baining of Papua New Guinea* (Chicago: University of Chicago Press, 1997), 119.

[8] Greg Urban, 'Ritual Wailing in Amerindian Brazil', *American Anthropologist*, 90/2 (1988), 385–400, here 385. See also Mark Münzel, 'Tränengruß und weinendes Lied bei den Tupi in Südamerika', in August Nitschke, Justin Stagl, and Dieter R. Bauer (eds), *Überraschendes Lachen, gefordertes Weinen: Gefühle und Prozesse: Kulturen und Epochen im Vergleich* (Vienna: Böhlau, 2009), 221–36.

[9] Unni Wikan, 'Managing the Heart to Brighten Face and Soul: Emotions in Balinese Morality and Health Care', *American Ethnologist*, 16/2 (1989), 294–312, here 297.

faints'.[10] A 12-year-old in the *Laxdæta Saga* is 'swollen with grief' every time that he thinks of his murdered father.[11] 'Swelling bodies' as a sign of emotion? That is something we today find hard to imagine. Whoever thinks Icelandic sagas too literary, and that swelling bodies seem to be more a metaphor than 'genuine' somatic consequences of feeling, should consider *Le Dictionnaire des précieuses* (1660–1) by Antoine Beaudeau de Somaize, a contemporary of Molière. He shows how what was in the past supposedly authentic love could instead be the product of calculation and artifice. This Baroque collection offers 'a typology of the sigh', both description of feeling and guidance on its expression, presenting twelve variants of 'the sigh', to be used as occasion demanded: the sigh of love, the sigh of friendship, the sigh of grief, the sigh of jealousy, the sigh of sympathy, the sigh of uncertainty, and so on. And each of these had its own sub-variants.[12]

Moreover, even if emotions remained essentially the same, in the course of time their objects altered quite considerably. Objects of fear—fear of what?—have undergone enormous historical changes. Joanna Bourke has shown very clearly how the fear of being buried alive spread like wildfire at the end of the nineteenth and into the twentieth century. An American sociological survey published in 1897 reported that a fear of being buried alive came at the top of a list of reasons to be fearful.[13] Both in the USA and in Europe, civil movements quickly developed in response to what was thought to be an excessively casual treatment of the dead. They collected hundreds of eyewitness reports of people who had 'come back from the dead' in their coffin, the implication being that there were also those who did not come back at all. There was no statistical evidence for this mass panic: during the 1860s and 1870s 1,200 bodies were exhumed in New York cemeteries, and only six showed signs of premature burial.[14] But the panic was stoked up by cases such as Eleanor Markham from Sprakers, in the state of New York. Markham had complained of heart problems, and 'died' on 8 July 1894. During her burial the coffin bearers and the doctor noticed that there was something moving within the coffin. They opened up the lid, and found 'poor Eleanor Markham lying on her back, her face white and contorted, and her eyes distended'. Markham cried out: ' "My God!" . . . "You are burying me alive!" ' Later she said,

---

[10] William.Ian Miller, *Humiliation: And Other Essays on Honor, Social Discomfort, and Violence* (Ithaca, NY: Cornell University Press, 1993), 102; see also 98, 101.

[11] Miller, *Humiliation*, 108.

[12] Antoine Beaudeau de Somaize, *Le Dictionnaire des précieuses*, ed. Charles-Louis Livet (repr. Paris: Jannet, 1856; Hildesheim: Olms, 1972), 131–9. The expression 'typology of the sigh' comes, along with the reference to *Le Dictionnaire des précieuses*, from Niklas Luhmann, *Love as Passion: The Codification of Intimacy* (Cambridge, MA: Harvard University Press, 1986) [Ger. orig., *Liebe als Passion: Zur Codierung von Intimität*, 1982], 66.

[13] Joanna Bourke, *Fear: A Cultural History* (London: Virago, 2005), 34. See also Martina Kessel, 'Die Angst vor dem Scheintod im 18. Jahrhundert: Körper und Seele zwischen Religion, Magie und Wissenschaft', in Thomas Schlich and Claudia Wiesemann (eds), *Hirntod: Zur Kulturgeschichte der Todesfeststellung* (Frankfurt am Main: Suhrkamp, 2001), 133–66, and on the fear of apparent death in 19th-century continental Europe, 'Klingel im Sarg', *Der Spiegel*, 48 (1967), 177.

[14] Bourke, *Fear*, 34.

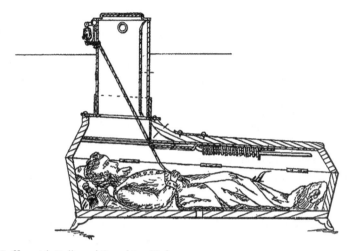

Fig. 5 Coffin with Bells and Breathing Tube

Source: Joanna Bourke, *Fear: A Cultural History* (London: Virago, 2005), between 244 and 245; US Patent No. 81,437 (25 August 1868), inventor: Franz Vester, Newark, NJ.

> I was conscious all the time you were making preparations to bury me . . . The horror of my situation is altogether beyond description. I could hear everything that was going on . . . and although I exerted all my will power, and made a supreme physical effort to cry out, I was powerless.[15]

For others, rescue came too late. When their coffins were opened their bodies were found huddled, with their fingernails broken and other signs of an unsuccessful attempt to free themselves, ending in death. Technical devices were soon found that would avoid the danger of being buried alive. Coffins with air shafts, or bells with which the 'undead' could attract attention, sold well (Fig. 5).

A bell system like this figures in Edgar Allan Poe's short story 'Premature Burial' of 1844, in which Poe takes pleasure in describing to his readers the horror of waking up inside a coffin:

> And now, amid all my infinite miseries, came sweetly the cherub Hope—for I thought of my precautions. I writhed, and made spasmodic exertions to force open the lid: it would not move. I felt my wrists for the bell-rope: it was not to be found. And now the Comforter fled for ever, and a still sterner Despair reigned triumphant; for I could not help perceiving the absence of the paddings which I had so carefully prepared—and then, too, there came suddenly to my nostrils the strong peculiar odor of moist earth.[16]

The outbreak of the First World War quickly blew this epidemic of fear away. But where did this panic come from, and why did it die out after two hundred years? One explanation can be found in the bitter struggle between experts from different

---

[15] Bourke, *Fear*, 34, 35.

[16] Edgar Allan Poe, 'The Premature Burial', in *The Works of Edgar Allan Poe*, ii (New York: Armstrong & Son, 1884), 484–505, here 502–3.

disciplines over the authority to declare someone dead. Funeral directors, doctors, scientists, representatives of organized religion—during these decades they all sought discursive hegemony. At first the result was simply cacophony; but then, more significantly, the blurring of the boundary between life and death, and with it the loss of certainty that burial marked the end of a life. It was the industrialized mass slaughter on the battlefields of the First World War that once more drew a clear line; paradoxically, however, just when trenches and bomb craters made being buried alive a serious problem.[17] Why this collective fear came to an end is not something we can pursue, for here we seek only to demonstrate just how mobile the objects of particular emotions can be.

A journey into past time is comparable with the journey that anthropologists make through space: both toss up differences, differences with what is here and now. It is no coincidence that anthropology and history should be used in parallel here. It was the exploration of other peoples by anthropologists during the 1970s that first uncovered expressions of emotion and conceptions of emotion which then, in turn, led historians to the assumption that emotions are socially constructed, and in variant ways. This chapter consequently reports the discoveries of anthropologists, including two excursions into sociology and linguistics; and it also considers more generally the social construction of feelings.[18]

2 EMOTIONS IN TRAVEL WRITINGS AND EARLY ANTHROPOLOGY

Historians like Herodotus and Tacitus already knew that across Europe there were not only different ways of speaking, eating, and living, but also different ways of feeling.[19] But the idea that far away from Europe people had different feelings, or at least expressed them differently (the distinction between feelings and their expression is dealt with below), first struck the European seafarers who embarked upon 'voyages of discovery'. Between 1772 and 1775 Georg Forster was part of the ship's company on James Cook's second circumnavigation of the globe, noting the manner in which the Tahitians showed 'their gentleness, their generosity, their

---

[17] Bourke, *Fear*, 37–9.

[18] Two readers collect together key texts from different disciplines on the social constructivist approach: Helena Wulff (ed.), *The Emotions: A Cultural Reader* (Oxford: Berg, 2007); Jennifer Harding and E. Deirdre Pribram (eds), *Emotions: A Cultural Studies Reader* (London: Routledge, 2009).

[19] Herodotus on the Agathyrsoi: 'The males of the Agathyrsoi are most luxurious and wear gold more than other men. They share their women in common for the purposes of intercourse, in order that they will all be brothers to one another, and they thus eliminate envy and hatred among one another, since they are all related'; Herodotus, *The Landmark Herodotus: The Histories*, iv, ed. Robert B. Strassler, trans. Andrea L. Purvis (New York: Anchor Books 2009), 325. Tacitus on the Germans during burials: 'They quickly put aside their lamentations and tears, their grief and sadness slowly. It is honorable for women to mourn, for men to remember'; Tacitus, *Agricola, Germany, and Dialogue on Orators*, trans. Herbert W. Benario (Indianapolis: Hackett, 2006), 76.

affectionate friendship, their tenderness, their pity'.[20] Even the expression of emotion that showed on the Tahitian's faces seemed different to that in Europe. Joseph Banks, who was a naturalist on the first circumnavigation between 1768 and 1771, wrote: 'few faces have I seen which have more expression in them than those of these people'.[21] To others, the expressiveness of Tahitian faces seemed suspicious. They sensed deception, like Cook himself, reporting on his departure from the island of Huahine during the second circumnavigation: 'The chief, his wife and daughter, but especially the two latter, hardly ever ceased weeping. I will not pretend to say whether it was real or feigned grief they showed on this occasion.'[22] William Bligh, Cook's Master, also wondered whether the display of feeling was genuine. He recorded in his diary that he had passed by a dead child's mother who was 'in a violent degree of distress'. As he got closer he was shocked to see that 'the mourner burst into a fit of laughter at seeing me. . . . Several young women were with her, but they all resumed a degree of cheerfulness, and the tears were immediately dried up.' Bligh explained to his companion that 'the woman had no sorrow for her child, as her grief could not so easily have subsided if it was the case she regretted the loss of it—when with some humor he [Bligh's companion] told her to cry again; however we left her without any visible marks of its return'.[23]

This problem of authenticity greatly exercised missionaries who in the early 1800s travelled to Tahiti, and who sought to read in the faces of the natives whether their conversion to Christianity had been successful. To begin with, the strength of expression in Tahitian faces was thought to be evidence of an especially deep and lasting Christianization; but this later turned out to be an illusion. In 1851 the missionary John Davis published an English–Tahitian dictionary, in which twenty-six entries attest to the divergence of feeling and expression of feeling, for example, '"fair and deceptive, as the speech of a hypocrite", "great in appearance only", "empty sympathy", "a fair exterior and that the only good quality"', together with 'to pretend faith or obedience in order to gain some end'.[24]

Following these 'voyages of discovery', the new discipline of anthropology began to develop in England in the mid-nineteenth century, subsequently spreading to Germany, Russia, France, the USA, and other countries. During the 1980s it played a vanguard role in the multidisciplinary study of emotions, revealing the lack of substance in the idea of human universals. In the early phases of its research—bracketing the various names applied to it, whether it be ethnology, anthropology, *etnografiia*, social and cultural anthropology—this new discipline paid little attention to the nature of emotions. It was primarily interested in social organization (including kinship), and above all the question of Man's origin. The variety of human appearance and customs was obvious, but how could one explain this variety? Did Man have a unique origin, or were there a variety of sources? Is

---

[20] Georg Forster, *A Voyage Round the World: In His Britannic Majesty's Sloop, Resolution, Commanded by Capt. James Cook, During the years 1772, 3, 4, and* 5, ii (London: White, 1777), 133.
[21] Cited in Robert I. Levy, *Tahitians: Mind and Experience in the Society Islands* (Chicago: University of Chicago Press, 1975), 97.
[22] Levy, *Tahitians*, 97.   [23] Levy, *Tahitians*, 98.   [24] Levy, *Tahitians*, 98.

mankind one or many? Monogenetic or polygenetic?[25] Universalism or particularism? Initially, these were the central questions posed by anthropology.

Monogenism, *ab uno sanguine*, and an emphasis upon universal mental structures was the progressive response of early British anthropologists who devoted themselves to the cause of anti-slavery—like James Prichard (1786–1848), the son of a Quaker preacher.[26] This approach bore some resemblance to the idea, widespread during the seventeenth and eighteenth centuries, of the 'noble savage', although distinguished from that idea by the absence of any Christian understanding of cyclical temporality. Philosophers like Anthony Ashley-Cooper and Jean-Jacques Rousseau regarded the 'noble savage' as being closer to the state of nature before the Fall, and so in many respects superior to the contemporary corruption of the European. This idea was also a response to Thomas Hobbes's conception of the state of nature as a war of all against all, and retained an emotional component, imagining that people from foreign cultures were possessed by purer, more primordial feelings.[27]

Charles Darwin's *On the Origin of Species* (1859) reshuffled the cards in this discussion. Evolutionary theory reinforced the linear dynamic of monogenism, lending it scientific validity. Darwin did away with the idea of divine creation entirely, and the principle of natural and sexual selection provided a temporal opening to the future, reducing those presently living to but one stage of evolution, which many others would later follow. Vulgarized versions of evolutionary theory were 'scientificized' as racist discourse and, together with the new technologies of destruction, would in the twentieth century lead to the worst genocides in human history. Darwin distanced himself from any idea of savages, noble or otherwise, and made 'savages' of us all. This was made very clear in his 1872 book *The Expression of the Emotions in Man and Animals*, in which he emphasized 'that fear was expressed from an extremely remote period, in almost the same manner as it now is by man'.[28] For Darwin, emotions were universal, since they had clearly been of advantage to all animals, from primates to *Homo sapiens*, in their struggle for existence. This universalization and its connection with the struggle for existence—natural fight-or-flight reactions—was an important precondition for experimental psychology, which had to presuppose the comparability of its subjects.

The connection between Darwin's own 'voyages of discovery' aboard HMS *Beagle* and his book *The Expression of the Emotions in Man and Animals* has been

---

[25] George W. Stocking, Jr, *Victorian Anthropology* (New York: Free Press, 1987), 67. On the history of anthropology see also Henrika Kuklick (ed.), *A New History of Anthropology* (Malden, MA: Blackwell, 2008).

[26] Stocking, *Victorian Anthropology*, 48–51; Fredrik Barth, Andre Gingrich, Robert Parkin, and Sydel Silverman, *One Discipline, Four Ways: British, German, French, and American Anthropology* (Chicago: University of Chicago Press, 2005), 4 (*ab uno sanguine*).

[27] Margrit Pernau, 'An ihren Gefühlen sollt Ihr sie erkennen: Eine Verflechtungsgeschichte des britischen Zivilitätsdiskurses (ca. 1750–1860)', *Geschichte und Gesellschaft*, 35/2 (2009), 249–81, here 250.

[28] Charles Darwin, *The Expression of the Emotions in Man and Animals*, with an introduction, afterword, and commentaries by Paul Ekman (3rd edn, New York: Oxford University Press, 1998), 356.

just as little investigated as has the impact of his book on contemporary anthropology. Nor has there been much in the way of interest in the effect that Wilhelm Wundt (1832–1920), a founder of a modern experimental psychology of emotions, had on the thinking of Adolf Bastian (1826–1905), who was in 1869 the first holder of a teaching position for *Völkerkunde*.[29] The twin lodestars Wundt and Bastian shone in two directions: towards France, where they influenced Émile Durkheim (1858–1942); and towards the USA, where Bastian's student Franz Boas (1858–1942) founded American anthropology after his immigration there in 1887—and it was from this source that, about one hundred years later, the anthropology of emotions developed as an independent field of study.

3 EMOTIONS IN THE ANTHROPOLOGICAL CLASSICS

While Durkheim did write about distant peoples, he did not himself undertake any great journeys. He based his work on existing anthropological studies. He was chiefly interested in what held society together, how groups were formed: 'collective representations', including rituals and their functions. In so doing he gave a new slant to the relationship between emotion and the expression of emotion—the question of authenticity that had bothered missionaries so much—and in 1912 he wrote:

> mourning is not the spontaneous expression of individual emotions. If the relatives weep, lament, and beat each other and themselves, it is not because they feel personally touched by the death of their kinsman. No doubt it may happen, in particular cases, that the sorrow expressed is sincerely felt. But more generally, there is no connection between the feelings experienced and the gestures performed by the actors of the rite. If, at the very moment when the mourners seem most overcome by pain, you speak to them about some secular interest of theirs, it often happens that they instantly change their expression and tone, take on a cheerful air, and talk with all the gaiety in the world. Mourning is not a natural impulse of the private sensibility bruised by a cruel loss; it is a duty imposed by the group. They lament, not simply because they are sad, but because they are obliged to lament. This is a ritual attitude they are compelled to adopt out of respect for custom, but which is in large measure independent of the affective state of individuals. Moreover, this obligation is sanctioned by mythic or social punishments. For example, they believe that when a relative does not mourn as he should, the soul of the dead person dogs his steps and kills him.[30]

---

[29] Barth et al., *One Discipline, Four Ways*, 84. See on Bastian in particular Klaus Peter Köpping, *Adolf Bastian and the Psychic Unity of Mankind: The Foundations of Anthropology in Nineteenth Century Germany* (Münster: Lit, 2005).

[30] Émile Durkheim, *The Elementary Forms of Religious Life*, trans. Carol Cosman (Oxford: Oxford University Press, 2001) [Fr. orig., *Forms élémentaires de la vie religieuse*, 1912], 295–6. This passage is cited time and again by anthropologists, usually to move beyond ritual and consider the reciprocal effect of ritual upon 'real' sensations. See e.g. Bruce Kapferer, 'Emotion and Feeling in Sinhalese Healing Rites', *Social Analysis*, 1/1 (1979), 153–76, here 153: 'In contrast to Durkheim, I make the assumption that when individuals or groups express anger, fear, love, sorrow, hate and happiness in the cultural medium of ritual, they often actually feel what they express.' For more about Durkheim

If we briefly fast-forward, we can see that the distinction made by Erving Goffman (1922–82) between social masks and 'real faces' or individuality bears the marks of not only Marx's theory of alienation, but also Durkheim's understanding of ritual.[31] At the same time, today's social constructivist anthropology of emotion is hard to conceive without Durkheim as a building block, especially his interpretation of emotions as ritualization.

But back to Durkheim and his studies of religion. For him, religion was not only something functional, not only the movement of social actors within fixed social rules that fostered community. Religion also meant 'effervescence' in ritual, collective emotional outbursts, and here it is hard to miss a trace of Gustave Le Bon, the rightist theorist of human crowds whose ideas were instrumentalized by those further to the right, like Benito Mussolini. We have already come across Le Bon in Chapter One, where we saw how he provided some basic ideas for Lucien Febvre.[32]

The undisputed No. 1 of French twentieth-century anthropology was Claude Lévi-Strauss (1908–2009). Like Marcel Mauss (1872–1950), he was influenced both by Durkheim and by the German tradition, mediated by Franz Boas while he was in the USA from 1941 to 1948. Lévi-Strauss was also influenced by Karl Marx and by structural linguistics. He worked closely with Roman Jakobson while he was in New York; and during that period he also read Saussure, the 'godfather' of structuralism.

Once back in France, at the end of the 1950s Lévi-Strauss set about examining totemism, and consequently the complex of religion and emotion. Various sociological and anthropological thinkers had developed theories of religion based on the relationship between 'primitive' peoples and a totem—a sign usually based upon animal origins. Durkheim had argued that the totem of Australian Aboriginals indicated that religious life always had a connection to community, involving an integrative, homogenizing moment.[33] Lévi-Strauss took the view that the use of totems did not indicate a 'different' way of thinking, but was instead an especially effective cognitive exercise in an environment in which abstraction was rare. According to Lévi-Strauss, all the important writers on totemism—Durkheim, Malinowski, Evans-Pritchard, Radcliffe-Brown, and Kroeber—traced the totem back to emotion, hence to the opposite of cognition, surrendering thereby any chance of constructing a scientific explanation. Lévi-Strauss noted that

> As affectivity is the most obscure side of man, there has been the constant temptation to resort to it, forgetting that what is refractory to explanation is *ipso facto* unsuitable for use in explanation. A datum is not primary because it is incomprehensible.[34]

and emotions see Helena Flam, *Soziologie der Emotionen: Eine Einführung* (Konstanz: UTB, 2002), 61–89.

[31] Erving Goffman, *The Presentation of Self in Everyday Life* (Garden City, NY: Doubleday, 1959).

[32] 'Still, the objection will be raised that even in this hypothesis religion is the product of a kind of delirium. What other name can we give to the burst of emotion in which men find themselves when, as the result of a collective effervescence, they believe they have been swept up into a world quite different from the one they see?'; Durkheim, *Elementary Forms of Religious Life*, 171. See also Barth et al., *One Discipline, Four Ways*, 175, 184.

[33] For a summary see Durkheim, *Elementary Forms of Religious Life*, 318.

[34] Claude Lévi-Strauss, *Totemism* (Harmondsworth: Penguin Books, 1969), 140.

Unlike Durkheim, who claimed that men constructed animalistic totems from feeling so that they might connect themselves with the community of their forefathers, the dead,[35] Lévi-Strauss argued against this 'affective theory of the sacred', maintaining that

> Actually, impulses and emotions explain nothing: they are always *results*, either of the power of the body or of the impotence of the mind. In both cases they are consequences, never causes.[36]

As far as emotions were concerned, Lévi-Strauss proved to be one more materialist in a long line of experimental psychologists, from which Carl Lange (1834–1900) and William James (1842–1910) developed the most promising theories, as will be shown in Chapter Three. They argued that emotions were not something internal to the body; instead, physical expression was itself the emotion. Later social constructivist writings have placed a different weight on this passage from *Totemism* about impulse and emotion as consequences rather than causes: some consider him to be an Aristotelian thinker who created room for a degree of evaluation or intentionalism;[37] others regard his apparent reduction of emotion to bodily movement as sufficient to make him an accomplice of the psychologist Silvan S. Tomkins (1911–91), the bête noire of all social constructivists and the spiritual father of Paul Ekman.[38]

In Britain the influence of structuralist anthropology in the style of Lévi-Strauss was first felt during the 1960s and 1970s, Victor Turner (1920–83) being the most prominent representative. Twentieth-century social anthropology, based on fieldwork, 'participant observation', and the learning of indigenous languages, had been initiated in Britain with the work of Bronisław Malinowski (1884–1942) in New Guinea from 1914 to 1918. Malinowski insisted that he had focused upon kinship relationships, but his diary eloquently testifies to the feelings experienced by anthropologists while engaged in their fieldwork.[39] Even in Australia he felt

---

[35] Durkheim, *Elementary Forms of Religious Life*, 176–7.

[36] Lévi-Strauss, *Totemism*, 142; emphasis in original.

[37] See e.g. Owen Lynch: 'Lévi-Strauss was, perhaps unwittingly, adverting to an alternative theory of emotion in Western culture, cognitive theory, with roots tracing back to Aristotle's *Rhetoric*. A cognitive theory is one that makes some aspect of mental activity—a belief, a thought, or a judgment—essential to emotion in general and to identifying separate emotions in particular.' Owen M. Lynch, 'The Social Construction of Emotion in India', in Lynch (ed.), *Divine Passions*, 3–34, here 7–8.

[38] Catherine A. Lutz introduces a quotation from the relevant passage in Lévi-Strauss as follows: 'The emphasis on this association between the emotional and the physical is especially strong in twentieth-century academic psychology. Take, for example, the definition given by Tomkins, whose view of emotion is one of the most influential of the contemporary psychological theories: "Affects are sets of muscular and glandular responses located in the face and also widely distributed throughout the body, which generate sensory feedback that is either inherently 'acceptable' or 'unacceptable'." Lévi-Strauss also draws on this cultural connection when he writes, "Emotions ... are always *results* either of the power of the body or the impotence of the mind" '; Catherine A. Lutz, *Unnatural Emotions: Everyday Sentiments on a Micronesian Atoll & Their Challenge to Western Theory* (Chicago: University of Chicago Press, 1988), 66, emphasis in original.

[39] Here we ignore the fact that Malinowski's diary has become the object of extensive critical reflection among anthropologists drawing upon post-structural ideas. One instance among many is

Strong fear of the tropics; abhorrence of heat and sultriness—a kind of panic fear of encountering heat as terrible as last June and July. . . . I was fairly depressed, afraid I might not feel equal to the task before me. . . . On Saturday, 9.12 [1914], arrival in New Guinea. . . . I felt very tired and empty inside, so that my first impression was rather vague. . . . 10.31 [1914] . . . Then, since there was no dance or assembly, I walked to Oroobo by way of the beach. Marvelous. It was the first time I had seen this vegetation in the moonlight. Too strange and exotic. The exoticism breaks through lightly, through the veil of familiar things. . . . Went into the bush. For a moment I was frightened. Had to compose myself. Tried to look into my own heart. 'What is my inner life?' No reason to be satisfied with myself.[40]

Malinowski's diary is also the founding document of self-reflection in the anthropology of emotion. Subsequently, anthropologists would come to see their own feelings as constitutive for the collection of 'data', hence the creation of emotion in an involvement with informants, since the feelings of the observed were always involved in a dialogue with the feelings of the observer (see below regarding Jean L. Briggs).

Another pioneer of British social anthropology was William Halse Rivers (1864–1922), who worked as an anthropologist up until the First World War and travelled widely. During the war he developed his medical interests and became a psychiatrist for soldiers suffering from 'shell shock', what would today be called post-traumatic stress disorder—a story immortalized in Pat Barker's *Regeneration Trilogy* (1991–5). Rivers's correspondence with Siegfried Sassoon and other inmates of Craiglockhart, the Scottish mental institution, has become one of the key sources of the First World War. The degree to which his conception of trauma was influenced by his fieldwork on Papua New Guinea has yet to be studied.[41]

Rivers's student Alfred Radcliffe-Brown (1881–1955)—in his 1922 study of the Andaman islanders—defined 'sentiment' as an 'organised system of emotional tendencies centred about some object'. He also held the view that 'A society depends for its existence on the presence in the minds of its members of a certain system of sentiments by which the conduct of the individual is regulated in conformity with the needs of the society', and that 'the sentiments in question are not innate but are developed in the individual by the action of the society upon him'.[42] Radcliffe-Brown was influenced by Durkheim and taught in the USA between 1931 and 1937. And so while German anthropology sank into relative

James Clifford, *The Predicament of Culture: Twentieth-Century Ethnography, Literature, and Art* (Cambridge, MA: Harvard University Press, 1988), ch. 3.

[40] Bronislaw Malinowski, *A Diary in the Strict Sense of the Term* (Stanford, CA: Stanford University Press, 1989), 4, 5, 7, 30–1.

[41] William H. Rivers, *The Todas* (London: Macmillan, 1906); also W. H. R. Rivers, 'Psychiatry and the War', *Science*, 49/1268 (18 April 1919), 367–9; William Halse R. Rivers, *Instinct and the Unconscious: A Contribution to a Biological Theory of the Pseudo-Neuroses* (Cambridge: Cambridge University Press, 1920). For the *Regeneration Trilogy* by Pat Barker: *Regeneration* (London: Viking, 1991); *The Eye in the Door* (London: Viking, 1993); *The Ghost Road* (London: Viking, 1995).

[42] A. R. Brown [Alfred Radcliffe-Brown], *The Andaman Islanders: A Study in Social Anthropology* (Cambridge: Cambridge University Press, 1922), 233–4.

obscurity, Bastian's influence upon American anthropology was—via Boas, Radcliffe-Brown, and Durkheim—significant.

Through Bastian's 'son' Franz Boas this line can be extended through to his 'granddaughter' Ruth Benedict (1887–1948), who directly after the defeat of Japan in 1945 published her epochal book *The Chrysanthemum and the Sword*, an ethnopsychological group portrait of an entire nation.[43] Benedict not only popularized the distinction between 'shame cultures' such as Japan and 'guilt cultures' like the USA, but more importantly examined those Japanese conceptions of feeling which guided social life, comparing them to similar North American conceptions. For example, the Japanese *on* is all-dominating. It involves a mixture of 'love' and 'respect', also implying duty and being indebted to someone: from newborn babies who are for ever in debt to their parents, to kamikaze pilots for whom the last cigarette given to them just before their final flight reminded them of their permanent indebtedness to the Emperor. 'Love, kindness, generosity, which we value just in proportion as they are given without strings attached, necessarily must have their strings in Japan.'[44] In a chapter on 'The Circle of Human Feelings', Benedict sketched Japanese ideas of the five senses and the practices related to them.[45]

Margaret Mead (1901–78) was Benedict's student at Columbia University, and so more or less Bastian's 'great-granddaughter'.[46] Mead's significance for American anthropology and the cultural history of twentieth-century America cannot be overestimated.[47] Not only did her fieldwork on the Samoa during 1925 and 1926 involve a strong version of cultural relativism that would later contribute to the reorganization of American education and race relations, but her image of the Polynesians, especially the women, also provided the groundwork for the sexual revolution. She observed that Polynesians had an

> unusual attitude towards the expression of emotion. The expressions of emotions are classified as 'caused' and 'uncaused'. The emotional, easily upset, moody person is described as laughing without cause, crying without cause, showing anger and pugnaciousness without cause. The expression 'to be very angry without cause' does not carry the implication of quick temper, which is expressed by the word 'to anger easily', nor

---

[43] Ruth Benedict, *The Chrysanthemum and the Sword: Patterns of Japanese Culture* (Boston: Houghton Mifflin, 1946). Among those influenced by Benedict is Eric Robertson Dodds, *The Greeks and the Irrational* (Berkeley and Los Angeles: University of California Press, 1951). See on this Ruth Leys, *From Guilt to Shame: Auschwitz and After* (Princeton: Princeton University Press, 2007), ch. 4, esp. 123; Barth et al., *One Discipline, Four Ways*, 296.

[44] Benedict, *The Chrysanthemum and the Sword*, 113.

[45] Benedict, *The Chrysanthemum and the Sword*, ch. 9.

[46] Between 1936 and 1950 Mead was married to Gregory Bateson (1904–80), a British anthropologist. They were one of several anthropological couples. Bateson, who later moved into cybernetics, understood *ethos* to be 'a culturally organized system of emotions'; Catherine A. Lutz and Geoffrey M. White, 'The Anthropology of Emotions', *Annual Review of Anthropology*, 15 (1986), 405–36, here 412. See also Gregory Bateson, *Naven: The Culture of the Iatmul People of New Guinea Tribe as Revealed Through a Study of the 'Naven' Ceremonial* (2nd edn, Stanford, CA: Stanford University Press, 1958).

[47] On Mead see Nancy C. Lutkehaus, *Margaret Mead: The Making of an American Icon* (Princeton: Princeton University Press, 2008).

the connotation of a disproportionate response to a legitimate stimulus, but means literally to be angry without cause, or freely, an emotional state without any apparent stimulus whatsoever.[48]

Generally speaking, Mead thought that 'The Samoan preference is for a middle course, a moderate amount of feeling.'[49] More explicitly than other anthropologists, Mead presented a mirror to American society through the study of other cultures. She suggested that there was a high price to be paid for the 'specialisation of affection' in the nuclear American family, since 'a larger family community, in which there are several adult men and women, seems to ensure the child against the development of the crippling attitudes which have been labelled Oedipus complexes, Electra complexes, and so on'.[50]

Many anthropologists later followed in Mead's footsteps—which is one reason why so many anthropologies of emotion are based in the South Seas, rather than for instance concerning themselves with Africa, South America, or the North American Indians. Conversely, Mead became a bugbear for psychologists like Paul Ekman, as will be shown in Chapter Three.

From the beginning of the 1960s a new hermeneutic strand of American anthropology developed, associated in particular with the Geertzes, Hildred and Clifford (1926–2006). We have only a few remarks from Clifford Geertz relating to emotions, such as: 'Not only ideas, but emotions too, are cultural artifacts in man' and 'In order to make up our minds we must know how we feel about things; and to know how we feel about things we need the public images of sentiment that only ritual, myth, and art can provide.'[51] The work of Clifford Geertz is constantly referred to in discussion of the description of the ritualistic character of the expression of feeling.[52] His first wife Hildred devoted more attention to emotions.

---

[48] Margaret Mead, *Coming of Age in Samoa: A Psychological Study of Primitive Youth for Western Civilisation* (New York: Morrow, 1928), 127.

[49] Mead, *Coming of Age in Samoa*, 128.

[50] Mead, *Coming of Age in Samoa*, 212, 212–13.

[51] Clifford Geertz, 'Chapter 3: The Growth of Culture and the Evolution of Mind', in *The Interpretation of Cultures* (New York: Basic Books, 1973), 81, 82; first published in Jordan M. Scher, *Theories of the Mind* (New York: Free Press of Glencoe, 1962), 713–40.

[52] Geertz influenced e.g. Bruce Kapferer, who can be called a post-Durkheimian Geertzian: 'Sinhalese healing rituals provide both a *model of* the reality as conceptualized by a patient and a *model for* how reality should be conceived. The organization of symbols and symbolic action into ritual form gives "objective conceptual form, to social and psychological reality both by shaping themselves to it and by shaping it to themselves"'; Kapferer, 'Emotion and Feeling in Sinhalese Healing Rites', 156; emphasis in original. See also Edward Schieffelin, who concludes his study of the Kaluli of Papua New Guinea with the following: 'Thus Kaluli emotions, however privately experienced (though Kaluli try to make anger, shame, and grief as public as possible), are socially located and have a social aim. To this degree they are located not only in the person but also in the social situation and interaction that, indeed, they help construct. One important message to come out of this analysis is that anthropologists interested in affect and culture may legitimately look outside the private interior of the individual to the processes of social interaction, not just for the sources that provoke feeling but for a substantial part of the form and significance of emotion as well. Geertz . . . has remarked that one does not have to look to the privacy of the individual to understand significant cultural symbols and beliefs: their meaning may be found in the marketplace. To a great extent, the same may be true of human feelings. Not only do socially shared meanings supply much of the significance and implications of feelings for individuals, the feelings are in part a social construction of the situation in which they participate'; Edward L. Schieffelin, 'Anger, Grief, and Shame: Toward a Kaluli Ethnopsychology', in Geoffrey M. White

While in the 1950s she did presuppose that every person was predisposed to express emotions that were culturally universal, she argued that this predisposition was modified in the course of childhood socialization by cultural variables that subjected it to differing influences and characteristics: some cultures encouraged particular kinds of emotion, while others tended to suppress them. Hildred Geertz tended to talk of 'the Javanese' in a general sense that now seems old-fashioned, even in comparison with ethnographies of the 1970s. She maintains that 'They dislike any strong expression of emotion and have few genuine friendship or love relationships. Javanese women are less quiet and subdued than the men; they are much more expressive.'[53] She also talks of how an Oedipal conflict is a natural part of growing up.[54] Nonetheless, she does go on to develop a sophisticated analysis of indigenous conceptions of emotion, all of which have in one way or another to do with respect, and which are communicated to children in their upbringing. From this Geertz concluded that 'child-training procedures' were an inherent component not only of emotional socialization, but also of the assumptions that a society made regarding inner emotional life.[55]

Other anthropologists who are today regarded as classics thought that emotions were even less closely tied to culture. Ernest Beaglehole (1906–65) argued in 1937 that there was no doubt that for the Ifaluk, a people living on an atoll in the Western Pacific, ritual formed a release for emotion otherwise usually suppressed for want of a private sphere in which it could find expression. He took the view that if there had not been specific socially-accepted means of expressing suppressed emotion, then the society would have broken down under the burden of its own neuroses.[56] In 1952 Melford Spiro argued that behind the Ifaluk's fear of ghosts there was suppressed aggression, direct expression of which was ruled out by their cultural obsession with harmony.[57] Elaborate psychoanalytical explanations were later added to this, as for instance, the 1967 study of George Morris Carstairs (1916–91) demonstrates.[58] Lutz and White argued that all of these approaches involved a 'two layers theory',

> in which universal emotions are located in an underlying layer of affect. Much like Freudian primary and secondary process thinking, the uniform or universal aspects of emotion are variously 'shaped', 'filtered', 'channeled', 'distorted', or 'masked' by cultural 'molds', 'filters', 'lenses', 'display rules', or 'defense mechanisms'.[59]

and John Kirkpatrick (eds), *Person, Self, and Experience: Exploring Pacific Ethnopsychologies* (Berkeley and Los Angeles: University of California Press, 1985), 168–82, here 180.

[53] Hildred Geertz, 'The Vocabulary of Emotion: A Study of Javanese Socialization Processes', *Psychiatry: Interpersonal and Biological Processes*, 22 (1959), 225–37, here 226.

[54] Geertz, 'The Vocabulary of Emotion', 232, 236.

[55] Geertz, 'The Vocabulary of Emotion', 236.

[56] Ernest Beaglehole, 'Emotional Release in a Polynesian Community', *Journal of Abnormal and Social Psychology*, 32/3–4 (1937), 319–28, here 320.

[57] Melford E. Spiro, 'Ghosts, Ifaluk, and Teleological Functionalism', *American Anthropologist*, 54/4 (1952), 497–503.

[58] G. M. Carstairs, *The Twice Born: A Study of a Community of High-Caste Hindus* (Bloomington: Indiana University Press, 1967).

[59] Lutz and White, 'Anthropology of Emotions', 412.

During the 1970s a comparative anthropological study concluded that there was a worldwide association of light and solid colours with more positive emotions, while dark and washed-out colours were linked to more negative emotions. This phenomenon, also known as 'synesthesia on the association between colors and emotion', led Roy D'Andrade and Michael Egan to suggest there existed 'innate reactions'.[60] And in 1978 Rodney Needham (1923–2006) expressed the view that

> A comparative study of emotions, in particular, indicates that these passions are not naturally so discrete or so numerous as are the names by which in different languages they are distinguished.[61]

4 EARLY ANTHROPOLOGY OF EMOTIONS IN THE 1970S

The Emotions of Inuits

So much for the classics of anthropology and the relatively little regard they gave to emotions. Jean L. Briggs devoted much more attention to emotions. Today, she is generally regarded as the pioneer of the modern anthropology of emotion.[62]

In the summer of 1963 Briggs joined the Utkuhikhalingmiut (Utku for short), a small group of Canadian Inuits whose shamanistic tribal religion she wanted to study during several years of fieldwork. At that time, the two or three dozen Utku lived about 150 miles from the nearest settlement, inhabiting an area of about 35,000 square miles, and living on fish and caribou. They had a nomadic seasonal existence, divided among eight households and three extended families, living during the summer in tents, and in igloos for the rest of the year. Briggs was assigned to the family of the Utku leader Inuttiaq and his wife Allaq, taking the role of an adopted daughter called Yiini alongside their three daughters Kamik, Raigili, and Saarak. A fourth daughter, Qayaq, was born in April 1964. Briggs took on this role despite the fact that she was at the time 34, about the same age as Allaq, and not that much younger that Inuttiaq, who was about 40.

---

[60] R. D'Andrade and M. J. Egan, 'The Colors of Emotion', *American Ethnologist*, 1/1 (1974), 49–63, here 49.

[61] Rodney Needham, *Essential Perplexities: An Inaugural Lecture Delivered before the University of Oxford on 12 May 1977* (Oxford: Clarendon Press, 1978), 20. Lutz on Needham: 'Needham, for example, sees diverse vocabularies of emotion developed in many societies as necessarily "wrong" about the feelings they purport to describe; this is so, he claims, because feelings, being natural and universal, exist at a level that is unaffected by the cultural modes of thought expressed in those vocabularies'; Lutz, *Unnatural Emotions*, 67. In 1981 Needham struck a more cautious note, and complained of the lack of anthropological studies of emotion: 'it is all the more remarkable that anthropologists have paid practically no systematic attention to the topic of emotion', asking then whether it was justified to conclude from the variety of linguistic expression of emotion that there was a variety of emotions, and then reviewed efforts to deduce basal emotions from Descartes to Ekman, concluding: 'and now with all the more power of perplexity, is that our emotional lives should be so obsessive and characteristic when so much about them is artificial and contingent'; Needham, *Circumstantial Deliveries* (Berkeley and Los Angeles: University of California Press, 1981), 99–102, quotations 99, 102.

[62] See e.g. Lutz and White, 'Anthropology of Emotions', 430.

It quickly transpired that the original project on shamanism was a non-starter, since the Utku had become Anglicans in the 1930s and now took the view that their shamans were all 'either in hell or in hiding'.[63] Instead, another topic presented itself: emotion. There were two levels to the question of emotions: on the one hand in the form of ethnographic observation, and on the other from Briggs's unintentional infringement on Utku norms about feelings. The latter slowly shifted her to the margin of Utku society, making her into an outsider who by the time of her premature departure could not wait for the arrival of the plane chartered for her by the Canadian government.

In time Briggs realized that one rule governing all Utku behaviour was that one should never become angry. Her book about her time with Inuttiaq's family was called *Never in Anger*. For the Utku, growing up meant acquiring *ihuma*, which can be translated as 'reason'. *Ihuma* was expressed primarily in emotional control. Only 'a child, an idiot, a very sick or an insane person' lacked *ihuma*.[64] The family accepted from little Saarak a great deal more selfishness and anger than would have been allowed an American child of the same age. Simply because she still lacked *ihuma*, the family expected little else than that she would quickly become enraged, was easily angered, screamed a great deal; they met more or less all of her demands. 'Steadfastness' as an ideal of parental education was foreign to the Utku in every respect.[65]

Saarak's pre-*ihuma* phase ended when she was about 3 years old, and a younger sister arrived. However, her mother's attention was not transferred from one day to the next, but more slowly, more carefully, and with greater tolerance for 'relapses' than would be conceivable in a contemporary American or European family. This was apparent most clearly in the fight over breast milk, for which Saarak, who was not yet weaned, and the newborn Qayaq competed. Briggs, living as an adoptive daughter in a corner of the same igloo, described the way in which Saarak first became aware of her new little sister shortly after her birth:

[Saarak] was allowed to sleep soundly, and when she did stir after a while, Inuttiaq rhythmically rubbed her back in an attempt to lull her back to sleep. His efforts were futile, and when he saw that she was really awake, he pointed out the baby to her. I held my breath. But there was no outburst, not for the first minute. Saarak chirped and cooed and poked at the baby with friendly interest. It was only when she saw her mother put the baby to her breast that the storm broke: a storm of wails and slaps. Allaq, holding the baby protectively, said in a tender voice, 'Don't hurt her.' Whereupon Saarak demanded her endangered right: to be nursed. Tactful as I knew Utku to be, I had never imagined that the crisis, when it came, could be handled as gently as it was. Allaq assumed a tone that I was to hear often in the next few days, a false but

---

[63] Jean L. Briggs, *Never in Anger: Portrait of an Eskimo Family* (Cambridge, MA: Harvard University Press, 1970), 3.

[64] Briggs, *Never in Anger*, 111.

[65] Briggs, *Never in Anger*, 112 commented: 'That first autumn my journal curtly noted that Saarak was one of the two least lovable children I had ever met, the other being Saarak's small cousin Rosi, whose moods were even more violent and who enjoyed similar freedom of expression.' Nonetheless, shortly afterwards even Briggs succumbed to Saarak's charm.

sympathetic tone of disgust. 'It tastes terrible,' she said. And the tone surrounded the words with affectionate protectiveness. But when Saarak continued to scream and slap at her mother and the baby, Allaq gave in, took her distressed daughter into the accustomed shelter of her parka, and nursed her, albeit briefly, at one breast while she nursed the baby at the other. I neglected to notice whether Saarak came away from the breast voluntarily or by persuasion; in any case, a little later she began to wail again. This time Inuttiaq took a hand. 'You're very much loved (*naklik*),' he assured his daughter, soothingly; but Saarak was too distressed to heed him. 'Go to sleep!' Inuttiaq then said, loudly and more gruffly. 'You're very sleepy!' And eventually she did cry herself to sleep. Inuttiaq looked at the little face on the pillow beside him, the cheeks still damply streaked and the small dark braids awry. 'Poor little thing (*naklik*)', he said, 'she realizes and she is troubled (*ujjiq*).'[66]

The parents broke off their attempts to wean Saarak several times, showing more patience than seemed at all practical to Briggs. Why should this be? Because *ihuma* is thought to emerge of its own accord in every Utku, without any parental involvement. And since it had not yet settled in little Saarak, this was accepted with equanimity.

The significance of emotional control became most strikingly and painfully apparent to Briggs not through her own observations, but through her own unintentional failure to conform to emotional norms. What happened did not occur suddenly and openly, but very gradually, arising from Briggs's difficulty in adapting to the Arctic cold, her difficulties with verbal communication, and her faulty interpretation of Utku behaviour. 'In retrospect, my relationship with the Utku seems to divide approximately into three phases, in which from the Utku point of view I was first a stranger and curiosity, then a recalcitrant child, and finally a confirmed irritant.'[67]

During the first phase Briggs lived in her own tent, which very quickly became a centre of attention for the Utku. She had visitors all day, and she yearned for nothing more than some privacy; although for the Inuit in the icy wastes in which they live, to be alone was the worst kind of punishment. Briggs was also linguistically and physically out of her league. She had to ask people to repeat themselves far more often than usual among the Utku, and even before the arrival of winter she was very worried about the cold, which had given her chilblains on her hands and her toes. Briggs then noticed that when she was visiting Utku they simply carried on with whatever they were doing, so she in turn ceased paying attention to her constant flow of visitors; this was apparently well received, but in fact taken as an infringement of norms, leading to her later marginalization as the *kapluna*, the Utku word for whites. At the same time Briggs was repeatedly irritable or weeping; emotional outbursts that were likewise freely accepted by the Utku:

as I later discovered, I was too easily reassured concerning the effects of my irritable lapses. When I succeeded in catching myself up, as I sometimes did after the first

---

[66] Briggs, *Never in Anger*, 157. *Naklik* is a barely translatable and ambiguous word that can be used as noun, verb, and adjective.
[67] Briggs, *Never in Anger*, 226.

aggressive impulse had spent itself, if I recounted the incident afterwards with amusement and heard others laugh with me, or if people seemed to accept the generous gestures with which I tried to dispel the chill that followed my transgression, then I was persuaded that no damage had been done. How wrong I was I learned only a year later when, on my return to Gjoa Haven, Ikayuqtuq told me of the reports that Utku had made of me that first winter.[68]

The situation came to a head during the winter when the temperature sank to $-50\,°C$ and Briggs moved into Inuttiaq's igloo. Briggs was only partially successful in behaving like an obedient adoptive daughter. She found Inuttiaq's behaviour arrogant, selfish, and patriarchal. Later she reported, 'I enjoyed also the respite that Inuttiaq's trips gave me from what I perceived as his "domineering self-centeredness".'[69] Her interests time and again clashed with those of Inuttiaq, 'when, for example, he destroyed the painfully achieved typing temperature of the iglu'.[70] But she also found the treatment of his wife and children unbearable:

> He seemed to have no compunctions about interrupting their activities, and occasionally even Allaq's sleep, to order them to do things for him: make tea, make bannock, fetch his pipe, help feed the dogs, chip the stalactites off the walls. If the wall developed a hole and snow began to accumulate on the bedding, or if a dog broke loose from its chain during the night, it would always be the soundly sleeping Allaq, not her wakeful husband, who had to go out and repair the damage.[71]

It slowly dawned on Briggs that control of one's emotion was a cardinal virtue for the Utku, but she found it increasingly hard to meet the ideal, the more that her relationship with Inuttiaq and the weather outside deteriorated, leaving her no recourse but retreat into her corner of the igloo. In such circumstances it was just too hard to control her emotions, the external stress was too great. Later she wrote: 'Applying Utku standards to my behavior, I felt each of these incidents as a personal reproach; but all too often my resolve to act in a way that Utku would consider exemplary was unequal to the situation.'[72] Her suppressed feelings 'had to get out', Briggs had to 'explode' like a volcano:

> The control required was much greater than that to which I was accustomed to discipline myself. At the same time, I was under considerably greater strain than I was used to, and the resulting tensions pressed for expression. Though I did my best to express them through laughter, as Utku did, laughter did not come naturally. Discouragingly often after hours, or even days, of calm, when I was congratulating myself on having finally achieved a semblance of the proper equanimity, the suddenness or the intensity of a feeling betrayed me. There was the coldness in my voice, which concealed a desire to weep with fatigue or frustration when I had to say for the thousandth time: 'I don't understand.' There was the time when, hurrying to leave the iglu, I unthinkingly moved Raigili aside with my hand instead of quietly telling her to move. There were the critical remarks I made in murmured English when the narrowed eyes and malicious whispers of Allaq and her sister, absorbed in a gossip

---

[68] Briggs, *Never in Anger*, 260.
[70] Briggs, *Never in Anger*, 106.
[72] Briggs, *Never in Anger*, 258.

[69] Briggs, *Never in Anger*, 106.
[71] Briggs, *Never in Anger*, 106.

session, irritated me beyond endurance. There was the burst of profanity (also in English) that I uttered when a lump of slush from the overheated dome fell for the third time in as many days into my typewriter and ended my work for the day.[73]

An open break came only following a specific incident. During the summer some white American and Canadian amateur fishermen arrived, and their arrogant manner shamed Briggs. When the fishermen borrowed two valuable Utku canoes on what Briggs considered unfair terms, she as translator let them know of her disapproval, thus implying that this disapproval was also shared by the Utku; she was heavily criticized by the Utku. This was seen as an infringement on the norm of emotional control, politeness, generosity, and also ultimately as a questioning of Inuttiaq's role as leader. Following this they continued to feed her, but they paid little attention to her any more. This in turn led Briggs to the onset of a period of depression that lasted months, during which her language ability also deteriorated. Her depression vanished only when the prospect of an early departure emerged. In addition to this, it finally became clear to the Inuit that she had in her work as a translator sought to help the Utku, and she was accepted by the family again. 'I consider Yiini a member of my family again': with these words Inuttiaq ended the conflict.[74]

Innutiaq became an exemplar of the meaning of emotional control for the Utku. In time, she came to regard him as 'not a typical Utku', as 'an unusually intense person. He, too, kept strict control of his feelings, but in his case one was aware that something was being controlled.'[75] The legitimacy of Innuttiaq as leader of the Utku flowed not least from the greater-than-average impulsiveness of his temperament, which made his self-control seem all the more titanic.[76] But this led in turn to a greater fear: 'They said that a man who *never* lost his temper could kill if he ever did become angry.'[77] Meanwhile Briggs had come to appreciate that the avoidance of expressions of extreme emotion, above all anger, was central to the Utku sense of self. 'Troublesome thoughts' (*ihumaquqtuuq*), as Briggs discovered, were thought to have an autonomous power. The Utku thought them capable of killing, or making someone ill. An Inuit told Briggs in Gjoa Haven that the Utku had said of her: 'If Yiini is angry, leave her alone. If an Eskimo gets angry it's something to remember, but a *kapluna* can get angry in the morning and be over it in the afternoon.'[78]

What is remarkable about this first major ethnography is the degree of self-reflection. Briggs explicitly included in the corpus of 'behavioral data' not only the 'description of Utku emotional patterns', her own observation of Utku emotions, and their statements about emotion, but also her own expressions of emotion, to which the Utku in turn reacted.[79] An example of Briggs's anthropological soul-searching is the following:

---

[73] Briggs, *Never in Anger*, 258–9.   [74] Briggs, *Never in Anger*, 302–3.
[75] Briggs, *Never in Anger*, 41, 42.   [76] Briggs, *Never in Anger*, 46.
[77] Briggs, *Never in Anger*, 47, emphasis in original.   [78] Briggs, *Never in Anger*, 261.
[79] Briggs, *Never in Anger*, 5. The novelty of such reflexive ethnographic observation was emphasized by Catherine A. Lutz: 'Briggs' description of her reactions to the igloo ceiling's dripping onto her

On my two previous field trips to Alaskan Eskimo villages I had identified strongly with the Eskimo villagers by contrast with such elements of the *kapluna* population as I had had occasion to meet. I had had no problems of rapport, and I expected the same to be true again. Indeed, never having felt very American in my outlook, I rather hoped I might discover myself essentially Eskimo at heart. I voiced no such romanticism aloud, however. I was rather ashamed of my 'unprofessional' attitude; and I had a number of qualms concerning the wisdom of being adopted, in terms of loss of 'objective' position in the community; drains on my supplies which would result from contributing to the maintenance of a family household; and loss of privacy with resultant difficulties in working. Therefore I was not—so I thought—seriously considering the idea of adoption. Nevertheless, when one day in Gjoa Haven Ikayuq-tuq asked me why I wanted to live at Back River for a year, I spontaneously told her that I wanted to be adopted by an Eskimo family in order to learn to live like an Eskimo. I put it this way partly because I wanted—I think now, wrongly—to conceal from her that I would be 'studying' the Eskimos. I was embarrassed by the scholarly analytical aspect of the enterprise, thinking she would consider it prying.[80]

The outcome of Briggs's time with Inuttiaq's family was the first book-length ethnography of emotion, exemplifying in oppressive detail the cultural contingency of the expression of emotion—emotional *expression*, and not feelings, for *Never in Anger* was never a work of social constructivism. The title is misleading, for in the book Briggs repeatedly emphasizes that the Utku did feel anger, but knew how to suppress it. In Briggs's view, for instance, Raigili really could not stand her tyrannical younger sister Saarak, but was not able to show this, these negative feelings emerging regularly as nightmares.[81] Briggs herself concisely summarized the object of her book as follows: it examined 'the ways in which feelings, both affectionate and hostile, are channeled [*sic*] and communicated, and the ways in which people attempt to direct and control the improper expression of such feelings in themselves and in others'.[82]

Emotions 'Hypercognized' and 'Hypocognized'

Robert Levy (1924–2003), another pioneer of the anthropology of emotion, was just as little prepared as Briggs to suggest that feelings are a cultural product. What also links him to Briggs is the fact that the central emotion with which he was concerned was anger. However, his fieldwork was located in warmer climes than that of Briggs: on Tahiti, the subject of extensive travel writings since the eighteenth century. From the very beginning Westerners focused upon the way that Tahitians lived out their 'natural feelings', especially love, creating a myth of sexual freedom. The myth was elaborated both by the early 'discoverers' such as Louis-Antoine de

typewriter keys, and to the expectation that the resident child's "imperious" demands for her own carefully hoarded raisins be met, introduces a novel view of fieldwork. It is one that at least implies that the emotional worldview of the anthropologist merits as much attention as that of the culture that we ostensibly go to "observe" '; Lutz, *Unnatural Emotions*, 12.

[80] Briggs, *Never in Anger*, 20.   [81] Briggs, *Never in Anger*, 144.
[82] Briggs, *Never in Anger*, 4.

Bougainville (1729–1811), who visited in 1767, and by artists such as Paul Gauguin (1848–1903), who lived on the island from the 1890s until his death. A high point of this interest in the sex life of Tahitians was reached in the 1960s, when the idea of a sexual revolution was associated with the work of Margaret Mead.[83]

Levy did his Tahitian fieldwork in the early 1960s. He originated the distinction between socially relevant (hypercognized) and socially irrelevant emotions (hypocognized). This does not imply that those emotions considered hypocognized were not felt; Levy was more interested in the differing weight put upon universal feelings from one collective to another. The question of the weight assigned to particular emotions in a wide range of social groups—from the family to the society—is central to the study of history. It is possible to go one step further and claim that even the question of whether in a specific historical period emotions were emphasized at all is an important historical question. Perhaps one day historians will conclude that 'emotion' and 'emotional' are today used as often, and as loosely, in the language of advertising, politics, and sport as 'psychology', 'psychic', or 'mental' once were during the 1980s. Today the relatives of a victim of a school shooting are expected to come to terms 'emotionally' with their loss; not 'mentally' or 'psychologically', which would have been the terms employed some twenty years ago. The team winning a basketball tournament is said to experience 'emotional' bonding; not to be 'mentally strong' or 'in good psychological shape'. Today there is even a vacuum cleaner on the market called 'Emotion'.[84] Where does this shift from 'mental' and 'psychological' to the 'emotional' come from? Which emotions count at a particular time and in specific circumstances as 'hypercognized'? This question demands historical analysis.

Briggs would have most likely regarded anger among the Utku as hypercognized. In any case, this is what Levy did with the Tahitian concept of anger, *riri*. The governing principle of Tahitian behaviour was not emotional control, but its opposite: verbally 'ridding' the human body of anger as quickly as possible—provided, that is, that anyone ever became angry, since 'a generalized and culturally valued timidity' ensured that this hardly ever happened.[85] Levy learned from his informant Tāvana that 'The Tahitians say that an angry man is like a bottle. When he gets filled up he will begin to spill over.' Suppressed rage 'has bad effects on one's body; it may give one trouble in one's head or heart. There are people who have died from anger.'[86] The Tahitian man Oro responded similarly to the question of what one should do if one felt angry: 'If you are angry at that man, don't procrastinate, go and talk to him, finish it. And afterward, things will be all right again between you.'[87] Flora added that suppressed anger turned your hair grey. And

---

[83] On Bougainville and Tahiti see Maurice Bloch and Jean H. Bloch, 'Women and the Dialectics of Nature in Eighteenth-Century French Thought', in Carol P. MacCormack and Marilyn Strathern (eds), *Nature, Culture and Gender* (Cambridge: Cambridge University Press, 1980), 25–41, esp. 31, 37.

[84] See 'Products: Special Cleaner: Rechargeable Vacuum Cleaner', *Fakir-Hausgeräte GmbH* <http://www.fakir.de/index.php/emotion-as-350.html> accessed 1 March 2014.

[85] Levy, *Tahitians*, 285.   [86] Levy, *Tahitians*, 285.   [87] Levy, *Tahitians*, 285.

Veve described sanctions that sound rather like the kind of sanctions one might find in a traditional Western village community: 'If somebody doesn't tell me when he is angry at me, he'll go and tell somebody else. He'll gossip about me, and exaggerate, and then trouble will start in the village.'[88]

In Tahiti, Levy also encountered extreme differences in dealing with emotions in comparison to Western societies. This is especially the case with grief, and the weeping which is supposed to be a universal human sign of grieving. The very first reports of Tahitian behaviour noted how suddenly the Tahitians switched during a burial from grief and weeping to happiness and laughter. The amount of demonstrative weeping—calibrating the expression of grief by the quantity of tears wept, and the volume of wailing—also had a different relationship to the immediate cause than was usual in Europe. One report from 1909 claimed that 'It is bizarre that the joy of seeing each other after a long separation is demonstrated in exactly the same manner . . . by the same crying and the same tears as are associated with the burial.'[89] Levy himself, during his fieldwork in the 1960s, was very disturbed by the way that the death of Tāvana's wife was dealt with. The first time he approached the house of the dying woman he heard 'loud, animated talking, joking, and laughter'. Once inside, he had the impression that he had crashed a family party, the dying woman having been pushed into a corner.[90] Tāvana's wife 'did not moan, cry out, or complain. She was dying in a restrained, low-key, matter-of-fact way.'[91] There was still laughter in the house shortly before she died; immediately after there were a few tears, but the merriment soon returned. 'Within a few days of the funeral, Tāvana's grandchildren had begun to play on Tāvana Vahine's tomb, sitting on the raised concrete, talking and laughing and rearranging the flowers which had been placed there.'[92] When Levy asked for an explanation for this obvious merriment in the face of the illness and death of a loved one, he was told that this was for the benefit of Tāvana: that he might think for a moment that his wife was recovering. It would thus be best of all if his wife could manage a smile.

Levy did not only establish great differences in the physical expression of feelings, but also in their location within the human body. This brings us back to a key problem already raised in the Introduction, and which we will encounter more than once again. Levy's informants told him that anger, desire, and fear, or their Tahitian equivalents, were located in the *ā'au*, or bowels. Some claimed that these emotions 'enter into the heart'. Levy thought this to be 'in part an introduced biblical form for the seat of the emotions, but it may also involve the perception of visceral emotional responses in the chest as well as in the abdomen'.[93] He also noted that the Tahitian language not only lacked equivalents for the particular types of feeling denoted in Western languages, but that there was a lack of comprehensive concepts such as 'affect', 'passion', 'feeling', or 'emotion'.[94] We will return to this absence of

---

[88] Levy, *Tahitians*, 286.

[89] Edmond de Bovis, *État de la société tahitienne à l'arrivée des européens* (Papeete: Impr. du gouvernement, 1909), 60, cited by Levy, *Tahitians*, 289.

[90] Levy, *Tahitians*, 291.   [91] Levy, *Tahitians*, 292.   [92] Levy, *Tahitians*, 298.

[93] Levy, *Tahitians*, 271.   [94] Levy, *Tahitians*, 271.

an emotional metalanguage as well. In the case of Levy, we should note that this is an instance of the anthropology of emotion *before* the development of social constructivism. While we found in Briggs elements of social constructivism *avant la lettre*, there is nothing like this in Levy; instead we find many statements that today ring ethnocentric alarm bells. Individual psychic distress—'depression'—is just as common among Tahitians as it is among us, writes Levy; but it is 'masked by being explained supernaturally' when calling upon the help of witch doctors. As for the notoriously early and promiscuous sexuality of the Tahitians, this is ascribed to their reluctance to commit to the married state. Levy considers that this reflects 'anxieties about being bound into a household and to a close relationship, as well as anxieties about relinquishing *taure'are'a* freedom'. Finally, Levy thought that some Tahitians 'frequently report fear of possible physical harm from other people in settings in which the fear does not seem to be objectively warranted'.[95]

5 THE LINGUISTIC TURN AND SOCIAL CONSTRUCTIVISM

Emotions have a uniform core but are expressed variously in different cultures—this summarizes the guiding assumption of the anthropology of emotions during the 1970s. It was in this period, however, that the human and social sciences underwent a paradigm shift, leading to the publication in the 1980s of emotional ethnographies that overturned this guiding assumption. Now it was argued that not only did the expression of emotion vary across cultures, but that people from different cultures had radically different feelings.

This paradigm change became known as the linguistic, or cultural, turn, the victory of postmodernism, the entry into the 'postmodern condition' as Jean-François Lyotard (1924–98) dubbed it in 1979. This was also associated with the work of Michel Foucault and Jacques Derrida (1930–2004), questioning the Enlightenment, scientific truth, and objectivity, master narratives of progress, any definite relationship between sign and meaning, the basic categories of gender and ethnicity, clear distinctions between high and low culture, the new architecture of pastiche, language games in science and literature.[96] Any kind of Hegelian or Marxian *telos*, novels, films, or histories with linear narratives, classical rigour or architectural modernism as with the Bauhaus, utopian social visions—after a decade of playful subversion and irony, all of these one-time certainties had been severely undermined, if not consigned to the dustbin of history. In 1988 the anthropologist Catherine A. Lutz argued that 'emotional experience is not

---

[95] Levy, *Tahitians*, 176, 198, 283. Another example of the universalistic anthropology of emotions of the 1970s—in this case inspired by the psychoanalyst and pioneer of attachment theory John Bowlby—is Charles Lindholm, *Generosity and Jealousy: The Swat Pukhtun of Northern Pakistan* (New York: Columbia University Press, 1982).

[96] See Barth et al., *One Discipline, Four Ways*, 322–7 for a brief account of the impact of post-structuralism on American anthropology.

precultural but pre*eminently* cultural'.[97] It is not insignificant that this statement was made by an anthropologist, and not by one of the master theorists of post-structuralism. For where could radical contingency be demonstrated any better than with emotions, which were at the time widely assumed to be prelinguistic, physical, and culturally universal? Perhaps a longstanding belief in the naturalness of emotions diverted post-structural criticism to Enlightenment rationality, over-looking the other side of a binary opposition that remains powerful today: emotion.

Headhunting for Pleasure

The starting shot for the decade of social constructivism in the anthropology of emotions was sounded with the publication of *Knowledge and Passion: Ilongot Notions of Self and Social Life* (1980) by Michelle Z. Rosaldo (1944–81). Together with her husband Renato Rosaldo she had carried out fieldwork during the later 1960s and the early 1970s among the Ilongot, a group of about 3,500 people living in woods in the Northern Philippines that covered about 600 square miles. The Ilongot were hunters and agriculturalists, living in large single-room houses in-habited by up to three nuclear families. During the twentieth century they were occupied by the Japanese during the Second World War, converted by American missionaries to Fundamentalist Christianity during the 1960s and 1970s, and from 1972 were the object of efforts by the Marcos military dictatorship to bring Philippine indigenous people under their control.

The Rosaldos had intended to observe how the Ilongot 'tell nightly myths, make intricate plans for ritual feasts, or in their daily lives reveal concern for detailed webs of ancient wisdom'—this was how Michelle Z. Rosaldo later ironically described it.[98] Instead of myths, rites, and ancient wisdom, the Rosaldos found a culture in which emotion had a special place, especially in connection with a practice that was known from older reports and from the diary of an early twentieth-century anthropologist, but which had been thought to have died out: headhunting. The Rosaldos only found out about this once they had established some familiarity with their informants. This knowledge made them rather anxious. Michelle Z. Rosaldo described what really happened when the Ilongot went hunting heads:

> A man (never a woman) chooses to go killing, talks to kin, and plans a raid because his heart is 'heavy'. Although he may have hopes to kill within particular kin groups or localities, the raider does not care about the personal identities of his victims or limit violence to opponents of his age or sex. Grieving for lost kin, envious of past beheadings, angry at an insult, and bent upon revenge, he and his fellows are concerned, primarily, to realize their *liget*. All feel a weight that is 'focused' and intensified as they progress, slowly and quietly, through wakeful nights, scant food, and unknown reaches of the forest, to an ambush whose general location is isolated in advance. Moving with tortured care and quiet, they talk only in whispers, and play reed

[97] Lutz, *Unnatural Emotions*, 5, emphasis in original.
[98] Michelle Z. Rosaldo, *Knowledge and Passion: Ilongot Notions of Self and Social Life* (Cambridge: Cambridge University Press, 1980), 14.

flutes to set their hearts on edge. Once near the place of ambush, they pound their heads to heighten *liget*; their vision dims and narrows toward a future victim; their eyes are burning red. After shooting, the raiders will rush upon their wounded and dead victims, slashing wildly with their knives. The men who will get credit for beheadings need not themselves kill or even cut off the heads of victims, but simply hold a head as it is severed and 'toss' it—the weight each killer would be rid of—on the ground. This accomplished, they shout in triumph, and others toss the heads and shout. Tense, intent, and cautious until that moment, the gay victors then abandon both the severed heads and the bodies. Purged of violence, they will seek out flowery reeds to wear like feathers signifying lightness, sweet-smelling leaves whose scent recalls the lives they stole. Finding these, they hurry home.[99]

During the first period of fieldwork, military controls and Christianization meant that the men only very rarely went headhunting. Nonetheless, a survey made by Rosaldo in 1968 showed that sixty-five out of seventy men who were older than 20 had, at some point in their life, killed someone and cut their head off.[100] She soon began to realize that the key to this practice was not be found in current anthropological ideas about its function as a rite of passage, but instead in the hunters' own explanation: that decapitating someone made 'their heavy heart light', an indigenous way of talking about feelings. She suggested that

> Men went headhunting, Ilongots said, because of their emotions. Not gods, but 'heavy' feelings were what made men want to kill; in taking heads they could aspire to 'cast off' an 'anger' that 'weighed down on' and oppressed their saddened 'hearts'.[101]

An internal perspective, rather than external observation, *emic* not *etic*: not the question, therefore, of the cosmology in which this *langue du cœur* was placed, but rather the meaning which these concepts had for the culture of the Ilongot—these were the questions that became central for Rosaldo:

> Whereas other anthropologists have been inclined to work 'from outside in', first describing a patterned social world and then asking how individuals are 'socialized' to work and live within it, I found it more illuminating to begin from the other pole of the analytical dialectic and ask how personal and affective life, itself 'socially constructed', is actualized in and orders the shapes of social action over time. This required an investigation of Ilongot words concerning hearts and motivations—especially, their words denoting 'energy/anger/passion' and civility, or 'knowledge'—and, at the same time, a discovery of local assumptions about the persons, relationships, and events to which such words were characteristically applied.[102]

What was going on in the 'hearts' (*rinawa*) of the Ilongot? It soon became clear that 'passion' or 'energy' (*liget*) and 'knowledge' (*bëya*) were key concepts, and stood in a dialectical relationship to each other. *Liget* was an expression of male autonomy which, before the first sexual encounter and entry into a monogamous relationship,

---

[99] Rosaldo, *Knowledge and Passion*, 55–6, emphasis in original.
[100] Rosaldo, *Knowledge and Passion*, 14.   [101] Rosaldo, *Knowledge and Passion*, 19.
[102] Rosaldo, *Knowledge and Passion*, 19–20.

had to be both put into practice and tamed.[103] Headhunting was the ritualized practice, perhaps the medium, through which this happened. Once the male was in a steady relationship he stopped going headhunting, and the *bēya* in his heart held *liget* in check. This therefore involves the emotional and ritual description and support of social institutions (marriage) and hierarchies (young/old, male/female).

During her second period of fieldwork in the 1970s, Rosaldo played tape recordings of headhunting songs to Ilongot men, who became sad, even irritated, not wanting to hear more. Most of them had recently converted to Christianity and had completely given up headhunting. The songs gave rise to 'nostalgia' for headhunting; more precisely, the songs touched their hearts, created bad *liget* that was no longer channelled by headhunting and could be directed to a particular end.[104] A similar kind of *liget* was created when a young unmarried man who had never been headhunting saw the headhunting earrings on another young man. This too associated the heart with weight, confusion, illness, effort, and frustration. By contrast, the ideal heart was 'weightless' and 'vibrant' in the wind, like the stems of upright plants. Headhunting 'eased the hearts' of headhunters:

> Finally, for the headhunter, there is joy in 'casting off' his burden; not murder or vengeance, but the loss of weight he feels in severing a human head and tossing it to the ground is what clears clouds and brings his heart new life.[105]

Rosaldo demonstrated that emotions were absolutely central for the construction of the Ilongot self. Emotional categories, especially *liget* and *bēya*, were thought to depend directly on external events (an animal sighted while hunting, seeking headhunting earrings, hearing a headhunting song). There was no internalized psychic control such as 'conscience' or understanding; emotions were self-determining: *liget* and *bēya* were, if you like, bound up within the heart into a self-regulating ecosystem. There were no 'emotions' as we understand them, but instead 'motions' of the heart.[106] As a result, they were not linked to an object, but had their own linguistic agency:

> In stories [which the Ilongots tell each other], the heart does not desire, reflect, or otherwise oppose itself to events that stand outside it. Narrators comment, 'My heart said "shoot it," and I shot it;' 'My heart said "he is coming", and he came.'[107]

This quite unusual construction of a self from the interplay of *liget* and *bēya* exemplified how the self and its relation to society is constructed, not given. The category of self or of subjectivity—what it means to be an individual—is known to be a central, if not *the* central, category of all post-structuralist theory. Showing its historicity and plasticity was what Foucault and the others were all about. If one

---

[103] 'Neither good nor evil in itself, *liget* suggests the passionate energy that leads young men to labor hard, to marry, kill, and reproduce; but also, if ungoverned by the "knowledge" of mature adults, to engage in wild violence. Ideally, "knowledge" and "passion" work together in the "heart" '; Rosdaldo, *Knowledge and Passion*, 27, emphasis in original.

[104] Rosaldo, *Knowledge and Passion*, 32–4.   [105] Rosaldo, *Knowledge and Passion*, 52.
[106] Rosaldo, *Knowledge and Passion*, 38.   [107] Rosaldo, *Knowledge and Passion*, 38.

had to name the one overall category dominating social constructivist anthropology of emotion, then it would be the self.

Moreover, the example of the Ilongot upsets Western ideas of especially strong female emotions. Since it was men who were seized by the *liget/bēya* dialectic, they felt more intensely than women.[108] In the West, by contrast, it is women who are 'emotional' and responsible for strong feelings.

Poetry, Not Tears, as the Medium of Authentic Feelings

The extent to which social constructivist anthropology of emotion reflects the gender issue is highlighted in the studies of Lila Abu-Lughod. She is probably the sole ethnologist of emotion—and one of a very few ethnologists in general—who was introduced to those among whom she would conduct her fieldwork by her father. Abu-Lughod, who grew up in America and now teaches there, is the daughter of Ibrahim Abu-Lughod (1929–2001), one of the best-known Palestin-ian-American intellectuals alongside Edward Said. She arrived in Cairo in October 1978, on her way to the Awlad 'Ali Bedouins in the Western Desert, near the Libyan border. Her father had insisted on personally introducing his daughter, knowing that in a traditional Muslim Arab society the protection of a father was vital to the social, and scholarly, success of an unmarried daughter. At the time she was 'a bit embarrassed' about this arrangement. But in retrospect she was grateful for her father's initiative, since if she had arrived without him,

> people as conservative as the Bedouins, for whom belonging to tribe and family are paramount and the education of girls novel, would assume that a woman alone must have so alienated her family, especially her male kin, that they no longer cared about her.[109]

This perception was of course only possible because she was herself seen as 'indigenous', as one of the Bedouins. How was that possible? The Awlad 'Ali regarded all Muslim and Arab non-Egyptians as 'one of us'. And so Abu-Lughod, who had an American mother, the sociologist Janet Lippman Abu-Lughod (1928–2013), who had been brought up in a secular family environment, spoke only basic Arabic, and who had spent only four years as a child in Egypt, spending summers as a child and young woman with relatives in Jordan, still had a better opportunity of being accepted as 'one of us' than an Egyptian who had lived all their life in Cairo would have had. This combination of distance and proximity has continued to drive Abu-Lughod, and she has written an influential article

---

[108] A similar example: Steven Feld, an American anthropologist who did fieldwork in Kaluli, Papua New Guinea during the 1970s, gained the greatest respect only when he wept uncontrollably in public; Feld, *Sound and Sentiment: Birds, Weeping, Poetics, and Song in Kaluli Expression* (2nd edn, Philadelphia: University of Pennsylvania Press, 1990), 233, see also 261–3.

[109] Lila Abu-Lughod, *Veiled Sentiments: Honor and Poetry in a Bedouin Society* (Berkeley and Los Angeles: University of California Press, 1986), 12.

describing the life of a 'halfie' in fieldwork: anthropologists who are in the field both their own self and an Other.[110]

In Alexandria, Abu-Lughod's father arranged a meeting with desert Bedouins and let them know about his daughter's intentions: perfecting her Arabic and learning something of the life of the Bedouin, for which reason she was looking for a family with which she could live. Hearing this, the tribal elder, the *haj*, offered to take Lila Abu-Lughod into his own family. She moved into the position of an 'adopted daughter', just like Briggs had done with the Utku—and of course Abu-Lughod had read Briggs's ethnography. This role gave her many insights, but at the same time greatly restricted her freedom of movement. The Bedouin lived in their tribe as patrilineal families, in which the senior male cousin (the oldest son of the uncle) had the first right of marriage to the daughter. Children were assigned to their male relatives, and Abu-Lughod recounted the case of a 5-year old boy who grew up with his mother after his parents had separated, until his paternal grandfather arrived to take him back to his proper family, that of the father:

> Although the boy had never seen him before, he ran to pack a few clothes, put his hand in his grandfather's, and left with hardly a glance back. His mother was heartbroken. Men who heard the story nodded their heads and did not seem surprised.[111]

After the Second World War the Awlad 'Ali had ceased being nomadic, living in simple houses, not in tents as they once had. They no longer worked as shepherds in a pastoral economy, but increasingly used their sheep for trading. They also made profits from the sale of land, and from smuggling, which flourished in the western part of Egypt, near the Libyan border and far from the capital and state authority. This transition to a settled existence was associated with an even greater degree of segregation between men and women. During their time as nomads, women had been relatively free to move between the tents of their families, but once they began living in houses they were more likely to be prevented from meeting their male relatives, or strangers. This resulted in restrictions to their freedom of movement, and an increase in the extent to which they were veiled. At the same time men who became wealthier could afford additional wives, which also had an impact on families' emotional economies.[112]

Abu-Lughod had not originally been interested in the issue of emotions, but it became central once she settled into the closed female world of her new family.[113] Arabic *ghinnāwas* (literally: 'little songs') were sung here, mostly improvised,

---

[110] Of course, for the social constructivist perspective Abu-Lughod claims to be writing from, categories like 'halfie' are inadmissible, since they presume the existence of fixed identities. And this contradiction does not disappear if one treats the identities as the product of a process of construction: 'What happens when the "other" that the anthropologist is studying is simultaneously constructed as, at least partially, a self?'; Lila Abu-Lughod, 'Writing against Culture', in Richard G. Fox (ed.), *Recapturing Anthropology: Working in the Present* (Santa Fe, NM: School of American Research Press, 1991), 137–62, here 140.

[111] Abu-Lughod, *Veiled Sentiments*, 53.   [112] Abu-Lughod, *Veiled Sentiments*, 70–3.

[113] Another reason for the shift of emotions to the centre of her interest was her use of unstructured interviews, which she hardly ever transcribed during the interview itself, but later from memory. Abu-Lughod, *Veiled Sentiments*, 23, 25.

sometimes in a rapidly shifting dialogue, songs which formally resembled Japanese haikus and, in their emotional content, American Blues songs. Voice and intonation were decisive to a successful presentation: successful *ghinnāwas* should, among other things, foster fellow-feeling among the women present. The oral literature of the *ghinnāwas* was, despite rules of genre and conventionalization, a place, in fact *the* place, for the Bedouin wives of the Awlad 'Ali to express their feelings. Emotionally-coloured verbal remarks were thought by the Awlad 'Ali to lack authenticity; such remarks were therefore not expected to be logical and consistent. They could indeed be entirely contradictory. *Ghinnāwas* by contrast were the 'poetry of personal life', dealing with sadness, troubled love and yearning, jealousy of the husband's second wife, desire for the husband who seemed to be entirely taken up with his third wife, love for someone other than the man with whom her marriage had been arranged; *ghinnāwas* therefore presented a window upon *'agl*, the Bedouin self, heart, consciousness, spirit, or—lacking all religious connotation—soul.[114]

What is in this context most alien from any Western viewpoint is that an ideal, 'truthful' idiom of feeling did not take the form of unmistakable bodily signs or informal speech, but instead took place in a literary genre which, even at the height of any improvisation, continued to adhere to fixed rules. *Ghinnāwas* were the prime means of authenticating feelings, as Abu-Lughod noticed. She heard the poems of a wife who may or may not have felt disdain towards the man she had been married off to. The family of the husband was unsettled by the situation, and Abu-Lughod broke her promise never to let men know about the poems she had heard; she told the brother-in-law of the wife in question about these poems. Up until then he had thought that this wife was simply fooling his brother and simulated her dislike so that her husband would present her with gifts. However, once the brother-in-law had heard about the poems he changed his mind. And the wife herself only admitted to Abu-Lughod that she loved another man from a hostile family in another tribe when the anthropologist reminded her of her own *ghinnāwas*.[115]

The social context in which *ghinnāwas* were sung was quite decisive, permitting general statements about the relationship between genders, social hierarchy, and the kind of emotions found among the Awlad 'Ali. For men, the public realm was governed by a rigid code of honour: proud, invincible, autonomous Bedouin males with a high level of emotional and physical self-control mostly kept to themselves; if they encountered women, their behaviour was regulated by a no less rigid code of shame, *hasham*. This was the honour of the weak, meaning something like 'shame' and 'shyness'. It was closely related to veiling. Ultimately, *hasham* meant fear of being dominated by a superior person, undermining the Awlad 'Ali ideal of autonomy and freedom.[116] This code of *hasham* prevented women from speaking

---

[114] Abu-Lughod, *Veiled Sentiments*, 31, 181. The Bedouin construction of the soul is very similar to the Western idea of a physical inner space for feelings.

[115] Abu-Lughod, *Veiled Sentiments*, 220–1.

[116] Abu-Lughod, *Veiled Sentiments*, 103–8, 117.

publicly, let alone in front of men, about true and ideal love (as opposed to love in an arranged marriage), and about jealousy of the husband's other wives.

To give an example, when Mabrūka, married to her husband for sixteen years and mother of six children, discovered that her husband planned to take a second wife, she seemed untroubled, and simply said: 'Let him get married, I don't care. But he should buy me nice things. He's worthless, he always was. A real man asks after his family, sees to it that they have everything they need.'[117] Even when her husband spent more than the usual seven days with his new wife after the wedding she reacted stoically, seemingly uninterested. On the tenth day after the second marriage he at last turned up again, bringing her food from the market. Mabrūka only complained that he had forgotten some things. Then her husband Rashīd took his gun and went hunting, about which Mabrūka said to Abu-Lughod, who was visiting her at the time: 'It's been ages [literally, years] since we saw him.' Abu-Lughod asked gently whether she missed him. She got the harsh response: 'No way. Do you think he is dear to me? I don't even ask about him. He can come and go as he pleases.'[118] Shortly afterwards she began reciting emotional poems which spoke of sadness and disappointment, as in the following:

> They always left me
> stuffed with false promises . . .
>
> dīmā khallō l-ʿagl
> ʿāmrāt bimwāʿīdhum.[119]

Did this mean that Mabrūka had 'lied' to her family, or misled them, while in her poem speaking the truth about her feelings? Not at all, argued Abu-Lughod. This kind of cynical reading would be like Erving Goffman's idea that people in their dealings with each other in public wear 'masks', keeping their true faces 'backstage', where they can show their true selves.[120] Abu-Lughod maintains that we should instead reject the Western chimera of the authentic self, and ascribe the same degree of authenticity to the female public utterance as we do to the poem uttered in private, treating both discourses equally (Abu-Lughod explicitly draws upon Foucault here).[121] In this light, Abu-Lughod would also reject the view expressed above that emotionally-coloured verbal statements were thought to lack authenticity.

At the same time, Abu-Lughod considered that the *ghinnāwas* were formally and aesthetically suited to the articulation of feelings that could not be verbally expressed in the framework of the *hasham* code. *Ghinnāwas* were both formalized and improvised; this created ambiguity and space for the expression of emotion. It was always possible to hide behind the poetic form and claim that one was

---

[117] Abu-Lughod, *Veiled Sentiments*, 229.   [118] Abu-Lughod, *Veiled Sentiments*, 230.
[119] Abu-Lughod, *Veiled Sentiments*, 230. Hence the proper reaction of a wife to an insult was not tears or a verbal counter-attack, but the recitation of a poem; see Abu-Lughod, *Veiled Sentiments*, 196–7.
[120] Goffman, *Presentation of Self in Everyday*. Goffman's metaphor is clearly based upon Marx's conception of alienation.
[121] Abu-Lughod, *Veiled Sentiments*, 237–8.

constrained by the genre, that one was only following a tradition. Of course, the *ghinnāwas* were an old art form, associated in the minds of the Awlad ʿAli with glorious times before the Egyptian state began the creeping modernization of the Western Desert.[122]

The Height of Social Constructivism

When people talk about a social constructivist approach to the anthropology of emotion, the name that usually comes up, along with and often even before that of Abu-Lughod, is Catherine A. Lutz.[123] In 1977 Lutz went to conduct fieldwork on Ifaluk Atoll in the South West Pacific. The two main islands which comprise Ifaluk Atoll together made up less than 1 square mile; they had been 'discovered' by the British in 1797 and belonged to Japan until the end of the Second World War. In 1945 they were then assigned to the USA as a strategic trust territory by the United Nations. At the time of Lutz's research there were 430 Ifaluk living in single-roomed thatched huts, with an average thirteen people per house.[124] Like the other ethnologies we have considered, Lutz's monograph betrayed a high level of self-reflection, and made her own position quite plain: she tells us that she was looking for a culture in which feelings were not automatically associated with femininity—a Western stereotype which she had repeatedly encountered during the course of the 1970s, despite the advance of women in American universities to professorial and other senior posts. At the same time she emphasized that the matrilocal system practised by the Ifaluk, in which families live in the household of the wife's parents, or nearby, led her to expect a greater degree of gender equality, and a less significant gendering of emotion. She also disclosed her romantic vision of the South Seas as the stronghold of a 'better', more peaceful society, as Paul Gauguin had depicted.[125]

The social constructivist approach has never been expressed more pointedly, neither before Lutz's work nor afterwards. The first sentences of her book read as follows:

> At first blush, nothing might appear more natural and hence less cultural than emotions, nothing more private and hence less amenable to public scrutiny, nothing more inchoate and less compatible with the logos of social science. These views can be treated, however, as items in a cultural discourse whose traditional assumptions about human nature and whose dualisms—body and mind, public and private, essence and appearance, and irrationality and thought—constitute what we take to be the self-evident nature of emotion.[126]

---

[122] Abu-Lughod, *Veiled Sentiments*, 239–40, 251–2, 256–7.
[123] Abu-Lughod and Lutz have also edited a book together: Catherine A. Lutz and Lila Abu-Lughod (eds), *Language and the Politics of Emotion* (Cambridge: Cambridge University Press, 1990).
[124] Lutz, *Unnatural Emotions*, 3, 22, 26, 29, 39, 151.
[125] Lutz, *Unnatural Emotions*, 14–17.
[126] Lutz, *Unnatural Emotions*, 3.

Correspondingly, one of her aims was to

> to deconstruct emotion, to show that the use of the term in both our everyday and social-scientific conversation rests on a network of often implicit associations that give force to statements that use it.[127]

But what she also sought was a greater emphasis upon emotions, and women, in Western cultures:

> While words like 'envy', 'love', and 'fear' are invoked by anyone who would speak about the self, about the private, about the intensely meaningful, or about the ineffable, they are also used to talk about devalued aspects of the world—the irrational, the uncontrollable, the vulnerable, and the female.[128]

Ultimately, Lutz stated that she was concerned with treating 'emotion as an ideological practice rather than as a thing to be discovered or an essence to be distilled'.[129]

Deconstruction and de-essentialization would, according to Lutz, open up an undistorted perspective upon local emotional constructs. For the Ifaluk these were said to be more intersubjective, rather than individual, as in the West; more external, rather than interior to the body, sometimes with physical effects; and marked social status, rather than inner conditions. Lutz therefore made the claim 'that emotional experience is not precultural but pre*eminently* cultural. The prevalent assumption that the emotions are invariant across cultures is replaced here with the question of how one cultural discourse on emotion may be translated into another.'[130]

This focus upon translation distinguished her project from the kind of hermeneutic approach typical of Clifford Geertz, who according to Lutz always asked 'what they are feeling'.[131] Her understanding of 'translation' was certainly not semantic and referential, but rather pragmatic and performative: she was not interested in aligning the meanings of emotional words, but instead in studying emotional signs embedded in human action, both verbal and non-verbal (gestures, facial expressions, bodily movements, and so on).

To take an example: translated in terms of reference and semantics, the Ifaluk word *song* means something like 'justifiable anger'. But what does that say about the Ifaluk? More or less nothing, for the practice of *song* involves no discharge, no loss of control, no *angry outburst* of a kind that the Western idea of anger might imply. The Ifaluk have a face-to-face society that manages without written law, and *song* functioned as a comprehensive form of cultural regulation. Whoever declared *song* was referring to a moral infringement on the part of a fellow islander, but also to his own social position, since access to the resources needed to make *song* valid were limited and asymmetrical: more powerful Ifaluk were able to declare *song* more frequently than the less powerful. However, the Ifaluk were a cooperative people,

---

[127] Lutz, *Unnatural Emotions*, 3.   [128] Lutz, *Unnatural Emotions*, 3–4.
[129] Lutz, *Unnatural Emotions*, 4.   [130] Lutz, *Unnatural Emotions*, 5, emphasis in original.
[131] Lutz, *Unnatural Emotions*, 8.

and so this did not involve a desire for social advancement or a struggle over the distribution of social resources. Instead, chiefs who invoked *song* were, according to Lutz, more concerned with the welfare of the collective: *pars pro toto* they expressed the will of all Ifaluk. In favour of this interpretation was the fact that chiefs were thought to possess in the highest degree the emotion which the Ifaluk considered to have the highest standing: *fago*, a mixture of sympathy, love, and melancholy. Hence chiefs should be like real Ifaluk and only have a slightly greater access to emotion than the others—emotion primarily involving *fago*, and only *song* if other Ifaluk infringed taboos.[132]

While on Ifaluk Atoll Lutz found herself confronted again and again with her own culture of origin whose contingency became clearer the more it came into contact with another culture. Once she was asked by the Ifaluk if she had ever seen a person without toes. Lutz talked of a homeless man she had seen in New York, who not only had no toes, but no legs either, and who moved around on a board with wheels. 'I would *fago* him if I saw him', said a perplexed, even appalled Ifaluk, and others asked where the family of this homeless man was, and why were they not looking after him.[133] They reacted in much the same way to Hollywood films that US Marines brought when visiting the island. A woman told Lutz that she looked away during violent scenes, 'because my *fago* is very strong for the ones who are killed'.[134]

Having gone into the field with 'a variant of the everyday and implicit emotional theories of my culture, class, and gender, wanting to know, for example, how islanders "really felt", and assuming that their emotional lives were essentially private matters, that fear and anger were things to be "conquered" and love to be publicly avowed', she came back with two emotional models: her own middle-class European-American model, and an Ifaluk ethnopsychology.[135] The first assumed emotion to be Janus-faced: emotion was both semi-pathological and also the 'seat of the true and glorified self', both good and bad.[136] If feelings are thought to be bad, then they are impulses (not intentional), value judgements (not facts), childish (not adult), subjective (not objective), from the heart (not the head), irrational (not rational), chaotic (not orderly), to do with nature (not culture)—and these are all associated with women, the poor, and blacks. But there are always a few among these who reverse the signs, and use emotionality in a positive way, like the Black Panther Party, which used anger for emancipatory political projects.[137] If by contrast emotion was to be considered good, then it is full of life (instead of aseptic and bloodless), as well as individual and autonomous—so much so that feelings become the last refuge of an authentic, untouched self, an idea articulated in the common saying, 'you cannot imagine how I feel'.[138]

[132] Less powerful Ifaluk who wished to sanction an infringement by one of their fellow islanders always talked of the chief's *song*, and not of the infringement of a taboo; Lutz, *Unnatural Emotions*, 169, 158. On *song* generally see Lutz, *Unnatural Emotions*, ch. 6.
[133] Lutz, *Unnatural Emotions*, 120, 134.   [134] Lutz, *Unnatural Emotions*, 136.
[135] Lutz, *Unnatural Emotions*, 215, 55.   [136] Lutz, *Unnatural Emotions*, 56.
[137] Lutz, *Unnatural Emotions*, 56–7, 62, 67, 73.
[138] Lutz, *Unnatural Emotions*, 61, 71–2.

Among the Ifaluk however, as described by Lutz, the metaconcepts were more holistic: *nunuwan* denoted mental feelings which were neither directly created by *tip* (will, desire), nor determined *tip*, but were the same thing as *tip*. *Nunuwan* were relational and intersubjective: they were talked about in the first person plural, rather than in the singular, and one emotion determined another—*song* from one person brought forth *metagu* (fear) in another. *Nunuwan* was brought about by social interaction as well as external events, the latter having a direct effect, and not involving deeper internalization. They were embedded in an understanding of the self that included three entities: people (*yaremat*), spirits (*yalus*), and the Catholic God (likewise *yalus*, or *got*). Ifaluks imagined that dead people became spirits and could cause sickness and nightmares.[139]

How did Lutz explain these cultural differences? As in all works of post-structuralism, there was little emphasis upon causality. All the same, holistic Ifaluk emotions were ascribed to an origin: a society based on face-to-face contact, and the absence of capitalism, with all its negative alienating aspects—this was what accounted for the healthy emotional world of the Ifaluk.[140] Naturally, one can argue about that, just as one can argue about the distillation of two monolithic cultural models of emotion, the middle-class European-American model on the one hand, and Ifaluk ethnopsychology on the other. The question that poses itself is: are these two cultures of emotion really without contact to one another? What about transfers and mutual influence, which are well illustrated by the introduction of the Catholic *got*? Furthermore, how timeless are these two emotional models?[141] Here we need historical scholarship to introduce some element of temporal and spatial difference.

6 SOCIAL CONSTRUCTIVISM ALONGSIDE ROSALDO, ABU-LUGHOD, AND LUTZ

During the 1980s Rosaldo, Abu-Lughod, and Lutz were not isolated researchers, but rather part of a broader social constructivist trend in anthropology. This work was centred not only on Oceania, but also South Asia—not least because in India there had been a complex aesthetic theory organizing emotional expression even

---

[139] Lutz, *Unnatural Emotions*, 92–4, 88–9, 82, 102–3, 87–8.

[140] Lutz, *Unnatural Emotions*, 128, 149, 152, 219.

[141] Many historians will stumble when they encounter the photographs in these ethnographies; they are very much of their time, with the anthropologists in old-fashioned jeans, 1970s shirts, and long hair standing alongside the 'aboriginals'. The photographs are also subject to remarkably little analysis, something which will strike a historian with even a passing interest in the visual. The captions that Lutz gives to a series of photographs with emotional facial expressions suddenly seem reductionist, as for example when a photograph of a smiling bare-breasted mother protectively holding her naked child is captioned: 'A mother smiles at the fright of her daughter, who has been told that the photographer has a hypodermic needle in her carrying basket'; Lutz, *Unnatural Emotions*, 50. For an important de-essentialization of older (and not recent) ethnographic photography see Christopher Pinney, *Photography and Anthropology* (London: Reaktion Books, 2011).

Rasa	Color	Deity
shringara (love in union and separation)	*shyama* (green)	Vishnu
hasya (humour)	*sita* (white)	Pramatha
karuna (pathos, sorrow)	*kapota* (dove-colored)	Yama
raudra (anger, wrath)	*rakta* (red)	Rudra (later Shiva)
vira (heroism)	*gaura* (wheat brown)	Mahendra
bhajanaka (fear/panic)	*krishna* (black)	Kala
bibhatsa (distaste/recoil/disgust)	*nila* (blue)	Mahakala
abdhuta (wonderment/surprise)	*pita* (yellow)	Brahma

Fig. 6 *Rasas* and Their Associations with Colours and Deities According to *Natyashastra*
Source: Susan L. Schwartz, *Rasa: Performing the Divine in India* (New York: Columbia University Press, 2004), 15.

before the time of Christ: *rasa*.[142] This related primarily to dance and theatre. The word literally means 'juice', hence also 'flavour', but is extremely difficult to define, Sanskrit dictionaries having over thirty entries for the term.[143] Each *rasa* is related in dance theatre with a particular facial expression and a hand gesture. But it is also associated with a colour, a divinity, and what Phillip Zarrilli calls 'states of being/ doing the actor embodies' (*bhava*).[144] The best known codification of *rasas* can be found in *Natyashastra*, which is thought to have been written between 200 BC and 400 AD.[145] In her study of *rasas* Susan Schwartz has summarized the subdivisions of the sixth book of *Natyashastra* in Fig. 6.

The connection of *rasa* to *bhava* is primarily described through metaphors of eating; *rasa* 'has the same relation to the *bhava* as wine has to the grapes, sugar and herbs which compose it and which dissolve and blend completely in an intoxicant of entirely different character'.[146] Or, *rasas* are when the audience 'tastes' the *bhavas*, the 'states of being/doing the actor embodies'.[147] Besides the basic *bhavas* (depending on how they are counted, there are eight or more) there are more than thirty intermediate conditions (*vyabhichari bhava*) that could during a short period accompany and influence the *bhavas*. If one looks at the photographs of the

---

[142] Not to be confused with *raasa* or *raas*, the dance song in honour of Krishnas und Shivas. See Susan L. Schwartz, *Rasa: Performing the Divine in India* (New York: Columbia University Press, 2004; repr. Delhi: Motilal Banarsidass, 2008), 20.

[143] Schwartz, *Rasa*, 8.

[144] Phillip B. Zarrilli, 'Pychophysical Acting in India', in Zarrilli, Jerri Daboo, and Rebecca Loukes (eds), *Acting: Psychophysical Phenomenon and Process* (Basingstoke: Palgrave Macmillan, 2013), 72. Also see Phillip B. Zarrilli, *Kathakali Dance-Drama: Where Gods and Demons Come to Play* (London: Routledge, 2000).

[145] Schwartz, *Rasa*, 4. There are many commentaries on *Natjashastra*; Schwartz, *Rasa*, 17.

[146] Balwant Gargi, *Theatre in India* (New York: Theatre Arts Books, 1962), 12; cited by Schwartz, *Rasa*, 15.

[147] Zarrilli, 'Pychophysical Acting in India', 72.

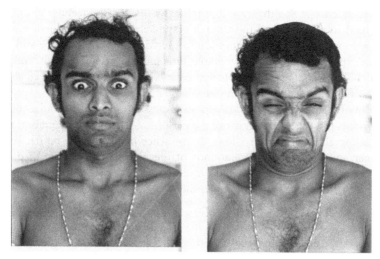

Fig. 7 Facial Expression for *raudra rasa* (Anger)
Source: Susan L. Schwartz, *Rasa: Performing the Divine in India* (New York: Columbia University Press, 2004), 64, photo: Phillip Zarrilli.

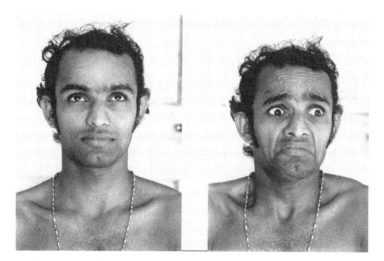

Fig. 8 Facial Expression for *bhayanaka rasa* (Fear/Panic)
Source: Susan L. Schwartz, *Rasa: Performing the Divine in India* (New York: Columbia University Press, 2004), 66, photo: Phillip Zarrilli.

theatrical representation of the facial expressions associated with the *rasas* (Figs. 7 and 8) it becomes apparent that we have here a quite different conception of emotion than the one we are familiar with in the West. One of the faces represents fear or panic (*bhayanaka*), the other anger (*raudra*). Few would probably guess that the man in Fig. 7 is making an angry face, and the man in Fig. 8 a panic-stricken face.

The prevalence of *rasa* theory and its influence on everyday feelings in India is of course hard to assess, but all the same, it is unlikely that these aesthetic emotions have developed without any connection to everyday life. What can be said is that the facial expressions in these photographs fundamentally differ from the supposedly culturally universal and transhistorical basic emotions that we can read about in Silvan S. Tomkins or Paul Ekman (see Chapter Three).[148]

In many Indian dance traditions—for example, in south Indian Kathakali dance theatre—it is presumed that in dance the performer and the representation merge, transcending all dualism; this allows the presence of divinity to be felt both by performer and public.[149] The emotions of the watcher are 'transformed into a purely aesthetic, transcendental, and universal one, a *rasa*'.[150] According to Lewis Rowell, an ethnomusicologist, *rasa* becomes

> a transcendent mode of emotional awareness by which all aspects of a performance are integrated, an awareness that rises above the circumstances which awakened it . . . and generalizes the individual emotional states of the spectators into a single emotional 'field'.[151]

Because of this, and drawing upon Rosaldo, Frédérique Apffel-Marglin treated *rasa* as embodied thought, rather than emotion.[152] To define *shringara rasa* as 'erotic emotion' would be false; instead, the audience 'taste' *shringara rasa* in an experience that is equally physical, spiritual, and emotional—what could also be called 'body-emotions-thoughts'.[153]

The aesthetic success of *rasa* is testified historically. Originating in classical Sanskrit and Hindu texts, it diffused through dance and theatre into the most diverse literary and aesthetic traditions, and all Indian religions, including Islam and Christianity. Some scholars even see its late echo in other domains, such as Bollywood films.[154]

As with so many social constructivist case studies in the anthropology of emotion, those relating to India and *rasas* once more disturb our settled sense of self. Some scholars go so far as to relate the Hindu Indian self not with the

---

[148] See Richard A. Shweder and Jonathan Haidt, 'The Cultural Psychology of the Emotions: Ancient and New', in Michael Lewis and Jeannette M. Haviland-Jones (eds), *Handbook of Emotions* (2nd edn, New York: Guilford Press, 2000), 397–414, here 401.

[149] Schwartz, *Rasa*, 97. She also emphasizes: 'performance thus has a special status, not only within but also beyond the boundaries of religious observance. It is through performative modes that the sacred becomes palpable in India'; Schwartz, *Rasa*, 6.

[150] Lynch, 'Social Construction of Emotion', 18.

[151] Lewis Rowell, *Music and Musical Thought in Early India* (Chicago: University of Chicago Press, 1992), 328.

[152] Frédérique Apffel Marglin, 'Refining the Body: Transformative Emotion in Ritual Dance', in Lynch (ed.), *Divine Passions*, 212–36, here 212. See also Frédérique Apffel Marglin, *Wives of the God-King: The Rituals of the Devadasis of Puri* (New Delhi: Oxford University Press, 1985).

[153] Apffel Marglin, 'Refining the Body', 212, 220.

[154] Matthew Jones, 'Bollywood, Rasa and Indian Cinema: Misconceptions, Meanings and Millionaires', review of Danny Boyle, dir., *Slumdog Millionaire*, in *Visual Anthropology*, 23/1 (2010), 33–43; also see Darius Cooper, *The Cinema of Satyajit Ray: Between Tradition and Modernity* (Cambridge: Cambridge University Press, 2000).

individual, but with 'dividual'.[155] Others concluded that *rasa* theory involved 'no emphasis on emotions being the lower part of the self or upon the search to know oneself through one's unique, individual feelings; rather, one's emotions are one's true self and "the" essence of true reality'.[156] This represents a final renunciation of what Charles Taylor has called the 'culture of authenticity' that arose in Western Europe during the eighteenth century, also involving an emphasis upon 'the strength and the genuineness of the feelings'.[157] Geertz has characterized this as a 'Western conception of the person as a bounded, unique, more or less integrated motivational and cognitive universe, a dynamic center of awareness, emotion, judgment, and action organized into a distinctive whole', creating an artificial separation between convention and authenticity, mask and face.[158] Finally, Indian examples suggest a different arrangement of gender relations. According to Owen M. Lynch, the 'Western equation of female gender with nature and emotion and male gender with culture and reason would probably not be found in India in the same way, if at all'.[159]

Ultimately, social constructivism even destabilizes the Western idea that authenticity is linked to particular media. The work of Niko Besnier, which lies on the border between linguistic and social anthropology, has shown that in non-Western societies letters can become the central medium of expressing emotion. In Western societies letters are by contrast just one among several possible forms of emotional communication, and it is mostly verbal or non-verbal communication that is the major medium of expression. Besnier found that the 310 members of the Nuku-laelae on the South Sea Tuvalu atoll, who had been literate for about a century, used letters to express their feelings:

> Thus, even when addressing topics that are not essentially affect-oriented, letter writers bring out the emotional aspects of what they describe. The overtness of this affect contrasts sharply with the covertness with which affect permeates everyday discourse in most face-to-face contexts, including damaging gossip.[160]

This overturns the Western association of oral communication with emotion, and written with rational communication. Besnier's findings contradicted not only everyday Western assumptions, but also the mainstream of sociolinguistics, where 'it is commonly assumed that spoken language is universally more "involved",

---

[155] McKim Marriott, 'The Open Hindu Person and Interpersonal Fluidity', Paper presented to the Annual Meeting of the Association of Asian Studies, Washington, DC, 1980; cited by John Leavitt, 'The Shapes of Modernity: On the Philosophical Roots of Anthropological Doctrines', *Culture* 11/1–2 (1991), 29–42, here 33. McKim Marriott's argument about the Hindu 'dividual' has given rise to a great deal of criticism, e.g.: Steve Barnett, Lina M. Fruzzetti, and Ákos Östör, 'On a Comparative Sociology of India: A Reply to Marriott', *Journal of Asian Studies*, 36/3 (1977), 599–601.
[156] Lynch, 'Social Construction of Emotion in India', 18.
[157] Charles Taylor, *Varieties of Religion Today: William James Revisited* (Cambridge, MA: Harvard University Press, 2002), 88, 99.
[158] Clifford Geertz, *Local Knowledge: Further Essays in Interpretive Anthropology* (New York: Basic Books, 1983), 59.
[159] Lynch, 'Social Construction of Emotion in India', 19.
[160] Niko Besnier, *Literacy, Emotion, and Authority: Reading and Writing on a Polynesian Atoll* (Cambridge: Cambridge University Press, 1995), 109.

"emotional", and better suited for the representation of emotions than written language'.[161] The prevailing view in sociolinguistics is that face-to-face interaction facilitates a higher level of affective communication. Besnier on the other hand emphasized that

> most of these claims have been supported with data from contemporary mainstream Western contexts, where writing is viewed as being less 'subjective', less 'emotional', and generally more 'reliable' than speaking. The literacy practices associated with Western, school-oriented, middle-class settings, particularly academia and other loci of cultural reproduction, are particularly prone to such characterizations.[162]

7 THE SOCIAL CONSTRUCTIVIST ANTHROPOLOGY OF EMOTIONS: SOME PRELIMINARY CONCLUSIONS

If one seeks to summarize the conditions favouring the emergence of the anthropology of emotion, the most obvious are to be found in academic and social developments that were interrelated. Roughly stated, it could be said that as far as the first goes, it was the diffusion during the 1970s of post-structuralism from literary studies to other disciplines that was decisive. Wider social factors included the rise of new social movements, such as the women's movement and gay rights, to name just a few. Together, these two forces undermined the assumption that gender and self had a natural basis, shifting the emphasis to the manner in which they were socially and historically constructed. The category of emotion followed in the wake of these changes.

Anthropology was therefore in the vanguard of social constructivist approaches to feelings, during the 1980s presenting a number of interesting studies on the nature of emotions. How far one can draw a parallel between travels in space and time, between anthropology and history, and what historical studies might take from anthropology, cannot be settled here. Nonetheless, the anthropological practice of self-reflection must be emphasized. Anthropologists have done wonders in illuminating what Max Weber called 'being bound to a particular location'. We have seen how Jean L. Briggs revealed her personal hopes for her fieldwork, and treated her own experiences as 'data' to be included as part of her studies, given the fact that the emotions of the Inuit emerged in dialogue with her. We have also seen with what kind of romantic ideas Michelle Rosaldo embarked upon her work; how embarrassing it was for Abu-Lughod to be introduced by her father; and how Catherine A. Lutz selected the Ifaluk because of her dream of equality between men and women in the American university.[163]

---

[161] Besnier, *Literacy, Emotion, and Authority*, 115.

[162] Besnier, *Literacy, Emotion, and Authority*, 115.

[163] We can also here mention Steven Feld, who in the 2nd edn of *Sound and Sentiment* described the reactions of the Kaluli when his book about them arrived. See the photograph with the caption: 'Kiliye and the author witness the arrival of *Sound and Sentiment*, July 1, 1982'; Feld, *Sound and Sentiment*, 243. Feld's statement of his reasons for selecting the Kaluli is informative: 'Indeed, it does

These are all examples of intense self-reflection. In the meantime, the emotional content of fieldwork has itself become a subject of study.[164] There is of course some contradiction between the postulates of social constructivism and self-reflection. For to direct post-structuralism towards what is 'one's own' leads straight into an aporia: if descriptions are constructions, then so are self-descriptions. Nevertheless, it would be of great benefit if historical study oriented itself more in accordance with the self-reflection of anthropology. Historians do not take the objects of their studies from thin air, nor are they in any respect 'dispassionate' in their work. Why should historians not record their experiences in a kind of fieldwork diary: regarding one's own encounter with documents; the first olfactory and tactile impression when opening files; accidental discoveries; the cigarette break outside the library entrance during which, when talking to a colleague, one unravelled the plan of a book; drinking tea with the archivist who had put one on the right track?[165]

Naturally there are problems in the convergence of anthropology and history. Many of these are well known: first of all, the difference between synchronic anthropology and diachronic history, but one would expect that a dedicated social constructivist anthropologist would at least be aware of the problem. Then there are the different sources: anthropology deals with living people, and is therefore able to observe their non-linguistic forms of expression, whereas history has perforce to rely mainly upon written evidence stemming from a small group of people existing in a former era, and has only very limited access to human expression. One exception here is oral history, which is addressed in Chapter Four.

There are, however, two central problems with social constructivism that call for discussion. Social constructivism was preceded by the emancipatory movements of the 1960s which, rather like the Enlightenment, established cultural universals and attributed an equal value to all cultures. Franz Boas's notion of the psychic unity of

---

not take long to figure out that Kaluli are quick to speak up and quicker to overlap what someone else is saying. You don't have to be like me, Jewish and from the urban American Northeast, to enjoy and engage in Kaluli interactions, but I think my background helps me easily interpret the polyphonies of this lively interpersonal and verbal style as collaborative engagement rather than pushy abrasiveness. To pursue the crude stereotype that underlies this comment, I'll recount a joke I heard at an anthropological convention. It is said that there are two kinds of ethnographies about Papua New Guinea. In one type the people are portrayed as rough, pragmatic, rational, pushy, overbearing, intense, and calculating. These are the books written by white Australian and British men and male American WASPs. In the other kind of ethnography Papua New Guineans are portrayed as sentimental, warm, bubbly, engaging, hospitable, emotional, and sensitive. These are the books written by women and Jewish men.' He continued: 'Put aside for the moment that even a brief scrutiny of the Papua New Guinea ethnographic literature would disprove the generalization presented by the joke. What is more important here is how perceptions of stylistic excess form the basis for ethnic, gender, and national stereotypes. Every ethnographer carries a cultural background that includes a set of behaviors and values surrounding interpersonal style'; Feld, *Literacy, Emotion, and Authority*, 250.

[164] James Davies and Dimitrina Spencer (eds), *Emotions in the Field: The Psychology and Anthropology of Fieldwork Experience* (Stanford, CA: Stanford University Press, 2010); George W. Stocking, Jr, *Glimpses into My Own Black Box: An Exercise in Self-Deconstruction* (Madison: University of Wisconsin Press, 2010).

[165] See Arlette Farge, *The Allure of the Archive*, trans. Thomas Scott-Railton (New Haven: Yale University Press, 2013) [Fr. orig., *Le goût de l'archive*, 1989]; Randolph Starn, 'Truths in the Archives', *Common Knowledge*, 8/2 (2002), 387–401.

mankind presupposes that this is invariant for all peoples of the world, independent of culture, colour of skin, gender, or passport—at first sight, an emancipatory idea. Social constructivists maintain, however, that such concepts demonstrate a lack of respect for other cultures, for these universals are European in origin, only subsequently transferred to the rest of the world. Universal conceptions such as these are, they argue, only constructs of one particular culture, just as the local conceptions of non-European cultures are. What has to be done, therefore, is to reconstruct the inner logic of each culture, recognizing the true, non-universal (non-Western imperialist) nature of its tradition. But, and here we identify the first problem: how is anthropological knowledge possible, if not within the framework of a Western scholarly tradition? Is it not true, as Valentin Mudimbe suggests, that it is 'impossible to imagine any anthropology without a Western epistemological link'?[166] Do we not constantly stumble upon what James Clifford calls 'the dilemma of culture', 'a state of being in culture while looking at culture'?[167] Besides that, the demand for a common epistemological denominator has further-reaching ethical and political consequences. It harbours the dangers of an indifferent *je ne sais quoi*: what is strange and alien is strange and alien, the Other is Other. The difference between this indifferent way of characterizing the Other and seeing the other as 'savage' is very small. There is the further danger that one might become blind to possible similarities. Why should one not, even starting out from social constructivist principles, finally come to the conclusion that universals do exist, after all?

Secondly, and related to this initial problem, we have to recognize that social constructivism is, strictly speaking, impossible. Ian Hacking made the point well in the title of his book, *The Social Construction of What?* Taken to its logical conclusion, social constructivism reduces the relationship between signifier and signified, the assumption of a multiplicity of languages, including the language of science, to the uncertainties of nominalism.[168] To be consistent, a social constructivist would have to maintain that the statement 'the social construction of X' is meaningless; the anthropology of emotion would not be able to employ any metaconcepts, including 'emotion', in the description of alien cultures. For 'emotion' is Western and has a particular meaning that cannot be aligned with

---

[166] V. Y. Mudimbe, *The Invention of Africa: Gnosis, Philosophy, and the Order of Knowledge* (Bloomington: Indiana University Press, 1988), 19.

[167] Clifford, *Predicament of Culture*, 9.

[168] Ian Hacking, *The Social Construction of What?* (Cambridge, MA: Harvard University Press, 2000). For an introduction to nominalism see Gonzalo Rodriguez-Pereyra, 'Nominalism in Metaphysics', *The Stanford Encyclopedia of Philosophy (Fall 2011 Edition)* <http://plato.stanford.edu/archives/fall2011/entries/nominalism-metaphysics> accessed 2 March 2014; Martin Jay, 'Magical Nominalism: Photography and the Re-enchantment of the World', *Culture, Theory & Critique*, 50/2–3 (2009), 165–83. Also see Carla Hesse, who writes that 'realism, as a philosophical stance, is a necessary foundation for any empirical claim to be able to reconstruct facts from evidence and to claim that language (and more broadly any system of signification—visual, textual or aural) has a denotative as well as a connotative function. That language is at some level referential (that it refers to something outside itself, albeit contingently) is critical, moreover, if one is to be able to make sustainable general claims—about culture, or about any other aspect of human existence'; Carla Hesse, 'The New Empiricism', *Cultural and Social History*, 1/2 (2004), 201–7, here 202.

conceptions found in local cultures. Hence Lutz should, in writing about the Ifaluk, talk exclusively about *nunuwan*, since to talk of Ifaluk 'emotions' betrays a decided ethnocentrism. Seen in this light, a radical social constructivism is an impossibility, since this would mean that any anthropology was impossible, surrendering us to unintelligible difference and cultural contingency.

Lutz's book *Unnatural Emotions* was published in 1988, in the midst of the culture wars between conservatives and leftists—and raised the issues just mentioned. For if everything is socially constructed, then so are the aesthetic and formal criteria according to which the quality of literature is judged. If formerly underprivileged groups—women, ethnic minorities, and gays—gained the upper hand in the literary and critical establishment, then they would be able to apply different canonical principles, demoting the work of Dead White European Males and elevating work assessed according to different criteria.[169] If everything is socially constructed, then so is the distinction between polite speech and dialect. Hence some American high schools, in adopting an Afrocentric approach, introduced lessons in Ebonics, or 'black English'. At the root of the culture wars was the question of whether, underlying all cultural relativism, there remained something shared in common, whether, as stated on the American coat of arms and on its currency, *e pluribus unum* was still valid. It was this contrast that lent structure to the study of emotion, and hence to this book: social constructivism versus universalism.[170]

Excursus I: Sociology

You might say that culture is to anthropology as social is to sociology. Whatever the merits of this formulation, it points to the way in which anthropology deals with movements across geographical space, while sociology deals with movements in social space, up and down the social ladder. There is of course the Anglo-American difference between social and cultural anthropology, but no discipline has developed a more sensitive set of instruments to calibrate the social than has sociology. It has as a consequence become an important source of ideas for the study of history. This excursus on the sociology of emotion will first of all introduce some older

---

[169] The debate over the literary canon was initiated by Alan Bloom's *The Closing of the American Mind* (New York: Simon and Schuster, 1987), which blamed the loss of a literary canon on the backwash of '1968' in the American university, and bemoaned the pluralization of American culture. See also Gregory S. Jay, *American Literature & the Culture Wars* (Ithaca, NY: Cornell University Press, 1997).

[170] On the culture wars, see e.g. James Davison Hunter, *Culture Wars: The Struggle to Define America* (New York: Basic Books, 1992); Clifford Geertz, 'Culture War', *New York Review of Books*, 42/19 (30 November 1995), 4–6; Richard Jensen, 'The Culture Wars, 1965–1995: A Historian's Map', *Journal of Social History*, 29/1 supplement (1995), 17–37. On Afrocentrism, see the founding text by Molefi Kete Asante, *Afrocentricity* (Trenton: Africa World Press, 1988), but also the debate over Martin Bernal, *Black Athena: The Afroasiatic Roots of Classical Civilization*, i. *The Fabrication of Ancient Greece, 1785–1985* (New Brunswick, NJ: Rutgers University Press, 1987), e.g. Mary R. Lefkowitz, *Not Out of Africa: How Afrocentrism Became an Excuse to Teach Myth as History* (New York: Basic Books, 1997); Jonathan Zimmerman, *Whose America? Culture Wars in the Public Schools* (Cambridge, MA: Harvard University Press, 2002).

sociological ideas, and then turn to the sociological studies of Arlie Hochschild and Eva Illouz.

If we go through the writings of classical sociologists looking for references to emotion, then we find them in Marx, Durkheim, Weber, and Simmel, as well as in Vilfredo Federico Pareto (1848–1923), George Herbert Mead (1863–1931), Pitirim Sorokin (1889–1968), and Talcott Parsons (1902–79). Simmel's studies on the social bonds of loyalty, as well as his typology of the ways in which people dealt with money—the miserly, the wasteful, the ascetic, the cynical, the blasé—all had an emotional component.[171] According to Max Weber, the Protestants that got capitalism going were driven by a fear of damnation.[172] Pitirim Sorokin thought that society swung between poles, from a culture open to emotion to a culture closed to emotion, from sensate to ideational.[173] And even when there is some dispute over the degree to which emotions were central to his thinking, Mead was in constant dialogue with some key figures in experimental psychological work on emotions, William James and Wilhelm Wundt.[174]

Even in the early post-war years, Talcott Parsons's first pattern variable during his structural-functionalist phase was the opposition affectivity/affective neutrality. Parsons believed that an individual had to choose between these alternatives if she wished to define a situation. The individual could in this way satisfy immediate needs (affectivity), or postpone such satisfaction in order to meet a long-term need (affective neutrality).[175] Nonetheless, as Helena Flam has noted, during the post-war years emotions enjoyed 'an extremely marginal and impoverished existence in the American social sciences, and in those European social sciences that came under their sway'. She supposed that, under the twin pressures of war and Fascism, there was a desire to believe 'that man was basically rational and normative, or that formal organisations were capable of compelling the individual to behave in a rational way'.[176] It was only during the 1970s that there was a detectable increase in the sociology of emotion, with the loss of interest in grand theory (and the emergence of doubt that such theories might be formulated), and a turn to microsociology. There is one name clearly identified with this shift: Arlie Hochschild.

---

[171] Flam, *Soziologie der Emotionen*, 16–43, 232–6.

[172] Flam, *Soziologie der Emotionen*, 44–51.

[173] Flam, *Soziologie der Emotionen*, 98–101.

[174] David Franks suggested 'that Mead's major thrust is once again not an investigation of emotions per se' and 'the task of developing a systematic theory of emotion remains for his followers'; David D. Franks, 'Introduction to the Special Issue: On the Sociology of Emotions', *Symbolic Interaction*, 8/2 (1985), 161–70, here 163, 164. Nevertheless, he considers that emotions were more central to Mead than does Arlie Hochschild: 'In the same way, George Herbert Mead did not talk about emotion, but he further cleared a path for doing so from an interactional perspective'; Arlie Russell Hochschild, *The Managed Heart: Commercialization of Human Feeling* (Berkeley and Los Angeles: University of California Press, 1983), 212. See more recently Jonathan H. Turner, 'The Sociology of Emotions: Basic Theoretical Arguments', *Emotion Review* 1/4 (2009), 340–54, here 340.

[175] Flam, *Soziologie der Emotionen*, 107–10.

[176] Flam, *Soziologie der Emotionen*, 114, 115.

'On PSA Our Smiles are Not Just Painted On': Arlie Hochschild

There was an American radio advertisement in the early 1980s which ran:

> On PSA our smiles are not just painted on.
> So smile your way
> From L.A.
> To San Francisco.[177]

In 1980 at a Delta Airlines Training Centre for Stewardesses the trainer, 'a crew cut pilot in his early fifties', demanded in a Southern drawl: 'Now girls, I want you to go out there and really *smile*. Your smile is your biggest *asset*. I want you to go out there and use it. Smile. *Really* smile. Really *lay it on*.'[178]

In the early 1980s Hochschild labelled this competence of not only being able to display emotion at work, but to 'really' feel it, 'emotional labour'. Bringing one's 'true' feelings into line with those which are demanded might or might not work in practice. If it does not, then there is '*emotive dissonance*, analogous to the principle of cognitive dissonance'.[179] Many techniques were employed in the world of work during the 1980s to avoid this problem, and to render emotional labour successful. Stewardesses were encouraged to treat the flight cabin not as their workplace, but instead as their home. 'Trainees were asked to think of a passenger *as if* he were a "personal guest in your living room".'[180] One stewardess described this as follows:

> You think how the new person resembles someone you know. *You see your sister's eyes in someone sitting at that seat.* That makes you want to put out for them. I like to think of the cabin as the living room of my own home. When someone drops in [at home], you may not know them, but you get something for them. You put that on a grand scale—thirty-six passengers per flight attendant—*but it's the same feeling.*[181]

This technique is comparable to American method acting, an approach that as a 'psychotechnique', or an as-if method, goes back to the work of the Russian director Constantin Stanislavsky (1863–1938). He told actors to develop their emotional memory, so that emotional events from their own life could be recalled at will. Stanislavsky once witnessed how a beggar was run over by a bus and killed. But in his memory he had stored another, stronger image.

> It was long ago—I came upon an Italian, leaning over a dead monkey on the sidewalk. He was weeping and trying to push a bit of orange rind into the animal's mouth. It would seem that this scene had affected my feelings more than the death of the beggar. It was buried more deeply into my memory. I think that if I had to stage the street accident I would search for emotional material for my part in my memory of the scene of the Italian with the dead monkey rather than in the tragedy itself.[182]

---

[177] PSA (Pacific Southwest Airlines) Hochschild, *Managed Heart*, 89. See also Arlie Russell Hochschild, 'Emotion Work, Feeling Rules, and Social Structure', *American Journal of Sociology*, 85/3 (1979), 551–75.

[178] Hochschild, *Managed Heart*, 4, emphasis in original.

[179] Hochschild, *Managed Heart*, 90, emphasis in original.

[180] Hochschild, *Managed Heart*, 105, emphasis in original.

[181] Hochschild, *Managed Heart*, 105, emphasis in original.

[182] Hochschild, *Managed Heart*, 42.

Like Stanislavsky's own pupils, flight attendants should also store their memories. Experienced stewardesses reported that they were taught the following techniques on training courses: 'If I pretend I'm feeling really up, sometimes I actually get into it. The passenger responds to me as though I were friendly, and then more of me responds back.' It can also be useful in times of stress to breathe deeply and relax your neck and shoulder muscles, or talk yourself out if it: 'Watch it. Don't let him [the anger] get to you'—and then 'talk to my partner and she'll say the same thing to me. After a while, the anger goes away.'[183]

Emotional labour or 'emotion management' have on the other hand only a small purchase when difficult passengers and their own anger are involved. In such cases, stewardesses working in the 1980s learned to empathize with the troublesome passenger and explain his behaviour. In such cases a stewardess sought to remember that

> if he's [the passenger] drinking too much, he's probably scared of flying. I think to myself, 'he's like a little child.' Really, that's what he is. And when I see him that way, I don't get mad that he's yelling at me. He's like a child yelling at me then.[184]

If that does not work, then one should imagine ways of getting away from the source of the trouble. A trainer advised: 'You can say to yourself, it's half an hour to go, now it's twenty-nine minutes, now it's twenty-eight.' If even this does not work, one should try to distract oneself, or indulge in aggressive fantasies. These can both work: one flight attendant reported that 'I chew on ice, just crunch my anger away.' Another admitted that: 'I think about doing something mean, like pouring Ex-Lax into his coffee.'[185] But despite all this, all control can be lost, leading to retaliation like the following:

> There was one time when I finally decided that somebody had it coming. It was a woman who complained about absolutely everything. I told her in my prettiest voice, 'We're doing our best for you. I'm sorry you aren't happy with the flight time. I'm sorry, you aren't happy with our service.' She went on and on about how terrible the food was, how bad the flight attendants were, how bad her seat was. Then she began yelling at me and my co-worker friend, who happened to be black. 'You nigger bitch!' she said. Well, that did it. I told my friend not to waste her pain. This lady asked for one more Bloody Mary. I fixed the drink, put it on a tray, and when I got to her seat, my toe somehow found a piece of carpet and I tripped—and that Bloody Mary hit that white pants suit![186]

Revenge of this kind might represent a failure in emotional labour, but it can also be seen as successful resistance, for emotional labour is work after all, and according to Hochschild this leads to alienation:

> Beneath the difference between physical and emotional labor there lies a similarity in the possible cost of doing the work: the worker can become estranged or alienated from an aspect of self—either the body or the margins of the soul—that is *used* to do the work.[187]

[183] Hochschild, *Managed Heart*, 55.   [184] Hochschild, *Managed Heart*, 55.
[185] Hochschild, *Managed Heart*, 113–14.   [186] Hochschild, *Managed Heart*, 114.
[187] Hochschild, *Managed Heart*, 7, emphasis in original.

And formulated even more drastically: 'Outside of Stanislavski's parlor, out there in the American marketplace, the actor may wake up to find himself actually operated upon.'[188]

It would be fitting here to talk of an actress, rather than an actor, since emotional labour is highly gender-specific. The jobs that call for emotional labour are in the female domain: secretaries, social workers, primary school teachers, nurses, and of course flight attendants. According to Hochschild, there are several reasons for these being 'women's jobs'. First of all, in the early gender socialization of little girls there is an emphasis upon feelings, rather than action. Secondly, 'the different childhood training of the heart that is given to girls and to boys', tends to encourage aggression in boys and the suppression of aggression in girls. Third, the numerical superiority of men in well-paid employment pushes women into those areas of work requiring a greater commitment of feeling.[189] Men only dominate where negative emotional labour is needed, for example in collection agencies, which Hochschild considers to be the polar opposite of airlines.

Even the training these two areas received in the 1980s could not be more different: while much time was devoted in training air hostesses in the finer points of emotional labour, recruits to collection agencies were given an hour's introductory talk and then set to work. The assumption was therefore that these recruits already came with the requisite degree of aggression. One employee said: 'I'd rather do eight hours of collecting than four hours of telephone sales. In telephone sales you've got to be nice no matter what, and lots of times I don't feel like being nice. To act enthusiastic is hard work for me.'[190] At work stewardesses wore name badges, while debt collectors remained anonymous. One collections agency that Hochschild visited was 'guarded by two Great Danes', and 'Offstage, and visible only to the collectors, was a sign in the window, a prompting card that read: "Catch your customer off guard. Control the conversation."'[191] One employee, who had not worked for very long as a debt collector, told her: 'My boss comes into my office and says, "Can't you get madder than *that*?" "Create alarm!"—that's what my boss says.'[192] Surprise tactics, attacks on the personal honour of the debtor, threats, and insults are still today all part of the repertoire of the debt collector. The law only prevents explicit swearing. Since the publication of *The Managed Heart* in 1983, emotional labour has become even more important, and the number of positions and workers has increased. In 2009 Hochschild described this development as follows:

> Over the last 40 years, the number of service sector jobs has rapidly grown all over the world. By my estimate, some six out of ten of those service jobs in the United States call for substantial amounts of emotional labor. This work falls unequally on men and women; only a quarter of men, but half of women work in jobs heavy in emotional

---

[188] Hochschild, *Managed Heart*, 55.   [189] Hochschild, *Managed Heart*, 163.
[190] Hochschild, *Managed Heart*, 139.   [191] Hochschild, *Managed Heart*, 140.
[192] Hochschild, *Managed Heart*, 146, emphasis in original.

labor—as elementary school teachers, nurses, social workers, child and elder care workers.[193]

Moreover, emotional labour is becoming ever more globalized:

> Emotional labor is going more and more global. Increasingly, we've seen what I call a South-to-North 'heart transplant'. A growing number of care workers leave the young and elderly of their families and communities in the poor South to take up paid jobs 'giving their hearts to' the young and elderly in families and communities in the affluent North.[194]

What is the conceptual basis for Hochschild's studies on emotional labour? Alienation and emotional dissonance—these rest upon a distinction between an authentic and an inauthentic emotional self. The most important inspiration was in the work of Erving Goffman, who, as has been already mentioned, assumed that the social world was like a stage, upon which people wore 'social masks'.[195] For Hochschild, an adopted smile was a social mask of this kind: she called it 'surface acting'. But she went further than Goffman in her emphasis that emotional labour involved the engagement of authentic feelings, of 'deep acting'. Goffman once wrote to her that when uniforms were handed out, so was skin. She developed this idea:

> We enact a new role (put on new uniform) let's say, and so speak with more authority, we change our emotive appearance. That's what Goffman meant by 'skin'. But, we ourselves engage our deep feelings in new ways—that's what I mean by 'two inches of flesh'. The 'social' goes far deeper than our current images of self lead us to suppose.[196]

Hochschild also maintained that it was the demand for authentic feelings that led to alienation, especially in a society like that of the United States in which such value was placed upon a 'true', 'authentic', and 'autonomous' self.

But can it be right to describe the culture of authenticity in American society in the singular?[197] What role do migrants—who come from cultures with different notions of authenticity, subcultures, and individual differences—play? Even if it is right to talk of an American culture of authenticity, this does not imply that it makes analytical sense to talk in terms of a true and a false self as an a priori given. A more exact analysis of particular historical situations, and of the variable role played within them by authenticity as a value, will also provide historically specific indicators regarding the degree of alienation brought about by emotional labour. This rather robs Hochschild's indignation of its point—indeed, robs *The Managed Heart* of its moral superiority. For a sociological study of traditional factory work

---

[193] Arlie Russell Hochschild, 'Introduction: An Emotions Lens on the World', in Debra Hopkins, Jochen Kleres, Helena Flam, and Helmut Kuzmics (eds), *Theorizing Emotions: Sociological Explorations and Applications* (Frankfurt am Main: Campus, 2009), 29–37, here 32.

[194] Hochschild, *Managed Heart*, 32.

[195] On Goffman see Hochschild, *Managed Heart*, 214–18.

[196] Hochschild, 'Introduction', 30–1.

[197] Further criticisms of Hochschild are summarized by Flam, *Soziologie der Emotionen*, 202–4.

would certainly reveal a similar alienation effect: if there were a comparable study of a Vietnamese shoe factory in which 16-year-old girls worked twelve-hour shifts making trainers, then the emotional dimensions of a programme for training flight attendants might well appear in a different light.

Quite apart from these objections, the publication of *The Managed Heart* marked something: the emergence of an autonomous field of study in the sociology of emotion.[198] This can be registered institutionally in the creation of new sections in national sociological associations: in 1986, for example, the Section for the Sociology of Emotion was formed as a part of the American Sociological Association.[199] The research that has developed since then has been divided by Jonathan Turner into seven main areas.

The first is 'evolutionary biology'. This tendency within the sociology of emotion believes that emotions are sited in the older evolutionary part of the brain beneath the cortex, and consequently indicate that they pre-existed language as a means of communication between people. Turner summarized this perspective as follows:

> Only much later, perhaps only with *Homo sapiens* did an auditory (verbal) language emerge, but this language was piggy-backed onto the language of emotions. Yet once auditory language existed, the behavioral capacities for emotions, language, and enhanced cognition all fed off each other to generate the cultural systems that are critical to human social organization.[200]

The second area is, according to Turner, 'symbolic interactionism'. This tendency, which runs back to Mead, argues that interpersonal human communication involves the maintenance of an individual self—an identity—in which emotions also play a role.[201]

The third area includes under 'dramaturgy' all approaches that can be traced back to Goffman, who

---

[198] Subsequently the following have been published: Jürgen Gerhards, 'Soziologie der Emotionen: Ein Literaturbericht', *Kölner Zeitschrift für Soziologie und Sozialpsychologie*, 38/4 (1986), 760–71; Rom Harré (ed.), *The Social Construction of Emotions* (Oxford: Blackwell, 1986); Peggy A. Thoits, 'The Sociology of Emotions', *Annual Review of Sociology*, 15/1 (1989), 317–42; Rom Harré and W. Gerrod Parrott (eds), *The Emotions: Social, Cultural and Biological Dimensions* (London: Sage Publications, 1996); W. Gerrod Parrott and Rom Harré, 'Princess Diana and the Emotionology of Contemporary Britain', *International Journal of Group Tensions*, 30/1 (2001), 29–38; Ansgar Klein and Frank Nullmeier (eds), *Masse, Macht, Emotionen* (Opladen: Westdeutscher Verlag, 1999); J. M. Barbalet, *Emotion, Social Theory, and Social Structure: A Macrosociological Approach* (Cambridge: Cambridge University Press, 2001); Jack Barbalet (ed.), *Emotions and Sociology* (Oxford: Blackwell, 2002); Sara Ahmed, *The Cultural Politics of Emotions* (Edinburgh: Edinburgh University Press, 2004); Dirk Baecker, 'Einleitung: Wozu Gefühle?', *Soziale Systeme*, 10/1 (2004), 5–20; Rainer Schützeichel (ed.), *Emotionen und Sozialtheorie: Disziplinäre Ansätze* (Frankfurt am Main: Campus, 2006); Patricia Ticineto Clough (eds), *The Affective Turn: Theorizing the Social* (Durham, NC: Duke University Press, 2007); Jonathan H. Turner, *Human Emotions: A Sociological Theory* (London: Routledge, 2007); Monica Greco and Paul Stenner (eds), *Emotions: A Social Science Reader* (London: Routledge, 2008); Jan E. Stets, 'Future Directions in the Sociology of Emotions', *Emotion Review*, 2/3 (2010), 265–8.

[199] Flam, *Soziologie der Emotionen*, 9. [200] Turner, 'Sociology of Emotions', 344.

[201] Turner, 'Sociology of Emotions', 344–5.

argued that individuals' behaviors always involve the presentation of self to audiences of others. In making a dramatic presentation, individuals use a cultural script of ideologies, values, and norms, along with staging props (wardrobes, spacing, and objects), to present the self not only dramatically but also strategically.[202]

Peggy Thoits also belongs, besides, the 'Goffmanite' Hochschild, to the rubric of 'dramaturgy'; her findings very much resemble those of Barbara H. Rosenwein (and also, as we shall see in Chapter Four of this book, those of the historian of emotion William M. Reddy) in that she treats individuals as belonging to different but overlapping emotional communities.[203]

Turner's fourth area is 'interaction ritual'. This is associated with the influential sociologist Randall Collins. He suggests that individuals in face-to-face meetings make use of ritualized greetings, gestures, and forms of speech that combine to produce an emotionally loaded voice which is modulated in the course of an encounter. If more than two individuals are involved, group solidarity arises. If the rituals are infringed on by outsiders it is able to turn against them, such that the group becomes angry with them, which in turn reinforces group solidarity.[204]

The fifth approach, 'exchange theory', treats social interaction as a kind of economic exchange relationship, in which social actors invest (e.g. time), and either win or lose (e.g. positive emotions).[205] The sixth and seventh tendencies, 'power and status', or 'stratification', are perhaps of greatest interest to historians, since they seek a theoretical approach to the core category of sociology, social inequality.[206] One could assign to this final tendency a scholar who moves between sociology, cultural studies, and critical theory: Eva Illouz.[207]

'Florists Turn Feelings into Flowers': Eva Illouz

'Florists turn feelings into flowers'—so runs an advertising line cited by Eva Illouz.[208] The slogan might at first seem rather amusing, but this feeling quickly

---

[202] Turner, 'Sociology of Emotions', 346.

[203] Turner on Thoits: 'Peggy Thoits (1990) ['Emotional Deviance: Research Agendas', in T. D. Kemper (ed.), *Research Agendas in the Sociology of Emotions* (Albany, NY: State University of New York Press), 180–203] extended Hochschild's theory by emphasizing the sources of discrepancy between actual feelings and feeling rules, the various emotional management strategies employed by individuals, and the conditions under which emotion management fails. The discrepancy between actual feelings and feeling rules is likely to increase, Thoits argues, when individuals occupy multiple roles (thus setting up potential role conflicts among emotions), when the subculture of a person is marginal to the mainstream culture (thus creating conflict between the two sets of cultural expectations), when individuals are caught in role transitions that can produce emotional stress or ambiguity that clashes with feeling rules, and when feeling rules and rituals affirming them are rigid and do not allow for even minor deviations'; Turner, 'Sociology of Emotions', 346.

[204] Turner, 'Sociology of Emotions', 347.

[205] Turner, 'Sociology of Emotions', 351.

[206] Turner, 'Sociology of Emotions', 347–51.

[207] The fact that Illouz moves between disciplines probably explains why she does not appear in Flam's otherwise comprehensive *Soziologie der Emotionen*.

[208] Eva Illouz, *Consuming the Romantic Utopia: Love and the Cultural Contradictions of Capitalism* (Berkeley and Los Angeles: University of California Press, 1997), 112. See also Eva Illouz, *Gefühle in Zeiten des Kapitalismus: Adorno-Vorlesungen 2004* (Frankfurt am Main: Suhrkamp, 2006); Eva Illouz,

dissipates as Illouz gets stuck into the way that people today meet each other and conduct their relationships. Illouz seeks to take apart the commercialization of love, together with its idealization as the most 'private', 'intimate' of all feelings, immune to commerce and market; and she questions the capacity of a supposedly 'classless' market to reproduce and reinforce existing social inequalities through the commercialization of feelings.

According to Illouz, the image that we have of romantic love has remained constant for more than a century: 'irrational rather than rational, gratuitous rather than profit-oriented, organic rather than utilitarian, private rather than public. In short, romantic love seems to evade the conventional categories within which capitalism has been conceived.'[209] Likewise, as Karl Marx prophesied, 'capitalism has implacably invaded the most private corners of our interpersonal and emotional lives', with the result, according to Illouz, that today love is closely bound up with the market mechanism and advertising.[210] This paradox—the 'collective utopia' of non-capitalistic romantic love combined with an almost complete commercialization of romantic love—renders this an 'arena within which the social divisions and the cultural contradictions of capitalism are played out'.[211]

Illouz's book *Consuming the Romantic Utopia* begins with a historical sketch of romantic love from the early 1900s to the Second World War, continuing then in the 1980s with a study of postmodern love, based on interviews and an analysis of magazines, advertising, and personal advice. If one examines the trends in advertising during the first period of the study, it is possible to detect a break at the end of the 1920s: adverts aimed at the middle classes were before that point distinct from those aimed at the working classes. The former draw clear spatial and gender boundaries—women in the kitchen, men 'at work', hardly ever presenting any physical or romantic proximity between genders. By contrast, advertising aimed at the working classes blurs these boundaries, and, for example, shows male and female workers embracing. From the 1930s the more hedonistic working-class morality becomes prevalent and is elevated into a generally valid ideal. Access to this ideal is now open to all, through consumption. Love, if you like, has now become something that can be bought—or in Illouz's words:

> During the first quarter of the twentieth century, the theme of romance became increasingly associated with consumption. At the same time, although at a slower pace, the romance–consumption link became an integral part of the middle-class lifestyle. During the same period, ads for ego-expressive products promoting new models of romance not only disentangled that emotion from domesticity, the ideology of the separate spheres, and religion, but were actually opposed to marriage. By

---

Saving the Modern Soul: Therapy, Emotions, and the Culture of Self-Help (Berkeley and Los Angeles: University of California Press, 2008).

[209] Illouz, *Consuming the Romantic Utopia*, 2.
[210] Illouz, *Consuming the Romantic Utopia*, 146.
[211] Illouz, *Consuming the Romantic Utopia*, 2.

contrasting the 'dullness of marriage' to the 'thrill of romance', these ads presented a negative image of the married state.[212]

This negative representation of marriage by advertising media was indicative of a general shift in perception. Towards the end of the interwar period it was increasingly work that was seen as the bond for life, which in turn prompted utopian thinking: in the collective imagination love became non-work, leisure, holiday, and ultimate love were the utopian constructs of the holidays that would never end. We still have this concept of love today: one of Illouz's interviewees told her, 'If you have had a long wonderful weekend trip somewhere, or you have gone some place romantic, Hawaii or something, and you come back and your luggage was lost, I find that very unromantic.' Illouz maintained that this respondent 'captured the essence of the opposition between the romantic and unromantic. Romantic is exotic (Hawaii), fun (the trip, the party), affluent (a plane ticket, dressy clothes), magic (the "spell"), and relaxed. The romantic stands above and outside the stream of everyday life conceived of as effortful, practical, routine, and unplayful.'[213]

Because of the shift in the image of marriage, many of Illouz's respondents considered short affairs to involve more intensive 'love' than long-lasting relationships.[214] It is plain to see that this phenomenon is culturally 'made' if one takes into account that breakfasting together on a daily basis and the intimacy it engenders can also be understood as 'love'. Moreover, a large part of advertising that makes us think of 'love' is today linked to holiday products, emphasizing the non-everyday nature of the product. We thus have on the one hand the advertisement for a holiday in the Caribbean, pictured with a lonely palm-fringed beach, or a sunset, while on the other hand,

> Romance—as well as the products that signify it and are signified by it—takes place in an idealized, timeless utopia of intimacy and consumption. The imbibing of alcohol condenses all the feelings of celebration; smoking cigarettes signifies relaxation and withdrawal into a private world; in diamonds love goes on forever.[215]

There is also a counter-discourse from the therapeutic era following the Second World War:

> In this view, making a marriage last, even keeping its passion alive, required 'hard work'. The new ideal thus attempted to combine attitudes and activities not otherwise

---

[212] Illouz, *Consuming the Romantic Utopia*, 37.

[213] Illouz, *Consuming the Romantic Utopia*, 119, 120.

[214] Illouz on her interviews: 'All the experiences of my respondents had a clear beginning and a tight dramatic structure. Events happen quickly and have a strong emotional effect on the protagonists. All stories have obstacles which prevent the protagonists from carrying on the love story into marriage or a long-lasting bond. Finally, they differ from the ongoing and fuzzier plots of everyday life in coming to a sharply marked end: almost all these memorable love stories have a strong narrative closure. Only three out of the fifty interviewees cited a relationship that was under way at the time of the interview as their most memorably romantic; all the others had been brought to a clear closure'; Illouz, *Consuming the Romantic Utopia*, 169.

[215] Illouz, *Consuming the Romantic Utopia*, 84–5.

easily reconciled. To be successful, a couple now had to combine spontaneity and calculation, the ability to negotiate with a taste for 'hot romance'. The hedonistic-therapeutic model that emerged was characterized by such phrases as 'having a good time together', 'sharing common interests', 'talking', 'getting to know each other', 'understanding the other person's needs', and 'compromising'.[216]

The contrast between calculation and spontaneity was only one of the many contradictions that capitalism produced. The purposively rational optimization of profits is also in tension with the ideal of disinterestedness: 'The paradox of the romantic bond is that although it can be motivated by self-interest, it is fully convincing only if at a certain point the individual proves his or her disinterestedness.'[217] The greatest contradiction is certainly that between the equalizing logic of the market and the remarkable capacity of love to be anything but 'blind', rather enabling one to attach oneself with dreamlike certainty and alarming precision to members of one's own social stratum. Once open inequality and the Victorian model of love had been done away with, a fresh paradox was generated: 'The postmodern romantic utopia contains the classless dream of leisure and authenticity at the same time that it affirms new class divisions and class identities.'[218] For, as Illouz asks, 'How do we come to love the personal qualities, rather than the market value, of our mates and yet make choices that are congruent with our social and economic positions?'[219] One explanation for this mechanism is offered by Pierre Bourdieu's conception of habitus: potential partners make use of established physical markers, habitual markers such as clothing and language, to signal the stratum to which they belong. This happens implicitly, or 'metaintentionally', below the threshold of consciousness, so that the ideal of a free choice of partners, decisional autonomy, and principles of originality and individuality might remain untainted.[220] However, Illouz never manages to completely resolve this contradiction; in fact, this is not possible, since the idea of 'contradiction' is here taken directly from Marx.

The problem of the medial structuration of love assumes a particular importance in postmodernity. The ideal of any originality and authenticity in signs of love is hard to fulfil in times that these signs are suffused by cliché. Illouz cites Umberto Eco on this:

---

[216] Illouz, *Consuming the Romantic Utopia*, 53.

[217] Illouz, *Consuming the Romantic Utopia*, 240.

[218] Illouz, *Consuming the Romantic Utopia*, 100.

[219] Illouz, *Consuming the Romantic Utopia*, 210–11.

[220] Illouz, *Consuming the Romantic Utopia*, 214, cites Bourdieu from his text 'Marriage Strategies as Strategies of Social Reproduction': 'a happy love, that is, a socially approved and success-bound love, [is] the same thing as *amor fati*, love of one's own social destiny, which brings together socially compatible partners by way of free choice that is unpredictable and arbitrary in appearance only.' (Bourdieu's text was published in Robert Forster and Orest Ranum (eds), *Family and Society: Selections from the Annales, Économies, Sociétés, Civilisations*, trans. Elborg Forster and Patricia M. Ranum (Baltimore: Johns Hopkins University Press, 1972), 117–44 [Fr. orig., 'Les Stratégies matrimoniales dans le système de reproduction', 1972], quotation 140.)

I think of the post-modern attitude as that of a man who loves a very cultivated woman and knows he cannot say to her, 'I love you madly', because he knows that she knows (and that she knows that he knows) that these words have already been written by Barbara Cartland. Still, there is a solution. He can say, 'As Barbara Cartland would put it, I love you madly.' At this point, having avoided false innocence, having said clearly that it is no longer possible to speak innocently, he will nevertheless have said what he wanted to say to the woman: that he loves her, but he loves her in an age of lost innocence.[221]

A logical consequence of these contradictions and their warping is the popular diagnosis of 'commitment phobia'—perhaps it will soon be included in the *Diagnostic and Statistic Manual of Mental Disorders*. Illouz argues that this is not a 'genuine' illness, but rather a hypertrophied variant of the capitalist model of love. She argues that commitment phobia is the impossibility of making a decision when faced with an oversupply of options. In the market for love there always seems to be something better, even more transient:

One might even venture to suggest that the 'commitment phobia' . . . is a by-product of an identity largely based on the affirmation of autonomy through lifestyle choices, resulting in a reluctance to give up the freedom to choose and the prospect of 'finding a better mate'.[222]

What kind of sociology of emotion did Illouz practise, and what method did she employ? Theoretically she was rather eclectic, drawing both upon the classical writings of Weber, Marx, and Durkheim, and upon structuralism, the Frankfurt School, and post-structuralism. Illouz often introduces a theoretical quotation, applies it to her material, and concludes by modifying the position from which she had started. Her methods included qualitative interviews and experiments—subjects chose one of three 'romantic' postcards and gave reasons for their choice. She also compared a sample of magazine advertisements from the 1920s and 1930s with some from the period 1989–91, making no claim to any comprehensive analysis and drawing upon both magazines and various forms of counselling literature. If the book had any claim to the kinds of conventions encountered in historical studies, this chronological disorder, the leap from the interwar years to the 1980s, would be cause for concern. Besides that, *Consuming the Romantic Utopia* is not the first sociological study of romantic love.[223] Nonetheless, what is very striking in Illouz's book is the effect of disillusion. She guides her sociological scalpel with such a sure hand, unrelentingly revealing a socio-economic framework of love, so that at the conclusion of her book there is hardly anything left of romance.

---

[221] Umberto Eco, 'Reflections on "The Name of The Rose"', *Encounter* (April 1985), 7–18, here 17.

[222] Illouz, *Consuming the Romantic Utopia*, 175.

[223] See Luhmann, *Love as Passion*.

8 THE 1990s I: THE ANTHROPOLOGY OF EMOTIONS AFTER SOCIAL CONSTRUCTIVISM

Let us return to anthropology from this digression into sociology, and once more address the crucial question of the culture wars: *e pluribus unum* or *e pluribus plures*? While during the 1980s it was mostly conservatives like Gertrude Himmelfarb or William F. Buckley Jr who opted for *unum*, during the 1990s the pendulum swung the other way. The liberal David Hollinger and the former student activist Todd Gitlin are representative of those who joined forces with conservatives to argue that identity politics threatened to go too far, and appeared to have lost sight of the point of it all: social inequality.[224] Gays might be able to celebrate spectacular successes, and encounter in public less discrimination than ever before in American history, but what use was this when the infant mortality rates in some areas of New York or Detroit was above that in Bangladesh? What was the point of Ivy League universities such as Harvard and Cornell hiring the academic superstars of African American or Postcolonial Studies, like Henry Louis Gates Jr. and Homi Bhabha, if in the South Side of Chicago poverty was passed from generation to generation? Did America's ruling class simply play the diversity game on the campuses of the top universities in order to avoid the problem of the equal distribution of wealth? The analytic categories of the trinity of class, race, and gender were clearly not to be dealt with equally. Ultimately it was class that predominated, since socio-economic circumstances were primary. Hence, universalism rather than particularism. At the same time, post-structuralism slowly lost impetus, and as already noted in Chapter One, across all disciplines there developed a shift away from the humanities and the social sciences to life sciences such as neurobiology, biochemistry, and study of the brain.

It was in this context that Margot Lyon published a paper in 1995 with the programmatic title: 'Missing Emotion: The Limitations of Cultural Constructionism in the Study of Emotion'.[225] For Lyon, emotion was central to a more general settling of accounts with social constructivist anthropology. She suggested that 'The cultural constructionist approach to emotion has real limitations. I say this because emotion is more than a domain of cultural conception, more than mere construction.'[226] Following a thorough critique of Geertz's conception of the symbol, she came back to the question of what emotion really was asking: 'So "where" is emotion?'[227] She was dissatisfied with its location both in a public symbolic space and within an internal, psychological space. She felt that the key category for a convincing conception of emotion was that of the body. However, the physical aspects of emotion had hitherto been insufficiently taken into account, both in terms of the body itself and in terms of their cultural 'construction'. In a

[224] David A. Hollinger, *Postethnic America: Beyond Multiculturalism* (New York: Basic Books, 1995); Todd Gitlin, *The Twilight of Common Dreams: Why America is Wracked by Culture Wars* (New York: Metropolitan Books, 1995).
[225] Margot L. Lyon, 'Missing Emotion: The Limitations of Cultural Constructionism in the Study of Emotion', *Cultural Anthropology*, 10/2 (1995), 244–63.
[226] Lyon, 'Missing Emotion', 247.   [227] Lyon, 'Missing Emotion', 251.

section on the 'Re-embodiment' of anthropology she therefore outlined the role
that a new 'embodied' anthropology could play:

> The study of emotion can provide an expanded understanding of the place of the body
> in society through a consideration of the agency of the body. Emotion has a central role
> in bodily agency, for by its very nature it links the somatic and the communicative
> aspects of being and thus encompasses bodily as well as social and cultural domains.[228]

From this she concluded:

> An expanded understanding of emotion and its social and biological ontology is
> required to move beyond the limitations of cultural constructionism. We must seek
> to take account of the formal social relations, such as power and status, which function
> in a structural manner irrespective of cultural context, in regrounding our study of
> emotion in society. And, we must overcome our fear of biology and, thus, seek to re-
> embody anthropology.[229]

What this would actually look like Lyon did not say. Her paper remained programmatic, and did not even make any reference to the life sciences. And as far as
the conception of body was concerned, it was as though social constructivism had
never happened: the body was untouched by language or culture, and so became
elevated into a new essence, or nature.

Excursus II: The Linguistics of Emotion

Here we can make another digression, this time into linguistics. During the 1990s
an autonomous field of research developed which relied on social constructivist
anthropology of emotion and at the same time went beyond it. It also engaged in
direct dialogue with psychologists using universal models.

Anna Wierzbicka and a Culturally-Universal
Natural Semantic Metalanguage (NSM)

Anna Wierzbicka disputed the argument of psychologists like Paul Ekman that
emotional words had no necessary relation to emotions, and that the content of
a basic emotion was best represented by images of facial expression (see Chapter
Three). Even if the same argument was dressed up in neuroscience, and sought a
universal content not in the face, but through brain-imaging techniques, Wierzbicka disagreed. She considered Steven Pinker, an evolutionary psychologist using
neuroscientific methods, to be 'naive and ethnocentric' when he suggested 'that
mental life goes on independently of particular languages', or that English concepts
'will be thinkable even if they are nameless'. Wierzbicka cited evidence from
linguistics, anthropology, and psychology (e.g. the Ekman critic James Russell)
which demonstrated that emotional words do indeed have something to do with
emotion. Moreover, she drew attention to the inconsistency that theorists of basic

---

[228] Lyon, 'Missing Emotion', 256.   [229] Lyon, 'Missing Emotion', 258–9.

emotions caption images of facial expressions not with neutral descriptions such as dilated pupils and open mouth, but with fear.[230] Nonetheless, in contrast to the social constructivist anthropology of emotion, Wierzbicka adhered to the idea of universal emotions. She believed that a culturally universal metalanguage existed, identified from lengthy research in many languages, and which she called Natural Semantic Metalanguage (NSM). What it looks like is shown in Fig. 9.

According to Wierzbicka, these are the building blocks used by every existing human language. Her intention is nothing less than to confirm, via a metalanguage, earlier philosophical conceptions of 'innate ideas' (Descartes), of an 'alphabet of human thought' (Leibniz), a 'midpoint around which all languages revolve' (Wilhelm von Humboldt), and a 'psychic unity of mankind' (Franz Boas).[231] She believes that this canon of conceptual primitives and lexical universals is associated with universal grammatical structures.[232] This universal language and grammar enables the expression of emotions that are universally valid. She maintains that 'The NSM approach seeks above all to distinguish the essential from the optional, to capture the invariant, and to break complex concepts into maximally simple ones, relying exclusively on independently established conceptual primes and lexico-grammatical universals.'[233] What would the cultural universality of emotion look like when brought into line with NSM? Wierzbicka proposed the following hypothetical canon:

1. All languages have a word for FEEL.

2. In all languages, some feelings can be described as 'good' and some as 'bad' (while some may be viewed as neither 'good' nor 'bad').

3. All languages have words comparable, though not necessarily identical in meaning, with cry and smile; that is words referring to bodily expression of good and bad feelings.

4. In all cultures people appear to link some facial gestures with either good or bad feelings, and in particular, they link the raised corners of the mouth with good feelings whereas turned down corners of the mouth or a wrinkled nose appear to be linked with bad feelings.

5. All languages have 'emotive' interjections (i.e. interjections expressing cognitively based feelings).

6. All languages have some 'emotion terms' (i.e. terms designating some cognitively based feelings).

7. All languages have words linking feelings with (i) the thought that 'something bad can happen to me', (ii) the thought that 'I want to do something', and (iii) the thought that 'people can think something bad about me', that is words overlapping (though not identical) in meaning with the English words afraid, angry, and ashamed.

---

[230] Wierzbicka, *Emotions across Languages and Cultures*, 26–8, 47–8.
[231] Wierzbicka, *Emotions across Languages and Cultures*, 36.
[232] Wierzbicka, *Emotions across Languages and Cultures*, 36.
[233] Wierzbicka, *Emotions across Languages and Cultures*, 40.

Substantives   I, YOU, SOMEONE (PERSON), SOMETHING (THING), PEOPLE, BODY

Determiners   THIS, THE SAME, OTHER

Quantifiers   ONE, TWO, SOME, MANY/MUCH, ALL

Attributes   GOOD, BAD, BIG, SMALL

Mental predicates   THINK, KNOW, WANT, FEEL, SEE, HEAR

Speech   SAY, WORD, TRUE

Actions, events, movements   DO, HAPPEN, MOVE

Existence and possession   THERE IS, HAVE

Life and death   LIVE, DIE

Logical concepts   NOT, MAYBE, CAN, BECAUSE, IF

Time   WHEN (TIME), NOW, AFTER, BEFORE, A LONG TIME, A SHORT TIME, FOR SOME TIME

Space   WHERE (PLACE), HERE, ABOVE, BELOW, FAR, NEAR, SIDE, INSIDE

Intensifier, augmentor   VERY, MORE

Taxonomy, partonomy   KIND OF, PART OF

Similarity   LIKE

Spanish Version

Substantives   YO, TÚ, ALGUÉN, ALGO, GENTE, CUERPO

Determiners   ESTE, EL MISMO, OTRO

Quantifiers   UNO, DOS, ALGUNOS, MUCHOS, TODOS

Attributes   BUENO, MALO, GRANDE, PEQUENO

Mental predicates   PENSAR, SABER/CONOCER, QUERER, SENTIR, VER, OÍR

Speech   DECIR, PALABRA, VERDAD

Actions, events, movements   HACER, SUCEDER, MOVERSE

Existence and possession   HAY (EXISTIR), TENER

Life and death   VIVIR, MORIR

Logical concepts   NO, QUIZÁS, PODER, PORQUE, SÍ

Time   CUANDO, AHORA, ANTES, DESPUÉS, MUCHO TIEMPO, POCO TIEMPO, POR UN TIEMPO

Space   DÓNDE, ACQUÍ, SOBRE, DEBAJO, LEJOS, CERCA, LADO, DENTRO

Intensifiers, augmentor   MUY, MÁS

Taxonomy, partonomy   GÉNERO, PARTE

Similarity   COMO

Fig. 9 Conceptual Primitives and Lexical Universals

Source: Anna Wierzbicka, *Emotions across Languages and Cultures: Diversity and Universals* (Cambridge: Cambridge University Press, 1999), 36–8.

8. In all languages, people can describe cognitively based feelings via observable bodily 'symptoms' (that is, via some bodily events regarded as characteristic of these feelings).

9. In all languages, cognitively based feelings can be described with reference to bodily sensations.

10. In all languages, cognitively based feelings can be described via figurative 'bodily images'.

11. In all languages, there are alternative grammatical constructions for describing (and interpreting) cognitively based feelings.[234]

She summarizes this as follows:

> Clearly, the ways of thinking and talking about feelings in different cultures and societies (and also different epochs) exhibit considerable diversity; but neither can there be any doubt about the existence of commonalities and indeed universals. The problem is how to sort out the cultural-specific from the universal; how to comprehend the former through the latter; and, also, how to develop some understanding of the universal by sifting through a wide range of languages and cultures rather than by absolutizing modes of understanding derived exclusively from one's own language. For all this, I have claimed, we need a well-founded *tertium comparationis*; and such a *tertium comparationis* is provided by the mini-language of universal human concepts, derived from empirical cross-linguistic investigations.[235]

A number of points can be made here. It could be that the expression of emotions in language and mimicry can be reduced to universals, at least to some extent. None-theless, the discipline of history works according to different rules, and with a different epistemology. It is ultimately uninterested in such universals, since historians place an emphasis upon cultural variation. Truths of the kind that Wierzbicka advances are for historians 'trivially true', as Daniel Gross has put it so well.[236] But the conceptual history of the future will make use of linguistics, above all lexical linguistics, and for the time being Wierzbicka's theories are the most well grounded.

Zoltán Kövecses and Metaphors

Zoltán Kövecses, a specialist on metaphor, went beyond the lexica of words for emotion. For him, the content of 'anger' was not exhausted by the word 'anger'. In an article much cited in connection with the new history of emotions and written at the end of the 1980s with George P. Lakoff, he showed that the term 'anger' includes a greater number of metaphors within which the word itself does not occur—for example, 'let off steam', 'blow up', 'making one's blood boil', 'foam at the mouth'. In abstract terms, these images can be captured by metaphoric formulae such as 'anger is heat' (e.g. 'hothead' for a person who is easily aroused

[234] Wierzbicka, *Emotions across Languages and Cultures*, 275–6.
[235] Wierzbicka, *Emotions across Languages and Cultures*, 306–7.
[236] Daniel M. Gross, *The Secret History of Emotion: From Aristotle's Rhetoric to Modern Brain Science* (Chicago: University of Chicago Press, 2006), 34.

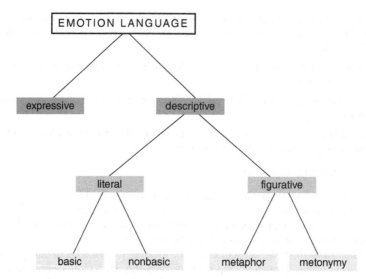

Fig. 10 Summary of Types of Emotion Language

Source: Peter Palm based on an illustration in Zoltán Kövecses, *Metaphor and Emotion: Language, Culture, and Body in Human Feeling* (Cambridge: Cambridge University Press, 2000), 6.

to anger); 'anger is a dangerous animal' (e.g. 'He has a ferocious temper'); or 'anger is a burden' (e.g. 'after I lost my temper, I felt lighter'). The most widely used is the image that 'anger is the heat of a fluid in a container'. This 'central metaphor focuses on the fact that anger can be intense, that it can lead to a loss of control, and that a loss of control can be dangerous'.[237] Over the years Kövecses has further developed his theory of metaphor, arriving at the scheme in Fig. 10.

Moreover, according to Kövecses there are hardly any 'pure' emotional metaphors; instead, common metaphors are applied to emotions.[238] The preponderant metaphors are power, energy, or force: 'Emotion is force'. There is therefore a metaphor to which all others are subordinate, and 'Emotion metaphors are not isolated and unrelated specific-level metaphors, but form a large and intricate system that is organized around the generic concepts of force'—a new insight in the study of the linguistics of emotion.[239]

Even Kövecses sees the study of emotion as trapped between social constructivism and universalism, considering this dichotomy to be unproductive and instead requiring some kind of mediation—between on the one hand radical

---

[237] George Lakoff and Zoltán Kövecses, 'The Cognitive Model of Anger Inherent in American English', in Dorothy Holland and Naomi Quinn (eds), *Cultural Models in Language and Thought* (Cambridge: Cambridge University Press, 1987), 195–221, here 197, 200.

[238] Lakoff and Kövecses, 'Cognitive Model of Anger Inherent in American English', 197, 200.

[239] Zoltán Kövecses, *Metaphor and Emotion: Language, Culture, and Body in Human Feeling* (Cambridge: Cambridge University Press, 2000), 61, 85. In the specialized language of linguistics: 'The general conclusion I would like to offer is that most source domains of emotion metaphors are not specific to the domain of emotion, though some are'; Kövecses, *Metaphor and Emotion*, 49.

constructivists like Rom Harré, who believes that emotions are primarily constructed in language, and on the other, Joseph LeDoux, for whom emotions occur
unconsciously in the brain, the expression of emotion in language merely being
'the frills that have added icing to the emotional cake'.[240] How does Kövecses
envisage the marriage of these two approaches? Universality, or the 'near-universal',
is argued to be the embodiment of emotion.[241] On this basis 'near-universal'
metaphors are formulated. The physiological dimension of anger sets certain
boundaries to the conceptualization of anger. For instance, anger is associated
with an increase in skin temperature, and this is obviously a cultural universal.[242]
This physiological observation provides the framework within which the metaphors
of anger can emerge. One almost universal metaphor for anger is that of the
'pressurized container'. Kövecses concedes that there is no causal relationship
between physiology and metaphor, so that bodily experiences do not necessarily
give rise to metaphors; however, 'it makes a large number of other possible
metaphorical conceptualizations either incompatible or unnatural. It would be
odd to conceptualize anger as, say, softly falling snow, an image completely
incompatible with what our bodies are like and what our physiology does in
anger.'[243]

Finally there is the attempt to adopt a mediating position between the poles of
social constructivism and universalism.

> [People] can choose to conceptualize their emotions in many different ways *within the
> constraints* imposed on them by universal physiology. These limits leave a lot of room
> for speakers of very different languages to conceptualize their intense emotions in
> sometimes very different ways.[244]

The 'new synthesis' of emotion language is called 'body-based constructionism',
and presumes

> that some aspects . . . are universal and clearly related to the physiological functioning
> of the body. Once the universal aspects of emotion language are parsed out, the very
> significant remaining differences in emotion language and concepts can be explained
> by reference to differences in cultural knowledge and pragmatic discourse functions

---

[240] Joseph E. LeDoux, *The Emotional Brain: The Mysterious Underpinnings of Emotional Life*
(New York: Simon and Schuster, 1996), 302. On Rom Harré see Kövecses, *Metaphor and Emotion*,
184–5.

[241] *Near-universals* and *near-universality* in Kövecses, *Metaphor and Emotion*, 139.

[242] Raised skin temperature as a culturally-universal physiological response to anger was postulated
by Kövecses, using experimental measurements made by Levenson, Ekman, Heider, and Friesen for
North Americans and also for the Minangkabau on Western Sumatra; Kövecses, *Metaphor and
Emotion*, 159. Kövecses refers to Robert W. Levenson, Paul Ekman, Karl Heider, and Wallace
V. Friesen, 'Emotion and Autonomic Nervous System Activity in the Minangkabau of West
Sumatra', *Journal of Personality and Social Psychology*, 62/6 (1992), 972–88.

[243] Kövecses, *Metaphor and Emotion*, 160. Kövecses moves more cautiously in the direction of
cultural universalism than we can do here. He includes the possibility that the universal dissemination
of anger metaphors occurred by 'sheer coincidence', or that 'it may have been transmitted from one
culture to the others', but he believes that the universal and physical provides a more certain
foundation; Kövecses, *Metaphor and Emotion*, 162.

[244] Kövecses, *Metaphor and Emotion*, 165, emphasis in original.

that work according to divergent culturally defined rules or scenarios. This approach also allows us to see points of tension where cultural interests might contradict, suppress, or distort innate tendencies of expression. Thus, we need not be forever aligned in opposing camps, the innatists pitted against the social constructionists.[245]

Hence for Kövecses as a specialist in linguistics, the most important 'source' for emotion is speech, especially figurative speech. He finally comes to the conclusion that the linguistic and imagistic expression of emotion is in part embodied and universal, and in part cultural. So far, so good. But to what extent is the body reducible to physiology? What happens if even the body is cultural?

9 THE 1990s II: THE SUPERSESSION OF THE SOCIAL CONSTRUCTIVISM–UNIVERSALISM DUALITY?

The body: nature or culture? For a long time this discussion has been conducted in ever newer variations. Pascal Eitler and Monique Scheer responded with 'culture' in one recent round of the debate, demonstrating how a culturalized conception of the body drawn from 1990s history of the body and of genders could be of benefit to the historical study of emotions. Instead of assuming, as is so often done, that the body is a refuge of unchanging nature, implicitly assigning the 'physical' share of emotion to a timeless and pancultural dimension, Eitler and Scheer treat the embodiment of emotion in terms of historicization. As they say, culture is inscribed in the body in many different ways:

> Once capacities, impairments, or habits have been acquired, whether unconsciously assumed or deliberately cultivated, they are hard to shed. They mark the body: in shortened tendons that no longer allow someone to sit in a particular way; through raised blood pressure, or sudden fainting spells; in a pounding heart, or shedding tears.[246]

Eitler and Scheer are critical of the logocentrism of the linguistic turn:

> Feelings are not only culturally signified, as is claimed, but also and quite literally materially produced. They are not only represented physically, they first have to be physically practised, or fabricated. . . . To trace the body in its 'process of materialization' requires that we pay close attention to the materiality of permanent, and quite possibly minimal, changes . . . It is assumed that, in its physical form, there is nothing about the daily treatment of the body that is not to some extent affected and marked by particular social conditions: from the pitch of a voice to the density of bone, from the production of insulin to the rate of respiration.[247]

---

[245] Kövecses, *Metaphor and Emotion*, 183.

[246] Pascal Eitler and Monique Scheer, 'Emotionengeschichte als Körpergeschichte: Eine heuristische Perspektive auf religiöse Konversionen im 19. und 20. Jahrhundert', *Geschichte und Gesellschaft*, 35/2 (2009), 282–313, here 285.

[247] Eitler and Scheer, 'Emotionengeschichte als Körpergeschichte', 290–1.

This also applies to that part of the body which has, following the bio-revolution, become identified as the ultimate essence, the most unchanging human matter: the brain. Eitler and Scheer emphasize that 'psychology and the neurosciences no longer confront the historiography of emotion with timeless factors, but with contemporary structures and processes within the brain'.[248] Neuroscientists readily talk of the 'plasticity' of the brain, but the epistemological charge of this capacity has seldom been so clearly spelled out as it is in Eitler and Scheer. It amounts to this: literary scholars who push their experimental subjects into an MRI scanner, read them passages from *Anna Karenina*, and interpret the increased blood flow through the amygdala (which shows up as yellow on the screen) as 'fearsome arousal' are dealing not only with brains that have evolved through aeons of time, but also with brains that are the product of individual biography and short-term changes. Hence any statistical inference is made from one experimental subject only: n = 1.

Moreover, 'processes of materialization' and practices of inscription are temporally open and unstable:

> Constant repetition is required not only for the signification of feelings, but also for their embodiment. Consequently, processes of materialization are best treated as processes of sedimentation. Crucial to this idea is that body and feelings gain or lose materiality, or stability, in this respect. Constant repetition also ineluctably involves 'the possibility of failure'.[249]

Eitler and Scheer continue by emphasizing that post-structuralist approaches accordingly break

> with the prevailing linguistic or cognitive reductionism within the study of emotion, directing attention less to discourse as theory, and more to discourse as practice. Instead of speaking or thinking emotion being the point of central attention, doing emotion, or better, trying emotion, moves centre stage. Within this framework particular bodies facilitate or foster, further, block or hinder particular feelings; while feelings relate to, shape or change bodies—whether this be in the form a tiny laughter lines or a twisted spine, whether in the context of a high level of serotonin or a developing stomach ulcer.[250]

This represents for the time being the current position in debate over the natural characteristics of the body in the context of the historical study of emotion. From this standpoint in the early 2000s we can look back upon the state of discussion during the 1990s.

At that time, calls for the supersession of dichotomous emotional constructs were not limited to linguistics and Zoltán Kövecses. During the 1990s they became louder in anthropology itself. As early as 1987, Nancy Scheper-Hughes and Margaret M. Lock saw in emotion an object of study that promised to lead medical

---

[248] Eitler and Scheer, 'Emotionengeschichte als Körpergeschichte', 291.
[249] Eitler and Scheer, 'Emotionengeschichte als Körpergeschichte', 292–3.
[250] Eitler and Scheer, 'Emotionengeschichte als Körpergeschichte', 293. Eitler and Scheer take this from Judith Butler's performance theory and Pierre Bourdieu's concept of habitus or hexis.

anthropology out of a cul-de-sac composed of a whole battery of binary opposi-
tions: 'mind/body, seen/unseen, natural/supernatural, magical/rational, rational/
irrational, and real/unreal'.[251] Emotion was an important medium for overcoming
this Cartesian heritage, providing 'an important "missing link" capable of bridging
mind and body, individual, society, and body politic'.[252] In particular, ethnographies of illness in non-Western cultures were especially illuminating because 'It is
sometimes during the experience of sickness, as in moments of deep trance or sexual
transport, that mind and body, self and other become one.'[253] The anthropology of
emotion rendered the outlines of a mindful body visible.

    The studies that Unni Wikan conducted on Bali went beyond this. Balinese in
the northern province of Buleleng had a 'double-anchoredness' for the self, in both
heart and face, but according to Wikan these two dimensions were linked, one
being constantly present in the other.[254] She argued that it was ethnocentric to treat
the heart as the refuge of the 'true' and 'authentic' self, while the face was merely a
mask—an approach that was broadly accepted in the pantheon of anthropology
from Margaret Mead to Clifford Geertz. Wikan by contrast insisted on the
indigenous 'holistic view of the person', a self which included the dimensions of
both heart and face, without the one being treated as fundamental and the other as
superficial.[255]

    At the same time, Wikan distanced herself from the social constructivist van-
guard of the 1980s. While their achievements were very great, the focus upon
emotion was ultimately owing to the women's movement of the 1970s and the
consequent re-evaluation of 'female' characteristics such as emotionality. Consequently, according to Wikan, the dichotomy between irrational emotion and
rational cognition was simply replicated. The time had therefore come to leave
behind emotions as the object of study, and instead take more seriously the
significance of meta-emotional conceptions like those of the northern Balinese,
really understanding their *keneh* as 'feeling-thoughts'. For this, a new focus upon
'people' and 'lived experience' was necessary. Anthropologists had to completely
immerse themselves in alien culture and 'empathize'. The work of translation
would enable them to then understand their own culture, for in the absence of
such work an alien culture would forever and irrevocably remain 'the Other';
indeed, the 'exotic Other'. To thoroughly rid oneself of this exoticism it was
necessary to immerse oneself, tracing and identifying what humans shared in
common.[256] Only in this way might 'resonance' emerge. In sum: if one fails to
engage with the other *plures*, one will never discover what *unum* is. Wikan herself

---

[251] Nancy Scheper-Hughes and Margaret M. Lock, 'The Mindful Body: Prolegomenon to Future
Work in Medical Anthropology', *Medical Anthropology Quarterly*, 1/1 (1987), 6–41, here 7.
[252] Scheper-Hughes and Lock, 'The Mindful Body', 28–9.
[253] Scheper-Hughes and Lock, 'The Mindful Body', 29.
[254] Unni Wikan, *Managing Turbulent Hearts: A Balinese Formula for Living* (Chicago: University of
Chicago Press, 1990), 104–7. See also her influential essay, 'Managing the Heart to Brighten Face and
Soul'.
[255] Wikan, *Managing Turbulent Hearts*, 114.
[256] Wikan, *Managing Turbulent Hearts*, 281 ('deexotization').

had 'lived experience[s]', placing renewed emphasis upon the 'participant' side of 'participant observation'. She finally realized that she believed in black magic and had developed facial cramp from so much smiling, although the cramps eventually wore off—this reminds us of the sedimentation processes that produce 'trying emotion', as noted by Scheer and Eitler.[257]

An *unum* cannot be defined a priori, but emerges from confrontation with the *plures* in Bali. There it proved to be laughter and weeping. Wikan established that the Balinese saw tears as a sign of sadness inaccessible to the will, a more-or-less automatic reaction. In terms of Austin's theory of speech acts (of which William M. Reddy makes use, as we shall see), this reaction is constative, or descriptive of the world, whereas laughter changes the world, it is performative. Laughter made the world look better, according to the Balinese,

> Laughter *makes* happiness, it takes sadness out. . . . The relationship [between laughter and happiness] is not abstract; it is experientially known and perceived. Just as getting one's feet wet and cold makes one shivering and dizzy. . . . Laughter helps one forget, makes one feel good, and strengthens the spirit. It also preserves youthfulness of face and body.[258]

According to Wikan, it is here that a perspective opens up on unanticipated common features, upon elective affinities. For the connection between laughter and happiness is something that 'Western bio-medicine is just beginning to acknowledge and use for therapeutic effect'.[259] There is therefore common ground between Balinese and Western medical knowledge, 'a steadily growing clinical literature that confirms the effects of emotions and mental state on health'.[260] The advantages of a broad perspective that takes as much as possible into view and initially excludes nothing, were not something that only Wikan, and anthropology in general, recognized.[261] Around the same time voices began to be heard in historical scholarship emphasizing the productivity of broadly based comparisons which revealed not only differences but unsuspected similarities. In turn, these made it possible to clarify the specificity of similar objects.[262]

---

[257] Wikan, *Managing Turbulent Hearts*, 270–2.
[258] Wikan, *Managing Turbulent Hearts*, 123, emphasis in original.
[259] Wikan, *Managing Turbulent Hearts*, 123.
[260] Wikan, *Managing Turbulent Hearts*, 148.
[261] As an example from anthropology, see the practice of *disentangling* found both in Bali and many South Seas societies; discussed and resolved in the context of a group, 'tangled feelings' (i.e. interpersonal conflict) are dealt with in a manner that at first sight looks very much like Western strategies of conflict resolution. On closer comparative examination there are however two striking differences: first of all, in Bali there is no idea of the authentic individual self, as in the West, a self that can be invoked by the patient in psychotherapy or the legal person before a court of law. Instead, we always have persons in the plural, people who only exist 'in a matrix of social relations'. Secondly, these disentangling practices are not associated with 'bodily displays of felt emotion', as in cathartic weeping in psychotherapy; Geoffrey M. White and Karen Ann Watson-Gegeo, 'Disentangling Discourse', in Karen Ann Watson-Gegeo and Geoffrey M. White (eds), *Disentangling: Conflict Discourse in Pacific Societies* (Stanford, CA: Stanford University Press, 1990), 3–49, here 8, 12.
[262] For historical comparison, see Heinz-Gerhard Haupt and Jürgen Kocka (eds), *Geschichte und Vergleich: Ansätze und Ergebnisse international vergleichender Geschichtsschreibung* (Frankfurt am Main: Campus, 1996); Hartmut Kaelble, *Der historische Vergleich: Eine Einführung zum 19. und 20.*

Parallel to the work of Wikan, and developing through the later 1990s and the 2000s, there has been innovative empirical work that goes beyond the dichotomy of social constructivism and universalism. One example is a study by Lisa Mitchell, who used the perspective of emotion to provide a new explanation for the 1950s south Indian phenomenon of suicide out of love of one's language. Some historical background is necessary here. Following independence in 1947, India was divided into a federal structure, using the old British administrative boundaries. These boundaries had never respected linguistic divisions, and Potti Sriramulu was the first to starve himself to death in protest against them. In 1953 and under the rule of Nehru, the first federal state based on linguistic borders (Andhra) was founded, in the wake of which large numbers of people in the south Indian states followed Sriramulu's example. Suicide for the love of one's language became notorious, and for years it was interpreted as 'a rational, matter-of-fact issue for members of the educated middle classes. The participation of anyone other than a member of the middleclass was explained to me either as false consciousness or elite manipulation, or with the assertion that some "people want their names to be published in papers.... That's all".'[263]

Lisa Mitchell did not find explanations of this kind satisfactory. She asked herself: 'What conditions must exist in order for someone to be willing to die, not for a nation, but for a language?'[264] Her answer was that, first of all, during the nineteenth century linguistic ideas had been imported from Europe that equated languages with living things, and which stood in complex relationships with other languages. In particular, the phases of life typical of biological beings—birth, childhood, maturity, death—were transferred to languages. It was this importation that first made it possible to be anxious about the death of a language. Secondly, language was personified as an Indian god who was to be worshipped. The mother-tongue of the Tamils was worshipped as a mother, as a female god, and *tamilpparru* was coined as a Tamil concept for 'devotion to Tamil'.[265] Thirdly, there was a steady

Jahrhundert (Frankfurt am Main: Campus, 1999); Hartmut Kaelble and Jürgen Schriewer (eds), *Vergleich und Transfer: Komparatistik in den Sozial-, Geschichts- und Kulturwissenschaften* (Frankfurt am Main: Campus, 2003); for criticism, see Margrit Pernau, *Transnationale Geschichte* (Stuttgart: Vandenhoeck & Ruprecht, 2011), esp. 30–5.

[263] Lisa Mitchell, *Language, Emotion, and Politics in South India: The Making of a Mother Tongue* (Bloomington: Indiana University Press, 2009), 32.

[264] Mitchell, *Language, Emotion, and Politics in South India*, 1.

[265] Mitchell, *Language, Emotion, and Politics in South India*, 12; see also 69: 'The Telugu language, like many other languages used in India, increasingly came to be personified more elaborately than had ever previously been the case. It also, for the first time, began to be imagined and described as having a life of its own independent of the speakers and writers who used it. Although sometimes metaphorically portrayed as an eroticized maiden in which a poet might take pleasure, the Telugu language was experienced up to the nineteenth century primarily as a medium for written and oral communication; for linguistic play, artistic and musical pleasure, and the demonstration of technical virtuosity; for religious and literary education; and for inscriptions, record keeping, and accounting. By the end of the nineteenth century, however, the Telugu language also began to be experienced as a new personified object of adoration, pride, and devotion, as a specific subject of study, pedagogy, and attention in its own right, and as a marker of identity. During the nineteenth century, the Telugu language acquired a number of new attributes, including a birth and, as Rama Mantena has argued in her work on language and historical time, stages of development and a progressive life narrative. It also gained a family tree,

increase in the circulation of print media, and then the development of audio media, spreading the love of language among ever more people. It is just this practical grounding which is an important aspect of the study, which asks 'how languages came to be viewed during the twentieth century as primary and natural foundations for the reorganization of a wide range of forms of knowledge and everyday practice. These include such practices as history writing, literary production, canon (re)formation, pedagogy, political organization, and the representation of sociocultural identities.'[266]

In the late nineteenth century the writer Gurujada Sriramamurti (1851–99) sought support for the publication of the second edition of his text *Lives of [Telugu] Poets*, a book about those who wrote in Telugu, a south Indian language. He opened his preface with an appeal to 'those having affection for or pride in the language of the Telugu country'.[267] In the mid-twentieth century, according to Mitchell, the combined effect of the three factors noted earlier rendered affective adherence to the language even stronger. Added to this was the fear of Hindi dominance in south India following Indian Independence, which was spoken in most of the central and northern Indian states. Moreover, the boundaries of the federal states paid as little regard to the love of language as those drawn by the British, but the foundation of Andhra created a precedent. All of these factors led to a radicalization in affective attachment to Telugu, and ultimately to the spectacular cases of suicide for the love of a language. In their own way these acts of protest were successful, since 'Within just a few short years of Andhra State's pathbreaking formation, mounting pressure nationwide resulted in the States Reorganisation Act of 1956, which redrew much of the map of India on linguistic lines. As a result, linguistic states became the new norm within the Indian nation rather than the exception.'[268] And with this, the wave of suicides came to an end.

Mitchell's study is an inspiration for the historical study of nationalism and its relation to emotion. Combining anthropology and history, she brought together the methods of the history of communication (the analysis of new dictionaries, radio, and so forth), linguistic anthropology (the evaluation of dictionaries and grammars, plus interviews), and history (archival research, interviews). The result was a multicausal and original explanation for events that had been difficult to explain: the waves of suicides in south India motivated by a love of language.

---

kinship relations with other languages, and the possibility of its own death. All of these acquisitions led eventually to a new full-fledged personification of the Telugu language by the early decades of the twentieth century. From this point onward, the Telugu language began to appear in a new personified and gendered form as *Telugu Talli*, "Mother Telugu", represented in human-like form—often as a goddess—in descriptive narratives, poems, songs, and artistic renderings.' See further Rama Sundari Mantena, 'Vernacular Futures: Colonial Philology and the Idea of History in Nineteenth-Century South India', *Indian Economic and Social History Review*, 42/4 (2005), 513–34.

[266] Mitchell, *Language, Emotion, and Politics in South India*, 11.
[267] Mitchell, *Language, Emotion, and Politics in South India*, 11.
[268] Mitchell, *Language, Emotion, and Politics in South India*, 7.

10 RECENT UNIVERSALIST ANTHROPOLOGY
OF EMOTIONS

During the social constructivist 1980s a parallel development in the anthropology of emotion occurred which was marked by its universalistic tendency. While admittedly a minority development, we need to take note of it here, given the ground covered in Chapter Three on the life sciences. Some of these scholars took up work from psychoanalytic literature. For them it was axiomatic that there was a 'structure of emotion' or a 'universal pattern of emotions, a dialectic between love and hate, union and separation, community and individual, that must find expression in every society'.[269] Others, for the most part linguistic anthropologists, used data from their fieldwork to confirm Paul Ekman's postulate of culturally-universal basic emotions, such as happiness, anger, disgust, fear, contempt, sadness, and surprise.[270] One of these was Karl Heider.

Heider had worked together with Ekman since 1968, and in 1986 they undertook a joint one-month-long field trip to Bukittinggi, West Sumatra.[271] Heider's central question was posed as follows:

> How does culture influence emotion? Obviously, different languages have different words for emotions. But beyond that, how much of emotion behavior is culturally variable? How much overlap is there between, say, Americans' 'anger' and Indonesians' *marah*?[272]

Since Heider adopted Ekman's theory as the starting point of his own work, the answer to this question seems obvious. According to Heider, Ekman's work on facial expression had revealed the universals that bound cultures together. Henceforth, the task of anthropologists was to distil cultural differences—Ekman's 'display rules'—from the established half-dozen basic emotions (this is further discussed in Chapter Three). There was a division of labour here which united psychology and anthropology: 'The task of the anthropologist examining emotion

---

[269] Lindholm, *Generosity and Jealousy*, 273; see also 267: 'Despite the complexities and ambiguities, despite disputes over the source of human duality, there is nonetheless a very striking correspondence of terms, and I take it as a given that human beings do indeed have an emotional structure, visualized as dialectical, and consisting of sentiments associated with separation and independence on the one hand and attachment and interdependence on the other. This emotional structure, which may derive from the experience of extended nurturance and an intense mother-child tie, or from innate instincts, or a combination of both, is seen as existing independently of any particular social structure, though it can be modified in its expression by social circumstances. All humans everywhere will need to feel autonomy, and all will need to experience attachment. This is implicit in the definition of humanity offered by the psychoanalytic literature.'

[270] Another universalistic study of emotional terminology from the 1990s, using a comparative linguistic-anthropological approach is A. Timothy Church, Marcia S. Katigbak, Jose Alberto S. Reyes, and Stacia M. Jensen, 'Language and Organisation of Filipino Emotion Concepts: Comparing Emotion Concepts and Dimensions Across Cultures', *Cognition and Emotion*, 12/1 (1998), 63–92.

[271] Karl G. Heider, *Landscapes of Emotion: Mapping Three Cultures of Emotion in Indonesia* (Cambridge: Cambridge University Press, 1991), xiv. On the joint work of Heider and Ekman, see Paul Ekman, 'Afterword: Universality of Emotional Expression? A Personal History of the Dispute', in Darwin, *Expression of the Emotions in Man and Animals*, 363–93, here 383–4.

[272] Heider, *Landscapes of Emotion*, 3.

is to look for differences: to identify and to account for culturally variable emotion behavior that takes place against the pan-cultural background.'[273] Or, as Heider systematically formulated it at the beginning of his Indonesian study:

> **Assumption 3.** *Emotion behavior is a mix of pan-cultural and culture-specific behavior.* It is shaped by both pan-cultural influences (perhaps species-common biology) and culture-specific norms.
>
> **Assumption 4.** *Since the culture-specific patterns exist in a context with the pan-cultural, both must be considered concurrently.* A noncomparative ethnography of emotion runs the risk of not recognizing much that is in fact pan-human behavior, while an approach that ignores cultural contributions may count as experimental errors some behavior that is in fact normative specific.
>
> **Assumption 5.** *The prime task of anthropology is to work out the role of culture-specific influences on emotion.*[274]

Heider believed that

> Emotion behavior is culturally constructed on a pan-cultural base, and so it follows that an ultimate goal of research is to tease apart the two.[275]

In Heider's representation of the opposition between social constructivism and universalism, an anthropologist like Catherine A. Lutz becomes a social constructivist extremist, and a psychologist like Jerry Boucher an extreme universalist. From this perspective, Ekman's position could be presented as a happy medium, having a place for universalism (basic emotions) and for the culturally specific ('display rules'). Heider contrasted 'pan-culturalists, who thought that all emotions everywhere were the same', with 'the culture-specific proponents, who thought that everything was always different'.[276] In other words: on the one hand there was the *'pan-cultural universalism* of those who simply ignore the possible effect of different cultures. Here are found especially psychologists'. On the other hand there was '*cultural relativism* of those who simply ignore or reject the pan-cultural findings of the facial expression research. . . . Here I include most ethnographers.' By contrast, superior to these two poles and the extremist who inhabited them were the '*compromise positions,* such as Ekman's, of those who hold that pan-cultural facial expressions are mediated by cultural display rules'.[277]

Heider's approach rests upon one major assumption: the existence of universal basic emotions, as revealed by Ekman's experiments on facial expression. These will be dealt with in greater detail in Chapter Three. We can nonetheless say here that Ekman's assumption is anything but definitively proven; that it is, on the contrary, vigorously disputed within even experimental psychology, let alone by other fields of study. But does Heider's own empirical work in linguistic anthropology fall to pieces if Ekman's rug, on which it supposedly stands, is pulled away? Not at all. For

---

[273] Heider, *Landscapes of Emotion*, 3.
[274] Heider, *Landscapes of Emotion*, 13, emphasis in original.
[275] Heider, *Landscapes of Emotion*, 55. [276] Heider, *Landscapes of Emotion*, 7.
[277] Heider, *Landscapes of Emotion*, 87–8, emphasis in original.

his work does not necessarily rely upon Ekman's theory of basic emotion. In fact, he presents a classical linguistic study of the anthropology of emotion, rather like Niko Besnier's studies, or Catherine A. Lutz's investigation of *fago* and *song*.[278]

Heider took four languages for which he supposed there were differing degrees of cultural connection: Minangkabau, Minangkabau-Indonesian, High Indonesian, and American English. In this selection he saw a greater degree of cultural variation than in a similar comparative study—which he considered to be the most ambitious to date—of six languages in Europe and Israel among which the cultural differences were thought to be much less significant.[279] From his four languages, Heider gathered up words that could be classified as emotional in their respective cultures, and drafted 'cognitive maps' for their semantics, graphic representations of relationships of meaning within one language and between different languages. In this way he rendered semantic similarities between lexical expressions of emotion— emotional words—visible. For example, in the three Indonesian languages the word *takut*, which roughly means 'fear', is more strongly connected with 'guilt' than are English concepts for fear; it is always also a feeling of 'contempt, shame'.[280]

Even the conception of emotion that Heider developed on the basis of this 'cognitive cartography' is actually more complex than his introductory remarks on Ekman might lead one to think. First of all, for Heider emotions were always mixed conditions, which to some extent went against the grain of Ekman's idea of basic emotions, and also involved a convergence with other branches of psychology.[281] Secondly, Heider did not see emotion as a condition, but as a process. He presented this graphically as a 'flow of emotion' (Fig. 11).

He described this flow of emotion as follows:

> *Antecedent events* can be described neutrally: for example, 'the death of a child.' The event is given emotional coloring by, first, the *cultural definition* through culture-specific rules that produce simple or complex emotional *inner states*. A second culture-specific intervention, the reaction rules, or display rules, of that culture for that emotion determine whether the emotion of the inner state is altered in its public performance through intensification, diminution, neutralization, or masking by the behavior (usually the facial expression) of another emotion.... An Indonesian display rule, for example, is reported by the musicologist Mantle Hood: 'Among the many refinements of Javanese society is the ideal of concealing the emotions—it is sometimes said that there is a Javanese smile for every emotion.' In other words, in Java every

[278] Heider explicitly refers to Lutz's linguistic work; Heider, *Landscapes of Emotion*, 88.
[279] Heider, *Landscapes of Emotion*, 57–8. The study of six European languages can be found in Klaus R. Scherer, Harald G. Wallbott, and Angela B. Summerfield (eds), *Experiencing Emotion: A Cross-cultural Study* (Cambridge: Cambridge University Press, 1986).
[280] Heider, *Landscapes of Emotion*, 113, 119.
[281] For example, the developmental psychologist Jerome Kagan maintained that emotional words are impoverished by comparison with emotional reality, since they represent a unitary category, and not mixed forms involving two or three conditions. See Jerome Kagan, *What Is Emotion? History, Measures, and Meanings* (New Haven: Yale University Press, 2007), 8. He went on: 'Let us agree to a moratorium on the use of single words, such as fear, ... and write about emotional processes with full sentences rather than ambiguous, naked concepts'; Kagan, *What Is Emotion?*, 216.

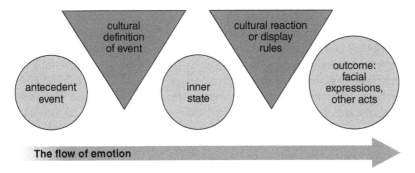

Fig. 11 The Flow of Emotion by Karl G. Heider

Source: Peter Palm based on an illustration in Karl G. Heider, *Landscapes of Emotion: Mapping Three Cultures of Emotion in Indonesia* (Cambridge: Cambridge University Press, 1991), 7.

emotion is to be masked with a smile. However, one suspects that the real meaning of the saying is that the Javanese have a different smile for each emotion.[282]

The flow of emotion was thus

> A very general model that admits the complexity of real emotion behavior recognizes both the simultaneous synchronic combination of several emotions and the diachronic succession of emotions. This is a kaleidoscope model that, like that children's toy, allows for a complicated mixture of emotions changing over time.[283]

It can be said that this is ultimately just a stimulus-response model that suppresses the possibility that emotions are produced purely 'internally', for instance, the fear of a snake placed in the context of otherwise positive stimuli such as sunshine on a spring day.[284] Nonetheless, Heider's flow of emotions remains one of the most promising approaches.

At the end of this chapter we can return to the trend in the anthropology of emotion that can serve as a symbol of the social constructivist pole in the general study of emotion. This equation of anthropology with social constructivism, and even the dichotomy of social constructivism and universalism, of course works only up to a point. The chaos of reality is stronger than any principle of order, however much it seeks to structure this chaos. We have seen in the cases discussed in this chapter that even the anthropology of emotion oscillates between social constructivism and universalism, and that many of its representatives see their own domain as being trapped between these two poles. Dichotomous distinctions like this prove simplistic, as is their temporal placement between the 1970s and the 1990s. Typifying the flux of history through this or that 'decade' has never been a

---

[282] Heider, *Landscapes of Emotion*, 7, emphasis in original.

[283] Heider, *Landscapes of Emotion*, 98.

[284] One can also criticize Heider's book for occasionally politically incorrect remarks, as when he excludes the Dani (an Indonesian tribe) on the grounds that they 'are preliterate and quite nonintellectual and I wanted to try an intellectual, literate culture'; Heider, *Landscapes of Emotion*, 21.

satisfactory business, and the problem is exacerbated in anthropology because of the many years that fieldwork often takes from the original idea to the final publication of description and conclusions. Work in the human and social sciences, not to mention the life and natural sciences, typically has a much shorter interval between inception and conclusion. It would have been possible to organize this chapter on emotion in anthropology quite differently: for example, around the topic of weeping as a social practice. Ultimately, however, perception and historical-scientific effectivity won out. The studies of Rosaldo, Abu-Lughod, and Lutz are considered by other disciplines, even in historical studies, as the most prominent formulation of social constructive positions. Finally, one thing matters here: no discipline has done so much to shatter the idea that feelings are timeless and everywhere the same as has anthropology.

Three

Universalism
Life Sciences

1 PAUL EKMAN AND BASIC EMOTIONS

Fig. 12 shows three faces. Please caption each of them as expressing sadness, anger, or disgust, and make a note of which image belongs to which emotion. We will return to this later.

In early 2009 the first episodes of the TV series *Lie to Me* were screened in the United States. Eventually, fifty other countries bought the rights to screen the series. The programme was fronted by a psychologist, Dr Carl Lightman, who headed a private business which helped police and security services carry out criminal investigations. The firm specialized in a very particular line of work: it detected liars by studying 'micro-expressions', which revealed true intentions and feelings. Particularly legible through body language, but above all in facial expressions, these micro-expressions shine through all efforts made by professional swindlers to mislead their questioners. Despite all mutual agreements, those working for the firm tend to take their techniques home with them. Lightman had, for example, just promised his teenage daughter Emily not to use any covert scientific techniques on Dan, her boyfriend, that night. But when Dan turned up to take Emily out, Lightman, the mobile lie-detector, opens the door and greets him with the question: 'Are you going to try and have sex with my daughter tonight?' and then studies Dan's reaction in the usual way.[1]

Lightman is modelled on Paul Ekman who has worked as a psychologist at the University of California, San Francisco since the late 1950s. He is also the CEO of the Paul Ekman Group Ltd. In 2009 Ekman was ranked among the hundred most globally influential people by *Time* magazine, and he is a pivotal figure in the anthropology, sociology, and linguistics of emotion. He has also authored books and articles with the anthropologist Karl G. Heider, as we saw at the end of

---

[1] The original dialogue runs: 'Emily Lightman: "No, we're not doing this. You just go let Dan in while I finish getting ready and you better not do some covert scientific technique to find out what we're doing or not doing tonight. Promise!" Cal Lightman: "No covert science, I promise." Cal Lightman [opening the front door]: "Hi Dan!" Dan: "Hi Dr. Lightman!" Cal Lightman: "Are you going to try and have sex with my daughter tonight?"'; *Lie to Me*: Pilot (#1.1) (Fox, 2009) [TV series].

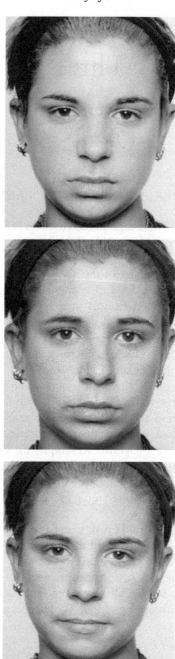

Fig. 12 Sadness, Anger, or Disgust? Please, Make a Note!
Source: © Paul Ekman 2003, Paul Ekman Group, LLC.

Chapter Two.[2] Ekman advised on the script for *Lie to Me*, and the extent to which Lightman could resemble Ekman was detailed contractually, from biographical details such as the suicide of his mother to any physical similarities between Ekman and the actor Tim Roth. Consultation did not end when the series was broadcast: on an accompanying blog, 'Dr. Paul Ekman' explained 'the scientific bases of each episode'.[3] Of decisive importance here is the use of intellectual property, for the whole idea of the series comes from Ekman's work on emotions. So what does this work involve?

Ekman is best known for his theory of the basic emotions that people of all cultures are said to have, and which they are able to recognize in others. The basic emotions are happiness, anger, disgust, fear, sadness, and surprise. What these conceptions might mean in the English language as opposed to their translations in other languages seems to be of little relevance, since for Ekman the expression of emotion is not something that occurs in language, but is instead physical, to be read in the face. For every basic emotion there is a corresponding unmistakable facial expression which no one is capable of concealing. If someone sets out to deceive, or when 'display rules' (in Ekman's terminology) prohibit the display of basic emotions, micro-expressions always give them away. Micro-expressions might last only fractions of a second, but they still 'leak' through any attempt to mask one's feelings.[4]

Universal facial expressions, or more generally 'distinctive universal signals', are the leading characteristic of basic emotions. Whatever shifts in definition Ekman might have made, this idea has remained a constant in his thought.[5] The selection and number of basic emotions has changed over the years. In 1992, for instance, Ekman wrote that there were six basic emotions—happiness, anger, disgust, fear, sadness, and surprise—and another five which might prove to be part of this group. He considered the possibility that contempt, shame, guilt, embarrassment, and awe

---

[2] See 'Paul Ekman' Paul Ekman Group, <http://www.paulekman.com/paul-ekman/> accessed 5 March 2014; 'The 2009 TIME 100: The World's Most Influential People', *TIME Magazine* (27 April 2009). In a ranking of the most influential 20th-century psychologists Ekman was placed 59th; Steven J. Haggbloom, René Warnick, Jason E. Warnick, Vinessa K. Jones, Gary L. Yarbrough, Tenea M. Russell, Chris M. Borecky, Reagan McGahhey, John L. Powell III, Jamie Beavers, and Emmanuelle Monte, 'The 100 Most Eminent Psychologists of the 20th Century', *Review of General Psychology*, 6/2 (2002), 139–52, here 147.

[3] < http://community.fox.com/drpaulekman/blog> accessed 28 January 2011; the link does not work anymore but the content of blog can be found here: 'Lie to Me Blog', *Lie to Me Now* <http://www.lie-to-me-now.com/blog> accessed 6 March 2014.

[4] The concept of leakage used here comes from Ekman. See Paul Ekman, 'Afterword: Universality of Emotional Expression? A Personal History of the Dispute', in Charles Darwin, *The Expression of the Emotions in Man and Animals* (3rd edn, New York: Oxford University Press, 1998), 363–93, here 373.

[5] In different phases of his long career Ekman has given varying definitions of basic emotions. For example, in the later 1980s and early 1990s he added eight further characteristics to his universal facial expressions: 1. 'Presence in other primates', 2. 'Distinctive physiology', 3. 'Distinctive universals in antecedent events', 4. 'Coherence among emotional response', 5. 'Quick onset', 6. 'Brief duration', 7. 'Automatic appraisal', and 8. 'Unbidden occurrence'; Paul Ekman, 'An Argument for Basic Emotions', *Cognition and Emotion*, 6/3–4 (1992), 169–200, here 175. Basic emotions are 'basic' in another sense as well: 'Emotions evolved for their adaptive value in dealing with *fundamental life-tasks*'; Ekman, 'An Argument for Basic Emotions', 171, emphasis in original. The function of fear, for instance, was to prepare the body for flight, and in this way helped the species to survive.

might be added.[6] Two years later and he was talking about five proven and three potential basic emotions:

> There is consistent evidence for pan-cultural facial expressions for five emotions: anger, fear, sadness, enjoyment, and disgust. There is still disagreement about whether there is a pan-cultural signal for surprise, contempt, and shame/guilt.[7]

Such a sudden change of mind might come as a surprise for anyone working in the humanities, raising doubts about the robustness of changing ideas about basic emotions which are supposedly so fixed; but from the standpoint of the natural sciences there is nothing much amiss here. Since the 1980s the impact of post-structuralism on the study of history has promoted pluralism. Epistemic systems have overlaid each other, and even where the logic of progress continues to reign, it is relatively slow progress (once something is established, it can take years—in the human sciences often decades—before it is superseded). By contrast, the natural sciences have since the mid-nineteenth century worked with a short-term idea of progress.[8] Here each piece of knowledge that has been gained remains valid only until it is superseded by new knowledge; indeed, knowledge is defined by the fact that it is something that will be superseded. According to the natural sciences, it is quite possible to refine experiments while leaving the question of any true and final result open. Hence, from the standpoint of the natural sciences, there was nothing going against Ekman, when he took into consideration the possibility of 'complex' emotions comprised of a 'mixture' of basic emotions. For Ekman, the test case was 'smugness . . . considered to be a blend of the two elemental emotions, happiness and contempt'.[9] He later restricted the definition of basic emotions, and argued that only basic emotions could properly be called 'emotions'.[10]

How did Ekman arrive at the idea of basic emotions? Ruth Leys, a historian of science, has critically examined the path that Ekman has taken, and constructed a kind of 'genealogy of the present' that she explicitly links to the work of Michel Foucault. Leys understands by this a diagnosis of present intellectual trends—in this case, the 'emotional turn' taken by many of those working in the human and life sciences—identifying the structure that unites them, and seeking their sources.[11] With Ekman, Leys develops a history in which the lines along which

---

    [6] Ekman, 'An Argument for Basic Emotions', 170.
    [7] Paul Ekman and Richard J. Davidson, 'Epilogue—Affective Science: A Research Agenda', in Ekman and Davidson (eds), *The Nature of Emotion: Fundamental Questions* (New York: Oxford University Press, 1994), 409–30, here 413.
    [8] A genealogy of the idea of progress in the natural sciences can be found in Lorraine Daston, 'Fear and Loathing of the Imagination of Science', *Daedalus*, 127/1 (1998), 73–95.
    [9] Paul Ekman, 'Basic Emotions', in Tim Dalgleish and Mick J. Power (eds), *Handbook of Cognition and Emotion* (Chichester: Wiley, 1999), 45–60, here 46–7.
    [10] Paul Ekman, 'All Emotions Are Basic', in Ekman and Davidson (eds), *Nature of Emotion*, 15–19, here 19.
    [11] Leys writes of her approach: 'I consider myself an intellectual historian who writes in the mode of what I call the "genealogy of the present", by which I mean that I tend to write about contemporary developments or paradigms in the human sciences that have a relatively recent (also a relatively dense) history or lineage. My aim is simultaneously to write the history of those developments or paradigms (or concepts or issues) that interest me and to make an intervention in the present by situating current

scientific practice develops (for example, the use of photography in laboratory experiments) run together with intellectual and cultural trends.

In his own account, Ekman developed an interest in psychology at the age of 14, prompted by the suicide of his mother, who he later realized suffered from depression. His reading of Freud led him into psychoanalysis. He went into analysis himself, and even in his mid-twenties he was still committed to a career involving group and individual therapy. While working on his doctoral dissertation he encountered the methods of experimental psychology as articulated in B. F. Skinner's behavioural psychology. Added to this were his interests in photography and modern dance; later, photographs and non-verbal communication were to play an important part in his studies of emotion. After completing his undergraduate degree in Chicago and his doctorate in New York, Ekman moved to San Francisco in 1957, where he has worked as a psychologist at the University of California, San Francisco ever since, first as a research assistant and then as a professor, with a period in the army working as a military psychologist.[12] Initially 'committed to a cultural relativist social learning view', Ekman recalls that he was 'totally convinced that everything about expression and gesture was learned.'[13]

In the mid-1960s this conviction changed, influenced by the work of another experimental psychologist, Silvan S. Tomkins (1911–91), who had broken away from the mainstream of behaviourism and psychoanalysis. Influenced by Darwin's writings on emotion, Tomkins postulated the existence of 'affect programmes'. These were particular physical reactions and ways of behaving that were prompted by external stimuli and set in motion independent of culture or individual biography, volition, or imagination. Tomkins argued that external stimuli triggered reactions in those parts of the brain that were oldest in evolutionary terms, these reactions automatically taking the form of particular behaviours and particular bodily movements. Leys described Tomkins's approach as follows:

> If I run from a snake I do not do so because I believe there is a dangerous object in front of me and desire or intend not to be bitten by it. I run because I am terrified of snakes. The threat of the snake lies out there in the object: snakes make me frightened because they were once terrifying to our ancestors in evolutionary history.[14]

---

debates genealogically and critically commenting on them'; Ruth Leys and Marlene Goldman, 'Navigating the Genealogies of Trauma, Guilt, and Affect: An Interview with Ruth Leys', *University of Toronto Quarterly*, 79/2 (2010), 656–79, here 656–7. See also Ruth Leys, *Trauma: A Genealogy* (Chicago: University of Chicago Press, 2000), 10; Ruth Leys, *From Guilt to Shame: Auschwitz and After* (Princeton: Princeton University Press, 2007), 13; and of course Michel Foucault, 'Nietzsche, Genealogy, History', in Paul Rabinow (ed.), *The Foucault Reader* (New York: Pantheon Books, 1984), 76–100.

[12] These details of Ekman's life and career are taken from the most detailed of his autobiographical texts: Paul Ekman, 'A Life's Pursuit', in Thomas A. Sebeok and Jean Umiker-Sebeok (eds), *The Semiotic Web 1986* (Berlin: Mouton de Gruyter, 1987), 3–45.

[13] Ekman, 'A Life's Pursuit', 16, 10.

[14] Ruth Leys, 'How Did Fear Become a Scientific Object and What Kind of Object Is It?', *Representations*, 110 (2010), 66–104, here 69.

Emotions are treated as part of a stimulus-response sequence, whereby we humans respond to stimuli in ways which today quite probably do not enhance our chances of survival, but which did improve those of our forefathers. This model allows no room for other narratives, such as: I run from a snake because that is what I like to do; or because I was bitten by a snake as a child; or because it reminds me of the penis of the uncle who raped me when I was a little girl; or, indeed, I do not run away from the snake because I love reptiles. Ruth Leys calls this position 'non-intentionalist'. The contrary, intentionalist position includes very different approaches such as that of psychoanalysis, in which objects such as the snake do not automatically trigger the same reaction in everyone, but instead variable responses shaped by the meanings formed in an individual's biography; or that of cognitive psychology, in which emphasis is placed upon the moment of appraisal. For the time being, we can say that, for Leys, intentionalism and non-intentionalism are the two poles around which later twentieth-century psychological research into emotions has organized itself.[15] Ekman adopted Tomkins's hypothesis, and then began to consider the kind of experimental design that might confirm it. First of all, he showed experimental subjects photographs that Tomkins had made of facial expressions, and asked them to ascribe a selection of feelings to the emotions there depicted. Since these ascriptions for the most part agreed with each other, Ekman believed that this constituted initial proof of the hypothesis of universalism.[16]

Next, Ekman prepared his own set of photographs showing expressions of human emotions. For this, he photographed experimental subjects who had been asked to show a particular emotion. Then, he says, 'photographs were selected from over 3000 pictures to obtain those which showed only the pure display of a single affect'—as Ruth Leys observed, this was a highly dubious procedure, given that emotions made on command were treated as authentic and not simulated. Moreover, the process of picking out 'pure' and universal basic emotions was not subject to any control, but instead left entirely to the intuition of Ekman and his

[15] Leys, 'How Did Fear Become a Scientific Object and What Kind of Object Is It?', 69, 88–9.

[16] It is not clear how far Ekman here modelled himself on Darwin, who showed eleven photographs, chosen from more than five dozen taken by the physiologist Duchenne de Boulogne, to twenty-four visitors to his home, asking them to ascribe to each photograph a particular emotion. The outcome of this domestic experiment was that his visitors only agreed on a few emotions such as pleasure, sadness, and fear, while opinions on other photographs diverged greatly. Darwin, who was in regular correspondence with Duchenne, thought that this confirmed his scepticism of Duchenne's thesis that individual muscles controlled over sixty different facial expressions. The connection between Darwin and Duchenne has been well known for many years, and is summarized in Leys, 'How Did Fear Become a Scientific Object and What Kind of Object Is It?', 70–5. Not until 2010 were the details of Darwin's domestic experiments made known, archival research showing that shortly after receiving Duchenne's photographs he scribbled on the back: 'I don't believe this. This isn't true.' See Peter J. Snyder et al., 'Charles Darwin's Emotional Expression "Experiment" and his Contribution to Modern Neuropharmacology', *Journal of the History of the Neurosciences*, 19/2 (2010), 158–70; Ferris Jabr, 'The Evolution of Emotion: Charles Darwin's Little-Known Psychology Experiment', *Scientific American Observations Blog* (24 May 2010) <http://blogs.scientificamerican.com/observations/2010/05/24/the-evolution-of-emotion-charles-darwins-little-known-psychology-experiment> accessed 6 March 2014.

colleagues.[17] A third point that can be added here is that this collection of several thousand photographs did not form a representative spectrum of facial emotional expression, insofar as the emotions were simulated on an uttered command. It must be pointed out that the command reduces a complex and multifaceted emotional reality to one of several emotion words. Ekman's use of language thus attests to the overly reductionist nature of the experiment. The developmental psychologist Jerome Kagan has suggested that we should 'agree to a moratorium on the use of single words, such as *fear* . . . and write about emotional processes with full sentences rather than ambiguous, naked concepts', summarizing his own work on emotion going back sixty years.[18] Applied to Ekman's procedures, this poses the question: If I ask a subject to express 'fear', how do I tell the difference between a soldier's fear of imminent death when staring down his enemy's gun-barrel, and the kind of self-induced fear experienced by someone riding through a ghost tunnel at the funfair, which could be called a 'thrill'?[19]

To prove the universal validity of these emotions, and thus their basic or 'primary' character, as Tomkins called them, Ekman and his team showed a selection of the 'emotions in their pure state' to university students across the world (see Fig. 13). Most such experiments use university students as their subjects, and in this case they took ninety-nine students from the USA, twenty-nine from Japan, forty from Brazil, plus thirty-two illiterate subjects from New Guinea, and fifteen from Borneo. The procedure was as follows:

> The observers' task was to select a word from a list of six affects for each picture. In the United States, Brazil, and Japan, slides were projected one at a time for 20 seconds each to groups of freshmen college students from whom the foreign-born had been eliminated. The photographic prints (13 by 18 cm) were shown one at a time to each observer in New Guinea and Borneo. The affect words were translated into the locally understood languages (Japanese, Portuguese, Neo-Melanesian Pidgin, Fore, and Bidayuh). There were no Neo-Melanesian Pidgin equivalents for disgust-contempt or surprise, and in these cases a phrase was submitted (looking at something which stinks, looking at something new).[20]

The outcome: all the test subjects ascribed the same descriptions of emotion to the same photographs. That is no real surprise, given the tautological manner in which the experiment was constructed. Each subject had been presented with a face which was supposed to represent a pure form of fear—if Ekman did not think it did so properly, then he excluded it—together with a list of six concepts of emotion, among which was the concept 'fear', which the subject had been asked to represent.

---

[17] Paul Ekman, E. Richard Sorenson, and Wallace V. Friesen, 'Pan-Cultural Elements in Facial Displays of Emotion', *Science*, 164/3875 (1969), 86–8, here 87. See also Leys, 'How Did Fear Become a Scientific Object and What Kind of Object Is It?', 75–9.

[18] Jerome Kagan, *What Is Emotion? History, Measures, and Meanings* (New Haven: Yale University Press, 2007), 216.

[19] I am not referring here to 'thrill' in the psychoanalytic sense of Michael Balint, *Thrills and Regressions* (London: Hogarth, 1959).

[20] Ekman, Sorenson, and Friesen, 'Pan-Cultural Elements in Facial Displays of Emotion', 87.

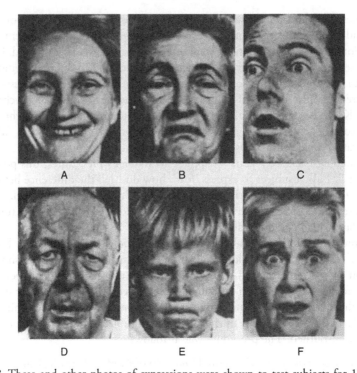

Fig. 13 These and other photos of expressions were shown to test subjects for 10 to 15 seconds one after another. The viewer had to choose between anger, fear, sadness, disgust, surprise, and pleasure, and decide which term best fitted each picture. The transcultural finding is that A shows pleasure, B disgust, C surprise, D sadness, E anger, and F fear.

Source: Paul Ekman, 'Afterword: Universality of Emotional Expression? A Personal History of the Dispute', in Charles Darwin, *The Expression of the Emotions in Man and Animals* (3rd edn, New York: Oxford University Press, 1998), 363–93, here 376 © Paul Ekman Group, LLC.

It was not long before there was criticism of Ekman's experimental design. Margaret Mead (1901–78), an anthropologist known to be a cultural relativist, emphasized the artificiality of the expressions which Ekman had collected, and attacked the argument that it 'is a culturally unmodified *expression* of emotion, rather than a simulation of emotion'.[21] All Ekman had demonstrated was that, 'Given a limited range of semantically designated emotions—grief, happiness, anger, disgust, it is possible to persuade members of different cultures to produce simulations which are mutually intelligible between these cultures.'[22] To reinforce this idea, her review was illustrated with theatre masks expressing different feelings. This detailed criticism was combined with a general attack on experimental

[21] Margaret Mead, 'Margaret Mead Calls "Discipline-Centric" Approach to Research an "Example of the Appalling State of the Human Sciences"', review of Paul Ekman (ed.), *Darwin and Facial Expression: A Century of Research in Review* (New York: Academic Press, 1973), in *Journal of Communication*, 25/1 (1975), 209–13, here 212, emphasis in original.

[22] Mead, 'Margaret Mead Calls "Discipline-Centric" Approach to Research', 212.

psychology as practised by Ekman, in which 'members of each discipline treat their specialized approach as the only approach'.[23] Mead's former husband, Gregory Bateson (1904–80), an anthropologist and cybernetics specialist, emphasized the social and communicative functions of facial emotional expression. He argued that these did not convey in a direct and unfiltered manner true emotions of the kind that Ekman saw, but served instead to communicate with other people, and so were subject to all the various influences to which communication is subject—intentional, volition, context. There was also criticism from Ray Birdwhistell (1918–94), a linguist and anthropologist who shared a great deal with Mead and Bateson. He had himself carried out anthropological fieldwork on the expression of emotion, and had come to the conclusion that there were no culturally-universal facial expressions, but a very great cultural diversity in the non-verbal communication of emotion. When Ekman's first studies appeared, Birdwhistell maintained that Ekman had not in fact been dealing with uncontaminated cultures: the aboriginals in the New Guinea rain forest were simply imitating John Wayne and Charlie Chaplin, whose films they had seen.[24]

To rebut such criticism, Ekman extended his experiment to more cultures, among which in particular there was one more culture that was non-Western and lacked a written language: the Dani in Western New Guinea, which is today part of Indonesia. Karl G. Heider was preparing for another field study of these people at the beginning of the 1970s, and he expressed his willingness to conduct a study based upon a modification of Ekman's methods. Rather than reading out a list of supposedly basic emotions translated into the local language and ascribing emotion to image, 'a translator told a story and the New Guinean picked the expression which fitted the story' (see Fig. 14).[25]

According to Ekman, Heider started off thinking that Ekman's results could not be confirmed, since the Dani had no corresponding terms that might relate to the English concepts which expressed supposedly universal basic emotions. Ekman thought that this initially negative predisposition was resounding proof of the reliability of Heider's results, which almost exactly matched those of Ekman. Subsequently, Ekman suggested that

> The one exception was that the Dani did not differentiate between anger and disgust expressions, although they did distinguish these from all the other emotions. Heider had predicted this finding, as he had observed that the Dani avoid expression of anger and often mask it with disgust.[26]

Likewise in retrospect, Ekman noted the absence of any empirical proof for display rules, the overlaying of 'true' basic emotions by socially standardized modes of expression. This involved the reconciliation of nature (basic emotion) and culture (display rule). Ekman and his team thought up the following experiment: American and Japanese college students would be shown film of the circumcision of

[23] Mead, 'Margaret Mead Calls "Discipline-Centric" Approach to Research', 210.
[24] The positions of Bateson and Birdwhistell are here described as in Ekman, 'Afterword', 364–77.
[25] Ekman, 'Afterword', 383. The psychologist Carroll Izard carried out similar experiments; Ekman, 'Afterword', 375.
[26] Ekman, 'Afterword', 383.

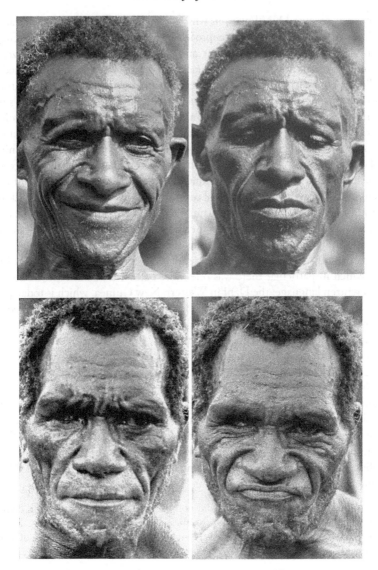

Fig. 14 The instructions were to show how your face would look if you were the person in the story. A = your friend has come and you are happy. B = your child has died. C = you are angry and about to fight. D = you see a dead pig that has been lying there a long time.

Source: Paul Ekman, 'Afterword: Universality of Emotional Expression? A Personal History of the Dispute', in Charles Darwin, *The Expression of the Emotions in Man and Animals* (3rd edn, New York: Oxford University Press, 1998), 363–.93, here 380 © Paul Ekman Group, LLC.

Australian aboriginal youths, together with film of surgical procedures; all of these films would be disturbing and stressful.[27] Test subjects would be shown these films

---

[27] Ekman, 'Afterword', 384.

individually, and covertly filmed; as a control, they would also be filmed while viewing 'neutral' films that did not provoke stress. The images recorded in this way would then be shown to a second group of subjects, each group belonging to a third culture. Both groups concluded that Japanese and American students showed the same emotional reaction at the same points—even the supposedly 'inscrutable Orientals', the Japanese students who, according to the usual stereotype, masked their feelings, which had been the precise reason for selecting Japanese students as a contrasting culture for the experiment.

The covert recordings were then studied using FAST (Facial Action Scoring Technique; later known as FACS, Facial Action Coding System), the method developed and patented by Ekman and his closest colleague Wallace V. Friesen for the analysis of facial muscle movements. This again confirmed the result that the same basic emotions could be detected beneath the acculturated surface.[28] Finally, the experiment was repeated, the test subject being first filmed individually with a hidden camera while watching 'stressful' films, and then a second time in the presence of an 'authority figure' from his or her own culture—in fact, a doctoral student dressed in surgical whites. This second experiment revealed that the test subjects showed 'entirely different facial expressions. The Japanese showed more smiling than the Americans to mask their negative emotional expressions.'[29] Culture did therefore play a role, although nature remained basic, Ekman concluding that 'It is never a question only of nature or only of nurture.'[30]

Ekman's thesis attracted ever greater support among psychologists, and his increasing prestige was crowned at the beginning of the 1980s by his replacing Birdwhistell as advisor to the National Institute of Mental Health on research proposals relating to non-verbal communication. 'Ekman's triumph over Birdwhistell', wrote Leys, 'a triumph at once methodological, intellectual, and institutional—sealed the destiny of emotion research in the United States for the next several decades.'[31] Ekman's own retrospective judgement was that this represented a triumph of science over speculation, of objectivity over subjectivity, of empirically-based experimental psychology over the hermeneutic interpretations of an anthropology based upon participant observation, defining the status of the observer as standing both within and without observed human behaviour.[32] Leys's own perspective was that of a historian of science, and what she saw here was the triumph of the suggestive power of photographic and filmic images over honest and serious science; a triumph of convenience, since the experiments could easily be repeated using a set of the facial photographs available online from Ekman's firm; a triumph of strategic action, and a victory ending in the successful marginalization of dissenting voices. In particular, it was a victory of emotion as an imagined category of a 'hard' universal physicality, itself related to a growing need on the part

---

[28] For this experiment see Ekman, 'Afterword', 381.
[29] Ekman, 'Afterword', 385.   [30] Ekman, 'Afterword', 393.
[31] Leys, 'How Did Fear Become a Scientific Object and What Kind of Object Is It?', 97 n. 49.
[32] Ekman, 'Afterword', 365–6, 372–3.

of other sciences for such a category.[33] As we shall see, from the 1990s, and especially in the early 2000s, it became more common in the human sciences to adopt Ekman's conception of emotion and its neurobiological offshoots.

It is because of this assimilation of Ekman's work by the human sciences that so much space here is devoted to his research. In the life sciences, Ekman has in many respects been superseded by the neurosciences; the play of emotions is now sought in the brain, not in the face.[34]

From the standpoint of the natural sciences, and according to the principles of scientific procedure and verity, Ekman's research is bankrupt. More exactly: empirical proof for his hypotheses could be said to be very weak, leaving open the possibility that someone, somewhere, could produce other evidence that would still confirm the hypotheses. Let us recapitulate the reasons for this conclusion:

1. The experimental construction using photographs of emotional states is circular. First of all, emotional complexity is reduced through selecting concepts denoting basic emotions. It is by no means clear that these concepts do actually coincide with basic emotions rather than with other emotions, which are however excluded a priori on the grounds that they are 'more complex'. It is also not evident why only English emotional concepts are employed, and why no attempt was made to extract basic emotions using other languages. Secondly, test subjects were asked to mimic through facial expression the selected, and supposedly basic, English emotional concepts. Third, using FAST, the photos were sorted, and only those images were chosen which seemed to correspond to the basic emotions that had been verbally requested. But FAST had been developed using the original, posed photographs. Searching for 'pure' photos with FAST therefore involved circularity. Finally, other test subjects were shown the selected photographs displaying what were supposed to be basic emotions, and were then asked to assign them to the same set of concepts that had been originally used in their production. Even with such a tautological experimental design, no complete match between concepts and expression was established when the experiment was carried out in the American culture from which it originated. And another thing: did you, the reader, correctly identify the emotions in the Ekman faces at the beginning of this chapter? Give it a try! The picture at the top is supposed to show disgust; the one in the middle sadness; and the one at the bottom anger. As soon as one leaves the USA, agreement declines. Some

---

[33] On Ekman and the power of images see Anne Schmidt, 'Showing Emotions, Reading Emotions', in Ute Frevert et al., *Emotional Lexicons: Continuity and Change in the Vocabulary of Feeling 1700–2000* (Oxford: Oxford University Press, 2014), 62–90.

[34] For instance, consider just one neurobiological version of the theory of basic emotions: Jaak Panksepp and Lucy Biven, *The Archaeology of Mind: Neuroevolutionary Origins of Human Emotions* (New York: Norton, 2012). The publisher's blurb states that 'Jaak Panksepp's lifework has revealed that all mammalian brains are composed of seven common emotional systems—seeking, lust, rage, fear, care, grief, and play. This book provides an easy-to-understand explanation of the way in which these common systems guide emotional life in all mammals, including humans.'

allegedly basic emotions are simply not registered, there being non-American cultures that do not have a concept—or anything close to one—for a particular basic emotion.

2. Experiments conducted in cultures without a written language were based upon narration—stories that were made up about the photographs—and the translation of these narratives from English into the local language and then back into English. Both narration and translation weaken the link between image and emotion.

3. There are no longer any cultures that are truly untouched. If an Ekman experiment were conducted in an untouched culture, then a second could not take place, since the culture would no longer be untouched. This infringes on the scientific principle of the replicability of experiments.

4. There is no explanation of why the face, and only the face, has been deemed to express a particular set of supposedly basic emotions. Ekman's choice of the face is part of a long tradition going back to Aristotelian ideas of facial expression, and on through Le Brun's *Méthode pour apprendre à dessiner les passions* (1668) and Lavater's writings on physiognomy, to Darwin and Duchenne's photographs.[35] This tradition is also indebted to the demands of experimental psychology, its epistemology and technical possibilities. The selection of one physical site for emotions has changed over time: this much is clear from the way that today, after the advent of brain-imaging techniques in the 1990s, it is the brain that is the privileged site when conducting experimental psychological research on emotions. It was demonstrated in Chapter Two that there are different answers, varying from culture to culture, to the question of where exactly emotions are located in the body. We saw that *rasa* theory and Indian dance theatre did not presume that one looked to the face for the fullest emotional authenticity; instead the face was deliberately employed for theatrical effect. There are also forms of expression of emotion that are entirely neglected by our fixation on image and sight: smell is for instance never mentioned at all in these experiments, despite the fact that in many cultures fear, for instance, is linked to sweating, and so has an olfactory component.

5. As Ruth Leys has demonstrated, Ekman's use of photographs of emotional states is riven by an internal contradiction between authenticity and simulation. On the one hand, Ekman criticized earlier studies on the facial expression of emotion for using posed photographs. He considered this to be inauthentic, devaluing the photographs used. But then he shifted his ground, and claimed that photographs that are most likely to have been posed are the purest and most authentic.[36]

---

[35] See Leys, 'How Did Fear Become a Scientific Object and What Kind of Object Is It?'; Alan J. Fridlund, *Human Facial Expression: An Evolutionary View* (San Diego, CA: Academic Press, 1994).
[36] Leys, 'How Did Fear Become a Scientific Object and What Kind of Object Is It?', 77–8.

6. The idea that emotions can be captured photographically at the instant of the purest expression presupposes that everything happens instantaneously. Yet even the most modern photographic apparatus has a slight delay when taking a photo, partly to do with the apparatus itself, and partly because a finger has to press a button to release the shutter. The idea that everything can be captured in real time is therefore chimerical. This hesitation is problematic for an experimental model which assumes that the most natural reaction will immediately follow a given stimulus, without any hesitation; that a sudden verbal command (for example, fear!) will yield an emotion least contaminated by a display rule.

7. Leys has also examined the contradiction between how one feels when alone and unobserved, and how one feels in the presence of an authority figure and observed. To start with, the original photographs were made with a subject conscious of the presence of the photographer. Even when Ekman took his photographs and shot footage in New Guinea, those being filmed and photographed were always conscious of the presence of Ekman as a photographer and film-maker. However, Ekman concedes that the ideal circumstance for the realization of 'genuine' facial expressions of feeling is to be alone, and under the impression that one is unobserved. It was for this reason that the experiments were continued using a hidden camera.[37]

8. The comparative study of American and Japanese students using a hidden camera was decisive for Ekman's triumph. Many critics of the photographic experiments were silenced by this. However, during the 1990s the study was criticized in detail by Alan Fridlund, a renegade member of Ekman's laboratory. The following points of criticism carried most weight: first of all, Fridlund criticized Ekman's assumption that the viewing of films in a laboratory context was in any way comparable with how the test subjects felt when alone in their own home. Just because the test subject is physically alone, argued Fridlund, does not at all mean that they are psychologically alone, because the person directing the experiment is always an implicit public, and the lab itself is the stage on which an experiment plays out.[38] Secondly, Fridlund pointed out that when the Japanese subjects were shown films in the company of someone supposed to be an authority figure, they did not react unemotionally because of display rules, but rather because of the general demands of politeness in Japanese society, directing their attention to the other person present and not to the screen. Thirdly, Fridlund criticized the assumption in Ekman's experimental design that in the course of the experiment it was only the face that expressed emotion. This was demonstrably not the case, since facial muscles are also used to create speech. The FAST method did not allow for any distinction between movements of facial

---

[37] Leys, 'How Did Fear Become a Scientific Object and What Kind of Object Is It?', 74–5.
[38] Fridlund, *Human Facial Expression*, 291.

muscles in order to express emotion and movements linked to the articulation of speech. This contaminated the results.[39]

Taken together, the internal contradictions and methodological problems of Ekman's theory of emotion are very striking. I repeat: most of the criticism of Ekman does not come from the humanities; instead, the deficiencies of the basic emotion approach have been demonstrated by psychologists using the standard criteria of experimental psychology.[40]

Ekman sceptics have increasingly formed networks and become institutionalized; a clear sign of the latter trend is the foundation in 2009 of the journal *Emotion Review* by the well-known critics of Ekman, Lisa Feldman Barrett and James Russell—this is a journal which also publishes articles on the history of emotions. All the same, Ekman has gained in popularity in other areas of academia, as well as in politics and popular culture. American politics has undergone a tectonic shift since 9/11, being dominated by a virulent debate on national security. If before 9/11 these debates followed fairly predictable paths that could be generally called 'democratic', arguments being exchanged in public and compromises forged, the debate after 9/11 has taken a turn in which differences of opinion seem no longer tolerable, focused on a vision of total, rather than relative, security. There are clear parallels between the logic of this new era and the logic of Ekman's laboratory experiments: Ekman's approach assumes that the emotions of others can be unambiguously read from their faces, quite independent of the individual person who feels such emotions, quite independent of what they feel, and quite independent of the way in which they manage and guide what they feel, the conscious or unconscious influence they assume over their own emotions.

Given all this, it is no real surprise that after 9/11 Ekman became the godfather of the anti-terror programme SPOT (Screening Passengers by Observational Techniques). After a test phase ending in 2004, there were by the beginning of 2012 SPOT machines installed at 161 American airports. These machines pick up 'micro-expressions' of the emotion that shows in the face, and are used to select those in queues who are thought to have something to hide, or who lie.[41] Ekman wrote in an article that critics of the SPOT programme

> have said that it [SPOT] is an unnecessary invasion of privacy, based on an untested method of observation, that is unlikely to yield much in the way of red-handed terrorists set on blowing up a plane or flying it into a building, but would violate fliers' civil rights. I disagree. I've participated in four decades' worth of research into deception and demeanor, and I know that researchers have amassed enough knowledge

---

[39] Fridlund, *Human Facial Expression*, 285–93.

[40] See the most recent criticism of Ekman: Rachael E. Jack et al., 'Facial Expressions of Emotion Are Not Culturally Universal', *Proceedings of the National Academy of Sciences*, 109/19 (2012), 7241–4.

[41] See Benjamin Carlson, 'The Daily Exclusive: Facing Reality', *The Daily* (27 May 2012) [daily news application] <http://www.thedaily.com/page/2012/05/27/052712-news-tsa-behavior-detection-1-3> accessed 2 August 2012 (dead link; *The Daily* ceased operations on 15 December 2012); Ben Buchwalter, 'Forget Your "Junk": The TSA Wants to Feel Up your Mind', *Mother Jones* (2 February 2011) <http://www.motherjones.com/politics/2011/02/tsa-spot-scan-paul-ekman> accessed 7 March 2014.

about how someone who is lying looks and behaves that it would be negligent not to use it in the search for terrorists. Along with luggage checks, radar screening, bomb-sniffing dogs and the rest of our security arsenal, observational techniques can help reduce risks—and potentially prevent another deadly assault like the attacks of Sept. 11, 2001.[42]

Certainty in the laboratory is obtained by an epistemology specific to experimental psychology: the reduction of reality to a small number of dependent and independent variables, securing internal validity by the proven causal connection of two variables, external validity by the fact that results can be generalized, and also ecological validity, that outside the laboratory in a natural environment the results would be the same. These are the rules governing experimental psychology, and the results gained in this way may well be true enough in the very limited domains where they might have some application. But external validity is crucial: it is very dangerous to export laboratory practices into the chaos of practical politics in general, and especially into those dominated by security discourse, for here there is no way of creating the kinds of boundaries the natural sciences require. However seductive the certainty manufactured in a laboratory might be, it cannot be reproduced in the world of security policy. Neither SPOT, nor the five levels of alerts used by the Department of Homeland Security (which represent the threat level as a particular colour), will ever be capable of creating absolute security—all that they can do is present the *promise* of absolute security.

The creation of this promise eats up large amounts of public money that could be used for other purposes. Whether it is worth spending so much money on SPOT is a question increasingly raised in the USA, and related to the demand that the debate on national security be once more made answerable to the logic of politics, rather than the logic of security discourse. Resistance has developed in various political circles and among a new expert culture. The former strip down pseudo-scientific security rhetoric in the tradition of the Enlightenment, while the latter maintain that cost-benefit calculations—does the high cost of preventing terrorism justify its relative use?—must be used and applied.[43]

Recently, transfer from the logic of the laboratory to the field of politics has become less of a one-way street, and more like a mutual process of exchange. Ekman now cloaks his own research in the logic of security, claiming that he will no longer publish in specialist journals because he might reveal state secrets.[44] Such scientific opacity is combined with increasingly public and popular visibility. *Lie to Me* is just the most recent scene in a long sequence of media appearances and

[42] Paul Ekman, 'How to Spot a Terrorist on the Fly', *Washington Post* (29 October 2006), B03. The first critical assessment of SPOT is by Sharon Weinberger, 'Intent to Deceive? Can the Science of Deception Detection Help to Catch Terrorists?', *Nature*, 465/7297 (2010), 412–15.

[43] Peter N. Stearns, *American Fear: The Causes and Consequences of High Anxiety* (London: Routledge, 2006); Corey Robin, *Fear: The History of a Political Idea* (Oxford: Oxford University Press, 2004); Marc Siegel, *False Alarm: The Truth about the Epidemic of Fear* (Hoboken, NJ: John Wiley & Sons, 2005); Cass R. Sunstein, *Laws of Fear: Beyond the Precautionary Principle* (Cambridge: Cambridge University Press, 2005).

[44] Weinberger, 'Intent to Deceive?', 413.

interviews. From his first impression of Bill Clinton during the presidential campaign of 1992 ('This is a guy who wants to be caught with his hand in the cookie jar, and have us love him for it anyway'), to the claim that he could see in Clinton's face that he was lying at a 1998 press conference when he denied having had any relationship with Monica Lewinsky; and more recently, co-authoring a feel-good self-help guide with the Dalai Lama.[45]

2 ROAD MAP FOR CHAPTER THREE

As might by now be clear from these introductory remarks, this third chapter pursues a particular idea. It has a mission. It seeks to warn Clio of the dangers of following the path of other human sciences and thoughtlessly borrowing from experimental psychology, especially in its neuroscientific incarnation. The tone will therefore become rather more shrill than hitherto, but this is I think justified by the way in which other human sciences have adopted the findings of experimental psychology. All the same, the principle formulated in the Introduction to this book retains its validity: the discipline of history has to remain as open as possible and admit of no taboos in dealing with neighbouring disciplines, including the life sciences.

So where are we headed? First of all, I will shed some light on Darwin's psychology of emotion. Then we will move back to the theological origins of the psychological study of emotion, then shift chronologically forwards, encountering along the way William James (1842–1910), Carl Lange (1834–1900), and Wilhelm Wundt (1832–1920). Following that are sections on laboratory practice around the turn of the century, the influence of social hierarchies on the spatial conception of the brain, and the absence of a theory of emotion in the work of Freud. I will then discuss the 'emotional boom' in psychology since the 1960s, introducing influential paradigms such as Schachter and Singer's approach and the appraisal school. After that I deal with the neuroscience boom and brain-imaging techniques from the 1990s onwards. Three central neuroscientific hypotheses will then be subjected to critical examination: LeDoux's two paths of fear, Damasio's Somatic Marker Hypothesis, and Rizzolatti's, Gallese's, and Iacoboni's mirror neurons, together with their application in the human and social sciences. In conclusion I will sketch the emergence of a loose coalition called the 'critical neurosciences', including not only neuroscientists, but also representatives from the human and social sciences, all of whom have moved beyond the contrast of social constructivism to universalism.

---

[45] For Ekman's comment about the cookie jar: Malcolm Gladwell, 'The Naked Face: Can You Read People's Thoughts just by Looking at them?', *New Yorker* (5 August 2002), 38–49, here 43. On Ekman and the Lewinsky scandal, Robin Marantz Henig, 'Looking for the Lie', *New York Times Magazine* (5 February 2006), 47–53, 76, 80. The book written with the Dalai Lama: Paul Ekman (ed.), *Emotional Awareness: Overcoming the Obstacles to Psychological Balance and Compassion: A Conversation between The Dalai Lama and Paul Ekman* (New York: Times Books, Henry Holt and Co., 2008).

3 CHARLES DARWIN'S *THE EXPRESSION OF THE EMOTIONS IN MAN AND ANIMALS* (1872), OR, HOW ONE BOOK BECAME A BATTLEFIELD BETWEEN SOCIAL CONSTRUCTIVISTS AND UNIVERSALISTS

Darwin's *The Expression of the Emotions in Man and Animals* was published in 1872 in both English and German, and later became one of the most important sites where the conflict between social constructivists like Margaret Mead and universalists such as Paul Ekman was fought out. Each camp repeatedly sought interpretative advantage over the other in dealing with 'the most important book on emotions yet written', as a psychology textbook put it.[46] In 1955, Mead published an edition for which she wrote an introduction. Ekman succeeded in being appointed editor of the 1972 centenary edition, whose appearance was delayed until 1973.[47] In 1998, Ekman published a revised third edition of *The Expression of the Emotions in Man and Animals*, which marked the triumph of his approach: it was the most editorialized version ever, Ekman inserting whole paragraphs into the original edition in square brackets where he gave his opinion about where Darwin was on the right track, where he had erred, where Ekman confirmed Darwin, where Darwin confirmed Ekman, and where he did not. In addition, Ekman wrote an afterword which was a partisan blow-by-blow account of his battles with Mead, Bateson, and Birdwhistell, all recounted from the victor's perspective—that of Ekman.

Let us try to unravel this argument over the interpretation of Darwin's book, starting with its most recent phase: from Ekman's victorious perspective. Ekman says that Mead's 1955 edition distorts Darwin's book almost to the point of making it unrecognizable:

> In a 1955 edition of *Expression*... prepared by Margaret Mead, she included pictures from a conference on kinesics, showing Birdwhistell, herself and others who were drawn to this approach. In her introduction to this edition, Mead did not say anything of Darwin's proposal that expressions are universal, nor did she mention the word 'emotion'. Instead she praised Birdwhistell's new science of kinesics, and recommended substituting the term 'communication' for Darwin's term 'expression'. I wonder how Darwin would have felt had he known that his book was introduced by a cultural relativist who had included in his book pictures of those most opposed to his theory of emotional expressions.[48]

In other words: according to Ekman, the cultural relativist Mead makes out the universalist Darwin to be a fellow cultural relativist. Ekman maintained that his

---

[46] Dacher Keltner, Keith Oatley, and Jennifer M. Jenkins, *Understanding Emotions* (3rd edn, Hoboken, NJ: Wiley, 2014), 5.

[47] The edition was published as Paul Ekman (ed.), *Darwin and Facial Expression: A Century of Research in Review* (New York: Academic Press, 1973). The delay was caused by the failure of Silvan S. Tomkins to provide a promised supplementary chapter on his own theory of emotion; Paul Ekman, 'Preface to New Edition', in Paul Ekman (ed.), *Darwin and Facial Expression: A Century of Research in Review* (Los Altos, CA: Malor Books, 2006), vii–ix, here vii.

[48] Ekman, 'Afterword', 370.

1973 anniversary edition had put a stop to this annexationist propaganda, even though at the time Mead was a powerful Goliath and he but a weedy, if fearless, David. Thanks to his untiring scientific struggle over the following twenty-five years, his own interpretation of Darwin—the one true interpretation—had finally triumphed over all others preceding it. The 1998 edition was framed by Ekman's introduction and afterword, his detailed additional comments setting in stone the sole valid reading of the text for all time.

Some of Ekman's additions to this edition need to be savoured. Here are two very striking examples, retaining the format of the original with Ekman's commentary in square brackets:

> There is another obscure point, namely, whether the sounds which are produced under various states of the mind determine the shape of the mouth, or whether its shape is not determined by independent causes, and the sound thus modified. When young infants cry they open their mouths widely, and this, no doubt, is necessary for pouring forth a full volume of sound; but the mouth then assumes, from a quite distinct cause, an almost quadrangular shape, depending, as will hereafter be explained, on the firm closing of the eyelids, and consequent drawing up of the upper lip. How far the square shape of the mouth modifies the wailing or crying sound, I am not prepared to say; but we know from the researches of Helmholtz and others that the form of the cavity of the mouth and lips determines the nature and pitch of the vowel sounds which are produced.
>
> [Scherer and I did some preliminary work in which I tried to emit a continuous sound while changing the contraction of different muscles around my mouth. Scherer's analysis of the vocalizations I produced showed that tensing different parts of the muscle which orbits the mouth (*orbicularis oris*) had an appreciable effect on the power spectrum. Regrettably, we did not continue or publish that work.][49]

Ekman here tries to confirm one of Darwin's theses by describing one of his own experiments. We can wonder whether he did either Darwin or himself a favour in describing a casual experiment directed by a psychologist friend (Scherer) in which the subject was Ekman himself, the results never being published and hard to replicate. In the second example Ekman corrects Lamarckian ideas about the inheritance of acquired characteristics that, somewhat paradoxically, crop up in Darwin's book, even though Darwin opposed Lamarck's project:

> A start from a sudden noise, when the stimulus is conveyed through the auditory nerves, is always accompanied in grown-up persons by the winking of the eyelids. I observed, however, that though my infants started at sudden sounds, when under a fortnight old, they certainly did not always wink their eyes, and I believe never did so. The start of an older infant apparently represents a vague catching hold of something to prevent falling. I shook a pasteboard box close before the eyes of one of my infants, when 114 days old, and it did not in the least wink; but when I put a few comfits into the box, holding it in the same position as before, and rattled them, the child blinked its eyes violently every time, and started a little. It was obviously impossible that a carefully-guarded infant could have learnt by experience that a rattling sound near its eyes indicated danger to them. But such experience will have been slowly gained at a

---

[49] Darwin, *Expression of the Emotions in Man and Animals*, 96.

later age during a long series of generations; and from what we know of inheritance, there is nothing improbable in the transmission of a habit to the offspring at an earlier age than that at which it was first acquired by the parents.

[This is an especially blatant example of how completely Darwin accepted the now discredited idea of the inheritance of acquired characteristics. Habits learned by parents cannot be inherited by their offspring.][50]

There is a strategy at work here: Ekman is able to assume the mantle of detached and balanced objectivity by inserting comments that are not uniformly positive, but rather criticize and correct from a standpoint one hundred years after the fact, during which time Darwin's many hypotheses could be tested. Further, he presents himself as a young scientist loyal to the values of empiricism and truth, bravely defying the 'soft' and politically established giants (Mead, Bateson) and their puppet (Birdwhistell). Critics are mentioned in passing, as scientific fairness requires, but presented as unrelated to Ekman's experiments. For example, he writes of Alan Fridlund, a former member of his own laboratory but more recently a renegade:

In the last five years, however, the argument against Darwin's *Expression* has been renewed. The American psychologist Alan Fridlund attacked Darwin for not emphasizing that expressions were selected because of their communicative value.... Fridlund has echoed the position of Bateson and some ethologists who claim that it is not useful to think of expressions in terms of emotion, but only as communicative signals ...I have explained why this is a false dichotomy.[51]

Not a word about Fridlund's inside knowledge—he worked alongside Ekman for years and published joint work—and a crude dismissal of Fridlund's solid criticism.

Another theme relevant to Ekman takes us back to the question upon which Chapter Two turned: *e pluribus unum* or *e pluribus plures*? The identification of culturally universal emotions prompted vigorous criticism from the very first, sometimes presented in very drastic from. At one conference an anthropologist shouted Ekman down and dismissed his research as 'fascist'.[52] Cultural relativists like Mead and Bateson did observe the usual academic niceties, but were substantively just as hard on Ekman. Since they were old enough to have witnessed the instrumentalization of eugenics during the period of National Socialism, they could well see the dangers inherent in the postulation of universal human standards, deviations from which by, for example, the disabled, led to marginalization, and potentially to pathologization and criminalization. It seems to me that they kept in mind the catastrophic history of the first half of the twentieth century in considering it socially and politically desirable that differences should not be made the grounds for unequal treatment. This was, if you like, a kind of weak universalism, understood as the sum of its parts. At the same time Mead, Bateson, and their allies saw in the way Ekman's research led to universalistic conclusions a threat to American reforms of the 1960s, which all presupposed the plasticity of disadvantaged

---

[50] Darwin, *Expression of the Emotions in Man and Animals*, 44–5.
[51] Ekman, 'Afterword', 389.   [52] Ekman, 'A Life's Pursuit', 18.

social groups and their capacity for change. 'That's what they are like, the African Americans, you can't change that'—this poisonous universal argument seemed to them to run through Ekman's work as well. But advocates of cultural hierarchy also felt themselves under attack. Not only white racists, who had since the time of Darwin opposed the idea that humans of all colours and cultures felt the same; extremist and separatist elements of the civil rights' movement reacted in the same way. Ekman recalls being attacked during the later 1960s 'by a Black radical activist' who accused him 'of being racist for claiming that Black facial expressions of emotion were no different from white expressions'.[53]

Ekman has always maintained that he was motivated from the very beginning by the anti-racist and universalist impetus of the civil rights movement—arguing that insofar as his research had political implications, they involved unity and fraternity.[54] Ultimately he sought to emphasize Darwin's anti-racism, which was he thought far ahead of its time. We can find in the 1998 edition of *The Expression of the Emotions in Man and Animals* the following passage, again with Ekman's comments in square brackets:

> The various species and genera of monkeys express their feelings in many different ways; and this fact is interesting, as in some degree bearing on the question, whether the so-called races of man should be ranked as distinct species or varieties; for, as we shall see in the following chapters, the different races of man express their emotions and sensations with remarkable uniformity throughout the world.
>
> [In Darwin's time some who claimed that Caucasians were superior to other races had proposed that the different races had descended not from one but from different progenitors—the Caucasians from more advanced progenitors than the negroid race. Darwin's evidence that the expression of emotions is the same for all mankind was strong evidence for the opposite view—that all human beings have common progenitors—challenging the opinion that any race is superior to another. Nevertheless, the American historian Frederick Burkhardt pointed out that Darwin does speak of 'higher' and 'lower' races in *Descent of Man*.][55]

This brings us back to Darwin's book, and the question of whose interpretation is more plausible: Mead's or Ekman's? What is this book about? What explains its remarkable adaptability, being taken up by different disciplines and diametrically opposed positions? On Darwin's own account, he had formed the original idea for the book in 1840, when his first child was born:

> I attended to this point in my first-born infant, who could not have learnt any thing by associating with other children, and I was convinced that he understood a smile and received pleasure from seeing one, answering it by another, at much too early an age to have learnt anything by experience.[56]

It was only later that Darwin began to examine emotions as a scientist, and started collecting data. He had originally intended that this work would find a place in his

[53] Ekman, 'A Life's Pursuit', 19.   [54] Ekman, 'A Life's Pursuit', 18–19.
[55] Darwin, *Expression of the Emotions in Man and Animals*, 130–1.
[56] Darwin, *Expression of the Emotions in Man and Animals*, 353.

The Descent of Man, and Selection in Relation to Sex (1871), but that book became very large during the composition process, and so he excluded the material. After finishing it, he then wrote up *The Expression of the Emotions in Man and Animals* in just four months. Later, Ekman never tired of presenting himself as the rediscoverer of a forgotten key text by a brilliant prophet: the 1998 edition was described as the 'first definitive edition' of 'Darwin's forgotten masterwork'. Powerful voices supported this idea. Steven Pinker talked of Darwin's empirical research results, which had been more or less ignored for a century until Paul Ekman's investigation of the universal expression of emotion revived interest in it. But *The Expression* had never been ignored, but had rather even been a best-seller in the nineteenth century. Since its publication in 1872 it had been continually in print in English, and by 1976 there had been seventy-three editions.[57]

Darwin had collected material for years, and pursued an inductive method. The general conclusions that he arrived at inductively he placed at the front of his book. He starts with three principles, which at first sight are not necessarily related to emotion, but which in his view underlie all expressions of emotion. The first principle concerns 'the principle of serviceable associated habits', which states that

Certain complex actions are of direct or indirect service under certain states of the mind, in order to relieve or gratify certain sensations, desires, etc.; and whenever the same state of mind is induced, however feebly, there is a tendency through the force of habit and association for the same movements to be performed, though they may not then be of the least use.[58]

And so dogs, 'after voiding their excrement often make with all four feet a few scratches backwards, even on a bare stone pavement, as if for the purpose of covering up their excrement with earth'.[59] People scratch their heads if they are stuck for an idea, as though they could get hold of an idea in their brain, even if such a thing is a physiological impossibility.[60]

The second principle is the 'principle of antithesis'; it supposes that each emotion has its opposite. The friendly wagging of a dog's tail is explained by Darwin as the antithesis of the unmoving tail of a dog ready to attack. The cause of the wagging is not an external stimulus, but an opposed expression of emotion. Darwin explains the way people shrug their shoulders in the same way, linking it to

[57] See the well-meaning review of Ekman's 1998 edition by Eric Korn, 'How Far Down the Dusky Bosom?', *London Review of Books*, 20/23 (1998), 23–4. 'How Far Can Darwin Take Us? Adam Gopnik with Steven Pinker', *New York Public Library* (20 May 2009) <http://www.nypl.org/audiovideo/how-far-can-Darwin-take-us-adam-gopnik-steven-pinker> accessed 10 March 2014. Pinker talked of 'an empirical body of research that basically lay ignored for another century until Paul Ekman revived the study of the universalism of expression'. Testimony to the general success of *The Expression of the Emotions in Man and Animals* is provided by the fact that, only three years after its simultaneous publication in English and German, it was included in German home encyclopedias; Pascal Eitler, 'The "Origin" of Emotions: Sensitive Humans, Sensitive Animals', in Frevert et al., *Emotional Lexicons*, 91–117.
[58] Darwin, *Expression of the Emotions in Man and Animals*, 34.
[59] Darwin, *Expression of the Emotions in Man and Animals*, 50.
[60] This example has been changed slightly; see Darwin, *Expression of the Emotions in Man and Animals*, 37.

a questioning face, raised eyebrows, and an inclination of the head; this is the opposite of the aggressive pose in which the chin is thrust forward, the eyebrows furrowed, and the head held straight.[61]

The third principle is the 'direct action of the nervous system'. This is 'due to the constitution of the nervous system, independently from the first of the will, and independently to a certain extent of habit'.[62] Darwin means by this the diversion of excess nervous energy to the extremities and other parts of the body, which then express emotion. It is not only trembling from fear that illustrates this principle, but also this example:

> The most striking case, though a rare and abnormal one, which can be adduced to the direct influence of the nervous system, when strongly affected, on the body, is the loss of colour in the hair, which has occasionally been observed after extreme terror or grief.[63]

Having presented these three principles Darwin introduces masses of examples upon which they are based, but which are not always unambiguously attributable to them. *The Expression of the Emotions in Man and Animals* is also a challenge to the modern reader for other reasons. It does not really have a single argument running through it. When Darwin tries to summarize his theses it becomes apparent how contradictory and ambiguous his best-seller is. On top of this, there are the prejudices of later writers who are responsible for putting into circulation clichéd ideas about Darwin's theses. One of these, spread by Ekman and others, is the idea that Darwin is the founding father of cultural universalism in the study of emotion. 'Darwin argues that our expressions of emotion are universal (that is, innate not learned) and the product of our evolution', says Ekman.[64] It is true that *The Expression* presumes a universalism, in one breath talking of bared teeth, closed eyes, and the tensing of the leg muscles in both man and animals. In so doing, Darwin humanizes animals and 'animalizes' humans. His contemporaries found the former touching, but were not amused by the latter. Christian anthropocentrists would not have taken to Darwin's argument about the evolutionary origins of bared teeth: for the baring of teeth did not after all enhance the chances of survival of nineteenth-century British citizens, who rarely resorted to biting their foes. Darwin therefore argued that this habit had its evolutionary origins in animals that fought with their teeth, as hyenas and dogs still did in his time (Fig. 15).

There was also concern expressed about Darwin's argument that the blush of a young woman was not related to her natural God-given embarrassment, but could be explained through evolution.[65] Darwin seemed to be aware of the controversial

---

[61] Darwin, *Expression of the Emotions in Man and Animals*, 55–6, 265–72, esp. 271.

[62] Darwin, *Expression of the Emotions in Man and Animals*, 34.

[63] Darwin, *Expression of the Emotions in Man and Animals*, 69–70.

[64] Paul Ekman, 'Introduction to the Third Edition', in Darwin, *Expression of the Emotions in Man and Animals*, xxi–xxxvi, here xxii.

[65] 'The belief that blushing was *specially* designed by the Creator is opposed to the general theory of evolution'; Darwin, *Expression of the Emotions in Man and Animals*, 335, emphasis in original.

Fig. 15 Baring of Teeth in a Human as an Evolutionary Remnant
Source: Charles Darwin, *The Expression of the Emotions in Man and Animals* (3rd edn, New York: Oxford University Press, 1998), 246.

nature of such arguments, but in *The Expression* he places remarkably little emphasis upon the evolutionary point of emotion—that the expression of emotion confers advantage in natural selection, since it enables warnings to be given and threats made.

The equation of humans and animals privileged non-verbal and physical expressions of emotion, while discounting linguistic expression. In this Darwin was less exceptional than has often been claimed, since he was part of a larger trend in experimental psychology. Laboratory conditions downgraded the attention paid to linguistic expressions of emotion. Subjective experience—how a patient responded to the psychologist's question how he or she felt, or had felt, and how exactly they had felt—was no longer of any interest. In the same way, any question concerning deliberate, wilful control of emotion ('intentionalism', to use Ruth Leys's term) also became irrelevant. To investigate emotion in a laboratory setting, and produce results that satisfied the epistemological demands of the young science of experimental psychology, emotion had to be emptied of language and reduced to physical movements of the body.

In parallel to this universalistic ground bass, *The Expression* is full of examples that seem to imply instead an anti-universalist, culturally relative standpoint, and which point up Darwin's stance as an empiricist, proceeding inductively, collecting what he could and only then describing what he had collected. It often seems here as though Darwin became stuck at the first descriptive stage, making little headway on the second, barely developing the generalizations made in the principles that he had initially presented. The empirical examples are drawn from a wide range of sources, including observations of the behaviour of children, the mentally ill, older people, people from non-European cultures, domestic pets, and animals in the wild. Darwin drew upon his own observations (including of his own children and domestic pets), the descriptions of animals made by other researchers, the knowledge of the director of a mental institution, and also the results of thirty-six questionnaires in which colonial officials and missionaries recorded what had struck them about people of other cultures. Almost without missing a beat Darwin combines this material with comments on fine art and quotes from ancient authors, the Bible, and Shakespeare—without making any comment on the differences in these very diverse 'sources'.

If we take the example of New Zealand we see how Darwin could be labelled more as a cultural relativist than a universalist. He emphasizes 'that the women can voluntarily shed tears in abundance', even though weeping 'seems to be the primary and natural expression, as we see in children, of suffering of any kind, whether bodily pain short of extreme agony, or mental distress'.[66] In another counter-proof of the thesis that tears are always and everywhere an expression of suffering, he notes that with the inhabitants of the Sandwich Islands, 'according to [Louis de] Freycinet, tears are actually recognized as a sign of happiness'.[67] And the following sentence sounds rather similar: 'Mr. [Robert] Swinhoe informs me that he has often seen the Chinese, when suffering from deep grief, burst out into hysterical fits of laughter.'[68] Then Darwin commented on kissing:

> We Europeans are so accustomed to kissing as a mark of affection, that it might be thought to be innate in mankind; but this is not the case. . . . Jemmy Button, the Fuegian, told me that this practice was unknown in his land. It is equally unknown with the New Zealanders, Tahitians, Papuans, Australians, Somals of Africa, and the Esquimaux.[69]

So we can be quite certain: these cases of cultural contingency in the expression of emotion were not ignored or suppressed by Darwin, but by Ekman's interpretation of Darwin.

We cannot here deal with the question of how much *The Expression of the Emotions in Man and Animals* is influenced by Lamarckism and how much by 'classical' Darwinian evolutionary theory. Even the psychology textbook cited at the beginning of this section admits to confusion, for we can read there that

> you might imagine that Darwin would have proposed that emotions had functions in our survival. Indeed many psychologists and biologists assume, that this is what he said. But he didn't.[70]

For the time being there is no sign of a ceasefire on the battlefield of *The Expression*. On the contrary: quite recently Daniel M. Gross published an article entitled 'Defending the Humanities with Charles Darwin's *The Expression of the Emotions in Man and Animals* (1872)'. Here he reclaims Darwin as a theoretician whose

---

[66] Darwin, *Expression of the Emotions in Man and Animals*, 158, 157–8.
[67] Darwin, *Expression of the Emotions in Man and Animals*, 174–5.
[68] Darwin, *Expression of the Emotions in Man and Animals*, 207.
[69] Darwin, *Expression of the Emotions in Man and Animals*, 213.
[70] Keltner, Oatley, and Jenkins, *Understanding Emotions*, 5.

subtle thinking could not be more indebted to the human sciences.[71] According to Gross, Darwin's conception of emotion 'accounts for the emotion's medium, occasion, and social situation'.[72]

Darwin did not, like Ekman, try to brush under the carpet diverging interpretations of emotional expression in the Duchenne photos by invoking the variation of 'display rules'; instead, he openly noted the differing results following from showing the photos with or without the written explanation. In Darwin's own words:

> This exhibition was of use in another way, by convincing me *how easily we may be misguided by our imagination*; for when I first looked through Dr Duchenne's photographs, reading at the same time the text, and thus learning what was intended, I was struck with admiration at the truthfulness of all, with only a few exceptions. Nevertheless, if I had examined them without any explanation, no doubt I should have been as much perplexed, in some cases, as other persons have been.[73]

Unlike Ekman, who limited emotions to short-lived, automatic, physiological events, allowing for only half-a-dozen basic emotions, Gross noted that Darwin laid emphasis on imagination, as well as emotions such as love, sympathy, hatred, mistrust, jealousy, envy, meanness, pride, and so on.[74] In place of Ekman's precise and distinct emotional categories, Darwin was conscious of the mixed circumstances that emotions usually represent.[75] And unlike Ekman's like-minded colleague, the brain scientist Antonio Damasio, who employs cultural products from Shakespeare and the rest as textual decoration and illustrations for his own theses, these sources served Darwin as examples of human behaviour, and thus called for explanation.[76] According to Gross, Ekman 'obfuscates the subtlety of Darwin's work', and palms the world off with an 'impoverished Darwinian model'. Gross concludes with the statement that 'As Darwin understood over a century ago we need the arts and humanities for many reasons, including for a science that can account both for the basic ways we are and the ways we can be.'[77] That is directed more against Ekman than Darwin, and goes too far, however honourable the sentiment may be. But it once again indicates the real meaning of *The Expression*, beyond its actual content: it remains a work over which opinions divide very sharply.

---

[71] Daniel M. Gross, 'Defending the Humanities with Charles Darwin's "The Expression of the Emotions in Man and Animals" (1872)', *Critical Inquiry*, 37/1 (2010), 34–59, here 35–6.

[72] Gross, 'Defending the Humanities', 48.

[73] Darwin, *Expression of the Emotions in Man and Animals*, 21, emphasis from Gross, 'Defending the Humanities', 48.

[74] Gross, 'Defending the Humanities', 49.   [75] Gross, 'Defending the Humanities', 50.

[76] Gross, 'Defending the Humanities', 51–2. See Darwin, *Expression of the Emotions in Man and Animals*, 21–2.

[77] Gross, 'Defending the Humanities', 44, 59. Sarah Winter also presents Darwin as a bridge-builder between the human and natural sciences in her 'Darwin's Saussure: Biosemiotics and Race in Expression', *Representations*, 107/1 (2009), 128–61.

4 THE BEGINNINGS OF PSYCHOLOGICAL RESEARCH INTO
EMOTIONS, OR, HOW FEELINGS, PASSIONS, AND CHANGES
OF MOOD MIGRATED FROM THEOLOGY TO PSYCHOLOGY
AND IN THE PROCESS BECAME 'EMOTIONS'

Darwin's *The Expression of the Emotions in Man and Animals* was not written in a vacuum. Thomas Dixon has outlined its prehistory by tracing the rise of the meta-category 'emotion' in the English language. He presents this as a process of reduction, during which complexity emerged as the loser in many respects: the semantic field 'emotion' sucked in a whole series of differentiated meanings that had been conveyed by the older, individual concepts of 'passion', 'affection of the soul', 'sentiment', 'desire', and 'lust'.[78] Dixon argues that this reduction to a single meta-category began during the 1730s with the Scottish moral philosophers, 'reaching a decisive point in the *Lectures* of the physician-philosopher Thomas Brown', a native of Edinburgh whose most influential writings were published between 1810 and 1820.[79] This process was closely connected with the historical development we call secularization, although this implies too great a linearity. Concepts such as 'passion' and 'affection of the soul' were biblical and theological, whereas the category 'emotion' came from a scientific lexical field involving conceptions of organisms and nature. This displacement made it possible for feelings to be treated as being independent of metaphysical influences, and later as purely physical processes devoid of any volitional or intentional influence. Secularization, and this decoupling from the will, in turn made possible the animalization of feelings that humans and animals shared in common. This was a further nail in the coffin of Christian cosmology, for which the capacity to feel was the mark of human nature—'along with reason, hallmarks of what was especially dignified, superior and noble about the human mind'.[80]

Working within intellectual history, Dixon established that early psychologists or physiologists of emotion who thought in terms of evolution—like Herbert Spencer (1820–1903) and Alexander Bain (1819–1903)—were, together with Darwin, closely interconnected with the Scottish moral philosophers: they were all in dialogue with Christian theology; indeed, this was their starting point. Spencer, for instance, rebelled against the idea that the intellectual development of humans was guided by a metaphysical instance, including in this the development of the brain and of feelings. In his view, intellectual development did involve a process of perfection, but this was an autonomous process following the laws of evolution.[81] Unlike Spencer and Darwin, Bain did not categorically deny the existence of the will and the idea that it could influence emotion. He integrated it, however, into a triangular model that encompassed, along with the will, cognition and emotion. He defined the will and its influence as a kind of mental

---

[78] Thomas Dixon, *From Passions to Emotions: The Creation of a Secular Psychological Category* (Cambridge: Cambridge University Press, 2003), 2.
[79] Dixon, *From Passions to Emotions*, 133.   [80] Dixon, *From Passions to Emotions*, 136.
[81] Dixon, *From Passions to Emotions*, 149.

motor driving the movement of muscles, including those muscles responsible for the expression of emotion. This motor was fuelled by the energy provided by food, or as Dixon puts it: 'Food had replaced God as the prime mover of the will. Christian readers of Bain such as John Grote, unsurprisingly, took exception to this new scientific psychology.'[82]

While Spencer and Bain enjoyed a broad reception among an Anglo-American public during their own lifetimes—primarily between the 1850s and 1870s—Darwin's reputation has lasted much longer. He is also quite definitely the most complicated case. How might we explain his remarkably 'non-Darwinist' procedure in *The Expression*, where he not only associated emotions with physical attributes useful for survival, but also drew attention to their lack of utility and superfluity? It could be said that Darwin was a victim of his own anti-Christian polemics, which tended to overshadow his evolutionary and biological arguments. He had devoted such great energy to the criticism of a few earlier texts—chiefly Charles Bell's *Essays on the Anatomy and Philosophy of Expression* (1824), which propagated the idea of the providence of an all-knowing Creator (so that the blushing of a young woman is a God-given mechanism which protects her from immoral actions[83])—that he simply lost sight of the possible evolutionary advantages of emotional expression.[84] Dixon disputes this. Through a close reading of the relevant texts he argues that Darwin took more from Charles Bell (1774–1842), Thomas H. Burgess, and the rest than is usually supposed. In truth, suggests Dixon, *The Expression* is structured by analogy with the biblical story of the fall of man: while Adam and Eve had originally controlled their behaviour and feelings, this was all lost with Eve's bite of the apple. Dixon's revisionist thesis is that Darwin's book involves a de-Christianized version of the Augustinian story of the fall of man, presenting the expression of feeling as 'malfunctions of the human machine'.[85]

The idea that Christian theological elements were diverted and rechannelled, reappearing in a new guise, is much more appealing than that of a linear secularization process in which Christian thought gradually faded out.[86] Moreover, this framework of diversion and revalorization also provides a partial explanation as to why all those studying emotion from the 1860s to the 1880s, like Darwin and others whom we will consider shortly, tried so hard to separate emotion from free will, or intention.[87] During this period the new science of psychology was emerging, and it became necessary for it to set itself apart from other competing sciences, especially theology, creating its own domain and form of legitimacy. It also had to distinguish itself clearly from 'anti-science'—Christian cosmology. The fact that

---

[82] Dixon, *From Passions to Emotions*, 159.

[83] See Thomas H. Burgess, *The Physiology or Mechanism of Blushing: Illustrative of the Influence of Mental Emotion on the Capillary Circulation* (London: John Churchill, 1839).

[84] This standard explanation of the anti-Darwinist aspects of Darwin's *The Expression* is summarized in Dixon, *From Passions to Emotions*, 169.

[85] Dixon, *From Passions to Emotions*, 87.

[86] On this process of diversion and rechannelling, see Friedrich Wilhelm Graf, *Die Wiederkehr der Götter: Religion in der modernen Kultur* (Munich: Beck, 2004).

[87] For details of this process, see Roger Smith, *The Norton History of the Human Sciences* (New York: Norton, 1997), 492–501.

during this process elements of Christian ideology continually resurfaced—as Dixon has shown in his reading of Darwin's *The Expression*—makes plain the continuing subterranean influence of the long tradition of Christian thought about feelings. That the separation of emotion from free will took place during these decades of the later nineteenth century can be explained by the reductionist epistemology and practice of the laboratories of experimental psychology.[88] Modern psychological experimental design, invented at this time, finds it difficult to measure how humans and animals feel what they do; how humans evaluate, deal with, and influence their emotions. The process through which experimental design developed was indeed reciprocal: epistemology determined experiments, and vice versa; emotional experiments determined conceptions of emotion, and vice versa.

Around the same time, representatives of the new science of psychology developed a physiological conception of emotion, detached from free will and intention, which could be applied to the study of both humans and animals. This particular idea diffused very quickly because of the emergence of a transnational scientific community whose members corresponded with each other, met at conferences, sent each other books and offprints, and exchanged doctoral students. This transnational networking makes it impossible to determine where exactly the decoupling of emotion from intention originated, since it is often associated with one particular psychologist (at most two—see below): William James. In 1884 James wrote his essay 'What Is an Emotion?', which is, alongside Darwin's *The Expression*, probably the most-read psychological text on emotion:

> My thesis on the contrary is that *the bodily changes follow directly the* PERCEPTION *of the exciting fact, and that our feeling of the same changes as they occur* IS *the emotion.* Common sense says, we lose our fortune, are sorry and weep; we meet a bear, are frightened and run; we are insulted by a rival, are angry and strike. The hypothesis here to be defended says that this order of sequence is incorrect, that the one mental state is not immediately induced by the other, that the bodily manifestations must first be interposed between, and that the more rational statement is that we feel sorry because we cry, angry because we strike, afraid because we tremble, and not that we cry, strike, or tremble, because we are sorry, angry, or fearful, as the case may be. Without the bodily states following on the perception, the latter would be purely cognitive in form, pale, colourless, destitute of emotional warmth. We might then see the bear, and judge it best to run, receive the insult and deem it right to strike, but we could not actually *feel* afraid or angry.[89]

---

[88] Excluded here is Wilhelm Wundt, who in the 5th rev. edn of his *Grundzüge der physiologischen Psychologie* (1902–3) developed an 'emotional theory of the will'; Claudia Wassmann, 'The Science of Emotion: Studying Emotions in Germany, France, and the United States, 1860–1920', PhD diss, University of Chicago, Chicago, 2005, 110–11; Claudia Wassmann, 'Emotion into Science: How Our Modern Ideas about Emotion Were Created in the Nineteenth Century', *Emotional Studies (HIST-EX)* [online journal] (29 November 2011) <http://historiadelasemociones.wordpress.com/2011/11/29/emotion-into-science-how-our-modern-ideas-about-emotion-were-created-in-the-nineteenth-century-claudia-wassmann/> accessed 11 March 2014.

[89] William James, 'What Is an Emotion?', *Mind*, 9/34 (1884), 188–205, here 189–90, emphasis in original.

We do not therefore run away from the snake (or the bear) because we feel fearful, but the physical reactions (dilation of pupils, rapid respiration, tensing of muscles, raised pulse) following from the stimulus (discovery of the snake or of the bear) *are* the emotion. Perception and evaluation, the subjective and personal aspects of emotion, can from this point of view be discounted. James went on:

> A purely disembodied human emotion is a nonentity. . . . The more closely I scrutinise my states, the more persuaded I become, that whatever moods, affections, and passions I have, are in very truth constituted by, and made up of, those bodily changes we ordinarily call their expression or consequence; and the more it seems to me that if I were to become corporeally anæsthetic, I should be excluded from the life of the affections, harsh and tender alike, and drag out an existence of merely cognitive or intellectual form. Such an existence, although it seems to have been the ideal of ancient sages, is too apathetic to be keenly sought after by those born after the revival of the worship of sensibility, a few generations ago.[90]

There is a historicizing element here: as understood at the time that James was writing, emotion had to be thought about in terms of physical signs, although this did not exclude the possibility that in other periods—James alludes to the Greek Stoics and their alleged ideal of lack of feeling—a non-physical definition might well be accepted in the understanding of emotion for both everyday life and for science. Once again, the discovery of such historicizing elements shows how much work there is still to do even on the texts of classical psychological work on emotion. If the history of emotion is to avoid reproducing clichéd ideas about these classical sources, it urgently needs a reliable 'intrinsic' intellectual history of the psychology of emotion. James has not entered the annals of emotional research because of his historicizing approach but rather by virtue of his formulation 'priority of the bodily symptoms to the felt emotion'.[91] This approach 'is indeed enjoying something of a renaissance by virtue of the emphasis it places on the embodiment of emotions, which sits well with broader frameworks of embodied cognition'.[92] The priority of physical symptoms is today called 'Jamesian', and those who consider themselves disciples are called 'neo-Jamesians'.

This approach is often referred to as the 'James–Lange theory of emotion', since the Dane Carl Georg Lange arrived at a similar idea at the same time. Lange is the other psychologist to whom the uncoupling of emotion and intention has been attributed. In 1885 he published in Danish his major work on emotions, which was later translated into other languages.[93] The similarity between the arguments of James and Lange can be seen in this key quotation:

[90] James, 'What Is an Emotion?', 194.   [91] James, 'What Is an Emotion?', 199.

[92] Tim Dalgleish, Barnaby D. Dunn, and Dean Mobbs, 'Affective Neuroscience: Past, Present, and Future', *Emotion Review*, 1/4 (2009), 355–68, here 356.

[93] Carl Georg Lange, 'The Emotions: A Psychophysiological Study', trans. Istar A. Haupt from the authorized German translation of H. Kurella, in Carl Georg Lange and William James, *The Emotions* (Baltimore: Williams and Wilkins, 1922), i. 33–90. [Da. orig., *Om Sindsbevägelser*, 1885].

Take away the bodily symptoms from a frightened individual; let his pulse beat calmly, his look be firm, his color normal, his movements quick and sure, his speech strong, his thoughts clear; and what remains of his fear?[94]

But as Claudia Wassmann has shown, if one looks more carefully there are differences between Lange and James. The texts involved are for one thing quite different: Wassmann considers that James's short theoretical essay is a 'masterpiece of scientific rhetoric', while Lange's book is a detailed monograph filled with clinical descriptions of patients. The physiological explanations of how emotion functions are themselves also quite different in James and in Lange.[95] While James did search for 'centres in the brain' that process emotion, he ultimately rejected the idea that these existed, and instead outlined a model in which emotion is the stimulation of nerves in the sense organs, the extremities, and inner organs.[96] Here the signals from the organs are directed to the brain (and are thus 'afferent'), but 'only' bring about cognition, the 'cold' idea of fear or love. Nothing travels in the opposite direction: no signals travel from the brain to the organs. This theory has quite properly been called a 'peripheral' theory of emotion, since what happens on the periphery of the body is decisive. But Lange has been wrongly associated with this line of thinking. For him, there is a conglomeration of nerve cells, a 'vasomotor centre' in the brain, which serves as a switchboard for signals from the nerves and which both sends and receives, hence is both efferent and afferent. Thus a visual stimulus (seeing the snake, for instance) moves via the eye and the 'optical nerve' to the brainstem above the spinal cord, or more exactly to the medulla oblongata; nervous stimulation then causes the relevant blood vessels to dilate (for instance, the heart, so that one might run from the snake) or to contract.[97] This model was proposed a long time before the exact functioning of nerves was established, quite apart from any knowledge of the neurochemical processes in the brain. Around 1900, a good decade after Lange, Sir Charles Scott Sherrington (1857–1952) conducted an experiment in which he separated a dog's spinal cord and an important nerve from the vasomotor centre. The dog continued to react 'emotionally' to the same stimulus, allowing Sherrington to draw the conclusion that Lange's vasomotor centre played no part in the production of emotion.[98] As far as we know, Lange was nonetheless the first modern experimental psychologist to seek a location in the brain for emotion, and so in a part of the body that, for Darwin and many twentieth-century psychologists like Ekman, was forgotten in favour of the face, until the rapid rise of contemporary neuroscience revived the idea.

Generally speaking, this early phase of research in experimental psychology has been overlooked, and it was barely treated in more conventional history of science.

---

[94] Lange, 'The Emotions: A Psychophysiological Study', 66.

[95] Claudia Wassmann, 'Reflections on the "Body Loop": Carl Georg Lange's Theory of Emotion', *Cognition and Emotion*, 24/6 (2009), 974–90, here 975.

[96] See for James's unsuccessful search for the 'centres in the brain' responsible for emotion, Claudia Wassmann, 'Physiological Optics, Cognition and Emotion: A Novel Look at the Early Work of Wilhelm Wundt', *Journal of the History of Medicine and Allied Sciences*, 64/2 (2009), 213–49, here 247.

[97] Wassmann, 'Reflections on the "Body Loop"', 976, 980–4.

[98] Wassmann, 'Reflections on the "Body Loop"', 987.

There is not one competent study based on a reading of the original texts in their original language—a study which would have to include, among others, the English writings of Charles Bell, Charles Darwin, and Walter Cannon (1871–1945), the German writings of Wilhelm Wundt, the French writings of Claude Bernard (1813–78), the Italian writings of Paolo Mantegazza (1831–1910) and Angelo Mosso (1846–1910), the Russian writings of Ivan Pavlov (1849–1936) and Vladimir Bekhterev (1857–1927), and the Danish writings of Carl Lange. Only a study of this kind could begin to disentangle the ideas and mutual intellectual influences of an expanding international network.

Claudia Wassmann has also rediscovered another giant of the early psychology of emotion: Wilhelm Wundt—not the later Wundt, whose *Grundriss der Psychologie* (1896) is known to students of the history of emotions, but instead the earlier, pre-Darwinist Wundt of the *Vorlesungen über die Menschen- und Thierseele* of 1863. Wundt came to emotions through his study of sense perception. Having first formed a theory of the genesis of the senses, he then turned to their processes and functioning, extending his interest to the entire psychic-mental apparatus and in this way arriving at emotions.[99] In his *Vorlesungen* he made a distinction between brief 'emotions' and longer-lasting, more complex 'affects', involving 'complex emotions' which were also relevant to the domain of aesthetics.[100] No matter how confused the definition of feelings is today, this would now be seen as back to front: affect is associated with quick reaction to external stimuli, whereas emotions are generally thought to be more complex longer-term processes. But fundamental to Wundt's position was that he treated feelings, and also impressions of images, as being processed in the brain. He considered feelings to be subjective, that is, related to the feeling subject and not associated with the distinction between 'subjective = personal, hence inaccessible' and 'objective = external, hence natural'. Moreover, for Wundt emotions were critical to cognition, and he maintained that even newborn babies were capable of distinguishing between 'sweet' and 'sour', between pleasant and unpleasant feelings. Fame came to Wundt neither as a result of these early studies on emotion, now rediscovered, nor for his better-known work on emotion from the turn of the century, but because in 1879 he founded in Leipzig the first psychological laboratory, which revolutionized the scientific practice of psychology the whole world over.

5 EMOTION LABORATORIES AND LABORATORY EMOTIONS, OR, THE BIRTH OF PSYCHOLOGICAL CONCEPTIONS OF EMOTION FROM THE EXPERIMENTAL SPIRIT

If one looks in recent psychology textbooks for a historical outline of the study of emotions in the life sciences, one finds the following standard narrative: everything

---

[99] Wassmann, 'Physiological Optics, Cognition and Emotion'. See also Wassmann, 'Science of Emotion', 26–112.

[100] Wassmann, 'Physiological Optics, Cognition and Emotion', 231–2.

started with Darwin, who by publishing *The Expression of the Emotions in Man and Animals* in 1872 laid the foundations for the idea of basic emotions, treating emotion as a mental state to which a specific physical expression corresponded. In the mid-1880s William James and Carl Lange revolted against Darwin, reversing the order and declaring that physical expression was itself emotion. In turn, Walter Cannon and Philip Bard (1898–1977) positioned themselves against James and Lange in the later 1920s, objecting that physical movements could not be emotions, because such movements were too slow and ambiguous; they occurred not only under emotional conditions, but under conditions that had nothing to do with emotion. Cannon and Bard therefore supplanted the James–Lange duo. After that, the textbook story goes on, came behaviourism, which treated emotion according to a model of human behaviour based on physical reflex and so 'ontologically reduced emotion to something else'.[101] With the emergence of behaviourism the Dark Ages set in. The gloom was only broken by some flashes from early research into the brain—James Papez, for example, and the 1937 discovery of a connection between the cortex and the hypothalamus, which provided a new explanation for emotional control. It was only in the 1960s that the psychological study of emotion experienced a rebirth with three almost simultaneous developments: Silvan S. Tomkins's elaboration of Darwin's basic emotion approach; Magda B. Arnold's founding of the appraisal school in cognitive psychology, which retains a value dimension in the study of emotion; and the creation by Stanley Schachter (1922–97) and Jerome Singer (1934–2010) of a model which integrated physiological arousal and cognitive labelling. The psychological study of emotion has, since the 1960s, turned on the poles of basic emotion and appraisal. And it is flourishing.[102]

So much for the standard story. It is clear, but far too simple. We have already seen how much more complicated the early phases were. We will see in a moment that things got no better after the 1880s, and we switch from the history of ideas to that of practices. The question here is: how have the practices of experimental psychology constituted conceptions of emotion? In what way did the laboratory of Wilhelm Wundt influence the model of emotion, and the emotions of those working in it?

We can find a striking example in Angelo Mosso:

> The phenomenon which had most surprised me in my first experiments in Italy was the great instability of the blood-vessels of the hand, in consequence of which it changed in volume under the slightest emotions in the most surprising manner, whether the subject were awake or asleep. A few days after having installed myself in the laboratory in Leipzig, I was making an experiment in a room near that of the professor, my colleague, Professor Luigi Pagliani, helping me in everything with the devotion of a friend. Our first object was to establish the relation between respiration and change of volume in the hands. While Professor Pagliani was standing before the

---

[101] Maria Gendron and Lisa Feldman Barrett, 'Reconstructing the Past: A Century of Ideas about Emotion in Psychology', *Emotion Review*, 1/4 (2009), 316–39, here 330.
[102] Gendron and Barrett, 'Reconstructing the Past', 316–17.

registering apparatus, with his arms in the glass cylinders filled with water, Professor [Carl] Ludwig walked into the room. Immediately the two pens indicating the volume of the arms, descended, as though a vertical line, ten centimetres in length, were drawn down this page. It was the first time that I had seen such a considerable decrease in the volume of the hand and fore-arm, produced by an apparently slight emotion. Professor Ludwig himself was very much astonished, and, with that affability which made him so beloved by his pupils, took a pen and wrote on the paper at that point where the plethysmograph had marked the disturbance in the circulation caused by his appearance, *Der Löwe kommt* ('Enter the lion').[103]

A scientist is standing in the laboratory conducting an experiment on himself which measures the volume of his hands and arms. When his much-respected teacher comes in, the volume of his extremities decreases, and the measuring apparatus shows it; the experimental subject literally shrinks with fear.

At the end of the nineteenth century there spread among some parts of the scientific community the view that emotions were not interior to the body, and that they could not be studied through the verbal description of subjectively felt feelings. Instead, emotions were to be made physically measurable in the laboratory or clinic, using animals and humans as test subjects and a new, specially developed apparatus. The correspondence between measured values and emotions was so close that it often seemed as though emotions *were* heart rates, blood pressure, the pH of saliva, or the sugar content of urine.

To measure physical emotion, bodies had to be aroused; and to arouse them, they had first to be placed in a non-aroused state. It was no simple matter to find a non-emotional body, a baseline, a zero value in diagram, table, or graph, as the historian of science Otniel Dror has demonstrated in his pioneering works based on laboratory records, correspondence between scientists, and the research diaries. First of all, it was a matter of finding the right animals or persons to test. Physiologists thought that animals and people existed who were basically unsuitable for emotional experiments, because a species or an ethnicity, age, or gender group were emotional per se—hares, young animals, black people, women. According to a doctoral dissertation submitted to Harvard in 1921, the last had a 'less controlled and therefore more constantly active emotional life'.[104] Within each category physiologists also assumed a hierarchic order, such that dogs were always better experimental subjects than cats, and cats always better than hares.[105] And even within the prior assumption that white men and dogs, both in middle age, were the ideal experimental subjects, there was still a selection made on the basis of temperament and character. One scientist favoured a fox terrier cross because of its 'marked emotional characteristics', and a psychologist 'distinguished between

[103] Angelo Mosso, *Fear*, trans. E. Lough and F. Kiesow (London: Longmans, Green, and Co., 1896), 94–5.

[104] William Moulton Marston, 'Systolic Blood Pressure and Reaction Time Symptoms of Deception and Constituent Mental States', PhD diss., Harvard University, Ann Arbor, 1921, 5–6, cited in Otniel E. Dror, 'The Scientific Image of Emotion: Experience and Technologies of Inscription', *Configurations*, 7/3 (1999), 355–401, here 386.

[105] Otniel E. Dror, 'The Affect of Experiment: The Turn to Emotions in Anglo-American Physiology, 1900–1940', *Isis*, 90/2 (1999), 205–37, here 220.

"Blackey", an "extremely highly strung" dog, and "Tilley III", who was "of a temperament diametrically opposite"'.[106]

Once the experimental subject had been found, the zero level had to be produced, all emotion switched off. There was a whole spectrum of procedures the scientist could use to bring this about: animals, for instance, were introduced to the laboratory and experiments gradually, habituation being equated to an absence of emotion.[107] Experiments were also adapted to the test animals, and set up so as to minimize stress, so that several hours before taking some blood 'the skin is shaved and cleaned', then 'the animal is gently tied . . . to a comfortable board' and 'a *sharp* medium sized needle' is used.[108] Other animals were stroked and calmed, or spent the entire experiment in the lap of one of the scientists: 'This proved very satisfactory, except for the attendant. It is irksome, to say the least, to sit still for two to eight hours at a stretch.'[109] During the 1920s test animals were decorticated, a process by which the cortex is surgically removed. Since this was the region of the brain considered central for emotional control, decortication was supposed to bring about 'more pure' emotions, and 'authentic' zero values.[110]

Once one had a zero value, the experiment could finally get going. All experiments began with stimuli, and the list was simply endless. Visual stimuli ranged from pornography, snakes (live or rubber), photos of skin ailments, human intestines, alcohol put on the table in front of the subject, all the way to the New Testament. For acoustic stimuli pistol shots were used, as well as jumping jacks, laughter, screaming, barking dogs, meaningless syllables, reading very loud from Henri Barbusse's *Under Fire*, or shouting 'Socialist!'[111]

Then there were two basic procedures: either to observe the reaction of the body to the stimulation, or to take a sample from the body and measure it. Self-observation was one version of the first approach. In the late nineteenth century Angelo Mosso subjected himself to a strong emotional stimulus and measured a rise in his body temperature of 0.7 ºC rectally.[112] Later, male psychologists 'read "the more pornographic selections" from *The Thousand and One Nights*', but failed to register any emotional reaction, which they blamed either on their cortex or their 'critical, intellectual attitude'.[113] Scientists also measured themselves, for example, before, during, and after a game of American football—a form of sport that during the 1920s in the US became the most important refuge for the unrestrained expression of emotion.[114] Here the older instruments proved unsuitable, since they did not meet the expectation of researchers for objective and standardized

---

[106] Dror, 'The Affect of Experiment', 221.   [107] Dror, 'The Affect of Experiment', 223–5.
[108] Dror, 'The Affect of Experiment', 225, emphasis in original.
[109] Dror, 'The Affect of Experiment', 230; see also 226.
[110] Otniel E. Dror, 'Techniques of the Brain and the Paradox of Emotions, 1880–1930', *Science in Context*, 14/4 (2001), 643–60, here 649–53.
[111] Dror, 'Fear and Loathing in the Laboratory and Clinic', in Fay Bound Alberti (ed.), *Medicine, Emotion and Disease, 1700–1950* (New York: Palgrave Macmillan, 2006), 125–43, here 131.
[112] Dror, 'Scientific Image of Emotion', 358.   [113] Dror, 'Scientific Image of Emotion', 394.
[114] Otniel E. Dror (Dror, Otniel Yizhak), 'Afterword: A Reflection on Feelings and the History of Science', *Isis*, 100/4 (2009), 848–51; Otniel E. Dror, 'Modernity and the Scientific Study of Emotions, 1880–1950', PhD diss., Princeton University, Princeton, 1998, 166.

measurements of emotion. There was a boom in inventions after 1900. The pneumograph measured breathing, the cardiograph the heartbeat, the sphygmograph blood pressure, the galvanometer the pH value of various bodily secretions, and the thermometer the body's temperature (Figs. 16 and 17).

These were standard instruments, or as Otniel Dror puts it, 'inexpensive, and unsophisticated' devices, which 'directly measured relatively mundane aspects of

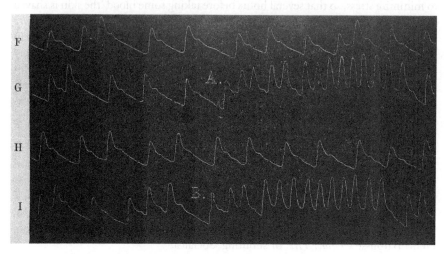

Fig. 16 Acceleration of the Heart Rate under the Influence of Fear (in A and B)
Source: Angelo Mosso, *Fear*, trans. E. Lough and F. Kiesow (London: Longmans, Green, and Co., 1896), 115.

Fig. 17 Robert Dudgeon's Sphygmograph for the Recording of Blood Pressure
Source: Dudgeon sphygmograph by James Coxeter and Son, London, 1885–1930 (© Science Museum/Science & Society Picture Library).

Fig. 18 Kiss-O-Meter

Source: © Awe Inspiring Images/Shutterstock Images, New York.

human physiology', to which then mythical powers were attributed in the unrav-elling of the emotional life of humans and animals.[115] By the early 1930s, measurement had become commercialized, as instruments for the measurement of emotion were being mass-produced.[116] Soon the affectometer, the emotograph, and the emotion meter made it into the popular press: using the Kiss-O-Meter, the degree of love between two people during a kiss could be 'objectively' measured on a scale of 0 to 120 (Fig. 18). One study involving the Kiss-O-Meter concluded that the intensity of kisses diminished with age and years of marriage. In addition, ten husbands were persuaded to kiss their mother-in-law; the machine registered no more than a 6, and it was suggested that it might be worthwhile extending the scale to include negative values.[117]

[115] Dror, 'Scientific Image of Emotion', 364.
[116] Dror, 'Scientific Image of Emotion', 359.
[117] Dror, 'Fear and Loathing in the Laboratory and Clinic', 136.

Scientists extended their experiments to ever more objects and test persons, moving outside the laboratory to include, for example, the emotional state of death-row inmates shortly before their execution.[118] Basically, one measured fear and anger in animals, while the spectrum of emotions measured in humans was much greater.[119] On human test subjects there was a greater belief in the prospect of objective access to prelinguistic emotions detached from volition. Beyond that, measurements were also made covertly—at last one was certain that the test subject was unaware of being measured: 'the patient sits at ease with hands on the electrodes, which may be so concealed in the arms of his chair that he is unaware that the most intimate processes of his soul are being registered'.[120] The process of recording seemed here automatic, as though the emotion recorded itself.[121] Faith in machinery found a depressing zenith when a famous psychologist argued in 1908 for the use of psychological expertise in court proceedings: 'We must bring the man before a registering apparatus to find out . . . whether sun-shine or general cloudiness prevails in his mind.'[122]

The second method was to take a sample of secretions from the stimulated body (blood, sweat, saliva, urine) and measure it. An example from 1931:

> A cat in a small cage was placed in front of a large dog. The dog tried to get at the cat, and being prevented by the cage became more and more enraged. The cat inside the cage became more and more frightened. A sample of the blood of both animals was procured both before and after.[123]

Two techniques were used in the analysis of bodily secretions. First of all, one could measure 'emotional' secretions: the pH value of saliva, for instance, or glucose in urine (sugar content), or the number of red blood cells in a blood sample. Secondly, one could introduce the emotional secretion by injecting the 'unemotional' tissue of an animal or a person, and then measure the emotionalization of this tissue, which, as a researcher wrote about an experiment on rage, worked like a 'rage-thermometer'.[124] Less common was the analysis of tissue samples from an animal that had died from emotion—for instance, a bird that had died from fear. Here a microscope would be used to locate signs of strong emotion within the cells.[125]

This all went to minimize the subjective and linguistic aspects of emotion. Feelings were de facto demystified. Edward Wheeler Scripture (1864–1945) summed things up in 1908 when he said: 'some people have objected to the sweat glands being dignified into organs of the emotions. But dignity does not exist for science.'[126] Even dreams could be objectified, since the recordings made by

---

[118] Dror, 'Scientific Image of Emotion', 359.
[119] Dror, 'Fear and Loathing in the Laboratory and Clinic', 131–2.
[120] Dror, 'Scientific Image of Emotion', 367.   [121] Dror, 'Scientific Image of Emotion', 357.
[122] Hugo Münsterberg, *On the Witness Stand: Essays on Psychology and Crime* (New York: Doubleday, 1908), 122–3.
[123] Dror, 'Techniques of the Brain and the Paradox of Emotions', 648.
[124] Dror, 'Scientific Image of Emotion', 370–1.
[125] Dror, 'Scientific Image of Emotion', 371.
[126] E. W. Scripture, 'Detection of the Emotions by the Galvanometer', *JAMA: Journal of the American Medical Association*, 50/15 (1908), 1164–5, here 1164.

an instrument attached to a test subject while they were asleep appeared to provide better information about dreaming than unreliable memory.[127] Scientists internalized a belief in the scientific nature of emotion, and expressed this in their diaries and notebooks. Walter Cannon, for example, wrote to his colleague Smith Ely Jelliffe (1866–1945) in 1932: 'I have just seen in the September issue of the *Journal of Mental and Nervous Diseases* a review of my book, "The Wisdom of the Body", that has tickled my diencephalon [a region of the brain beneath the thalamus] in just the right spot to give me a feeling of pleasure!'[128]

In sum, it can be said that from 1900 on there were four major processes in the constitution of laboratory emotions in emotion laboratories—and this was, by the way, no insignificant field of scientific activity, about a quarter of leading American psychologists having conducted experiments involving emotion during the years from 1900 to 1940.[129] Firstly, emotions were separated from other phenomena—primarily pain—that often brought about similar physical reactions, so that these emotions might be maintained in a pure state. Secondly, emotions were placed on a scale, establishing a zero point as an unstimulated state against which data could be ordered. Third was an effort to standardize experiments so that emotion might be made capable of replication, internalizing a principle of modern experimental science that experiments be repeatable, and that under the same conditions the same results should be obtained. Fourth, there was a continuing effort to render emotions graphically visible, the trace of a needle across a roll of graph paper replacing linguistic self-description of subjectively felt emotion as the guarantee of truth.[130]

These processes were never fixed or certain, but remained unstable, involving a range of paradoxes; emotions researchers did notice this, for in 1925 Walter Cannon and Sydney William Britton wrote that those studying emotion saw themselves 'confronted by almost insuperable difficulties'.[131] Paul D. MacLean (1913–2007), the 'discoverer' of the limbic system, responded to the question of why James Papez (1883–1958) had only written one paper on emotion by saying that Papez had sensed 'that you were showing a soft side talking about emotion—not being a really hard scientist'.[132] What then were the real ambiguities of studying emotion in a laboratory setting around 1900? Firstly, as Dror writes, there was the 'schizoid status of the study of emotions', which 'created a fundamental paradox: emotion as an object of knowledge was studied only by violating the laboratory's status as an emotion-free space, a status that was essential for the

---

[127] Dror, 'Scientific Image of Emotion', 399.   [128] Dror, 'Scientific Image of Emotion', 396.
[129] Dror, 'Affect of Experiment', 208; Dror, 'Modernity and the Scientific Study of Emotions', 14–15. Claudia Wassmann disputes Dror's argument that graphic representations had supplanted linguistic self-description, citing among others Rudolf Schulze's *Aus der Werkstatt der experimentellen Psychologie und Pädagogik* (1909) and his 'impression method'. In this, test subjects were exposed to an external stimulus and then asked about their personal sensations; see Wassmann, 'Science of Emotion', 226–8.
[130] Dror, 'Fear and Loathing in the Laboratory and Clinic', 129.
[131] Dror, 'Techniques of the Brain and the Paradox of Emotions', 649.
[132] Otniel E. Dror, 'Counting the Affects: Discoursing in Numbers', *Social Research*, 68/2 (2001), 357–78, here 370.

very act of producing knowledge'.[133] Furthermore, it was never clear whether what was measured was really emotion, and not something else. Did a particular number of white blood cells really represent 'emotional arousal', rather than an infection? Did particular kinds of heartbeats really mean 'fear' and 'anxiety', or did they indicate that something was wrong with the valves of the test subject's heart?[134] Above all, in experiments upon human subjects it was never evident whether these individuals deliberately sought to distort the experiment, learning by watching the measuring needle to control their own blood pressure—biofeedback *avant la lettre*.[135] The ideal human reactive body was really one which had rendered itself wilfully unemotional, which had eliminated free will, and this was of course a contradiction in terms. Ultimately instability and ambiguity, the aporias and paradoxes, lay in the nature of emotion itself—as Dror writes:

> And emotion was, by definition, an accidental event that was often unpredictable—even in the sanctuary of the laboratory. Emotion signified the collapse of the laboratory's ideal of the animal-machine, of reliable control, predictability, replicability, and standardization.[136]

Along with Wilhelm Wundt, William James, Walter Cannon, and others, the writer Robert Musil, a keen observer of experimental psychology, even took the view that

> Because they are constantly fluid, emotions cannot be stopped; nor can they be looked at 'under the microscope'. This means that the more closely we observe them, the less we know what it is we feel. Attention is already a change in the emotion.[137]

6 HOW IDEAS OF SOCIAL ORDER ALSO ORDERED THE INTERIOR OF THE BRAIN

An empirically rich, praxis-theoretical history of the study of emotion in laboratories is a worthwhile undertaking. If this kind of history finds more supporters, then we might hope that some light will be shed on the genealogy of the spatial representations those studying emotions in the brain today bring to their work.[138] Two examples will show the degree of implicit evaluation contained in these conceptions of space, employing culturally formed concepts like higher and lower, right and left. One of the most influential neuroanatomists of the later nineteenth century, John Hughlings Jackson (1835–1911), was sure that cognitive

---

[133] Dror, 'Techniques of the Brain and the Paradox of Emotions', 644.
[134] Dror, 'Scientific Image of Emotion', 373–4.
[135] Dror, 'Scientific Image of Emotion', 380–1.
[136] Dror, 'Affect of Experiment', 237.
[137] Robert Musil, *The Man Without Qualities*, trans. Sophie Wilkins and Burton Pike (New York: Knopf, 1995) [Ger. orig., *Der Mann ohne Eigenschaften*, 3 vols, 1930–43], ii. 1277.
[138] Fundamental to this: Michael Hagner, *Homo cerebralis: Der Wandel vom Seelenorgan zum Gehirn* (Frankfurt am Main: Suhrkamp, 2008); Erhard Oeser, *Geschichte der Hirnforschung: Von der Antike bis zur Gegenwart* (2nd enl edn, Darmstadt: Wissenschaftliche Buchgesellschaft, 2010).

functions were located mainly in the frontal cortex, with emotional functions by contrast in the lower cortex. To treat Jackson's finding as metaphorical would be inadequate. It was more a social conception of order which reached deep into the supposedly objective domain of brain research: in the higher regions of the cortex sat the 'government', composed of the most capable men available, while below in the subcortical regions was to be found the masses. Mental illnesses that were rooted in brain pathologies, such as schizophrenia, were no more than class struggle run out of control, or an anarchic attempt to overthrow the natural order of higher and lower:

> The higher nervous arrangements evolved out of the lower keep down those lower, just as a government evolved out of a nation controls as well as directs that nation. If this be the process of evolution then the reverse process of dissolution is not only a 'taking off' of the higher, but is at the very same time a 'letting go' of the lower. If the governing body of this country were destroyed suddenly, we should have two causes for lamentation: 1, the loss of the services of eminent men; and 2, the anarchy of the now uncontrolled people.[139]

'[E]minent men' and 'uncontrolled people', or as it had been earlier, master and slave, heaven and hell—these are only some of the images that animated the cerebral imagination of medicine and psychology, and, in fact, still do. We can, for instance, read a passage that the brain researcher Joseph LeDoux published in 1996: 'Traditionally, the sensory processing structures below the cortex are viewed as slaves to the cortical master.'[140]

A second example: in 1912 the American neurologist Charles K. Mills (1845–1930) hypothesized that the right-hand side of the brain was solely responsible for emotion. Even in the 1970s this 'hypothesis of the right-hand hemisphere' had adherents, and this lateralization—the question of whether each half of the brain performs different functions in neuronal emotional activity, or whether they interconnect in some way—is a leading preoccupation of affective neuroscience today.[141] Quite probably the same sort of spatial ideas, linguistic images, and ideas of social order influenced Mills as had influenced John Hughlings Jackson. Nobody

---

[139] J. Hughlings Jackson, 'The Croonian Lectures on Evolution and Dissolution of the Nervous System: Lecture II', *British Medical Journal*, 1/1214 (1884), 660–3, here 662. An analysis of Jackson's ideas of the organization of the brain can be found in Anne Harrington, *Medicine, Mind, and the Double Brain: A Study in Nineteenth-Century Thought* (Princeton: Princeton University Press, 1987), ch. 7, esp. 210–12, 217.

[140] Joseph E. LeDoux, *The Emotional Brain: The Mysterious Underpinnings of Emotional Life* (New York: Simon and Schuster, 1996), 152. See also Andreas Heinz, 'Wie böse ist die Impulsivität?', *Arcadia*, 44/1 (2009), 24–30, here 29; Andreas Heinz, 'Irre Lüste und Lustloses Irren: Konstruktionen von Lust und Begierde im 20. Jahrhundert', in Detlev Schöttker (ed.), *Philosophie der Freude: Von Freud bis Sloterdijk* (Leipzig: Reclam, 2003), 175–86, here 176–7.

[141] See Harold A. Sackeim and Ruben C. Gur, 'Lateral Asymmetry in Intensity of Emotional Expression', *Neuropsychologia*, 16/4 (1978), 473–81; Harold A. Sackeim, Ruben C. Gur, and Marcel C. Saucy, 'Emotions are Expressed More Intensely on the Left Side of the Face', *Science*, 202/4366 (1978), 434–6; Gary E. Schwartz, Geoffrey L. Ahern, and Serena-Lynn Brown, 'Lateralized Facial Muscle Response to Positive and Negative Emotional Stimuli', *Psychophysiology*, 16/6 (1979), 561–71; Gary E. Schwartz, Richard J. Davidson, and Foster Maer, 'Right Hemisphere Lateralization from Emotion in the Human Brain: Interactions with Cognition', *Science*, 190/4211 (1975), 286–8; Ralph

has yet pursued the question—although it would seem reasonable to do so—that the idea of two halves of the brain, the left for cognition and the right for emotion, simply tips Jackson's vertical topography on its side. 'That this duality of action is in any sense complete cannot be maintained, but for certain well developed functions..., as language, music, emotion..., it is altogether probable, and indeed is well known as regards language, that one hemisphere, the left, plays the leading role.'[142] As proof, Mills cited 'involuntary or explosive laughing or weeping, and one case of Jacksonian epilepsy with a peculiar laughing or smiling aura, in which the lesion present was in the right half of the brain'.[143]

Basically it was lesions—damage to, and hence the closing-down of, specific areas of the brain—that served as the typical medical indicators in the brain research of this period. If a particular zone ceased to function, and at the same time abnormal behaviour was observed, the two elements were brought together into a causal relationship, it being concluded that the damaged area was responsible for the dysfunction; and in reverse, that in a healthy state this area was responsible for the corresponding function. This is today still a usable experimental procedure, and we will come to this shortly. But for the moment, all we need to understand is that indicating the important influence of spatial valencies, linguistic images, and underlying conceptions of social order does not mean that Jackson and Mills had no experimental evidence, or that they did not arrive at their hypotheses through experimental induction. Nevertheless, sociocultural conceptions of space and the metaphors employed to express this always determine which experiments are in fact completed, how they are set up, and what is actually measured. Given the primitive means of measurement in the early twentieth century, Mills was drawn entirely off the mark and could thus posit completely untenable hypotheses.

7 RESEARCH INTO THE EMOTIONAL RESPONSE OF THE BRAIN

We have seen how with Jackson, Mills, and Lange—the last of whom introduced the idea of the 'vasomotor centre'—experimental psychologists investigating emotion always came back to the brain. Clinicians had already sensed that the brain could have something to do with emotions, seeing patients who had suffered brain damage and had subsequently displayed abnormal emotional expressions. In the annals of medical history in general, and the history of emotion in particular, there is one spectacular case: Phineas Gage. Gage was a foreman who in 1848, in the course of an accident while working on the construction of a railway in Vermont,

---

Adolphs et al., 'Cortical Systems for the Recognition of Emotion in Facial Expression', *Journal of Neuroscience*, 16/23 (1996), 7678–87.

[142] Charles K. Mills, 'The Cortical Representation of Emotion, with a Discussion of Some Points in the General Nervous Mechanism of Expression and its Relation to Organic Nervous Mental Disease and Insanity', *Proceedings of the American Medico-Psychological Association*, 19 (1912), 297–300, here 298.

[143] Mills, 'The Cortical Representation of Emotion', 298.

Fig. 19 Phineas Gage and His Iron Bar

Source: Cabinet-card portrait of brain-injury survivor Phineas P. Gage (1823–60), shown holding the tamping iron which injured him; image cropped to remove much of surrounding card. From the Gage family of Texas photo collection.

had an iron bar 1.1 m long and 3 cm thick pass through his head. The rod shot up with such force that it entered his head under his left eyebrow, exited through the top of his skull, and landed 15 m away. Despite heavy bleeding and an infection, Gage retained consciousness and recovered, with only his left eye terminally damaged. Very quickly his friends noticed that he had become irritable and moody, that he was 'no longer Gage', and John Harlow, the doctor who treated him, noted that Gage was 'capricious and vacillating, devising many plans of future operation, which are no sooner arranged than they are abandoned'.[144] Gage lost his job, and henceforth earned a living as a fairground curiosity, the iron bar always close at hand (Fig. 19).

---

[144] John M. Harlow, 'Recovery from the Passage of an Iron Bar through the Head: Read before the Massachusetts Medical Society 3 June 1868', *History of Psychiatry*, 4/14 (1993), 274–81, here 277.

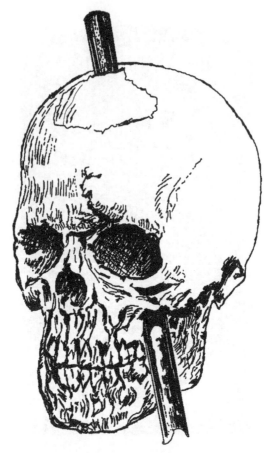

Fig. 20 The Position of the Iron Bar in Phineas Gage's Skull

Source: Birgit Jackel, 'Zur Bedeutung der Hirnforschung für Entwicklung und Lernen im Elementar-und Primarbereich' (2006) <http://www.birgit-jackel.de/kongresse/duisburg2006/text01.html> accessed 11 March 2014

When Gage died in 1860 in San Francisco, Harlow obtained the permission of his relatives for his body to be transferred to Harvard University for study. Harlow and his colleagues were there able to examine the skull; afterwards, both skull and iron bar were given to the university's medical museum, where they went on permanent display.

Investigation of Gage's skull showed that the bar had damaged his brain's orbitofrontal cortex and the prefrontal cortex (Fig. 20). Harlow concluded that 'The equilibrium or balance, so to speak, between his intellectual faculties and animal propensities, seems to have been destroyed.' Here too we can see the influence of Jackson's idea that cortex and intellect are 'above', the remainder below, and that emotions are animal.[145]

Phineas Gage remains of interest to neuroscientists and philosophers today.[146] Historical accounts of the study of emotion in experimental psychology treat his case as the origin of one of the most important approaches to emotions, via the study of lesions.[147] It is assumed that damage to a particular area of the brain allows conclusions to be drawn regarding the functions of that area. Subsequently, lesions were deliberately made in the brains of test animals, and humans with particular kinds of emotional disorders were 'healed' by the removal of specific parts of the brain. In the USA from 1936 to 1955 between 40,000 and 50,000 psychiatric patients diagnosed with psychoses and schizophrenia were subjected to a prefrontal lobotomy. It was hoped that this operation would bring about the opposite of the effect that Phineas Gage had experienced, and in fact this drastic intervention did calm the patients in question, although the operation itself quickly became discredited.[148]

Cases like that of Phineas Gage directed attention to the brain as the site of emotional processes. And so, before we turn to psychoanalysis, we should first review three milestones in the study of emotion and the brain—all from the first half of the twentieth century, and so from a time long before the invention of computer-imaging procedures in the 1990s.

The Cannon–Bard Theory

In the early 1920s Henry Head (1861–1940) showed that those who had sustained an injury to the thalamus just on one side of the brain subsequently showed overtly strong reactions to painful stimulation—a pin prick or heat, for instance—applied to the body on the side of the injury.[149] Around the same time, Walter R. Hess (1881–1973) carried out experiments on cats in which he stimulated the hypothalamus with electrodes, bringing about non-specific emotional responses such as a raised heart rate and defensiveness (he called the latter an 'affective defence reaction').[150] In time, he refined his methods, and could eventually bring about specific emotions like anger, fear, curiosity, or lethargy simply by stimulating a

---

[145] Harlow, 'Recovery from the Passage of an Iron Bar through the Head', 277.

[146] See e.g. Hanna Damasio et al., 'The Return of Phineas Gage: Clues about the Brain from the Skull of a Famous Patient', *Science*, 264/5162 (1994), 1102–5; Richard David Precht, *Who am I? And If so, How Many?: A Journey Through Your Mind*, trans. Shelley Frisch (London: Constable, 2011) [Ger. orig., *Wer bin ich—und wenn ja wie viele?: Eine philosophische Reise*, 2007], 121–4.

[147] Keltner, Oatley and Jenkins, *Understanding Emotions*, 23.

[148] Walter Freeman, 'Frontal Lobotomy in Early Schizophrenia: Long Follow-up in 415 Cases', *British Journal of Psychiatry* 119/553 (1971), 621–4; Elliot S. Valenstein, *Brain Control: A Critical Examination of Brain Stimulation and Psychosurgery* (New York: Wiley, 1973).

[149] Henry Head, 'Croonian Lecture: Release of Function in the Nervous System', *Proceedings of the Royal Society of London. Series B. Containing Papers of a Biological Character (1905–1934)*, 92/645 (1921), 184–209.

[150] W. R. Hess and M. Brügger, 'Das subkortikale Zentrum der affektiven Abwehrreaktion', *Helvetica physiologica et pharmacologica acta*, 1 (1943), 33–52.

particular part of the brain. He also suspected that the brain was functionally subdivided according to rewards, or, more precisely, pleasure and the avoidance of stress. From these findings and his own experiments Walter Cannon, joined later by Philip Bard, concluded that the thalamus region was key to emotions, and that there was a circuit connecting the cortical parts of the brain (which were, from the evolutionary point of view, younger) to the subcortical of the thalamus.[151] (In Bard's most important experiment he removed a cat's cortex, which led to sudden and erratic aggression, what he called 'sham rage'. By process of elimination he came to the conclusion that emotion could not be located exclusively in the cortex.[152])

The Cannon–Bard Theory is often treated as a counterpart to James and Lange, since it shifts the location of emotional process from the periphery of the body (blushing, sweating) into the brain. In fact, Cannon and Bard sought in part to clearly distinguish their own work from that of James and Lange, pointing to the difficulty of clearly attributing particular emotions to peripheral movements of the body (how do I know that my blushing is related to embarrassment, and not to sexual arousal?). The history of emotion is still at too early a stage of development to adopt such simplified stories about psychological treatises as the replacement of James–Lange by Cannon–Bard. In any case, as was made clear above, once one looks more closely at the James–Lange tandem it turns out that they are not coupled together in the way usually assumed.

The Papez Circuit

Before the invention of neuroimaging it was James Papez who made the second significant move in locating emotion in the brain. He built upon Cannon and Bard's finding that the subcortical thalamus, combined with the cortex, represented an important emotional system based upon excess and control. In a key paper of 1937 Papez refined this connection: he argued that the thalamus was a switchboard dealing with the input from stimuli, directing this input either to an upper cognitive path or to a lower emotional path. The upper path was linked to the sense region of the cortex, especially the cingulum, and divided sense impressions among perceptions, thoughts, and memories. The stimulus then returned to the thalamus via a complicated path, passing through the cingulum, the hippocampus, the fornix, and the mamillary bodies. The lower path was by contrast much

[151] The key article for the Cannon–Bard Theory is Walter B. Cannon, 'The James–Lange Theory of Emotions: A Critical Examination and an Alternative Theory', *American Journal of Psychology*, 39/ 1–4 (1927), 106–24; Walter B. Cannon, 'Again the James–Lange and the Thalamic Theories of Emotions', *Psychological Review*, 38/4 (1931), 281–95; Philip Bard, 'A Diencephalic Mechanism for the Expression of Rage with Special Reference to the Sympathetic Nervous System', *American Journal of Physiology*, 84 (1928), 490–513; David M. Rioch and Philip Bard, 'A Study of Four Cats Deprived of Neocortex and Additional Portions of the Forebrain', *Bulletin of the Johns Hopkins Hospital*, 60 (1937), 73–153.

[152] Dalgleish, Dunn, and Mobbs, 'Affective Neuroscience', 356–7.

quicker, leading directly to the mamillary bodies, activating them and prompting the expression of emotion.[153]

The Papez Circuit is still today regarded as a milestone in the neurosciences, and we can see an echo of Papez's work in that of LeDoux and the two roads to fear already mentioned in the Introduction. It is also significant in regard to the history of science that the interwoven and multidirectional paths that Papez proposed suggest a perspective on the brain that today looks increasingly likely: as a dynamic and interactive entity. Long before the neuronal and neurochemical breakthroughs of the 1980s and 1990s, Papez perhaps sensed that there were more connections and paths to be found, that one would even come to the conclusion in the future that brain activity really involved the interaction of everything, even if there were different levels of intensity in this activity and different centres of concentration. This perspective now competes with one that has prevailed for a very long time: that the individual regions are exclusively responsible for particular functions—this is dealt with below.

The Limbic System

The third development of importance here is the 'discovery' of the limbic system (Fig. 21). Besides building on Cannon and Papez, this work also made use of the Klüver–Bucy Syndrome: Heinrich Klüver (1897–1979) and Paul Bucy (1904–92) had noted that after surgically removing the temporal lobe from apes, they became less emotionally responsive, hyper-sexualized, used their mouths to explore objects, and increasingly ate their own excrement. From all this Paul D. MacLean created a new and comprehensive model of the brain's anatomy and its relationship to emotion.[154] He suggested that the brain was composed of three mutually-related parts. 'Primitive' emotion, such as fear, could be located in the oldest part of the brain, the 'reptile brain', to which the striatum and the basal ganglia belong. Aggression and more complex social emotions are located in the 'old' mammalian parts of the brain, which include many regions of the Papez Circuit (hypothalamus, thalamus, hippocampus, and cingulum), but also the amygdala and the prefrontal cortex. The 'new' mammalian brain, primarily composed of the neocortex, was first and foremost responsible for the cognitive control of emotions. MacLean went on to argue that emotion was a process that took place in all three parts of the brain; the sum of participating areas was the 'limbic system', so called after Broca's *Le Grand Lobe limbique* (1878). In particular, the hippocampus in the 'older' mammalian brain was an active switchboard which received incoming external stimuli, passing them on to give rise to physical reactions, which were themselves refracted and perceived as emotion.

Although MacLean's original hypotheses were often doubted in his lifetime, today one still speaks of the limbic system whenever the question is raised of the

[153] Dalgleish, Dunn, and Mobbs, 'Affective Neuroscience', 357.

[154] Paul D. MacLean, 'Psychosomatic Disease and the "Visceral Brain": Recent Developments Bearing on the Papez Theory of Emotion', *Psychosomatic Medicine*, 11/6 (1949), 338–53.

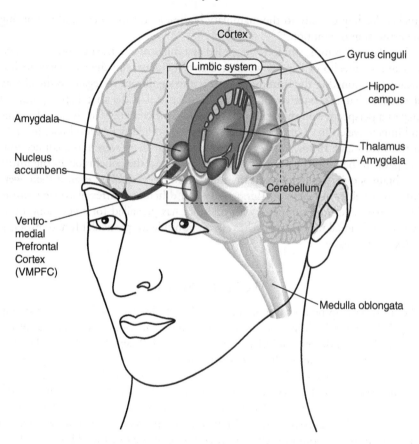

Cortex:	complex cognition, language, memory, consciousness
Gyrus cinguli:	emotional learning, emotional memory
Hippocampus:	transfer of information from short- to long-term memory, spatial memory
Thalamus:	switchboard for the brain's incoming information
Amygdala:	(negative) emotions, esp. fear, anxiety
Nucleus accumbens:	reward, sexual arousal, addiction
Cerebellum:	motor coordination
VMPFC:	decision-making, risk-taking behaviour
Hypothalamus:	body temperature, hunger, thirst, tiredness
Medulla oblongata:	heart rate, breathing and other autonomous functions

Fig. 21 Regions of the Brian (including the Limbic System) and Their Functioning
Source: Peter Palm.

localization of emotion in the brain. However, such discussion does not presume that there is a processual interaction between different regions of the brain in the sense MacLean meant, but rather that there is a loose and changing group of areas, among which the amygdala and the prefrontal cortex are those most often included.[155]

Despite there being many other foci for experimental psychological work on emotion during the first half of the twentieth century, it was the Cannon–Bard Theory, the Papez Circuit, and the limbic system that laid the foundations for the brain-based study of emotion. As with all other initial approaches in the study of emotion, these were always refracted through the prism of contemporary conceptions of space and order, gender and racial stereotypes. The same goes for another great tradition in psychological research during the first half of the twentieth century: psychoanalysis.

8 FREUD'S MISSING THEORY OF FEELING

One of the most popular English-language textbooks on the psychology of emotion states baldly: 'Sigmund Freud did not propose a theory of emotions as such.'[156] But questions arise at once: are not psychological illnesses such as neuroses and psychoses emotional pathologies? Does not anxiety, as opposed to object-related fear, involve an aimless and diffuse—and so dangerous—feeling that runs amok in someone's soul? Surely the conception of trauma involves the positing of disordered emotions? And do not Freud's writings on cultural theory relate very closely to emotions, for example, when there is reference to 'discontent' in a culture? The paradox that psychoanalysis seems to lack a specific theory of emotion, while emotions are at the same time an eminent preoccupation of psychoanalytic thought, can be approached through a reading of the case of Katharina, one of the most famous of Freud's *Studies in Hysteria* [Ger. orig., *Studien über Hysterie*, 1895].

During an Alpine walking holiday Freud stopped at an inn. The young waitress, Katharina, soon found out that Freud was a doctor, and asked him if he could help her. She suffered from shortage of breath and panic attacks:

> I always think I'm going to die. I'm brave as a rule and go about everywhere by myself—into the cellar and all over the mountain. But on a day when that happens I don't dare to go anywhere; I think all the time someone's standing behind me and going to catch hold of me all at once.[157]

Freud's first diagnosis: 'So it was in fact an anxiety attack, and introduced by the signs of a hysterical "aura"—or, more correctly, it was a hysterical attack the content of which was anxiety.' But this was merely a superficial description, behind

[155] See Dalgleish, Dunn, and Mobbs, 'Affective Neuroscience', 357–8.

[156] Keltner, Oatley and Jenkins, *Understanding Emotions*, 7.

[157] Sigmund Freud, 'Case 4: Katharina', in Josef Breuer and Sigmund Freud, *Studies on Hysteria*, trans. and ed. James Strachey and Anna Freud (London: Hogarth, 1955), 125–34, here 126.

which more must be hidden. Freud asked himself: 'Might there not probably be some other content as well?'[158] Here we can glimpse the beginning of an explanation as to why it is that in psychoanalysis emotions are paradoxically both present and absent: feelings often arise, but they are only epiphenomena of a psychic condition.

Katharina went on to say that during her panic attacks she always saw a frightening man's face, which she could not however recognize. Freud wrote that in a case like this he would have normally used hypnosis, but since he was at a mountain inn he could only ask more questions: 'I should have to try a lucky guess. I had found often enough that in girls anxiety was a consequence of the horror by which a virginal mind is overcome when it is faced for the first time with the world of sexuality.'[159] So he said to Katharina that he suspected the panic attacks had begun after she had experienced something distressing—he was aiming here at the domain of sexuality. Katharina suddenly recalled that she had seen her own uncle through a window lying on top of her cousin Franziska. At the time she had not understood what was happening, but for the first time she found it hard to catch her breath. Shortly afterwards she chronically vomited. Her aunt noticed and forcefully questioned her about it. She, Katharina, had described everything that she had seen, the aunt had questioned the uncle about the matter, and Franziska had become pregnant by her uncle, which then brought about an open break and divorce. The aunt had moved out with Katharina and opened the inn in which she now worked, and which the Viennese doctor had come across during his walking tour.

While Katharina was talking about her aunt's divorce, Freud describes how, 'to my astonishment she dropped these threads and began to tell me two sets of older stories, which went back two or three years earlier than the traumatic moment'.[160] These stories all related to the attempted sexual abuse of Katharina by the uncle, the first time being when she was 14, and

she had once gone with him [the uncle] on an expedition down into the valley in the winter and had spent the night in the inn there. He sat in the bar drinking and playing cards, but she felt sleepy and went up to bed early in the room they were to share on the upper floor. She was not quite asleep when he came up; then she fell asleep again and woke up suddenly 'feeling his body' in the bed. She jumped up and remonstrated with him: 'What are you up to, Uncle? Why don't you stay in your own bed?' He tried to pacify her: 'Go on, you silly girl, keep still. You don't know how nice it is.'—'I don't like your "nice" things; you don't even let one sleep in peace.' She remained standing by the door, ready to take refuge outside in the passage, till at last he gave up and went to sleep himself. Then she went back to her own bed and slept till morning. From the way in which she reported having defended herself it seems to follow that she did not clearly recognize the attack as a sexual one. When I asked her if she knew what he was trying to do to her, she replied: 'Not at the time.' It had become clear to her much later

[158] Freud, 'Case 4: Katharina', 126.   [159] Freud, 'Case 4: Katharina', 127.
[160] Freud, 'Case 4: Katharina', 129.

on, she said; she had resisted because it was unpleasant to be disturbed in one's sleep and 'because it wasn't nice'.[161]

Katharina seemed to have been healed by the recollected memory: 'At the end of these two sets of memories she came to a stop. She was like someone transformed. The sulky, unhappy face had grown lively, her eyes were bright, she was lightened and exalted.'[162] For Freud, the solution lay in the connection of the Franziska episode with the previous attempt at sexual abuse by her uncle. For when Katharina saw her uncle having sex with Franziska, the consciousness of the threat that had existed for her literally cut off her breath. The only loose end was the terrible face that regularly accompanied her panic attacks, which had not been identified. But even this puzzle could be cleared up, for Katharina said:

> Yes, I know now. The head is my uncle's head—I recognize it now—but not from *that* time. Later, when all the disputes had broken out, my uncle gave way to a senseless rage against me. He kept saying that it was all my fault: if I hadn't chattered, it would never have come to a divorce. He kept threatening he would do something to me; and if he caught sight of me at a distance his face would get distorted with rage and he would make for me with his hand raised. I always ran away from him, and always felt terrified that he would catch me some time unawares. The face I always see now is his face when he was in a rage.[163]

Freud closed the epicrisis of the case with the following:

> The anxiety from which Katharina suffered in her attacks was a hysterical one; that is, it was a reproduction of the anxiety which had appeared in connection with each of the sexual traumas. I shall not here comment on the fact which I have found regularly present in a very large number of cases—namely that a mere suspicion of sexual relations calls up the affect of anxiety in virginal individuals.[164]

In 1924, almost twenty-four years later, he supplemented his remarks:

> I venture after the lapse of so many years to lift the veil of discretion and reveal the fact that Katharina was not the niece but the daughter of the landlady. The girl felt ill, therefore, as a result of sexual attempts on the part of her own father.[165]

The states of anxiety to which Freud referred—today we call them panic attacks—had therefore an especially dramatic aspect. The case of Katharina seems to prove that while psychoanalysis constantly turns on emotions, emotions never find their way into an explanation, and that for Freud the decisive level of causal interpretation was always that of sexuality.

That is of course too crude a generalization. Uffa Jensen has shown that in psychoanalysis emotions are not only the 'central marker' for underlying psychic processes, but that there are 'two threads running through Freud's life and work':

[161] Freud, 'Case 4: Katharina', 129–30.   [162] Freud, 'Case 4: Katharina', 131.
[163] Freud, 'Case 4: Katharina', 132.   [164] Freud, 'Case 4: Katharina', 134.
[165] Freud, 'Case 4: Katharina', 134 n. 2.

'the ambivalence of feelings and the condition of anxiety'.[166] The incomplete and complex affect theory of the early Freud—he talks of 'affects'—was in fact more biological and mechanical than his later thinking on emotion and anxiety, on the role of emotions in the psychic development of the child, and on the connection between emotions and culture. To take only one aspect of the earlier theory of affect: Freud presupposed a psychic economy involving drives, undifferentiated affects (without demarcating fear, hatred, or love), and differentiated sensations. In 1915 he wrote in 'Repression':

> The quantitative factor of the instinctual representative has three possible vicissitudes, as we can see from a cursory survey of the observations made by psycho-analysis: either the instinct is altogether suppressed, so that no trace of it is found, or it appears as an affect which is in some way or other qualitatively coloured, or it is changed into anxiety.[167]

Here we have the triangle of drives, affects, and an individual feeling. 'The affective condition', writes Jensen, 'consisted of an element of energy which within the psychic apparatus functioned according to the law of the conservation of energy.' He goes on: 'An affect forced its way through an incomplete repression in the form of a distortion or displacement from the unconscious to the conscious, and in this way could be felt as an emotion.'[168] This reminds us of something: there is an echo of Freud's theory of affects in Norbert Elias. He talked of an 'economy of affects', and accused modernity of having overlaid the expression of feeling, still unfiltered in the Middle Ages, with taboos, so that at best emotions could be lived out on the artificial stage of sport, at worst repressed, creating neuroses, compulsions, and other disorders. Jensen attributes the biological and mechanical character of Freud's affect theory to the influence of physiology on the early Freud, to the internalization of bourgeois and manly values such as rationalism, understood as emotional control, and to excessive scientism, which provided some kind of shield against accusations of scientific deficiencies. Those studying emotions in general, and psychoanalysis in particular, were accused precisely of being 'unscientific'.

The thread of ambivalence about feelings that Jensen identifies in Freud is revealed, for example, with compulsive neurotics, who admit one feeling (for instance, love) while repressing another which is also present (for instance, hate), driving them to compulsive behaviour. But ambivalence about feelings also had for

---

[166] Uffa Jensen, 'Freuds unheimliche Gefühle: Zur Rolle von Emotionen in der Freudschen Psychoanalyse', in Jensen and Daniel Morat (eds), *Rationalisierungen des Gefühls: Zum Verhältnis von Wissenschaft und Emotionen 1880–1930* (Munich: Fink 2008), 135–52, here 141, 138. See also Mai Wegener, 'Warum die Psychoanalyse keine Gefühlstheorie hat', in Johannes Fehr and Gerd Folkers (eds), *Gefühle zeigen: Manifestationsformen emotionaler Prozesse* (Zurich: Chronos, 2009), 143–62; Nancy J. Chodorow, *The Power of Feelings: Personal Meaning in Psychoanalysis, Gender, and Culture* (New Haven: Yale University Press, 1999).

[167] Sigmund Freud, 'Repression', in *The Standard Edition of the Complete Psychological Works of Sigmund Freud*, xiv. *1914–1916*, trans. and ed. James Strachey and Anna Freud (London: Hogarth, 1957), 141–58, here 153.

[168] Jensen, 'Freuds unheimliche Gefühle', 142.

Freud a biographical dimension: as he later recalled, as a child he had a nephew who was a year older, whom he worshipped but also hated for his superiority:

> All my friends have in a certain sense been re-incarnations of this first figure . . . My emotional life has always insisted that I should have an intimate friend and a hated enemy. I have always been able to provide myself afresh with both, and it has not infrequently happened that the ideal situation of childhood has been so completely reproduced that friend and enemy have come together in a single individual.[169]

According to Jensen, the second thread is the increasing importance of anxiety in Freud's thinking. 'However that may be, there is no question', wrote Freud, 'that the problem of anxiety is a nodal point at which the most various and important questions converge, a riddle whose solution would be bound to throw a flood of light on our whole mental existence.'[170] As soon as he had prised the conception of anxiety from the iron jaws of his earlier 'economy of affect', Freud put together the theory of the primal anxiety of the child at birth, the blueprint for all other anxieties, related to an 'immense increase of stimulation owing to the interruption of the renovation of the blood (internal respiration)' at the moment of birth: 'The name *"Angst"*—*"angustiae" [sic]*, *"Enge"*—emphasizes the characteristic of restriction in breathing which was then present as a consequence of the real situation and is now almost invariably reinstated in the affect.'[171] All anxieties in the later development of a person could be traced back to this primal situation. Freud emphasized that 'With the depersonalization of the parental agency from which castration was feared, the danger becomes less defined. Castration anxiety develops into moral anxiety—social anxiety—and it is not so easy now to know what the anxiety is about.'[172] Freudian anxiety was located at the level of the ego, and from there worked on the superego, rendering anxiety, according to Uffa Jensen, the 'central culturally-creative feeling'.[173] Seeking an individual sense of well-being, the ego transmitted signals of anxiety that were translated into ethics, as well as powerful super-individual, collective, and social cultural achievements. 'In the failure that manifested itself at the level of an individual as a symptom there could be discerned that which drove culture onwards: a feeling whose rational mastery had to become the task of each individual, and of all individuals together.'[174]

There would be little point in following through the role of emotion in all the variations, further developments, and revisions that psychoanalysis has undergone

---

[169] Sigmund Freud, 'The Interpretation of Dreams (Second Part)', in *The Standard Edition of the Complete Psychological Works of Sigmund Freud*, v. *1900–1901*, trans. and ed. James Strachey and Anna Freud (London: Hogarth, 1953), 339–508, here 483.

[170] Sigmund Freud, 'Introductory Lectures on Psycho-Analysis (Part III)', in *The Standard Edition of the Complete Psychological Works of Sigmund Freud*, xvi. *1916–1917*, trans. and ed. James Strachey and Anna Freud (London: Hogarth, 1963), 393.

[171] Freud, 'Introductory Lectures on Psycho-Analysis (Part III)', 396–7.

[172] Sigmund Freud, 'Inhibitions, Symptoms and Anxiety', in *The Standard Edition of the Complete Psychological Works of Sigmund Freud*, xx. *1925–1926*, trans. and ed. James Strachey and Anna Freud (London: Hogarth, 1959), 77–178, here 139.

[173] Jensen, 'Freuds unheimliche Gefühle', 151.

[174] Jensen, 'Freuds unheimliche Gefühle', 151.

since Freud. But to make plain what goes on in this domain we can introduce two current examples for the purpose of illustration. First of all, there has recently been the development of neuropsychoanalysis, combining emotions as understood by neuroscience with psychoanalytical conceptions. The psychiatrist and neuroscientist Yoram Yovell put Freud's theory of drives together with the Emotional Command Systems (ECS) developed by the neuroscientist Jaak Panksepp, who had in 1998 coined the term 'affective neuroscience'. The outcome proposed by Yovell was a neuropsychoanalytical model of love.[175] Panksepp's ECS are universal neurochemical processes that lead to advantages in survival, and so are based functionally on evolutionary biology. The ECS 'search', 'fear', 'rage', and 'desire' are located in the deepest palaeocortical regions of the brain, in and around the brain stem. These ECS are responsible in humans and animals for basic activities, such as dealing with threats or reproduction. Other ECS in higher, but still subcortical, regions of the brain regulate simple social behaviour ('panic', 'care', 'play') involving social ties and fear of separation. Although Panksepp was himself not in favour of the blending of his ECS with the theory of drives, arguing that it was much too multifaceted to be matched up with Freudian conceptions of libido and the self- or sex-drive, this process is now fully engaged in the new field of neuropsychoanalysis.[176]

Yovell has addressed, of all things, romantic love, which is both object-related (who to love?) and culturally contingent (many cultures lack the concept of romantic love), linking in this context ECS and the theory of drives. Or better: Yovell seeks to rewrite Freud using ECS as a corrective. A generalized drive of desire that underpins everything cannot, according to Yovell, be applied directly to romantic love. Only by combining different ECS is that possible: the ECS 'search', which comes closest to the libido, together with the ECS 'panic' and 'care', which would most closely correspond to the appetitive aspects of Freud's drives, coincide in romantic love. These last two elements accounted for anxieties linked to attachment and fear of separation, the specific aspects of romantic love. 'Either way, drive theory may now be revised to include the contribution of nonlibidinal instinctual/emotional systems such as the attachment system. It may then serve as a useful link between psychoanalysis and the cognitive and affective neurosciences in their combined efforts to study and understand romantic love.'[177] Felicity

[175] Yoram Yovell, 'Is There a Drive to Love?', *Neuro-Psychoanalysis*, 10/2 (2008), 117–44; Jaak Panksepp, *Affective Neuroscience: The Foundations of Human and Animal Emotions* (New York: Oxford University Press, 1998). Here I am relying on Constantina Papoulias and Felicity J. Callard, 'The Rehabilitation of the Drive in Neuropsychoanalysis: From Sexuality to Self-Preservation', in Christine Kirchhoff and Gerhard Scharbert (eds), *Freuds Referenzen* (Berlin: Kulturverlag Kosmos, 2012), 189–215. See also on neuropsychoanalysis Giselher Guttmann and Inge Scholz-Strasser (eds), *Freud and the Neurosciences: From Brain Research to the Unconscious* (Vienna: Verlag der Österreichischen Akademie der Wissenschaften, 1998); Mark Solms and Edward Nersessian, 'Freud's Theory of Affect: Questions for Neuroscience', *Neuro-Psychoanalysis*, 1/1 (1999), 5–14; Eric R. Kandel, *Psychiatry, Psychoanalysis, and the New Biology of Mind* (Washington, DC: American Psychiatric Publishing, 2005).

[176] Papoulias and Callard, 'Rehabilitation of the Drive in Neuropsychoanalysis', 196–7.

[177] Yovell, 'Is There a Drive to Love?', 140–1.

J. Callard and Constantina Papoulias have argued that this only works if one assumes a particular neuroscientific reading of Freud which above all interprets the pleasure principle (*Lustprinzip*) functionally within the framework of evolutionary biology—a reading which, one might add, could hardly be further from everyday conceptions of romantic love.[178]

Secondly, there is today an increasing emphasis on the healing power of storytelling in therapeutic practice dealing with trauma and other emotional ailments, even where psychoanalysis remains a strong influence. The aim is not, as with earlier psychoanalytic practice, to trace the origin of a trauma and reveal its trigger. The therapist does not seek the verbalization of dreadful experiences that have as a consequence been repressed; rather, it is the character of narration itself that is thought to have therapeutic properties. Storytelling has an iterative, performative power, making a coherent whole of fragmentary memories. Furthermore, narration creates a distance with respect to something terrible. The process of narration defuses emotions by removing their immediacy.[179] Some therapies presuppose a staged process, in which even the identification of feelings is healing. Narrative Exposure Therapy (NET), for instance, invokes the neuroscientific principle that 'Affect-labeling, not just the recognition of the emotion as such, disrupts the affective responses and diminishes activity in the limbic system that would otherwise occur in the presence of negative experiences.'[180] But narration is ultimately decisive here too:

> the main goal of therapy is to construct a consistent . . . representation of the sequence of events experienced by the patient. . . . This process allows for habituation and reduces fear responses over time. The task of a therapist is to encourage the activation of painful memories and to prevent the patient's learned strategies of avoiding or ending the activation of these memories and physical sensations. . . . The patient will habituate in the process and will become accustomed to remembering the events without activating strong emotional responses.[181]

9 THE BOOM IN THE PSYCHOLOGY OF EMOTION FROM THE 1960S ONWARDS

From the 1960s 'the number of conceptual and empirical works on emotion increased exponentially'.[182] It is still not clear why that happened. Part of the

---

[178] Papoulias and Callard, 'Rehabilitation of the Drive in Neuropsychoanalysis', 203.

[179] See e.g. the writings of Tilmann Habermas: Tilmann Habermas, Michaela Meier, and Barbara Mukhtar, 'Are Specific Emotions Narrated Differently?', *Emotion*, 9/6 (2009), 751–62; Tilmann Habermas and Verena Diel, 'The Emotional Impact of Loss Narratives: Event Severity and Narrative Perspectives', *Emotion*, 10/10 (2010), 312–23; Tilmann Habermas and Nadine Berger, 'Retelling Everyday Emotional Events: Condensation, Distancing, and Closure', *Cognition and Emotion*, 25/2 (2011), 206–19.

[180] Maggie Schauer, Frank Neuner, and Thomas Elbert, *Narrative Exposure Therapy: A Short-Term Treatment for Traumatic Stress Disorders* (2nd rev. and enl. edn, Cambridge, MA: Hogrefe, 2011), 32.

[181] Schauer, Neuner, and Elbert, *Narrative Exposure Therapy*, 33.

[182] Gendron and Barrett, 'Reconstructing the Past', 335.

explanation has to do with internal developments in psychology, together with trends in other sciences. One major influence was the importance of emotions in the philosophy of existentialism, which was exerting a global impact. Quite probably general social developments played a part in changing the relationship to emotion. The rise of the women's movement and the entry of women into universities and professional life certainly raised the profile of stereotypical female qualities such as emotionality. Another factor during the 1970s and the 1980s was the enhancement of emotions in the broader society through the influence of therapeutization, self-help groups, and New Age talk about one's own feelings.[183] The Peace Movement also made a contribution to the fading of any negative connotation in the idea of the 'emotional'; indeed, men who had trouble expressing their anxiety had a hard time in groups related to the Peace Movement.[184] This, together with other shifts whose history has yet to be written, brought about a real explosion in the psychological study of emotion. Let us examine the results of this by considering some of its most successful paradigms.

10 A SYNTHETIC COGNITIVE-PHYSIOLOGICAL THEORY OF EMOTION: THE SCHACHTER–SINGER MODEL

At the end of the 1950s two psychologists, Stanley Schachter and Jerome E. Singer, formulated the hypothesis that people who were in a state of general physical arousal could identify this state of arousal in terms of differing emotional descriptors, according to circumstance. According to Schachter and Singer, therefore, there are no physical signals that have an exclusive relationship to one emotion. Rather, general physical signals find an emotional nomenclature only after an evaluation procedure has taken place. Anger, envy, or pleasure are therefore not states of the body, but learned ascriptions, applied based on situation. Conversely, they argued, people who had an illuminating physiological explanation for a non-specific physical arousal ('they were injected with adrenalin') did not use emotional labels for these states at all. At the same time, there could be no emotional description without physical arousal.[185]

---

[183] Pascal Eitler, 'Der "Neue Mann" des "New Age": Emotion und Religion in der Bundesrepublik Deutschland 1970–1990', in Manuel Borutta and Nina Verheyen (eds), *Die Präsenz der Gefühle: Männlichkeit und Emotion in der Moderne* (Bielefeld: Transcript, 2010), 279–304. Also Sabine Maasen, Jens Elberfeld, Pascal Eitler, and Maik Tändler (eds), *Das beratene Selbst: Zur Genealogie der Therapeutisierung in den 'langen' Siebzigern* (Bielefeld: transcript, 2011).

[184] Susanne Schregel, 'Konjunktur der Angst: "Politik der Subjektivität" und "neue Friedensbewegung", 1979–1983', in Bernd Greiner, Christian Th. Müller, and Dierk Walter (eds), *Angst im Kalten Krieg* (Hamburg: Hamburger Edition, 2009), 495–520; Jörg Arnold, ' "Kassel 1943 mahnt...".': Zur Genealogie der Angst im Kalten Krieg', in Greiner, Müller, and Walter (eds), *Angst im Kalten Krieg*, 465–94.

[185] Stanley Schachter and Jerome E. Singer, 'Cognitive, Social, and Physiological Determinants of Emotional State', *Psychological Review*, 69/5 (1962), 379–99, here 381–2.

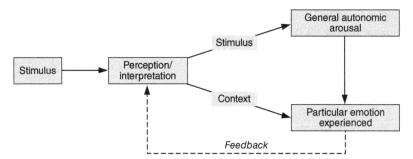

Fig. 22 The Schachter–Singer Model of Emotion

Source: Peter Palm, based on an illustration in 'The Schachter–Singer Theory of Emotion', *Psychwiki.com* <http:// www.psychwiki.com/wiki/The_Schachter-Singer_Theory_of_Emotion> accessed 12 March 2014.

To verify their hypothesis Schachter and Singer designed a model in which 184 male test subjects, all of them college students, were told that they were to be injected with a vitamin to test their sight. In fact, they were injected with an adrenalin solution which, as a rule, led to a raised heart rate and blood pressure, an increased blood sugar level, and accelerated breathing. During the entire experiment all test subjects were encouraged to think that these effects were the result of the vitamin used to test their vision; but one part of the group was given an explanation of the effects of the supposed vitamin injection. Then the group was divided roughly in two, one of which was asked to simulate euphoria with the help of some actors, the other rage. All test subjects had their heart rate monitored afterwards, and all of them filled in a questionnaire regarding their physical state (heart rate, trembling, deafness, itching, headache), as well as their own impressions of their emotional state. The results confirmed the hypothesis: all of those who had been given a physiological explanation for their physical condition ('the injection of the vitamin led to an increased heart rate, shaking hands, etc.') described themselves as unemotional and as simply having had a reaction to the injected solution. Those subjects who had not been told of the physical effects of the injection reacted either euphorically or angrily and described their physical reactions as either euphoria or anger. This created the 'probably most influential emotion theory in academic psychology' for at least 'the 20 years following its publication'.[186] The Schachter–Singer Model, also known as the Two-Factor Model or the Cognitive-Physiological Model, considers emotion and physical movement to be always intertwined (there is no such thing as emotion without a body), learned cognitions being responsible to interpretation and specification of the particular emotion involved (Fig. 22).

Because of its synthetic nature, the Schachter–Singer Model has been linked with both (neo-)Jamesian and cognitive psychology (Schachter himself once called

[186] According to the psychologist Rainer Reisenzein, 'Schachter–Singer Theory', in David Sander and Klaus R. Scherer (eds), *The Oxford Companion to Emotion and the Affective Sciences* (Oxford: Oxford University Press, 2009), 352–3, here 352.

his theory 'modified Jamesianism').[187] It is today this synthesis of cognition and physiology that is always positively emphasized, even if criticism is made of the details of the model.[188]

11 EVALUATING EMOTIONS: COGNITIVE PSYCHOLOGY AND APPRAISAL MODELS

A few years before Schachter and Singer the American psychologist Magda B. Arnold had elaborated a model of emotion that left room for evaluation of the stimulus which prompted the emotion process, or of the object to which the emotion was directed. According to Arnold and her co-author John A. Gasson, an emotion is a 'felt tendency toward an object judged suitable, or away from an object judged unsuitable, reinforced by specific bodily changes according to the type of emotion'.[189] Unlike stimulus-response models (I run away from the snake because it represents *eo ipso* a dangerous stimulation), judgements also can influence matters: I run away from the poisonous snake because I know it is dangerous, but not from the slow-worm since I know it is harmless. In other words:

> To arouse an emotion, the object must be appraised as affecting me in some way, affecting me personally as an individual with my particular experience and my particular aims. If I see an apple, I know that it is an apple of a particular kind and taste. This knowledge need not touch me personally in any way. But if the apple is of my favorite kind and I am in a part of the world where it does not grow and cannot be bought, I may want it with a real emotional craving.[190]

The model can be reduced to the following simple schema:

Perception $\rightarrow$ Appraisal $\rightarrow$ Emotion

Although Arnold built an element of appraisal into her model, she did concur with the view taken by psychologists of emotion working in the Darwinian tradition that emotions were necessary to the struggle for survival. And while this appraisal component left a great deal of space for cultural, group-specific, or individual influences, Arnold was certain that 'there will always be a core that is similar from person to person or even from man to animal', since we could not otherwise decode the emotional expression of fellow humans and animals.[191]

---

[187] Schachter on his model as 'modified Jamesianism': Stanley Schachter, 'The Interaction of Cognitive and Physiological Determinants of Emotion State', *Advances in Experimental Social Psychology*, 1 (1964), 49–80, here 70; Schachter as a representative of cognitive psychology: Ruth Leys, 'The Turn to Affect: A Critique', *Critical Inquiry*, 37/3 (2011), 434–72, here 469.

[188] Reisenzein, 'Schachter–Singer Theory', 353.

[189] Magda B. Arnold and John A. Gasson, 'Feelings and Emotions as Dynamic Factors in Personality Integration', in Arnold and John A. Gasson (eds), *The Human Person: An Approach to an Integral Theory of Personality* (New York: Ronald Press, 1954), 294–313, here 294.

[190] Magda B. Arnold, *Emotion and Personality*, i. *Psychological Aspects* (New York: Columbia University Press, 1960), 171.

[191] Arnold, *Emotion and Personality*, i. 179. See also Randolph R. Cornelius, *The Science of Emotion: Research and Tradition in the Psychology of Emotion* (Upper Saddle River, NJ: Prentice Hall, 1996), 119.

In the following decades one of the largest schools of research into emotions developed around 'appraisal'. Among the most important institutions here is the journal *Cognition and Emotion*, founded in 1987; the leading specialists today are Phoebe C. Ellsworth, Nico Frijda, Batja Mesquita, and Klaus R. Scherer. The success of the appraisal approach coincided with the 'cognitive revolution' and the 'demise of radical behaviorism in the late 1970s and early 1980s'.[192] While the appraisal school is today divided into many different subgroups with ever more complex models, one is typical of its experimental culture: 'self-report'—verbal or written estimation by test subjects of their own emotions—here plays a major role. This does not mean that no measurements are made of sweat production, pulse, and the dilation of pupils, but physical values are not an exclusive source. The appraisal approach is constantly compared with the philosophy of emotion, especially Aristotelian thinking on the subject for, as we saw in the Introduction to this book, that also has an evaluative aspect. This dimension opens the way for an assessment of the impact of culture, and so also for history. It is therefore no surprise that those working in the human sciences have long found the appraisal approach to the study of emotion the most accessible of experimental psychology.[193]

At the beginning of the 1980s interest developed in an issue that was related to a controversy that arose in the later neurosciences—the question of how fast appraisal processes were. Arnold had herself emphasized that cognition did not arise instantaneously, and that as a rule appraisal was 'direct, immediate, nonreflective, non-intellectual, automatic'. She cited baseball in which the player has to decide in fractions of a second the direction from which the ball is travelling towards him, and then coordinate his own movements so that he can catch it. If the player stopped to think about his own movements or that of the ball, 'he would never stay in the game'.[194] This aspect of the Arnold approach was simply bypassed in an article written by the psychologist Robert Zajonc (1923–2008), which led to a fierce debate with another psychologist, Richard S. Lazarus (1922–2002). Zajonc presented a model of emotion which was in many respects rather like the appraisal approach, although it was not related to the older Arnold school, but was oriented by a polemic with cognitive psychology, as though the appraisal approach had never happened.[195] Zajonc wrote that emotion was 'postcognitive'.[196] For him, emotion played a leading, unconscious, and temporally precognitive role in all human behaviour, in particular where decision-making was involved: '"Do you like this person?" "How do you feel about capital punishment?" "Which do you prefer, Brie or Camembert?"'[197] Affective responses were, 'in contrast with cold cognition... effortless, inescapable, irrevocable, holistic, more difficult to verbalize, yet easy to

---

[192] Cornelius, *Science of Emotion*, 114.
[193] See e.g. William M. Reddy, *The Navigation of Feeling: A Framework for the History of Emotions* (Cambridge: Cambridge University Press, 2001).
[194] Arnold, *Emotion and Personality*, i. 175.
[195] According to Zajonc: 'Contemporary cognitive psychology simply ignores affect', only social psychology paid emotion proper attention; R. B. Zajonc, 'Feeling and Thinking: Preferences Need no Inferences', *American Psychologist*, 35/2 (1980), 151–75, here 152 n. 3.
[196] Zajonc, 'Feeling and Thinking', 151.   [197] Zajonc, 'Feeling and Thinking', 152.

communicate and to understand'.[198] In this, Zajonc still presumed a strict separation of cognition and emotion. The cognitive system was, he considered, slower, more complex, and more precise, since it employed culturally contingent language. By contrast, the emotional system was older in evolutionary terms, it created advantages in survival, and it was prelinguistic, faster, and less conscious, hence more universal. Ultimately, emotions could easily be communicated across cultural borders. Read in terms of what we know today, this characterization of emotion as a non-verbal process, combined with the fact that Zajonc talked consistently of 'affect', anticipated definitions of emotion typical of later research in the neurosciences. It would therefore be anachronistic to project today's neuroscience back on to the later 1970s, as is clear in Zajonc's own position, and also because he did himself see an affinity with the Freudian conception of the unconscious: 'The separation of affect and cognition, the dominance and primacy of affective reactions . . . are all very much in the spirit of Freud, the champion of the unconscious.'[199]

    The appraisal theorist Richard S. Lazarus responded that 'the most serious mistake in Zajonc's analysis lies in his approach to cognition'.[200] Lazarus maintained that Zajonc had defined cognition in too restricted a fashion, as higher-level cognition of the kind involved in considering the solution of a difficult mathematical equation, or the meaning of a complicated philosophical text. In so doing he had made use of a widespread, but false, conception modelled on a computer, in which cognition was a mode of calculation employing meaningless bits. In this model, it was only at the conclusion of a chain of calculations that something as meaningful as emotion could emerge, and that seemed to Zajonc to be too late. If one instead used the broader definition of cognition employed by the appraisal school, which involved the production of meaning from the very beginning, it was possible to treat appraisal procedures that were mostly unconscious as cognition. Appraisal, according to Lazarus, was not necessarily 'rational, and conscious'.[201] Cognition defined in this way would therefore precede emotion temporally, and not the other way around. The controversy between Zajonc and Lazarus did create a fuss in the early 1980s, but even ten years later it seemed obsolete, as newer neuroscientific methods and approaches revolutionized the study of emotion in the brain.

12 THE NEUROSCIENCES, fMRI SCANNING, AND OTHER IMAGING PROCEDURES

At the end of the 1980s psychologists, medical scientists, biologists, and physicists in Britain and America together developed a new procedure that made brain activity visible: functional magnetic resonance imaging. This provided the neurosciences with the chance of a breakthrough, and secured the dominance of the life

---

[198] Zajonc, 'Feeling and Thinking', 169.   [199] Zajonc, 'Feeling and Thinking', 172.
[200] Richard S. Lazarus, 'Thoughts on the Relations between Emotion and Cognition', *American Psychologist*, 37/9 (1982), 1019–24, here 1020.
[201] Lazarus, 'Thoughts on the Relations between Emotion and Cognition', 1019.

sciences. The rise of fMRI scanning was quite fabulous. On the basis of yellow spots in a grey brain scan, bold hypotheses were put forward about love, free will, the human capacity for empathy, the way in which children acquired language, the feel for rhythm, and truthfulness. Of course, criticism of the broad and simplistic interpretations made of these brain photos followed very quickly, there was talk of the 'New Phrenology', 'brain porn', 'neurobabble', and 'blobology', the 'science' of coloured spots on a brain scan.[202] But before we explore the limits of the new imaging procedures, we need to explain how they work.

Magnetic resonance imaging measures changes in the oxygen content of blood in the brain, and from that draws conclusions about neuronal activity. The procedure is based on knowledge that red blood cells have differing magnetic properties according to their oxygen content. The difference between greater or less oxygen content in the blood is called the BOLD contrast (blood-oxygen-level dependent contrast). During the simplest kind of activity in nerve cells, the transmission of an electrical impulse (the 'firing' of nerve cells or neurons that we hear so much about), oxygen is used, changing the oxygen content in the blood. Of course, this happens with a delay which varies, and which is either given a fixed value by the measuring software or estimated using mathematical models.[203] This means that an fMRI scanner has to measure neuronal activity indirectly, and with a time lag.[204]

So how does an experiment take place? The test subject first of all removes all metal objects and puts on headphones to insulate himself from noise (the scanner creates a strong magnetic field and loud noises). He puts on video spectacles, is given a keyboard, and is pushed into the scanner. Depending on the kind of machine, either the whole body, the upper body and head, or only the head lies in the tunnel (Fig. 23). A control group is used to exclude the possibility that emotions like claustrophobia will not be triggered by the experimental situation. To get the best possible pictures of the brain, the test subject has to lie motionless in

---

[202] For 'New Phrenology': William R. Uttal, *The New Phrenology: The Limits of Localizing Cognitive Processes in the Brain* (Cambridge, MA: MIT Press, 2001); for 'brain porn' and 'neurobabble': Christopher F. Chabris and Daniel J. Simons, *The Invisible Gorilla: And Other Ways our Intuitions Deceive Us* (New York: Crown, 2009), 139–43; for 'blobology': Cordelia Fine, *Delusions of Gender: How Our Minds, Society, and Neurosexism Create Difference* (New York: Norton, 2010), 153. Critical of fMRI scanning and its (bio)political implications: Joseph Dumit, *Picturing Personhood: Brain Scans and Biomedical Identity* (Princeton: Princeton University Press, 2004); Kelly A. Joyce, *Magnetic Appeal: MRI and the Myth of Transparency* (Ithaca, NY: Cornell University Press, 2008).
[203] The most popular of these mathematical models at the moment is the Dynamic Causal Modelling (DCM) developed by Karl Friston and others—this was published in K. J. Friston, L. Harrison, and W. Penny, 'Dynamic Causal Modelling', *NeuroImage*, 19/4 (2003), 1273–1302.
[204] One of the inventors of the fMRI scanner, Peter A. Bandettini, summarized the limits of the scanner in 2004 as follows: 'Functional MRI cannot map transient activity on the order of milliseconds. It cannot map brain activity on a spatial scale smaller than about 2 mm². Because of baseline drift, it cannot map very slow "state" changes. It cannot differentiate activity resulting from excitatory vs. inhibitory input. It cannot map baseline activity and metabolic state. It cannot temporally resolve cascaded communication between sequentially activated brain regions. Calibration procedures are relatively crude. It cannot draw inferences about individual activation maps as they relate to averaged population brain activation maps'; 'Peter A. Bandettini, Ph.D., Investigator', *Neuroscience@NIH* <http://neuroscience.nih.gov/Lab.asp?Org_ID=160> accessed 11 March 2014.

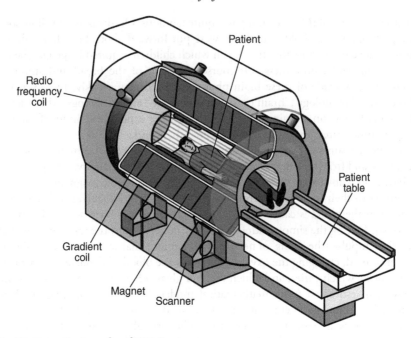

Fig. 23 Cross-Section of an fMRI Scanner

Source: Peter Palm based on an illustration from Neuroskeptic, 'fMRI in 1000 Words', *Discover Magazine* (24 May 2010) <http://blogs.discovermagazine.com/neuroskeptic/2010/05/24/fmri-in-1000-words/> accessed 11 March 2014.

the scanner for stretches of up to 15 minutes during an experiment that can last between 30 and 60 minutes.[205]

In each experiment the test subject is stimulated in one way or another.[206] This can be done acoustically through the headphones, visually through the spectacles, tactilely by touching the body, or through olfactory stimuli. These stimuli are usually associated with the completion of a task. Among the most important experimental designs in the study of emotion are first of all the colouring of emotions through stimulation—what is called 'priming'—and subsequent examination of the way in which this emotional colouring has influenced the decision behaviour. Is it important if, for example, I am 'primed' with mournful music, a

---

[205] A description of the external and technical aspects of experimental design gives 'fMRI Research Project Participant Information', *Sanford School of Medicine at University of South Dakota* <http://www.usd.edu/medical-school/biomedical-sciences/fmri-research-project-participant-information.cfm> accessed 11 March 2014.

[206] For descriptions of the usual experiments on emotion see Hugo Critchley, 'Emotion and Its Disorders: Imaging in Clinical Neuroscience', *British Medical Bulletin*, 65 (2003), 35–47; Tom Johnstone, Carien M. van Reekum, Terrence R. Oakes, and Richard J. Davidson, 'The Voice of Emotion: An FMRI Study of Neural Responses to Angry and Happy Vocal Expressions', *Social Cognitive and Affective Neuroscience*, 1/3 (2006), 242–9; Kateri McRae, Kevin N. Ochsner, Iris B. Mauss, John J. D. Gabrieli, and James J. Gross, 'Gender Differences in Emotion Regulation: An fMRI Study of Cognitive Reappraisal', *Group Processes and Intergroup Relations*, 11/2 (2008), 143–62.

photo of a sad Ekman face, or a request to recall a sad episode from my own life, and then shown pictures of a smiling and a serious-looking politician, being asked to decide which I would rather trust? Secondly, test subjects can be stimulated with cultural products through the spectacles or headphones—a passage from *Anna Karenina*, a clip from *Dracula*, or a Beatles song. From the region of the brain that has been stimulated, one can identify the specific emotion, or emotions, that have been prompted by this means. If, for instance, the amygdala lights up, then this is proof that the cultural product prompts fear, since it has been shown in many previous experiments that the amygdala is responsible for fear. If the amygdala and the nucleus accumbens are both activated, then the stimulus involves both fear and sexual arousal, since among other thing the nucleus accumbens is susceptible to sexual stimulation.

A variant of this experimental design tests whether particular regions of the brain are stimulated by particular objects. For example, do Chinese people feel as much empathy for non-Chinese, like white Europeans, as they do for their fellow countrymen? An fMRI experiment has shown that empathy depends on the ethnic membership of the object of the empathy, and that members of one's own ethnic group are always favoured. Test persons from Beijing were shown through the spectacles film of Chinese and European people who were either touched with a cotton bud or injected with a needle. When Chinese people were injected, their anterior cingular cortex (ACC, which is responsible for empathy) together with their insular cortex was always more strongly activated than was the case when Europeans were injected. 'Our findings', stated the scientists involved, 'have significant implications for understanding real-life social behaviors and provide a neurocognitive mechanism for stronger intentions to help racial in-group than out-group members.'[207]

One of the great advantages of fMRI scanning over other procedures is that no harm is inflicted on the test subject. In positron emission tomography (PET) the spatial resolution is more or less similar to that in fMRI scanning, but as with X-ray procedures radiation is released. Among non-harmful procedures—electroencephalography (EEG), magnetoencephalography (MEG), and transcranial magnetic stimulation (TMS)—the temporal resolution is a great deal better than with fMRI scanning, but inferior to fMRI scanning when it comes to the spatial localization of brain functions. A clear recent trend is the combination of different procedures: multimodal imaging.

---

[207] Xiaojing Xu et al., 'Do You Feel My Pain? Racial Group Membership Modulates Empathic Neural Responses', *Journal of Neuroscience*, 29/26 (2009), 8525–9, here 8528. See also an Italian study which showed using transcranial magnetic stimulation (thus not fMRI) that the region of the brain responsible for empathy is activated less strongly in test subjects disposed to be racist if they see a black hand being pricked with a needle than they are when they see a white hand being pricked; Alessio Avenanti, Angela Sirigu, and Salvatore M. Aglioti, 'Racial Bias Reduces Empathic Sensorimotor Resonance with Other-Race Pain', *Current Biology*, 20/11 (2010), 1018–22, extended in Joan Y. Chiao and Vani A. Mathur, 'Intergroup Empathy: How does Race Affect Empathic Neural Responses?', *Current Biology*, 20/11 (2010), R478–80.

From the very beginning, neuroscientists themselves have pointed out the limits of imaging procedures. First of all, no direct measurements are made, not even of any causal relationship between the oxygen content of the blood and neuronal activity; instead a correlation is established. A haemodynamic signal is no more than a 'surrogate', as a prominent neuroscientist has written.[208] Secondly, there are problems with the specification of the signal: 'The fMRI signal cannot easily differentiate between function-specific processing and neuromodulation, between bottom-up and top-down signals, and it may potentially confuse excitation and inhibition.'[209] Thirdly, the spatial resolution of the blobs, the coloured representations of the oxygen content of the blood, is too poor to map them precisely to the supposed spatial extensions of individual regions of the brain. Remember the point made about the amygdala in the Introduction to this book: conglomerated nerve cells that are called 'the amygdala' are very difficult to distinguish from those that border on it, the transition is blurred and not precise. If we put together these two issues—the lack of precision in localizing the oxygen content of blood and in clarifying the exact extent of regions of the brain—then any attempt to link activity to any one particular region of the brain is questionable. Fourthly, it is becoming increasingly clear that where brain activity is concerned, really the whole brain is engaged; but since the initial point of the scale of activity for BOLD has to be set somewhere, the activity of other regions is simply below whatever this point happens to be, and is consequently not recorded. Many more sites are active than the brain scan shows to be active, and so one has a distorted idea of brain activity as a whole.[210] Fifthly, and lastly, fMRI scanning involves serious statistical and software problems, as the following experiment made plain. In 2009 an American neuroscientist put a salmon in an fMRI scanner and showed it photographs of people in different social situations that had differing emotional valencies, both positive and negative. Then he asked the salmon 'which emotion the individual in the photo must have been experiencing'. The salmon was, as he laconically remarked, 'approximately 18 inches long, weighed 3.8 lbs, and was not alive at the time of scanning'.[211] Nonetheless, the brain scan showed blobs that indicated brain activity (Fig. 24).

[208] Nikos K. Logothetis, 'What We Can Do and What We Cannot Do with fMRI', *Nature*, 453/7197 (2008), 869–78, here 869.

[209] Logothetis, 'What We Can Do and What We Cannot Do with fMRI', 877.

[210] Felicity Callard and Daniel S. Margulies, 'The Subject at Rest: Novel Conceptualizations of Self and Brain from Cognitive Neuroscience's Study of the "Resting State"', *Subjectivity*, 4/3 (2011), 227–57.

[211] Craig M. Bennett, Abigail A. Baird, Michael B. Miller, and George L. Wolford, 'Neural Correlates of Interspecies Perspective Taking in the Post-Mortem Atlantic Salmon: An Argument for Multiple Comparisons Correction', *Journal of Serendipitous and Unexpected Results*, 1/1 (2010), 1–5, here 2. See also Daniel S. Margulies, 'The Salmon of Doubt: Six Months of Methodological Controversy within Social Neuroscience', in Suparna Choudhury and Jan Slaby (eds), *Critical Neuroscience: A Handbook of the Social and Cultural Contexts of Neuroscience* (Chichester: Wiley-Blackwell, 2011), 273–86. Apart from the case of the salmon, two other papers by users of fMRI scanners caused a worldwide stir in 2009. On the statistical problem of *double dipping*: Nikolaus Kriegeskorte, W. Kyle Simmons, Patrick S. F. Bellgowan, and Chris I. Baker, 'Circular Analysis in Systems Neuroscience: The Dangers of Double Dipping', *Nature Neuroscience*, 12/5 (2009), 535–40.

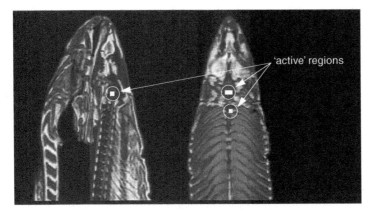

Fig. 24 Brain Activity Relating to Emotion in a Dead Salmon?
Source: Craig M. Bennett et al., 'Neural Correlates of Interspecies Perspective Taking in the Post-Mortem Atlantic Salmon: An Argument for Multiple Comparisons Correction', *Journal of Serendipitous and Unexpected Results*, 1/1 (2010), 1–5, here 4.

How could that happen? Scan images are subdivided into units that are like pixels, three-dimensional, and dice-shaped: so-called voxels. One scan image often consists of over 100,000 voxels. With so much data there is always the risk of statistical noise—voxels that look active although the corresponding region of the brain is completely inactive. An algorithm is used to filter out this statistical noise. If the wrong algorithm is selected, then one gets false positives—and so follow signs of activity in the brain scan of a dead fish, which seems to be posthumously giving its assessment of human expressions of feeling.

Despite these reservations from the neuroscientific perspective, fMRI scanning has experienced resounding success. This much is apparent from the raw numbers: a search of ISI/Web of Science shows that the publication of the first paper on fMRI procedures in 1991 was followed by four in 1992, and that since then an exponential increase set in, so that by 2007 there were about eight such papers published every day.[212] Imaging procedures are 'sexy', something you hear again

---

On the so-called *voodoo correlations* see Edward Vul et al., 'Puzzlingly High Correlations in fMRI Studies of Emotion, Personality, and Social Cognition', *Perspectives on Psychological Science*, 4/3 (2009), 274–90. Torsten Heinemann, a sociologist of science, explained the lack of any scandal surrounding *voodoo correlations*, which really should have been enough to 'shake the discipline of neuroscience to its foundations', by the conscious and 'demonstrative use of self-criticism and self-reflection', which was however merely superficial. Heinemann considered that this instance once again showed up the 'great strength of the neurosciences: the popularization of scientific knowledge with regard to different publics. They are adept at reinterpreting even critical work produced within the discipline as part of their own superior work, and maintain closed ranks with respect to the outside world'; Torsten Heinemann, *Populäre Wissenschaft: Hirnforschung zwischen Labor und Talkshow* (Göttingen: Wallstein, 2012), 144–5.

[212] Logothetis, 'What We Can Do and What We Cannot Do with fMRI', 869.

and again in the life sciences.[213] At the beginning of the twenty-first century virtually every hospital and every experimental psychology laboratory that thought they counted for something in the world equipped themselves with scanners. This cost millions—the current standard scanner has as a rule 3 tesla, the unit indicating the strength of the magnetic field, and in 2011 cost from US$3–4 million. The biggest machines that can be bought are 7 tesla, and cost three or four times as much; currently 15 tesla machines are coming on stream. On top of the purchase price, around US$500,000 are needed for associated equipment and for personnel to run it all. Self-critical neuroscientists have noted that the introduction of scanners has drastically reduced the range and quality of innovation in experimental design; laboratories have spent years transferring their old experiments onto the scanning machines, without engaging in thinking up any fundamentally new experiments: 'Perhaps the most common mistake of newcomers to brain imaging is to take a well-established paradigm that has been used with other techniques (for example, cognitive psychology or neurophysiology) and simply to run *exactly* the same paradigm in the scanner, without optimizing the design or considering whether the possible outcomes can enlighten theories about the process in question.'[214]

The suggestive power of brain images has had an especially magical impact outside the life sciences: renowned professors of English and Art History in leading American universities have simply forgotten three decades of post-structuralism, and seem prepared to attribute essential qualities to the colour yellow (or red) as though people with their own subjective agendas had not decided what is yellow, and where it should be placed on the scale built into the scanning software (see below for more about this). Everywhere there is the most extraordinary fog of confusion which, at the same time, endows these grey brain scans with metaphysical properties. Not until the fuss is all over, when a degree of scientific sobriety returns, when disciplines retreat back to their own way of doing things, will we be able to judge what advances in our scientific knowledge fMRI scanning has brought.

What are the most frequent neuroscientific experiments that are made and which relate to emotion?[215] These will now be introduced; a neutral account of each experiment will be followed by a critique.

13 JOSEPH LEDOUX AND THE TWO ROADS TO FEAR

In the Introduction to this book I mentioned one of the best-known theories regarding the way in which supposedly basic emotions function: that of Joseph

[213] See e.g. an interview with the psychologist Alan Baddeley from 2010: 'The Promise of Neuroimaging', *Go Cognitive* <http://gocognitive.net/interviews/promise-neuroimaging> accessed 12 March 2014.

[214] Jody C. Culham, 'Functional Neuroimaging: Experimental Design and Analysis', in Roberto Cabeza and Alan Kingstone (eds), *Handbook of Functional Neuroimaging of Cognition* (2nd edn, Cambridge, MA: MIT Press, 2006), 53–82, here 59, emphasis in original.

[215] For an introduction, see Gary G. Berntson and John T. Cacioppo (eds), *Handbook of Neuroscience for the Behavioral Sciences* (Hoboken, NJ: Wiley, 2009) vol. i, ch. 16; vol. ii, chs. 32–42.

LeDoux. Just to recap, a stimulus passes into the amygdala, which within about 12 milliseconds places the body in a state of alarm (raised pulse, and muscles readied to run away from the snake); the stimulus also simultaneously passes into the cortex, where a rapid decision is made by the higher cognitive functions as to whether the stimulus is really a threat. If the cortex decides that the stimulus is in fact threatening, the body responds with a fight-or-flight reaction; if, on the other hand, it is determined that there is no threat, the body stands down and returns to a state of rest. This is the theory of the two roads to fear: one pathway involving the subcortical region of emotion in the amygdala, which is on an evolutionary scale very old, and the other a cortical region where cognition occurs—the theory also includes the joint functioning of these two separate regions. LeDoux's theory has become well known beyond the neurosciences because of its appealing symmetry, embodied in the concrete example of the poisonous snake and imagery associated with it, probably the most frequently cited example when the issue of emotion is discussed. A second reason for the success of this theory is its very extensive potential for application in an era when emotional disturbance—phobias, post-traumatic stress disorders, depression—has become a common condition. LeDoux has devoted an entire chapter to these ailments and the potential uses of his research in dealing with them.[216] Ultimately, LeDoux's theory is so widely known outside the neurosciences because he has been, apart from Damasio, the best-known popularizer of the neurology of emotion, having written two best-sellers that have also been translated into many languages.[217]

While an ever-broader public has become acquainted with LeDoux's twin road theory and the connection of the amygdala with fear, there are increasing signs within the neurosciences that it does not work. On the one hand, an increasing number of studies question whether there is a 'fast' road via the amygdala, and whether there is any temporal difference at all in the emotional processes triggered by emotional stimuli. On the other hand, it turns out that the amygdala is not especially sensitive to visual stimuli, and is not especially well connected to the visual thalamus. This had been a constant claim in the experiments made in LeDoux's laboratory, despite the fact that the dominant model of Pavlovian conditioning functioned with acoustic rather than visual or olfactory stimuli. It became clear in further studies made in the neurosciences that the connections between the amygdala and the cortex were much more numerous and complex than LeDoux's model suggested, and that neuronal circuits were much more prominent than had hitherto been thought. In any case, the amygdala is not responsible for 'quick and dirty' functions, as LeDoux called them, but is instead more like a switchboard from which various inputs are distributed. Among others,

---

[216] LeDoux, *Emotional Brain*, ch. 8.

[217] I use the terms 'popularizer' and 'popularization' in a looser and less analytic sense than, e.g. Andreas W. Daum, *Wissenschaftspopularisierung im 19. Jahrhundert: Bürgerliche Kultur, naturwissenschaftliche Bildung und die deutsche Öffentlichkeit, 1848–1914* (2nd enl. edn, Munich: Oldenbourg 2002), 25–9.

one important input is the pulvinar, a conglomeration of nerves in the centre of the thalamus, which is clearly another important stage in the work of processing.[218]

The results of this re-examination of LeDoux's two roads theory effectively amount to its refutation, and so represent real progress in the scientific sense; but if this forward shift is not taken up by others, including the human and social sciences, then the latter will face serious problems.

14 ANTONIO R. DAMASIO AND THE SOMATIC MARKER HYPOTHESIS

Another best-selling author whose influence runs way beyond the neurosciences is the brain researcher Antonio R. Damasio. Along with Eric R. Kandel, Steven Pinker, Vilayanur S. Ramachandran, Oliver Sacks, Frans de Waal, and a few others, he is a neuroscientific star. He can probably be described as *the* leading neuroscientist linked to the study of emotion. His work has been taken up within the human sciences, in particular his Somatic Marker Hypothesis (SMH), which became known to a wider public through his book *Descartes' Error: Emotion, Reason, and the Human Brain* (1994).

SMH states that higher cognitive processes such as decision-making are simplified, accelerated, and improved by emotional signals in the body. Somatic markers are impressions or traces of expression of physical emotion stemming from the body's periphery (the skin, the hands, the hair) that are left in a particular region of the brain, the Ventromedial Prefrontal Cortex (VMPFC). When an impending decision has several possible outcomes this colours a promising option with a positive emotion. This exclusion of negative options improves decision-making and speeds it up. Also important is that somatic markers can function through a direct body loop, physically marking a behavioural option with a potentially positive outcome, and so rendering the subject aware of this through, for instance, an accelerated pulse. Besides this, they can make use of an as-if loop to draw attention to promising behavioural options without employing physical signals, using thoughts as elements of higher cognition.

SMH is based on the famous Iowa Gambling Task (IGT) experiment, in which test subjects choose playing cards from four different decks. They are instructed to draw one card at a time, attempting to maximize wins while minimizing losses. After drawing a card, one receives either a reward or a penalty. The players do not know that each deck is associated with a different schedule of rewards and penalties. With some decks, one wins often at the beginning, but then later faces higher losses, resulting in a net loss at the end. Other decks involve lower gains, but then

[218] LeDoux, *Emotional Brain*, 163. See Luiz Pessoa and Ralph Adolphs, 'Emotion Processing and the Amygdala: From a "Low Road" to "Many Roads" of Evaluating Biological Significance', *Nature Reviews Neuroscience*, 11/11 (2010), 773–82; Luiz Pessoa, 'Emotion and Cognition and the Amygdala: From "What Is It?" to "What's to Be Done?"', *Neuropsychologia*, 48/12 (2010), 3416–29. Also critical of LeDoux, Ian Hacking, 'By What Links Are the Organs Excited?', *Times Literary Supplement*, 4970 (17 July 1998), 11–12.

also lower losses with a net gain as the final outcome. The experiment is set up so that test subjects have to quickly recall the decks that initially involve high gains, but which ultimately lead to higher losses (Figs. 25 and 26).

Even before they became famous, Antonio and Hanna Damasio had built up at the University of Iowa the world's largest databank of patients with unusual neurological damage—mostly lesions, but also loss of brain tissue as a result of brain tumours. The IGT experiment was conducted with two groups: one of patients who had a lesion in the region of the prefrontal cortex, and the other a control group whose brains were undamaged. It turned out that the patients with lesions in the prefrontal cortex sought higher gains without regard to the eventual negative outcome, whereas the healthy patients always kept in view the outcome and were prepared to accept smaller wins. Patients with VMPFC lesions suffered from what the experiment's designer, Antoine Bechara, a colleague of Damasio, called '"myopia" for the future'.[219] The scientists also discovered that measurements of the Anticipatory Skin Conductance Response (SCR) and other physical values all began to increase when the first high wins were made.

The IGT experiment has been replicated many times, and has been run even more frequently to test other hypotheses—since 1994 over one hundred papers have been published whose results are based on IGT. The conclusions drawn from these experiments go far beyond decision-making in card games. For example, an experiment was run with test subjects from Chicago who were HIV positive and had severe drug-dependency issues, and they ended up with results just as bad as those with VMPFC lesions. The authors of this study concluded that drug dependency damaged the VMPFC in a similar way to lesions incurred through accident or a brain tumour. There was a further point that could be made: just as the VMPFC patients only thought of quick wins at the cost of long-term profit, and so drew cards linked to a higher risk, those with severe drug dependencies engaged in very risky sexual behaviour and so contributed to the spread of HIV.[220] The biopolitical potential of this application of IGT is very great. Since this suggests that highly risky sexual behaviour (which is itself very costly for the health system) is not the result of 'character weaknesses', 'lethargy', or 'indecisiveness', but is instead wired into the brain, it would be possible to regulate the sexual practice of those dependent on drugs and severely punish infringements. IGT results have not yet

---

[219] Antoine Bechara et al., 'Insensitivity to Future Consequences Following Damage to Human Prefrontal Cortex', *Cognition*, 50/1–3 (1994), 7–15, here 14.

[220] Marvin Zuckerman and D. Michael Kuhlman, 'Personality and Risk-Taking: Common Biosocial Factors', *Journal of Personality*, 68/6 (2000), 999–1029; Antonio Verdejo-García et al., 'Executive Dysfunction in Substance Dependent Individuals during Drug Use and Abstinence: An Examination of the Behavioral, Cognitive and Emotional Correlates of Addiction', *Journal of the International Neuropsychological Society*, 12/3 (2006), 405–15; Margaret C. Wardle et al., 'Iowa Gambling Task Performance and Emotional Distress Interact to Predict Risky Sexual Behavior in Individuals with Dual Substance and HIV Diagnoses', *Journal of Clinical and Experimental Neuropsychology*, 32/10 (2010), 1110–21. Criticism can be found in William A. Schmitt, Chad A. Brinkley, and Joseph P. Newman, 'Testing Damasio's Somatic Marker Hypothesis with Psychopathic Individuals: Risk Takers or Risk Averse?', *Journal of Abnormal Psychology*, 108/3 (1999), 538–43.

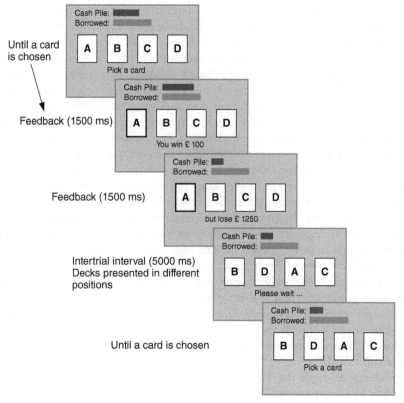

Fig. 25 The Iowa Gambling Task (IGT) Experiment

Source: Peter Palm, based on an illustration from Anna Pecchinenda, Michael Dretsch, and Paul Chapman, 'Working Memory Involvement in Emotions-Based Processes Underlying Choosing Advantageously', *Experimental Psychology*, 53/3 (2006), 191–7, here 194.

been used in this way, but they have been used in tests to determine whether there might be a pharmacological treatment for obsessive compulsive disorder.[221] Besides that, IGT has many possibilities for the economic neurosciences.[222] IGT also has fans in the human and social sciences who respond to the idea of embodied cognition, a synthesis of mind and body. We will come to this shortly.

There has been a great deal of criticism of SMH.[223] First of all it was questioned whether there was actually anything novel about it. William M. Marston

[221] Paolo Cavedini, Tommaso Bassi, Claudia Zorzi, and Laura Bellodi, 'The Advantages of Choosing Antiobsessive Therapy According to Decision-Making Functioning', *Journal of Clinical Psychopharmacology*, 24/6 (2004), 628–31.

[222] See e.g. Martin Reimann and Antoine Bechara, 'The Somatic Marker Framework as a Neurological Theory of Decision-Making: Review, Conceptual Comparisons, and Future Neuroeconomics Research', *Journal of Economic Psychology*, 31/5 (2010), 767–76.

[223] An overview of the criticisms made of SMH can be found in Barnaby D. Dunn, Tim Dalgleish, and Andrew D. Lawrence, 'The Somatic Marker Hypothesis: A Critical Evaluation', *Neuroscience and*

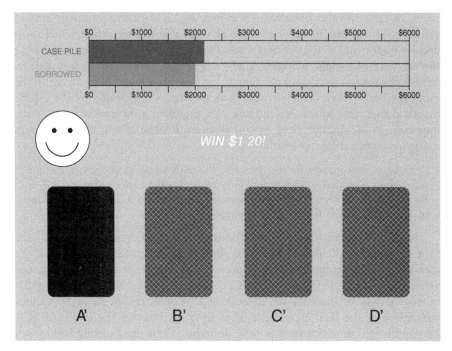

Fig. 26 The BASIS Glossary
Source: 'The BASIS Glossary', *The Brief Addiction Science Information Source (BASIS)* <http://basisonline.org/basis. glossary.html> accessed 13 March 2014.

(1893–1947) had advanced similar arguments in 1928; and when in 1971 the neuroscientist Walle J. H. Nauta (1916–94), on the basis of MacLean's limbic system, postulated that the frontal lobe created connections between sensory impressions at the body's periphery and complicated decisions, this was very close to what Damasio argued some twenty years later.[224] This first line of criticism involved the reinstatement of experimental psychology's institutional memory. The second line of attack was to question whether IGT really did activate emotional memory, and was 'cognitively impenetrable'.[225] Damasio had claimed that a 'key ingredient that distinguishes the task of Bechara and colleagues from other tasks of probabilistic reasoning' was 'that subjects discriminate choices by feeling; they develop hunches that certain choices are better than others'.[226] The experiment

---

Biobehavioral Reviews, 30/2 (2006), 239–71. See also Eric-Jan Wagenmakers and Sander Nieuwenhuis, 'Damasio's Error: De somatic marker hypothese onder vuur', *Neuropraxis*, 9/6 (2005), 159–63; Hideki Ohira, 'The Somatic Marker Revisited: Brain and Body in Emotional Decision Making', *Emotion Review*, 2/3 (2010), 245–9.

[224] Walle J. H. Nauta, 'The Problem of the Frontal Lobe: A Reinterpretation', *Journal of Psychiatric Research*, 8/3–4 (1971), 167–87.

[225] Dunn, Dalgleish, and Lawrence, 'Somatic Marker Hypothesis', 249.

[226] Antonio R. Damasio, Ralph Adolphs, and Hanna Damasio, 'The Contributions of the Lesion Method to the Functional Neuroanatomy of Emotion', in Richard J. Davidson, Klaus R. Scherer, and

stands or falls with this question: if it is only higher cognitive processes without emotional signals that are activated when playing cards are being chosen, and are of decisive importance to the decision made, then the experiment says nothing about the existence of somatic markers. A whole series of studies have in fact demonstrated that test subjects grasp the general logic of rewards and punishment in the card experiment more completely and quickly than is anticipated by the experimental design, and so execute the task at a cognitive meta-level which is more important to the decision than somatic markers, if these exist at all.[227] A survey article has summed this up as follows:

> there seems little support for the claim that the reward/punishment schedule of the IGT is fully cognitively impenetrable. This means that the assertion that the IGT in the early stages involves covert, non-conscious somatic markers to regulate decision-making can no longer be confidently endorsed.[228]

The third line of criticism relates to the interpretation of the emotion signal—the Skin Conductance Response (SCR). As already noted, according to Damasio the capacity to make cognitive decisions improves because in the body loop a real change in the SCR is registered in the VMPFC; or, as with an as-if body loop, a pseudo-impression will be made in the absence of a genuine change in SCR. Various replications of the IGT experiment failed to clarify whether the measured SCR were really signs of anticipatory positive decisions. These signals might just as well be 'a response to feedback, an indicator of risk, a marker of post-decision emotion state, or a signal of how good or bad a particular response option is'.[229]

A fourth point of criticism concerns the healthy control group with undamaged VMPFC. Replications of the experiment showed that a constant proportion, about one-fifth, of all the supposedly healthy test subjects in the control group performed just as badly in the experiment as those test subjects with VMPFC lesions. This places a large question mark over the reliability of IGT as a proxy for real life: if a large group of healthy people do as badly in IGT as those with lesions, but on the other hand have no problems in dealing with their everyday lives—what then does IGT tell you about real life?[230] Moreover, and fifthly, some scientists have pointed out that even clean results involve at best a correlation—and not a causal relationship—between skin conductivity response and decision-making behaviour.[231] The sixth and final line of criticism that will be raised here concerns the neuroanatomy of the VMPFC. Damasio and his colleagues treat this as a particular organization of nervous cells that has, so far, not been charted in the brain. Not only the connectivity of these cells, that is, the outline of the supposed VMPFC, has

H. Hill Goldsmith (eds), *Handbook of Affective Sciences* (Oxford: Oxford University Press, 2003), 66–92, here 84.

[227] This critique is summarized in Dunn, Dalgleish, and Lawrence, 'Somatic Marker Hypothesis', 248–9.
[228] Dunn, Dalgleish, and Lawrence, 'Somatic Marker Hypothesis', 249.
[229] Dunn, Dalgleish, and Lawrence, 'Somatic Marker Hypothesis', 251.
[230] Dunn, Dalgleish, and Lawrence, 'Somatic Marker Hypothesis', 252.
[231] Dunn, Dalgleish, and Lawrence, 'Somatic Marker Hypothesis', 252–3.

been questioned, but also the claim that they function as somatic markers in IGT. It has since become apparent that lesions in other areas of the brain—in the equally ill-defined amygdala, for instance—likewise limit the chances of success in IGT. It has also become clear that the region in the left-hand side of the brain that the Damasio laboratory calls VMPFC plays hardly any role; it is the right hemisphere which is decisive, if any one side is.[232]

15 GIACOMO RIZZOLATTI, VITTORIO GALLESE, MARCO IACOBONI, MIRROR NEURONS, AND SOCIAL EMOTIONS

In 2010 two neuroscientists said that 'It is hard to imagine a class of neurons that has generated more excitement than mirror neurons'; at the end of the same year the German weekly *Die Zeit* summed this up with the words: 'mirror neurons are pop'.[233] Neither is an exaggeration. What hasn't been explained by reference to normal mirror neurons and dysfunctional mirror neurons? Smiling, yawning, empathy, love, the child's acquisition of language, religion, Theory of Mind (ToM), even culture in general;[234] and then also hair loss, impotence, and autism (the 'broken mirror neuron hypothesis').[235] Vilayanur S. Ramachandran, a star

[232] Dunn, Dalgleish, and Lawrence, 'Somatic Marker Hypothesis', 258–62.

[233] Gregory Hickok and Marc Hauser, '(Mis)understanding Mirror Neurons', *Current Biology*, 20/14 (2010), R593–4, here R593; Werner Siefer, 'Die Zellen des Anstoßes', *Die Zeit*, 51 (16 December 2010). See also Ruth Leys, '"Both of Us Disgusted in My Insula": Mirror Neuron Theory and Emotional Empathy', *nonsite.org*, 5 (18 March 2012) <http://nonsite.org/article/%E2%80%9Cboth-of-us-disgusted-in-my-insula%E2%80%9D-mirror-neuron-theory-and-emotional-empathy> accessed 13 March 2014.

[234] See on mirror neurons, smiling, and yawning: G. Rizzolatti et al., 'Resonance Behaviors and Mirror Neurons', *Archives italiennes de biologie: A Journal of Neuroscience*, 137/2–3 (1999), 85–100; on empathy: Giacomo Rizzolatti and Corrado Sinigaglia, *Mirrors in the Brain: How Our Minds Share Actions and Emotions*, trans. Frances Anderson (Oxford: Oxford University Press, 2008) [It. orig., *So quel che fai: Il cervello che agisce e i neuroni specchio*, 2006], 173–93; love: Maddalena Fabbri-Destro and Giacomo Rizzolatti, 'Mirror Neurons and Mirror Systems in Monkeys and Humans', *Physiology*, 23/3 (2008), 171–9; language acquisition in children: Lisa Aziz-Zadeh et al., 'Congruent Embodied Representations for Visually Presented Actions and Linguistic Phrases Describing Actions', *Current Biology*, 16/18 (2006), 1818–23; religion: Vilayanur S. Ramachandran, 'Mirror Neurons and the Brain in the Vat', *Edge* (9 January 2006) <http://edge.org/conversation/mirror-neurons-and-imitation-learning-as-the-driving-force-behind-the-great-leap-forward-in-human-evolution> accessed 13 March 2014; Theory of Mind: Vittorio Gallese and Alvin Goldman, 'Mirror Neurons and the Simulation Theory of Mind-Reading', *Trends in Cognitive Sciences*, 2/12 (1998), 493–501; culture: Gerhard Lauer, 'Spiegelneuronen: Über den Grund des Wohlgefallens an der Nachahmung', in Karl Eibl, Katja Mellmann, and Rüdiger Zymner (eds), *Im Rücken der Kulturen* (Paderborn: Mentis-Verlag, 2007), 137–63. See also Joachim Bauer, *Warum ich fühle, was du fühlst: Intuitive Kommunikation und das Geheimnis der Spiegelneurone* (Hamburg: Hoffmann und Campe, 2005).

[235] On hairloss: E. Bruce Goldstein, *Sensation and Perception* (8th edn, Belmont, CA: Wadsworth Cengage Learning, 2010), 277–80; impotence: H. Mouras et al., 'Activation of Mirror-Neuron System by Erotic Video Clips Predicts Degree of Induced Erection: An fMRI Study', *NeuroImage*, 42/3 (2008), 1142–50; autism: Mirella Dapretto et al., 'Understanding Emotions in Others: Mirror Neuron Dysfunction in Children with Autism Spectrum Disorders', *Nature Neuroscience*, 9/1 (2006), 28–30.

among the popularizers of neuroscience, predicted in 2000 that 'that mirror neurons will do for psychology what DNA did for biology'.[236]

But what are mirror neurons? They were discovered in Parma in 1995/6 by Giacomo Rizzolatti, Vittorio Gallese, and others.[237] Rizzolatti and Gallese were searching for the neuronal events in the physical movements made by Southern pigtailed macaques (*Macaca nemestrina*). They observed what happened at the level of nerve cells when the monkey reached for a nut and put it in its mouth. By accident, they found out from electrodes attached to the brain that neurons fired in a specific region (the premotor cortex) not only when the monkeys made the movement themselves, but also when the monkeys watched the same movement being made by humans or other monkeys. Nobody had expected to find visual perception in the premotor cortex, which had previously been associated only with movement. To take account of the dual function of the nerve cells whose firing they observed, Rizzolatti and Gallese dubbed these 'mirror neurons'. This was the origin of a hypothesis concerning the unconscious, neuronal connection between bodily movement and cognition, a neuronal correlate of unconscious imitation and higher-level understanding—not so very different to Damasio's Somatic Marker Hypothesis.

Shortly after the beginning of the new millennium evidence began to accumulate that comparable nerve cells could be found in humans, bound into a similar firing circuit; in 2010 there was significant proof that this was indeed so.[238] In the meantime a number of laboratories claimed to have discovered, using the non-invasive procedures of transcranial magnetic stimulation and fMRI scanning, that mirror neurons fire in regions other than those in the premotor cortex responsible for movement, and are tied into a similar firing sequence with those in the cortex responsible for higher cognition.[239] It seemed to be clear that the acquisition of language (and much more) functioned in a similar automatic and unconscious manner. From all this journalists and popularizers drew the conclusions mentioned

[236] V. S. Ramachandran, 'Mirror Neurons and Imitation Learning as the Driving Force behind "the Great Leap Forward" in Human Evolution', in John Brockman (ed.), *The Mind: Leading Scientists Explore the Brain, Memory, Personality, and Happiness* (New York: HarperCollins, 2011), 101–11, here 101. This publication is based on an interview given on 1 June 2000; 'MIRROR NEURONS and Imitation Learning as the Driving Force behind "The Great Leap Forward" in Human Evolution', *Edge* (1 June 2000) <http://www.edge.org/3rd_culture/ramachandran/ramachandran_index.html> accessed 13 March 2014.

[237] See L. Fadiga et al., 'Motor Facilitation during Action Observation: A Magnetic Stimulation Study', *Journal of Neurophysiology*, 73/6 (1995), 2608–11; Giacomo Rizzolatti et al., 'Premotor Cortex and the Recognition of Motor Actions', *Cognitive Brain Research*, 3/2 (1996), 131–41; Vittorio Gallese et al., 'Action Recognition in the Premotor Cortex', *Brain*, 119/2 (1996), 593–609.

[238] See Giacomo Rizzolatti and Laila Craighero, 'The Mirror-Neuron System', *Annual Review of Neuroscience*, 27 (2004), 169–92; Roy Mukamel et al., 'Single-Neuron Responses in Humans during Execution and Observation of Actions', *Current Biology*, 20/8 (2010), 750–6; Christian Keysers and Valeria Gazzola, 'Social Neuroscience: Mirror Neurons Recorded in Humans', *Current Biology*, 20/8 (2010), R353-4.

[239] When working with humans, neuroscientists employ different ethical norms to the ones in use when studying monkeys, and refrain from drilling through skulls to implant electrodes directly on the groups of neurons, or individual neurons, in which they are interested; the sole exception are patients who are in any case subject to brain surgery, because, for example, of epilepsy or chronic depression.

at the beginning of this section. One example is an experiment described by the neuroscientist Marco Iacoboni:

> In a series of experiments, one group of participants was asked to think about college professors, who are typically associated with intelligence, and write down everything that came to mind, and a second group was asked to do the same regarding soccer hooligans—those unruly and destructive fans who are typically associated with stupidity (or at least with very stupid behavior). Then both groups were asked a series of 'general knowledge' questions, a task ostensibly unrelated to the first one. But it turned out that there was a relationship: the participants who had concentrated earlier on college professors outperformed the participants who had been thinking about soccer hooligans. Indeed, the 'college professor' participants outperformed a control group that came fresh to general knowledge questions, and this control group in turn outperformed the 'soccer hooligans' participants.
>
> Conclusion: just thinking about college professors makes you smarter, whereas thinking about soccer hooligans makes you dumber! Ap Dijksterhuis summarizes his research by saying: 'Relevant research has shown by now that imitation can make us slow, fast, smart, stupid, good at math, bad at math, helpful, rude, polite, long-winded, hostile, aggressive, cooperative, competitive, conforming, nonconforming, conservative, forgetful, careful, careless, neat, and sloppy.' That's quite a list, and I believe that this constant automatic mimicry is indeed an expression of some form of neural mirroring.[240]

Hence people become more clever not only through cognitive achievement, but also through second-degree imitation—thinking about other clever people. And this is because mirror neurons bring about a kind of doubling of other neurons (here responsible for cognition). This is the core statement of the experiment. This is not the place to go into the detail of this experiment, but from a historical perspective there is obviously a critical point here: how is change possible in such a closed imitative circuit? How is it possible for people to be clever who have never ever associated with clever people, whom they might have imitated? And how do differences arise in human behaviour if everyone is imitating everyone else?

But Iacoboni goes further. In a chapter entitled 'Existential Neuroscience and Society' he writes:

> The second reason why there is resistance to the idea of neuroscience affecting policy has to do with the perceived threat to our notion of free will that is obviously linked to the argument on imitative violence. The research on mirror neurons implies that our sociality—perhaps the highest achievement of humans—is also a limiting factor of our autonomy as individuals. This is a major revision of long-standing beliefs. Traditionally, biological determinism of individual behavior is contrasted by a view of humans capable of rising above their biological makeup to define themselves through their ideas and their social codes. Mirror neuron research, however, suggests that our social codes are largely dictated by our biology. What should we do with this newly acquired

---

[240] Marco Iacoboni, *Mirroring People: The New Science of How We Connect with Others* (New York: Farrar, Straus, and Giroux, 2008), 200–1.

knowledge? Deny it because it is difficult to accept it? Or use it to inform policy and make our society a better one? I would obviously vote for the latter.[241]

What follows from this? Should we bar from society children who have proved to be aggressive in kindergarten, locking them up, so that their peers do not emulate their behaviour? Should we severely censor the representation of violence in the media and everyday language, since such films as well as the linguistic expression of violence necessarily invite imitation (at lunch I loudly express a wish to use physical violence on a tyrannical boss, and in so doing bring myself closer not only to the neuronal threshold for violent action, but to all those sharing lunch with me as well)?

A more differentiated and critical perspective upon the study of mirror neurons came in 2012, around one-and-a-half decades after Rizzolatti and Gallese's original discovery. Gregory Hickok and his colleagues, who were studying the neurological foundations of language, did not question the existence of new forms of neurons. But they doubted that higher cognition was part of neuronal processes. Reviewing the original experiments, and setting up new ones of their own, they demonstrated that semantic analysis in the temporal lobe was not part of the firing circuit. Mirror neurons were in reality sensorimotoric neurons that play an important part in the choice between different behavioural options. For example, it was observed that rhesus monkeys could distinguish between someone who threw a stone at them and someone who threw them food, although they could not themselves throw either stones or food. According to Hickok and his colleagues, mirror neurons resembled other, associative cells which were 'object-oriented': they made it possible for a connection to be made between the movement of throwing and the object thrown.[242] Hickok and others maintained that Rizzolatti and Gallese should have stuck with their original problem and thought more about the processes of movement, instead of taking the mirror quality of the neurons they had discovered for cognition.

Other neuroscientists argued that the temporal and spatial resolution of imaging procedures with instruments like the fMRI scanner was far too crude to prove the existence of something as fast and small as the firing of mirror neurons. In an fMRI brain scan it was likely that only the simultaneous firing of different cells—some responsible for motor functions, others for cognition—could be observed. In the absence of invasive procedures it was not possible to identify the firing of an individual nerve cell which simultaneously assumed motor and cognitive functions. Above all, this made the existence of human mirror neurons questionable.[243]

[241] Iacoboni, *Mirroring People*, 269–70.
[242] Hickok and Hauser, '(Mis)understanding Mirror Neurons', R593. See also Vittorio Gallese et al., 'Mirror Neuron Forum', *Perspectives on Psychological Science*, 6/4 (2011), 369–407, here 370–1, 373–5. Finally, see the critical blog moderated by Gregory Hickok und David Poeppel; 'Talking Brains: News and Views on the Neural Organization of Language' <http://www.talkingbrains.org> accessed 13 March 2014.
[243] Ilan Dinstein, Justin L. Gardner, Mehrdad Jazayeri, and David J. Heeger, 'Executed and Observed Movements Have Different Distributed Representations in Human aIPS', *Journal of Neuroscience*, 28/44 (2008), 11231–9; Ilan Dinstein et al., 'A Mirror Up to Nature', *Current Biology*, 18/1 (2008), R13-8.

Finally, some neuroscientists pointed out that even at the beginning of the twentieth century scientists had considered the cerebral connection between ideas and motor functions. For example, in 1908 Hugo Liepmann made a distinction between ideational and ideomotor apraxia, based upon his studies of patients who had become apraxic due to brain damage, and who had problems with executing learned purposeful movements. He argued that ideational apraxia was connected to the loss of ability to connect ideas together, while ideomotor apraxia involved the loss of capacity to coordinate movements.[244] Once again, the furore surrounding a 'new' paradigm, attracting new researchers and funding, was countered by voices pointing to long-established knowledge that had been neglected by the institutional memory of experimental psychology.

The case of mirror neurons is, however, instructive about the popularization of the neurosciences. The fact that established scientists like Rizzalotti and Iacoboni could get away with promoting such apparently implausible ideas is in part related to the generally high level of interest in the life sciences, which together with the hubris and florid imagination of science journalists seduces some neuroscientists. Many of them will think: if a poorly informed journalist can write a best-seller about mirror neurons and the battle of the sexes, then I can too, instead of working day in day out in the lab, or endlessly writing grant applications to keep my people in work. This is really a new form of commerce involving a new publication model, which is closely related to the name of John Brockman and his New York literary agency.

Brockman first made a name for himself in the 1960s, when he was linked to Andy Warhol and John Cage in the New York avant-garde scene. During the 1970s he developed work as a literary agent, representing Fritjof Capra and other New Age writers. Today his agency specializes in the natural sciences, his authors including Joseph LeDoux, Marco Iacoboni, and Steven Pinker. Popular science books that use vivid, everyday examples, with a narrative reaching far beyond experimental research, sometimes seeking to explain the world in general, are a relatively new phenomenon. None of them would have been conceivable without the surprising world success of Stephen Hawking's *A Brief History of Time* (1988). In most cases it is Brockman who has made these laboratory scientists into authors. His agency is more deeply involved in the conception and composition of books than is the case with other disciplines, for example, history, whose specialized language is closer to everyday language and which has long been represented in the domain of academic popularization. Brockman's agents keep very close track of laboratory developments, assessing marketing potential and the degree of media-friendliness of researchers (not every scientist is as eloquent and telegenic as Steven Pinker, or can, like Joseph LeDoux, claim that in his spare time he plays electric guitar in a band). They then approach a selected life scientist and offer help in

---

[244] Doreen Kimura, *Translations from Liepmann's Essays on Apraxia* (London, CA-ON: Department of Psychology, University of Western Ontario, 1980) [Ger. orig., *Drei Aufsätze aus dem Apraxiegebiet*, 1908]. For a discussion of Liepmann see Georg Goldenberg, 'Apraxia and Beyond: Life and Work of Hugo Liepmann', *Cortex* 39/3 (2003), 509–24.

completing a short proposal (rarely more than two pages) for a popular science book. The proposal is then auctioned off to the highest-bidding publishing house—in 1999 Brockman scored a US$2-million advance for a book by the physicist Brian Greene. As Brockman has said, 'what is wrong with an evolutionary biologist earning as much as a rock star?'[245] Once the book is printed the publisher's marketing machine gets to work, with YouTube clips, talk shows, an appearance on breakfast TV as an expert on mirror neurons and empathy in connection with famine in Africa, and on evening TV as an expert on mirror neurons and violence after a school shooting. This all pushes up sales and recovers the advance that had been made. The same pattern then plays out in the many countries where the rights have been bought, and whose publishing houses likewise have an interest in at least breaking even. The author is then put on a cycle, as the jargon has it: if he manages to turn out a new manuscript every three years, this cycle gives him a higher market value than a writer with a seven-year cycle, for whom the half-life of public attention sets in more quickly. In other words, the brand name of an author with a three-year cycle is stronger than one with a seven-year cycle.

In the publishing world this is all quite usual, and functions in exactly the same way with the historians represented by the literary agency of Andrew Wylie—Richard J. Evans, Niall Ferguson, Ian Kershaw, or Peter Longerich, whose books can be bought in almost every airport throughout the world. The difference between Brockman and Wylie is that Brockman's agency invests more time in the author, both in composition and production, for the simple reason that the writing of accessible descriptive books is not one of the core competences of the average life scientist. But this increased investment clearly pays off, for the sales figures achieved by Damasio, Pinker, and LeDoux, let alone the numbers typical of science journalism in the style of Malcolm T. Gladwell, are much higher than those achieved by historians engaged in popularization. This also has to do with the way that life scientists claim to be dealing with the really big issues—the sorts of things one used to hear from the likes of Jean-Paul Sartre or Susan Sontag—employing more user-friendly language than they ever managed.

It is partly on account of Brockman and his agency that the life sciences were able to rise to such dominance. Brockman created an important media platform for life scientists with his Internet forum at edge.org, where they can express themselves on the great problems of humanity. Alluding to C. P. Snow's idea of the two cultures—the natural sciences on the one hand and the literary human sciences on the other—Brockman proclaimed a 'third culture' to which belong 'scientists and other thinkers in the empirical world, who, through their work and expository writing, are taking the place of the traditional intellectual in rendering visible the deeper meanings of our lives, redefining who and what we are'.[246]

---

[245] Andrew Brown, 'The Hustler', *The Guardian* (30 April 2005). Brockman's comment in Ulrich Schnabel, 'Wie Agenten, Verleger und Autoren mit populärer Welterklärung Gewinn machen: Trendsurfer der Wissenschaft', *Die Zeit*, 6 (29 January 1998), 43.

[246] John Brockman, *The Third Culture* (New York: Simon & Schuster, 1995), 17.

16 ON THE SHOULDERS OF DWARVES, OR, THE NEUROSCIENCES AS A 'TROJAN HORSE' FOR THE HUMAN AND SOCIAL SCIENCES

Today, LeDoux, Damasio, Rizzolatti, and their experiments are cited in a growing number of works in the human and social sciences no less frequently than Nietzsche, Heidegger, Derrida, and Foucault were in the 1980s.[247] Brain scans and coloured dendrites decorate the covers of new books in literary criticism and political science. New fields of research have sprung up using 'neuro' as a prefix: neuropolitics, neuroeconomics, neuroethics, neuroaesthetics, neuroliterary criticism, neurotheology. While philosophy and linguistics were all-dominant during the postmodern phase, the neurosciences have become the chief resource for all those disciplines that address themselves to the analysis of text and image. Sometimes this triumph is heralded as the sign of a new, post-postmodern era, as yet without its own name. Even in the historical sciences the orientation to literature and anthropology that followed the linguistic turn is now thought in part to have been superseded, and the first books on neurohistory have begun to appear, such as Johannes Fried's *Der Schleier der Erinnerung: Grundzüge einer historischen Memorik* (2004; 'The Veil of Memory: Features of a Historic Memory') and Daniel Lord Smail's *On Deep History and the Brain* (2008). Emotions—or more precisely affects, as strong physical and unconscious feelings are called in the neurosciences—are central to the neuroscientific literature that today sets the pace. How did this orientation to the neurosciences come about? And why do affects play such a prominent role?

One explanation is that the neurosciences have triumphed in the natural sciences themselves. New knowledge and new procedures—we have seen that fMRI scanning is among the most exciting—have for the first time made possible the visualization of brain processes. These breakthroughs have been associated in science policy with large-scale research initiatives like the American 'Decade of the Brain' (1990–9), leveraged economically by the deregulation of financial markets, the Internet, easier access to venture capital, and generally with the biotechnology boom that accompanied the dotcom boom. By the beginning of the new millennium, with the decoding of the human genome, it did in many places seem as though one could begin afresh with the search for answers to the big questions of human history—the acquisition of language, free will, consciousness, and feelings. On the day that the sequence of the human genome was announced in the White House, on 27 June 2000, the first six pages of the culture section of the German daily *Frankfurter Allgemeine Zeitung* were plastered with the letters A, C, G, and T—the final sequence of the 3.2 billion pairs that makes up the human genome. This was an iconic turning point.

---

[247] The term 'Trojan horse' has been used in this context by Gross, 'Defending the Humanities', 35–6: 'In this essay I recall how Darwin's *Expression* foregrounds the inherent rhetoricity of emotion . . . that claims to follow in its wake and which has recently infiltrated the humanities like a Trojan horse settling in the new critical subfield of Cognitive Approaches to Literature (CAL).'

In the USA there are other factors which play a role: support for Christian fundamentalism, the rise of creationism and intelligent design, and a general retreat from Enlightenment ideas. As Daniel Smail wrote:

> In an age when biblical literalism is on the rise, when presidents doubt the truth of evolution, when the teaching of evolutionary biology in the United States is being dumbed down and school boards talk seriously about creation science and intelligent design, it is all the more important for historians to support their colleagues in the biological sciences.[248]

Also of importance were immanent developments in the human sciences, first and foremost the decline of post-structuralism. This in part had to do with the logic of scientific production, which constantly seeks the 'new', resulting in a sequence of 'turns'; it was also related to politics and ethics.[249] In her book *Touching Feeling: Affect, Pedagogy, Performativity* (2003), the influential Queer theorist, Eve Kosofsky Sedgwick (1950–2009), wrote:

> I daily encounter graduate students who are dab hands at unveiling the hidden historical violences that underlie a secular, universalist, liberal humanism. Yet these students' sentient years, unlike the formative years of their teachers, have been spent entirely in a xenophobic Reagan-Bush-Clinton-Bush America where 'liberal' is, if anything, a taboo category; and where 'secular humanism' is routinely treated as a marginal religious sect, while a vast majority of the population claims to engage in direct intercourse with multiple invisible entities such as angels, Satan, and God.[250]

In other words: in the later 1970s and early 1980s Sedgwick's generation jumped on the post-structuralist bandwagon, having fought for one or possibly two decades for classical Enlightenment ideals such as the emancipation of blacks, women, and gays. They made this move because they had thought the Enlightenment through to its logical conclusion, and become clear about the violent, totalizing potential of humanistic universalism. This shift in thinking is still best exemplified in Michel Foucault's *Discipline and Punish* (1977; Fr. orig., *Surveiller et punir*, 1975). The book opens with two snapshots of sentencing practice in France. In 1757, punishing Robert-François Damiens for his attempt on the king's life, the gravity of the crime was inscribed upon the body—Damiens was tortured, quartered, the sections of his body burned and scattered, his house destroyed, his relatives forced to change their names—all told, a clear instance of the 'cruelty' of punishment in premodern times. Foucault contrasts Damiens's fate with the rules of a prison for young offenders from 1838. Here the ordered daily round prevails: school lessons, work, religion. This means that while in premodern times it was the body which was punished, in modern times one punishes the soul. This was a shift from the macrophysics to the

---

[248] Daniel Lord Smail, *On Deep History and the Brain* (Berkeley and Los Angeles: University of California Press, 2008), 11.

[249] Doris Bachmann-Medick, *Cultural Turns: Neuorientierungen in den Kulturwissenschaften* (Reinbek bei Hamburg: Rowohlt-Taschenbuch-Verlag, 2006).

[250] Eve Kosofsky Sedgwick, *Touching Feeling: Affect, Pedagogy, Performativity*, (Durham, NC: Duke University Press, 2003), 139–40.

microphysics of power, and by the end of the book hardly any readers will be left in any doubt about which form of punishment is worse. Progress turns out to be a chimera.

If we follow Sedgwick's reasoning, the younger generation born between 1960 and 1980 have benefited from emancipatory struggles, but have never learned themselves how to fight for Enlightenment projects. Nor have they learned to understand Enlightenment as a value. The majority of the American population, the Christian fundamentalist 'Middle America' ('flyover territory' for leftist bicoastal liberals), had broken with the Enlightenment—even if teachers like Sedgwick had not, one should add. In other words: it makes a difference if one arrives at postmodernism via modernism, and if one is simply born into it.

How much longer must identities remain fluid, borders porous, discourses shifting, without knowing why something has shifted? According to Sedgwick and Co., what is needed is a more solid anchor in the world: a more robust conception of reality and much clearer causal relationships. Why Sedgwick lighted on emotions in their Silvan Tomkins variant would itself be worth the attention of intellectual history and the history of the sciences. But the fact is that Sedgwick opted for Ekman's forerunner as her theoretical source, the pioneer for the theory of basic emotions revealed in the human face. And her students also seemed to think that the theory inspired by Tomkins and experimental psychology was useful for thinking about political change: 'her readings of Tomkins (along with the work of Tomkins himself) were incredibly enabling for a graduate student suspicious of the political nihilism that seemed inherent to successful scholarly practice'.[251]

For others it could have been the security radiating from this supposed anchor in genetics or the neurosciences—in the form of Silvan S. Tomkins's psychology of emotions—that was reassuring on the personal and existential level. What if the 'gay gene', a genetic disposition to homosexuality, really exists? Then it would be immutable, and I need no longer worry about the circumstances, the milieu, the upbringing, childhood experiences, that led to my being gay. I cannot even 'convert', as did American same-sex loving Christians who, influenced by the 'ex-Gay' movement, married someone of the opposite gender and began to found families.[252] Ironically, this movement had been started off at the other end of the political spectrum, by progressive post-structuralists like Judith Butler and Eve Kosofksy Sedgwick. Unlike culture, nature can be an enormous relief.

---

[251] Gregory J. Seigworth and Melissa Gregg, 'An Inventory of Shimmers', in Melissa Gregg and Gregory J. Seigworth (eds), *The Affect Theory Reader* (Durham, NC: Duke University Press, 2010), 1–25, here 22.

[252] Tanya Erzen, *Straight to Jesus: Sexual and Christian Conversions in the Ex-Gay Movement* (Berkeley and Los Angeles: University of California Press, 2006); Michelle Wolkomir, 'Emotion Work, Commitment, and the Authentication of the Self: The Case of Gay and Ex-Gay Christian Support Groups', *Journal of Contemporary Ethnography*, 30/3 (2001), 305–34; Michelle Wolkomir, *Be Not Deceived: The Sacred and Sexual Struggles of Gay and Ex-Gay Christian Men* (New Brunswick, NJ: Rutgers University Press, 2006). A self-help book intended to assist young homosexuals during their 'conversion', written by a priest, a pioneer of the American ex-Gay movement, is Alan Medinger, *Growth into Manhood: Resuming the Journey* (Colorado Springs: Waterbrook Press, 2000).

And for many, the security provided by genes and neurons was a source for answers to the most pressing questions they had pursued through years of study and argument: passing through the 'death of the author', the discrediting of Marxism by the collapse of real existing socialism, and the demolition of psychoanalysis. It is possible to account in this way for the route to the neurosciences taken by the art historian David Freedberg, author of a well-regarded book on iconoclasm, even if he accounts for this in a different way—more on this shortly.[253] Freedberg is interested in the question of why some works of art successfully retain their power over hundreds of years, evoking in their viewers the same emotions, while other works of art fail to achieve this. Using the Somatic Marker Hypothesis and the mirror neuron hypothesis, he claims that successful works make possible physical emotional empathy, and that this is brought about by underlying universal neurobiological conditions.

We can best understand Freedberg's thesis with reference to a particular work of art, Rogier van der Weyden's *The Descent from the Cross* (painted between 1435 and 1438 for a church in Louvain) (Fig. 27). This is a frontal image of the dead Jesus Christ, who seems to be being lifted down from the cross, held under the arms by Nicodemus and by the feet by Joseph of Arimathea. To the side, and below Jesus, the Virgin Mary is collapsing to the ground, supported by John the Baptist and Mary of Cleophas. According to Freedberg,

> The painting shows how emotion can only be fully expressed through the body itself. Previously, painters had shown the Virgin standing or kneeling beside the cross, but in the *Descent*, she collapses in exactly the way Christ descends from the Cross. Rogier gave literal and physical expression to centuries of sentiment about her *compassio*, her sympathetic grieving for her Son by showing how she feels the wounds to His body in her own. Today the *Descent* hangs in the Early Flemish galleries of the Prado. In every respect, it is far from its original context—yet it continues to exert a powerful hold on its viewers. It is surely the sense of bodily presence (of Christ in particular) along with the gestural and physiognomic indices of emotion those bodies so powerfully convey, that continues to draw the attention of viewers of this work. When we see Christ's body slumping down from the Cross, we sense a slumping in our own bodies, and we notice how precisely the Virgin reenacts that same movement, as if to express her grief at the sight of her Son.[254]

Moreover, Freedberg is a declared disciple of Paul Ekman's theory of universal basic emotions, which express themselves in particular in the face:

> Furthermore, when we see the gamut of emotions that are so poignantly registered both by the tears on the faces of protagonists of this drama and by the movements of their hands and limbs, we have an immediate sense of the muscular forces that drive these expressions of emotion.[255]

---

[253] David Freedberg, *The Power of Images: Studies in the History and Theory of Response* (Chicago: University of Chicago Press, 1989).

[254] David Freedberg, 'Memory in Art: History and the Neuroscience of Response', in Suzanne Nalbantian, Paul M. Matthews, and James L. McClelland (eds), *The Memory Process: Neuroscientific and Humanistic Perspectives* (Cambridge, MA: MIT Press, 2011), 337–58, here 344–5.

[255] Freedberg, 'Memory in Art', 345.

Fig. 27 Rogier van der Weyden, *The Descent from the Cross* (1435–8)

Source: © akg-images/Erich Lessing, <http://www.museodelprado.es/de/besuchen-sie-das-museum/15-meisterwerke/grundlegende-werksangaben/obra/die-kreuzabnahme>, accessed 13 March 2014.

What can we say about this? On the one hand, Freedberg universalizes the success of works of art by claiming that physical and emotional empathy with the representation of movement is the central criterion of response, accessible to all people of all cultures in all eras. On the other, he leaves a back door open through which he can smuggle experts in the history of art back in, or simply connoisseurship, thereby leaving a space for particularism. He cites a well-known mirror neuron experiment in which dancers and non-dancers watched ballet and capoeira dance videos, the dancers experiencing a stronger activation of their sensorimotoric nerve cells than the non-dancers, which according to Freedberg 'made it clear that the effects of viewing on motoric circuits are enhanced by prior skill and training'.[256] From this, Freedberg takes away for his own research the fact that expertise in the body movements performed in 'great' art cultivates a highly developed sense of physical empathy. But is this true? Any proof would require that canonical works of art be re-examined with respect to their representation of movement and its importance

---

[256] Freedberg, 'Memory in Art', 351–2. The mirror neuron article to which Freedberg refers is B. Calvo-Merino et al., 'Action Observation and Acquired Motor Skills: An fMRI Study with Expert Dancers', *Cerebral Cortex*, 15/8 (2005), 1243–9.

to the work in question, and whether the movements depicted lead to the firing of neurons in all people, and especially strong firings in experts. Besides, even the fact that over time canons change tends to speak against the idea that physical empathy with movement should be a leading criterion for the impact of art. And what about the results of countless sociological studies seeking to measure how much art is liked? According to these studies, the elaborate representations of movement that one can find in Leonardo and Michelangelo are unpopular; the art that has real impact on the lay public shows mountains, the sea, the sky, roaring stags, and above all, the colour blue.[257] Quite apart from all that, Freedberg's basic idea—that art with an impact has a universal impact—is illogical, since he also maintains that for some people (experts, connoisseurs) it has a greater impact, implying that they are more universal than everyone else.

Moreover, despite promising otherwise, Freedberg still owes us some kind of neuroscientific proof that realistic, natural photos like those made at Abu Ghraib in 2004 have a lesser impact than Rogier van der Weyden's painted picture.[258] This separation of 'artistic art' from 'realistic photography'—hard to understand from the standpoint of modern visual studies—is indispensable to Freedberg's reinforcement of the supposed impact of older, canonically 'higher' art. Otherwise, the images with the greatest impact would always be those which were realistic, and universally seen as such. Last of all, the most serious problem is that Freedberg relies upon experiments—those discussed in Sections 13–15, such as LeDoux's hypothesis of the two roads of fear, Damasio's Somatic Marker Hypothesis, Rizzolatti's and Gallese's mirror neuron hypothesis—all of which are now regarded as questionable within the neurosciences. Even if Freedberg is a better and more careful reader of neuroscience literature than the neuropolitical scientists, to whom we will shortly turn, and even though he has in the meantime conducted neuroscientific experiments himself, as we shall likewise soon see, the plausibility of his ideas depends on their underlying neuroscientific hypotheses.

Ultimately, Freedberg is interested in nothing less than a defence of 'great' art, or even the idea of a canon as such. Are there not after all absolute criteria that make particular works of art 'great', art which has appealed to humankind for centuries, and which will continue to appeal to future generations? It could well be, as the postmodern mantra goes, that great art is only that which those in power—patrons, connoisseurs, art historians—say is great art; it could be that the canon is always the

---

[257] See the series *The Most Wanted Paintings* by the Sots Artists Komar & Melamid based on surveys made in various countries, and presenting the locally most (and least) favourite work: Komar & Melamid, 'The Most Wanted Paintings on the Web', <http://awp.diaart.org/km/index.html> accessed 13 March 2014. See also 'The Search for a People's Art', *The Nation*, 258/10 (14 March 1994), 334–48; Andrew Ross, 'Poll Stars: Komar & Melamid's "The People's Choice"', *ArtForum* (January 1995), 72–7, 109.

[258] 'Indeed, for reasons that I intend to set out elsewhere, this "hyperaesthetic" response may be even greater in the case of images than of reality, depending, in the end, on the intuitive understanding artists may have of such possibilities.'; David Freedberg, 'Empathy, Motion and Emotion', in Klaus Herding and Antje Krause-Wahl (eds), *Wie sich Gefühle Ausdruck verschaffen: Emotionen in Nahsicht* (Berlin 2007), 17–51, here 41.

product of political negotiation and conflict. But what if the formal and aesthetic criteria for 'great' art came not from a secularized religious conception of culture, but from the hard neurosciences?[259] Here is Freedberg once again writing about Rogier van der Weyden's *Descent from the Cross*: 'Lesser artists may simply be less good at evoking the motor responses that underlie appropriate emotion.'[260] And more generally:

> Forms of direct and unmediated response (provisional labels for a variety of immediate and unconscious responses) offer a way of thinking about the continued hold of a centuries-old work of art on contemporary viewers, even in the absence of any particular knowledge or conscious recollection of its subject.[261]

How did Freedberg come upon the neurosciences? In his own account, his reading of nineteenth-century art historians—Robert Vischer, Theodor Lipps, and Heinrich Wölfflin—introduced him to the universal substrate in ways of seeing works of art: 'in *Das optische Formgefühl* of 1873, Robert Vischer distinguished between sensation and feeling in a way that anticipates recent neuroscientific distinctions between emotions and conscious feelings'.[262] (The use of the word 'emotion' shows how little even adepts adhere to the neuroscientific distinction between physical, unconscious 'affects' and less physical, conscious 'emotion'.) According to Freedberg, these nineteenth-century art historians were already on the right lines, although their legacy was suppressed in the process of forming the new discipline of art history. This new discipline had to look solid and serious; it could not afford to be doing with feelings. Ernst H. Gombrich's *Art and Illusion* (1960), 'perhaps the finest attempt ever made to bring art and scientific psychology together, scarcely referred to the emotions'.[263] Later Freedberg became interested in the neurosciences, even performing experiments together with neuroscientists such as Vittorio Gallese, one of the discoverers of mirror neurons.[264] Freedberg's most recent neuroscience experiments indicate that our mirrored perception is especially marked with the representation of movement, but not with regard to the representation of unmoving bodies. This supports Hickok's revision of the mirror neuron hypothesis, which implies that mirror neurons are more sensorimotoric than 'cognitive'.[265] Freedberg is probably the most prominent neuro-convert in the study of the visual arts, but he is by no means alone. Various art historians have worked with the neuroscientist Semir Zeki, who coined the concept of

---

[259] See also Tomohiro Ishizu and Semir Zeki, 'Toward a Brain-Based Theory of Beauty', *PLoS ONE*, 6/7 (2011), e21852: 1–10.

[260] Freedberg, 'Memory in Art', 347–8.   [261] Freedberg, 'Memory in Art', 337.

[262] Freedberg, 'Empathy, Motion and Emotion', 27.

[263] Freedberg, 'Empathy, Motion and Emotion', 23.

[264] David Freedberg and Vittorio Gallese, 'Motion, Emotion and Empathy in Esthetic Experience', *Trends in Cognitive Sciences*, 11/5 (2007), 197–203.

[265] Fortunato Battaglia, Sarah H. Lisanby, and David Freedberg, 'Corticomotor Excitability during Observation and Imagination of a Work of Art', *Frontiers in Human Neuroscience*, 5 (2011), 79: 1–6. Freedberg follows developments in neuroscience, and is well aware that the mirror neuron hypothesis is disputed: 'Although mirror neurons cannot live up to many of the claims currently made on their behalf'; Freedberg, 'Memory in Art', 341.

'neuroaesthetics', and who designs experiments using stimuli taken from 'great' art.[266] This is clearly a trend.

There is no space here to pursue the comparable trend towards the neurosciences in the study of literature.[267] Instead, let us take a look at neuropolitics, and so at a social science. Here too there was initially an intention to demarcate oneself from post-structuralism. The problem with post-structuralism is its logocentrism, and its lack of capacity to deal jointly with language and physicality, cognition and emotion. William E. Connolly writes:

> You will have noticed neuroscience on the list of topics to address. Because it is, the following question is often posed to me these days, particularly by friends: 'But, Bill, doesn't that venture drive you to the very reductionism (or scientism, phrenology, sociobiology, genetic determinism, behaviorism, eliminative materialism, barefoot empiricism, depreciation of language, etc.) you have heretofore fought against?' I don't think so. My sense is that in their laudable attempt to ward off one type of reductionism too many cultural theorists fall into another: they lapse into a reductionism that ignores how biology is mixed into thinking and culture and how other aspects of nature are folded into both.[268]

Brian Massumi argues in much the same way. He describes the expressionist ontology of Gilles Deleuze (1925–95) and Félix Guattari (1930–92)—'A less fashionable concept, for late twentieth-century European thought, would also be hard to find'—as marginal, and claims that 'All of these assumptions have been severely tested by structuralist, poststructuralist, postmodern, and postpostmodern thought'.[269] In contrast to the ontological status of expression in Deleuze and Guattari, 'The "postmodern" is an image of communication out of control. Seeming to have lost its mooring in objective conformity or correspondence, it appears uncaused, unmotivated, in endless, unguaranteed "slippage".'[270] And the editors of the *The Affect Theory Reader* inform their readers that

---

[266] Semir Zeki, *A Vision of the Brain* (Oxford: Blackwell Scientific Publications, 1993); Semir Zeki, *Inner Vision: An Exploration of Art and the Brain* (Oxford: Oxford University Press, 1999); Semir Zeki, *Splendors and Miseries of the Brain: Love, Creativity, and the Quest for Human Happiness* (Chichester: Wiley-Blackwell, 2009). See also Whitney Davis, 'Neurovisuality', *Nonsite.org*, 2 (12 June 2011) <http://nonsite.org/issues/issue-2/neurovisuality> accessed 14 March 2014; John Oinans, *Neuroarthistory: From Aristotle and Pliny to Baxandall and Zeki* (New Haven: Yale University Press, 2008); *Journal of Neuroesthetics; Arts and Neurosciences Review*.

[267] A few titles will have to do: Sianne Ngai, *Ugly Feelings* (Cambridge, MA: Harvard University Press, 2007); Jane F. Thrailkill, *Affecting Fictions: Mind, Body, and Emotion in American Literary Realism* (Cambridge, MA: Harvard University Press, 2007); Barbara Johnson, *Persons and Things* (Cambridge, MA: Harvard University Press, 2008); Raoul Schrott and Arthur Jacobs, *Gehirn und Gedicht: Wie wir unsere Wirklichkeiten konstruieren* (Munich: Hanser, 2011). See also Andreas Lambert, Oliver Kauselmann, and Boris Kleber, *Cognitive Poetics: Visualisierung von emotionalen Reaktionen auf Literatur* [web installation] <http://cognitive-poetics.net> accessed 14 March 2014.

[268] William E. Connolly, *Neuropolitics: Thinking, Culture, Speed* (Minneapolis: University of Minnesota Press, 2002), 3.

[269] Brian Massumi, 'Introduction: Like a Thought', in Massumi (ed.), *A Shock to Thought: Expression after Deleuze and Guattari* (London: Routledge, 2002), xiii–xxxix, here xiii.

[270] Massumi, 'Introduction: Like a Thought', xv.

This is the point at which we would want to mark a limit for theory's usefulness, and offer these essays as incitements to *more than* discourse. We want them to touch, to move, to mobilize readers. Rather than offering mere words, we want them to show what affect can *do*.[271]

Of course, these intentions were expressed in words, not acoustically or visually: there is no change in typeface, it is not embossed, and there is nothing to scratch to release a smell. Nonetheless, this delimiting move against post-structuralism does not stop neuropolitical theorists of 'vitalism' or the 'new materialism', as they call their new approach, making use of post-structural conceptions in a typically eclectic post-structural way—taking over, for instance, Foucault's use of 'biopolitics'.

Neuropolitical theorists say that they are different and ahead of most of us, but above all they demarcate themselves from post-structuralism. Their first, and most important, move is the separation of unconscious physical affect from conscious emotion, although affect and emotion remain linked and emotion is not conceivable without affect (whereas affect without emotion certainly is). Emotion is a form of cognition, and always has an affective component. Here are a few tries at definition, starting with Connolly:

> Affective pressures travel from a variety of human and nonhuman sources—sunlight, electrical shocks, insulting statements, magnetic fields, a raging sea, inspirational actions, and so on—into the human sensorium. The latter affective states then become organized into feelings and higher emotions. Affect, in its most elementary human mode, is an electrical-chemical charge that jolts or nudges you toward positive or negative action before it reaches the threshold of feeling or awareness. Its action invoking pressure arrives before it takes the shape of culturally infused feelings, emotions, or moods. The affective charge, consisting of vibrations running through different parts of the nervous system, provides the initial, fast, subliminal response to something arriving from the outside. A painting of glistening sunflowers by Van Gogh, sunlight bathing the body, an unexpected caress, a screeching sound, a pungent smell, a dancing body in motion, a bolt of lightning—all these affect the sensorium before being organized by it into conscious perceptions, feelings, and reactions. The organization, indeed, results from a set of resonances between the new vibrations and sensorial habits already there, unless the affect overwhelms those habits. Affectively imbued action is underway even before a perception crystallizes. As when a driver is jolted into making a sharp turn even before a visual image is formed or a conscious feeling of danger arises.[272]

John Protevi emphasizes 'that cognition and affectless rational calculation performed on representation can no longer be identified'.[273] And finally Massumi states that 'Thought strikes like lightning, with sheering ontogenetic force. It is *felt*.'[274]

---

[271] Seigworth, 'Inventory of Shimmers', 24, emphasis in original.

[272] William E. Connolly, *A World of Becoming* (Durham, NC: Duke University Press, 2011), 150–1.

[273] John Protevi, *Political Affect: Connecting the Social and the Somatic*, Posthumanities 7 (Minneapolis: University of Minnesota Press, 2009), 25.

[274] Massumi, 'Introduction', xxxi, emphasis in original. See also Shaviro on Massumi's distinction between affect and emotion: 'For Massumi, affect is primary, non-conscious, asubjective or

The next step involves the scope for action, or agency. Given the embodiment and weakening of the cognitive dimension, agency is ascribed to a broad spectrum and a great number of organisms, even to things. According to Connolly it is

> plausible to construe human agency as an emergent phenomenon, with some nonhuman processes possessing attributes bearing family resemblances to human agency and with human agency understood by reference to its emergence from non-human processes of proto-agency.[275]

There follows discussion about the proto-agency of bacteria ('possesses *some* characteristics of agency'; 'It is attracted to sugar; it pursues it as an end; it adjusts its behavior to pursue its end; and it feels satisfaction when it achieves the end intended')[276] and about the agency of monkeys and dung beetles:

> Even at some of these levels of complexity, it is not clear that agency is entirely restricted to human beings. According to Giacomo Rizzolatti—the neuroscientist who discovered mirror neurons and triggered a revolution in neuroscience that is still unfolding—monkeys with culturally infused mirror neurons and without complex linguistic skills read the intentions of other monkeys and other living beings rather well. They then incorporate some of those intentions into their own repertoires of action. They can also adjust their behavior toward others according to the initial reading of those intentions. They are invested with a degree of cultural agency before and below language. Even a dung beetle adjusts a first order desire to move a piece of dung when it meets a barrier, if not by changing the end, at least by altering the means to it.[277]

With such a broad conception of agency very many more objects and living things become worthy of protection than would normally be the case.[278]

Ultimately, at the centre of all neuropolitical thought is the issue of resistance. It should be said that neuropolitical science is an enterprise run by leftists (or liberals, in the American sense) who believe that, since the 1980s, there has been an ever greater affective and cognitive danger from Christian fundamentalist conservatives, especially since the foundation of conservative radio stations and, above all, the TV channel Fox News. They maintain that these new TV formats address media consumers in a more subtle, unconscious manner: 'Today programs such as *The*

---

presubjective, asignifying, unqualified, and intensive; while emotion is derivative, conscious, qualified, and meaningful, a "content" that can be attributed to an already-constituted subject . . . , or tamed and reduced to the extent that it becomes commensurate with that subject. Subjects are overwhelmed and traversed by affect, but they *have* or *possess* their own emotions'; Steven Shaviro, *Post-Cinematic Affect* (Winchester: Zero Books, 2009), 3, emphasis in original.

[275] Connolly, *World of Becoming*, 23.

[276] Connolly, *World of Becoming*, 24, emphasis in original.

[277] Connolly, *World of Becoming*, 26.

[278] The vitalist, or rather new materialist neuropolitical thinker Jane Bennett has thought about the agency of things amd drawn mostly political and ecological conclusions. See Jane Bennett, *Vibrant Matter: A Political Ecology of Things* (Durham, NC: Duke University Press, 2010); also Andrew Barry, 'Materialist Politics: Metallurgy', in Bruce Braun and Sarah J. Whatmore (eds), *Political Matter: Technoscience, Democracy, and Public Life* (Minneapolis: University of Minnesota Press, 2010), 89–117; Gay Hawkins, 'Plastic Materialities', in Braun and Whatmore (eds), *Political Matter*, 119–38.

Hannity Report, *Glenn Beck*, and *The O'Reilly Factor* infiltrate the tonalities of political perception. . . . As a result resentment and dogmatic cynicism are now coded into the very color of perception.'[279] Given such circumstances, which could be called 'cogaffective', 'rationally based' resistance is not enough. Opposition on the basis of 'objective' class position, subjective belief, or ideology is helpless in the face of this new threat, and understanding this is the first step in resistance. '[N]o single social category or creedal confession', Connolly writes, 'corresponds neatly to the existential disposition you seek to expose, resist, or overcome.'[280] And further:

> A stated change in personal or constituency *belief* is not enough since the layered embodiment of belief and the actual performance of roles are so closely bound together. *A belief is an embodied tendency to performance; concerted practices of perform-ance help to alter or intensify beliefs; and new intensities of belief fold back into future desires, performative priorities, and potentialities of political action.*[281]

Hence Connolly recommends particular actions which automatically shape resist-ant interlinked bodies and movements:

> If you are in the middle class, buy a Prius or a Volt and explain to your friends and neighbors why you did; write in a blog; attend a pivotal rally; ride your bike to work more often; consider solar panels; introduce new topics at your church. As you do those things, you may note how an array of hesitant beliefs and desires now becomes more solid and how other tendencies begin to melt away. You may now be prepared to participate in larger political assemblages in more robust ways, joining others whose beliefs, role perfomances, and desires have also been moving. You can call such a combination micropolitics if you want, a dimension of life that must be joined at many junctures to macropolitics if either is to work in a positive way. Today it is urgent to forge a counter-resonance machine composed of several constituencies who diverge along lines of creedal faith, class position, racial or ethnic identification, sexual affiliation, and gender practice. It is to enlarge the cohort who give priority to the earth, however they themselves otherwise interpret the most fundamental terms of existence.[282]

This is leftist political science with ambitions for application, distinguishing itself from rational choice political science, which lacks any such ambition (since it lacks a physical-affective dimension), and from Marxist political science and Marxist political movements, which do have ambitions for application (since these are founded only on ideology and belief, and likewise lack a physical-affective dimen-sion). Finally, it also distinguishes itself from postmodern identity politics with ambitions for application (because this tendency lacks an *unum* to follow on from *e pluribus*).[283] It is however not clear, to use rather old-fashioned terminology, from

---

[279] Connolly, *World of Becoming*, 54–5.   [280] Connolly, *World of Becoming*, 90.
[281] Connolly, *World of Becoming*, 145, emphasis in original.
[282] Connolly, *World of Becoming*, 91.
[283] Other disciplinary branches also steer clear of rational choice approaches because of their lack of an affective-physical dimension; see the work of the neuroeconomist Ernst Fehr, or that of the decision psychologist Gerd Gigerenzer on *bounded rationality*: Colin F. Camerer and Ernst Fehr, 'When Does "Economic Man" Dominate Social Behavior?', *Science*, 311/5757 (2006), 47–52; G. Gigerenzer and R. Selten (eds), *Bounded Rationality: The Adaptive Toolbox* (Cambridge, MA: MIT Press, 2001); Gerd Gigerenzer, *Gut Feelings: The Intelligence of the Unconscious* (New York: Viking, 2007). See also the

what affective and cognitive sources the *content* of this resistance might draw. Given this form of materialist and vitalist empathy—from bacteria to fellow human beings, since we are all part of the greater universe—it is no longer possible to make any decision that privileges human beings. Not when animal experiments are made under strict conditions for the development of new medicines; nor if genetically-modified, robust, and high-yielding seeds are used which, while their use has unforeseen consequences, could help feed a growing world population. Nor does neuropolitics provide any foundation for the redistribution of property (through, for instance, radically progressive taxation) that goes beyond securing a minimum existence for the poorest. And, finally, this kind of neuroscientific argumentation does not help overthrow a tyrant, nor bring an end to genocide. It is the limited vision of a kinder, gentler middle-class America; and with that a central claim, that of universality, is driven to absurdity.

Neuropolitics relies upon the findings of the life sciences. Two things can be said about how neuropolitical theorists deal with the life sciences. First of all, they draw upon a small number of popularizing texts: counting generously, in Connolly's *A World of Becoming* it is eleven, in Bennett's *Vibrant Matter* eighteen. Most of these references are not articles, but books by the popularizers, and they are all based on LeDoux's hypothesis of the two roads to fear, on Damasio's Somatic Markers, on mirror neurons, and also sometimes on the Libet experiment.[284] All these hypotheses are very dubious. All of them, as well as the basic distinction between unconscious affect and conscious emotion (which runs back to Tomkins and Ekman), have been subjected to critical review by historians of science, for example, in the work of Ruth Leys, who has a background in the natural sciences. There has been careful and detailed work done on experimental design, sample size, and epistemological premises; but neuropolitics ignores all of this substantive criticism entirely.[285] Instead, its proponents take refuge in philosophical generalities, as does Connolly in a response to Leys, arguing that too much is at stake in times of right-wing blogs, Fox News, and the Tea Party. They claim that rational discourse no longer works when faced with such developments.[286] Secondly, the work of the life sciences is dealt with in the classic casual postmodern manner: for Connolly, Damasio's *Spinoza Effect* is 'a fine study in neuroscience that draws upon both

sociology of economic organization approached from a similar perspective: Helena Flam, *Soziologie der Emotionen: Eine Einführung* (Konstanz: UTB, 2002), 178, 187–8.

[284] In Benjamin Libet's experiment subjects are asked to make a small bodily movement—e.g. crook the finger—and record the time that they decided upon making this physical movement. Simultaneously brain activity is measured with an EEG. It turns out that the area of the cortex responsible for movement (motorcortex) 'prepares itself' before the conscious decision and the execution of the movement; there is therefore a preconscious brain-body circuit. This experiment is used to cast doubt on the theory of free will, among other things. For criticism of the Libet experiment, see e.g. Daniel C. Dennett, *Freedom Evolves* (New York: Viking, 2003); Christine Zunke, *Kritik der Hirnforschung: Neurophysiologie und Willensfreiheit* (Berlin: Akademie Verlag, 2007), 110–28.

[285] See Leys, 'The Turn to Affect'.

[286] William E. Connolly, 'Critical Response I: The Complexity of Intention', *Critical Inquiry*, 37/4 (2011), 791–8; Ruth Leys, 'Critical Response II: Affect and Intention: A Reply to William E. Connolly', *Critical Inquiry*, 37/4 (2011), 799–805.

Spinoza's philosophy of parallelism and his idea that affect always accompanies perception, belief, and thinking'.[287] In the neurosciences there is no 'fine', nor finest, very fine, less fine—only true or false, the only qualification that its cast-iron binary epistemological rules permit.[288]

Lastly, a word about the literary style of neuropolitics and the hype surrounding it. Stylistically, neuropolitical texts are a mix of statements of personal feeling—since of course writing always has a physical and affective dimension—and descriptions of laptops, computer keyboards, and the lead of a pencil, because there is equally a material dimension to writing. There are also New Age-ish comparisons and pictures, together with a complete absence of irony, as though writers had just completed a creative writing course the day after post-structuralism had been completely erased from the world's memory.

17 AFFECTARIANS OF ALL LANDS, UNITE! THE NEUROSCIENCES AS REPRESENTED BY HARDT, NEGRI, & CO.

Neuroscientific thinking has also spread beyond academia into political movements. The most influential texts among groups critical of globalization, besides Naomi Klein's *No Logo!* (1999), are by Michael Hardt and Antonio Negri. Their book *Empire* (2000) has already been called a 'Communist Manifesto for the Twenty-First Century': it presents a picture of a global, post-industrial capitalism with flat hierarchies, networked, computerized production, decentralized states, private police forces and armies; there is no room for retreat, or at least not from those niches dominated by biopower.[289] In *Empire*, and in particular its sequel *Multitude: War And Democracy in the Age of Empire* (2004), as well as in a number of smaller pieces, Hardt and Negri describe how work has changed in the new globalized world: work, the products of which are said to be immaterial, is becoming ever more important, even '*hegemonic in qualitative terms*'. On the one hand, we have the knowledge professions—the economists and sociologists of work talk about a new 'cognitariat'; while on the other hand there is 'affective labor' (no one has yet talked about an 'affectariat').[290] Affective work, first

---

[287] William E. Connolly, 'Materialities of Experience', in Diana H. Coole and Samantha Frost (eds), *New Materialisms: Ontology, Agency, and Politics* (Durham, NC: Duke University Press, 2010), 198 n. 6.

[288] Nor can one defend, as John Protevi does, SMH from a strictly philosophical perspective: 'Shaun Gallagher will say that the details of Damasio's proposal "either inflate the body to the level of ideas in a phenomenologically untenable way, or reduce it to neuronal processes". But if we take into account Colombetti and Thompson's reminder that as-if loops require constant somatic updating and hence are not mere neurocentric representations, we can retain the "somatic marker" hypothesis'; Protevi, *Political Affect*, 198 n. 35.

[289] Slavoj Žižek, 'Have Michael Hardt and Antonio Negri Rewritten the Communist Manifesto for the Twenty-First Century?', *Rethinking Marxism*, 13/3–4 (2001), 190–8.

[290] Michael Hardt and Antonio Negri, *Multitude: War And Democracy in the Age of Empire* (New York: Penguin Books, 2005), 109, emphasis in original. See also Michael Hardt, 'Affective Labor',

studied by the feminist sociologist Arlie Hochschild, whom we encountered in Chapter Two,

> is labor that produces or manipulates affects such as a feeling of ease, well-being, satisfaction, excitement, or passion. One can recognize affective labor, for example, in the work of legal assistants, flight attendants, and fast food workers (service with a smile). One indication of the rising importance of affective labor, at least in the dominant countries, is the tendency for employers to highlight education, attitude, character, and 'prosocial' behavior as the primary skills employees need. A worker with a good attitude and social skills is another way of saying a worker adept at affective labor.[291]

Hardt and Negri's conception of affect comes from Spinoza, Deleuze, Massumi, and Damasio.[292] Hardt writes:

> On the one side we have reason, actions of the mind, along with actions of the body, which one might call provocatively corporeal reason; on the other side are the passions both of the mind and the body. The perspective of the affects does not assume that reason and passion are the same, but rather poses them together on a continuum. ... One way of understanding this complex set of propositions, then, is simply to say that the perspective of the affects requires us constantly to pose as a problem the relation between actions and passions, between reason and the emotions. We do not know in advance what a body can do, what a mind can think—what affects are capable of. The perspective of the affects requires an exploration of these as yet unknown powers. Spinoza thus gives us a new ontology of the human or, rather, an ontology of the human that is constantly open and renewed.[293]

For Hardt and Negri, affect is supposed to be the source upon which resistance can feed. It is therefore stated in general that the affective perspective opens 'avenues for political organizing and collective practices of refusal and liberation'.[294] More exactly, following a sketch of Foucault's conception of biopower—for Hardt and Negri a 'top-down' conception:

> These dangers, however—important though they might be—do not negate the importance of recognizing the potential of labor as biopower, a biopower from below. This biopolitical context is precisely the ground for an investigation of the productive relationship between affect and value. ... On one hand affective labor, the production and reproduction of life, has become firmly embedded as a necessary foundation for capitalist accumulation and patriarchal order. On the other hand, however, the production of affects, subjectivities, and forms of life present an enormous potential for autonomous circuits of valorization, and perhaps for liberation.[295]

Boundary 2, 26/2 (1999), 89–100; Michael Hardt, 'Foreword: What Affects Are Good For', in Patricia Ticineto Clough and Jean Halley (eds), *The Affective Turn: Theorizing the Social* (Durham, NC: Duke University Press, 2007), ix–xiii. See as well Michael Hardt and Antonio Negri, *Empire* (Cambridge, MA: Harvard University Press, 2000).

[291] Hardt and Negri, *Multitude*, 108.
[292] Spinoza, Deleuze, Massumi: see Hardt, 'Foreword', xiii n. 2; Damasio: see Hardt and Negri, *Multitude*, 374 n. 9.
[293] Hardt, 'Foreword', x.   [294] Hardt, 'Foreword', xii.
[295] Hardt, 'Affective Labor', 100.

It never gets any more specific than this.

Many have little objection to Hardt and Negri's analysis, although they do reject the idea of basing resistance in the emotional. One line of criticism comes from Lacanian psychoanalysis. A neuroscientific nature, as configured by Damasio, simply cannot exist because 'nature' always presupposes symbolic signification. Hence as soon as people agree about anything—about 'nature', for instance—they denaturalize it through the use of the contingent means available to them, primarily language.[296] From another direction, leftists criticize the approach taken by Hardt and Negri and insist on the primacy of objective socio-economic factors. For Walter Benn Michaels, a literary scholar, Hardt and Negri's neuroscientific and affective foundation of resistance (which by the way he considers a by-product of postmodernism, rather than of post-postmodernism as I do here) involves an ontologization, through which resistance undermines itself:

> Replacing the question of what people believe with the question of what they want, [Francis] Fukuyama's posthistoricism repeated the [Paul] de Manian replacement of the cognitive with the affective. And this turn to affect at the end of history produced the same result as the turn to affect at the beginning of history: the primacy of the subject. Liberals and socialists have different beliefs about the world, and the disagreement between them necessarily transcends their subject positions, which is just to say that if the liberals are right, then the socialists must be wrong. But once what people believe is replaced (as Fukuyama says) by what they want or (as de Man says) by what they see, the difference between them requires no disagreement. The difference between what you want and what I want is just a difference between you and me; the difference between what you see and what I see is just the difference between where you're standing and where I'm standing—literally, a difference in subject position.[297]

There is a sarcastic edge to Michaels's criticism of Hardt and Negri, suggesting that they write tracts for a self-pitying middle class. He claims, for instance, that post-structuralist identity politics simply allows social inequality to be forgotten: 'And because the poor are not marginalized, and because they are victimized by capitalism rather than by "oppressive definitions of the subject", writers committed to [Judith] Butler's version of "a Left political project" have tended more or less to ignore them.' Furthermore:

> The great merit of Hardt and Negri is thus to reclaim the poor for the Left, and their great ingenuity is to do so by ontologizing poverty, treating it as if it were not so much a lack of money as a way of being. It's no wonder, then, that Saint Francis emerges as the 'communist' hero of *Empire*; he turns the project of getting rid of poverty into the project of becoming poor.
>   Or, perhaps more precisely, into the project of outing ourselves as the poor people we all potentially are. For once we turn poverty into a structure of identification, a

[296] Adrian Johnston, 'The Misfeeling of What Happens: Slavoj Žižek, Antonio Damasio and a Materialist Account of Affects', *Subjectivity*, 3/1 (2010), 76–100; Slavoj Žižek, 'Some Concluding Notes on Violence, Ideology and Communist Culture', *Subjectivity*, 3/1 (2010), 101–16.
[297] Walter Benn Michaels, *The Shape of the Signifier: 1967 to the End of History* (Princeton: Princeton University Press, 2004), 9–10.

relation to identity rather than to money, we can begin to think that our problem is that we're all insufficiently 'poor'. It's for this reason that [Slavoj] Žižek, as hostile to the usual forms (cultural, national, racial) of identitarianism as Hardt and Negri, nonetheless finds himself reproducing their ontologizing commitments

... More generally, we might say that *we*—the middle class, not as alive as Saint Francis, not as alive as Palestinian suicide bombers—are the victims. And, more generally still (but this is a slightly different topic), we might also say that the Left today obsessively interests itself in a set of essentially liberal issues—from racism to gay marriage—as a way of not interesting itself in the problem of economic inequality.[298]

Michaels's insistence upon ideological rather than affective-ontological difference finds support from the way that conservative circles likewise make use of the category of affect, although in an opposite, affirmative manner, explaining away poorly-paid post-industrial labour by claiming that the main thing should be that it 'feels good'. This is the programme of compassionate conservatism in the USA under Reagan and Bush, and in David Cameron's conception of the 'Big Society' in Britain.[299] One could, then, go a step further and point to the parallels between the universalism of the neurosciences and the universalism of global capitalism. After the dominance of pluralism in the post-structuralist 1980s, globalization has discovered in the neurosciences the kind of universalism with which it can do business.[300]

18 BORROWINGS FROM THE NEUROSCIENCES: AN INTERIM BALANCE

The spectacular neuroscientific experiments of which human and social scientists have made such daring use turn out as a rule to be dubious, or even entirely untenable. Criticism of these experiments and hypotheses is made in the neurosciences itself. Should enthusiastic amateur users of the neurosciences bother themselves about this? Could they not treat a hypothesis based on an experiment as 'an interesting reading', in much the same way that deconstructionist literary criticism lists various interpretations of the same passage, implying the ambiguity of the sign and the openness of interpretation?

I do not know how that would be possible. The human and social sciences have, following a phase of post-structural pluralism and relativism, gone back to the search for universal truths, and seem to think they have hit on a suitable source with the neurosciences. If some neuroscientific finding which was thought to be true is

---

[298] Michaels, *The Shape of the Signifier*, 180–1, emphasis in original.

[299] Jacob Weisberg, *The Bush Tragedy* (New York: Random House, 2008). 'Compassionate conservatism' is outlined, for example, in Marvin Olasky, *Compassionate Conservatism: What it is, What it Does, and How it Can Transform America* (New York: Free Press, 2000); Arthur C. Brooks, *Who Really Cares: The Surprising Truth About Compassionate Conservatism* (New York: Basic Books, 2006).

[300] That seems appropriate: Patricia T. Clough, 'The Affective Turn: Political Economy, Biomedia and Bodies', *Theory, Culture & Society*, 25/1 (2008), 1–22, esp. 15–17.

now thought to be false, there is no relativist lifebelt that can save it, suggesting that today's truth is just one possible reading. Sink or swim, true or false: that is how the epistemology of the natural sciences works.[301]

The majority of human and social scientists choose to adhere to this natural scientific epistemology when confronting natural scientific findings which they do not like: whether dealing with phrenology, eugenics, the physiognomics of the nineteenth and early twentieth century, or the racist implications of the Bell Curve in the later twentieth century—none of these are treated as one interesting 'reading' among others, but as false, completely obsolete, insufficiently proven, unambiguously refuted.[302] Neuroscientists by contrast have no problem with their own epistemology. They are used to truths being quickly superseded, and to the Damocles sword of replicability that hangs over every experiment.

From all of this one thing follows for the human and social sciences: if one uses findings from the neurosciences, one cannot avoid a more thorough engagement with them. One needs an idea of experimental design, sample size, of internal, external, and ecological validity. One should have a deep-seated scepticism with regard to the popularizers like LeDoux and Damasio, who mostly present just one hypothesis, dressed up with quotations from Descartes, Spinoza, or Shakespeare, all put handily between two book covers for those who are not neuroscientists. William M. Reddy has said that 'My principal frustration with reading popularizers is that they offer a candidate theory to explain the trends in research as if this candidate were already recognized as the unchallenged, new explanation of brain and mind functioning. They systematically downplay the diversity of the research, in order to extrapolate dramatic answers from a select number of recent, fashionable breakthroughs.'[303] How right he is. How particular supposedly universal theories really are becomes quickly apparent if one considers the work of popularization in different countries. In Germany it would seem that Gerhard Roth and Wolf Singer—perhaps also Hans J. Markowitsch and Manfred Spitzer—had claimed for themselves the market in neuroscientific truth; but in the USA they and their

---

[301] The epistemology of the natural sciences, and especially the question of falsification, is a domain of research in itself. Here we can only note that the philosopher of science Imre Lakatos refined Karl Popper's falsificationism in the following way (and defended him against Thomas Kuhn): as a rule, only particular statements and predictions are falsified, and it is very rare for a research programme to be negated as a whole. See Imre Lakatos, *The Methodology of Scientific Research Programmes* (Cambridge: Cambridge University Press, 1978), 8–101; Imre Lakatos, *Proofs and Refutations: the Logic of Mathematical Discovery* (Cambridge: Cambridge University Press, 1976). On the debate see also Gunnar Andersson, *Kritik und Wissenschaftsgeschichte: Kuhns, Lakatos' und Feyerabends Kritik des Kritischen Rationalismus* (Tübingen: Mohr, 1988). A useful article summarizing the epistemological similarities and differences between the social and the neuerosciences is John Cromby, 'Integrating Social Science with Neuroscience: Potentials and Problems', *BioSocieties*, 2/2 (2007), 149–69.

[302] The Bell Curve is the bell-shaped graph of the distribution of IQ in the population, and is the title of a book by Herrnstein and Murray which suggested that black Americans had on average a lower level of intelligence than white Americans; Richard J. Herrnstein and Charles Murray, *The Bell Curve: Intelligence and Class Structure in American Life* (New York: Free Press, 1994).

[303] Jan Plamper, 'The History of Emotions: An Interview with William Reddy, Barbara H. Rosenwein, and Peter Sterns by Jan Plamper', *History and Theory*, 49/2 (2010), 237–65, here 248.

findings are more or less unknown.[304] As the philosopher Thomas Metzinger has said, 'the completely commercialized pop intellectuals of the twenty-first century' could end up making their own contribution to high-level 'dumbing-down'.[305] It is for this reason that one should bear in mind the differing temporalities involved: the delay between the publication of laboratory research in scientific journals and its presentation in popularizations contracted by the Brockman Agency is considerable (even if much less than the time it takes for historical archival research to reach publication). As a layperson, therefore, a reliance on popularizations runs the risk that one depends upon knowledge that is already obsolete. One should also be sceptical about sensational new neuroscientific findings as presented in the press, on the radio, or on TV. Very often these supposedly new discoveries rest upon a single article whose findings have been interpreted and summarized by science journalists.

A sceptical and more responsible approach to the neurosciences should begin with the reading of meta-analyses, articles that systematically compare the findings of sometimes hundreds of papers on one topic, for example, mirror neurons. In the neurosciences themselves these meta-analyses are treated as the gold standard. But it will also be necessary to read very many individual papers. And if one is attracted to one particular finding, then one should remember the temporalities involved and ask oneself, more than once, whether this finding would really satisfy the criterion of robustness employed in the study of history: that the domain of any statement is carefully restricted, that the object about which such statements are made is neither unique nor aberrant, and that any conclusion has been considered valid for some time. Historical studies are at an advantage when considering whether something has been considered valid for a long time. While many neuroscientists complain about the lack of institutional memory in their discipline, that experiments done

---

[304] While popular Anglo-American texts in the neurosciences are almost always quickly translated into German, hardly any comparable German work has been translated into English; see Gerhard Roth, *Fühlen, Denken, Handeln: Wie das Gehirn unser Verhalten steuert* (Frankfurt am Main: Suhrkamp, 2001); Gerhard Roth, *Aus Sicht des Gehirns* (Frankfurt am Main: Suhrkamp, 2003); Gerhard Roth, *Persönlichkeit, Entscheidung und Verhalten: Warum es so schwierig ist, sich und andere zu ändern* (Stuttgart: Klett-Cotta, 2007); Michael Pauen and Gerhard Roth, *Freiheit, Schuld und Verantwortung: Grundzüge einer naturalistischen Theorie der Willensfreiheit* (Frankfurt am Main: Suhrkamp, 2008); Wolf Singer, *Der Beobachter im Gehirn: Essays zur Hirnforschung* (Frankfurt am Main: Suhrkamp, 2002); Wolf Singer, *Ein neues Menschenbild? Gespräche über Hirnforschung* (Frankfurt am Main: Suhrkamp, 2003); Wolf Singer, *Vom Gehirn zum Bewußtsein* (Frankfurt am Main: Suhrkamp, 2006); Hans J. Markowitsch and Werner Siefer, *Tatort Gehirn: Auf der Suche nach dem Ursprung des Verbrechens* (Frankfurt am Main: Campus, 2007); Hans J. Markowitsch, *Das Gedächtnis: Entwicklung, Funktionen, Störungen* (Munich: Beck, 2009); Manfred Spitzer, *Nervensachen: Geschichten vom Gehirn* (Frankfurt am Main: Suhrkamp, 2005); Manfred Spitzer, *Dopamin & Käsekuchen: Hirnforschung à la carte* (Stuttgart: Schattauer, 2011); Manfred Spitzer, *Nichtstun, Flirten, Küssen und andere Leistungen des Gehirns* (Stuttgart: Schattauer, 2012); Manfred Spitzer, *Digitale Demenz: Wie wir uns und unsere Kinder um den Verstand bringen* (Munich: Droemer, 2012). The exceptions are: Hans J. Markowitsch and Harald Welzer, *The Development of Autobiographical Memory*, trans. David Emmans (Hove: Psychology Press, 2010) [Ger. orig., *Das autobiographische Gedächtnis: Hirnorganische Grundlagen und biosoziale Entwicklung*, 2005]; Birgitt Röttger-Rössler and Hans J. Markowitsch (eds), *Emotions as Bio-Cultural Processes* (New York: Springer, 2009); the first appeared five years after the German original, the second is a collection based on papers by a mostly Anglophone research group.

[305] Thomas Metzinger cited in Schnabel, 'Wie Agenten, Verleger und Autoren mit populärer Welterklärung Gewinn machen', 43.

five years ago are as good as forgotten, this recursive function is the core business of history. If one fails to adhere to this precept, then much the same thing can happen as it did to Jean Delumeau, the author of a classic book on fear in early modernity whom we encountered in Chapter One. At one point he allows himself to make a universal statement borrowed from experimental psychology which today, more than twenty years after the publication of the book, is hopelessly dated: 'once alerted, the hypothalamus responds by generally mobilizing the organism, giving rise to various kinds of somatic behaviour and, notably, prompts endocrinal changes'.[306]

19 BEYOND ALL DIVIDES: THE CRITICAL NEUROSCIENCES AND GENUINE POSSIBILITIES FOR COOPERATION

Over the past ten years the scenery has shifted. There are increasing numbers of neuroscientists who are themselves critical of their discipline, or who have taken to heart criticism from the human sciences and from those in the humanities who have approached the neurosciences sceptically, although with an open mind. Neuroscientists have begun to develop an institutional memory for their discipline so that they might help prevent the wheel being reinvented yet again, and so that they might learn from the mistakes of the past. They have accepted philosophical criticism, based upon a long tradition and logical consistency. Conversely, those working in the human sciences have had to admit that, for all their scepticism, progress has been made in the neurosciences, refining and ultimately improving procedures, images, and models of the brain. They take this progress seriously, as they do any other kind of scientific achievement; when their tonsils are inflamed they take penicillin, they keep their food in the fridge, and hope for a cure for cancer. We could call this loose coalition 'critical neurosciences'.[307] The borders of this coalition are of course porous, and it is not easy to draw sharp distinctions: the neuroscientist Richard J. Davidson has, for example, worked a great deal with Ekman, but in 2003 published a fundamental critique of the 'Seven Sins in the

---

[306] Jean Delumeau, *La Peur en Occident (XVIe–XVIIIe siècles): Une cité assiégée* (Paris: Fayard, 1978), 13. See also the Stearns, who summarized the position of the life sciences on emotion in the early 1980s as 'glandular or hormonal reactions'; Peter N. Stearns and Carol Z. Stearns, 'Emotionology: Clarifying the History of Emotions and Emotional Standards', *American Historical Review*, 90/4 (1985), 813–36, here 834.

[307] Borrowing from the network based on the Berlin Max Planck Institute for the History of Science: <http://www.critical-neuroscience.org>; see also Choudhury and Slaby, *Critical Neuroscience*; William R. Uttal, *Mind and Brain: A Critical Appraisal of Cognitive Neuroscience* (Cambridge, MA: MIT Press, 2011), ch. 4 on emotion. See also the critical blogs: Michael Anderson, 'After Phrenology: Will we Ever Understand the Brain', *Psychology Today* <http://www.psychologytoday.com/blog/after-phrenology>; Luiz Pessoa, 'Emotion & Cognition and the Brain', <http://cognitionemotion. wordpress.com>; Michelle Greene, *NeurRealism* <http://neurealist.blogspot.de>); *The Neurocritic: Deconstructing the Most Sensationalistic Recent Findings in Human Brain Imaging, Cognitive Neuroscience, and Psychopharmacology* <http://neurocritic.blogspot.de>; 'Neuroskeptic', *Discover* <http://blogs.discovermagazine.com/neuroskeptic/>; all accessed 16 March 2014.

Study of Emotion'; Ralph Adolphs cooperates with Damasio, but also publishes together with the neuroscientist Luiz Pessoa, a sharp critic of his own discipline.[308]

The extent to which neuroscientific results can be linked to neighbouring fields remains therefore an open question, but at the very least there is no a priori reason why knowledge of the brain should fail to have an impact upon the study of mind, culture, and history. It is this approach, beyond entrenched thinking, which I find personally the most productive. Three topics that currently pre-occupy critical neuroscientists will be sketched out here: functional specification, the idea that particular regions of the brain are responsible for particular functions; plasticity, the question of the scope for change in the brain; and social neurosciences, studies that go beyond the individual person and take into account individuals in interaction with other individuals, or even in groups. None of these can be dealt with here in any detail; the object is simply to indicate the areas where neurosciences, human sciences and social sciences converge, where there is clear epistemological overlap, and what this intersection might mean for the study of history.

Functional Specification, also Known as Functional Segregation

Not so very long ago it was thought that particular regions of the brain were responsible for defined functions, and that when executing a particular function only one region was activated; ergo, those regions not involved were inactive. This topographical perspective of the brain still today determines a great deal of brain research, as well as almost the entire spectrum of the popular science presented in the media: 'God discovered in the temporal lobe'; 'the amygdala takes control of social life in the brain', and so on.[309]

The critical neurosciences have concluded from a growing number of studies that functional specification and the topographical perspective on the brain is an incomplete description of reality, especially when these ideas become fixed absolutes. There is increasing doubt that the brain is a space that 'lights up' when activated in one particular area, then settling back to repose.[310] This resting state was the first thing to be questioned. Then towards the end of the 1990s brain

---

[308] Ekman and Davidson (eds), *Nature of Emotion*; Richard J. Davidson, 'Seven Sins in the Study of Emotion: Correctives from Affective Neuroscience', *Brain and Cognition*, 52/1 (2003), 129–32; Justin S. Feinstein, Ralph Adolphs, Antonio Damasio, and Daniel Tranel, 'The Human Amygdala and the Induction and Experience of Fear', *Current Biology*, 21/1 (2011), 34–8; Pessoa and Adolphs, 'Emotion Processing and the Amygdala'.

[309] 'They Found God and Other Spiritual Phenomena in the Temporal Lobe', *Personality Cafe* <http://personalitycafe.com/science-technology/21574-they-found-god-and-other-spiritual-phenomena-temporal-lobe-o.html> accessed 16 March 2014; see Martin Haidinger, 'Die Amygdala regelt im Gehirn das Sozialleben', in *Wissen aktuell* (OE1 on ORF, 27 December 2010, 1.55 p.m.) [broadcast].

[310] Typical of this trend is the meta-analysis of Luiz Pessoa, 'Emergent Processes in Cognitive-Emotional Interactions', *Dialogues in Clinical Neuroscience*, 12/4 (2010), 433–48. Or, Dalgleish, Dunn, and Mobbs, 'Affective Neuroscience', 363: 'a historical analysis of the development of affective neuroscience reveals that many more brain regions than initially supposed are involved in the processing of emotion and mood'.

activity was discovered that was not directly related to the solution of experimental tasks.[311] Today such activity is generally considered purposeful, but oriented towards specific long-term future aims rather than short-term spurts related to the solution of specific immediate tasks.[312] This parallel brain activity related to the solution of tasks was called Default Mode Network (DMN).[313] Moreover, 'previously dispersed research on stimulus-independent thoughts, task-unrelated thoughts and "zone outs" has been gathered together under the umbrella term of "mind-wandering"'.[314] Mind-wandering is, however, also a form of activity. This was noticed when dealing with problems of calculation in the processing of data generated by brain scans, in the form of 'the spontaneous activity that was discarded as noise in analytic models'.[315] Finally, studies involving lesions showed that regions that had never been thought capable of doing so could assume the functions of damaged areas.[316] More recently, critical neuroscience has talked of 'integration', and of an interactive, dynamic, and networked perspective. The brain scientist Ernst Pöppel summed this up in an interview:

Question: Feelings are important for our thinking and learning. How do you make difficult decisions yourself? According to your intuition, or your understanding?

Pöppel: That is the wrong question, but that is not the fault of either of us. We use concepts like intelligence, consciousness, feeling, free will—that has been our tradition for 2,500 years—but these concepts conceal the fact that such functions do not exist independently of each other. There is no such thing as feeling in itself, perception in itself, no memory as such, they all derive from the anatomy of the brain; it is all unbelievably closely networked. Every feeling is also perception and memory, every rational process is embedded in emotional evaluation, every intuition is linked to behavioural intention.

Question: But surely the imaging procedures of brain research show that particular activities in the brain are linked to a specific location?

Pöppel: That is an illusion. These regions are always embedded in a larger structure. The so-called insular cortex, the island in the brain, lights up during experiments when someone eats chocolate, feels pain, has sex, has a strong desire—so what else? If you look more carefully, there are always several areas in the brain as a whole that take part when we perform a particular activity.[317]

---

[311] Gordon L. Shulman et al., 'Common Blood Flow Changes across Visual Tasks: II. Decreases in Cerebral Cortex', *Journal of Cognitive Neuroscience*, 9/5 (1997), 648–63.

[312] R. Nathan Spreng, Raymond A. Mar, and Alice S. N. Kim, 'The Common Neural Basis of Autobiographical Memory, Prospection, Navigation, Theory of Mind, and the Default Mode: A Quantitative Meta-Analysis', *Journal of Cognitive Neuroscience*, 21/3 (2009), 489–510.

[313] Marcus E. Raichle et al., 'A Default Mode of Brain Function', *Proceedings of the National Academy of Sciences*, 98/2 (2001), 676–82. See also Marcus E. Raichle and Abraham Z. Snyder, 'A Default Mode of Brain Function: A Brief History of an Evolving Idea', *NeuroImage*, 37/4 (2007), 1083–90.

[314] Callard and Margulies, 'The Subject at Rest', 235.

[315] Callard and Margulies, 'The Subject at Rest', 236.

[316] Laurent A. Renier et al., 'Preserved Functional Specialization for Spatial Processing in the Middle Occipital Gyrus of the Early Blind', *Neuron*, 68/1 (2010), 138–48.

[317] Martina Keller, 'Wie kriege ich den Kopf frei? Interview mit Ernst Pöppel', *Brigitte*, 8 (25 March 2009), 127. See also Anthony Randal McIntosh, 'From Location to Integration: How Neural Interactions Form the Basis for Human Cognition', in Endel Tulving (ed.), *Memory, Consciousness, and the Brain: The Tallinn Conference* (Philadelphia: Psychology Press, 2000), 346–62.

It can of course be objected that there are, all the same, gradations of intensity in local brain activity, and that this variability in intensity justifies the assumption of functional specification. Marco Iacoboni, for example, argues along these lines:

> In one way, of course, every cell is connected to every other cell, just as the tiniest town in this vast country—the United States—is connected to every other town by the road system. You can get from A to Z; the route may be circuitous, but you can do it. Likewise in the brain, but in theory only, because the maze of connections is exponentially—infinitely, it is fair to say—more complex than the U.S. or any other road system. In order for one region of the brain to talk with another, a pretty direct pathway is required—an interstate of some sort, if you will.[318]

And yet the procedures available today—fMRI scanning and so forth—are too imperfect even to pick up traffic on Iacoboni's interstate, let alone simultaneously take account of traffic on highways and byways. But these procedures are subject to constant refinement, and great progress is being made in linking them together: for example, the combination of fMRI, PET, and EEG/MEG. Based on current knowledge, we can form the following picture: a constantly active brain in which, during specific functions, several regions are strongly involved, and within these, one or more with a greater degree of intensity than others. There is a gradient of functionally specific activity, without any part being completely inactive.

From all of this it could well be that for the study of history the relationship between concepts like 'emotion', 'cognition', and 'consciousness' will be shaken up once more, as Pöppel rightly observes. Even if one insists on the way in which these constructs constitute reality, it makes a difference if it should really turn out that these cognitive regions can barely be separated one from another. This could, for example, shed light upon the ideologization of individuals, and their path to ideologies would then be more difficult to describe than if they were treated entirely rationally. Why did so many West European and American students turn to Marxism in the 1960s and 1970s? Citing exclusively rational reasons (reading Marxist texts) would be either unsatisfactory or even absurd, and given the fact that at that time most students came from the upper and middle classes, rational choice theory has nothing to say about this, since it presumes that the maximization of profit is a constant motivation. When interviewed, those involved talk of a murky sense of injustice and consequent anger. What we have here is a 'cogmotive' or 'cogaffective' mixture. But such concepts are still tied to the dichotomous structure of the two separate domains of 'cognition' and 'emotion' (or 'affect'). If the interactive perspective on the brain develops, and historical study seeks to draw from this an analytical concept distinct from the usual sources, there will be no avoiding the introduction of a holistic neologism.

The dissolution of the functional specification paradigm and its replacement by an integrated understanding of the brain provides a space for the history of the sciences. Much of what counts as radically new in this understanding of the brain had already been developed in cybernetics. The cybernetic model of active

---

[318] Iacoboni, *Mirroring People*, 117.

homeostasis—a stable, constant condition in a living organism, one instance of which is the maintenance of body temperature—can serve as a blueprint for the constantly active brain, and lead us away from the idea of an entirely inactive brain.[319] The interaction of different regions of the brain also has parallels with cybernetic network theory.[320] Finally, if one asks why we should today have arrived at the dissolution of the functional specification paradigm and the associated idea of a condition of brain inactivity, then there are analogies with today's world of work that seem fairly obvious. Networking through the Internet, digital communications media, multitasking, smartphones, and globalized 24/7 supply-chain management correspond to the image of an interactive brain; the fact that even while sleeping our brains and bodies are active, rather than inactive, corresponds to modern-day lives, where borders between work and leisure, work and unemployment have become indistinct, where work is a constant through rapidly shifting sources of income, from regular employment with full social contributions, minimum wages, and cash in hand to unpaid labour.

Neuroplasticity

For a long time the idea prevailed that the brain, with respect to neurogenesis (the building of nerve cells) and wiring (the connection between nerve cells), was after a certain age more or less a fixed entity. The mature brain had a fixed number of nerve cells, and no great changes in their connectivity were envisaged. Recent work has however shown that the mature brain does continue to produce nerve cells, and that new forms of connection are made.[321] In other words, even the hardware of the brain changes during the entire lifespan of the person.[322] Cultural differences, life phases (most of all puberty), disruptive experiences ('traumas'), psychotropic influences (drugs, but also ecstatic dancing at a club): these all leave traces in the architecture of the brain. It could be that there are in this regard differences between the various regions, with less plasticity in subcortical areas, the region of the brain that is oldest on an evolutionary scale. All the same, this conception of neuroplasticity opens up possibilities for a human science like history: life is constantly inscribed into the brain; the brain becomes the object of historical variability. We will have to assume historicized and acculturated brains; no longer can we treat the brain as a bastion of unchanging nature. This also presents an enormous challenge to the neurosciences, since the universal claim of many

[319] Callard and Margulies, 'Subject at Rest', 231; Norbert Wiener, *Cybernetics: Or Control and Communication in the Animal and the Machine* (2nd edn, Cambridge, MA: MIT Press, 1961), 115.

[320] Michael A. Arbib, *The Metaphorical Brain: An Introduction to Cybernetics as Artificial Intelligence and Brain Theory* (New York: Wiley, 1972); Michael A. Arbib (ed.), *The Handbook of Brain Theory and Neural Networks* (2nd edn, Cambridge, MA: MIT Press, 2003); Viktor K. Jirsa and A. R. McIntosh, preface in *Handbook of Brain Connectivity* (Berlin: Springer, 2007), v–vii.

[321] Beatrix P. Rubin, 'Changing Brains: The Emergence of the Field of Adult Neurogenesis', *BioSocieties*, 4/4 (2009), 407–24; Tobias Rees, 'Being Neurologically Human Today: Life Science and Adult Cerebral Plasticity (An Ethical Analysis)', *American Ethnologist*, 37/1 (2010), 150–66.

[322] Martin Lövdén et al., 'A Theoretical Framework for the Study of Adult Cognitive Plasticity', *Psychological Bulletin*, 136/4 (2010), 659–76.

statements regarding 'the' brain is placed in question; domains are drastically reduced, representativeness reduced to n = 1. If neuroscientists carry out a brain scan they will need to take greater account of the fact that they are not scanning 'the brain', but are scanning one individual brain, one with an individual biography, belonging to a particular group, from a particular culture, at a particular time.[323] In the investigation of group-specific, generational, historically-formed brains, historians must become partners in dialogue with neuroscientists.

Social Neurosciences

This is a relatively new area of research, and it takes up the advances made in understanding the plasticity of the brain. Its aim is to 'overcome the trap of individuality in neuroscientific research' and secure its ecological validity—the significance of experiments outside the narrow confines of the laboratory.[324] In 2010 an experimental psychologist put together a top ten of 'hot topics' in the study of emotion; here are numbers 7 and 8: 'individual differences in emotion-related processes, with an eye to genetic and epigenetic factors' and 'cultural differences and similarities in emotion-related processes'.[325] Of course, social psychology has for a long time dealt with emotions in intersubjective situations.[326] The concept of 'social neuroscience' was coined by social psychologists as early as 1992.[327] Empathy quickly became a fashionable research topic in the neurosciences. Unlike the Theory of Mind, empathy does not presuppose that it has a claim to 'the recognition of the thoughts, convictions, and intentions of other people'.[328] It is a matter of emotion, as the following definition by the historian Ute Frevert and the social neuroscientist Tania Singer makes clear:

> We feel empathy if (1) we find ourselves in an emotional condition, (2) this situation is isomorphic with the emotional condition of another person, (3) this condition is

[323] Ulman Lindenberger, Shu-Chen Li, and Yvonne Brehmer, 'La Variabilité dans le vieillissement comportemental: Conséquence et agent du changement ontogénétique', in Jacques Lautrey, Bernard Mazoyer, and Paul van Geert (eds), *Invariants et variabilités dans les sciences cognitives* (Paris: Éditions de la Maison des sciences de l'homme, 2002), 315–34.
[324] Ute Frevert, 'Was haben Gefühle in der Geschichte zu suchen?', *Geschichte und Gesellschaft*, 35/2 (2009), 183–208, here 192 n. 33.
[325] James J. Gross, 'The Future's So Bright, I Gotta Wear Shades', *Emotion Review*, 2/3 (2010), 212–16, here 215.
[326] Brian Parkinson, Agneta H. Fischer, and Antony S. R. Manstead, *Emotion in Social Relations: Cultural, Group, and Interpersonal Processes* (New York: Psychology Press, 2005), and a textbook that emphasizes social psychological approaches: Paula M. Niedenthal, Silvia Krauth-Gruber, and François Ric, *Psychology of Emotion: Interpersonal, Experiential, and Cognitive Approaches* (New York: Psychology Press, 2006).
[327] The concept 'social neuroscience' was coined by John T. Cacioppo and Gary G. Berntson, 'Social Psychological Contributions to the Decade of the Brain: Doctrine of Multilevel Analysis', *American Psychologist*, 47/8 (1992), 1019–28, here 1025. See also Ralph Adolphs, 'Conceptual Challenges and Directions for Social Neuroscience', *Neuron*, 65 (2010), 725–67, here 752.
[328] Ute Frevert and Tania Singer, 'Empathie und ihre Blockaden: Über soziale Emotionen', in Tobias Bonhoeffer and Peter Gruss (eds), *Zukunft Gehirn: Neue Erkenntnisse, neue Herausforderungen* (Munich: Beck, 2011), 121–46, here 135. See also Romana Snozzi and Tania Singer, 'Empathie aus der Sicht der sozialen Neurowissenschaften', in Fehr and Folkers, *Gefühle zeigen*, 97–113.

brought about by the emotional condition of another person, and (4) we are conscious that the other person is the trigger for 'our' condition.[329]

In the empathy experiments conducted by social neuroscientists there is an increasing tendency to take several people into the scanning room. An example:

> Singer and her colleagues invited couples into the laboratory with the aim of studying the neuronal foundations of empathy with pain. The women lay for the duration of the experiment in the scanner so that her brain activity could be measured. Both subjects were then stimulated with electrodes attached to their hands, so that for both it either tickled a bit, or was painful. Lying in the scanner, the woman was able to see through a set of mirrors her own hand and that of her partner, with the electrodes attached. She also saw a screen which displayed arrows showing which of them was to receive a stimulation, and whether this would be strong or weak. This made it possible to compare the activation of the brain brought about by real pain with that brought about through empathy.... This study of couples showed that the affective components of the pain matrix were activated not only when the women herself received a painful shock, but also when she knew that her partner would get one too.... Those who, according to questionnaires were more empathetic, also showed stronger activation in both pain-related areas.[330]

This is only one experiment on empathy. Others are directed to the blocking of empathy—with respect to ethnic minorities for racists, for instance—to the competition of different motivational systems, to the phenomenon of the surplus of empathy, and more.

There are epistemological crossovers in these three fields between the neurosciences and the human and social sciences. Currently the work that is being done seems robust, but not of course as robust as Pythagoras' theorem or Kepler's laws. These have proved themselves over centuries, and withstood countless tests. It will take time to see how these three fields stand up to the tests of time.

I would like to conclude this section on what might be thought a frivolous note, noting that some neuroscientists now consider that art is still the best way of depicting human animals in their full dimensions. No experiment can model the chaos of human reality. Anyone who wants to understand memory should read Marcel Proust, whoever wants to understand emotional complexity should read Walt Whitman—these are the recommendations of Jonah Lehrer, who as a student of the neurosciences once worked in the laboratory of Eric R. Kandel, an expert on memory and a Nobel Prizewinner.[331]

We have arrived at the end of the chapter on the universalist pole of emotion, embodied in the life sciences. I could have told the history of the study of emotion in the life sciences differently. Psychologists like Maria Gendron and Lisa Feldman

---

[329] Frevert and Singer, 'Empathie und ihre Blockaden', 136.
[330] Frevert and Singer, 'Empathie und ihre Blockaden', 137.
[331] Jonah Lehrer, *Proust Was a Neuroscientist* (Boston: Mifflin, 2007), 1–24 (I thank Slava Gerovitch for this reference); 'Chimera of Experience: A Conversation with Jonah Lehrer', Edge (21 May 2009) <http://edge.org/3rd_culture/lehrer09/lehrer09_index.html> accessed 17 March 2014.

Barrett, in an article on the history of their discipline, assume that there are three ideal-typical 'traditions'—basic emotion, *appraisal*, and psychological constructionism. Randolph Cornelius talks of four 'perspectives'—Darwinist, Jamesian, cognitive, and social constructivist—and organizes all research since the nineteenth century retrospectively into these ideal types, even presenting deviations from these pure forms graphically.[332] Ruth Leys has herself chosen a genealogical approach, tracing the beginnings of paradigms that spill over from psychology into other sciences, and in which she detects a strong element of anti-intentionalism. Thomas Dixon and Claudia Wassmann have written the intellectual history of the psychological study of emotion, and have examined the connection of ideas— which idea was taken up by whom, and how?—and Otniel E. Dror has studied the laboratory practice of experimental psychology's engagement with emotion and its influence on conceptions of emotion.

I could also have foregrounded the genealogy of conceptions—hedonic valence and its associated guiding distinctions—basic and complex, pleasant and unpleasant, object-related and non-object-related, conscious and unconscious. I could have introduced other experiments which, if they related to emotion indirectly, were nonetheless significant: on Benjamin Libet and unconscious behaviour in decision-making, or the missing half-second; on the nucleus accumbens, the reward system, and neurotransmitters; on memory and the emotional foundation for remembering. I could have discussed other sciences which have borrowed from the neurosciences, for instance, neuroeconomics. And I could have cleared up other myths, such as the following claim from Silvan S. Tomkins: 'That Behaviorism slighted the role of affects is obvious.'[333] This claim did the rounds and for a long time before the 1960s distorted understanding of the study of emotions. I could have here dealt with the different threads of behaviourism, the Russian reflexology of Ivan Pavlov and Vladimir Bekhterev, together with their studies on emotional stimuli. But I would still end up with the question that seems to me the most urgent: should the discipline of history borrow from the life sciences? And if yes, then how? In Chapter 4 we will turn to the most interesting attempt to answer these questions, and in this way leave the opposition of social constructivism and universalism behind.

---

[332] Gendron and Barrett, 'Reconstructing the Past'; Cornelius, *Science of Emotion*. The psychologist Ilse Kryspin-Exner distinguishes between four ideal types: general psychological theories of emotion, neuropsychological approaches, emotions in the face, and cognitive theories of emotion; Ilse Kryspin-Exner, 'Ich fühle, also bin ich: Emotionen und "Rationalität" aus einer psychologischen Perspektive', in Heinrich Schmidinger and Clemens Sedmak (eds), *Der Mensch—ein 'animal rationale'?: Vernunft— Kognition—Intelligenz* (Darmstadt: Wissenschaftliche Buchgesellschaft, 2004), 216–38.

[333] Silvan S. Tomkins, *Affect, Imagery, Consciousness*, i. *The Positive Affects* (New York: Springer, 1962), 5.

Four

Perspectives in the History of Emotions

1 *THE NAVIGATION OF FEELING*: WILLIAM M. REDDY'S ATTEMPT TO MOVE BEYOND SOCIAL CONSTRUCTIVISM AND UNIVERSALISM

William M. Reddy, an American historian and anthropologist, was the first to make productive use of the life sciences in his own study of emotions, in particular cognitive psychology. He examined the concept of honour in early nineteenth-century France, while also keeping track of the new anthropological literature on emotion.[1] In the process he became increasingly dubious of the social constructivist direction this work was taking. In 1997 he published a programmatic essay, 'Against Constructionism: The Historical Ethnography of Emotions', and it is worth here revisiting the arguments he put forward there.[2]

Reddy opens with the dilemma posed by the way in which the anthropological-relativist perspective obstructs the development of a normative stance, even if the author wishes to take such a stance. He gives an example from the anthropology of emotion: Benedicte Grima has shown how *gham*, a kind of sadness, is the most intensive—and more or less the only—emotion that Pashtun women in Pakistan are supposed to express in public. The open display of *gham* is something that is particularly expected of them when they get married. If a person close to them, for instance, a son, is injured, Pashtun women gather together and weep and wail—show each other *gham*—away from the injured party, ignoring the injured person entirely. These are therefore two social situations in which female expression of emotion is different from that prevailing in Western culture, where a bride is supposed to feel happy, or where the injury of a close friend or relative is supposed to prompt concern and an intensive fixation on this person. As in Chapter Three, we once again see that studies like that of Grima overturn the idea that emotions are universal. Emotion is socially constructed. As Grima writes herself, 'emotion is culture'.[3]

---

[1] William M. Reddy, *The Invisible Code: Honor and Sentiment in Postrevolutionary France, 1814–1848* (Berkeley and Los Angeles: University of California Press, 1997).

[2] William M. Reddy, 'Against Constructionism: The Historical Ethnography of Emotions', *Current Anthropology*, 38/3 (1997), 327–51.

[3] Benedicte Grima, *The Performance of Emotion among Paxtun Women: 'The Misfortunes Which Have Befallen Me'* (Austin: University of Texas Press, 1992), 6.

Reddy then points to passages in Grima's book where a universalist and essentialist perspective creeps in. For instance, Grima describes how marriages are arranged and the bride moves into the home of the husband, involving an immense loss of status, since she has to do a very great deal of housework there, and must accept the lowest position in the hierarchy of the house. Mothers and sisters-in-law—and, in polygamous families, older wives—push the new arrival around for years, both verbally and in any other way they can find. Grima argues that *gham* is no social construct, but simply an epiphenomenon of what is specific to Pashtun family structure. She is critical of this form of 'oppression' in particular, and the 'gerontocracy' of 'Muslim culture' in general.[4]

But Reddy maintains that whoever has embarked on the path of social constructivist cultural relativism must abjure any resorting to value judgements. You have to decide between relativism and universalism. You cannot have both at once. This dilemma runs right through not only the social constructivist anthropology of emotion, but post-structuralism in general. So how to recover a vantage point from which value judgements can be made? Reddy proposes a translation of the two poles of social constructivism and universalism into John Austin's theory of speech acts: universalism is comparable with the *constative*, a descriptive statement about the world, while social constructivism is comparable with the *performative*, a statement that changes the world. 'The fir branch is green' is consequently a *constative* statement, while saying 'I will' in a registry office is *performative*. Statements about emotions would therefore possess both *constative* and *performative* properties, describing the world and at the same time changing it. 'I am sad' is partly a description of a condition, partly the intensification of one among several emotions (and so a diminution or overwriting of other emotions). Many of us are familiar with the idea from everyday life that a smile prompts positive emotions. To do justice to the mixed character of statements about emotions, Reddy suggests the concept *emotive*.

He would extend this concept by introducing a cognitive psychological dimension, experimentally reinforcing the world-altering force of statements about emotions—more on this soon. In his 1997 essay Reddy at first only used the term *emotive* to reconcile social constructivism and universalism, so that he might regain a normative position. Reddy's position was this: by describing a condition of the world using emotion, we also seek to influence this condition; thus, we are adopting an evaluative stance. It was probably too much to link to this the hope

[4] Grima, *The Performance of Emotion among Paxtun Women*, 163. A similar contradiction runs through Abu-Lughod's *Veiled Sentiments*. One reviewer has written that the singing of *ghinnāwas* by the Bedouin wives was a 'privileged vehicle of emotional expression of things denied in ordinary discourse, as therefore a potent strategic device for the cunning of the weak (a tool to upset normal relations of power)', suspecting that Abu-Lughod's sympathy lay with the wives and their subversive singing. From a strictly social constructivist and culturally relative perspective, Abu-Lughod should have been neutral with respect to the patriarchal order of the Awlad 'Ali Bedouin; Michael M. J. Fischer, 'Aestheticized Emotions & Critical Hermeneutics', review of Lila Abu-Lughod, *Veiled Sentiments: Honor and Poetry in a Bedouin Society* (Berkeley and Los Angeles: University of California Press, 1986), in *Culture, Medicine and Psychiatry*, 12/1 (1988), 31–42, here 31.

that by using the category 'emotion' it would be possible to liberate the sign from its post-structuralist, free-floating state and provide it with a 'real world-anchor'— the hope that *emotion* 'generates *parole* against the backdrop of *langue*', using *emotive* to trump Foucault's 'discourse', Derrida's critique of *présence*, and Habermas's theory of communicative reason, all of which supposedly do not permit political resistance.[5] This argument prompts many questions. First of all: to what extent can the model of statements about emotion be transferred to statements that have nothing to do with emotions? Put in the terms of social science: how large is the domain of the *emotive*, where are its boundaries? Or put another way: can such a central problem like the relation between language and reality be resolved through a conceptual innovation taken from the sphere of the study of emotion?

The journal in which Reddy's essay was published invited comments from five anthropologists and a historian. The general criticism was that Reddy had not really given a true picture of the current state of anthropological research, and that it was not as social constructivist as he suggested. Particular criticism was directed at Reddy's understanding of emotion and memory. Taking, for example, historical sources such as documents recording a trial held thirty years after the events in question, the emotions of the actors involved as described in the documents were not identical with the emotions they had thirty years previously: *emotive* was treated too synchronically, there was a missing analytical step, namely that of memory.[6] In addition, two anthropologists accused Reddy of ignoring the difference between fieldwork and historical research: in the former the participant observer influences the emotions of the observed subject, whereas in the latter the presence of the historian has no impact upon the *emotives* of historical actors.[7] Catherine Lutz wrote that one should not emulate Reddy, for whom 'in the name of progressive anticonstructionism, psychobiological research is simply slapped on to ethnographic work', but instead examine the socially constructed nature of the laboratory work done in cognitive psychology, the pharmacological companies financing it, and their influence upon contemporary debate, taking columns in women's magazines on Premenstrual Tension (PMT) and depression as an example.[8] And yet these reactions all bore the marks of a certain helplessness in formulating fundamental criticism. Might this have been something to do with Reddy's innovativeness—the vague sense that here someone was starting up a paradigm change, and that soon any discussion of emotion would either be pre-Reddy, or qua Reddy? Other commentators were prepared to acknowledge Reddy's achievement. Lynn Hunt,

---

[5] Reddy, 'Against Constructionism', 331; on Habermas see 332.

[6] See the reaction of Linda C. Garro, 'Comment on William M. Reddy, Against Constructionism: The Historical Ethnography of Emotions', *Current Anthropology*, 38/3 (1997), 341–2.

[7] See reactions by Signe Howell, 'Comment on William M. Reddy, Against Constructionism: The Historical Ethnography of Emotions', *Current Anthropology*, 38/3 (1997), 342–3; and Chia Longman, 'Comment on William M. Reddy, Against Constructionism: The Historical Ethnography of Emotions', *Current Anthropology*, 38/3 (1997), 344–5.

[8] Catherine Lutz, 'Comment on William M. Reddy, Against Constructionism: The Historical Ethnography of Emotions', *Current Anthropology*, 38/3 (1997), 345–6, here 345.

an expert on French history, declared that 'Once again, William Reddy is at least two steps ahead of the pack.'[9]

During the following years Reddy put one brick on top of another as he constructed his theoretical approach. In 2001 his book *The Navigation of Feeling: A Framework for the History of Emotions* was published.[10] This was a major shift forward, and will be outlined in detail here. Reddy's ambitious aim was to bridge the gap between the social constructivism of work in the anthropology of emotions and the universalism of cognitive psychology. This is even apparent in the dialectical architecture of his book: in part one, the first chapter on cognitive psychology (thesis) is followed by one on anthropology (antithesis)—a contrast that is in the following two chapters superseded by his own theory of emotion (synthesis). In part two, Reddy devotes four chapters to an application of his new theory to French history, following the deductive social science principle that first of all a theory (hypothesis) is advanced, which is then tested upon empirical material.[11] This structure corresponds to the way in which Reddy, crossing boundaries, formulates his claim: in clear language, free of any of the irony or playfulness of post-structuralist writing, he insists on the necessity of creating a position from which values such as freedom and justice can be defended. These are values which he shares with post-structuralist feminists, but which in the wake of post-structuralist deconstruction have become denaturalized and so untenable, just like the category of gender. If everything is socially constructed then so too are my values, and they are of only local validity; so, for example, I cannot really have anything against female genital mutilation (clitoridectomy) in parts of Africa. This dilemma is a familiar one for post-structuralist feminists, gone over many times, as Reddy himself emphasizes.

In the first chapter of his book on the universalism of cognitive psychology, Reddy first of all emphasizes that it is not possible to unambiguously define emotions; they cannot be clearly separated one from another, nor reduced to a handful of basic emotions together with other emotions. From the perspective of cognitive psychology, it was likewise impossible to separate emotion from cognition, or emotions from reason. In truth, emotion is *cogmotion*, in the words of Douglas Barnett and Hilary Horn Ratner.[12] They suggest that emotions should really be understood as 'overlearned cognitive habits', which were not of course always learned, changed, or forgotten through conscious decisions, but were always constrained in two respects:

[9] Lynn Hunt, 'Comment on William M. Reddy, Against Constructionism: The Historical Ethnography of Emotions', *Current Anthropology*, 38/3 (1997), 343–4, here 343.

[10] William M. Reddy, *The Navigation of Feeling: A Framework for the History of Emotions* (Cambridge: Cambridge University Press, 2001).

[11] Reddy has himself rejected my characterization of his approach as 'deductive-social scientific'; Jan Plamper, 'The History of Emotions: An Interview with William Reddy, Barbara H. Rosenwein, and Peter Stearns', *History and Theory*, 49/2 (2010), 237–65, here 246–7.

[12] Reddy, *Navigation of Feeling*, 15. *Cogmotion* comes from Douglas Barnett and Hilary Horn Ratner, 'The Organization and Integration of Cognition and Emotion in Development', *Journal of Experimental Child Psychology*, 67/3 (1997), 303–16.

(1) Most psychologists agree that emotions have a special relationship to goals. They have a 'valence' or 'hedonic tone' that renders them either inherently pleasant or inherently unpleasant; and they have an 'intensity' that determines how easy or difficult it is for a person to override them. (2) New work on the nature of mental control shows that there are special constraints on the kind of learning or unlearning that involves emotion.[13]

The first constraint relates to the strength of an emotion and the consequent prospect of conscious influence. The second constraint is more complex. It is related to the knowledge about mental control (for example, that of the psychologist Daniel Wegner) prevalent at the time, knowledge that evidences the paradoxical nature of this control. For instance, if I sit in a plane and want to suppress my fear of flying, I have to maintain it in an active part of my brain so that I might constantly keep it under control. I cannot make it disappear completely since I have to be able to keep an eye on it, to prevent it entering my 'consciousness'. This is 'ironic monitoring'.[14]

For Reddy, the overview of recent cognitive psychological research on emotions serves chiefly to outline a position which is very similar to that of post-structuralist anthropological work on emotions, in this way enabling seemingly opposed academic disciplines to be brought closer together:

> In sum, psychologists have moved away from linear models of cognition toward models involving multiple pathways, multiple levels of activation and types of activation, involving complex combinations of suppression and enhancement. Departure from linear models has forced psychologists to drop, as well, neat dividing lines between conscious and unconscious, supraliminal and subliminal, controlled and involuntary processes. These shifts have brought in their train a sweeping reconceptualization of the nature of emotion—a 'revolution in the study of emotions'... Traditionally, emotion was associated both with nonlinear (free-associational, poetic, or symbolic) thinking and with physiological arousal (blushing, adrenaline flow, changes in heart rate, and so on). These two types of phenomena were linked in that they both departed from a vision of conscious, rational, voluntary action that was believed to be the hallmark of human intelligence. Symbolic thinking is not strictly rational; physiological arousal is not strictly under voluntary control. But as notions of 'voluntary' and 'conscious' have broken down, and as thinking has increasingly been regarded as reflecting multiple levels of activation, attention, and coherence, it has become difficult to sustain the distinction between thought and affect.[15]

The jury is still out on whether the consensus that Reddy describes does exist among psychologists, together with the question of how influential cognitive psychology and its 'appraisal'-based theses are at a time of neuroscientific boom. For him, this description of the existing state of affairs is nonetheless the

---

[13] Reddy, *Navigation of Feeling*, 21.

[14] Daniel M. Wegner and Laura Smart, 'Deep Cognitive Activation: A New Approach to the Unconscious', *Journal of Consulting and Clinical Psychology*, 65/6 (1997), 984–95, here 987. Also see Daniel M. Wegner, 'Ironic Processes of Mental Control', *Psychological Review*, 101/1 (1994), 34–52.

[15] Reddy, *Navigation of Feeling*, 31.

precondition for any reconciliation between psychology and anthropology, or between universalism and social constructivism.

While cognitive psychology has not reflected upon this last polarity to any great extent, Reddy thinks that the anthropology of emotions has been confronted with it since the very beginning:

> From the very beginning to this day, the anthropology of emotions has been caught on the horns of this dilemma: how much influence to attribute to culture, how much to attribute to underlying universal psychic factors. Does death bring grief everywhere, or just in those cultures where the individual is highly valued? Is romantic love a universal human experience, celebrated in some cultures, suppressed in others—or is it just the creation of Western individualism? Is depression a neurological illness that can strike down anyone, anywhere, or is it a cultural artifact of modern, clinical treatment and modern social isolation?[16]

There is a correspondence here with work in the life sciences, but there discussion of, for example, intelligence or schizophrenia is merely treated as a variation of the classical dichotomy of nature versus culture. Reddy thinks that there are bigger stakes in anthropology. The question of whether emotions are social constructs or universal, and what the relationship might be between these two poles, goes to the epistemological heart of the discipline. If one adopts the expansive conception of culture of Clifford Geertz, which allows for no extra-cultural space, then there is no longer any possibility of an independent position from which differences between culturally formed expressions of emotion can be registered. It also becomes impossible to conceive how emotions might change over time; or rather, such change is so radically contingent that it admits of no analysis.[17] In this view, the floods of tears accompanying a medieval act of subordination (*deditio*), such as the Walk to Canossa, are just as radically culturally-contingent as the tears of a young hopeful auditioning for a casting show in the twenty-first century; one would only be able to talk of a change if these tears had the same emotional core.[18]

This choice between the universal and the socially constructed goes to the ethical heart of anthropology, according to Reddy. If everything is culturally determined, then there is no position from which emotional variants can be ethically differentiated. Reddy cites two examples from classical studies in the anthropology of emotions. Michelle Z. Rosaldo, a pioneer of American cultural anthropology and the study of emotion, whom we first encountered in Chapter Two and who spent years studying the Ilongot in the mountains of the Philippines, described in 1980 how the Philippine state forbade the usual male practice of headhunting, and how the Ilongot as a whole began converting to Christianity. The male Ilongot experienced a great deal of grief as a result. As a cultural relativist, Rosaldo is able to take

---

[16] Reddy, *Navigation of Feeling*, 37–8.   [17] Reddy, *Navigation of Feeling*, 41.
[18] On the tears shed during medieval rituals of subordination and submission see Gerd Althoff, 'Empörung, Tränen, Zerknirschung: "Emotionen" in der öffentlichen Kommunikation des Mittelalters', *Frühmittelalterliche Studien*, 30 (1996), 60–79; Gerd Althoff, 'Gefühle in der öffentlichen Kommunikation des Mittelalters', in Claudia Benthien, Anne Fleig, and Ingrid Kasten (eds), *Emotionalität: Zur Geschichte der Gefühle* (Cologne: Böhlau, 2000), 82–99.

no position on this: she cannot say either that she morally condemns headhunting, and so welcomes the government's new law, or that she rejects such intervention into an ethnic group whose way of life is worth preserving. Catherine A. Lutz, author of the best-known anthropological study of emotion from the standpoint of social constructivism, develops a critique of Western ideas of emotion on the basis of her study of the Ifaluk, a group of people living on a Polynesian atoll. She noted that the Ifaluk gave political authority figures the right to *song*, a kind of justified anger. But, she went on, *song* was not a male preserve, it was gender-neutral, and belonged to a politics generally conducted in a far more egalitarian manner than was usual in the West. However, the Western evaluation of publicly expressed rage—for men rage is positive, for women negative ('hysteria')—is no less culturally determined and thereby justified than it is for the Ifaluk. And so Reddy suggests that Lutz's post-structuralism ultimately robs her of the possibility of criticizing her own culture on the basis of a comparison with the Ifaluk.

> Even if the Western view was 'wrong' because it 'constructed' the domain of emotion as a 'natural' one, and women as especially emotional, this could not change the fact that, for Westerners, it thereby became a natural domain. If it made no sense for Rosaldo to criticize her Ilongot informants for feeling grief over the end of headhunting, then it made no sense for Lutz or Abu-Lughod to criticize Western social science for being male-centered and for seeing emotions as natural and peculiarly female.[19]

How then can a political and ethical vector be built into the conception of emotion? The building bricks that Reddy uses are the terms emotion, *emotive*, emotional regime, emotional navigation, emotional refuge, emotional suffering, and emotional liberty. But what do these concepts mean? Emotion is activated cognitive material which is always directed towards a particular end, and which also has to be 'translated' at such high speed that it remains below the threshold of 'attention'. (To remind ourselves once again of the older theories and principles of which Reddy is seeking to rid himself, we can try to express this last sentence in familiar psychoanalytical terminology: emotions are cognitive activities that have an object, and often remain unconscious.) *Emotives* first appeared in Reddy's 1997 essay, but we need to bear in mind here that *emotives* are speech acts which both describe and change. If I say 'I am happy', that can simply be a description of a state of affairs, but can also overwrite other emotions (anger, grief) that I feel at the same time, also of course at the non-linguistic level.[20] An 'emotional regime' is the ensemble of prescribed *emotives* together with their related rituals and other symbolic practices. An open declaration of patriotism—swearing on the flag in the army—would be an *emotive* of this kind, and part of a modern national emotional regime. Every

---

[19] Reddy, *Navigation of Feeling*, 42.
[20] See also Ahmed: 'The feeling does not simply exist before the utterance, but becomes "real" as an effect, shaping different kinds of actions and orientations. To say, "the nation mourns" is to generate the nation, *as if it were a mourning subject*. The "nation" becomes a shared "object of feeling" through the orientation that is taken towards it. As such, emotions are performative . . . and they involve speech acts . . . , which depend on past histories, at the same time as they generate effects'; Sara Ahmed, *The Cultural Politics of Emotions* (Edinburgh: Edinburgh University Press, 2004), 13, emphasis in original.

political regime is supported by an emotional regime. 'Emotional navigation' has to do with manoeuvring between different and conflicting emotional objectives. Here there are often emotional conflicts: for example, a non-Jewish German sympathizer with National Socialism might be torn in 1938 between love for her Jewish husband and her enthusiasm for a 'racially pure' people's state. The greater the conflict between different orientations, and the fewer 'emotional refuges' there are, the greater the 'emotional suffering'. Finally, 'emotional liberty' means the minimization of 'emotional suffering'. According to Reddy, the conception of emotional liberty 'will point toward a form of political engagement that is not reductionist, condescending, or ethnocentric'.[21] The greatest possible degree of emotional liberty is the ideal. One can therefore measure against this ideal the emotional regimes in all cultures in all historical periods, and evaluate them morally—without relapsing into aggressive universal norms, and hence ethnocentrism. In practice, emotional regimes stretch across the following spectrum:

> At one extreme are strict regimes which require individuals to express normative emotions and to avoid deviant emotions. In these regimes, a limited number of emotives are modeled through ceremony or official art forms. Individuals are required to utter these emotives in appropriate circumstances, in the expectation that normative emotions will be enhanced and habituated. Those who refuse to make the normative utterances (whether of respect for a father, love for a god or a king, or loyalty to an army) are faced with the prospect of severe penalties.... At the other end of the spectrum are regimes that use strict emotional discipline only in certain institutions (armies, schools, priesthoods) or only at certain times of the year or certain stages of the life cycle.[22]

Reddy goes on:

> Thus, very roughly, one might generalize that strict regimes offer strong emotional management tools at the expense of allowing greater scope for self-exploration and navigation. Loose regimes allow for navigation and allow diverse sets of management tools to be fashioned locally, individually, or through robust subgroup formation. Why should we favor one type of regime over another? Against the strict regimes, two points may be made: (1) They achieve their stability by inducing goal conflict and inflicting intense emotional suffering on those who do not respond well to the normative emotives. (2) When such regimes pronounce anathemas on all deviation, they set themselves against an important human possibility—or vulnerability, the vulnerability to shifting purposes or goals, to conversion experiences, crisis, doubt.[23]

Now one might object that this ideal of the greatest possible emotional liberty is nothing but a biologically modified form of neo-humanism, and ask: who then decides what 'greatest possible' and 'liberty' mean? The standpoint from which this can be judged is just as much socially constructed and relative as anything else. But this would be to do Reddy's theory an injustice. For if one takes *emotive* seriously, the emotional statements historical actors make cannot be separated from their

---

[21] Reddy, *Navigation of Feeling*, 129, 113.   [22] Reddy, *Navigation of Feeling*, 125.
[23] Reddy, *Navigation of Feeling*, 126.

emotions. Rather there is instead a feedback loop connecting their expressed and felt emotion. An example: Pavlik Morozov, the peasant son who in Stalin's Soviet Union at the beginning of the 1930s denounced his parents to the secret police, could have suffered from greater emotional conflict than can be registered using the usual methods of historical analysis. His emotional regime could have pitched him into an emotional conflict between his love for his parents and his love for the state which 'little father' Stalin embodied. For a long time historians could only config-ure the emotional world of the 10-year-old Pavlik in terms of either lip-service to Stalin and true love for his parents, or exclusive devotion to Stalin; the simultaneity of two emotional objectives, and the potential for conflict between them, had previously been almost impossible to capture adequately.

After Reddy introduces his theory in part one of *The Navigation of Feeling*, he turns in the empirical part of his book to historical 'data', to France in the age of sensibility. He raises the question of whether French people felt differently before the onset of sensibility, and before the introduction of emotional words such as *émotion* and *sentiment*, terms which had displaced an emotionally charged *civilité*. Reddy thinks so, and he considers that *emotives* are the key to this: 'The concept of emotives suggests that when words change their meaning, their emotive effects change as well'; the conception of *emotives* 'allows us to say this without requiring us to say exactly what any given person did feel'.[24] What impact did the new emotional words of sentimentalism have? Reddy's answer is an ambitious one, promising nothing less than a new explanation for the Terror during the French Revolution.

As Reddy argues, in absolutist France under Louis XIV there was an aristocratic code of honour which regulated external representation of emotion in an extremely hierarchical manner, and whose prime aim was to avoid giving offence.[25] As a reaction, during the early eighteenth century emotional refuges developed: salons and Freemasons' lodges, correspondence and novels imbued with feeling, marriages based upon romantic love—all of which were marked by warmth, intimacy, and honesty. The emotions expressed in letters were not only conventions but also expressive, real emotions. The feedback effect of *emotives* ultimately doomed sentimentalism. There was a radicalizing dynamic inherent in sentimentalism's public display of emotion—love in letters became increasingly intimate, hatred ever deeper. In addition to this, these emotions were understood as natural and authen-tic, and all men and women were capable of feeling them intensively.

In time, the scope of sentimentalism extended ever further into social life. Political virtuosity was also supposed to be anchored in emotions. Reddy empha-sizes how strongly classical writers of the Enlightenment (Montesquieu, Voltaire, Condorcet) relied upon emotions, that Rousseau's *La Nouvelle Héloïse* was more the rule than the exception; in this way Reddy readjusts the perspective upon the 'Age of Reason', and calls the years between 1700 and 1794 an 'era of sensibility'.

---

[24] Reddy, *Navigation of Feeling*, 143–4.   [25] Reddy, *Navigation of Feeling*, 145, 148.

The French Revolution was for Reddy an attempt to render the entire society an emotional refuge organized according to sentimentalist logic.[26] Robespierre and his associates were sentimentalists who believed that tears and other bodily signs were authentic expressions of emotion. If they had known about *emotives* they would have understood that their permanent expression of emotion would lead to a kind of overheating, that the intensive experiencing of emotion was unsustainable for longer periods. In any case, emotions are so multifaceted that more and more emotions are always co-present. This co-presence of emotions with an exaggerated emphasis upon an emotion (or several emotions) led to 'goal conflicts'. During the Terror the spiral of this emotional regime wound itself up to the greatest intensities. First of all, the expectation that one would continuously feel extreme and genuine emotions was followed by the realization that this was impossible, and this in turn led to doubt regarding the authenticity of felt emotions. Second, the co-presence of other emotions (for example, fear of the guillotine, which one really should as a Jacobin only welcome with pleasure, as a positively connoted sword of virtue) prompted doubt about one's own emotions and their authenticity. And finally, this led to emotional suffering that was so enormous that it eventually could only spell the end of the sentimentalist emotional regime.[27] Reddy goes on:

> Because no one knows precisely what her emotions are, and because attempting to express them changes them, sometimes predictably, sometimes unpredictably, a requirement to have certain 'natural' feelings or else face the death penalty is likely to inspire furtive doubts in most people. Am I being sincere? It is always hard to say.[28]

And:

> Far from providing an emotional refuge, the Revolution had turned into an emotional battleground, where everyone's sincerity was suspect, and where working to deflect suspicion, however essential it was to survival, was itself a proof of insincerity.[29]

The attempt to replace absolutism with a Republic of Virtue broke on false *emotives*:

> If the theory of emotives is right, then sentimentalism's view of human nature was wrong in interesting ways. (And in saying it was 'wrong' I am purposefully breaking with a relativist stance vis-à-vis the subject matter of my research.)[30]

---

[26] Reddy, *Navigation of Feeling*, 169.

[27] See Reddy, *Navigation of Feeling*, 326. It was precisely the language of late sentimentalism spoken during the Revolution (see the example of Marat in Reddy, *Navigation of Feeling*, 189; or another example in Reddy, *Navigation of Feeling*, 193) that 'was also well suited for raising doubts about the sincerity of these emotions—just because they were supposed to be, but never could be, "natural"'; Reddy, *Navigation of Feeling*, 185.

[28] Reddy, *Navigation of Feeling*, 197.

[29] Reddy, *Navigation of Feeling*, 198. Here also 'there is plentiful evidence that the leading Jacobins themselves were in the grip of gnawing anxiety about their own status, that they could not admit to such anxiety or address it directly, and that the safest response was often seen as the deflection of suspicion onto others'.

[30] Reddy, *Navigation of Feeling*, 146.

'Correct' *emotives* permitted the navigation of feeling, the successful manoeuvring between different orientations. The 'false' *emotives* of sentimentalism, however, led to a self-radicalizing expression of all emotions, immobilizing the navigation of feeling, thus destroying the earlier equilibrium between contradictory objectives of emotion.

The remainder of the book traces the dying away of the sentimental emotional regime in the conflagration of 1794. Reddy thinks that until the mid-nineteenth century France had little but scepticism and pessimism regarding the public expression of emotion. Sentimentalist *emotives* could have had a chance in a particular sphere: in the sphere of the private, domestic, or the feminine; in art; in early socialism.[31] George Sand was a kind of sentimentalist aftershock; her lack of success gives Reddy proof that the sentimental emotional regime was replaced by a post-sentimentalist regime.[32] The strict separation between liberal reason and romantic emotion can be traced back before the Revolution; it is this, and not so much Descartes, that is responsible for the dualism of *emotio* and *ratio* that still holds today. The connection of reason and emotion in the sphere of politics during the eighteenth century was successfully erased from any collective memory.[33] The incision made by emotional overkill during the Terror was too great.

Reddy's book is so far the most important theoretical work dealing with the history of emotion. He is one of the very few historians capable of judging the quality of the basic research presented in a paper from the life sciences. At the same time he has an excellent knowledge of anthropological work. The combination of these two qualities with decades of study of French eighteenth- and nineteenth-century sources is unique. Nonetheless, there is scope for criticism. First of all, there is a suspicion that Reddy's keystone, the *emotive*, certainly his most important innovation, is logocentric. Reddy derives *emotives* from John Austin's theory of speech acts. Nevertheless, it is not clear whether the feedback effect with non-linguistic practices works in a similar way with speech acts. Does the unspoken thought 'I am happy' prompt the same emotionally-influenced consequences as the utterance of the sentence 'I am happy'? Does a deliberate smile have the same effect as saying 'I am happy'? And if we, like Barbara H. Rosenwein, transfer these ideas to history: 'Reddy's "emotives" privilege words over other forms of emotional behavior, but in some cultures (for example, that of medieval Iceland) reddening, trembling, and swelling play a more important role than utterances.'[34] Even in the speech act the social situation of speaking remains obscure: does the same feedback mechanism come into play if I say 'I am happy' when I am with my psychotherapist whom I have paid to help me find happiness, or when I am with my mother and she is trying to prove to me that I am locked in an unhappy relationship, and so I say truculently: 'I am happy'?

[31] Reddy, *Navigation of Feeling*, 237–48.   [32] Reddy, *Navigation of Feeling*, 248–56.
[33] Reddy, *Navigation of Feeling*, 143.
[34] Barbara H. Rosenwein, review of William M. Reddy, *The Navigation of Feeling: A Framework for the History of Emotions* (Cambridge: Cambridge University Press, 2001), in *American Historical Review*, 107/4 (2002), 1181–2, here 1182. See also Plamper, 'History of Emotions', 241.

Also problematic is the close connection that Reddy makes between an emotional regime and a political regime. He seems to think that the typical political regime is the modern nation state. But this is a relatively new invention. During most eras of human existence there was no dominant state organization that ruled over large sections of society. Instead, a historical actor belonged to several communities, and even in the era of the centralized state, there were, to cite Rosenwein again,

> varieties and localisms. Is it not likely, for example, that eighteenth-century salons, marital beds, and law courts—let alone the homes of the laboring poor (the latter a point raised by Reddy himself)—constituted their own emotional communities, whose relations to the emotives prescribed by 'sentimentalism' (or courtly civility, for that matter) varied?[35]

Quite probably, if one wants to be consistent, 'emotional regime' must be used in the plural.

One can also be doubtful of the manner in which Reddy seeks to resolve the post-structuralist dilemma: the impossibility of regaining an ethical, evaluative position once one has adopted a relativist standpoint. This is true above all of its scope, for the post-structuralist dilemma is not limited to emotion, but affects many more questions, like those of truth and objectivity. Of course, one can adopt the description Reddy himself gives of his book, and argue that emotions are an essential part of the self, like 'thought, memory, intention, or language'.[36] And since questions of ontology, of the self, of subjectivity, are all central to the post-structuralist dilemma, then Reddy's way out must also apply here. Yet the question of reality and truth does seem to be fundamentally different from that of minimizing emotional suffering by maximizing the navigation of emotion, so that conflicts over the objects of emotion might be reduced. Do emotions dramatize the post-structuralist dilemma in a particular way? Is it only about emotion, or about emotion as one of several domains that suffer from the post-structuralist dilemma; or can we really find a way out of the post-structuralist dilemma altogether?

It is also perplexing that the closest thing to Reddy's idea of emotional liberty is liberal democracy within a market economy and solid protection of minority rights, and that the transhistorical and transcultural position that Reddy has created so that it might once more be possible to establish persuasive political valuations turns out to match precisely the utopia that provides orientation to many progressive forces in Western democracies—namely, Reddy's own contemporary political reality. I should stress here that Reddy is not bewailing the loss of all values from a conservative position, but is rather seeking to liberate post-structuralism from its radical consequences. Having begun by destroying for political reasons a dominant orientation to the West and to male culture, it ended by becoming radically disoriented, lacking any ethical core. Reddy responded to one reviewer by arguing that his utopia would look more like that of Judith Butler than that of Martha

---

[35] Rosenwein, Review of William M. Reddy, 1182. See also Plamper, 'History of Emotions', 242.
[36] Reddy, *Navigation of Feeling*, 315.

Nussbaum.[37] But to what extent is cognitive psychology linked to a particular time and place, its research 'proving' the existence of conflicts between the objects of emotion? What would a history of the social construction of cognitive psychological knowledge look like? Might Reddy's entire thinking be circular?

This suspicion cannot be easily disposed of, even if he dismisses it as misleading:

> [Question to Reddy:] One might wonder why you chose to first lay out a specific cognitive psychological theory of emotions and then to say that a certain type of polity best fits this theory because it allows for a maximum of emotional refuge, navigation, and liberty, creating a minimum of suffering. An alternative would have been to first spell out your political-ethical values and then to say that a certain brand of cognitive psychology best fits these political-ethical values. What do you think?
>
> W[illiam] R[eddy]: My intention has been to find, rather than to lay out *a priori*, my political-ethical values through a process of critical reading of neuroscience research, motivated by a sense of frustration with the landscape left us by poststructuralism. I have tried to share this process with interested readers.[38]

At a public event Reddy said, even if firmly tongue-in-cheek, that he only chooses the life science that confirms his political convictions.[39] Why then bother with deviation through the life sciences? Does it serve only to naturalize contingent political positions? If this is true, then it cannot represent any kind of progress with respect to post-structural relativism. The same question can be asked of Ruth Leys, although she has never, like Reddy, claimed that she sought to create a new theory of emotion for historical studies, but instead through her critique of Damasio and Ekman limited herself to distinguishing 'good' from 'bad' natural scientific research.[40] As an example of 'good' natural science she cites among others Lisa Feldman Barrett and James Russell, both critics of Ekman. Nonetheless, it is doubtful whether the conception of 'core affect' would stand up to serious criticism from Leys, and show itself to be 'good' natural science: 'core affects' are ultimately basic emotions à la Tomkins and Ekman, and rather like Massumi's 'pure

---

[37] William M. Reddy, Response to Jeremy D. Popkin's review of William M. Reddy, *The Navigation of Feeling: A Framework for the History of Emotions* (Cambridge: Cambridge University Press, 2001), in *H-France Review*, 2/119 (2002), 477–80, here 479.

[38] Plamper, 'History of Emotions', 246.

[39] Most recently during the period for questions following his keynote lecture, 'Are Emotions Like Language?' at the conference on 'Learning to Feel', Van Leer Institute, Jerusalem (14 April 2011).

[40] 'Throughout his response, Connolly appears to want to portray me as someone who, in a conservative and reactionary way, is trying to defend humanistic cultural theory from the encroachment of scientifically minded thinkers from the "outside", whereas he is someone who is generously open to the findings of neuroscientists. But this portrait is false. I am far from saying that humanists have nothing to learn from scientists; my engagement with the work of Alan Fridlund, James A. Russell, Lisa Feldman Barrett, and many others speaks for itself on this point. The issue here is not in which discipline a particular idea originates but whether the idea is a good one—indeed, whether it is correct. It is precisely because I appreciate science that I draw the line at bad science—as well as at the predictable appeal to the latter by humanists who have adopted the theoretical assumptions I argue against in my essay. ("Does any contemporary neuroscientist make a positive contribution to [Leys's] reading of culture?" Connolly asks (p. 799). Indeed, some do, by challenging the false reductionism of so many of their peers and by emphasizing instead the role of contextual meaning in emotional states)'; Ruth Leys, 'Critical Response II: Affect and Intention: A Reply to William E. Connolly', *Critical Inquiry*, 37/4 (2011), 799–805, here 803.

intensity', insofar as they have no object and are not immediately accessible to intentions.[41] There are also 'genetically based individual differences in average levels of core affect, its volatility, and its responsiveness to types of stimuli'.[42] This raises the suspicion that Leys needs an objective distinction between 'good' and 'bad', false and true, so that she might be able to criticize crude appropriations of the life sciences by those working in the human sciences from the standpoint of the life sciences, while however not using the same criteria in selecting her own conceptions of emotion.

But back to Reddy: ultimately his theory will be measured against the empirical results that it produces. For a book oriented towards the social sciences, and constructed in like fashion, the logic of the social scientific production of knowledge has to apply. The anthropologist Signe Howell made the point in 1997: 'However, as it stands, the argument [regarding *emotives*] is suggestive rather than convincing. . . . Ultimately, the anthropological contribution to the study of cognition and emotion must be founded in empirical fieldwork.'[43] But even after Reddy has applied his theory to historical material, historians still have many doubts. His central break points are the same as in the conventional histories, Jeremy Popkin remarking that Reddy's narrative of French history is not an unfamiliar one.[44] Not only not entirely unfamiliar, but slightly disturbing, it could be added. For Reddy's kind of historical writing can seem one-dimensional: the philological nuances of the new cultural history—sensitivity to metaphor, metonymy, synecdoche, genres, and the rest—recede into the background in Reddy's history of emotions.

It remains to be seen whether criticism of Reddy damages, or even destroys, his theoretical structure. He certainly remains influential. Even if many historians

---

[41] For Feldman Barrett and Russell, 'Core affect is defined as a neurophysiological state consciously accessible as a simple primitive nonreflective feeling most evident in mood and emotion but always available to consciousness. Although one feeling, it can be characterized by two pan-cultural bipolar dimensions: pleasure–displeasure (valence; feeling good versus bad) and activation (arousal; feeling energetic versus enervated). The phrase "core affect" was chosen because it (unlike *emotion, mood, anger*, etc.) is not an everyday lay concept. Core affect can remain constant (as in mood) or change rapidly (as in emotion). It is subject to many causes, some internal, some external, some obvious, some beyond human ability to perceive. Functionally, core affect is an aspect of the core self, a barometer of one's state and, as such, influences psychobiological processes from reflexes to complex cognitions. Individuals often attribute core affect to something, and they are often correct but also sometimes mistaken. Although a person is always in some state of core affect, even when not conscious of it, interest in core affect stems partly from its role in our emotional lives. Core affect per se is free-floating (i.e. not about something). Strong free-floating core affect occurs in such object-free mood disorders as anxiety or depression. Core affect is the mental heat in an emotional episode. A rapid change in core affect perceived as due to something is a key ingredient in such object-directed emotions as anger: to be angry is, in part, to feel bad because of someone's offence. (Prototypically, anger also includes appraisal, action, and so on.) Core affect is part of, not the whole of, moods and emotions'; James A. Russell and Lisa Feldman Barrett, 'Core Affect', in David Sander and Klaus R. Scherer (eds), *The Oxford Companion to Emotion and the Affective Sciences* (Oxford: Oxford University Press, 2009), 104.
[42] James A. Russell, 'Core Affect and the Psychological Construction of Emotion', *Psychological Review*, 110/1 (2003), 145–72, here 148.
[43] Howell, 'Comment on William M. Reddy', 342–3.
[44] Jeremy D. Popkin, Review of William M. Reddy, *The Navigation of Feeling: A Framework for the History of Emotions* (Cambridge: Cambridge University Press, 2001), in *H-France Review*, 2/118 (2002), 470–6.

would not want to follow him through all the rooms of his theoretical construction, some elements have already become detached and vulgarized, as so often happens in scholarship. Emotional regime, cogmotion, *emotive*—these terms are today heard in many places. The term 'emotional regime' is, for example, seldom employed in its full meaning—the ensemble of prescribed *emotives* together with the appropriate rituals and other symbolic practices. It is mostly understood as 'emotional norms', as a synonym for the Stearns' 'emotional standards' or Hochschild's 'feeling rules'.

2 EMOTIONAL PRACTICES

The ethnohistorian Monique Scheer is responsible for a promising development of Reddy's theory. We encountered her in Chapter Two, in the context of an essay inspired by the work of Pierre Bourdieu that she co-authored with Pascal Eitler. She is not interested in the retrieval of a post-structuralist vantage point from which ethical judgements can once more be made, but instead with overcoming dualisms such as that of mind and body, structure and agency, and, above all, the opposition of the external expression of emotion to inner, 'authentic' emotional experience. Scheer seeks to develop a holistic history of emotions, in which there is space for both the body and 'authentic' emotional experience, together with culture and history. This will only work if the body is acculturated and historicized.

Starting from the new philosophy of consciousness (especially Extended Mind Theory [EMT] and approaches associated with 'situated cognition'), Scheer begins by disputing the idea that cognition can only ever take place in the brain.[45] She cites the philosopher Alva Noë, one of the leading representatives of the new philosophy of consciousness, who argues that thinking, feeling, and perception are 'not something the brain achieves on its own. Consciousness requires the joint operation of brain, body, and world. Indeed, consciousness is an achievement of the whole animal in its environmental context.'[46] Scheer points to the sensorimotor systems, to gestures and ways of holding the body, concluding that 'The socially and environmentally contextualized body thinks along with the brain.'[47]

---

[45] Extended Mind Theory treats cognitive processes as processes that transcend the brain and even the human body. The environment is not treated as something separate and outside the body, but as part of cognitive processes. Situated cognition likewise argues that cognitive processes are always embedded in the environment and situations that sometimes change quickly change; Batja Mesquita, Lisa Feldman Barrett, and Eliot R. Smith (eds), *The Mind in Context* (New York: Guilford Press, 2010).

[46] Alva Noë, *Out of Our Heads: Why You Are Not Your Brain, and Other Lessons from the Biology of Consciousness* (New York: Hill and Wang, 2009), 10.

[47] Monique Scheer, 'Are Emotions a Kind of Practice (and Is That What Makes Them Have a History)? A Bourdieuan Approach to Understanding Emotion', *History and Theory*, 51/2 (2012), 193–220, here 197. See also Monique Scheer, 'Empfundener Glaube: Die kulturelle Praxis religiöser Emotionen im deutschen Methodismus des 19. Jahrhunderts', *Zeitschrift für Volkskunde*, 105 (2009), 185–213. And see the sociological convergence with Bourdieu on emotion in Andreas Reckwitz, 'Umkämpfte Maskulinität: Zur Historischen Kultursoziologie männlicher Subjektformen und ihrer Affektivitäten vom Zeitalter der Empfindsamkeit bis zur Postmoderne', in Manuel Borutta and Nina Verheyen (eds), *Die Präsenz der Gefühle: Männlichkeit und Emotion in der Moderne* (Bielefeld: Transcript, 2010), 57–79; Andreas Reckwitz, 'Affective Spaces: A Praxeological Outlook',

By latching on to a new philosophy engaged with the neurosciences—Noë, for example, has taken part in neuroscientific experiments—historians could better recover the body as an object of study than with 'appraisal' cognitive psychology, which had been their favourite because of its equation of emotion with cognition and the space this seems to open for temporal change. That is not all, however. This new philosophy of consciousness has in fact very little to say about the way in which the body has been shaped by culture and history. Scheer considers that it is best to think in terms of a 'knowing body', as did Bourdieu.[48] Drawing upon Bourdieu, she talks of 'emotional practices'—this is her own theoretical contribution—which she defines as 'manipulations of body and mind to evoke emotions where there are none, to focus diffuse arousals and give them an intelligible shape, or to change or remove emotions already there'.[49] She identifies four kinds of emotional practices: mobilizing, naming, communicating, and regulating.

Mobilizing Emotional Practices

These often involve the use of media, and are typically more communal in character than isolated, as, for example, with courtship. Anthropological and historical research has shown that there is great variability here: 'changing technologies (from love letters to the cell phone and the internet) and changing venues (from supervised visits to dates to parties)'.[50] These contexts and technologies do not frame emotions that are always the same, but instead play a significant part in shaping emotions and the feelings 'between potential marriage partners—which can range from dutiful obedience, to honor, to passion, admiration, familiarity, or respect. Courtship, then, is not just a behavior but has performative effects on the constitution of feelings and the (gendered) self.'[51]

The consumption of drugs, often combined with dancing and music, is another example. This promotes the speedy realization of emotion. It would however be wrong to deal with this in terms of a simple stimulus-response model, as though a chemical substance has always and everywhere prompted exactly the same emotion. This approach has been shown to be mistaken by the existence of a placebo effect, which is also capable of producing emotions. Moreover, the use of mind-altering drugs is often embedded in ritual and cultural codes.[52]

The practice of confession which is found in some Catholic cultures is a final example of mobilizing emotional practices. The emotion of remorse does not have to be present before the act of confession, but can arise in the course of making a confession, and through the related physical techniques—kneeling, or the wearing

Rethinking History, 16/2 (2012), 241–58; Andreas Reckwitz, *Das hybride Subjekt: Eine Theorie der Subjektkulturen von der bürgerlichen Moderne zur Postmoderne* (Weilerswist: Velbrück Wissenschaft, 2006).

[48] Scheer, 'Are Emotions a Kind of Practice?', 199.
[49] Scheer, 'Are Emotions a Kind of Practice?', 209.
[50] Scheer, 'Are Emotions a Kind of Practice?', 209.
[51] Scheer, 'Are Emotions a Kind of Practice?', 209–10.
[52] Scheer, 'Are Emotions a Kind of Practice?', 211–12.

of a headscarf or a cilice. Combined with these techniques, confession can create the desired emotion, can 'mobilize' it. The emphasis here lies on 'can': Scheer maintains that emotional practices are always unpredictable to some extent, and can fail—and if they fail too often, they are abandoned.[53]

Naming Emotional Practices

These are primarily speaking and writing, but also silent memory in thought. Hence *emotives* are also naming emotional practices, and Scheer's practices go beyond Reddy's *emotives* by placing greater emphasis upon the form of naming. The naming of emotional practices therefore questions whether the naming involves writing, speaking, or thinking: for writing, whether this is done with the hand, or with a computer; for speaking, who the addressee is, the emphases given, in what language situation it takes place. With naming emotional practices it is always a question of producing meaning, or as Scheer says: 'Like snowflakes, every emotion is unique and gets put into a category—is typified—only through naming.'[54] The 'work of *signifying* and *resignifying* emotions' is highly commercialized, from the afternoon talk show to the therapeutic 'industries' that convey emotional know-how.[55]

Scheer emphasizes that the reconstruction of naming emotional practices permits historians to grasp 'authentic' emotional experiences. In India, for instance, it was only through Bollywood films that a sentence from anglophone culture—'I love you'—first gained broad recognition. It seeped into Hindi and became, hitherto more or less unknown, part of courtship and marriage rituals. 'If naming emotions makes them available to experience, then charting changes in naming means writing a history of feeling in the fullest sense.'[56]

Communicating Emotional Practices

The prime aim of these practices is exchange with others. If a politician wishes to communicate his or her concern on TV after a natural catastrophe, this happens 'on a multisensory level and involves different modes of knowledge', including 'faces, gestures, vocal patterns, bodily postures, or manifestations such as tears, changing skin color, or heavy breathing'.[57] Scheer argues that it is essential for successful emotional communication that messages are received in the manner intended; here again it is very important that the sender takes proper account of the situation's context, the participating actors, and their social expectations.

The key point of Scheer's communicating emotional practices is that presuppositions from the domain of the a priori—for example, did emotional communication fail because the social actor did not feel authentically?—are thereby recovered as

[53] Scheer, 'Are Emotions a Kind of Practice?', 210.
[54] Scheer, 'Are Emotions a Kind of Practice?', 213.
[55] Scheer, 'Are Emotions a Kind of Practice?', 213, emphasis added.
[56] Scheer, 'Are Emotions a Kind of Practice?', 214.
[57] Scheer, 'Are Emotions a Kind of Practice?', 214.

objects of scholarly investigation. The central questions are therefore: were the conditions of communication in a particular historical setting such as to elevate the authenticity of feeling as an ideal? Or was there instead in this setting no distinction made between 'authentic' and 'simulated', so that this differentiation played no role in the success of emotional communication, or lack of it? Or did the setting perhaps privilege simulation, so that the expression of emotion became entirely conventionalized?

Regulating Emotional Practices

At first glance this seems to account for most of the history of emotions written so far: emotional norms and their oversight, along with punishment for their infringement. Seen in this light the emotionology of the Stearns would be regulatory emotional practices, and self-help books on etiquette *the* source for its historical investigation. But that would be too hasty, since then the distinction between norms accessible to historical study and 'genuine' emotions that remain inaccessible would prevail. In Scheer's understanding, regulating emotional practices do not only control emotion, they *make* emotion. They are closely related to 'orders of knowledge, to use Foucault's term, such as that which constitutes emotion and reason as opposites'.[58] Other dichotomies follow from this, for example, male and female, inner and outer, civilized and uncivilized, private and public. The fact that young boys rarely cry and that young girls often swallow their anger is the result of concrete regulating emotional practices, both open (explicit directions in a book of etiquette) and covert (practices prescribed by teachers or others in authority).

Besides these four emotional practices there is also habitus, a concept of Bourdieu's upon which Scheer places a great deal of weight. Habitus describes 'body knowledge' that has become sedimented and absorbed. Musicians whose fingers dart across their instruments unconsciously, and in so doing internalize music faster than is the case with slower forms of cognition, or athletes whose bodies habitually perform quick and complex movements—these are the classic examples used to clarify what habitus means.[59] Habitus involves the inscription of, among other things, social and cultural differences, and of gender: that one is cultured and educated is shown not only by the ability to interject a quote from a canonical novel, instantly recognize an opera aria, or know the correct plural form of a word derived from ancient Greek, but also by knowing just how loudly to laugh at a joke, or exactly how close to stand to someone one is talking to at a reception after a doctoral examination, and so on. That can of course all be learned relatively quickly, but mistakes will be made if one has not paid sufficient attention, or one could give oneself away by being self-conscious and trying too hard.

Habitus is of course unconscious, it has to be 'static and binding to a certain extent', but it is not a prison from which there is no escape. Habitual dispositions

---

[58] Scheer, 'Are Emotions a Kind of Practice?', 216.
[59] Scheer, 'Are Emotions a Kind of Practice?', 202.

always need 'confirmation in everyday practices'.[60] Habitus 'leaves space for behaviors not entirely and always predictable, which can also instantiate change and resistance rather than preprogrammed reproduction'.[61] It therefore permits the contrast 'between social structure and individual agency or between cultural demands and the timeless, universal "truth" of a body whose functions and structures remain untouched by their uses'.[62] For as Scheer emphasizes,

> The skillful use of the body in automatic movements, impulses, and activations is a learned practice, acquired through mimesis, making lasting changes in the body and brain. Habitual postures and movements build up muscle tissue, innervation, and blood vessels in one area and not another, shorten some tendons, lengthen others, affect bone density and shape, and induce specific development of brain tissue.[63]

All the same, our bodies set us absolute limits, and 'no human society will develop a dance step that requires five feet or a musical instrument made for a hand with eight digits'.[64]

Emotions as habitus are never just a linear response to stimuli, but are always circular.[65] They are never merely 'pure intensity', as in Brian Massumi, who defines affect as entirely unconscious and physical, and so lends it an autonomous status.[66] Scheer thinks that there is always a physical dimension to emotion, even if this is drenched with culture and history. One does not 'have' emotions; it is more like trying them out, or doing emotion, 'along a continuum from wholly conscious and deliberate to completely inadvertent, shifting in the course of their [emotions] execution along this continuum'.[67] In the same way, one 'is' not an emotional subject, or 'has' an emotional self, 'this feeling subject is not prior to but emerges in the *doing of emotion*'.[68]

What does all this mean for the study of history? First of all, the range of sources is extended, or the analysis of existing sources gains a new dimension. Apart from explicitly emotional words and biographical data, attention shifts to bodily language—'boiling blood', for example. Traces of *all* forms of physical feeling in writing, sound, and image are important—shaking with rage, a trembling voice, fear, suppressed anger, through to fainting from shame—and there are also of course the extended or broadened eyebrows (*yang-shou shen-mei*) that were mentioned in the Introduction of this book, which for the Chinese denote happiness and contentment. Here Scheer goes far beyond Reddy, whose attention is primarily fixed upon verbal speech acts. Of especial interest are conflicts, since they say something about the failure of 'doing', and so reveal the unspoken, implicit rules of

[60] Scheer, 'Are Emotions a Kind of Practice?', 204.
[61] Scheer, 'Are Emotions a Kind of Practice?', 204.
[62] Scheer, 'Are Emotions a Kind of Practice?', 204.
[63] Scheer, 'Are Emotions a Kind of Practice?', 202.
[64] Scheer, 'Are Emotions a Kind of Practice?', 201.
[65] Scheer, 'Are Emotions a Kind of Practice?', 206.
[66] Scheer, 'Are Emotions a Kind of Practice?', 207.
[67] Scheer, 'Are Emotions a Kind of Practice?', 207.
[68] Scheer, 'Are Emotions a Kind of Practice?', 220, emphasis added.

'doing'. In conflicts, different regulating emotional practices collide, thus making it possible to draw conclusions about more extensive cultures of emotion.

3 NEUROHISTORY

Scheer's 'cogaffective' conception of consciousness is linked to Extended Mind Theory, and Reddy also knew very well what he was doing when, at a time when hardly any historians took an interest in the life sciences, he opted for cognitive psychology and the appraisal school, with its intentionalist dimension.[69] Since Reddy's reception of experimental psychology there has been a neuroscientific wave that washed over many other human sciences before it finally reached history. And so there it is today: neurohistory.[70] Its most prominent representative is the medievalist Daniel Lord Smail, whose well-regarded book *On Deep History and the Brain* (2008), which touches on emotion at a central point, has been critically reviewed by Reddy. But let us turn first of all to Smail's book.

Smail wants to extend the chronological bounds of what counts as 'history', moving the starting point back way beyond the Mesopotamian invention of writing in *c.*4000 BC. Hence he begins by revealing what got lost with the development of history in the nineteenth century as an enterprise based upon written sources. This became 'prehistory', the history of the Sumerians and their cuneiform script, the Palaeolithic era becoming 'a timeless dystopia whose unchangingness was only broken, *deus ex machina*, by some ill-defined catalytic event that created movement and history'—the introduction of writing technologies.[71]

If one bids goodbye to the study of history as it developed in the later nineteenth century, based upon the written document, and instead extends the concept of sources (Smail prefers to call them 'traces') to include stone fragments, fossils, traces

---

[69] Reddy built upon a postdoctoral year in developmental psychology at the end of the 1970s with Jerome Kagan, and more than twenty years of accumulated knowledge of the life sciences. For Reddy's time studying with Kagan, see Reddy, *Navigation of Feeling*, xiv; Plamper, 'History of Emotions', 237. Moreover, during 1975 and 1976 Reddy was at the Institute for Advanced Study in Princeton at the invitation of Clifford Geertz, together with Ellen and William Sewell, and the anthropologists Michelle and Renato Rosaldo. If Reddy's work contains the results of neuroscience research, this material is far better grounded than in the works of popularizers like LeDoux and Damasio, and testifies to his extensive readings on the subject; William M. Reddy, 'Saying Something New: Practice Theory and Cognitive Neuroscience', *Arcadia: International Journal for Literary Studies*, 44/1 (2009), 8–23.

[70] Edmund P. Russell, 'Neurohistory', *Rachel Carson Center at Ludwig-Maximilians-Universität München* <http://www.carsoncenter.uni-muenchen.de/download/staff_and_fellows/projects/project_russel.pdf> accessed 17 March 2014; Edmund Russell, *Evolutionary History: Uniting History and Biology to Understand Life on Earth* (Cambridge: Cambridge University Press, 2011). The best-known German-language examples, which deal more with collective memory than emotion, are Johannes Fried, *Der Schleier der Erinnerung: Grundzüge einer historischen Memorik* (Munich: Beck, 2004); Niels Birbaumer and Dieter Langewiesche, 'Neuropsychologie und Historie—Versuch einer empirischen Annäherung: Posttraumatische Belastungsstörung (PTSD) und Soziopathie in Österreich nach 1945', *Geschichte und Gesellschaft*, 32/2 (2006), 153–75.

[71] Daniel Lord Smail, *On Deep History and the Human Brain* (Berkeley and Los Angeles: University of California Press, 2008), 4. See also Andrew Shryock and Daniel Lord Smail (eds), *Deep History: The Architecture of Past and Present* (Berkeley and Los Angeles: University of California Press, 2011).

of DNA, isotopes, models of behaviour, pottery fragments, and phonemes; if one recalls 'the great historical disciplines, including geology, evolutionary biology and ethology, archeology, historical linguistics, and cosmology'—then, according to Smail, we arrive at a better and more profound understanding of history: deep history.[72] There emerges 'a grand historical narrative that links the Paleolithic to the Postlithic and can coalesce, in part, around the continuous interplay between human culture, on the one hand, and the human brain, behavior, and biology, on the other'.[73]

If one looks at 'traces' more carefully, then the parallels to textual sources becomes obvious. 'A trace', says Smail, 'is anything that encodes some sort of information about the past.'[74] He goes on:

A phoneme, uttered today, is a living fossil, though the lineage fades into oblivion after a few thousand years. So is DNA. Although population geneticists do occasionally extract DNA from ancient remains, they more commonly work with modern DNA borrowed from the inside of a cheek or from a drop of blood. Modern DNA is uncannily similar to an edited text. It consists of lines of code, written in an alphabet of four letters, that faithfully reproduce an original. Like a text, it carries information that can be read by future generations. It must be read to have any meaning. The only difference—and to some this will be important—is that DNA is not the product of anyone's intention.[75]

But, Smail argues, it is exactly this absence of authorial intention that brings biology close to some branches of historical study. In the social history of the 1960s and 1970s, for example, intentionality was neglected in favour of anonymous structures; social history paid no attention to the agency of individuals.[76] There were also other ways in which biology, together with other life and geosciences, was not so distant from history. Both history and evolutionary biology had an open conception of time: phylogenesis, the evolutionary development of relationships within a group (as opposed to ontogenesis, the origin and development of a particular individual), presumes open beginnings and open ends; in short, infinity.[77] And the idea that neuropsychology imputes agency to neuronal events is not such a strange idea. For ultimately 'historians habitually think with psychology anyway. We are prone to making unguarded assumptions about the psychological states of the people we find in our sources.'[78]

Emotions are dealt with in the fourth chapter, 'The New Neurohistory'. Smail defines emotions as 'relatively automated' and, following LeDoux and Damasio, distinguishes between emotions which are unconscious and physical, and feelings as a product of consciousness and physical emotions (as we have seen in

[72] Smail, *On Deep History and the Human Brain*, 48.
[73] Smail, *On Deep History and the Human Brain*, 8.
[74] Smail, *On Deep History and the Human Brain*, 48–9.
[75] Smail, *On Deep History and the Human Brain*, 49.
[76] Smail, *On Deep History and the Human Brain*, 72.
[77] Smail, *On Deep History and the Human Brain*, 80.
[78] Smail, *On Deep History and the Human Brain*, 159.

Chapter Three, most neuroscientists would call the first 'affect' and the second 'emotion').[79] This definition of emotion is essential to Smail's approach, since he believes that emotions determine human action, but are unconscious and ancient—they are the connection that runs far back into former times. Without an anti-intentionalist conception of emotion, to make use of Ruth Leys's distinction again, Smail would not be able to create a lengthy chronology for human behaviour. He puts it like this:

> And then there are all the noncognitive features of the brain. Many of the things we do are shaped by behavioral predispositions, moods, emotions, and feelings that have a deep evolutionary history. These body states are not ghostly things flitting mysteriously through consciousness. Recent work in neuropsychology and neurophysiology has shown that they are physiological entities, characteristically located in specific parts of the brain and put there by natural selection. Some of them, including emotions, are relatively automated, no different from the other areas of life governance—basic metabolism, reflexes, pain, pleasure, drives, motivations—that are routinely handled by the brain in all hominoids. Most, perhaps all, are also associated with an array of hormones and neurotransmitters such as testosterone and other androgens, estrogen, serotonin, dopamine, endorphins, oxytocin, prolactin, vasopressin, epinephrine, and so on. Produced in glands and synapses throughout the body, these chemicals facilitate or block the signals passing along neural pathways. They induce the somatic states revealed on and in our bodies and help determine how feelings actually feel. We share virtually all of these chemicals with other animals, though the nervous system of an iguana, say, will not necessarily use testosterone in the same way ours does. In a sense, each of these chemicals has its own natural history.[80]

The outcome: 'The existence of brain structures and body chemicals means that predispositions and behavioral patterns have a universal biological substrate that simply cannot be ignored.'[81]

Smail constantly emphasizes that he has left the dichotomy of nature and nurture behind him. So given so much universalism, where does variability come in?[82] He treats emotions as patterns of stimulus and response; variability comes from historically changing stimuli. Fear of the snake is founded upon millions of years of the threat from the stimulus 'snake'. Today, this 'deep historical trace', the fear of a snake, no longer provides a chance of survival for the majority of the world's population, since most people do not encounter snakes in the wild. What would be evolutionarily useful would be a fear of cars, and individuals who were frightened of cars should be favoured by natural selection. It is entirely possible that, in a few million years, there will be other stimuli that will determine evolutionarily advantageous behaviour, and the fear of cars will be nothing but another deep-seated

[79] Smail, *On Deep History and the Human Brain*, 113, 150–1.
[80] Smail, *On Deep History and the Human Brain*, 113.
[81] Smail, *On Deep History and the Human Brain*, 114.
[82] Smail's rejection of the nature-nurture dichotomy can be found in Smail, *On Deep History and the Human Brain*, 118.

historical trace.[83] In any case, this is how Smail envisages the place for any dynamic influence.

Of course, this dynamic has in no respect left behind the dichotomy of nature and nurture, but is laced into this particular corset as tightly as ever. For according to Smail, emotions—and to repeat, these are defined, with LeDoux and Damasio, as unconscious and physical phenomena contrasted to conscious emotions—are unchanging: 'emotions . . . form a structural backdrop for many things we do and have done'.[84] Smail reproduces the old affect programme that we have already encountered in Tomkins and Ekman. It is only the objects of emotion (snakes, cars) that can change. Smail writes that 'The medieval female saint who ate lice and licked pus from infected wounds and leper sores knew, on some level, just what sort of effect she would have on those who watched', meaning that it is only the cultural response to disgust-stimuli that changes, not however the universality of these stimuli.[85] Hence Smail does not consider whether emotions themselves can change, that the 'hardware' of the brain is itself changeable.

A contradiction arises here, and it runs through the whole book. On the one hand, since the dawn of time animals and humans have influenced the conditions of their brains with 'psychotropic mechanisms', defined as 'the mood-altering practices, behaviors, and institutions generated by human culture'.[86] Moreover, it is not only humans who have such psychotropic mechanisms, for

> Many animals do this to a certain degree. Horses who get bored or lonely while isolated in a paddock sometimes take pleasure in startling themselves. A lively snort causes a chemical feedback that induces a startle reflex and an exciting wash of neurochemicals. Birds who flock around trees bearing fruit that is somewhat past its prime and eat the alcohol-laden fruit have found a way to ingest, rather than manufacture, a mood-altering substance. Cats are drawn to catnip.[87]

People dance and drink, work themselves up into religious ecstasy, and have recreational sex. Just like emotion, therefore, the use of psychotropy, the inclination to stimulate oneself, seems to be universal (although it is not clear at which organism Smail would draw the line).

On the other hand, according to Smail, the agricultural revolution around 5000 BC brought about lasting change, since it produced an immense range of new psychotropic mechanisms. And there were always periods of acceleration, as in eighteenth-century Europe 'with its caffeinated culture, its sentimental novels and pornographic works, and its growing array of consumer goods'.[88] Today, in our global consumer culture, psychotropic mechanisms are ever more numerous and ever stronger, with the result—here Smail makes a quick shift that he needs in order

---

[83] Smail, *On Deep History and the Human Brain*, 139–40.
[84] Smail, *On Deep History and the Human Brain*, 117.
[85] Smail, *On Deep History and the Human Brain*, 115.
[86] Smail, *On Deep History and the Human Brain*, 161.
[87] Smail, *On Deep History and the Human Brain*, 127.
[88] Smail, *On Deep History and the Human Brain*, 155.

to introduce historical change—that we become increasingly dulled.[89] How can that happen? Why do we become more numb, in spite of ever-greater access to psychotropic mechanisms? This about-face is the only possibility Smail has of bringing historical variability into his schema, and do what historians usually do: classify changes and transformations. He is a historian after all, and this is indeed his claim: to develop a new periodization. Of course, his approach does not explain why some people make use of certain psychotropic mechanisms and others do not.[90] And if we follow Smail here, we can no longer refer to some psychotropic mechanisms as 'mildly addictive'. For, according to Smail, in time all psychotropic mechanisms lead to diminishing dependency and dullness.

Smail's anchoring of an unchanging nature in emotions becomes a real problem for him. The distinction of emotion from cognition keeps breaking down, as with his example of the African tracker, who shows by his ability to detect lions on the far horizon that he is better adapted to his environment than people who do not live in the savannah:

> Anyone who has seen an African tracker scan a featureless plain and locate a distant pride of lions, invisible to everyone else in the car, will appreciate the impoverished nature of the synapses in his or her own visual cortex.[91]

Why does cognitive adaptation to the environment here become inscribed in the cortex, but not when reading a novel in the era of sensibility (according to Smail, reading novels is purely an affective-psychotropic practice)?[92]

And how—this is the central question—does this add to historical explanation? Consider Smail's explanation of terrorist political regimes:

> Practices that instill a capacity to feel submission can be found in primate societies. Studies of matriarchal baboon societies, for example, show that high-ranking female baboons routinely terrorize subordinate females. As with chimpanzees, a key feature of this terrorism is that it is often random and unpredictable. Since they cannot predict abuse, subordinate females suffer very high levels of stress, which in turn reduces their fertility. This generates a clear biological advantage for the dominant females. . . . Post-lithic societies saw an increase in the range or density of devices and mechanisms that generated stress hormones in the bodies of subordinates. Political elites could not have been aware of the precise physiological consequences of their actions and behaviors. Instead, political behaviors converged on these solutions because this is how power was most effectively maintained.[93]

---

[89] 'Beyond that, we grow numb to the mechanisms that stimulate our moods and feelings on a daily basis, a neurochemical insensitivity that may help explain why one decade's excitement is another decade's boredom'; Smail, *On Deep History and the Human Brain*, 188.

[90] Smail writes: 'Drugs like heroin and cocaine appeal to some of us because they mimic the effects of serotonin and dopamine in the brain and therefore serve to alter body states artificially'; Smail, *On Deep History and the Human Brain*, 151.

[91] Smail, *On Deep History and the Human Brain*, 137.

[92] Smail, *On Deep History and the Human Brain*, 118, 128, 155, 161, 175, 180, 182.

[93] Smail, *On Deep History and the Human Brain*, 166–7.

And Smail writes about the behaviour of one of Jane Goodall's young female chimpanzees in the Gombe National Forest:

> On several occasions, Passion, abetted by her daughter Pom, snatched away and ate the babies of other mothers. The grisly meal complete, Passion then consoled the distressed mothers with hugs and pats. The behavior looks positively pathological. As political behavior, however, it makes a great deal of sense: how better to build or maintain power than to create stress as well as offer the means to alleviate it?[94]

Smail here refers explicitly to 'fascist regimes of the twentieth century'.[95] Such explanations quite plainly fail to meet the standard of complexity even of grand sociological theories of fascism and totalitarianism, let alone the wealth of detailed microstudies. They are, as Daniel Gross has said, 'trivially true'.[96] Smail's reductionism becomes most evident when dealing with particular cases, and so it is perhaps no accident that he provides no studies of his own in which he could apply his ideas to historical 'data', unlike Reddy in *The Navigation of Feeling*.

Reviewing Smail, William M. Reddy accused him of functionalism. He demonstrates that, while Smail claims to have abandoned evolutionary psychology in favour of non-functionalist neuroscience, his deficient neuroscientific knowledge leads him again and again into the classical traps of functionalism. For example:

> According to Smail, humans in the presence of social superiors commonly, and unconsciously, 'speak with a higher voice, carry a submissive grin on their faces, and laugh immoderately at the bad jokes made by those above them'. The module that codes for this kind of behavior, Smail surmises, 'may have been moribund' in small-scale societies prior to the agricultural revolution. But once large-scale agricultural societies emerged, parents, by acting according to the dictates of this module, shaped the synaptic configurations of their children. Primate studies support this conjecture, Smail believes. In this way, culture and genetic programming interacted to enhance a configuration of behaviors that was previously suppressed.... Of course, there is abundant evidence that early agricultural social orders were highly hierarchical. Of course, humans have known for millennia that training is crucial and that habit and custom are very powerful. Neuroscience research has shown that constant repetition of behaviors can alter synaptic structures—that, in effect, neural architecture is, in part, a product of learning and culture. But to say that high voices and submissive grins are 'adaptive' in a bureaucratic monarchy and can be passed on via learning is to rush far beyond what neuroscience can currently confirm or disprove. To take such speculation seriously is to open a Pandora's box of functional imaginings.[97]

One could also have taken the example of the African tracker. Along with Smail's stress upon the African roots of humanity, this example is in all likelihood the outcome of anti-racism on the part of a white, liberal, male American academic.[98]

---

[94] Smail, *On Deep History and the Human Brain*, 174.

[95] Smail, *On Deep History and the Human Brain*, 186.

[96] Daniel M. Gross, *The Secret History of Emotion: From Aristotle's Rhetoric to Modern Brain Science* (Chicago: University of Chicago Press, 2006), 34.

[97] William M. Reddy, 'Neuroscience and the Fallacies of Functionalism', *History and Theory*, 49/3 (2010), 412–25, here 414–15.

[98] On the African origins of humanity, see Smail, *On Deep History and the Human Brain*, 9–10, 15.

But if you reverse the example of the tracker, then it becomes evident that there are logical dangers hidden in this anti-racism: for taking Smail's line of argument, you could argue that Africans, lacking the inscription of cultural techniques in their brain, are not able to play classical music, nor would be able to appreciate the beauty of a piano concerto by Mozart or Beethoven, let alone a symphony by Shostakovich or Schnittke.

Naive neurohistory cannot therefore be the correct approach, or as a reviewer of *On Deep History and the Brain* put it:

> A more serious obstacle is the fact that historians lack the critical tools for the evaluation of biological and medical discoveries. I myself, for example, am unable to tell whether what I have written here about the findings of neuro-physiological research is correct, controversial, or total nonsense. It may be that the same is true for Smail as well. It is hard to imagine many scholars in the humanities developing the scientific expertise they would need in order to participate in this discourse and not just accept it on faith.[99]

4 PERSPECTIVES IN THE HISTORY OF EMOTION

'It might well be that we are programmed to respond to stimuli, and are washed by feedback waves, but how does this help us in historical studies?' This critic then answered his own question: 'From the historical perspective, the neuronal approach . . . is a reboot of determinism.'[100] Many share this basic criticism. To take the wind out of the sails of the neurosciences, one needs a sceptical approach informed by a thorough knowledge of the neurosciences, of the kind that William M. Reddy set out to achieve. It is also very true that it would be of little use if 'emotion' became yet another 'mentalité' or degenerated into a category like 'national character'.[101]

[99] Dror Wahrmann, 'Where Culture and Biology Meet', review of Daniel Lord Smail, *On Deep History and the Human Brain* (Berkeley and Los Angeles: University of California Press, 2008), in *Haaretz* (24 April 2008). I would like to thank Igal Halfin for bringing this review to my attention.

[100] Markus Völkel, 'Wohin führt der "neuronal turn" die Geschichtswissenschaft?', in Christian Geyer (ed.), *Hirnforschung und Willensfreiheit: Zur Deutung der neuesten Experimente* (Frankfurt am Main: Suhrkamp, 2004), 140–2, here 140. See also Christian Geyer, 'Frieds Brainstorming: Jetzt ist auch die Geschichte aufs Gehirn gekommen', in Geyer, *Hirnforschung und Willensfreiheit*, 134–9; Alexander Kraus and Birte Kohtz, 'Hirnwindungen—Quelle einer historiographischen Wende? Zur Relevanz neurowissenschaftlicher Erkenntnisse für die Geschichtswissenschaft', *Zeitschrift für Geschichtswissenschaft*, 55/10 (2007), 842–57; Michael L. Fitzhugh and William H. Leckie, Jr, 'Agency, Postmodernism, and the Causes of Change', *History and Theory*, 40/4 (2001), 59–81. On agency and the life science approach see the special issue 'The Return of Science: Evolutionary Ideas and History', *History and Theory* 38/4 (1999); also the special issue 'Agency after Postmodernism', *History and Theory*, 40/4 (2001); Gabrielle M. Spiegel (ed.), *Practicing History: New Directions in Historical Writing after the Linguistic Turn* (New York: Routledge, 2005).

[101] Also see Robert Solomon, who claims to have destroyed eight myths about emotion: 'Myth 1: Emotions Are Ineffable; Myth 2: Emotions Are Feelings; Myth 3: The Hydraulic Model; Myth 4: Emotions Are "in" the Mind; Myth 5: Emotions Are Stupid (They Have No Intelligence); Myth 6: Two Flavors of Emotion, Positive and Negative; Myth 7: Emotions Are Irrational; Myth 8: Emotions Happen to Us (They Are "Passions")'; Robert C. Solomon, *True to our Feelings: What our Emotions Are Really Telling Us* (Oxford: Oxford University Press, 2007), 127–200.

As with any historical fashion, there are free riders and oversimplification, and these are unavoidable; but that does not mean that one should ignore the threat that they pose. Emotion is not simply whatever doesn't fit into the anachronistic common-sense model of historical explanation. In other words, one should avoid invoking 'emotion' to label all human action that cannot be explained through 'interests' and 'rationality'—the classical rational-choice assumption of optimizing gain.

It is also not a good idea to make a distinction between positive and negative emotions. There is a long history to this kind of distinction, reaching back to the psychology of the early twentieth century and its methods of measurement, from which too many thinkers took the idea of hedonic valence; but this is of little use in the history of emotions. Nor are metaphors that equate emotion with the economy, nor the image of a stock of emotions and its current balance. Nearly always implicit here is the idea of a balanced budget, running back to a hydraulic model of the emotions. And finally, it is of little help to divide emotions into the basic and the synthetic, the simple and the complex. As Jerome Kagan never tires of saying, we need to keep in view the mixed nature of emotions; emotions are always more complex than the clear boundaries of emotional concepts—'fear', 'pleasure', 'shame'—suggest.[102]

Having issued these warnings, in the following I will highlight a few areas in which productive work in the history of emotions seems possible. In some cases these are established subfields of history that could profit from an 'emotional' perspective. Each field will be introduced with a historical vignette.

Political History, Social Movements, and Emotions

In October 1988 the American Food and Drug Administration (FDA) simplified the standards for medication so that AIDS-related drugs could pass more quickly through clinical trials and be made available to patients who needed them.[103] It was preceded by a demonstration of about one thousand mostly gay and lesbian activists on 11 October 1988 at the Washington FDA building, organized by the AIDS Coalition to Unleash Power (ACT UP). The building was closed for a day, and the demonstration had an enormous worldwide media impact (Fig. 28).[104]

---

[102] Jerome Kagan, *What Is Emotion? History, Measures, and Meanings* (New Haven: Yale University Press, 2007). See also Robert Musil, who entitled one chapter in the draft of *The Man without Qualities* 'Feeling and Behavior: The Precariousness of Emotion', and wrote: 'The peculiar manner in which the emotion is from the beginning both present and not present can be expressed in the comparison that one must imagine its development as the image of a forest, and not as the image of a tree. A birch, for example, remains itself from its germination to its death; but on the other hand, a birch forest can begin as a mixed forest; it becomes a birch forest as soon as birch trees—as the result of causes that can be quite varied—predominate in it and the departures from the pure stamp of the birch type are no longer significant', Robert Musil, *The Man without Qualities*, trans. Sophie Wilkins and Burton Pike (New York: Vintage International, 1996) [Ger. orig., *Der Mann ohne Eigenschaften*, 3 vols, 1930–43], ii. 1266, 1275–6.

[103] 'A Timeline of AIDS', *AIDS.gov (U.S. Department of Health & Human Services)* <http://aids.gov/hiv-aids-basics/hiv-aids-101/aids-timeline/> accessed 18 March 2014.

[104] James Wentzy, 'Detailed Scene List and Transcription: Fight Back, Fight AIDS: 15 Years of ACT UP', *ACT UP* (November 2002) <http://www.actupny.org/divatv/synopsis75.html> accessed 18 March 2014.

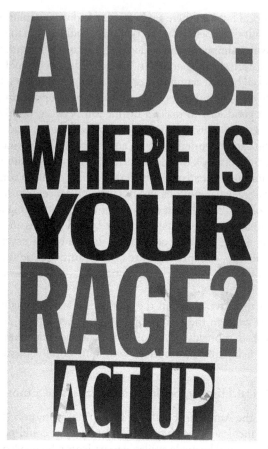

Fig. 28 ACT UP Poster

Source: Image Title: 'How Many of Us Will Be Alive for Stonewall 35?' Verso: 'AIDS: Where is your Rage? ACT UP', ACT UP New York records, 1969, 1982–97 (bulk 1987–95), posters and placards © Manuscripts and Archives Division, The New York Public Library, Astor, Lenox and Tilden Foundations.

Classical political history would describe this chain of events as the successful protest action of leading individual persons. The involvement of the FDA would be treated as the result of the tactical skill and charisma of the ACT UP founder, Larry Kramer. This conventional kind of history would foreground the interests of the activists—to achieve more effective treatment for AIDS, end the everyday and workplace discrimination of the infected and sick, promote medical research, and make existing drugs available to a wider public by reducing their prices.

However, the sociologist Deborah Gould has written this history quite differently. She treats ACT UP demonstrations like that on 11 October 1988 as models for the creative politics of affect-based social movements. Gould, herself a member of the Chicago ACT UP group and active in the movement, writes that 'our common sense was to "turn grief into anger"'.[105] The founding of ACT UP was linked to the invention of new, non-violent forms of protest with a media impact, for example, the storming of a news broadcast during the First Gulf War in January 1991 on a 'Day of Desperation', chanting slogans such as 'Fight AIDS, not Arabs; AIDS is news!' in front of the cameras. This and other events were a reaction to the hopelessness of a situation where mass death among the gay community was treated by politics, the churches, and large sections of the society at best with indifference, at worst with scorn.[106] To relate the history of ACT UP with an emotional focus did not mean, as would be the case in a conventional political history, that pragmatic interests were emphasized—the emotional language and actions of the actors involved being treated as epiphenomena of these interests—but instead that light was shed on the complex emotional processes of all participants, both the activists and the addressees in politics, government, and society. This also involved breaking with a sociological tradition in which social movements were treated as being led by reason.[107]

What can a political history augmented by the history of emotions accomplish? It can, for instance, consider the changing way of dealing with the public expression of emotion in politics. Before the 1972 US presidential election, it was generally thought that the Democrat Ed Muskie had the best chance of beating the incumbent Republican candidate, Richard Nixon. But after Muskie appeared to have cried in public he had to withdraw from the Democratic primary. A New Hampshire newspaper had published an article suggesting that Muskie's wife was an alcoholic—it later turned out that the story had been set up by Nixon's election team. Muskie held a meeting outside the newspaper offices in a snowstorm, vehemently denying the charge. While he spoke, it looked as though tears were running down his cheeks; Muskie later said it was melting snowflakes (Fig. 29).[108]

Three decades later America was ruled for eight years by George W. Bush, a president who again and again cried in front of the camera; for instance, on 11 January 2007, during a ceremony to posthumously honour a 22-year-old soldier who in 2005 had died trying to save his comrades (Fig. 30).[109] In the same year Bush admitted in an interview that 'I do a lot of crying in this job. I'll bet I've shed

[105] Deborah B. Gould, *Moving Politics: Emotion and ACT UP's Fight against AIDS* (Chicago: University of Chicago Press, 2009), 8.

[106] 'DIVA TV Program Synopsis: Day of Desperation', ACT UP New York <http://www.actupny.org/diva/synDesperation.html> accessed 18 March 2014.

[107] Sidney Tarrow, *Power in Movement: Social Movements, Collective Action and Politics* (Cambridge: Cambridge University Press, 1994); Doug McAdam, John D. McCarthy, and Mayer N. Zald, 'Introduction: Opportunities, Mobilizing Structures, and Framing Processes: Toward a Synthetic, Comparative Perspective on Social Movements', in McAdam, McCarthy, and Zald (eds), *Comparative Perspectives on Social Movements: Political Opportunities, Mobilizing Structures, and Cultural Framings* (Cambridge: Cambridge University Press, 1996), 1–20. See also Gould, *Moving Politics*, 14–15. See also Jeff Goodwin, James M. Jasper, and Francesca Polletta (eds), *Passionate Politics: Emotions and Social Movements* (Chicago: University of Chicago Press, 2001).

[108] 'Remembering Ed Muskie', *PBS Newshour* (26 March 1996) <http://www.pbs.org/newshour/bb/remember-jan-june96-muskie_03-26/> accessed 18 March 2014.

[109] Raymond Hernandez, 'Tears Are Shed at the White House for a Marine's Bravery in Iraq', *New York Times* (12 January 2007), B3.

Fig. 29 The Weeping Presidential Candidate? Edmund Muskie in a Snowstorm, 26 February 1972

Source: Corbis: U1731490; original caption: 'Manchester, New Hampshire: Muskie Rakes Publisher. Front-running Democratic presidential primary candidate Sen. Edmund Muskie (R) of Maine, campaigns in the snow, Feb 26th, in front of the *Union Leader*—New Hampshire's largest newspaper. He lashed out at the paper's publisher, William Loeb' © Bettmann/Corbis.

more tears than you can count, as president';[110] it did his popularity no harm at all. What changed between Muskie and Bush? Why was Muskie thought weak and unreliable for crying, and Bush was not? What are the boundaries upon the public expression of emotion, how does this boundary change, and why? What is the role played here by the gender, age, ethnicity, and religion of a politician?

It is also worthwhile examining political vocabulary from the standpoint of the history of emotion. The Introduction to this book touched on the use of emotionally coded language and action by diplomats. What happens with demonstrative anger, 'one of the most effective tactical resources, especially in the course of parliamentary business'?[111] Or during a memorial service, party congresses, meetings of monarchs, imperial marriages, and political stump speeches, addressing rabbit breeders or parish councils? What about the brand of politics that has emerged in the wake of the emotional turn, such as demonstrations and actions

---

[110] Robert Draper, *Dead Certain: The Presidency of George W. Bush* (New York: Free Press, 2007), 418.

[111] Christophe Prochasson, 'Le Socialisme des indignés: Contribution à l'histoire des émotions politiques', in Anne-Claude Ambroise-Rendu and Christian Delporte (eds), *L'Indignation: Histoire d'une émotion (XIXe–XXe siècles)* (Paris: Nouveau Monde, 2008), 173–90, here 174. See also Christophe Prochasson, *L'Empire des émotions: Les Historiens dans la mêlée* (Paris: Demopolis, 2008).

Fig. 30 The Crying President: George W. Bush, 11 January 2007

Source: Caption: 'Tears run from the eyes of U.S. President George W. Bush during a ceremony in honor of Medal of Honor winner Marine Cpl. Jason Dunham in the East Room of the White House in Washington, January 11, 2007. Cpl. Dunham was killed when he jumped on a grenade to save fellow members of his Marine patrol while serving in Iraq. REUTERS/Jim Bourg (UNITED STATES)' © JIM BOURG/X90054/Reuters/Corbis

of the 'International Parade of the Politically Depressed', 'Depress-ins', 'networks of desperation', and so on? What about the Chicago Feel Tank to which Deborah Gould belonged, and which often deliberately and ironically used emotional language?[112]

Ultimately of interest are 'those emotions that are decisive in motivating action in a political context'; but they are extremely inaccessible, and will for the most part remain a minor part of historical research.[113] If sources and means could be found to investigate them—one suggestion will be made at the end of this chapter—then one would obtain an emotional foundation for causal explanations of political decision-making.

---

[112] 'Feeltank Chicago' <http://feeltankchicago.net/01.html> <http://politicalfeeling.uchicago.edu/>; Jason Foumberg, 'Don't Fear the Reaper: The Museum of Contemporary Phenonmena Confronts the Angst of our Age', *Newcity Art* (September 2008) <http://art.newcity.com/2009/09/08/dont-fear-the-reaper-the-museum-of-contemporary-phenomena-confronts-the-angst-of-our-age/>; 'Pathogeographies', *Feel Tank* <http://pathogeographies.net/> all accessed 18 March 2014.

[113] José Brunner, editorial in *Politische Leidenschaften: Zur Verknüpfung von Macht, Emotion und Vernunft in Deutschland*, Tel Aviver Jahrbuch für deutsche Geschichte, 38 (Göttingen: Wallstein, 2010), 9. See also Alf Lüdtke, 'Emotionen und Politik: zur Politik der Emotionen', *Sozialwissenschaftliche Informationen/SOWI*, 30/3 (2001), 4–13.

Economic History and Emotions

The Wall Street Crash of 1929 had catastrophic consequences (the Great Depression; some even argue also the Second World War and the Holocaust), but its causes are still obscure. The causes of banking and economic crises in other countries (Japan 1927, Germany 1931, Great Britain 1931) are clear, but economists and economic historians still puzzle over the American crash. Paul Krugman has questioned how such a small cause could have such great effects, and the former chairman of the Federal Reserve, Ben Bernanke, has said that 'to understand the Great Depression is the Holy Grail of macroeconomics'.[114]

The economic historian Harold James has now deciphered the panic selling of shares and the collapse of the Dow Jones on 24 October 1929. James suggests that in panics like this, memories of similar catastrophic events surface, and combine with contemporary events. The confrontation with uncertainty appears to prompt a need for some kind of historical foothold; but by orienting their actions to the assumed historical precedent (past collapses of stock and commodity exchanges), actors just make everything worse, since no one crash is like another. James goes on:

> The historical reference is, in other words, a continuous and necessary driver of financial crises: in euphoric states, people are prepared to imagine futures that they can paint in utopian terms; when the euphoria collapses, they pick up memories of past disasters (that they may never have personally witnessed).[115]

With the Great Crash of 1929, the present mingled primarily with memories of the crash that happened on 24 September 1869, a Friday. The shadow of this past event hung over the present to such an extent that, by allusion, the crash on 24 October 1929, a Thursday, became known as 'Black Friday'.[116] And it was the same with every crash after 1929: in 1987, 2000, and 2008 the worst day of the crisis was qualified as 'black'. It is therefore typical of collective situations of crisis, like financial crashes, that meaning is sought in the past, and 'a febrile, temporal imagination' develops which blends differing temporalities.[117]

Classical writers in economic sociology were already aware that the economy often has little to do with what is commonly understood as 'rationality'. Max Weber, whom most people would associate with the concept of rationalization and the 'iron cage' of the modern bureaucracy and the working world, did not only write about piety and emotion, as we have seen in Chapter One. Ute Frevert has noted that 'if one examines Weber more closely, he turns out to be an analyst who did not neglect the power of emotions in modern capitalism to create values and

---

[114] Harold James, '1929: The New York Stock Market Crash', *Representations*, 110/1 (2010), 129–44, here 132–3.

[115] James, '1929: The New York Stock Market Crash', 140.

[116] James, '1929: The New York Stock Market Crash', 140.

[117] Jan Plamper and Benjamin Lazier, 'Introduction: The Phobic Regimes of Modernity', *Representations*, 110/1 (2010), 58–65, here 64. See also Benjamin Lazier and Jan Plamper, 'Introduction' in Plamper and Lazier (eds), *Fear: Across the Disciplines* (Pittsburgh: University of Pittsburgh Press, 2012), 9.

guide behaviour'.[118] 'Did he not', she asks, 'take account of the way in which the modern capitalist economic and social order was entirely based upon "affect", and that "acquisitive greed", "agonal passions" and "temperamental values" were genuine motivations for economic subjects?'[119]

During Weber's lifetime, the comparatively young psychological sciences began to take an interest in the emotions of industrial workers. A study based on a questionnaire given to over five thousand workers showed that affects related to disengagement predominated, and that a typical reaction to modern machine production was 'revulsion'.[120] One metalworker, who as a young man had worked in a domestic workshop, said that

> When machines took over my work, with foundries and mills employing between eighty and a hundred men, you can imagine how it feels if you have worked for forty-two years without such a din, and then suddenly there is so much racket and noise that it gets on an old man's nerves. I sweat all day long, feel anxious. Often I cry like a small child, and I can't sleep at night any more. I leave a light burning at night now, that helps me with my feelings.[121]

We can see here not only the possibilities for a history of the psychology of work and emotions, but also the outlines of a combined history of labour and emotion.[122]

What also seems very promising is to deal with consumption from the perspective of the history of emotions.[123] Advertising specialists developed early on an interest in the functions of mood and emotion, and set out to explore them.[124] There is great potential here in the development of the advertising business. Source material can also be found in the media products it has developed, posters and TV advertising, street advertising and web strips, decorated hot-air balloons, and leaflets distributed by people in foam costumes. Here the interconnection with the media history of emotions is quite plain. Also of great fascination is the connection to all forms of political 'advertising': from National Socialist propaganda to 'visual agitation' under real existing socialism to political advising in the TV democracies of the late twentieth centuries. What can be said about the role of emotion in the forerunners of public relations and political propaganda, from Gustave Le Bon to

---

[118] Ute Frevert, 'Gefühle und Kapitalismus', in Gunilla Budde (ed.), *Kapitalismus: Historische Annäherungen* (Göttingen: Vandenhoeck & Ruprecht, 2011), 50–72, here 51.

[119] Frevert, 'Gefühle und Kapitalismus', 50.

[120] Frevert, 'Gefühle und Kapitalismus', 54.

[121] Frevert, 'Gefühle und Kapitalismus', 54–5.

[122] Sabine Donauer, 'Job Satisfaction statt Arbeitszufriedenheit: Gefühlswissen im arbeitswissenschaftlichen Diskurs der siebziger Jahre', in Pascal Eitler and Jens Elberfeld (eds), *Eine Zeitgeschichte des Selbst* (Bielefeld: Transcript, forthcoming)

[123] On envy and consumption see Susan J. Matt, *Keeping Up with the Joneses: Envy in American Consumer Society, 1890–1930* (Philadelphia: University of Pennsylvania Press, 2003); on shopping see Erika Diane Rappaport, *Shopping for Pleasure: Women in the Making of London's West End* (Princeton: Princeton University Press, 2000); for criticism of consumption and shopping as topics of study, see Daniel Miller, *The Dialectics of Shopping* (Chicago: University of Chicago Press, 2001).

[124] See the project of Anne Schmidt, who is working on the history of emotions and advertising in the twentieth century at the Max Planck Institute for Human Development, Berlin.

The History of Emotions

Paul Bernays and on to Joseph Goebbels? What kind of psychological and other emotional resources did Charles de Gaulle's and Ronald Reagan's image-makers draw upon?

Legal History and Emotions

Hugo Münsterberg (1863–1916), a German-American psychologist, father of the lie-detector, and student of Wilhelm Wundt, took a close interest in the Dreyfus Affair in France, which was motivated by anti-Semitism. In 1894 the Jewish artillery captain Alfred Dreyfus was accused of passing secret military information to the Germans. Münsterberg noted that when the conspirators

> sought to manufacture evidence against him, they made much of the fact that he trembled and was thus hardly able to write when they dictated to him a letter in which phrases of the discovered treasonable manuscript occurred. Much of that which the police and the delinquents call the third degree consists of these bodily signs of a guilty conscience; to make the accused break down from his own inner emotion is the triumph of such maladministration of law.[125]

The physical movements of an accused person—in this case, shaking hands—were thought to provide indications of his inner emotions, and ultimately of his guilt or innocence.[126] As this example shows, the expression of physical emotion—at least in late nineteenth- and early twentieth-century France—had a fixed place in criminal procedure.

But combining legal and emotional history is not a possibility first presented in the late nineteenth century, and not only for France. Many sources on legal disputes talk of attacks on honour and insults—from offending a sovereign to procedures between private persons.[127] Sources dealing with marital disputes and the distribution of property after divorce are saturated with emotion.[128] And there are statutes that are exclusively concerned with emotions, such as crimes of passion. As with the use of drugs or alcohol, emotions can be used to mitigate punishment. If the history of emotion were to apply itself to the law and legal history, it could link up with an increased interest in emotion among lawyers themselves.[129]

---

[125] Hugo Münsterberg, *On the Witness Stand: Essays on Psychology and Crime* (New York: Doubleday, 1908), 115.

[126] Dreyfus maintained that his hands were shaking from the cold, but this was discounted; the physical sign was interpreted as being objective; Ruth Harris, *The Man on Devil's Island: Alfred Dreyfus and the Affair that Divided France* (New York: Penguin Books, 2010), 16.

[127] For Austria-Hungary: Philip Czech, *Der Kaiser ist ein Lump und Spitzbube: Majestätsbeleidigung unter Kaiser Franz Joseph* (Vienna: Böhlau, 2010); for Russia towards end of the Tsarist regime, Boris Kolonitskii, *'Tragicheskaia erotika': Obrazy imperatorskoi sem'i v gody Pervoi mirovoi voiny* (Moscow: Novoe Literaturnoe Obozrenie, 2010).

[128] Reddy, *Navigation of Feeling*, pt. 2.

[129] See the conference 'Law and the Emotions: New Directions in Scholarship', Berkeley (8–9 February 2007), as well as a preceding meeting in May 1998 at the University of Chicago Law School, its proceedings published in Susan A. Bandes (ed.), *The Passions of Law* (New York: New York University Press, 1999).

284

Media History and Emotions

In the early evening of Halloween in 1938, the American radio station CBS broadcast the play *The War of the Worlds*, a story by H. G. Wells from 1898 in which extraterrestrial beings invaded the earth. Orson Welles had adapted the story for radio and changed the location from England to New Jersey. The play was so realistic, and the comparatively new medium of radio was taken so seriously, that very many listeners rang up the station in a panic asking for more exact information about this attack from Mars.[130]

This example illustrates the importance of the media in the emotional history of modernity. Existing studies of the media can be used, seeking to operationalize its leading principle: media are more than containers that transport information; the structural properties of a medium shape the forms and mechanisms of the production of meaning. Many historians share this idea when dealing with literary products, that conventions of genre have a major influence on the production of meaning. They distinguish, for instance, between the behaviour-modifying intentions of a self-help guide and the way in which a crime thriller aims at tension and pleasure. But we have only just begun to transfer this insight to the study of mass media and emotions.[131]

It is certainly not enough to dub some media products 'emotional'—the treatment of Nazism on the History Channel, for instance—as though emotions can be switched on and off, and there is no more to be said than that.[132] Film and media studies, together with media philosophy, have probably gone furthest in considering emotions and their relation to the structural properties of a medium. The philosopher Christiane Voss sees the viewer in the cinema as a 'filmic surrogate body':

> My thesis is that it is only the spectator's body, in its mental and sensorial-affective resonance with the events on-screen, which (as I described earlier) 'loans' a three-dimensional body to the screen and thus flips the second dimension of the film event over into the third dimension of the sensing body. The spectator thus becomes a temporary 'surrogate body' for the screen, and this body is, for its part, a constituent feature of the filmic architecture.[133]

---

[130] Werner Faulstich, *Radiotheorie: Eine Studie zum Hörspiel 'The War of the Worlds' (1938) von Orson Welles* (Tübingen: Narr, 1981). Although there were stories of a mass hysteria across America, this did not in fact take place.

[131] Frank Bösch and Manuel Borutta (eds), *Die Massen bewegen: Medien und Emotionen in der Moderne* (Frankfurt am Main: Campus, 2006). See also Oliver Grau and Andreas Keil (eds), *Mediale Emotionen: Zur Lenkung von Gefühlen durch Bild und Sound* (Frankfurt am Main: Fischer Taschenbuch Verlag, 2005).

[132] On this also Barbara Rosenwein, *Emotional Communities in the Early Middle Ages* (Ithaca, NY: Cornell University Press, 2006), 1: 'a particularly simplistic notion of the emotions that makes passions not so much different from age to age as either "on" (impulsive and violent) or "off" (restrained)'.

[133] Christiane Voss, 'Film Experience and the Formation of Illusion: The Spectator as "Surrogate Body" for the Cinema', *Cinema Journal*, 50/4 (2011), 136–50, here 145. See also Christiane Voss, *Narrative Emotionen: Eine Untersuchung über Möglichkeiten und Grenzen philosophischer Emotionstheorien* (Berlin: de Gruyter, 2004).

This involvement of the viewer goes far beyond the idea that the film is a kind of stimulus to which the viewer responds. As a surrogate body the viewer participates, for example, in enormous chronological discontinuities in the film narrative, while 'we may regret the fact that our aesthetic entanglement will de facto soon end—at the latest when the lights go on again and the obligatory 90 to 120 minutes of real time in the movie theater are over'.[134]

Voss defines emotions as narrative phenomena. They need 'a certain period of time before all their components can be brought together'. It is also true that 'complex emotions display a sequential and not random character, having a particular dramatic structure'.[135] Films can have a very great impact upon us, since they involve the surrogate bodies of the viewer in parallel narrative emotions that are no longer read as representations, but are felt as one's own. According to Voss, borrowing from Aristotle, emotions always have a cognitive dimension. It is for this reason that cinema audiences do not completely involve themselves in what happens on the screen, but retain the sense of a separate self. But this 'background feeling, that one is sitting in the cinema and has a life whose complexity is far greater than that of the cinema' reinforces narrative and emotional involvement while the film is playing.[136]

Historians would certainly lend greater weight to other factors, for example, the historicity of audience reaction (in what culture, at what time, and from which gender is one expected to cry watching a melodrama?) and mutual influence (how does the presence of other feeling bodies in the cinema affect one's own feeling?). Nonetheless, a study like that of Christiane Voss gives a sense of what might be gained if historians of emotion took the properties of media into account.

Moreover, different media are thought to have different properties when it comes to education and conditioning. At different times in history soldiers have been prepared for battle through the use of media. It is certainly no coincidence that at a particular time it is one particular medium that is chosen. Soldiers were prepared for the Vietnam War with films; today, preparation for war is done with computer games and simulations. This implies that these media are thought to be more effective than others available in the given context (prose, poetry, marching songs). On the other hand, the use of film makes it easier to create a distance with respect to one's own use of violence: 'One part of me was doing something while the other part watched from a distance, shocked by the things it saw, yet powerless to stop them from happening', in the words of Philip Caputo, describing how he had killed Vietcong.[137]

The study of media scandals would especially benefit from the inclusion of emotion as a factor.[138] Besides this, the changing repertoire of reception is a

---

[134] Voss, 'Film Experience and the Formation of Illusion', 145.

[135] Christiane Voss, 'Die leibliche Dimension des Mediums Kino', in Bösch and Borutta (eds), *Die Massen bewegen*, 63–80, here 77.

[136] Voss, 'Die leibliche Dimension des Mediums Kino', 79.

[137] Philip Caputo, *A Rumor of War* (New York: Holt, Rinehart and Winston, 1977), 306.

[138] Daniel Siemens, 'Sensationsprozesse: Die Gerichtsreportage in der Zwischenkriegszeit in Berlin und Chicago', in Bösch and Borutta (eds), *Die Massen bewegen*, 142–71.

rewarding field of study for the history of emotion. Ol'ga Kuptsova, a scholar of Russian theatre, has written that in the eighteenth century audience reaction corresponded to the range of fifteen emotions typical of the Baroque period, and which the actors themselves employed. This changed with the spread of sensibility towards the end of the century. The public reactions began to diverge widely. While at one place they would sigh loudly or sob, others maintained the norm of keeping their emotions to themselves, and betrayed no external emotion at all. It took the broad dissemination of writings by well-known authors, such as the writer Nikolai Gogol and the critic Vissarion Belinskii, to unify the emotional reactions of theatre audiences on some kind of normative plane. Gogol dreamed of a public as a holistic collective body, 'who suddenly all share the same amazement, shed the same tears and are able to laugh one big collective laugh'.[139] Belinskii wrote of a performance of *Hamlet* in 1839: 'all these people with different titles, personalities, likes, tastes, genders, and different ages, and different education merge into a great mass, occupied with one thought, one feeling'.[140] During the second half of the nineteenth century, Russian theatre audiences did for the most part correspond to these ideas. They had learned from Gogol and Belinskii to align their expression of emotion to one common denominator.

Tabloid journalism, radio, film, TV, Internet—the sources for an emotionally inflected history of the media are many and various. A media history of this kind could shed new light on the existing history of emotions. It would be possible to ask what distinguished emotional communities à la Barbara H. Rosenwein, constituted exclusively through media, from those which were based on face-to-face contact. What changes have been brought about by modern mass media since the Middle Ages that Rosenwein studied? What weight should be given to the possibility of real-time communication over long distances?

Oral History, Memory, and Emotions

1.1 I: well, there was this woman, helga.

1.2 P: . . . I remember . . . the long dining table. it was something like a youth hostel

1.3 somehow I realized, (.) eh, (.) there is something bright between us

1.4 I think this entire thing with falling in love was easily like that for me. (pause) uhmm,

1.5 (pause) now with finding someone especially beautiful or something, that always only

1.6 comes later. initially, it is a feeling.

1.7 actually quite similar (.) to my very first, (.) eh, (.) erotic (.) experience

1.8 this woman and I, we did, we sat on the (.) sofa . . . and we

1.9 talked about something. (.) and, (laughs briefly)

[139] Ol'ga Kuptsova, ' "Ekzazheratsiia chuvstv": Osobennosti emotsional'nykh reaktsii russkoi teatral'noi publiki 1830-1840-kh godov', in Jan Plamper, Schamma Schahadat, and Marc Elie (eds), *Rossiiskaia imperiia chuvstv: Podkhody k kul'turnoi istorii emotsii* (Moscow: Novoe Literaturnoe Obozrenie, 2010), 131–43, here 136.

[140] Kuptsova, ' "Ekzazheratsiia chuvstv" ', 139.

1.10 and suddenly we look at each other and, and, and start and (.) get closer to each
      other
1.11 like that and start to (.) like (.) kissing each other
1.12 I can't actually explain it, really. I, (.) I wasn't in love with this woman,
1.13 . . . later, I was, but, . . . that has really, (.) really (.) at (.) tacked me
1.14 or so . . . it just happened like that, well (.) it is INexplicable to me . . . like, why
      that now
1.15 with THIS women in THIS moment, like, without me thinking, oh, you would
      like that at
1.16 some point or even, I do find her, (.) that I am feeling also something MORE,
      not just
1.17 a friend or so. All of that was NOT THERE AT ALL.
1.18 that's how it was, in the BROADEST SENSE with the other woman, too . . .
1.19 first looking, well, who is that and how do I like her . . . do I think she is then
1.20 also pretty . . . and then as well, that gazes started (.) to cling to each other like
      that . . .
1.21 and then you also realize (.) that the other one is looking, too.
1.22 that's how it was (.) with helga.[141]

History is sometimes said to be necrophiliac or necromantic because, unlike anthropology and the life sciences, it deals exclusively with the dead. Of course, this is not entirely true, because oral history is a part of contemporary history, and there have been some first attempts to move this into the history of emotion. Benno Gammerl recorded long interviews with seventeen men and fifteen women who identified themselves as gays or lesbians and who had responded to his call for testimonies of same-sex love, as part of his project 'Feeling Different: Homosexuality and Emotional Life in the West German Countryside (1960–1990)'. The interviews took the following form: on the first day a biographical narrative was established through interview, while on the second the subjects were interviewed according to set guidelines and questions. As the long quotation shows, the transcription of the interviews took account of emphasis and other prosodic characteristics—(.) means a short pause of about one second, and (pause) a longer pause.

Hence the oral history of emotions conforms to the elaborate rules of qualitative social research. First of all, it marks itself off from any starting assumption that if one allows people to speak directly then one gets closer to what has 'really been experienced'. Instead, as Gammerl emphasizes, it is especially in oral statements about what had been felt in the past that the basically irrecoverable nature of 'lived experience' becomes evident.

[141] Benno Gammerl, 'Erinnerte Liebe: Was kann eine Oral History zur Geschichte der Gefühle und der Homosexualitäten beitragen?', *Geschichte und Gesellschaft*, 35/2 (2009), 314–45, here 324–5; English translation of pseudonymized passages from the transcript: Mrs Fischer, interview 2, sequence 613: Benno Gammerl, 'Same Sex Intimacies in Transition', *History of Emotions—Insights into Research* (October 2013) <https://www.history-of-emotions.mpg.de/en/texte/same-sex-intimacy-in-transition> accessed 18 March 2014. (.) means a short pause of about one second, and (pause) a longer pause.

Accounts of recalled feelings make especially clear the lack of a distinction between objectivity and subjectivity. Even with current emotional experiences the interpretation of the psychophysical tangibility of feelings can hardly be separated off from their subjective value, 'inner' experience from 'external', sociocultural frameworks. Biographical accounts are just as ambiguous, or various, as feelings. They do not allow any definitive statement to be made about what the historical actors really felt.[142]

Contrary to the idea of a radical narrative construction of reality, Gammerl adheres to the 'plausibility' of contemporary statements made about memories of emotions during interviews. He regards a memory as plausible 'when there is a correspondence between the content and the narrative structure of a story'; when the way in which a contemporary witness talks—there is sophisticated linguistic and literary scholarship on this—corresponds with what he or she says.[143] Moreover, as a whole, biographical storytelling provides insights into 'self-fashioning', the self-representation of subjects in the interview process, and this in turn permits 'deductions to be made about the origins and development of these identities and the particular manner in which the narrating subject puts him- or herself together'.[144] And last of all, the way in which the interviewer and interviewee relate to sociocultural contexts can be more or less in tune. If, for instance, the interviewees are from a group of males who, in the early 1980s, were influenced by New Age and therapeutic cultures, while the interviewer is poorly acquainted with codes, patterns of speech, and metaphors drawn from this context but otherwise known from other sources, the dissonances that arise are themselves worth exploring.

As with oral history in general, the oral history of emotions raises in particular the question of representativeness. In choosing his interviewees Gammerl of course sought to ensure that they reflected as much as possible the full range of ways of life of West German rural homosexuals during the period of his study. It is not the aim of such a study to establish once and for all whether among West German gays in 1980 love or desire (think of 'hedonism' in gay culture) dominated, or whether the experience of AIDS in the mid-1980s was characterized by fear, grief, or anger. The attraction was much more in the detail: the 'ehs', 'uhmms', and emphases, conveying the fluid, ephemeral, hard-to-pin-down aspect of emotions. It is as though the feedback loops can be examined with a magnifying glass—missing verbs, the overwriting of a co-present emotion by the verbal expression of another—processes which Reddy himself has worked through theoretically, but which he cannot render so vividly with his sources in judicial history as can oral history.

The oral history of emotions also throws up the question of the relation between emotion and memory. To be sure, the neurosciences increasingly concern themselves with 'emotional memory'.[145] There is also the study of trauma which takes its

---

[142] Gammerl, 'Erinnerte Liebe', 317. [143] Gammerl, 'Erinnerte Liebe', 317–18.
[144] Gammerl, 'Erinnerte Liebe', 318.
[145] On neurosciences and emotional memory see Kevin S. LaBar and Roberto Cabeza, 'Cognitive Neuroscience of Emotional Memory', *Nature Reviews Neuroscience*, 7/1 (2006), 54–64; Ulrike Rimmele, Lila Davachi, Radoslav Petrov, Sonya Dougal, and Elizabeth A. Phelps, 'Emotion Enhances the Subjective Feeling of Remembering, Despite Lower Accuracy for Contextual Details', *Emotion*, 11/3 (2011), 553–62. A historical study of the politics of memory and the Holocaust that

inspiration from psychoanalysis, and this has been broadly accepted by historians. But however problematic it is to formulate a categorical distinction between 'then' and 'now'—between the experience of an emotion and the memory of an emotion, between falling in love and later writing down how one fell in love, between a murder done with a kitchen knife in a fit of rage and the handing down of a sentence mitigated by 'affect'—these lapses of time are sometimes considerable, and have so far hardly been considered in the history of emotions. It was for this reason that the anthropologist Signe Howell argued that Reddy paid no attention to the lapse of time when talking about his *emotives*. The emotion-saturated documents of a judicial process do not contain any *emotives*, no direct emotional speech act, but written records of them set down some time later. There are several intermediary instances between the speech act and its record. In short, Reddy is insensitive to diachrony; he works just as synchronically as an anthropologist involved in participant observation.[146] Historians who might want to exploit the resources of oral history would thus be well advised to keep in mind this temporal difference between the experience of an emotion and its memory.

Historians as Emotional Beings

It is well known that Tacitus (*c.* AD 58–120) maintained that he had written his history of Rome under the emperors Augustus and Tiberius 'sine ira et studio' (without anger or zeal).[147] During the nineteenth century the 'non-partisan view', as Leopold von Ranke (1795–1886) called it, was described with 'changing words, but always maintaining that "passions and interests" be excluded, something which was of course easier with phenomena which were removed in time than with those that reached right into the present', as Rudolf Vierhaus (1922–2011) wrote about the founder of historicism.[148] In 1946, the British historian Robin George Collingwood (1889–1943) wrote that 'irrational elements', 'sensation as distinct from thought, feelings as distinct from conceptions', were the 'subject-matter of psychology ... but ... not parts of the historical process'.[149] History and emotion might belong together, but the writing of history and emotion were mutually exclusive—that is clear in all these quotes, however different the times in which they were written. A lack of passion is what is expected of historians—and this is not simply a

---

gives a central place to emotion is Ulrike Jureit and Christian Schneider, *Gefühlte Opfer: Illusionen der Vergangenheitsbewältigung* (Stuttgart: Klett-Cotta, 2010).

[146] See the response of Howell, 'Comment on William M. Reddy, Against Constructionism'.

[147] P. Cornelii Taciti, *Annalum ab excessu divi augusti libri: The Annals of Tacitus*, i, ed. Henry Furneaux (2nd edn, Oxford: Clarendon Press, 1896), 180.

[148] Rudolf Vierhaus, 'Rankes Begriff der historischen Objektivität', in Vierhaus, *Vergangenheit als Geschichte: Studien zum 19. und 20. Jahrhundert*, ed. Hans Erich Bödeker, Benigna von Krusenstjern, and Michael Matthiesen (Göttingen: Vandenhoeck & Ruprecht, 2003), 358–69, here 361. See also Jörn Rüsen, 'Emotional Forces in Historical Thinking: Some Metahistorical Reflections and the Case of Mourning', *Historein: A Review of the Past and Other Stories*, 8 (2008), 41–53, here 42.

[149] R. G. Collingwood, 'Human Nature and Human History', in Collingwood, *The Idea of History* (Oxford: Oxford University Press, 1946; repr. 1962), 231.

consequence of the stellar rise of objectivity to the status of a central category as history developed into a scientific discipline during the nineteenth century.[150]

Daniela Saxer has studied the strategies used to neutralize emotions by selected German-speaking Swiss and Austrian historians around the turn of the century, using their correspondence and diary entries. From this it becomes very clear that acquaintance with the past in sources does not only mean that passion and enthusiasm must be tamed. Historians working in the late nineteenth century did hear a great deal about the discovery of unknown treasures, and the 'resulting triumphal feelings'; but they were themselves trained using the major printed editions of sources. Recording, ordering, copying—these everyday activities for historians after the making of spectacular discoveries were described in their letters as 'boring', 'making one want to give up', 'mind-numbing', and 'horrible'.[151]

Besides collections of sources, young historians were initially trained in the late nineteenth century in the method of 'empathy'. Well into the 1870s, young historians had to complete exercises in writing in the style of ancient and medieval authors and their chronicles. This 'bridge of feeling into the past' was based on the idea that there was no fundamental difference between the historical actors, the historiographers who had written about them, and the student of history in the nineteenth century.[152] This idea of empathy and the formalized training based upon it was increasingly displaced by the growing claims of objectivity in historical writing towards the end of the century. There could be no compromise between empathy and objectivity. Around 1900, empathy was no longer part of historical training; young historians now had to 'intuit' the nature of empathy.[153]

Roughly around the same time a new wave of historians began to treat emotions themselves as the object of scholarly attention; in his lecture from 1917, 'Science As a Vocation', Max Weber directed a rhetorical question to them: 'do you think that you can bear to see for year after year mediocrity promoted over your head without becoming embittered and damaged?' And he added: 'I . . . have known of only very few who can tolerate it without doing themselves harm.'[154] The wearisome path to a tenured professorship which then permitted one to practise science as a vocation on a permanent basis found its compensation only, Weber suggested, in the excitement of scientific discovery. This concerned 'what one may call the "experience" of science. Without this particular frenzy which is ridiculed by every outsider, without this passion . . . one has no vocation for science and should do something else.'[155]

---

[150] Peter Novick, *That Noble Dream: The 'Objectivity Question' and the American Historical Profession* (Cambridge: Cambridge University Press, 1988).

[151] Daniela Saxer, 'Geschichte im Gefühl: Gefühlsarbeit und wissenschaftlicher Geltungsanspruch in der historischen Forschung des späten 19. Jahrhunderts', in Uffa Jensen und Daniel Morat (eds), *Rationalisierungen des Gefühls: Zum Verhältnis von Wissenschaft und Emotionen 1880–1930* (Munich: Fink, 2008), 79–98, here 90.

[152] Saxer, 'Geschichte im Gefühl', 92.   [153] Saxer, 'Geschichte im Gefühl', 95.

[154] Max Weber, 'Science As a Vocation', in Peter Lassman, Irving Velody, and Herminio Martins (eds), *Max Weber's 'Science As a Vocation'* (London: Unwin Hyman, 1989), 3–32, here 8.

[155] Weber, 'Science As a Vocation', 9.

The history of the relationship between those writing history and their own emotions has not been studied for the twentieth century. We only know that the emancipatory history of the 1960s and 1970s was to a great extent driven by the outrage and anger of young historians about the injustices of their own day— segregation in the American South and the Vietnam War. Even 'objectivity', a distanced lack of engagement, can have different intentions, functions, and aspects. In the works of the historian of the Holocaust Raul Hilberg (1926–2007), who fled the Nazis from Vienna in 1939 at the age of 13, one can sense what an enormous effort this reticence took—we sense a kind of engaged disengagement. Hilberg wrote that

> My training in the social sciences took place in the 1940s. The methodological literature that I read emphasized objectivity and neutral or value-free words. . . . I added charts and numbers, which added an air of cool detachment to my writing [of the book *The Destruction of the European Jews*]. I did yield to some temptations. Herman Wouk said to me that the work contained a suppressed irony, in other words, an irony *recognizably* suppressed.[156]

Hilberg sought inspiration in music:

> Writing, like music, is linear, but there are no chords or harmonies in literature. For this reason I concentrated more and more on chamber music, which is sparse, and in which I could hear every instrument and every note distinctly. The Schubert Quintet in C—a Germanic work—gave me the insight that power is not dependent on simple mass or even loudness, but on escalations and contrasts. Beethoven's *Appassionata*, that supreme achievement of piano music, which proves that one keyboard can be the equivalent of an orchestra, showed me that I could not shout on a thousand pages, that I had to suppress sonority and reverberations, and that I could loosen my grip only selectively, very selectively.[157]

After Hilberg came post-structuralism, which adopted a different form of distance—an ironic distance—between the historian and the object of study. In the past few years the complaint has been raised that the principles of post-structuralism could never make headway among the majority of historians because they were already overwhelmed by emotion, touch, and smell working with source material in the archives. The immediacy of excitement in the discoveries they made would always be stronger than the distancing strategies of post-structuralism. On top of this came 'Machiavelli's perception of conversing with the dead and being "received by them lovingly"'.[158] Others objected that the dominant emotion

[156] Raul Hilberg, *The Politics of Memory: The Journey of a Holocaust Historian* (Chicago: Dee, 1996), 87–8, emphasis added.

[157] Hilberg, *The Politics of Memory*, 85.

[158] Emily Robinson, 'Touching the Void: Affective History and the Impossible', *Rethinking History*, 14/4 (2010), 503–20, here 513. See also Arlette Farge, *The Allure of the Archives*, trans. Thomas Scott-Railton (New Haven: Yale University Press, 2013) [Fr. orig., *Le Goût de l'archive*, 1989]; see also the interview of Arlette Farge by Dominique Dupart and Claude Millet: 'Entretien avec Arlette Farge', *Écrire l'histoire: Dossier émotions*, 1 (2008), 89–95.

during archival work was boredom.[159] But whether being overwhelmed or bored, what is undisputed is that more self-reflection upon their emotions in archival work, and historical work in general, would do historians no harm. Here anthropology is way ahead of the study of history. Why should historians not keep a kind of fieldwork diary about their emotions during archival work?

5 PROSPECTS

So much for a few selected fields in which a future history of emotions can be written. This by no means exhausts all possibilities. A conceptual history of emotions could study the shifts of meaning in individual emotions such as fear over long periods,[160] as well as temporal changes in, say, 'German words for feeling' in general,[161] or in a particular source, for example, in dictionaries.[162] One could also explore the genealogy of national stereotypes of emotion and ask, for instance, where the ideas come from for the British 'stiff upper lip'; for *saudade*, a particular Portuguese form of listlessness; for the Russian *khandra*, a comparable kind of bittersweet melancholia tinged with idleness; or for the German *angst*.[163] What determines the stereotypes one applies to oneself and to others? Another interesting question along these lines would be: what about collective emotions, when bodies can at least see one another in a circumscribed space? The mutual affectation of bodies in a football stadium or at Nazi Party rallies has not yet been made into a topic of study for the history of emotions.[164] Only very preliminary work has been done so far on combining the study of nationalism with the history of emotion.[165]

---

[159] Benno Gammerl, 'Introduction: Emotional Styles—Concepts and Challenges', *Rethinking History*, 16/2 (2012), 161–75, here 171.

[160] Henning Bergenholtz, *Das Wortfeld 'Angst': Eine lexikographische Untersuchung mit Vorschlägen für ein großes interdisziplinäres Wörterbuch der deutschen Sprache* (Stuttgart: Klett-Cotta, 1980).

[161] Ludwig Jäger (ed.), *Zur historischen Semantik des deutschen Gefühlswortschatzes: Aspekte, Probleme und Beispiele seiner lexikographischen Erfassung* (Aachen: ALANO, 1988).

[162] Ute Frevert et al., *Emotional Lexicons: Continuity and Change in the Vocabulary of Feeling 1700–2000* (Oxford: Oxford University Press, 2014).

[163] On German *angst* see the interview with Frank Biess, 'Die Deutschen und ihre Krisen: "Angst war ein Leitmotiv"', *Der Stern* (26 February 2009) <http://www.stern.de/wirtschaft/news/maerkte/die-deutschen-und-ihre-krisen-angst-war-ein-leitmotiv-656061.html> accessed 19 March 2014; Frank Biess, ' "Everybody Has a Chance": Nuclear Angst, Civil Defence, and the History of Emotions in Postwar West Germany', *German History*, 27/2 (2009), 215–43; Frank Biess, 'Die Sensibilisierung des Subjekts: Angst und "neue Subjektivität" in den 1970er Jahren', *WerkstattGeschichte*, 49 (2008), 51–71.

[164] This kind of work could begin from Hans-Ulrich Thamer, 'The Orchestration of National Community: The Nuremberg Party Rallies of the NSDAP', in Günter Berghaus (ed.), *Fascism and Theatre: Comparative Studies on the Aesthetics and Politics of Performance in Europe, 1925–1945* (Providence: Berghahn Books, 1996), 172–90; Alf Lüdtke, 'Love of State—Affection for Authority: Politics of Mass Participation in Twentieth Century European Contexts', in Luisa Passerini, Liliana Ellena, and Alexander C. T. Geppert (eds), *New Dangerous Liaisons: Discourses on Europe and Love in the Twentieth Century* (New York: Berghahn Books, 2010), 58–74.

[165] Roger D. Petersen, *Understanding Ethnic Violence: Fear, Hatred, and Resentment in Twentieth-Century Eastern Europe* (Cambridge: Cambridge University Press, 2002); Karen Hagemann, 'Aus Liebe zum Vaterland: Liebe und Hass im frühen deutschen Nationalismus', in Birgit Aschmann (ed.), *Gefühl und Kalkül: Der Einfluss von Emotionen auf die Politik des 19. und 20. Jahrhunderts* (Cologne: Steiner,

Nor has the history of 'warmth' in the societies of real existing socialism yet been written.[166] Socio-economic explanations—that the states of the Eastern bloc were societies based on shortage, which made more intense and denser social communication necessary so as to compensate for the structural problems of provision—by no means exhaust what can be said about the emotion in the kitchen of a Soviet-era flat belonging to members of the intelligentsia, which today many recall with nostalgia. Besides that, there is virtually no comparative emotional history, although the specific quality of emotion is often best revealed through transnational comparison, or in longitudinal studies.[167]

Just as long as the list of possible fields for studying the history of emotion is that of the possible sources. In memoriam notices, the choreography of May Day in Moscow in 1939, the radio broadcast of the closing phases of the Football World Cup in Bern in 1954, normative texts such as laws or advice manuals, the interviews of oral history—these are all relevant to a history of emotion.[168] Photos and film of Protestants at worship in the 1960s, as well as photos, engravings, and written descriptions of religious rituals in the nineteenth century—for example, of the German Methodists in the mid-West of the United States, whose own sinfulness was 'felt' through Jacob's struggle with God, and which was expressed by trembling bodies and shrieking—all these can serve as sources.[169] Works of literature—from Laurence Sterne's *A Sentimental Journey through France and Italy* (1768), via Leo Tolstoy's *Sevastopol Sketches* (1887; Russ. orig., *Sevastopolskie rasskazy*, 1855), to Marcel Proust's *In Search of Lost Time* (1922–31; Fr. orig., *A la recherche du temps perdu*, 1913–27), right down to the 'penny dreadful'—are all good sources for the history of emotions. Besides written sources, there are visual and audio sources, even smell, which is usually connected to written texts—all of

2005), 101–23; Ronald Grigor Suny, 'Thinking about Feelings: Affective Dispositions and Emotional Ties in Imperial Russia and the Ottoman Empire', in Mark D. Steinberg and Valeria Sobol (eds), *Interpreting Emotions in Russia and Eastern Europe* (DeKalb: Northern Illinois University Press, 2011), 102–27; Nicole Eustace, *1812: War and the Passions of Patriotism* (Philadelphia: University of Pennsylvania Press, 2012); but also the early work of Thomas J. Scheff, *Bloody Revenge: Emotions, Nationalism, and War* (Boulder: Westview Press, 1994); Étienne François, Hannes Siegrist, and Jakob Vogel (eds), *Nation und Emotion: Deutschland und Frankreich im Vergleich, 19. und 20. Jahrhundert* (Göttingen: Vandenhoeck & Ruprecht, 1995).

[166] See Dale Pesmen, *Russia and Soul: An Exploration* (Ithaca, NY: Cornell University Press, 2000).

[167] Susanne Michl and Jan Plamper, 'Soldatische Angst im Ersten Weltkrieg: Die Karriere eines Gefühls in der Kriegspsychiatrie Deutschlands, Frankreichs und Russlands', *Geschichte und Gesellschaft*, 35/2 (2009), 209–48.

[168] For memoriam notices: Angela Linke, 'Trauer, Öffentlichkeit und Intimität: Zum Wandel der Textsorte "Todesanzeige" in der zweiten Hälfte des 20. Jahrhunderts', in Ulla Fix, Stephan Habscheid, and Josef Klein (eds), *Zur Kulturspezifik von Textsorten* (Tübingen: Stauffenberg-Verlag, 2001), 195–223; on the World Cup broadcast: Rudolf Oswald, 'Emotionale "Volksgemeinschaften": Das "Wunder von Bern" 1954 als Rundfunkereignis in Ungarn und Deutschland', in Bösch and Borutta (eds), *Die Massen bewegen*, 369–86; also on the gestures made by athletes: Angela Linke, 'Sprache, Körper und Siegergesten: Eine Skizze zur historischen Normiertheit von sprachlichem wie körperlichem Gefühlsausdruck', in Johannes Fehr and Gerd Folkers (eds), *Gefühle zeigen: Manifestationsformen emotionaler Prozesse* (Zurich: Chronos, 2009), 165–202.

[169] Pascal Eitler and Monique Scheer, 'Emotionengeschichte als Körpergeschichte: Eine heuristische Perspektive auf religiöse Konversionen im 19. und 20. Jahrhundert', *Geschichte und Gesellschaft*, 35/2 (2009), 282–313, esp. 296–304; Monique Scheer, 'Empfundener Glaube'.

these are most closely associated with emotions, and can be of significance for its history.[170] Images provide a broad spectrum, from instructions for the artistic depiction of affects by Leon Battista Alberti (1404–72) to the paintings themselves. The interpretation of the expression of emotion in one single painting—Mona Lisa's smile—at different times says a great deal about the cultural assumptions of those doing the interpreting.[171]

Finally, even the gaps and the silence of the sources can be productive: 'the absence of evidence is not necessarily evidence of absence'. Through what I would like to call a hermeneutics of silence, it might be possible to decode noise and rupture at the microlevel of language, as well as the ersatz discourse that has to stand in for emotional language when the description of emotions is taboo.[172] It is possible to go further conceptually towards psychoanalysis and talk about repression and the unconscious, but that seems neither necessary nor desirable given the theoretical and methodological problems with which one would then become involved. For example: assume that, while reading the description of a battle by a Russian officer—a familiar genre in the First World War—I come across a passage in which the depiction of the course of the battle suddenly no longer makes logical sense. As a historian who wants to understand the course and outcome of the battle, I can look for other sources, and find, perhaps from a soldier's memoir or an article by a psychiatrist based on the records of traumatized soldier, that at a certain point

---

[170] A few examples which link the history of the senses with the history of emotion: Alain Corbin, *Time, Desire and Horror: Towards a History of the Senses*, trans. Jean Birrell (Cambridge: Polity Press, 1995) [Fr. orig., *Le Temps, le désir et l'horreur*, 1991]; Daniel Wickberg, 'What Is the History of Sensibilities? On Cultural Histories, Old and New', *American Historical Review*, 112/3 (2007), 661–84; Alexander M. Martin, 'Sewage and the City: Filth, Smell, and Representations of Urban Life in Moscow, 1770–1880', *Russian Review*, 67/2 (2008), 243–74; Constance Classen, *The Deepest Sense: A Cultural History of Touch* (Urbana: University of Illinois Press, 2012).

[171] On Mona Lisa see Zirka Z. Filipczak, 'Poses and Passions: Mona Lisa's "Closely Folded" Hands', in Gail Kern Paster, Katherine Rowe, and Mary Floyd-Wilson (eds), *Reading the Early Modern Passions: Essays in the Cultural History of Emotion* (Philadelphia: University of Pennsylvania Press, 2004), 68–88. See also Claudia Schmölders, 'Affekte', in Uwe Fleckner, Martin Warnke, and Hendrik Ziegler (eds), *Handbuch der politischen Ikonographie*, i. *Abdankung bis Huldigung* (Munich: Beck, 2011), 29–35. Early on Norbert Elias sought to establish in medieval paintings the boundary of what was thought to be distressing; Norbert Elias, *The Civilizing Process: Sociogenetic and Psychogenetic Investigations*, trans. Edward Jephcott, ed. Eric Dunning, Johan Goudsblom, and Stephen Mennell (rev. edn, Oxford: Blackwell, 2010) [Ger. orig., *Über den Prozeß der Zivilisation*, 2 vols, 1939], 173–80.

[172] See also Barbara Rosenwein, who after writing 'Read the silences', states: 'Some sources are unemotional in tone and content. These are as important as overtly emotional texts. Emotional communities generally avoid some emotions while stressing others. Or they avoid certain emotions in particular contexts. This is all grist for the historian's mill'; Barbara H. Rosenwein, 'Problems and Methods in the History of Emotions', *Passions in Context: International Journal for the History and Theory of Emotions* [online journal], 1 (2010) <http://www.passionsincontext.de> accessed 19 March 2014. Hermeneutics of silence has nothing to do with Lucian Hölscher's concepts, 'the semantics of emptiness' and the 'hermeneutics on non-understanding'; the former relates to the import of the number zero from Indian and Arabic linguistic culture into the European measurement of time in the thirteenth century, and so connected to a conception of an open future; the latter to the irreducible 'otherness' of human action in the past, which nonetheless has to be theorized; Lucian Hölscher, 'Semantik der Leere', in Hölscher, *Semantik der Leere: Grenzfragen der Geschichtswissenschaft* (Göttingen: Wallstein, 2009), 13–32; Lucian Hölscher, 'Hermeneutik des Nichtverstehens', in Hölscher, *Semantik der Leere*, 226–39.

on the battle the soldiers panicked and ran in a different direction from the one in which they were supposed to. This led to an unexpected turn in the battle—and then to the logical holes in the description of the battle by the officer.

But if I have neither the soldier's memoir, nor the article written by the military psychiatrist, the outcome of the battle will remain a puzzle. Here we need new methods. First of all, I could reconstruct so far as was possible the local emotional culture(s); in this case, collecting information about the generic conventions of descriptions of battle. In so doing I would discover that the depiction of fear—and in particular collective fear that ended in panic—was a taboo subject in descriptions of the battles of the First World War. In addition to this, I would need to put together information on emotional constructs, if possible according to rank, religion, and ethnicity. Then I would reread the text of the officer very carefully. Is there ersatz language—comments on the weather, or long descriptions of a soldier who repeatedly cleaned his weapon? Does this disturb the inner logic of the text; is there, for instance, a sudden and unexpected shift in tempo; does a preposition appear that is not used in the remainder of the text; does the author undermine the logic of his narrative? If other writings by the same officer are available, then the methods of literary studies might be useful, such as stylometric software with which the authenticity of a text can be checked, so that it can be determined whether one particular text was really written by this author. Such software compares texts, and can show whether a particular word or use of a comma in a phrase occurs for the first time in a passage.[173]

At the conclusion of the contextual and reconstructive work I would assume that, at the point where the officer's description of the battle breaks down logically, there should be a description of the soldiers' panic. The outcome of the battle would now be understandable. This would be a relatively reliable method of reading between the lines. Certainly, this kind of method involves an analytical leap. But it would be a far more transparent leap than most historians make when they make casual use of conceptions of emotion from their own time and apply them to the past, and so fall into the trap of anachronism.

---

[173] See the freeware programme The *Signature* Stylometric System (by Peter Millican) or JGAAP (the Java Graphical Authorship Attribution Program by Patrick Juola).

Conclusion

In the foregoing I have sought to create some kind of order in the study of the history of emotions. I have put all of its pieces in place. Others might have arranged them differently, and the components will continue to be shifted around. I am writing during a boom in the history of emotions; there is gold rush fever in the air.[1] So, once more, how did it all come to this?

Looking back, we can say: if there is a starting point for this boom, then it would be 11 September 2001, an event that catalysed a process already under way. Even before this date one could sense a general dissatisfaction with post-structuralism, and a new hunger for 'authentic reality', but 9/11 was like a reality shock that made old categories and concepts redundant, obsolete. 'Experience' had become regarded as a moribund category; it now underwent a thoroughgoing revival. Historians sought to revive 'an idea of experience as a pretheorized, prediscursive, direct encounter with others, with society, or with the past'.[2] To cite only a few prominent instances: in 2005 the medievalist Gabrielle Spiegel wrote that 'the new master concepts in post-linguistic turn historiography' were 'experience and practice'. Among other issues, at stake was a 'new conceptualization of the body, no longer seen as an "instrument" used by an agent in order to act, but the place where mental, emotional, and behavioral routines are inscribed'.[3] In 2009 Lynn Hunt, one of the leading historians of the French Revolution, published an essay with the significant title 'The Experience of Revolution', in which she argued that it was necessary to switch 'the text or linguistic metaphor for the social, the cultural, and the historical'. But with what, one might ask? '[I]f I knew with what, I would tell you', Hunt wrote with disarming honesty.[4] Her own investigations ran through Antonio Damasio's conception of embodiment: 'The world is not just discursively constructed. It is also built through embodiment, gesture, facial expression, and feelings, that is, through nonlinguistic modes of communication that have their own logics.' And: 'The rational and the emotional cannot be clearly separated, and

[1] Nina Verheyen, 'Geschichte der Gefühle, Version: 1.0', *Docupedia-Zeitgeschichte* (18 June 2010) <http://docupedia.de/docupedia/index.php?title=Geschichte_der_Gef%C3%BChle&oldid=74436> accessed 19 March 2014.

[2] Harold Mah, 'The Predicament of Experience', *Modern Intellectual History*, 5/1 (2008), 97–119, here 99. The best-known example of this revival is Frank Ankersmit, *Sublime Historical Experience* (Stanford, CA: Stanford University Press, 2005).

[3] Gabrielle M. Spiegel, 'Introduction' in *Practicing History: New Directions in Historical Writing after the Linguistic Turn* (New York: Routledge, 2005), 18, 19.

[4] Lynn Hunt, 'The Experience of Revolution', *French Historical Studies*, 32/4 (2009), 671–8, here 674.

the latter is essential to the functioning of the former.'[5] Other examples could be cited, all of which can be said to share a search 'for an objective way out of the crisis of objectivism', in the words of Václav Havel.[6]

Hence 9/11 promoted a retreat from the linguistic turn, a retreat which in part took shape as a new emotional turn. In other disciplines, this went along with borrowings from the neurosciences, which had by the late 1990s become leading forces in the world of science. Apart from isolated examples, the history of emotions has yet to come under the influence of the neurosciences. Why that is a good thing, and why casual borrowings from the neurosciences are dangerous, should by this stage be clear: most historians know too little about the neurosciences to be capable of telling which hypotheses are plausible, which results are correct, and which are false. One can resort to popularizers like Damasio, but as a rule they present one striking finding from their own laboratory and use it to claim authorship of the sole valid theory. Apart from anything else, by the time such popularizing work gets published it is, often enough, already obsolete, given the lapse between what happens in laboratories and the representation of this in best-sellers.

There is, in principle, nothing against borrowing from the neurosciences. One just has to apply oneself, and read more than popular texts; read individual research papers as well as meta-analyses that review a wide range of papers. One need not be bashful, the technical vocabulary is easier to master than one would think; there is no need to engage in formal training. Even a modest investment of time can prove worthwhile, since most historians have so little idea about the neurosciences, nor of how far the latter have already penetrated American and European literary and visual studies. Trashing psychoanalysis is a respectable pastime among historians, since the discipline has still not fully recovered from the psychohistory of the 1970s. But the danger lies elsewhere: we need to guard against simplistic adaptations of the neurosciences. The epistemologies of the neurosciences and of history work according to different rules. In the former, causality, variables, internal, external, and ecological validity are important watchwords. Results are often only thought to have substance if the experiments from which they come can be frequently replicated; that repetition under the same conditions leads to the same results. For this reason, natural scientists are much more used to a rapid turnover of 'truths'. It is not for nothing that Nobel Prizes are awarded sometimes decades

---

[5] Hunt, 'The Experience of Revolution', 674, 673; on Damasio's influence on her work, 673 n. 5. Or again: 'New studies of emotion and over the embodiment of the self indicate a way out of this reduction of experience to discursive and social constructions'; 'to leave space for universals, however small it may be, means the radical rejection of social and cultural constructivism'; Lynn Hunt, 'Kulturgeschichte ohne Paradigmen?', *Historische Anthropologie*, 16 (2008), 323–40, here 337, 338. On Damasio: see Hunt, 'Kulturgeschichte ohne Paradigmen?', 339–40. Hunt has employed these insights in her study of human rights, *Inventing Human Rights: A History* (New York: Norton, 2007), in which she, as summarized by a critic, argues 'that certain sensual or embodied "experiences" of the late eighteenth century, including reading epistolary novels and viewing pictures in public exhibitions, gradually produced actual, physiological changes in French men's and women's brains that resulted in two collective psychological developments: an increase in the feeling of individual autonomy and an increase in empathy with unknown others'; Sophia Rosenfeld, 'Thinking about Feeling, 1789–1799', *French Historical Studies*, 32/4 (2009), 697–706, here 703.

[6] Vaclav Havel, 'The End of the Modern Era', *New York Times* (1 March 1992), section 4, 15.

after a discovery has been made. Historians who make use of neuroscientific findings should always keep these different temporalities in mind. For example, the Somatic Marker Hypothesis really is only a hypothesis, and neuroscientists would not lose any sleep if it were overthrown, as presently seems to be the case. For those working in the social sciences and humanities who are building interpretations and entire theories upon this foundation, it would be a rude awakening, however, if it turned out that the Somatic Marker Hypothesis was false. For neuroscientists there is really only true or false. Any other science that borrows from this source must also adopt this logic. Arguments like 'a reading which I personally find very exciting' or something similar will just not cut it. And any such openness of interpretation would undermine the new search for a 'solid reality' which has driven the human and social sciences to the neurosciences.

This is all very familiar to a small but growing multidisciplinary group—from the neurosciences, the social sciences, and the humanities—who set out to build 'critical neurosciences'. At present, areas of common endeavour are being developed, and this book has introduced three of these: neuroplasticity, the social neurosciences, and the functional integration of the brain. If this work continues and its foundations are really as solid as it presently appears, then there will be potential for cooperation with historians.

Since the nineteenth century the study of emotion has turned upon a polarity between social constructivism and universalism. While duly sceptical of all turns and fashions, and the current hunger for reality, even radical social constructivism has tossed up genuine problems. The impossibility of using meta-concepts—nominalism—would mean the end of scholarship, at least as we have known it. But in fact most social constructivists do not actually practise any radical social constructivism. Take an example raised earlier in this book, the medieval Icelandic sagas. When, in the thirteenth-century *Brennu-Njáls saga*, Thorhall Asgrimsson hears of the murder of his foster-father, 'his body swells up, blood flows from his ears, and he faints'.[7] We can all understand fainting, the swelling of the body is more problematic, but blood flowing from your ears when you get angry? Radical social constructivism would have to take the position that in the Middle Ages it was normal for blood to come out of one's ears in fits of rage, and that the boundaries of the body went beyond those which we imagine today. But from all that we know today about bodies it is clear that this is impossible, and could not have been possible in the thirteenth century. No evolutionary development over seven centuries is going to produce such a serious physiological change. Quite unconsciously, we treat the body here as an absolute limit. And we make implicit assumptions like this all the time: we constantly extrapolate current phenomena, the world as-is, even when we do not notice that we are doing so.

Social constructivism and universalism—this dichotomy also shapes the architecture of this book. But our declared aim was to move beyond this structure and open up perspectives on the study of emotion 'beyond the couch', to one last time

---

[7] William Ian Miller, *Humiliation: And Other Essays on Honor, Social Discomfort, and Violence* (Ithaca, NY: Cornell University Press, 1993), 102.

use Lorraine Daston's image of the need for collective psychotherapy. This is needed if a scientific discipline is to finally break out of the binary opposition of nature to culture. What will happen if psychotherapy fails? If a course of therapy has to be terminated, then there is only one thing to do: find a new therapist and start all over again.

Glossary

affect a bodily event (or as others would have it, intensity) usually considered autonomous, non-signified through language or other corporeal signs, and unconscious. Thus defined, affect precedes and is not influenced by intentionality, evaluation, volition, ideology, and cognitive operations in general.

affect programme a set of physical reactions (e.g. facial muscle movements) and ways of behaving prompted by external emotional stimuli. Associated with basic emotion paradigm.

affective neuroscience term to describe neuroscience on emotion. Coined in 1998 by neuroscientist Jaak Panksepp.

amygdala almond-shaped groups of subcortical nerve cells in both hemispheres of the brain; by many neuroscientists thought to be the site of negative emotions, esp. fear.

apatheia in ancient Greek Stoic philosophy, an emotionless or calm state that leads towards utmost tranquillity, *ataraxia*.

appraisal instantaneous (or nearly) evaluation of an emotional stimulus as good or bad for one's well-being. Typical of cognitive psychological approaches to emotion.

apraxia inability to carry out learned purposeful movements.

ataraxia in ancient Greek Stoic philosophy, a state of pure happiness or tranquillity to be attained by *apatheia*.

basic emotions paradigm that posits the existence of a set of cross-cultural emotions usually associated with distinct facial micro-expressions that 'leak' through display rules, e.g. sadness that can be read (with a special method of decoding muscle movements) through a mask of happiness in a social situation that requires people to seem happy. In 1992 six emotions were considered basic emotions: happiness, anger, disgust, fear, sadness, and surprise. Paradigm associated with psychologists Silvan S. Tomkins and, more recently, Paul Ekman.

Begriffsgeschichte field of historiography pioneered by Reinhart Koselleck et al. that studies shifts in meanings of concepts (*Begriffe*) such as 'liberty' or 'nation'. In its early incarnation, a precursor to linguistic turn and post-structuralism in that it clung to the belief that a 'hard' non-linguistic reality exists.

behaviouralism/behavioural psychology school of psychological thought particularly popular in the mid-twentieth century and represented by B. F. Skinner et al. United by belief (contra psychoanalysis) that psychology should exclusively concern itself with observable behaviour, not with hidden psychic processes. Saw emotion as part of human behaviour based on physiological reflex.

biofeedback a way to train physiological processes, such as heart rate or pain perception, by watching an instrument record these processes. To illustrate, when confronted with an unpleasant auditory stimulus (e.g. the sound of a siren), the subject learns to bring heart rate back to normal by observing it on a monitor.

biopower or biopolitics mechanisms of governing modern populations not by brute force but through subtle techniques, such as profiling them socially and ethnically in a census and then shaping discriminatory social policy on that basis. Terms associated with philosopher and historian Michel Foucault.

bio-revolution turn-of-the-millennium New Economy biotechnology boom linked with the general emergence of the life sciences as the leading discipline not only in the natural sciences (instead of physics), but also in the humanities.

BOLD contrast (blood-oxygen-level dependent contrast) in fMRI, measures changes in the oxygen content of blood in the brain, and on that basis draws conclusions about neuronal activity. Based on the knowledge that red blood cells have differing magnetic properties according to their oxygen content.

cogmotion signifies the inseparability of cognition and emotion. Term introduced by the psychologists Douglas Barnett and Hilary Horn Ratner.

cognitive psychology school of psychological thought since the 1960s that considers emotions as forms of cognition. Most models of emotion from cognitive psychology include a dimension of appraisal, in which an object (e.g. the snake in the woods) is evaluated (e.g. positive? negative? past experience associated with object?).

constative an utterance that describes the world, e.g. 'The grass is green'. Term coined by linguist John Austin.

core affect a multistage model of emotion developed by psychologists James Russell and Lisa Feldman Barrett. The initial stage is a core affect that has a merely hedonic valence (good to bad) and an intensity (strong to weak). Core affect is always present in living human beings. Only at later stages do signification, object-relatedness, and consciousness come into play, and only then can we speak of 'emotion'. In other words, emotions as such do not exist. The initial stage of core affect is not unlike philosopher and affect theorist Brian Massumi's 'pure intensity'.

cortex/cortical large structure in upper part of brain thought to have developed in evolution later than limbic system. Considered responsible for complex cognition, language, memory, and consciousness.

critical neuroscience loose coalition of neuroscientists, social scientists, and humanities scholars, united by a belief in the promises of neuroscience but sceptical towards facile usage with claims that extend far beyond the reach of the experiments. Tries to work beyond the nature v. culture divide. Term from a network of scholars founded in the late 2000s and coordinated from Berlin.

culturally contingent culturally conditioned, culturally relative, culturally specific, anti-determinist, malleable.

Default Mode Network (DMN) brain activity thought to be related not to immediate tasks of an experiment but to more long-term goals. Also associated with the brain's resting state and, more generally, with the emerging idea of a brain that is constantly active. Discovered in the late 1990s.

display rules social norms that shape the physical expression of emotions, esp. the facial expression. To illustrate, display rules can prohibit the showing of anger on a face, but micro-expressions (facial movements) will 'leak' the underlying anger anyway. Term associated with basic emotion paradigm of Silvan Tomkins, Paul Ekman et al. Arguably, display rules map onto the nature v. culture binary, basic emotion representing nature and display rules culture.

domain area of knowledge over which a life science or social science makes a statement.

ecological validity extent to which results of an experiment also apply outside the laboratory in a natural environment.

electroencephalography (EEG) technique of measuring and visualizing brain activity. Has the advantage of a better temporal resolution than fMRI but a worse spatial resolution; in other words, can show the brain's reaction to an external emotional stimulus with less of a time lag than fMRI but is not as precise in locating the site of that reaction in the brain.

emic/etic insider perspective on a culture (emic) v. an outsider perspective (etic). Terms from anthropology.

emotional labour management of feeling in the workplace, esp. in jobs that stipulate the actual feeling, not just the display, of an emotion. If this emotion is not felt, 'emotional dissonance' develops. The same kind of emotional management in a private context, without exchange value, is called emotion work. Concept developed by sociologist Arlie Hochschild.

Emotional Command Systems (ECS) universal neurochemical processes that lead to advantages in survival. The ECS 'search', 'fear', 'rage', and 'desire' are located in the deepest regions of the brain in and around the brain stem. These ECS are responsible in humans and animals for basic activities, such as dealing with threats or reproduction. Other ECS in higher, but still subcortical regions of the brain regulate simple social behaviour ('panic', 'care', 'play') involving social ties and fear of separation. Concept developed by neuroscientist Jaak Panksepp.

emotional community postulates that people live in these, i.e. people share with others in their 'community' (variously defined) certain emotional norms, valuations, and styles of expression. Each community may be a relatively small social group, such as a court or monastery; but equally a whole society may be considered an emotional community, although with some variant groups within it. There are normally many emotional communities at any one time. Term coined by historian Barbara Rosenwein.

emotional habitus concept which draws on sociologist Pierre Bourdieu's habitus, a set of mental and physical dispositions and habits acquired primarily through mimetic learning in a certain sociocultural milieu. The term 'emotional habitus' (arguably redundant) has been used to denote more specifically culturally expected and habituated patterns of feeling. Historical anthropologist Monique Scheer has suggested that emotions are not located in the body (as in the basic emotion paradigm) nor the mind (as in cognitive approaches) but in the habitus, which represents the socially conditioned body-and-mind.

emotional intelligence the capacity to understand and adequately react to emotions in others. Concept developed by psychologists John Mayer and Peter Salovey, popularized by psychologist Daniel Goleman.

emotional navigation the handling of *emotives* in an emotional regime. Term coined by historian William Reddy.

emotional liberty successful emotional navigation following out of a strong correspondence between an emotional regime and *emotives*, or, ultimately, between an emotional regime and the way in which emotions work in the human brain. Term coined by historian William Reddy.

emotional practices a concept developed by historical anthropologist Monique Scheer, who defines them as 'manipulations of body and mind to evoke emotions where there are none, to focus diffuse arousals and give them an intelligible shape, or to change or remove emotions already there'. Scheer builds on Pierre Bourdieu's practice theory and distinguishes between mobilizing, naming, communicating, and regulating emotional practices.

emotional refuge practices or institutions that allow for more emotional liberty than the dominant emotional regime. They help make emotional navigation more successful in an emotional regime that is otherwise hardly compatible with the way in which emotions function. Term coined by historian William Reddy.

emotional regime prescribed *emotives* with attendant rituals and other symbolic practices that prop up a political regime. All political regimes are also emotional regimes. Term coined by historian William Reddy.

emotional suffering suffering resulting from difficult emotional navigation because of lack of emotional liberty and emotional refuges. Caused, for instance, by emotional regimes that demand constant authenticity in emotional expression and thus do not correspond to real functioning of emotions, which always involves open-endedness and ambiguity. Ultimately caused by architecture of the brain which sets limitations on the way in which emotions work. Term coined by historian William Reddy.

emotionology dominant emotional norms that can be accessed via, e.g. advice literature on how to feel. What was actually felt (emotional experience) can be studied through first-person sources (e.g. diaries, letters). Changes in the emotional norms and dissonance between new norms and actual feelings will thus become apparent. Term coined by historian Peter Stearns and psychiatrist Carol Zisewitz Stearns.

emotive a (usually verbal) expression of an emotion that both describes the emotion (e.g. 'I am happy') and enacts a change not only in others but also upon that emotion by starting an open-ended self-exploratory process (e.g. by questioning one's happiness—is a co-present emotional state, such as sadness, not dominant?—or by overwriting co-present emotional states, amplifying the experience of happiness). An utterance possessing the qualities both of John Austin's constative and performative. Term coined by historian William Reddy.

essentialism/essentialist belief in a hard core of reality that exists independent of language, culture, and society. To 'de-essentialize' means making the construction of reality transparent—and thus showing the futility of essentialism.

ethnocentrism excessive concentration on one culture, nation, ethnic group, etc.

Extended Mind Theory (EMT) strand of philosophy, neuroscience, and related fields that emphasizes the distribution of cognition and consciousness throughout the entire body, not just in the mind or brain, in interaction with the exterior environment.

external validity results of an experiment that can be generalized, that are valid beyond the narrow confines of the experiment.

FAST (Facial Action Scoring Technique; later known as **FACS, Facial Action Coding System)** method developed and patented by psychologists Paul Ekman and Wallace Friesen for the analysis of facial muscle movements. Measurement technique for the basic emotions paradigm.

feeling rules social norms regulating the expression of emotion. When feeling rules and actual feelings do not correspond, 'emotional dissonance' arises. Term of sociologist Arlie Hochschild.

functional integration the interaction of various areas of the brain during brain function. Opposite of functional segregation/specificity.

functional magnetic resonance imaging (fMRI) neuroimaging technique with high spatial resolution.

functional segregation/specificity the notion that one area of the brain is active (and ultimately responsible) for one function. Associated with scans from neuroimaging (e.g. fMRI) that only show one active area through colouring. Opposite of functional integration.

hedonic valence the quality of an emotion on a spectrum of positive to negative.

hexis the bodily aspects of habitus (subconscious structures of thinking and acting in accordance with a social position), e.g. the professor's manner of crossing legs when seated in an armchair. Concept of sociologist Pierre Bourdieu.

hypercognized/hypocognized anthropologist Robert Levy's terminology to describe emotions prioritized (hypercognized) or downplayed (hypocognized) by a given culture. e.g. happiness = hypercognized in contemporary US culture.

intentionality/intentionalism diverse issue in (analytical) philosophy and other fields that, for emotions, concerns the existence of a dimension of volition, evaluation, or belief in the appraisal of emotion objects. Concept important in the thought of historian of science, Ruth Leys, and her critique of affect theory and basic emotion paradigm.

internal validity the coherence of an experiment—can the causal connection of variables be proven?

intersubjective relational, different persons interacting. Opposite of autonomous or individualistic conceptions of human action.

lateralization difference in brain function according to hemisphere (left or right).

lesion damage to, and hence the dysfunction of, specific areas of the brain. Important in neuroscience if a particular zone ceases to function, and at the same time abnormal behaviour is observed, the damaged area is assumed responsible for the dysfunction (and correspondingly, for its function in healthy individuals). One of the first cases of lesion method was Phineas Gage in 1848.

life sciences umbrella term for psychology, physiology, medicine, neurosciences, and related disciplines. The term dates to the 1980s as an extension of the more restricted sense of 'biology', introducing other fields that deal with living organisms, such as cognitive psychology, brain research, or computer-based neurological research.

limbic system subcortical brain area held to be evolutionarily old and comprising, among other things, the hippocampus, amygdala, and fornix. Thought to be responsible for the oldest, survival-related emotions, such as fear.

linguistic turn a late 1970s–early 1980s shift towards regarding language as the primary focus of historical analysis. Belief that linguistic formation of reality is primary and that there is no access to a prelinguistic essence. Associated with post-structuralism, postmodernism, and social constructivism.

logocentrism excessive concentration on verbal (written and oral) utterances.

magnetoencephalography (MEG) technique of measuring and visualizing brain activity. Has the advantage of a better temporal resolution than fMRI but a worse spatial resolution.

metaconcept term that describes a thing other than the thing itself, term that is referential in referring to something outside itself, e.g. describing the Ifaluk *nunuwan* as 'emotions' is to use 'emotion' as a metaconcept. In other words, an analytic category rather than everyday speech.

micro-expressions results of muscle movements in the face that involuntarily express authentic basic emotions. Will shine through social norms (display rules) and can be decoded with Facial Action Scoring Technique. Part of psychologist Paul Ekman's basic emotion paradigm.

mirror neurons special class of brain nerve cells thought to be responsible for mimicking the bodily movements of others in monkeys and of higher cognitive functions such as compassion in humans.

neuron nerve cell found in the brain. The basic operation of a neuron is to send electrical impulses, so-called 'firing'.

neuroplasticity ability of the brain to produce new nerve cells and to form connections between these (or existing, older) nerve cells throughout the lifespan. Recent hypothesis that many humanities scholars place hope in because it promises to make possible the inscription of history, culture, etc. into the brain, thus de-essentializing it.

new cultural history school of history-writing popular during 1980s and associated with emphasis on language and symbols in cultural construction of reality. Often considered successor to social history popular during 1960s and 1970s (after political history's eclipse). Influenced by linguistic turn and post-structuralism, esp. Michel Foucault. Name from 1989 landmark collection *The New Cultural History*, ed. Lynn Hunt.

new materialism/vitalism Post-post-structuralist theory seeking to conceptualize matter as lively and to endow it with agency, to arrive at a 'harder' notion of reality, and to downplay consciousness when it comes to defining entities (from things to small-scale organisms to human animals) that act in the world. Influenced by phenomenology, affect theory, etc. Driven partly by bio-revolution.

nominalism the exclusive usage of everyday or 'local' language (e.g. 'affection', 'sentiment', 'passion' in various periods) and concomitant renunciation of metaconcepts (e.g. 'emotion' for various periods).

performative an utterance that enacts a change upon the world, e.g. 'I will' at the registry office during a marriage ceremony. Term coined by linguist John Austin.

positron emission tomography (PET) neuroimaging technique involving coloured radioactive markers. Has the advantage of high spatial resolution and the disadvantage of emitting potentially harmful radioactive material.

post-structuralism/post-structuralist blanket term for theoretical approaches associated with uncertainty of meaning and construction of reality. Often used synonymously with 'postmodernism/postmodernist' and the 'postmodern condition' (Jean-François Lyotard, 1979). Emerged in 1970s and 1980s and is linked with theories of Jacques Derrida, Michel Foucault et al.

practice theory/praxeology approaches in social and cultural theory which seek to mediate between social structures and individual social action, to link the macro- and micro-levels of analysis. One of the important practice theorists is Pierre Bourdieu.

psychohistory school of history-writing associated with emphasis on the psychological dimension of historical actors, processes, and events. Popular during 1970s. Often criticized for ahistorically superimposing concepts from psychoanalysis etc. onto people from times and cultures in which psyches might have been shaped differently; and for not managing the difficult leap from the individual to the collective.

rasa aesthetic theory organizing emotional expression in India since antiquity. Primarily related to dance theatre. Each *rasa* is associated in dance theatre with a particular facial expression, a hand gesture, a colour, and a divinity.

qualia subjective, conscious experience. Experimental psychology seeks to access this data through self-report (e.g. via questionnaires or interviews).

reductionism pejorative term used by some humanities scholars when commenting on the experimental designs of psychology and other sciences. Refers to the reduction of reality to a small number of dependent and independent variables.

replicability the ability of an experiment to furnish the same results if repeated under exactly the same conditions.

Schachter–Singer model a model of emotion that posits the variable cognitive evaluation of physical emotion signs. Shortness of breath, for example, can thus be interpreted as fear, excitement, or sexual arousal. Also known as a synthetic cognitive-physiological model because it neither claims that emotions *are* physical signs nor that they are only cognitions. Developed by psychologists Stanley Schachter and Jerome Singer in the late 1950s.

sensorimotor neurons a class of nerve cells responsible for movements. (Alternatively spelled as sensory motor or sensory-motor neurons.)

situated cognition theory in neuroscience, philosophy, literary criticism, and related fields that holds that cognitive function does not just happen in the brain, but in relation with other humans beings, the larger environment, etc.

social constructivism or **constructionism/constructivist** or **constructionist** posits that reality (including emotion) is malleable because constituted by society, culture, and esp. language, rather than pre-existing in an essentialist fashion.

social neuroscience neuroscience based on experiments with more than one individual. Attempt to do justice to the relational nature of human subjectivity.

social psychology school of psychological thought premised on relational situatedness of individual. Influenced by sociology.

Somatic Marker Hypothesis (SMH) posits that higher cognitive processes such as decision-making are simplified, accelerated, and improved by emotional signals in the body. Based on Iowa Gambling Task (IGT) experiment. Developed by neuroscientist Antonio Damasio et al.

structuralism in various fields of knowledge, the belief in underlying deep structures that can be uncovered, e.g. through linguist Ferdinand de Saussure's or anthropologist Claude Lévi-Strauss's methods. Especially popular during 1960s and 1970s.

subcortical areas of the brain below the cortex (e.g. limbic system is subcortical). Thought to have developed earlier in evolution than the cortex.

transcranial magnetic stimulation (TMS) technique of measuring and visualizing brain activity. Has the advantage of a better temporal resolution than fMRI but a worse spatial resolution.

two roads to fear hypothesis that posits the existence of a fast (12-millisecond) path to fear via the amygdala that activates the body in a state of alarm (for fight-or-flight reactions) after a stimulus (e.g. a snake in the woods) is perceived. Meanwhile, neurochemical reactions travel in double the time to the cortex where cognitive operations take place (e.g. is the snake alive? Is it a poisonous snake?). Concept developed by neuroscientist Joseph LeDoux.

universalism/universalist belief in universal existence of phenomena or patterns in all cultures and all times. Often also associated with determinism, essentialism, hard-wiring, or an unchanging, basic, solid, and hard nature.

Select Bibliography

NB: The bibliography is based on English-language titles up until late 2011. Post-2011 titles are included here for reference only. The same goes for some titles published up until 2011: they were added after crowdsourcing calls in spring 2014 via the email-lists HIST-EMOTION and H-EMOTIONS. As a rule, if a chapter from a book (e.g. an edited volume) was used, only the title of the book is listed.

1 BOOK SERIES

Emotions and States of Mind in East Asia, Brill, eds Paolo Santangelo and Cheuk Yin Lee.
Emotions in History, Oxford University Press, eds Ute Frevert and Thomas Dixon.
Emotions of the Past, Oxford University Press, eds Robert A. Kaster and David Konstan.
History of Emotions, University of Illinois Press, eds Peter N. Stearns and Susan Matt.
Palgrave Studies in the History of Emotions, Palgrave Macmillan, eds David Lemmings and
    William M. Reddy.

2 JOURNALS

Emotion Review <http://emr.sagepub.com/> accessed 2 April 2014.
Passions in Context: International Journal for the History and Theory of Emotions <http://
    www.passionsincontext.de> accessed 2 April 2014.

3 BLOGS

Anderson, Michael, 'After Phrenology: Will We Ever Understand the Brain?', *Psychology
    Today* <http://www.psychologytoday.com/blog/after-phrenology> accessed 16 March
    2014.
Australian Research Council's Centre of Excellence for the History of Emotions, *Histories of
    Emotion: From Medieval Europe to Contemporary Australia* <http://historiesofemotion.
    com/> accessed 2 April 2014.
Dixon, Thomas, and Jules Evans (eds), *The History of Emotions Blog*, Queen Mary Centre
    for the History of the Emotions <http://emotionsblog.history.qmul.ac.uk/> accessed 5
    December 2013.
Greene, Michelle, *NeurRealism* <http://neurealist.blogspot.de> accessed 16 March 2014.
Hickok, Greg, and David Poeppel (moderators), *Talking Brains: News and Views on the
    Neural Organization of Language* <http://www.talkingbrains.org> accessed 5 December
    2013.
*The Neurocritic: Deconstructing the Most Sensationalistic Recent Findings in Human Brain
    Imaging, Cognitive Neuroscience, and Psychopharmacology* <http://neurocritic.blogspot.de>
    accessed 16 March 2014.
'Neuroskeptic', *Discover* <http://blogs.discovermagazine.com/neuroskeptic/> accessed 5
    December 2013.
Pessoa, Luiz, *Emotion & Cognition and the Brain* <http://cognitionemotion.wordpress.com>
    accessed 5 December 2013.

4 WEBSITES

Amsterdam Centre for Cross-Disciplinary Emotion and Sensory Studies, *ACCESS* <http://access-emotionsandsenses.nl/> accessed 10 April 2014.

Australian Research Council's Centre of Excellence for the History of Emotions, <http://historiesofemotion.com/> accessed 2 April 2014.

Critical Neuroscience Network <http://www.critical-neuroscience.org> accessed 5 December 2013.

Feel Tank, *Pathogeographies* <http://pathogeographies.net/> accessed 6 January 2014.

History of Emotions Working Group, Berkeley, *History of Emotions* <http://hoe-berkeley.squarespace.com/> accessed 5 April 2014.

Laukötter, Anja, and Margrit Pernau (eds), History of Emotions: Insights into Research, Centre for the History of Emotions at the Max Planck Institute for Human Development <http://www.history-of-emotions.mpg.de/en> accessed 5 December 2013.

Paul Ekman Group LLC <http://www.paulekman.com> accessed 5 December 2013.

Università degli Studi di Roma 'La Sapienza', Facoltà di Studi Orientali, *Emotions in History and Literature: An Interdisziplinary Research on Emotions and States of Mind in Ming-Qing China* <http://w3.uniroma1.it/santangelo/emotions.htm> accessed 9 April 2014.

5 HISTORY

Arnold, John H., 'Inside and Outside the Medieval Laity: Some Reflections on the History of Emotions', in Miri Rubin (ed.), *European Religious Cultures: Essays offered to Christopher Brookes on the Occasion of his Eightieth Birthday* (London: Institute of Historical Research, 2008), 107–30.

Bantock, G. H., 'Educating the Emotions: An Historical Perspective', *British Journal of Educational Studies*, 34/2 (1986), 122–41. doi: 10.2307/3121322

Barker-Benfield, G. J., *The Culture of Sensibility: Sex and Society in Eighteenth-Century Britain* (Chicago: University of Chicago Press, 1992).

Barker-Benfield, G. J., *Abigail and John Adams: The Americanization of Sensibility* (Chicago: University of Chicago Press, 2010).

Biess, Frank, '"Everybody Has a Chance": Nuclear Angst, Civil Defence, and the History of Emotions in Postwar West Germany', *German History*, 27/2 (2009), 215–43.

Blauvelt, Martha Tomhave, 'The Work of the Heart: Emotion in the 1805–1835 Diary of Sarah Connell Ayer', *Journal of Social History*, 35/3 (2002), 577–92. doi: 10.1353/jsh.2002.0003

Boddice, Rob, 'The Affective Turn: Historicising the Emotions', in Cristian Tileagă and Jovan Byford (eds), *Psychology and History: Interdisciplinary Explorations* (Cambridge: Cambridge University Press, 2014), 147–65.

Bourke, Joanna, *Fear: A Cultural History* (London: Virago, 2005).

Bracke, Maud Anne, 'Building a "Counter-Community of Emotions": Feminist Encounters and Socio-Cultural Difference in 1970s Turin', *Modern Italy*, 17/2 (2012), 223–36. doi: 10.1080/13532944.2012.665283

Broomhall, Susan (ed.), *Emotions in the Household, 1200–1900* (Basingstoke: Palgrave Macmillan, 2008).

Broomhall, Susan, and Jacqueline van Gent, 'Corresponding Affections: Emotional Exchange among Siblings in the Nassau Family', *Journal of Family History*, 34/2 (2009), 143–65. doi: 10.1177/0363199008330734

Bullard, Alice, 'Sympathy and Denial: A Postcolonial Re-reading of Emotions, Race, and Hierarchy', *Historical Reflections*, 34/1 (2008), 122–42. doi: 10.3167/hrrh2008.340108

Cairns, Douglas [L.], 'Honour and Shame: Modern Controversies and Ancient Values', *Critical Quarterly*, 53/1 (2011), 23–41. doi: 10.1111/j.1467-8705.2011.01974.x

Carrera, Elena (ed.), *Emotions and Health, 1200–1700*, Studies in Medieval and Reformation Traditions (Leiden: Brill, 2013).

Castillo, Greg, 'Making a Spectacle of Restraint: The Deutschland Pavilion at the 1958 Brussels Exposition', *Journal of Contemporary History*, 47/1 (2012), 97–119.

Chandler, James, 'Moving Accidents: The Emergence of Sentimental Probability', in Colin Jones and Dror Wahrman (eds), *The Age of Cultural Revolutions, Britain and France, 1750–1820* (Berkeley and Los Angeles: University of California Press, 2002), 137–77.

Chaniotis, Angelos (ed.), *Unveiling Emotions*, i. *Sources and Methods for the Studies of Emotions in the Greek World*, Heidelberger althistorische Beiträge und epigraphische Studien 52 (Stuttgart: Steiner, 2012).

Chaniotis, Angelos, and Pierre Ducrey (eds), *Unveiling Emotions*, ii: *Emotions in Greece and Rome: Texts, Images, Material Culture*, Heidelberger althistorische Beiträge und epigraphische Studien 55 (Stuttgart: Steiner, 2013).

Clark, Elizabeth B., '"The Sacred Rights of the Weak": Pain, Sympathy, and the Culture of Individual Rights in Antebellum America', *Journal of American History*, 82/2 (1995), 463–93.

Classen, Constance, *The Deepest Sense: A Cultural History of Touch* (Urbana: University of Illinois Press, 2012).

Cook, Hera, 'Emotion, Bodies, Sexuality and Sex Education in Edwardian England', *Historical Journal*, 55/2 (2012), 475–95. doi: 10.1017/S0018246X12000106

Cook, Hera, 'Getting "Foolishly Hot and Bothered"? Parents and Teachers and Sex Education in the 1940s', *Sex Education*, 12/5 (2012), 555–67. doi: 10.1080/14681811.2011.627735

Cook, Hera, 'From Controlling Emotion to Expressing Feelings in Mid-Twentieth-Century England', *Journal of Social History*, 47/3 (2014), 627–46. doi: 10.1093/jsh/sht107

Corbin, Alain, *The Village of Cannibals: Rage and Murder in France, 1870*, trans. Arthur Goldhammer (Cambridge, MA: Harvard University Press, 1992) [Fr. orig., *Le Village des cannibals* (1990)].

Corbin, Alain, *Time, Desire and Horror: Towards a History of the Senses*, trans. Jean Birrell (Cambridge: Polity Press, 1995) [Fr. orig., *Le Temps, le désir et l'horreur* (1991)].

Costigliola, Frank, '"Unceasing Pressure for Penetration": Gender, Pathology, and Emotion in George Kennan's Formation of the Cold War', *Journal of American History*, 83/4 (1997), 1309–39. doi: 10.2307/2952904

Costigliola, Frank, '"I Had Come as a Friend": Emotion, Culture, and Ambiguity in the Formation of the Cold War, 1943–1945', *Cold War History*, 1/1 (2000), 103–28. doi: 10.1080/713999913

Costigliola, Frank, *Roosevelt's Lost Alliances: How Personal Politics Helped Start the Cold War* (Princeton: Princeton University Press, 2012).

Crozier-De Rosa, Sharon, 'Popular Fiction and the "Emotional Turn": The Case of Women in Late Victorian Britain', *History Compass*, 8/12 (2010), 1340–51. doi: 10.1111/j.1478-0542.2010.00743.x

de Luna, Kathryn M., 'Affect in Ancient Africa: Historical Linguistics and the Challenge of "Emotion Talk"', in Gian Claudio Batic (ed.), *Encoding Emotions in African Languages* (Munich: Lincom Europa, 2011), 1–16.

de Luna, Kathryn M., 'Affect and Society in Precolonial Africa', *International Journal of African Historical Studies*, 46/1 (2013), 123–5.

deMause, Lloyd (ed.), *The History of Childhood* (New York: Harper & Row, 1974).

deMause, Lloyd, *Foundations of Psychohistory* (New York: Creative Roots, 1982).

Dixon, Thomas, 'The Tears of Mr Justice Willes', *Journal of Victorian Culture*, 17/1 (2011), 1–23. doi: 10.1080/13555502.2011.611696

Earle, Rebecca, 'Letters and Love in Colonial Spanish America', *Americas*, 62/1, (2005), 17–46.

Eustace, Nicole, *Passion Is the Gale: Emotion, Power, and the Coming of the American Revolution* (Chapel Hill: University of North Carolina Press, 2008).

Eustace, Nicole, *1812: War and the Passions of Patriotism* (Philadelphia: University of Pennsylvania Press, 2012).

Eustace, Nicole, Eugenia Lean, Julie Livingston, Jan Plamper, William M. Reddy, and Barbara H. Rosenwein, 'AHR Conversation: The Historical Study of Emotions', *American Historical Review*, 117/5 (2012), 1487–531. doi: 10.1093/ahr/117.5.1487

Febvre, Lucien, 'Sensibility and History: How to Reconstitute the Emotional Life of the Past', in Peter Burke (ed.), *A New Kind of History: From the Writings of Febvre*, trans. K. Folca (New York: Harper & Row, 1973), 12–26.

Flynn, Maureen, 'Blasphemy and the Play of Anger in Sixteenth-Century Spain', *Past and Present*, 149/1 (1995), 29–56. doi: 10.1093/past/149.1.29

Flynn, Maureen, 'The Spiritual Uses of Pain in Spanish Mysticism', *Journal of the American Academy of Religion*, 64/2 (1996), 257–78. doi: 10.1093/jaarel/LXIV.2.257

Flynn, Maureen, 'Taming Anger's Daughters: New Treatment for Emotional Problems in Renaissance Spain', *Renaissance Quarterly*, 51/3 (1998), 864–86.

'Forum: History of Emotions', *German History*, 28/1 (2010), 67–80.

Francis, Martin, 'Tears, Tantrums, and Bared Teeth: The Emotional Economy of Three Conservative Prime Ministers, 1951–1963', *Journal of British Studies*, 41/3 (2002), 354–87. doi: 10.1086/341153

Freier, Monika, 'Cultivating Emotions: The Gita Press and its Agenda of Social and Spiritual Reform', *South Asian History and Culture*, 3/3 (2012), 397–413. doi: 10.1080/19472498.2012.693711

Frevert, Ute, *Emotions in History: Lost and Found* (Budapest: Central European University Press, 2011).

Frevert, Ute, Monique Scheer, Anne Schmidt, Pascal Eitler, Bettina Hitzer, Benno Gammerl, Nina Verheyen, Christian Bailey, and Margrit Pernau, *Emotional Lexicons: Continuity and Change in the Vocabulary of Feeling 1700–2000* (Oxford: Oxford University Press, 2014).

Fulkerson, Laurel, *No Regrets: Remorse in Classical Antiquity* (Oxford: Oxford University Press, 2013).

Gammerl, Benno (ed.), *Emotional Styles—Concepts and Challenges* [Special Issue], *Rethinking History*, 16/2 (Abingdon: Routledge 2012).

Garro, Linda C., 'Comment on William M. Reddy, Against Constructionism: The Historical Ethnography of Emotions', *Current Anthropology*, 38/3 (1997), 341–2. doi: 10.1086/204622

Gay, Peter, *The Bourgeois Experience: Victoria to Freud*, 5 vols (New York: Oxford University Press and Norton, 1984–98).

Gertsman, Elina (ed.), *Crying in the Middle Ages: Tears of History* (New York: Routledge, 2011).

Gienow-Hecht, Jessica C. E., and Frank Schumacher (eds), *Culture and International History* (New York: Berghahn Books, 2003).

Gil, Daniel Juan, 'Before Intimacy: Modernity and Emotion in the Early Modern Discourse of Sexuality', *ELH: English Literary History*, 69/4 (2002), 861–87.

Harris, William V., *Restraining Rage: The Ideology of Anger Control in Classical Antiquity* (Cambridge, MA: Harvard University Press, 2001).

Hartman, Saidiya, *Scenes of Subjection: Terror, Slavery, and Self-Making in Nineteenth-Century America* (New York: Oxford University Press, 1997).

Hendy, David, 'Biography and the Emotions as a Missing "Narrative" in Media History: A Case Study of Lance Sieveking and the Early BBC', *Media History*, 18/3–4 (2012), 361–78. doi: 10.1080/13688804.2012.722424

Hendy, David, 'The Dreadful World of Edwardian Wireless', in Siân Nicholas and Tom O'Malley (eds), *Moral Panics, Social Fears, and the Media: Historical Perspectives* (New York: Routledge, 2013), 76–89.

Hendy, David, 'Representing the Fragmented Mind: Reinterpreting a Classic Radio Feature as "Sonic Psychology"', *Radio Journal: International Studies in Broadcast and Audio Media*, 11/1 (2013), 29–45.

Howell, Signe, 'Comment on William M. Reddy, Against Constructionism: The Historical Ethnography of Emotions', *Current Anthropology*, 38/3 (1997), 342–3. doi: 10.1086/204622

Huizinga, Johan, *The Autumn of the Middle Ages*, trans. Rodney J. Payton and Ulrich Mammitzsch (Chicago: University of Chicago Press, 1996). [Du. orig., *Herfsttij der middeleeuwen* (1921)].

Hunt, Lynn, 'Comment on William M. Reddy, Against Constructionism: The Historical Ethnography of Emotions', *Current Anthropology*, 38/3 (1997), 343–4. doi: 10.1086/204622

Hunt, Lynn, *Inventing Human Rights: A History* (New York: Norton, 2007).

Hunt, Lynn, 'The Experience of Revolution', *French Historical Studies*, 32/4 (2009), 671–8.

Ikegami, Eiko, 'Emotions', in Ulinka Rublack (ed.), *A Concise Companion to History* (Oxford: Oxford University Press, 2011), 333–53.

James, Harold, '1929: The New York Stock Market Crash', *Representations*, 110/1 (2010), 129–44. doi: 10.1525/rep.2010.110.1.129

Karant-Nunn, Susan C., *The Reformation of Feeling: Shaping the Religious Emotions in Early Modern Germany* (New York: Oxford University Press, 2010).

Keys, Barbara, 'Henry Kissinger: The Emotional Statesman', *Diplomatic History*, 35/4 (2011), 587–609. doi: 10.1111/j.1467-7709.2011.00968.x

Kietäväinen-Sirén, Hanna, '"The Warm Water in my Heart": The Meanings of Love among the Finnish Country Population in the Second Half of the 17th Century', *History of the Family*, 16/1 (2011), 47–61. doi: 10.1016/j.hisfam.2010.10.002

Laffan, Michael, and Max Weiss (eds), *Facing Fear: The History of an Emotion in Global Perspective* (Princeton: Princeton University Press, 2012).

Larrington, Carolyne, 'The Psychology of Emotion and Study of the Medieval Period', *Early Medieval Europe*, 10/2 (2001), 251–6. doi: 10.1111/1468-0254.00090

Lean, Eugenia, *Public Passions: The Trial of Shi Jianqiao and the Rise of Popular Sympathy in Republican China* (Berkeley and Los Angeles: University of California Press, 2007).

Leys, Ruth, *Trauma: A Genealogy* (Chicago: University of Chicago Press, 2000).

Liliequist, Jonas (ed.), *A History of Emotions, 1200–1800* (London: Pickering & Chatto, 2012).

Longman, Chia, 'Comment on William M. Reddy, Against Constructionism: The Historical Ethnography of Emotions', *Current Anthropology*, 38/3 (1997), 344–5. doi: 10.1086/204622

Lutz, Catherine, 'Comment on William M. Reddy, Against Constructionism: The Historical Ethnography of Emotions', *Current Anthropology*, 38/3 (1997), 345–6. doi: 10.1086/204622

Lyons, Martyn, 'Love Letters and Writing Practices: On *Écritures Intimes* in the Nineteenth Century', *Journal of Family History*, 24/2 (1999), 232–9. doi: 10.1177/036319909902400206

MacDonald, Michael, 'The Fearefull Estate of Francis Spira: Narrative, Identity, and Emotion in Early Modern England', *Journal of British Studies*, 31/1 (1992), 32–61. doi: 10.1086/385997

Mack, Phyllis, *Heart Religion in the British Enlightenment: Gender and Emotion in Early Methodism* (Cambridge: Cambridge University Press, 2008).

MacMullen, Ramsay, *Feelings in History, Ancient and Modern* (Claremont, CA: Regina Books, 2003).

Martin, Alexander M., 'Sewage and the City: Filth, Smell, and Representations of Urban Life in Moscow, 1770–1880', *Russian Review*, 67/2 (2008), 243–74. doi: 10.1111/j.1467-9434.2008.00483.x

Matt, Susan J., *Keeping Up with the Joneses: Envy in American Consumer Society, 1890–1930* (Philadelphia: University of Pennsylvania Press, 2003).

Matt, Susan J., 'Current Emotion Research in History: Or, Doing History from the Inside Out', *Emotion Review*, 3/1 (2011), 117–24. doi: 10.1177/1754073910384416

Matt, Susan J., *Homesickness: An American History* (New York: Oxford University Press, 2011).

Matt, Susan J., and Peter N. Stearns (eds), *Doing Emotions History* (Urbana: University of Illinois Press, 2014).

Medick, Hans, and David Warren Sabean (eds), *Interest and Emotion: Essays on the Study of Family and Kinship* (Cambridge: Cambridge University Press, 1984).

Mitchell, Timothy, *Passional Culture: Emotion, Religion, and Society in Southern Spain* (Philadelphia: University of Pennsylvania Press, 1990).

Mösslang, Markus, and Torsten Riotte (eds), *The Diplomats' World: A Cultural History of Diplomacy, 1815–1914* (Oxford: Oxford University Press, 2008).

Nash, David, and Anne-Marie Kilday, *Cultures of Shame: Exploring Crime and Morality in Britain 1600–1900* (Basingstoke: Palgrave Macmillan, 2010).

Nielsen, Phillip, 'Building Bonn: Democracy and the Architecture of Humility', *History of Emotions—Insights into Research* (2014) <http://www.history-of-emotions.mpg.de/en/texte/building-bonn-democracy-and-the-architecture-of-humility> accessed 2 April 2014.

Olsen, Stephanie, *Juvenile Nation: Youth, Emotions and the Making of the Modern British Citizen* (London: Bloomsbury, 2014).

Passerini, Luisa, Liliana Ellena, and Alexander C. T. Geppert (eds), *New Dangerous Liaisons: Discourses on Europe and Love in the Twentieth Century* (New York: Berghahn Books, 2010).

Pawlak, Nina (ed.), *Codes and Rituals of Emotions in Asia and African Cultures* (Warsaw: Elipsa, 2009).

Pernau, Margrit, 'Teaching Emotions: The Encounter between Victorian Values and Indo-Persian Concepts of Civility in Nineteenth-Century Delhi', in Indra Sengupta and Daud

Ali (eds), *Knowledge Production, Pedagogy, and Institutions in Colonial India* (New York: Palgrave Macmillan, 2011), 227–47.

Pernau, Margrit, 'Male Anger and Female Malice: Emotions in Indo-Muslim Advice Literature', *History Compass*, 10/2 (2012), 119–28. doi: 10.1111/j.1478-0542.2012.00829.x

Phillips, Mark Salber, *Society and Sentiment: Genres of Historical Writing in Britain, 1740–1820* (Princeton: Princeton University Press, 2000).

Plamper, Jan, Introduction in *Emotional Turn? Feelings in Russian History and Culture* [Special Section], *Slavic Review*, 68/2 (2009), 229–37.

Plamper, Jan, 'The History of Emotions: An Interview with William Reddy, Barbara H. Rosenwein, and Peter Stearns', *History and Theory*, 49/2 (2010), 237–65. doi: 10.1111/j.1468-2303.2010.00541.x

Plamper, Jan, and Benjamin Lazier, 'Introduction: The Phobic Regimes of Modernity', *Representations*, 110/1 (2010), 58–65. doi: 10.1525/rep.2010.110.1.58

Plamper, Jan, and Benjamin Lazier (eds), *Fear: Across the Disciplines* (Pittsburgh: University of Pittsburgh Press, 2012).

Popkin, Jeremy D., Review of William M. Reddy, *The Navigation of Feeling: A Framework for the History of Emotions* (Cambridge: Cambridge University Press, 2001), in *H-France Review*, 2/118 (2002), 470–6.

Reddy, William M., 'Against Constructionism: The Historical Ethnography of Emotions', *Current Anthropology*, 38/3 (1997), 327–51. doi: 10.1086/204622

Reddy, William M., *The Invisible Code: Honor and Sentiment in Postrevolutionary France, 1814–1848* (Berkeley and Los Angeles: University of California Press, 1997).

Reddy, William M., *The Navigation of Feeling: A Framework for the History of Emotions* (Cambridge: Cambridge University Press, 2001).

Reddy, William M., Response to Jeremy D. Popkin's review of William M. Reddy, *The Navigation of Feeling: A Framework for the History of Emotions* (Cambridge: Cambridge University Press, 2001), in *H-France Review*, 2/119 (2002), 477–80.

Reddy, William M., 'Historical Research on the Self and Emotions', *Emotion Review*, 1/4 (2009), 302–15. doi: 10.1177/1754073909338306

Reddy, William M., 'Saying Something New: Practice Theory and Cognitive Neuroscience', *Arcadia: International Journal for Literary Studies*, 44/1 (2009), 8–23. doi: 10.1515/ARCA.2009.002

Reddy, William M., 'Neuroscience and the Fallacies of Functionalism', *History and Theory*, 49/3 (2010), 412–25. doi: 10.1111/j.1468-2303.2010.00551.x

Reddy, William M., *The Making of Romantic Love: Longing and Sexuality in Europe, South Asia, and Japan, 900–1200 CE* (Chicago: University of Chicago Press, 2012).

Rizvi, M. Sajjad Alam, 'Conceptualizing Emotions: Perspectives from South Asian Sufism', *Economic and Political Weekly* (forthcoming).

Robb, Peter, 'Children, Emotion, Identity and Empire: View from the Blenchyndens' Calcutta Diaries (1790–1822)', *Modern Asian Studies*, 40/1 (2006), 175–201. doi: 10.1017/S0026749X06001946

Robinson, Emily, 'Touching the Void: Affective History and the Impossible', *Rethinking History*, 14/4 (2010), 503–20. doi: 10.1080/13642529.2010.515806

Rodman, Margaret Critchlow, 'The Heart in the Archives: Colonial Contestation of Desire and Fear in the New Hebrides, 1933', *Journal of Pacific History*, 38/3 (2003), 291–312. doi: 10.1080/022334032000154056

Roper, Lyndal, *Oedipus and the Devil: Witchcraft, Sexuality and Religion in Early Modern Europe* (London: Routledge, 1994).

Roper, Michael, 'Between Manliness and Masculinity: The "War Generation" and the Psychology of Fear in Britain, 1914–1950', *Journal of British Studies*, 44/2 (2005), 343–62. doi: 10.1086/427130

Roper, Michael, 'Slipping Out of View: Subjectivity and Emotion in Gender History', *History Workshop Journal*, 59 (2005), 57–72. doi: 10.1093/hwj/dbi007

Rosenfeld, Sophia, 'Thinking about Feeling, 1789–1799', *French Historical Studies*, 32/4 (2009), 697–706. doi: 10.1215/00161071-2009-018

Rosenwein, Barbara H. (ed.), *Anger's Past: The Social Uses of an Emotion in the Middle Ages* (Ithaca, NY: Cornell University Press, 1998).

Rosenwein, Barbara H., review of William M. Reddy, *The Navigation of Feeling: A Framework for the History of Emotions* (Cambridge: Cambridge University Press, 2001), in *American Historical Review*, 107/4 (2002), 1181–2. doi: 10.1086/532671

Rosenwein, Barbara H., 'Worrying about Emotions in History', *American Historical Review*, 107/3 (2002), 821–45. doi: 10.1086/532498

Rosenwein, Barbara H., *Emotional Communities in the Early Middle Ages* (Ithaca, NY: Cornell University Press, 2006).

Rosenwein, Barbara H., 'Problems and Methods in the History of Emotions', *Passions in Context: International Journal for the History and Theory of Emotions* [online journal], 1 (2010) <http://www.passionsincontext.de> accessed 5 December 2013.

Rosenwein, Barbara H., 'Thinking Historically about Medieval Emotions', *History Compass*, 8/8 (2010), 828–42. doi: 10.1111/j.1478-0542.2010.00702.x

Rothschild, Emma, *Economic Sentiments: Adam Smith, Condorcet, and the Enlightenment* (Cambridge, MA: Harvard University Press, 2001).

Rüsen, Jörn, 'Emotional Forces in Historical Thinking: Some Metahistorical Reflections and the Case of Mourning', *Historein: A Review of the Past and Other Stories*, 8 (2008), 41–53.

Santangelo, Paolo, 'Emotions in Late Imperial China: Evolution and Continuity in Ming-Qing Perception of Passions', in Viviane Alleton and Alexeï Volkov (eds), *Notions et perceptions du changement en Chine: Textes présentés au IXe Congrès de l'Association européenne d'études chinoises* (Paris: IHEC, 1994), 167–86.

Santangelo, Paolo, 'Emotions and the Origin of Evil in Neo-Confucian Thought', in Halvor Eifring (ed.), *Minds and Mentalities in Traditional Chinese Literature* (Beijing: Culture and Art Publishing House, 1999), 184–316.

Santangelo, Paolo, 'The Myths of Love-Passion in Late Imperial China', *Ming Qing Yanjiu*, 8 (1999), 131–95.

Santangelo, Paolo, *Sentimental Education in Chinese History: An Interdisciplinary Textual Research in Ming and Qing Sources*, Sinica Leidensia 60 (Leiden: Brill, 2003).

Santangelo, Paolo, 'A Textual Analysis for Capturing Data Concerning Emotions', in Lilie Suratminto and Munawar Holil (eds), *Rintisan Kajian Leksikologi dan Leksikografi: Pusat Leksikologi dan Leksikografi* (Jakarta: Fakultas Ilmu Pengetahuan Budaya, Universitas Indonesia, 2003), 87–98, 306–15.

Santangelo, Paolo, 'Evaluation of Emotions in European and Chinese Traditions: Differences and Analogies', *Monumenta Serica*, 53 (2005), 401–27.

Santangelo, Paolo, 'Emotions and Perception of Inner Reality: Chinese and European', *Journal of Chinese Philosophy* 34/2 (2007), 289–308. doi: 10.1111/j.1540-6253.2007.00414.x

Santangelo, Paolo, and Donatella Guida (eds), *Love, Hatred, and Other Passions: Questions and Themes on Emotions in Chinese Civilization* (Leiden: Brill, 2006).

Santangelo, Paolo, and Ulrike Middendorf (eds), *From Skin to Heart: Perceptions of Emotions and Bodily Sensations in Traditional Chinese Culture*, Lun-wen: Studien zur Geistesgeschichte und Literatur in China 11 (Wiesbaden: Harrassowitz, 2006).

Saillant, John, 'The Black Body Erotic and the Republican Body Politic, 1790–1820', *Journal of the History of Sexuality*, 5/3 (1995), 403–28.

Scheer, Monique, 'Are Emotions a Kind of Practice (and Is That What Makes Them Have a History)? A Bourdieuan Approach to Understanding Emotion', *History and Theory*, 51/2 (2012), 193–220. doi: 10.1111/j.1468-2303.2012.00621.x

Scheff, Thomas J., *Bloody Revenge: Emotions, Nationalism, and War* (Boulder, CO: Westview Press, 1994).

Schleyer, Maritta, 'Ghadr-e Dehli ke Afsane', *Annual of Urdu Studies*, 27 (2012), 34–56.

Shryock, Andrew, and Daniel Lord Smail (eds), *Deep History: The Architecture of Past and Present* (Berkeley and Los Angeles: University of California Press, 2011).

Smail, Daniel Lord, *On Deep History and the Brain* (Berkeley and Los Angeles: University of California Press, 2008).

Stearns, Carol Zisowitz, and Peter N. Stearns, *Anger: The Struggle for Emotional Control in America's History* (Chicago: University of Chicago Press, 1986).

Stearns, Carol Zisowitz, and Peter N. Stearns, *Emotion and Social Change: Toward a New Psychohistory* (New York: Holmes & Meier, 1988).

Stearns, Peter N., *Jealousy: The Evolution of an Emotion in American History* (New York: New York University Press, 1989).

Stearns, Peter N., *American Cool: Constructing a Twentieth-Century Emotional Style* (New York: New York University Press, 1994).

Stearns, Peter N., *American Fear: The Causes and Consequences of High Anxiety* (London: Routledge, 2006).

Stearns, Peter N., and Jan Lewis (eds), *An Emotional History of the United States* (New York: New York University Press, 1998).

Stearns, Peter N., and Carol Z. Stearns, 'Emotionology: Clarifying the History of Emotions and Emotional Standards', *American Historical Review*, 90/4 (1985), 813–36. doi: 10.2307/1858841

Steinberg, Mark D., and Valeria Sobol (eds), *Interpreting Emotions in Russia and Eastern Europe* (DeKalb: Northern Illinois University Press, 2011).

Tarlow, Sarah, 'Emotion in Archaeology', *Current Anthropology*, 41/5 (2000), 713–46. doi: 10.1086/317404

Tyson, Amy M., *The Wages of History: Emotional Labor on Public History's Front Lines* (Amherst: University of Massachussetts Press, 2013).

Valatsou, Despoina, 'History, Our Own Stories and Emotions Online', *Historein: A Review of the Past and Other Stories*, 8 (2008), 108–16.

Vincent-Buffault, Anne, *The History of Tears: Sensibility and Sentimentality in France* (New York: St Martin's Press, 1991).

Virág, Curie, 'Emotions and Human Agency in the Thought of Zhu Xi', *Journal of Song Yuan Studies*, 37 (2007), 49–88.

Wahrman, Dror, 'Where Culture and Biology Meet', review of Daniel Lord Smail, *On Deep History and the Human Brain* (Berkeley and Los Angeles: University of California Press, 2008), in *Haaretz* (24 April 2008) <http://www.haaretz.com/culture/books/where-culture-and-biology-meet-1.244504> accessed 5 December 2013.

Wickberg, Daniel, 'What Is the History of Sensibilities? On Cultural Histories, Old and New', *American Historical Review*, 112/3 (2007), 661–84. doi: 10.1086/ahr.112.3.661

Zeldin, Theodore, *France: 1848–1945*, 2 vols (Oxford: Clarendon Press, 1973–7).

Zeldin, Theodore, 'Personal History and the History of Emotions', *Journal of Social History*, 15/3 (1982), 339–47. doi: 10.1353/jsh/15.3.339

Zeldin, Theodore, *An Intimate History of Humanity* (New York: HarperCollins, 1994).

6 HISTORY OF SCIENCE

Alberti, Fay Bound, 'Angina Pectoris and the Arnolds: Emotions and Heart Disease in the Nineteenth Century', *Medical History*, 52/2, (2008), 221–36.

Alberti, Fay Bound, *Matters of the Heart: History, Medicine and Emotion* (Oxford: Oxford University Press, 2010).

Biess, Frank, and Daniel M. Gross (eds), *Science and Emotions after 1945: A Transatlantic Perspective* (Chicago: University of Chicago Press, 2014).

Boddice, Rob, 'Species of Compassion: Aesthetics, Anaesthetics and Pain in the Physiological Laboratory', *19: Interdisciplinary Studies in the Long Nineteenth Century*, 15 (2012), 1–22.

Boddice, Rob Gregory (ed.), *Pain and Emotion in Modern History*, Palgrave Studies in the History of Emotions (Basingstoke: Palgrave Macmillan, 2014).

Callard, Felicity, and Daniel S. Margulies, 'The Subject at Rest: Novel Conceptualizations of Self and Brain from Cognitive Neuroscience's Study of the "Resting State"', *Subjectivity*, 4/3 (2011), 227–57. doi: 10.1057/sub.2011.11

Choudhury, Suparna, and Jan Slaby (eds), *Critical Neuroscience: A Handbook of the Social, Political, and Cultural Contexts of Neuroscience* (Chichester: Wiley-Blackwell, 2011). doi: 10.1002/9781444343359

Dixon, Thomas, *From Passions to Emotions: The Creation of a Secular Psychological Category* (Cambridge: Cambridge University Press, 2003).

Dror, Otniel E. (Dror, Otniel Yizhak), 'Modernity and the Scientific Study of Emotions, 1880–1950', PhD diss., Princeton University, Princeton, 1998.

Dror, Otniel E., 'The Affect of Experiment: The Turn to Emotions in Anglo-American Physiology, 1900–1940', *Isis*, 90/2 (1999), 205–37. doi: 10.1086/384322

Dror, Otniel E., 'The Scientific Image of Emotion: Experience and Technologies of Inscription', *Configurations*, 7/3 (1999), 355–401. doi: 10.1353/con.1999.0025

Dror, Otniel E., 'Counting the Affects: Discoursing in Numbers', *Social Research*, 68/2 (2001), 357–78.

Dror, Otniel E., 'Techniques of the Brain and the Paradox of Emotions, 1880–1930', *Science in Context*, 14/4 (2001), 643–60. doi: 10.1017/026988970100028X

Dror, Otniel E., 'Fear and Loathing in the Laboratory and Clinic', in Fay Bound Alberti (ed.), *Medicine, Emotion and Disease, 1700–1950* (New York: Palgrave Macmillan, 2006), 125–43.

Dror, Otniel E., 'Afterword: A Reflection on Feelings and the History of Science', *Isis*, 100/4 (2009), 848–51. doi: 10.1086/652024

Gendron, Maria, and Lisa Feldman Barrett, 'Reconstructing the Past: A Century of Ideas about Emotion in Psychology', *Emotion Review*, 1/4 (2009), 316–39. doi: 10.1177/1754073909338877

Gouk, Penelope, and Helen Hills (eds), *Representing Emotions: New Connections in the Histories of Art, Music and Medicine* (Farnham: Ashgate, 2005).

Hayward, Rhodri, 'Enduring Emotions: James L. Halliday and the Invention of the Psychosocial', *Isis*, 100/4 (2009), 827–38.

Jabr, Ferris, 'The Evolution of Emotion: Charles Darwin's Little-Known Psychology Experiment', *Scientific American Observations Blog* (24 May 2010) <http://blogs.

scientificamerican.com/observations/2010/05/24/the-evolution-of-emotion-charles-darwins-little-known-psychology-experiment> accessed 5 December 2013.

Leys, Ruth, *From Guilt to Shame: Auschwitz and After* (Princeton: Princeton University Press, 2007).

Leys, Ruth, 'How Did Fear Become a Scientific Object and What Kind of Object Is It?', *Representations*, 110 (2010), 66–104. doi: 10.1525/rep.2010.110.1.66

Leys, Ruth, 'Critical Response II: Affect and Intention: A Reply to William E. Connolly', *Critical Inquiry*, 37/4 (2011), 799–805. doi: 10.1086/660994

Leys, Ruth, 'The Turn to Affect: A Critique', *Critical Inquiry*, 37/3 (2011), 434–72. doi: 10.1086/659353

Leys, Ruth, ' "Both of Us Disgusted in My Insula": Mirror Neuron Theory and Emotional Empathy', *Nonsite.org*, 5 (18 March 2012) [online journal] <http://nonsite.org/article/%E2%80%9Cboth-of-us-disgusted-in-my-insula%E2%80%9D-mirror-neuron-theory-and-emotional-empathy> accessed 5 December 2013.

Leys, Ruth, and Marlene Goldman, 'Navigating the Genealogies of Trauma, Guilt, and Affect: An Interview with Ruth Leys', *University of Toronto Quarterly*, 79/2 (2010), 656–79. doi: 10.1353/utq.2010.0227

Papoulias, Constantina and Felicity Callard, 'The Rehabilitation of the Drive in Neuropsychoanalysis: From Sexuality to Self-Preservation', in Christine Kirchhoff and Gerhard Scharbert (eds), *Freuds Referenzen* (Berlin: Kulturverlag Kadmos, 2012), 189–215.

Pfister, Joel, and Nancy Schnog (eds), *Inventing the Psychological: Toward a Cultural History of Emotional Life in America* (New Haven: Yale University Press, 1997).

Pilar, León-Sanz, 'Resentment in Psychosomatic Pathology (1939–1960)', in Bernardino Fantini, Dolores Martín Moruno, and Javier Moscoso (eds), *On Resentment: Past and Present* (Newcastle upon Tyne: Cambridge Scholars Publishing, 2013), 135–68.

Rees, Tobias, 'Being Neurologically Human Today: Life and Science and Adult Cerebral Plasticity (An Ethical Analysis)', *American Ethnologist*, 37/1 (2010), 150–66. doi: 10.1111/j.1548-1425.2010.01247.x

Richards, Graham, *Putting Psychology in Its Place: Critical Historical Perspectives* (3rd edn, London: Routledge, 2010).

Richardson, Angelique (ed.), *After Darwin: Animals, Emotions, and the Mind*, Clio Medica 93 (Amsterdam: Rodopi, 2013).

Riskin, Jessica, *Science in the Age of Sensibility: The Sentimental Empiricists of the French Enlightenment* (Chicago: University of Chicago Press, 2002).

Rose, Nikolas, and Joelle M. Abi-Rached, *Neuro: The New Brain Sciences and the Management of the Mind* (Princeton: Princeton University Press, 2013).

Rubin, Beatrix P., 'Changing Brains: The Emergence of the Field of Adult Neurogenesis', *BioSocieties*, 4/4 (2009), 407–24. doi: 10.1017/S1745855209990330

Snyder, Peter J., Rebecca Kaufman, John Harrison, and Paul Maruff, 'Charles Darwin's Emotional Expression "Experiment" and his Contribution to Modern Neuropharmacology', *Journal of the History of the Neurosciences*, 19/2 (2010), 158–70. doi: 10.1080/09647040903506679

Uttal, William R., *The New Phrenology: The Limits of Localizing Cognitive Processes in the Brain* (Cambridge, MA: MIT Press, 2001).

Uttal, William R., *Mind and Brain: A Critical Appraisal of Cognitive Neuroscience* (Cambridge, MA: MIT Press, 2011).

Wassmann, Claudia, 'The Science of Emotion: Studying Emotions in Germany, France, and the United States, 1860–1920', PhD diss., University of Chicago, Chicago, 2005.

Wassmann, Claudia, 'Physiological Optics, Cognition and Emotion: A Novel Look at the Early Work of Wilhelm Wundt', *Journal of the History of Medicine and Allied Sciences*, 64/2 (2009), 213–49. doi: 10.1093/jhmas/jrn058

Wassmann, Claudia, 'Reflections on the "Body Loop": Carl Georg Lange's Theory of Emotion', *Cognition and Emotion*, 24/6 (2009), 974–90. doi: 10.1080/02699930903052744

Wassmann, Claudia, 'Emotion into Science: How Our Modern Ideas about Emotion Were Created in the Nineteenth Century', *Emotional Studies (HIST-EX)* [online journal] (29 November 2011) <http://historiadelasemociones.wordpress.com/2011/11/29/emotion-into-science-how-our-modern-ideas-about-emotion-were-created-in-the-nineteenth-century-claudia-wassmann> accessed 5 December 2013.

Weinberger, Sharon, 'Intent to Deceive? Can the Science of Deception Detection Help to Catch Terrorists?', *Nature*, 465/7297 (2010), 412–15. doi: 10.1038/465412a

Winter, Sarah, 'Darwin's Saussure: Biosemiotics and Race in Expression', *Representations*, 107/1 (2009), 128–61. doi: 10.1525/rep.2009.107.1.128

7 ANTHROPOLOGY

Abu-Lughod, Lila, *Veiled Sentiments: Honor and Poetry in a Bedouin Society* (Berkeley and Los Angeles: University of California Press, 1986).

Apffel Marglin, Frédérique, *Wives of the God-King: The Rituals of the Devadasis of Puri* (New Delhi: Oxford University Press, 1985).

Besnier, Niko, *Literacy, Emotion, and Authority: Reading and Writing on a Polynesian Atoll* (Cambridge: Cambridge University Press, 1995).

Briggs, Jean L., *Never in Anger: Portrait of an Eskimo Family* (Cambridge, MA: Harvard University Press, 1970).

D'Andrade, R[oy], and M[ichael] Egan, 'The Colors of Emotion', *American Ethnologist*, 1/1 (1974), 49–63.

Fajans, Jane, *They Make Themselves: Work and Play among the Baining of Papua New Guinea* (Chicago: University of Chicago Press, 1997).

Feld, Steven, *Sound and Sentiment: Birds, Weeping, Poetics, and Song in Kaluli Expression* (2nd edn, Philadelphia: University of Pennsylvania Press, 1990).

Fish, Jonathan S., *Defending the Durkheimian Tradition: Religion, Emotion and Morality* (Aldershot: Ashgate, 2005).

Geertz, Clifford, *The Interpretation of Cultures* (New York: Basic Books, 1973).

Geertz, Clifford, *Local Knowledge: Further Essays in Interpretive Anthropology* (New York: Basic Books, 1983).

Geertz, Hildred, 'The Vocabulary of Emotion: A Study of Javanese Socialization Processes', *Psychiatry: Interpersonal and Biological Processes*, 22 (1959), 225–37.

Grima, Benedicte, *The Performance of Emotion among Paxtun Women: 'The Misfortunes which Have Befallen Me'* (Austin: University of Texas Press, 1992).

Heider, Karl G., *Landscapes of Emotion: Mapping Three Cultures of Emotion in Indonesia* (Cambridge: Cambridge University Press, 1991).

Kapferer, Bruce, 'Emotion and Feeling in Sinhalese Healing Rites', *Social Analysis*, 1/1 (1979), 153–76.

Leavitt, John, 'The Shapes of Modernity: On the Philosophical Roots of Anthropological Doctrines', *Culture*, 11/1–2 (1991), 29–42.

Leavitt, John, 'Meaning and Feeling in the Anthropology of Emotions', *American Ethnologist*, 23/3 (1996), 514–39.

Levy, Robert I., *Tahitians: Mind and Experience in the Society Islands* (Chicago: University of Chicago Press, 1975).

Lindholm, Charles, *Generosity and Jealousy: The Swat Pukhtun of Northern Pakistan* (New York: Columbia University Press, 1982).

Lutz, Catherine A., *Unnatural Emotions: Everyday Sentiments on a Micronesian Atoll & their Challenge to Western Theory* (Chicago: University of Chicago Press, 1988).

Lutz, Catherine A., and Lila Abu-Lughod (eds), *Language and the Politics of Emotion* (Cambridge: Cambridge University Press, 1990).

Lutz, Catherine, and Geoffrey M. White, 'The Anthropology of Emotions', *Annual Review of Anthropology*, 15 (1986), 405–36.

Lynch, Owen M. (ed.), *Divine Passions: The Social Construction of Emotion in India* (Berkeley and Los Angeles: University of California Press, 1990).

Lyon, Margot L., 'Missing Emotion: The Limitations of Cultural Constructionism in the Study of Emotion', *Cultural Anthropology*, 10/2 (1995), 244–63.

Michaels, Alex, and Christoph Wulf (eds), *Emotions in Rituals and Performances* (London, Routledge, 2012).

Mitchell, Lisa, *Language, Emotion, and Politics in South India: The Making of a Mother Tongue* (Bloomington: Indiana University Press, 2009).

Myers, Fred R., *Pintupi Country, Pintupi Self: Sentiment, Place, and Politics among Western Desert Aborigines* (Washington, DC: Smithsonian Institution Press, 1986).

Needham, Rodney, *Essential Perplexities: An Inaugural Lecture Delivered before the University of Oxford on 12 May 1977* (Oxford: Clarendon Press, 1978).

Needham, Rodney, *Circumstantial Deliveries* (Berkeley and Los Angeles: University of California Press, 1981).

Obeyesekere, Gananath, 'Depression, Buddhism, and the Work of Culture in Sri Lanka', in Arthur Kleinman and Byron Good (eds), *Culture and Depression: Studies in the Anthropology and Cross-Cultural Psychiatry of Affect and Disorder* (Berkeley and Los Angeles: University of California Press, 1985), 134–52.

Obeyesekere, Gananath, *The Work of Culture: Symbolic Transformation in Psychoanalysis and Anthropology* (Chicago: University of Chicago Press, 1990).

Ramaswamy, Sumathi, *Passions of the Tongue: Language Devotion in Tamil India, 1891–1970* (Berkeley and Los Angeles: University of California Press, 1997).

Rosaldo, Michelle Z., *Knowledge and Passion: Ilongot Notions of Self and Social Life* (Cambridge: Cambridge University Press, 1980).

Scheper-Hughes, Nancy, and Margaret M. Lock, 'The Mindful Body: Prolegomenon to Future Work in Medical Anthropology', *Medical Anthropology Quarterly*, 1/1 (1987), 6–41. doi: 10.1525/maq.1987.1.1.02a00020

Schwartz, Susan L., *Rasa: Performing the Divine in India* (New York: Columbia University Press, 2004).

Spiro, Melford E., 'Ghosts, Ifaluk, and Teleological Functionalism', *American Anthropologist*, 54/4 (1952), 497–503.

Straus, Anne S., 'Northern Cheyenne Ethnopsychology', *Ethos*, 5/3 (1977), 326–57.

Urban, Greg, 'Ritual Wailing in Amerindian Brazil', *American Anthropologist*, 90/2 (1988), 385–400.

White, Geoffrey M., and Karen Ann Watson-Gegeo, 'Disentangling Disourse', in Karen Ann Watson-Gegeo and Geoffrey M. White (eds), *Disentangling: Conflict Discourse in Pacific Societies* (Stanford, CA: Stanford University Press, 1990), 3–49.

Wikan, Unni, 'Managing the Heart to Brighten Face and Soul: Emotions in Balinese Morality and Health Care', *American Ethnologist*, 16/2 (1989), 294–312.

Wikan, Unni, *Managing Turbulent Hearts: A Balinese Formula for Living* (Chicago: University of Chicago Press, 1990).

8 LIFE SCIENCES (PSYCHOLOGY, NEUROSCIENCE, ETC.)

Adolphs, Ralph, 'Conceptual Challenges and Directions for Social Neuroscience', *Neuron*, 65 (2010), 752–67. doi: 10.1016/j.neuron.2010.03.006

Adolphs, Ralph, Hanna Damasio, Daniel Tranel, and Antonio R. Damasio, 'Cortical Systems for the Recognition of Emotion in Facial Expressions', *Journal of Neuroscience*, 16/23 (1996), 7678–87.

Adolphs, Ralph, Daniel Tranel, Hanna Damasio, and Antonio R. Damasio, 'Fear and the Human Amygdala', *Journal of Neuroscience*, 15/9 (1995), 5879–91.

Aggleton, John P. (ed.), *The Amygdala: A Functional Analysis* (2nd edn, Oxford: Oxford University Press, 2000).

Arnold, Magda B., *Emotion and Personality*, i. *Psychological Aspects* (New York: Columbia University Press, 1960).

Arnold, Magda B., and John A. Gasson, 'Feelings and Emotions as Dynamic Factors in Personality Integration', in Arnold and Gasson (eds), *The Human Person: An Approach to an Integral Theory of Personality* (New York: Ronald Press, 1954), 294–313.

Aziz-Zadeh, Lisa, Stephen M. Wilson, Giacomo Rizzolatti, and Marco Iacoboni, 'Congruent Embodied Representations for Visually Presented Actions and Linguistic Phrases Describing Actions', *Current Biology*, 16/18 (2006), 1818–23. doi: 10.1016/j. cub.2006.07.060

Barnett, Douglas, and Hilary Horn Ratner, 'The Organization and Integration of Cognition and Emotion in Development', *Journal of Experimental Child Psychology*, 67/3 (1997), 303–16. doi: 10.1006/jecp.1997.2417

Battaglia, Fortunato, Sarah H. Lisanby, and David Freedberg, 'Corticomotor Excitability during Observation and Imagination of a Work of Art', *Frontiers in Human Neuroscience*, 5 (2011), 79:1–6. doi: 10.3389/fnhum.2011.00079

Bechara, Antoine, Antonio R. Damasio, Hanna Damasio, and Steven W. Anderson, 'Insensitivity to Future Consequences Following Damage to Human Prefrontal Cortex', *Cognition*, 50/1–3 (1994), 7–15. doi: 10.1016/0010-0277(94)90018-3

Bennett, Craig M., Abigail A. Baird, Michael B. Miller, and George L. Wolford, 'Neural Correlates of Interspecies Perspective Taking in the Post-Mortem Atlantic Salmon: An Argument for Multiple Comparisons Correction', *Journal of Serendipitous and Unexpected Results*, 1/1 (2010), 1–5.

Berntson, Gary G., and John T. Cacioppo (eds), *Handbook of Neuroscience for the Behavioral Sciences*, i (Hoboken, NJ: Wiley, 2009).

Buchwalter, Ben, 'Forget Your "Junk": The TSA Wants to Feel Up your Mind', *Mother Jones* (2 February 2011) <http://www.motherjones.com/politics/2011/02/tsa-spot-scan-paul-ekman> accessed 7 March 2014.

Calvo-Merino, B., D. E. Glaser, J. Grezes, R. E. Passingham, and P. Haggard, 'Action Observation and Acquired Motor Skills: An fMRI Study with Expert Dancers', *Cerebral Cortex*, 15/8 (2005), 1243–9. doi:10.1093/cercor/bhi007

Cannon, Walter B., 'The James-Lange Theory of Emotions: A Critical Examination and an Alternative Theory', *American Journal of Psychology*, 39/1–4 (1927), 106–24. doi: 10.2307/1415404

Cannon, Walter B., 'Again the James-Lange and the Thalamic Theories of Emotions', *Psychological Review*, 38/4 (1931), 281–95. doi: 10.1037/h0072957

Cornelius, Randolph R., *The Science of Emotion: Research and Tradition in the Psychology of Emotion* (Upper Saddle River, NJ: Prentice Hall, 1996).

Curtis, Valerie, *Don't Look, Don't Touch, Don't Eat: The Science Behind Revulsion* (Oxford: Oxford University Press, 2013).

Dalgleish, Tim, Barnaby D. Dunn, and Dean Mobbs, 'Affective Neuroscience: Past, Present, and Future', *Emotion Review*, 1/4 (2009), 355–68. doi: 10.1177/1754073909338307

Damasio, Antonio R., *Descartes' Error: Emotion, Reason, and the Human Brain* (New York: Putnam, 1994).

Damasio, Antonio R., *The Feeling of What Happens: Body and Emotion in the Making of Consciousness* (New York: Harcourt Brace, 1999).

Damasio, Antonio R., *Looking for Spinoza: Joy, Sorrow, and the Feeling Brain* (Orlando, FL: Harcourt, 2003).

Damasio, Antonio R., Ralph Adolphs, and H. Damasio, 'The Contributions of the Lesion Method to the Functional Neuroanatomy of Emotion', in Richard J. Davidson, Klaus R. Scherer, and H. Hill Goldsmith (eds), *Handbook of Affective Sciences* (Oxford: Oxford University Press, 2003), 66–92.

Damasio, Hanna, Thomas Grabowski, Randall Frank, Albert M. Galaburda, and Antonio R. Damasio, 'The Return of Phineas Gage: Clues about the Brain from the Skull of a Famous Patient', *Science*, 264/5162 (1994), 1102–5. doi: 10.1126/science.8178168

Dapretto, Mirella, Mari S. Davies, Jennifer H. Pfeifer, Ashley A. Scott, Marian Sigman, Susan Y. Bookheimer, and Marco Iacoboni, 'Understanding Emotions in Others: Mirror Neuron Dysfunction in Children with Autism Spectrum Disorders', *Nature Neuroscience*, 9/1 (2006), 28–30. doi: 10.1038/nn1611

Darwin, Charles, *The Expression of the Emotions in Man and Animals* (London: John Murray, 1872).

Darwin, Charles, *The Expression of the Emotions in Man and Animals*, with an introduction, afterword, and commentaries by Paul Ekman (3rd edn, New York: Oxford University Press, 1998).

Davidson, Richard J., 'Seven Sins in the Study of Emotion: Correctives from Affective Neuroscience', *Brain and Cognition*, 52/1 (2003), 129–32. doi:10.1016/S0278-2626(03)00015-0

Dinstein, Ilan, Justin L. Gardner, Mehrdad Jazayeri, and David J. Heeger, 'Executed and Observed Movements Have Different Distributed Representations in Human aIPS', *Journal of Neuroscience*, 28/44 (2008), 11231–9. doi: 10.1523/JNEUROSCI.3585-08.2008

Dinstein, Ilan, Cibu Thomas, Marlene Behrmann, and David J. Heeger, 'A Mirror Up to Nature', *Current Biology*, 18/1 (2008), R13–8. doi: 10.1016/j.cub.2007.11.004

Dunn, Barnaby D., Tim Dalgleish, and Andrew D. Lawrence, 'The Somatic Marker Hypothesis: A Critical Evaluation', *Neuroscience and Biobehavioral Reviews*, 30/2 (2006), 239–71. doi:10.1016/j.neubiorev.2005.07.001

Edwards, Derek, 'Emotion Discourse', *Culture & Psychology*, 5/3 (1999), 271–91. doi: 10.1177/1354067X9953001

Ekman, Paul, 'A Life's Pursuit', in Thomas A. Sebeok and Jean Umiker-Sebeok (eds), *The Semiotic Web 1986* (Berlin: Mouton de Gruyter, 1987), 3–45.

Ekman, Paul, 'An Argument for Basic Emotions', *Cognition and Emotion*, 6/3–4 (1992), 169–200. doi: 10.1080/02699939208411068

Ekman, Paul, 'Basic Emotions', in Tim Dalgleish and Mick J. Power (eds), *Handbook of Cognition and Emotion* (Chichester: Wiley, 1999), 45–60. doi: 10.1002/0470013494.ch3

Ekman, Paul (ed.), *Darwin and Facial Expression: A Century of Research in Review* (Los Altos, CA: Malor Books, 2006).

Ekman, Paul, 'How to Spot a Terrorist on the Fly', *Washington Post* (29 October 2006), B03.

Ekman, Paul, and Richard J. Davidson (eds), *The Nature of Emotion: Fundamental Questions* (New York: Oxford University Press, 1994).

Ekman, Paul, Wallace V. Friesen, and Phoebe Ellsworth, *Emotions in the Human Face: Guidelines for Research and an Integration of Findings* (New York: Pergamon Press, 1972).

Ekman, Paul, E. Richard Sorenson, and Wallace V. Friesen, 'Pan-Cultural Elements in Facial Displays of Emotion', *Science*, 164/3875 (1969), 86–8. doi: 10.1126/science.164.3875.86

Fabbri-Destro, Maddalena, and Giacomo Rizzolatti, 'Mirror Neurons and Mirror Systems in Monkeys and Humans', *Physiology*, 23/3 (2008), 171–9. doi: 10.1152/physiol.00004.2008

Fadiga, L., L. Fogassi, G. Pavesi, and G. Rizzolatti, 'Motor Facilitation during Action Observation: A Magnetic Stimulation Study', *Journal of Neurophysiology*, 73/6 (1995), 2608–11.

Frank, Robert H., *Passions within Reason: The Strategic Role of the Emotions* (New York: Norton, 1988).

Fridlund, Alan J., *Human Facial Expression: An Evolutionary View* (San Diego, CA: Academic Press, 1994).

Frijda, Nico H., *The Emotions*, Studies in Emotion and Social Interaction (Cambridge: Cambridge University Press, 1986).

Gallese, Vittorio, Luciano Fadiga, Leonardo Fogassi, and Giacomo Rizzolatti, 'Action Recognition in the Premotor Cortex', *Brain*, 119/2 (1996), 593–609. doi: 10.1093/brain/119.2.593

Gallese, Vittorio, Morton Ann Gernsbacher, Cecilia Heyes, Gregory Hickok, and Marco Iacoboni, 'Mirror Neuron Forum', *Perspectives on Psychological Science*, 6/4 (2011), 369–407. doi: 10.1177/1745691611413392

Gallese, Vittorio, and Alvin Goldman, 'Mirror Neurons and the Simulation Theory of Mind-Reading', *Trends in Cognitive Sciences*, 2/12 (1998), 493–501. doi: 10.1016/S1364-6613(98)01262-5

Gigerenzer, Gerd, *Gut Feelings: The Intelligence of the Unconscious* (New York: Viking, 2007).

Gigerenzer, G[erd] and R. Selten (eds), *Bounded Rationality: The Adaptive Toolbox* (Cambridge, MA: MIT Press, 2001).

Goleman, Daniel, *Emotional Intelligence: Why It Can Matter More Than IQ* (New York: Bantam Books, 1995).

Gross, James J., 'The Future's So Bright, I Gotta Wear Shades', *Emotion Review*, 2/3 (2010), 212–16. doi: 10.1177/1754073910361982

Guttmann, Giselher, and Inge Scholz-Strasser (eds), *Freud and the Neurosciences: From Brain Research to the Unconscious* (Vienna: Verlag der Österreichischen Akademie der Wissenschaften, 1998).

Habermas, Tilmann, Michaela Meier, and Barbara Mukhtar, 'Are Specific Emotions Narrated Differently?', *Emotion*, 9/6 (2009), 751–62. doi: 10.1037/a0018002

Habermas, Tilmann, and Nadine Berger, 'Retelling Everyday Emotional Events: Condensation, Distancing, and Closure', *Cognition and Emotion*, 25/2 (2011), 206–19. doi: 10.1080/02699931003783568

Habermas, Tilmann, and Verena Diel, 'The Emotional Impact of Loss Narratives: Event Severity and Narrative Perspectives', *Emotion*, 10/10 (2010), 312–23. doi: 10.1037/a0018001

Herz, Rachel, *That's Disgusting: Unraveling the Mysteries of Repulsion* (New York: Norton, 2012).

Hickok, Gregory, and Marc Hauser, '(Mis)understanding Mirror Neurons', *Current Biology*, 20/14 (2010), R593–R594. doi: 10.1016/j.cub.2010.05.047

Hillman, James, *Emotion: A Comprehensive Phenomenology of Theories and Their Meaning for Therapy* (London: Routledge & Kegan Paul, 1960).

Iacoboni, Marco, *Mirroring People: The New Science of How we Connect with Others* (New York: Farrar, Straus and Giroux, 2008).

Ishizu, Tomohiro, and Semir Zeki, 'Toward a Brain-Based Theory of Beauty', *PLoS ONE*, 6/7 (2011), e21852: 1–10. doi: 10.1371/journal.pone.0021852

Jack, Rachael E., Oliver G. B. Garrod, Hui Yu, Roberto Caldara, and Philippe G. Schyns, 'Facial Expressions of Emotion Are Not Culturally Universal', *Proceedings of the National Academy of Sciences*, 109/19 (2012), 7241–4. doi: 10.1073/pnas.1200155109

Jackson, J. Hughlings, 'The Croonian Lectures on Evolution and Dissolution of the Nervous System: Lecture II', *British Medical Journal*, 1/1214 (1884), 660–3. doi: 10.1136/bmj.1.1214.660

James, William, 'What Is an Emotion?', *Mind*, 9/34 (1884), 188–205.

Johnstone, Tom, Carien M. van Reekum, Terrence R. Oakes, and Richard J. Davidson, 'The Voice of Emotion: An FMRI Study of Neural Responses to Angry and Happy Vocal Expressions', *Social Cognitive and Affective Neuroscience*, 1/3 (2006), 242–9. doi: 10.1093/scan/nsl027

Kagan, Jerome, *What Is Emotion? History, Measures, and Meanings* (New Haven: Yale University Press, 2007).

Kandel, Eric R., *Psychiatry, Psychoanalysis, and the New Biology of Mind* (Washington, DC: American Psychiatric Publishing, 2005).

Keltner, Dacher, Keith Oatley, and Jennifer M. Jenkins, *Understanding Emotions* (3rd edn, Cambridge, MA: Wiley, 2013).

Keysers, Christian, and Valeria Gazzola, 'Social Neuroscience: Mirror Neurons Recorded in Humans', *Current Biology*, 20/8 (2010), R353–R354. doi: 10.1016/j.cub.2010.03.013

Kleinginna Jun., Paul R., and Anne M. Kleinginna, 'A Categorized List of Emotion Definitions, with Suggestions for a Consensual Definition', *Motivation and Emotion*, 5/4 (1981), 345–79. doi: 10.1007/BF00992553

LaBar, Kevin S., and Roberto Cabeza, 'Cognitive Neuroscience of Emotional Memory', *Nature Reviews Neuroscience*, 7/1 (2006), 54–64. doi: 10.1038/nrn1825

Lange, Carl Georg, 'The Emotions: A Psychophysiological Study', trans. Istar A. Haupt from the authorized German translation of H. Kurella, in Carl Georg Lange and William James, *The Emotions*, i (Baltimore: Williams and Wilkins, 1922), 33–90. [Da. orig., *Om Sindsbevägelser* (1885)]. doi: 10.1037/10735-002

Lazarus, Richard S., 'Thoughts on the Relations between Emotion and Cognition', *American Psychologist*, 37/9 (1982), 1019–24. doi: 10.1037/0003-066X.37.9.1019

LeDoux, Joseph E., 'Emotion, Memory and the Brain', *Scientific American*, 270/6 (1994), 50–6. doi: 10.1038/scientificamerican0694-50

LeDoux, Joseph E., *The Emotional Brain: The Mysterious Underpinnings of Emotional Life* (New York: Simon and Schuster, 1996).

Lehrer, Jonah, *Proust Was a Neuroscientist* (Boston: Mifflin, 2007).

Levenson, Robert W., Paul Ekman, Karl Heider, and Wallace V. Friesen, 'Emotion and Autonomic Nervous System Activity in the Minangkabau of West Sumatra', *Journal of Personality and Social Psychology*, 62/6 (1992), 972–88. doi: 10.1037/0022-3514.62.6.972

Lewis, Michael, Jeannette M. Haviland-Jones, and Lisa Feldman Barrett (eds), *Handbook of Emotions* (3rd edn, New York: Guilford Press, 2008).

Logothetis, Nikos K., 'What We Can Do and What We Cannot Do with fMRI', *Nature*, 453/7197 (2008), 869–78. doi: 10.1038/nature06976

Lövdén, Martin, Lars Bäckman, Ulman Lindenberger, Sabine Schaefer, and Florian Schmiedek, 'A Theoretical Framework for the Study of Adult Cognitive Plasticity', *Psychological Bulletin*, 136/4 (2010), 659–76. doi: 10.1037/a0020080

McCosh, James, *The Emotions* (New York: Charles Scribner's Sons, 1880).

McGinn, Colin, *The Meaning of Disgust* (Oxford: Oxford University Press, 2012).

McIntosh, Anthony Randal, 'From Location to Integration: How Neural Interactions Form the Basis for Human Cognition', in Endel Tulving (ed.), *Memory, Consciousness, and the Brain: The Tallinn Conference* (Philadelphia: Psychology Press, 2000), 346–62.

McRae, Kateri, Kevin N. Ochsner, Iris B. Mauss, John J. D. Gabrieli, and James J. Gross, 'Gender Differences in Emotion Regulation: An fMRI Study of Cognitive Reappraisal', *Group Processes and Intergroup Relations*, 11/2 (2008), 143–62. doi: 10.1177/1368430207088035

Matthews, Gerald, Moshe Zeidner, and Richard D. Roberts, *Emotional Intelligence: Science and Myth* (Cambridge, MA: MIT Press, 2002).

Mead, Margaret, 'Margaret Mead Calls "Discipline-Centric" Approach to Research an "Example of the Appalling State of the Human Sciences"', review of Paul Ekman (ed.), *Darwin and Facial Expression: A Century of Research in Review* (New York: Academic Press, 1973), in *Journal of Communication*, 25/1 (1975), 209–13. doi: 10.1111/j.1460-2466.1975.tb00574.x

Mesquita, Batja, Lisa Feldman Barrett, and Eliot R. Smith (eds), *The Mind in Context* (New York: Guilford Press, 2010).

Mills, Charles K., 'The Cortical Representation of Emotion, with a Discussion of Some Points in the General Nervous Mechanism of Expression and its Relation to Organic Nervous Disease and Insanity', *Proceedings of the American Medico-Psychological Association*, 19 (1912), 297–300.

Mosso, Angelo, *Fear*, trans. E. Lough and F. Kiesow (London: Longmans, Green, and Co., 1896). [It. orig., *La paura* (1884; 5th edn, 1892)].

Mouras, H., S. Stoléru, V. Moulier, M. Pélégrini-Issac, R. Rouxel, B. Grandjean, D. Glutron, and J. Bittoun, 'Activation of Mirror-Neuron System by Erotic Video Clips Predicts Degree of Induced Erection: An fMRI Study', *NeuroImage*, 42/3 (2008), 1142–50. doi: 10.1016/j.neuroimage.2008.05.051

Mukamel, Roy, Arne D. Ekstrom, Jonas Kaplan, Marco Iacoboni, and Itzhak Fried, 'Single-Neuron Responses in Humans during Execution and Observation of Actions', *Current Biology*, 20/8 (2010), 750–6. doi: 10.1016/j.cub.2010.02.045

Nauta, Walle J. H., 'The Problem of the Frontal Lobe: A Reinterpretation', *Journal of Psychiatric Research*, 8/3–4 (1971), 167–87. doi: 10.1016/0022-3956(71)90017-3

Niedenthal, Paula M., Silvia Krauth-Gruber, and François Ric, *Psychology of Emotion: Interpersonal, Experiential, and Cognitive Approaches* (New York: Psychology Press, 2006).

Oatley, Keith, *Emotions: A Brief History* (Malden, MA: Blackwell, 2004).

Ohira, Hideki, 'The Somatic Marker Revisited: Brain and Body in Emotional Decision Making', *Emotion Review*, 2/3 (2010), 245–9. doi: 10.1177/1754073910362599

Ortony, Andrew, Gerald L. Clore, and Allan Collins, *The Cognitive Structure of Emotions* (Cambridge: Cambridge University Press, 1988)

Panksepp, Jaak, *Affective Neuroscience: The Foundations of Human and Animal Emotions* (New York: Oxford University Press, 1998).

Panksepp, Jaak, and Lucy Biven, *The Archaeology of Mind: Neuroevolutionary Origins of Human Emotions* (New York: Norton, 2012).

Parkinson, Brian, Agneta H. Fischer, and Antony S. R. Manstead, *Emotion in Social Relations: Cultural, Group, and Interpersonal Processes* (New York: Psychology Press, 2005).

Pessoa, Luiz, 'Emergent Processes in Cognitive-Emotional Interactions', *Dialogues in Clinical Neuroscience*, 12/4 (2010), 433–48.

Pessoa, Luiz, 'Emotion and Cognition and the Amygdala: From "What Is It?" to "What's to Be Done?"', *Neuropsychologia*, 48/12 (2010), 3416–29. doi: 10.1016/j.neuropsychologia.2010.06.038

Pessoa, Luiz, and Ralph Adolphs, 'Emotion Processing and the Amygdala: From a "Low Road" to "Many Roads" of Evaluating Biological Significance', *Nature Reviews Neuroscience*, 11/11 (2010), 773–82. doi: 10.1038/nrn2920

Plutchik, Robert, *The Emotions: Facts, Theories and a New Model* (New York: Random House, 1962).

Plutchik, Robert, *Emotion: A Psychoevolutionary Synthesis* (New York: Harper & Row, 1980).

Raichle, Marcus E., Ann Mary MacLeod, Abraham Z. Snyder, William J. Powers, Debra A. Gusnard, and Gordon L. Shulman, 'A Default Mode of Brain Function', *Proceedings of the National Academy of Sciences*, 98/2 (2001), 676–82. doi: 10.1073/pnas.98.2.676

Raichle, Marcus E., and Abraham Z. Snyder, 'A Default Mode of Brain Function: A Brief History of an Evolving Idea', *NeuroImage*, 37/4 (2007), 1083–90. doi: 10.1016/j.neuroimage.2007.02.041

Ramachandran, Vilayanur S., 'Mirror Neurons and Imitation Learning as the Driving Force behind the Great Leap Forward in Human Evolution', *Edge* (31 May 2000) <http://edge.org/conversation/mirror-neurons-and-imitation-learning-as-the-driving-force-behind-the-great-leap-forward-in-human-evolution> accessed 5 December 2013.

Ramachandran, Vilayanur S., 'Mirror Neurons and the Brain in the Vat', *Edge* (9 January 2006) <http://edge.org/conversation/mirror-neurons-and-the-brain-in-the-vat> accessed 5 December 2013.

Reimann, Martin, and Antoine Bechara, 'The Somatic Marker Framework as a Neurological Theory of Decision-Making: Review, Conceptual Comparisons, and Future Neuroeconomics Research', *Journal of Economic Psychology*, 31/5 (2010), 767–76. doi: 10.1016/j.joep.2010.03.002

Renier, Laurent A., Irina Anurova, Anne G. De Volder, Synnöve Carlson, John VanMeter, and Josef P. Rauschecker, 'Preserved Functional Specialization for Spatial Processing in the Middle Occipital Gyrus of the Early Blind', *Neuron*, 68/1 (2010), 138–48. doi: 10.1016/j.neuron.2010.09.021

Rimmele, Ulrike, Lila Davachi, Radoslav Petrov, Sonya Dougal, and Elizabeth A. Phelps, 'Emotion Enhances the Subjective Feeling of Remembering, Despite Lower Accuracy for Contextual Details', *Emotion*, 11/3 (2011), 553–62. doi: 10.1037/a0024246

Rizzolatti, Giacomo, and Laila Craighero, 'The Mirror-Neuron System', *Annual Review of Neuroscience*, 27 (2004), 169–92. doi: 10.1146/annurev.neuro.27.070203.144230

Rizzolatti, G[iacomo], L. Fadiga, L. Fogassi, and V. Gallese, 'Resonance Behaviors and Mirror Neurons', *Archives italiennes de biologie: A Journal of Neuroscience*, 137/2–3 (1999), 85–100.

Rizzolatti, Giacomo, L. Fadiga, Vittorio Gallese, and Leonardo Fogassi, 'Premotor Cortex and the Recognition of Motor Actions', *Cognitive Brain Research*, 3/2 (1996), 131–41. doi: 10.1016/0926-6410(95)00038-0

Röttger-Rössler, Birgitt, and Hans J. Markowitsch (eds), *Emotions as Bio-Cultural Processes* (New York: Springer, 2009).

Ruckmick, Christian Alban, *The Psychology of Feeling and Emotion* (New York: McGraw-Hill, 1936).

Russell, James A., 'Core Affect and the Psychological Construction of Emotion', *Psychological Review*, 110/1 (2003), 145–72. doi: 10.1037/0033-295X.110.1.145

Sackeim, Harold A., and Ruben C. Gur, 'Lateral Asymmetry in Intensity of Emotional Expression', *Neuropsychologia*, 16/4 (1978), 473–81. doi: 10.1016/0028-3932(78)90070-2

Sackeim, Harold A., Ruben C. Gur, and Marcel C. Saucy, 'Emotions are Expressed More Intensely on the Left Side of the Face', *Science*, 202/4366 (1978), 434–6. doi: 10.1126/science.705335

Salovey, Peter, and John D. Mayer, 'Emotional Intelligence', *Imagination, Cognition and Personality*, 9/3 (1989–1990), 185–211. doi: 10.2190/DUGG-P24E-52WK-6CDG

Sander, David, and Klaus R. Scherer (eds), *The Oxford Companion to Emotion and the Affective Sciences* (Oxford: Oxford University Press, 2009).

Schachter, Stanley, 'The Interaction of Cognitive and Physiological Determinants of Emotion State', *Advances in Experimental Social Psychology*, 1 (1964), 49–80. doi: 10.1016/S0065-2601(08)60048-9

Schachter, Stanley, and Jerome E. Singer, 'Cognitive, Social, and Physiological Determinants of Emotional State', *Psychological Review*, 69/5 (1962), 379–99. doi: 10.1037/h0046234

Schauer, Maggie, Frank Neuner, and Thomas Elbert, *Narrative Exposure Therapy: A Short-Term Treatment for Traumatic Stress Disorders* (2nd rev. and enl. edn, Cambridge, MA: Hogrefe, 2011).

Scherer, Klaus R., Angela Schorr, and Tom Johnstone (eds), *Appraisal Processes in Emotion: Theory, Methods, Research* (Oxford: Oxford University Press, 2001).

Scherer, Klaus R., Harald G. Wallbott, and Angela B. Summerfield (eds), *Experiencing Emotion: A Cross-Cultural Study* (Cambridge: Cambridge University Press, 1986).

Schmitt, William A., Chad A. Brinkley, and Joseph P. Newman, 'Testing Damasio's Somatic Marker Hypothesis with Psychopathic Individuals: Risk Takers or Risk Averse?', *Journal of Abnormal Psychology*, 108/3 (1999), 538–43. doi: 10.1037/0021-843X.108.3.538

Schoenbaum, Geoffrey, Andrea A. Chiba, and Michela Gallagher, 'Neural Encoding in Orbitofrontal Cortex and Basolateral Amygdala during Olfactory Discrimination Learning', *Journal of Neuroscience*, 19/5 (1999), 1876–84.

Schwartz, Gary E., Geoffrey L. Ahern, and Serena-Lynn Brown, 'Lateralized Facial Muscle Response to Positive and Negative Emotional Stimuli', *Psychophysiology*, 16/6 (1979), 561–71. doi: 10.1111/j.1469-8986.1979.tb01521.x

Schwartz, Gary E., Richard J. Davidson, and Foster Maer, 'Right Hemisphere Lateralization from Emotion in the Human Brain: Interactions with Cognition', *Science*, 190/4211 (1975), 286–8. doi: 10.1126/science.1179210

Scripture, E. W., 'Detection of the Emotions by the Galvanometer', *JAMA: Journal of the American Medical Association*, 50/15 (1908), 1164–5. doi: 10.1001/jama.1908.25310410004001a

Shulman, Gordon L., Julie A. Fiez, Maurizio Corbetta, Randy L. Buckner, Francis M. Miezin, Marcus E. Raichle, and Steven E. Petersen, 'Common Blood Flow Changes across Visual Tasks: II. Decreases in Cerebral Cortex', *Journal of Cognitive Neuroscience*, 9/5 (1997), 648–63. doi: 10.1162/jocn.1997.9.5.648

Slater, Mel, Angus Antley, Adam Davison, David Swapp, Christoph Guger, Chris Barker, Nancy Pistrang, and Maria V. Sanchez-Vives, 'A Virtual Reprise of the Stanley Milgram Obedience Experiments', *PLoS ONE*, 1/1 (2006), e39. doi: 10.1371/journal.pone.0000039

Solms, Mark, and Edward Nersessian, 'Freud's Theory of Affect: Questions for Neuroscience', *Neuro-Psychoanalysis*, 1/1 (1999), 5–14.

Spreng, R. Nathan, Raymond A. Mar, and Alice S. N. Kim, 'The Common Neural Basis of Autobiographical Memory, Prospection, Navigation, Theory of Mind, and the Default Mode: A Quantitative Meta-Analysis', *Journal of Cognitive Neuroscience*, 21/3 (2009), 489–510. doi: 10.1162/jocn.2008.21029

Strongman, K. T., *The Psychology of Emotion: From Everyday Life to Theory* (5th edn, Chichester: Wiley, 2003).

Swanson, Larry W., and Gorica D. Petrovich, 'What Is the Amygdala?', *Trends in Neurosciences*, 21/8 (1998), 323–31. doi: 10.1016/S0166-2236(98)01265-X

Tomkins, Silvan S., *Affect, Imagery, Consciousness*, i. *The Positive Affects* (New York: Springer, 1962).

Verdejo-García, Antonio, Antoine Bechara, Emily C. Recknor, and Miguel Pérez-García, 'Executive Dysfunction in Substance Dependent Individuals during Drug Use and Abstinence: An Examination of the Behavioral, Cognitive and Emotional Correlates of Addiction', *Journal of the International Neuropsychological Society*, 12/3 (2006), 405–15. doi: 10.10170S1355617706060486

Vul, Edward, Christine Harris, Piotr Winkielman, and Harold Pashler, 'Puzzlingly High Correlations in fMRI Studies of Emotion, Personality, and Social Cognition', *Perspectives on Psychological Science*, 4/3 (2009), 274–90. doi: 10.1111/j.1745-6924.2009.01125.x

Wardle, Margaret C., Raul Gonzalez, Antoine Bechara, and Eileen M. Martin-Thormeyer, 'Iowa Gambling Task Performance and Emotional Distress Interact to Predict Risky Sexual Behavior in Individuals with Dual Substance and HIV Diagnoses', *Journal of Clinical and Experimental Neuropsychology*, 32/10 (2010), 1110–21. doi: 10.1080/13803391003757833

Wegner, Daniel M., *White Bears and Other Unwanted Thoughts: Suppression, Obsession, and the Psychology of Mental Control* (New York: Viking, 1989).

Wegner, Daniel M., 'Ironic Processes of Mental Control', *Psychological Review*, 101/1 (1994), 34–52. doi: 10.1037/0033-295X.101.1.34

Xu, Xiaojing, Xiangyu Zuo, Xiaoying Wang, and Shihui Han, 'Do You Feel My Pain? Racial Group Membership Modulates Empathic Neural Responses', *Journal of Neuroscience*, 29/26 (2009), 8525–9. doi: 10.1523/JNEUROSCI.2418-09.2009

Yovell, Yoram, 'Is There a Drive to Love?', *Neuro-Psychoanalysis*, 10/2 (2008), 117–44.

Zajonc, R. B., 'Feeling and Thinking: Preferences Need no Inferences', *American Psychologist*, 35/2 (1980), 151–75. doi: 10.1037/0003-066X.35.2.151
Zuckerman, Marvin, and D. Michael Kuhlman, 'Personality and Risk-Taking: Common Biosocial Factors', *Journal of Personality*, 68/6 (2000), 999–1029. doi: 10.1111/1467-6494.00124

9 PHILOSOPHY

Aristotle, *On Rhetoric: A Theory of Civic Discourse*, trans. with introd., notes, and appendices by George A. Kennedy (New York: Oxford University Press, 1991) [Gr. orig., Téchnē rhētoriké].
Augustine, *The City of God against the Pagans*, ed. and trans. R. W. Dyson (Cambridge: Cambridge University Press, 1998) [Lat. orig., *De civitate dei* (426)].
Bagnoli, Carla (ed.), *Morality and the Emotions* (Oxford: Oxford University Press, 2011).
Braund, Susanna Morton, and Christopher Gill (eds), *The Passions in Romans Thought and Literature* (Cambridge: Cambridge University Press, 1997).
Brown, Wendy, *Regulating Aversion: Tolerance in the Age of Identity and Empire* (Princeton: Princeton University Press, 2006).
Brunschwig, Jacques, and Martha C. Nussbaum (eds), *Passions and Perceptions: Studies in Hellenistic Philosophy of Mind* (Cambridge: Cambridge University Press, 1993).
Byers, Sarah Catherine, *Perception, Sensibility and Moral Motivation in Augustine: A Stoic-Platonic Synthesis* (Cambridge: Cambridge University Press, 2013).
Colish, Marcia L., *The Stoic Tradition from Antiquity to the Early Middle Ages*, 2 vols, Studies in the History of Christian Thought 34 and 35 (Leiden: Brill, 1985).
Cooper, John M., *Reason and Emotion: Essays on Ancient Moral Psychology and Ethical Theory* (Princeton: Princeton University Press, 1999).
Cottingham, John, *Philosophy and the Good Life: Reason and the Passions in Greek, Cartesian and Psychoanalytic Ethics* (Cambridge: Cambridge University Press, 1998).
Cottingham, John, 'Sceptical Detachment or Loving Submission to the Good? Reason, Faith, and the Passions in Descartes', *Faith and Philosophy*, 28/1 (2011), 44–53. doi: 10.5840/faithphil201128115
Descartes, René, *The Passions of the Soul*, trans. Stephen M. Voss (Indianapolis: Hackett, 1989) [Fr. orig., *Les Passions de l'âme* (1649)].
de Sousa, Ronald, *The Rationality of Emotion* (Cambridge, MA: MIT Press, 1987).
Fitterer, Robert J., *Love and Objectivity in Virtue Ethics: Aristotle, Lonergan, and Nussbaum on Emotions and Moral Insight* (Toronto: University of Toronto Press, 2008).
Fortenbaugh, William W., *Aristotle on Emotion: A Contribution to Philosophical Psychology, Rhetoric, Poetics, Politics and Ethics* (2nd edn, London: Duckworth, 2002).
Gardiner, H. M. [*sic* Harry Norman], Ruth Clark Metcalf, and John G. Beebe-Center, *Feeling and Emotion: A History of Theories* (New York: American Book Company, 1937).
Goldie, Peter, *The Emotions: A Philosophical Exploration* (Oxford: Clarendon, 2000).
Goldie, Peter (ed.), *The Oxford Handbook of Philosophy of Emotion* (Oxford: Oxford University Press, 2010).
Graver, Margaret R., *Stoicism and Emotion* (Chicago: University of Chicago Press, 2007).
Harris, William V., *Restraining Rage: The Ideology of Anger Control in Classical Antiquity* (Cambridge, MA: Harvard University Press, 2004).

Hume, David, *A Treatise of Human Nature: Being an Attempt to Introduce the Experimental Method of Reasoning into Moral Subjects*, 3 vols (London: John Noon/Thomas Longman, 1739–40).

James, Susan, *Passion and Action: The Emotions in Seventeenth-Century Philosophy* (Oxford: Clarendon Press, 1997).

Kant, Immanuel, 'The Contest of Faculties', trans. H. B. Nisbet, in *Kant: Political Writings*, ed. Hans Reiss (2nd edn, Cambridge: Cambridge University Press, 1970), 176–90 [Ger. orig., *Der Streit der Fakultäten* (1798)].

Kant, Immanuel, *The Metaphysics of Morals*, trans. and ed. Mary Gregor (Cambridge: Cambridge University Press, 1996) [Ger. orig., *Metaphysik der Sitten* (1797)].

Kelly, Daniel, *Yuck!: The Nature and Moral Significance of Disgust* (Cambridge, MA: MIT Press, 2011).

Kenny, Anthony, *Action, Emotion and Will* (London: Routledge & Paul, 1963).

Keppler, Jan Horst, *Adam Smith and the Economy of the Passions* (London: Routledge, 2010).

Knuuttila, Simo, *Emotions in Ancient and Medieval Philosophy* (Oxford: Clarendon Press, 2004).

Kolnai, Aurel, *On Disgust*, ed. Barry Smith and Carolyn Korsmeyer (Chicago: Open Court, 2004).

Konstan, David, *Pity Transformed* (London: Duckworth, 2001).

Konstan, David, *The Emotions of the Ancient Greeks: Studies in Aristotle and Classical Literature* (Toronto: University of Toronto Press, 2006).

Konstan, David, *Before Forgiveness: The Origins of a Moral Idea* (Cambridge: Cambridge University Press, 2010).

Konstan, David, and N. Keith Rutter (eds), *Envy, Spite and Jealousy: The Rivalrous Emotions in Ancient Greece* (Edinburgh: Edinburgh University Press, 2003).

Korsmeyer, Carolyn, *Savoring Disgust: The Foul and the Fair in Aesthetics* (Oxford: Oxford University Press, 2010).

Lagerlund, Henrik, and Mikko Yrjönsuuri (eds), *Emotions and Choice from Boethius to Descartes* (Dordrecht: Kluwer Academic Publishers, 2002).

Lamb, Jonathan, *The Evolution of Sympathy in the Long Eighteenth Century* (London: Pickering & Chatto, 2009).

Levi, Anthony, *French Moralists: The Theory of the Passions, 1585 to 1649* (Oxford: Clarendon Press, 1964).

Lombardo, Nicholas E., *The Logic of Desire: Aquinas on Emotion* (Washington, DC: Catholic University of America, 2011).

Meyer, Michael, *Philosophy and the Passions: Toward a History of Human Nature* (University Park: Pennsylvania State University Press, 2000).

Miner, Robert, *Thomas Aquinas on the Passions: A Study of Summa Theologiae 1a2ae 22–48* (Cambridge: Cambridge University Press, 2009).

Misselhorn, Catrin, 'Empathy and Dyspathy with Androids: Philosophical, Fictional and (Neuro-)Psychological Perspectives', *Konturen*, 2 (2009), 101–23 <http://konturen.uoregon.edu/vol2_Misselhorn.html> accessed 5 December 2013.

Misselhorn, Catrin, 'Empathy with Inanimate Objects and the Uncanny Valley', *Mind and Machines*, 19/3 (2009), 345–59. doi: 10.1007/s11023-009-9158-2

Mori, Masahiro, 'The Uncanny Valley', trans. Karl F. MacDorman and Norri Kageki, *IEEE Robotics & Automation Magazine*, 19/2 (2012), 98–100 [Jap. orig., 'Bukimi no tani' (1970)]. doi: 10.1109/MRA.2012.2192811

Noë, Alva, *Out of Our Heads: Why You Are Not Your Brain, and Other Lessons from the Biology of Consciousness* (New York: Hill and Wang, 2009).

Nussbaum, Martha C., *Love's Knowledge: Essays on Philosophy and Literature* (New York: Oxford University Press, 1990).

Nussbaum, Martha C., *Upheavals of Thought: The Intelligence of Emotions* (Cambridge: Cambridge University Press, 2001).

Nussbaum, Martha C., *Political Emotions: Why Love Matters for Justice* (Cambridge, MA: Belknapp Press of Harvard University Press, 2013).

Roberts, Robert C., *Emotions: An Essay in Aid of Moral Psychology* (Cambridge: Cambridge University Press, 2003).

Rorty, Amélie Oksenberg, 'Structuring Rhetoric', in Amélie Oksenberg Rorty (ed.), *Essays on Aristotle's Rhetoric* (Berkeley and Los Angeles: University of California Press, 1996), 1–33.

Rousseau, Jean-Jacques, 'J. J. Rousseau, Citizen of Geneva, to M. d'Alembert: Letter to d'Alembert on the Theater', in *Letter to d'Alembert and Writings for the Theater*, trans. and ed. Allan Bloom, Charles Butterworth, and Christopher Kelly (Hanover, NH: University Press of New England, 2004), 251–352.

Rousseau, Jean-Jacques, *Émile, or, On Education (Includes Émile and Sophie, or, The Solitaries)*, trans. and ed. Christopher Kelly, and Allan Bloom (Lebanon, NH: Dartmouth College Press, 2010) [Fr. orig., *Émile, ou de l'éducation* (1762)].

Solomon, Robert C., *The Passions: Emotions and the Meaning of Life* (Indianapolis: Hackett, 1993).

Solomon, Robert C., *True to Our Feelings: What Our Emotions Are Really Telling Us* (Oxford: Oxford University Press, 2007).

Sorabji, Richard, *Emotion and Peace of Mind: From Stoic Agitation to Christian Temptation: The Gifford Lectures* (Oxford: Oxford University Press, 2000).

Spinoza, Baruch de, 'Ethics', in *Spinoza: Complete Works*, ed. Michael L. Morgan, trans. Samuel Shirley (Indianapolis: Hackett, 2002), 213–382 [Lat. orig., *Ethica: ordine geometrico demonstrata* (1674)].

Starr, G. A., 'Egalitarian and Elitist Implications of Sensibility', in Leon Ingber (ed.), *L'Égalité* (Brussels: Bruylant, 1984), 126–35.

Terada, Rei, *Feeling in Theory: Emotion after the 'Death of the Subject'* (Cambridge, MA: Harvard University Press, 2001).

10 LITERARY AND VISUAL STUDIES

Ahern, Stephen, *Affect and Abolition in the Anglo-Atlantic, 1770–1830* (Farnham: Ashgate, 2013).

Baum, Joan, *Mind-Forg'd Manacles: Slavery and the English Romantic Poets* (North Haven, CT: Archon, 1994).

Bell, Michael, *Sentimentalism, Ethics, and the Culture of Feeling* (Basingstoke: Palgrave Macmillan, 2000).

Berlant, Lauren, 'Poor Eliza', *American Literature*, 70/3 (1998), 635–68. doi: 10.2307/2902712

Berlant, Lauren, *The Female Complaint: The Unfinished Business of Sentimentality in American Culture* (Durham, NC: Duke University Press, 2008).

Braund Susanna, and Glenn W. Most (eds), *Ancient Anger: Perspectives from Homer to Galen*, Yale Classical Studies 32 (Cambridge: Cambridge University Press, 2003).

Burgett, Bruce, *Sentimental Bodies: Sex, Gender, and Citizenship in the Early Republic* (Princeton: Princeton University Press, 1998).

Burnham, Michelle, 'Between England and America: Captivity, Sympathy, and the Sentimental Novel', in Deidre Lynch and William B. Warner (eds), *Cultural Institutions of the Novel* (Durham, NC: Duke University Press, 1996), 47–72.

Burnham, Michelle, *Captivity and Sentiment: Cultural Exchange in American Literature, 1682–1861* (Hanover, NH: University Press of New England, 1997).

Cairns, Douglas L., *Aidōs: The Psychology and Ethics of Honour and Shame in Ancient Greek Literature* (Oxford: Clarendon Press, 1993).

Cairns, Douglas L., 'Hybris, Dishonour, and Thinking Big', *Journal of Hellenic Studies*, 116 (1996), 1–32. doi: 10.2307/631953

Cairns, D[ouglas] L., 'Anger and the Veil in Ancient Greek Culture', *Greece & Rome*, 48/1 (2001), 18–32. doi: 10.1093/gr/48.1.18

Cairns, Douglas [L.], 'Look Both Ways: Studying Emotion in Ancient Greek', *Critical Quarterly*, 50/4 (2008), 43–62. doi: 10.1111/j.1467-8705.2008.00853.x

Carey, Brycchan, *British Abolitionism and the Rhetoric of Sensibility: Writing, Sentiment, and Slavery, 1760–1807* (Basingstoke: Palgrave, 2005).

Carretta, Vincent, and Philip Gould (eds), *Genius in Bondage: Literature of the Early Black Atlantic* (Lexington: University Press of Kentucky, 2001).

Chandler, James, *An Archaeology of Sympathy: The Sentimental Mode in Literature and Cinema* (Chicago: University of Chicago Press, 2013).

Cohen, Margaret, 'Sentimental Communities', in Margaret Cohen and Carolyn Dever (eds), *The Literary Channel: The Inter-National Invention of the Novel* (Princeton: Princeton University Press, 2002), 106–32.

Coleman, Patrick, *Anger, Gratitude, and the Enlightenment Writer* (Oxford: Oxford University Press, 2011).

Cvetkovich, Ann, *Mixed Feelings: Feminism, Mass Culture, and Victorian Sensationalism* (New Brunswick, NJ: Rutgers University Press, 1992).

Denby, David J., *Sentimental Narrative and the Social Order in France, 1760–1820*, Cambridge Studies in French 47 (Cambridge: Cambridge University Press, 1994).

Dickey, Stephanie S., and Herman Roodenburg (eds), *The Passions in the Arts of the Early Modern Netherlands* (Zwolle: Waanders, 2010).

Dyson, Michael Eric, *Pride: The Seven Deadly Sins* (Oxford: Oxford University Press, 2006).

Ellis, Markman, *The Politics of Sensibility: Race, Gender and Commerce in the Sentimental Novel* (Cambridge: Cambridge University Press, 1996).

Ellison, Julie, *Cato's Tears and the Making of Anglo-American Emotion* (Chicago: University of Chicago Press, 1999).

Faflak, Joel, and Richard C. Sha (eds), *Romanticism and the Emotions* (New York: Cambridge University Press, 2014).

Festa, Lynn, *Sentimental Figures of Empire in Eighteenth-Century Britain and France* (Baltimore: Johns Hopkins University Press, 2006).

Fisher, Philip, *The Vehement Passions* (Princeton: Princeton University Press, 2002).

Fitzgerald, John T. (ed.), *Passions and Moral Progress in Greco-Roman Thought* (London: Routledge, 2008).

Fögen, Thorsten (ed.), *Tears in the Graeco-Roman World* (Berlin: de Gruyter, 2009).

Freedberg, David, 'Memory in Art: History and the Neuroscience of Response', in Suzanne Nalbantian, Paul M. Matthews, and James L. McClelland (eds), *The Memory Process: Neuroscientific and Humanistic Perspectives* (Cambridge, MA: MIT Press, 2011), 337–58.

Freedberg, David, and Vittorio Gallese, 'Motion, Emotion and Empathy in Esthetic Experience', *Trends in Cognitive Sciences*, 11/5 (2007), 197–203. doi: 10.1016/j.tics.2007.02.003

Gottlieb, Evan, *Feeling British: Sympathy and National Identity in Scottish and English Writing, 1707–1832* (Lewisburg, PA: Bucknell University Press, 2007).

Gross, Daniel M., *The Secret History of Emotion: From Aristotle's Rhetoric to Modern Brain Science* (Chicago: University of Chicago Press, 2006).

Gross, Daniel M., 'Defending the Humanities with Charles Darwin's "The Expression of the Emotions in Man and Animals" (1872)', *Critical Inquiry*, 37/1 (2010), 34–59. doi: 10.1086/656468

Hagstrum, Jean H., *Sex and Sensibility: Ideal and Erotic Love from Milton to Mozart* (Chicago: University of Chicago Press, 1980).

Halttunen, Karen, 'Humanitarianism and the Pornography of Pain in Anglo-American Culture', *American Historical Review*, 100/2 (1995), 303–34.

Hemmings, Clare, 'In the Mood for Revolution: Emma Goldman's Passion', *New Literary History*, 43/3 (2012), 527–45. doi: 10.1353/nlh.2012.0030

Hendler, Glenn, 'The Structure of Sentimental Experience', *Yale Journal of Criticism*, 12/1 (1999), 145–53.

Hendler, Glenn, *Public Sentiments: Structures of Feeling in Nineteenth-Century American Literature* (Chapel Hill: University of North Carolina Press, 2001).

Hinton, Laura, *The Perverse Gaze of Sympathy: Sadomasochistic Sentiments from Clarissa to Rescue 911* (Albany: State University of New York Press, 1999).

Juneja, Monica, 'Translating the Body into Image: The Body Politic and Visual Practice at the Mughal Court during the Sixteenth and Seventeenth Centuries', in Axel Michaels and Christoph Wulf (eds), *Images of the Body in India* (London: Routledge, 2011), 235–60.

Kanerva, K. T., 'Ógæfa as an Emotion in Thirteenth Century Iceland', *Scandinavian Studies*, 84/1 (2012), 1–26.

Kaster, Robert A., *Emotion, Restraint, and Community in Ancient Rome* (New York: Oxford University Press, 2005).

LeBrun, [Charles], *A Method to Learn to Design the Passions: Proposed in a Conference on the General and Particular Expression: Written in English, and Illustrated with a Great Many Figures Excellently Designed by M. Le Brun, Chief Painter to the French King, Chancellor and Director of the Royal Academy of Painting and Sculpture: Translated and all the Designs Engraved on Copper by, John Williams* (London: n.p., 1734).

Levecq, Christine, *Slavery and Sentiment: The Politics of Feeling in Black Atlantic Antislavery Writing, 1770–1850* (Durham, NH: University of New Hampshire Press, 2008).

Menninghaus, Winfried, *Disgust: Theory and History of a Strong Sensation*, trans. Howard Eiland and Joel Golb (Albany: State University of New York Press, 2003) [Ger. orig., *Ekel: Theorie und Geschichte einer starken Empfindung* (1999)].

Meyer, Richard (ed.), *Representing the Passions: Histories, Bodies, Visions* (Los Angeles: Getty Research Institute, 2003).

Michaels, Walter Benn, *The Shape of the Signifier: 1967 to the End of History* (Princeton: Princeton University Press, 2004).

Miller, William Ian, 'Emotions and the Sagas', in Gísli Pálsson (ed.), *From Sagas to Society: Comparative Approaches to Early Iceland* (Enfieldlock: Hisarlik Press, 1992), 89–110.

Miller, William Ian, *Humiliation: And Other Essays on Honor, Social Discomfort, and Violence* (Ithaca, NY: Cornell University Press, 1993).

Miller, William Ian, *The Anatomy of Disgust* (Cambridge, MA: Harvard University Press, 1997).

Mitchell, Robert [Edward], *Sympathy and the State in the Romantic Era: Systems, State Finance, and the Shadows of Futurity* (New York: Routledge, 2007).

Montagu, Jennifer, *The Epression of the Passions: The Origin and Influence of Charles Le Brun's 'Conférence sur l'expression générale et particulière'* (New Haven: Yale University, 1994) (PhD thesis, Warburg Institute, London, 1959).

Mullan, John, *Sentiment and Sociability: The Language of Feeling in the Eighteenth Century* (Oxford: Clarendon Press, 1988).

Munteanu, Dana LaCourse (ed.), *Emotion, Gender, and Genre in Classical Antiquity* (London: Bristol Classical Press, 2011).

Musil, Robert, *The Man without Qualities*, 2 vols, trans. Sophie Wilkins and Burton Pike (New York: Vintage International, 1996) [Ger. orig., *Der Mann ohne Eigenschaften*, 3 vols (1930–43)].

Nathans, Heather S., *Slavery and Sentiment on the American Stage, 1787–1861: Lifting the Veil of Black* (Cambridge: Cambridge University Press, 2009).

Ngai, Sianne, *Ugly Feelings* (Cambridge, MA: Harvard University Press, 2007).

Onians, John, *Neuroarthistory: From Aristotle and Pliny to Baxandall and Zeki* (New Haven: Yale University Press, 2008).

Paster, Gail Kern, *Humoring the Body: Emotions and the Shakespearean Stage* (Chicago: University of Chicago Press, 2004).

Paster, Gail Kern, Katherine Rowe, and Mary Floyd-Wilson (eds), *Reading the Early Modern Passions: Essays in the Cultural History of Emotion* (Philadelphia: University of Pennsylvania Press, 2004).

Pfau, Thomas, *Romantic Moods: Paranoia, Trauma, and Melancholy, 1790–1840* (Baltimore: Johns Hopkins University Press, 2005).

Pinch, Adela, *Strange Fits of Passion: Epistemologies of Emotion, Hume to Austen* (Stanford, CA: Stanford University Press, 1996).

Richardson, Alan, *The Neural Sublime: Cognitive Theories and Romantic Texts* (Baltimore: Johns Hopkins University Press, 2010).

Samuels, Shirley (ed.), *The Culture of Sentiment: Race, Gender, and Sentimentality in Nineteenth-Century America* (New York: Oxford University Press, 1992).

Sanders, Ed, *Envy and Jealousy in Classical Athens: A Socio-Psychological Approach* (New York: Oxford University Press, 2014).

Santangelo, Paolo, 'Emotions in History and Literature: An Interdisciplinary Research on Emotions and States of Mind in Ming-Qing Period', *Ming Qing Yanjiu*, 9 (2000), 237–308.

Shimamura, Arthur P., *Experiencing Art: In the Brain of the Beholder* (Oxford: Oxford University Press, 2013).

Soni, Vivasvan, *Mourning Happiness: Narrative and the Politics of Modernity* (Ithaca, NY: Cornell University Press, 2010).

Starr, G. Gabrielle, *Feeling Beauty: The Neuroscience of Aesthetic Experience* (Cambridge, MA: MIT Press, 2013).

Stern, Julia A., *The Plight of Feeling: Sympathy and Dissent in the Early American Novel* (Chicago: University of Chicago Press, 1997).

Thrailkill, Jane F., *Affecting Fictions: Mind, Body, and Emotion in American Literary Realism* (Cambridge, MA: Harvard University Press, 2007).

Vaught, Jennifer C., *Masculinity and Emotion in Early Modern English Literature*, Women and Gender in the Early Modern World (Aldershot: Ashgate, 2008).

Ward, Candace, *Desire and Disorder: Fevers, Fiction, and Feeling in English Georgian Culture* (Lewisburg, PA: Bucknell University Press, 2007).

Williams, Raymond, *Marxism and Literature* (Oxford: Oxford University Press, 1977).

Wood, Marcus, *Slavery, Empathy, and Pornography* (Oxford: Oxford University Press, 2002).

Zeki, Semir, *A Vision of the Brain* (Oxford: Blackwell Scientific Publications, 1993).

Zeki, Semir, *Inner Vision: An Exploration of Art and the Brain* (Oxford: Oxford University Press, 1999).

Zeki, Semir, *Splendors and Miseries of the Brain: Love, Creativity, and the Quest for Human Happiness* (Chichester: Wiley-Blackwell, 2009).

11 CULTURAL STUDIES, LAW, LINGUISTICS, POLITICAL SCIENCE, SOCIOLOGY, THEOLOGY

Ahmed, Sara, *The Cultural Politics of Emotions* (Edinburgh: Edinburgh University Press, 2004).

Ahmed, Sara, *The Promise of Happiness* (Durham, NC: Duke University Press, 2010).

Abruzzo, Margaret, *Polemical Pain: Slavery, Cruelty, and the Rise of Humanitarianism* (Baltimore: Johns Hopkins University Press, 2011).

Bailey, Joanne, *Parenting in England 1760–1830: Emotion, Identity, and Generation* (Oxford: Oxford University Press, 2012).

Bandes, Susan A. (ed.), *The Passions of Law* (New York: New York University Press, 1999).

Barbalet, J[ack] M., *Emotion, Social Theory, and Social Structure: A Macrosociological Approach* (Cambridge: Cambridge University Press, 2001).

Barbalet, Jack (ed.), *Emotions and Sociology* (Oxford: Blackwell, 2002).

Barclay, Katie, *Love Intimacy and Power: Marriage and Patriarchy in Scotland, 1650–1850* (Manchester: Manchester University Press, 2011).

Barreto, José-Manuel, 'Ethics of Emotions as Ethics of Human Rights: A Jurisprudence of Sympathy in Adorno, Horkheimer and Rorty', *Law and Critique*, 17/1 (2006), 73–106. doi: 10.1007/s10978-006-0003-y [repr. in Costas Douzinas and C. Perrin (eds), *Critical Legal Theory*, iv. *Critical Legal Themes* (London: Routledge, 2011), no. 56].

Barreto, José-Manuel, 'Rorty and Human Rights: Contingency, Emotions and How to Defend Human Rights Telling Stories', *Utrecht Law Review*, 7/2 (2011), 93–112.

Bennett, Jane, *Vibrant Matter: A Political Ecology of Things* (Durham, NC: Duke University Press, 2010).

Berendsen, Desiree, 'Religious Passions and Emotions: Towards a Stratified Concept of Religious Passions: Robert Solomon versus Thomas Dixon', in Lieven Boeve, Hans Geybels, and Stijn van den Bossche (eds), *Encountering Transcendence: Contributions to a Theology of Christian Religious Experience* (Leuven: Peeters, 2005), 201–12.

Berlant, Lauren (ed.), *Compassion: The Culture and Politics of an Emotion* (New York: Routledge, 2004).

Berthomé, François, and Michael Houseman, 'Ritual and Emotions: Moving Relations, Patterned Effusions', *Religion and Society: Advances in Research*, 1 (2010), 57–75. doi: 10.3167/arrs.2010.010105

Boltanski, Luc, *Distant Suffering: Morality, Media and Politics* (Cambridge: Cambridge University Press, 1999).

Callahan, Cornelia, *In Good Conscience: Reason and Emotion in Moral Decision Making* (San Francisco: HarperCollins, 1991).

Cates, Diana Fritz, *Aquinas on the Emotions: A Religious-Ethical Inquiry*, Moral Traditional Series (Washington: Georgetown University Press, 2009).

Cheng, Anne Anlin, *The Melancholy of Race: Psychoanalysis, Assimilation, and Hidden Grief* (New York: Oxford University Press, 2000).

Clough, Patricia T[icineto], 'The Affective Turn: Political Economy, Biomedia and Bodies', *Theory, Culture & Society*, 25/1 (2008), 1–22. doi: 10.1177/0263276407085156

Clough, Patricia Ticineto, and Jean Halley (eds), *The Affective Turn: Theorizing the Social* (Durham, NC: Duke University Press, 2007).

Coakley, Sarah (ed.), *Faith, Rationality, and the Passions* (Chichester: Wiley-Blackwell, 2012). doi: 10.1002/9781118321997

Cochrane, Tom, Bernardino Fantini, and Klaus R. Scherer (eds), *The Emotional Power of Music: Multidisciplinary Perspectives on Musical Arousal, Expression, and Social Control* (Oxford: Oxford University Press, 2013).

Connolly, William E., *Neuropolitics: Thinking, Culture, Speed* (Minneapolis: University of Minnesota Press, 2002).

Connolly, William E., 'Materialities of Experience', in Diana Coole and Samantha Frost (eds), *New Materialisms: Ontology, Agency, and Politics* (Durham, NC: Duke University Press, 2010), 178–200.

Connolly, William E., 'Critical Response I: The Complexity of Intention', *Critical Inquiry*, 37/4 (2011), 791–8. doi: 10.1086/660993

Connolly, William E., *A World of Becoming* (Durham, NC: Duke University Press, 2011).

Corrigan, John, '"Habits From the Heart": The American Enlightenment and Religious Ideas About Emotion and Habit', *Journal of Religion*, 73/2 (1993), 183–99.

Corrigan, John, *Business of the Heart: Religion and Emotion in the Nineteenth Century* (Berkeley and Los Angeles: University of California Press, 2001).

Corrigan, John (ed.), *Religion and Emotion: Approaches and Interpretations* (Oxford: Oxford University Press, 2004).

Corrigan, John, 'Cognition, Universals and Constructedness: Recent Emotions Research and the Study of Religion', in Willem Lemmens and Walter van Herck (eds), *Religious Emotions: Some Philosophical Explorations* (Newcastle: Cambridge Scholars Publishing, 2008), 34–47.

Corrigan, J[ohn] (ed.), *The Oxford Handbook of Religion and Emotion* (Oxford: Oxford University Press, 2008).

Corrigan, John, Eric Crump, and John M. Kloos, *Emotion and Religion: A Critical Assessment and Annotated Bibliography* (Westport: Greenwood Press, 2000).

Corten, André, *Pentecostalism in Brazil: Emotion of the Poor and Theological Romanticism*, trans. Arianne Dorval (Basingstoke: Macmillan, 1999) [Fr. orig., *Le Pentecôtisme au Brésil* (1995)].

Dalferth, Ingolf U. and Michael Rodgers (eds), *Passion and Passivity: Claremont Studies in the Philosophy of Religion* (Tübingen: Mohr Siebeck, 2011).

Dixon, Thomas, 'Revolting Passions', *Modern Theology*, 27/2 (2011), 298–312. doi: 10.1111/j.1468-0025.2010.01677.x

Egger-Wenzel, Renate, and Jeremy Corley (eds), *Emotions from Ben Sira to Paul*, Deutero-canonical and Cognate Literature Yearbook 2011 (Berlin: de Gruyter, 2012).

Elias, Norbert, *The Civilizing Process: Sociogenetic and Psychogenetic Investigations*, trans. Edward Jephcott, ed. Eric Dunning, Johan Goudsblom, and Stephen Mennell (rev. edn, Oxford: Blackwell, 2010) [Ger. orig., *Über den Prozeß der Zivilisation*, 2 vols (1939)].

Force, Pierre, *Self-Interest before Adam Smith: A Genealogy of Economic Science*, Ideas in Context 68 (Cambridge: Cambridge University Press, 2003).

Select Bibliography

Gondreau, Paul, *The Passions of Christ's Soul in the Theology of St. Thomas Aquinas* (Münster: Aschendorff, 2002).

González, Ana Marta (ed.), *The Emotions and Cultural Analysis* (Farnham: Asghate, 2012).

Goodwin, Jeff, James M. Jasper, and Francesca Polletta (eds), *Passionate Politics: Emotions and Social Movements* (Chicago: University of Chicago Press, 2001).

Gould, Deborah B., *Moving Politics: Emotion and ACT UP's Fight against AIDS* (Chicago: University of Chicago Press, 2009).

Greco, Monica and Paul Stenner (eds), *Emotions: A Social Science Reader* (London: Routledge, 2008).

Harding, Jennifer, and E. Deirdre Pribram (eds), *Emotions: A Cultural Studies Reader* (London: Routledge, 2009).

Hardt, Michael, 'Affective Labor', *Boundary 2*, 26/2 (1999), 89–100.

Hardt, Michael, and Antonio Negri, *Empire* (Cambridge, MA: Harvard University Press, 2000).

Hardt, Michael, and Antonio Negri, *Multitude: War and Democracy in the Age of Empire* (New York: Penguin Books, 2004).

Harré, Rom (ed.), *The Social Construction of Emotions* (Oxford: Blackwell, 1986).

Harré, Rom, and W. Gerrod Parrott (eds), *The Emotions: Social, Cultural and Biological Dimensions* (London: Sage Publications, 1996).

Hemmings, Clare, 'Affective Solidarity: Feminist Reflexivity and Political Transformation', *Feminist Theory*, 13/2 (2012), 147–61. doi: 10.1177/1464700112442643

Hesford, Victoria, *Feeling Women's Liberation* (Durham, NC: Duke University Press, 2013).

Hochschild, Arlie Russell, 'Emotion Work, Feeling Rules, and Social Structure', *American Journal of Sociology*, 85/3 (1979), 551–75.

Hochschild, Arlie Russell, *The Managed Heart: Commercialization of Human Feeling* (Berkeley and Los Angeles: University of California Press, 1983).

Hochschild, Arlie Russell, 'Introduction: An Emotions Lens on the World', in Debra Hopkins, Jochen Kleres, Helena Flam, and Helmut Kuzmics (eds), *Theorizing Emotions: Sociological Explorations and Applications* (Frankfurt am Main: Campus, 2009), 29–37.

Hoffman, W. Michael, 'The Structure and Origin of the Religious Passions', *International Journal for Philosophy of Religion*, 8/1 (1977), 36–50.

Illouz, Eva, *Consuming the Romantic Utopia: Love and the Cultural Contradictions of Capitalism* (Berkeley and Los Angeles: University of California Press, 1997).

Illouz, Eva, *Cold Intimacies: The Making of Emotional Capitalism* (Cambridge: Polity Press, 2007).

Illouz, Eva, *Saving the Modern Soul: Therapy, Emotions, and the Culture of Self-Help* (Berkeley and Los Angeles: University of California Press, 2008).

Illouz, Eva, *Why Love Hurts: A Sociological Explanation* (Cambridge: Polity Press, 2012).

Johnston, Adrian, 'The Misfeeling of What Happens: Slavoj Žižek, Antonio Damasio and a Materialist Account of Affects', *Subjectivity*, 3/1 (2010), 76–100. doi: 10.1057/sub.2009.36

Joyce, Kelly A., *Magnetic Appeal: MRI and the Myth of Transparency* (Ithaca, NY: Cornell University Press, 2008).

Juslin, Patrik N., and John A. Sloboda (eds), *Handbook of Music and Emotion: Theory, Research, Applications* (Oxford: Oxford University Press, 2010).

Kingston, Rebecca, *Public Passion. Rethinking the Grounds for Political Justice* (Montreal: McGill Queens University Press, 2011).

Kingston, Rebecca, and Leonard Ferry (eds), *Bringing the Passions Back In: The Emotions in Political Philosophy* (Vancouver: UBC Press, 2008).

Kövecses, Zoltán, *Metaphor and Emotion: Language, Culture, and Body in Human Feeling* (Cambridge: Cambridge University Press, 2000).

Lakoff, George, and Zoltán Kövecses, 'The Cognitive Model of Anger Inherent in American English', in Dorothy Holland and Naomi Quinn (eds), *Cultural Models in Language and Thought* (Cambridge: Cambridge University Press, 1987), 195–221.

Layton, Richard A., 'Propatheia: Origen and Didymus on the Origin of the Passions', *Vigiliae Christianae*, 54/3 (2000) 262–82.

Layton, Richard A., 'From "Holy Passion" to Sinful Emotion: Jerome and the Doctrine of Propassio', in Paul M. Blowers, Angela Russell Christman, David G. Hunter, and Robin Darling Young (eds), *In Dominico Eloquio—In Lordly Eloquence: Essays on Patristic Exegesis in Honor of Robert Louis Wilken* (Grand Rapids, MI: Eerdmans, 2002), 280–93.

Lemmings, David, and Ann Brooks (eds), *Emotions and Social Change: Historical and Sociological Perspectives*, Routledge Studies in Social and Political Thought (New York: Routledge, 2014).

Libby David J., Paul Spickard, and Susan Ditto (eds), *Affect and Power: Essays on Sex, Slavery, Race, and Religion in Appreciation of Winthrop D. Jordan* (Jackson: University Press of Mississippi, 2005).

Luhmann, Niklas, *Love as Passion: The Codification of Intimacy*, trans. Jeremy Gaines and Doris L. Jones (Cambridge, MA: Harvard University Press, 1986) [Ger. orig., *Liebe als Passion: Zur Codierung von Intimität* (1982)].

Lunt, Peter and Paul Stenner, 'The Jerry Springer Show as an Emotional Public Sphere', *Media, Culture & Society*, 27/1 (2005), 59–81. doi: 10.1177/0163443705049058.

McNamer, Sarah, *Affective Meditation and the Invention of Medieval Compassion*, Middle Ages Series (Philadelphia: University of Pennsylvania Press, 2010).

Madell, Geoffrey, *Philosophy, Music and Emotion* (Edinburgh: Edinburgh University Press, 2002).

Madigan, Kevin, *The Passions of Christ in High-Medieval Thought: An Essay on Christological Development* (Oxford: Oxford University Press, 2007).

Margolis, Diane Rothbard, *The Fabric of Self: A Theory of Ethics and Emotions* (New Haven: Yale University Press, 1998).

Massumi, Brian (ed.), *A Shock to Thought: Expression after Deleuze and Guattari* (London: Routledge, 2002).

Massumi, Brian, *Parables for the Virtual: Movement, Affect, Sensation* (Durham, NC: Duke University Press, 2002).

Moscoso, Javier, *Pain: A Cultural History* (Basingstoke: Palgrave Macmillan, 2012).

Parrott, W. Gerrod, and Rom Harré, 'Princess Diana and the Emotionology of Contemporary Britain', *International Journal of Group Tensions*, 30/1 (2001), 29–38. doi: 10.1023/A:1026649932173

Petersen, Roger D., *Understanding Ethnic Violence: Fear, Hatred, and Resentment in Twentieth-Century Eastern Europe* (Cambridge: Cambridge University Press, 2002).

Pettigrove, Glen, and Nigel Parsons, 'Shame: A Case Study of Collective Emotions', *Social Theory and Practice*, 38/3 (2012), 504–30.

Pinker, Steven, *How the Mind Works* (New York: Norton, 1997).

Protevi, John, *Political Affect: Connecting the Social and the Somatic*, Posthumanities, 7 (Minneapolis: University of Minnesota Press, 2009).

Rai, Amit S., *Rule of Sympathy: Sentiment, Race, and Power, 1750–1850* (New York: Palgrave, 2002).

Reckwitz, Andreas, 'Affective Spaces: A Praxeological Outlook', *Rethinking History*, 16/2 (2012), 241–58. doi: 10.1080/13642529.2012.681193

Roberts, Robert C., *Spiritual Emotions: A Psychology of Christian Virtues* (Grand Rapids: Eerdmans, 2007).

Robin, Corey, *Fear: The History of a Political Idea* (Oxford: Oxford University Press, 2004).

Roodenburg, Herman, '"Si vis me flere...": On Preachers, Passions and Pathos in Eighteenth-Century Europe', in Jitse Dijkstra, Justin Kroesen, and Yme Kuiper (eds), *Myths, Martyrs and Modernity: Studies in the History of Religions in Honour of Jan N. Bremmer* (Leiden: Brill, 2010), 609–28.

Rubin, Miri, *Emotion and Devotion: The Meaning of Mary in Medieval Religious Cultures* (Budapest: Central European University Press, 2009).

Scheff, Thomas J., *Microsociology: Discourse, Emotion, and Social Structure* (Chicago: University of Chicago Press, 1990).

Scheff, Thomas J., and Suzanne M. Retzinger, *Emotions and Violence: Shame and Rage in Destructive Conflicts*, Lexington Book Series on Social Theory (Lexington: Lexington Books, 1991).

Sedgwick, Eve Kosofsky, *Touching Feeling: Affect, Pedagogy, Performativity* (Durham, NC: Duke University Press, 2003).

Shaviro, Steven, *Post-Cinematic Affect* (Winchester: Zero Books, 2010).

Siegel, Marc, *False Alarm: The Truth about the Epidemic of Fear* (Hoboken, NJ: John Wiley & Sons, 2005).

Smith, J. Warren, *Passion and Paradise: Human and Divine Emotion in the Thought of Gregory of Nyssa* (New York: Crossroad, 2004).

Stets, Jan E., 'Future Directions in the Sociology of Emotions', *Emotion Review*, 2/3 (2010), 265–8. doi: 10.1177/1754073910361975

Stewart, Kathleen, *Ordinary Affects* (Durham, NC: Duke University Press, 2007).

Stump, Eleonore, 'The Non-Aristotelian Character of Aquinas's Ethics: Aquinas on the Passions', *Faith and Philosophy*, 28/1 (2011), 29–43.

Sussman, Charlotte, *Consuming Anxieties: Consumer Protest, Gender, and British Slavery, 1713–1833* (Stanford, CA: Stanford University Press, 2000).

Thoits, Peggy A., 'The Sociology of Emotions', *Annual Review of Sociology*, 15/1 (1989), 317–42.

Turner, Jonathan H., *Human Emotions: A Sociological Theory* (London: Routledge, 2007).

Turner, Jonathan H., 'The Sociology of Emotions: Basic Theoretical Arguments', *Emotion Review*, 1/4 (2009), 340–54. doi: 10.1177/1754073909338305

Voorwinde, Stephen, *Jesus' Emotions in the Gospels* (London: T&T Clark, 2011).

Walzer, Michael, *Politics and Passions: Toward a More Egalitarian Liberalism* (New Haven: Yale University Press, 2004).

Werbner, Pnina, and Helene Basu (eds), *Embodying Charisma: Modernity, Locality and the Performance of Emotion in Sufi Cults* (London: Routledge, 1998).

Wierzbicka, Anna, *Emotions across Languages and Cultures: Diversity and Universals* (Cambridge: Cambridge University Press, 1999).

Wolkomir, Michelle, 'Emotion Work, Commitment, and the Authentication of the Self: The Case of Gay and Ex-Gay Christian Support Groups', *Journal of Contemporary Ethnography*, 30/3 (2001), 305–34. doi: 10.1177/089124101030003002

Wulff, Helena (ed.), *The Emotions: A Cultural Reader* (Oxford: Berg, 2007).

Yu, Ning, 'Metaphorical Expressions of Anger and Happiness in English and Chinese', *Metaphor and Symbolic Activity*, 10/2 (1995), 59–92.

Yu, Ning, 'Body and Emotion: Body Parts in Chinese Expression of Emotion', *Pragmatics and Cognition*, 10/1 (2002), 341–67. doi: 10.1075/pc.10.12.14yu

Žižek, Slavoj, 'Have Michael Hardt and Antonio Negri Rewritten the Communist Manifesto for the Twenty-First Century?', *Rethinking Marxism*, 13/3–4 (2001), 190–8. doi: 10.1080/089356901101241875

Žižek, Slavoj, 'Some Concluding Notes on Violence, Ideology and Communist Culture', *Subjectivity*, 3/1 (2010), 101–16. doi: 10.1057/sub.2009.34

Index

Diagrams and pictures are given in italics. Notes are marked as 'n'.